HARRAP'S
LEARNERS
Spanish
MINI
DICTIONARY

HARRAP

HARRAP'S
LEARNER'S

Spanish

MINI
DICTIONARY

HARRAP

First published in Great Britain 1994
by Chambers Harrap Publishers Ltd
43-45 Annandale Street, Edinburgh EH7 4AZ, UK

This dictionary is a shortened version of Harrap's Spanish-English Mini
Dictionary. The project management was carried out by LEXUS Ltd.
El presente diccionario es una versión abreviada del Harrap's Spanish-
English Mini Dictionary. La dirección del proyecto corrió a cargo de
LEXUS Ltd.

Editors/Redactores:
Alicia de Benito Harland   Fernando León Solís   Hugh O'Donnell

ISBN 0 245 60525 8

Typeset by Hewer Text Composition Services, Edinburgh
Printed by Clays Ltd, St Ives plc

Contents/Materias

Trademarks
Words considered to be trademarks have been designated in this dictionary by (R). However, no judgement is implied concerning the legal status of any trademark by virtue of the presence or absence of such a designation.

Marcas Registradas
Las palabras consideradas marcas registradas vienen distinguidas en este diccionario con una (R). Sin embargo, la presencia o la ausencia de tal distintivo no implica juicio alguno acerca de la situación legal de la marca registrada.

Introduction

This dictionary, a shortened version of *Harrap's Mini Spanish-English Dictionary*, aims to provide a practical selection of the most frequently used words and expressions of the Spanish and English languages of today. An invaluable learning tool for beginners, the dictionary offers a usefulness and clarity of presentation unparalleled in a small-format work.

The new system for Spanish alphabetical order has been adopted. In this system 'ch' and 'll' are no longer considered as separate letters of the alphabet, but are each incorporated at their respective alphabetical positions under 'c' and 'l' - 'ñ', however, is listed after 'n'.

Phrasal verbs are indicated by a bullet point ● and are grouped after the word on which they are based.

Numbers are used to divide grammatical categories of headwords. For longer or more detailed entries a solid block ▌ is used to break up meaning categories.

A number code (1-7) against a Spanish verb means that the verb is irregular. The irregular forms of the verb can be discovered by looking at the model verbs on page 322. A list of regular Spanish verb conjugations and of some important verbs with irregular conjugations is given on pages 317–323.

An asterisk against an English verb means that it is irregular. The irregular forms of the verb can be found in the lists on pages 324–327.

A double asterisk against a Spanish noun means that the noun, although feminine, takes the singular definite article 'el', for example 'el agua'. The plural definite article for these words is 'las'.

Pronunciation for English words is given in the International Phonetic Alphabet. In order to save space, pronunciation is not given for derived forms. Stress is indicated in derived forms where it differs from the stress in the main form (for example, 'miracle', 'mi'raculous').

Broad coverage has been given to North American English and Latin American Spanish. Regular American English spelling variants ('theater', 'color' etc) are shown on the English-Spanish side of the dictionary only.

Introducción

El presente diccionario, una versión abreviada del *Harrap's Mini Spanish-English Dictionary*, tiene como objetivo proporcionar una selección de las palabras y expresiones más frecuentes del español y el inglés actuales. Este diccionario, un valioso instrumento de aprendizaje, es de una utilidad y una claridad de presentación sin parangón en el campo del pequeño formato.

Se ha adoptado la nueva ordenación alfabética del español. Según ésta, los dígrafos "ch" y "ll" no se consideran letras independientes, sino que ocupan el lugar que les corresponde alfabéticamente dentro de la "c" y "l", respectivamente . La "ñ", sin embargo, aparece tras la "n".

Los verbos frasales ingleses se indican con un punto en negrita • y vienen agrupados tras la palabra en que se basan.

Se utilizan números para dividir las categorías gramaticales de las palabras. En entradas más largas o más detalladas se usa un cuadrado en negrita ▌ para dividir los diferentes significados.

La presencia de un número en corchetes tras un verbo español indica que el verbo es irregular. Las formas irregulares de los verbos pueden averiguarse consultando los verbos modelo en la página 322. En las páginas 317–323 aparece una lista de la conjugación de verbos regulares del español y de algunos verbos importantes de conjugación irregular.

Un asterisco tras un verbo inglés indica que éste es irregular. Las formas irregulares del verbo se encuentran en las listas de las páginas 324–327.

Dos asteriscos tras un sustantivo español indican que éste, aun siendo femenino, requiere el artículo masculino "el" en el singular (por ejemplo, "el agua"); el plural sería "las aguas".

La pronunciación de las palabras inglesas viene dada en el Alfabeto Fonético Internacional. Para ahorrar espacio, la pronunciación de las formas derivadas no aparece. El acento de las formas derivadas se indica cuando es diferente del de la forma principal (por ejemplo, "miracle", "mi'raculous").

Se da una amplia cobertura del inglés americano y del español sudamericano. Las variantes ortográficas normales del inglés americano ("theater", "color" etc) sólo aparecen en la sección Inglés-Español del diccionario.

Guide to the Pronunciation of Spanish

Letter	Phonetic symbol	Examples	Approximate British English equivalent

Vowels:

a	[a]	gato, amar, mesa	as in father, but shorter
e	[e]	estrella, vez, firme	as in labour
i	[i]	inicuo, iris	as in see, but shorter
o	[o]	bolo, cómodo, oso	between lot and taught
u	[u]	turuta, puro, tribu	as in food, but shorter, but u in -que- or -qui- and -gue- or -gui- is silent (unless -güe- or -güe-)
y	[i]	y	as in see, but shorter

Diphthongs:

ai, ay	[ai]	baile, hay	as in life, aisle
au	[au]	fauna	as in fowl, house
ei, ey	[ei]	peine, ley	as in hate, feign
eu	[eu]	feudo	pronounce each vowel separately
oi, oy	[oi]	boina, hoy	as in boy

Semi-consonants:

u	[w]	buey, cuando, fuiste	as in wait
i	[j]	viernes, vicio, ciudad, ciar	as in yes
y	[j]	yermo, ayer, rey	as in yes

Consonants:

b	[b]	boda, burro, ambos	as in be
	[β]	haba, traba	a very light b
c	[k]	cabeza, cuco, acoso, frac	as in car, keep
	[θ]	cecina, cielo	as in thing, but in Andalusia and all of Latin America as s in silly
ch	[tʃ]	chepa, ocho	as in chamber
d	[d]	dedo, andar	as in day
	[ð]	dedo, ánade, abad	as in this (often omitted in spoken Spanish when at the end of a word)
f	[f]	fiesta, afición	as in for
g	[g]	gas, rango, gula	as in get
	[ɣ]	agua, agosto, lagar	a very light g
g	[x]	genio, legión	similar to Scottish [x] in loch
h	-	hambre, ahíto	Spanish h is silent
j	[x]	jabón, ajo, carcaj	similar to Scottish [x] in loch
k	[k]	kilo, kimono	as in car, keep
l	[l]	labio, hábil, elegante	as in law
ll	[ʎ]	lluvia, calle	similar to the sound in million
m	[m]	mano, amigo, hambre	as in man
n	[n]	nata, ratón, antes, enemigo	as in night
ñ	[ɲ]	año, ñoño	similar to the sound in onion
p	[p]	pipa, pelo	as in point
q	[k]	quiosco, querer, alambique	as in car
r(r)	[r]	pero, correr, padre	always pronounced, rolled as in Scots
	[rr]	reír, honrado, perro	rr is a lengthened r sound
s	[s]	sauna, asado, cortés	similar to the s in hissing

t	[t]	teja, estén, atraco	as in *t*ime
v	[b]	*v*erbena, vena	as in *b*e
	[β]	a*v*e, vi*v*o	a very light b
w	[b]	*w*agón, *w*aterpolo	as in *b*e
x	[ks]	é*x*ito, e*x*amen	as in e*x*ercise
	[s]	e*x*tensión	as in e*s*tate
z	[θ]	*z*orro, a*z*ul, ca*z*a, soe*z*	as in *th*ing, but in Andalusia and in all of Latin America as s in silly

Stress rules

If a word ends in a vowel, -n or -s, the stress falls on the second last syllable:

mano, examen, bocadillos

If a word has any other ending, the stress falls on the last syllable:

hablar, Madrid, ayer

Exceptions to these rules carry a written accent on the stressed syllable:

cómodo, legión, hábil

Fonética Inglesa

El acento primario se indica mediante un' delante de la sílaba acentuada.

Las consonantes

[p]	*p*en
[b]	*b*ill
[t]	*t*ent
[d]	*d*esk
[k]	*c*ar
[g]	*g*oal
[tʃ]	tea*ch*er
[dʒ]	a*g*e
[f]	*f*ish
[v]	ha*v*e
[θ]	me*th*od
[ð]	mo*th*er
[s]	i*c*y
[z]	ea*s*y
[ʃ]	*sh*oe
[ʒ]	mea*s*ure
[h]	*h*at
[m]	*m*ilk
[n]	*n*ame
[ŋ]	si*ng*
[l]	*fi*ght
[r]	*r*ead
[j]	*y*oghurt
[w]	*w*atch
[x]	lo*ch* (como en legión)
[ʳ]	se llama 'linking r' y se encuentra únicamente a final de palabra. Se pronuncia sólo cuando la palabra siguiente empieza por una vocal

Las vocales y los diptongos

[i:]	sh*ee*p
[ɪ]	sh*i*p, hous*e*s
[e]	b*e*d
[æ]	c*a*t
[ɑ:]	f*a*ther
[ɒ]	d*o*g
[ɔ:]	h*or*se
[ʊ]	w*o*man
[u:]	bl*ue*
[ʌ]	c*u*p
[ɜ:]	*ear*th
[ə]	*a*bout
[ə]	opcional. En algunos casos se pronuncia y en otros se omite: ['traɪfəl]
[eɪ]	t*a*ble
[əʊ]	g*o*
[aɪ]	t*i*me
[aʊ]	h*ou*se
[ɔɪ]	b*oy*
[ɪə]	f*ier*ce
[eə]	c*are*
[ʊə]	d*u*ring

vii

Abbreviations

Abreviaturas

adjective	*a*	adjetivo
abbreviation	*abbr, abr*	abreviatura
adverb	*adv*	adverbio
somebody, someone	*algn*	alguien
Latin American	*Am*	hispano americano
article	*art*	artículo
British	*Br*	británico
conjunction	*conj*	conjunción
definite	*def*	definido
demonstrative	*dem*	demostrativo
feminine	*f*	femenino
familiar	*fam*	familiar
figurative use	*fig*	uso figurado
feminine plural	*fpl*	plural femenino
future	*fut*	futuro
impersonal	*impers*	impersonal
indefinite	*indef*	indefinido
indeterminate	*indet*	indeterminado
indicative	*indic*	indicativo
infinitive	*infin*	infinitivo
interjection	*interj*	interjección
interrogative	*interr*	interrogativo
invariable	*inv*	invariable
irregular	*irreg*	irregular
masculine	*m*	masculino
masculine plural	*mpl*	plural masculino
noun	*n*	nombre
personal	*pers*	personal
plural	*pl*	plural
possessive	*pos, poss*	posesivo
past participle	*pp*	participio pasado
preposition	*prep*	preposición
present	*pres*	presente
preterite	*pret*	pretérito
pronoun	*pron*	pronombre
past tense	*pt*	pretérito
relative	*rel*	relativo
somebody, someone	*sb*	alguien
singular	*sing*	singular
something	*sth*	algo
subjunctive	*subj*	subjuntivo
auxiliary verb	*v aux*	verbo auxiliar
intransitive verb	*vi*	verbo intransitivo
impersonal verb	*v impers*	verbo impersonal
reflexive verb	*vr*	verbo reflexivo
transitive verb	*vt*	verbo transitivo
cultural equivalent	≈	equivalencia cultural

A

a [eɪ, *unstressed* ə] *indef art* (*before vowel or silent h* **an**) un, una; **he has a big nose** tiene la nariz grande; **half a litre/an hour** medio litro/media hora; **he's a teacher** es profesor; **60 pence a kilo** 60 peniques el kilo; **three times a week** tres veces a la semana.

abandon [əˈbændən] *vt* abandonar.

abbey [ˈæbɪ] abadía *f.*

abbreviation [əbriːvɪˈeɪʃən] abreviatura *f.*

ability [əˈbɪlɪtɪ] capacidad *f.*

able [ˈeɪbəl] *a* (*capable*) capaz; **to be a. to do sth** poder hacer algo.

abnormal [æbˈnɔːməl] *a* anormal.

abnormally *adv* anormalmente.

aboard [əˈbɔːd] **1** *adv* a bordo; **to go a.** (*ship*) embarcarse; (*train*) subir. **2** *prep* a bordo de.

abolish [əˈbɒlɪʃ] *vt* abolir.

abortion [əˈbɔːʃən] aborto *m*; **to have an a.** abortar.

about [əˈbaʊt] **1** *adv* **is he a. somewhere?** ¿está por aquí?; **there's nobody a.** no hay nadie; **to rush a.** correr de un lado para otro; **he's up and a. again** (*after illness*) ya está levantado. ‖ (*approximately*) más o menos; **he's a. 40** tendrá unos 40 años; **it's a. time you got up** ya es hora de que te levantes. **2** *prep* (*concerning*) acerca de; **a programme a. Paris** un programa sobre París; **to speak a. sth** hablar de algo; **what's it all a.?** ¿de qué se trata?; **how a. a game of tennis?** ¿qué te parece un partido de tenis? ‖ **it's a. to start** está a punto de empezar.

above [əˈbʌv] **1** *adv* arriba; **the flat a.** el piso de arriba; **a policy imposed from a.** una política impuesta desde arriba. **2** *prep* (*higher than*) encima de; (*greater than*) superior a; **100 metres a. sea level** 100 metros sobre el nivel del mar; **it's a. the door** está encima de la puerta; **a. all** sobre todo; **he's not a. stealing** es capaz incluso de robar.

above-mentioned *a* susodicho,-a.

abreast [əˈbrest] *adv* **to walk 3 a.** ir de 3 en fondo; **to keep a. of things** mantenerse al día.

abroad [əˈbrɔːd] *adv* en el extranjero; **to go a.** irse al extranjero.

abrupt [əˈbrʌpt] *a* (*manner*) brusco,-a; (*change*) súbito,-a.

abruptly *adv* (*act*) bruscamente; (*speak*) con aspereza.

abscess [ˈæbses] absceso *m.*

absence [ˈæbsəns] (*of person*) ausencia *f*; (*of thing*) falta *f.*

absent *a* ausente.

absent-'minded *a* distraído,-a.

absolute [ˈæbsəluːt] *a* absoluto,-a; (*failure*) total; (*truth*) puro,-a.

absolutely *adv* completamente; **a. not** en absoluto; **you're a. right** tienes toda la razón; **a.!** ¡desde luego!

absorb [əb'zɔːb] *vt* (*liquid*) absorber; **to be absorbed in sth** estar absorto, -a en algo.

absorbent cotton *US* algodón *m* hidrófilo.

absurd [əb'sɜːd] *a* absurdo,-a.

abuse [ə'bjuːs] **1** *n* (*ill-treatment*) malos tratos *mpl*; (*misuse*) abuso *m*; (*insults*) injurias *fpl*. **2** [ə'bjuːz] *vt* (*ill-treat*) maltratar; (*misuse*) abusar de; (*insult*) injuriar.

abusive [əb'juːsɪv] *a* (*insulting*) grosero,-a.

academic [ækə'demɪk] **1** *a* académico,-a; (*career*) universitario,-a; **a. year** año *m* escolar. **2** *n* académico,-a *mf*.

accelerate [æk'seləreɪt] *vi* acelerar.

accelerator acelerador *m*.

accent ['æksənt] acento *m*.

accept [ək'sept] *vt* aceptar; (*theory*) admitir.

acceptable *a* admisible.

access ['ækses] acceso *m*.

ac'cessible *a* accesible; (*person*) asequible.

accessory [ək'sesərɪ] (*to crime*) cómplice *mf*; **accessories** accesorios *mpl*; (*for outfit*) complementos *mpl*.

access time tiempo *m* de acceso.

accident ['æksɪdənt] accidente *m*; **by a.** por casualidad.

acci'dental *a* fortuito,-a; (*unintended*) imprevisto,-a.

acci'dentally *adv* (*by chance*) por casualidad.

accommodation [əkɒmə'deɪʃən] (*US also* **accommodations**) alojamiento *m*.

accompany [ə'kʌmpənɪ] *vt* acompañar.

accomplish [ə'kʌmplɪʃ] *vt* (*aim*) conseguir; (*task, mission*) llevar a cabo.

accord [ə'kɔːd] **of his own a.** espontáneamente.

accordance in a. with de acuerdo con.

according to *prep* según.

accordion [ə'kɔːdɪən] acordeón *m*.

account [ə'kaʊnt] (*report*) informe *m*; (*at bank, in business*) cuenta *f*; **on a. of** a causa de; **to take a. of, to take into a.** tener en cuenta; **accounts department** servicio *m* de contabilidad; **current a.** cuenta *f* corriente.

● **account for** *vt* (*explain*) explicar.

accountant contable *mf*.

accumulate [ə'kjuːmjʊleɪt] **1** *vt* acumular. **2** *vi* acumularse.

accurate ['ækjʊrɪt] *a* (*number*) exacto,-a; (*answer*) correcto,-a; (*observation*) acertado,-a; (*translation*) fiel.

accurately *adv* con precisión.

accu'sation acusación *f.*

accuse [ə'kjuːz] *vt* acusar.

accustomed [ə'kʌstəmd] *a* **to be a. to sth** estar acostumbrado a algo; **to get a. to sth** acostumbrarse a algo.

ace [eɪs] (*card & fig*) as *m*; (*in tennis*) ace *m.*

ache [eɪk] **1** *n* dolor *m.* **2** *vi* doler; **my back aches** me duele la espalda.

achieve [ə'tʃiːv] *vt* (*attain*) conseguir; (*accomplish*) llevar a cabo.

achievement (*attainment*) logro *m*; (*feat*) hazaña *f.*

acid ['æsɪd] **1** *a* ácido,-a. **2** *n* ácido *m.*

acid rain lluvia *f* ácida.

acknowledge [ək'nɒlɪdʒ] *vt* (*recognize*) reconocer; (*letter*) acusar recibo de; (*greet*) saludar.

acne ['æknɪ] acné *m.*

acorn ['eɪkɔːn] bellota *f.*

acoustics *npl* acústica *f sing.*

acquaint [ə'kweɪnt] *vt* **to be acquainted with sb** conocer a algn; **to be acquainted with sth** estar al corriente de algo.

acquaintance conocimiento *m*; (*person*) conocido,-a *mf*; **to make sb's a.** conocer a algn.

acquire [ə'kwaɪə^r] *vt* adquirir.

acre ['eɪkə^r] acre *m* (*approx* 40,47 áreas).

acrobatic *a* acrobático.

across [ə'krɒs] **1** *adv* a través; **to go a.** atravesar; **to run a.** atravesar corriendo. **2** *prep* a través de; (*at the other side of*) al otro lado de; **they live a. the road** viven enfrente; **to go a. the street** cruzar la calle.

acrylic [ə'krɪlɪk] *a* acrílico,-a.

act [ækt] **1** *n* (*action*) acto *m*; (*parliamentary*) ley *f*; (*of play*) acto *m*; **a. of God** caso *m* de fuerza mayor. **2** *vt* (*part*) interpretar; (*character*) representar; **to a. the fool** hacer el tonto. **3** *vi* (*pretend*) fingir; (*behave*) comportarse; (*take action*) actuar; (*work*) funcionar.

• **act for** *vt* obrar en nombre de.

• **act out** *vt* exteriorizar.

• **act up** *vi fam* (*machine*) funcionar mal; (*child*) dar guerra.

action ['ækʃən] (*deed*) acción *f*; (*in war*) acción *f* de combate; **to be out of a.** (*person*) estar fuera de servicio; (*machine*) estar estropeado,-a; **to take a.** tomar medidas.

action replay repetición *f.*

active ['æktɪv] *a* activo,-a; (*energetic*) vigoroso,-a; (*interest*) vivo,-a.

ac'tivity actividad *f*; (*on street etc*) bullicio *m.*

actor ['æktə^r] actor *m.*

actress ['æktrɪs] actriz *f.*

actual ['æktʃʊəl] *a* verdadero,-a.

actually *adv* (*really*) en efecto; (*even*) incluso.

acute [əˈkjuːt] *a* agudo,-a; (*pain*) intenso,-a; (*hearing*) muy fino,-a.

ad [æd] *fam* anuncio *m*.

AD [eiˈdiː] *abbr of* **Anno Domini** después de Cristo, d.C.

adapt [əˈdæpt] **1** *vt* adaptar (**to** a). **2** *vi* adaptarse.

adaptable *a* **he's very a.** se amolda fácilmente a las circunstancias.

adapter, adaptor (*plug*) ladrón *m*.

add [æd] **1** *vt* (*numbers*) sumar; (*one thing to another*) añadir. **2** *vi* (*count*) sumar.

add in *vt* (*include*) incluir.

● **add to** *vt* aumentar.

● **add together** *vt* (*numbers*) sumar.

● **add up 1** *vt* (*numbers*) sumar. **2** *vi* **it doesn't a. up** no tiene sentido.

addict [ˈædɪkt] adicto,-a *mf*; **drug a.** drogadicto,-a *mf*; **television a.** teleadicto,-a *mf*.

a'ddicted *a* adicto,-a.

a'ddiction (*to gambling etc*) vicio *m*; (*to drugs*) adicción *f*.

addition [əˈdɪʃən] adición *f*; **in a. to** además de.

additional *a* adicional.

additive [ˈædɪtɪv] aditivo *m*.

address [əˈdres] **1** *n* (*on letter*) dirección *f*; (*speech*) discurso *m*. **2** *vt* (*letter*) dirigir; (*speak to*) dirigirse (**to** a).

adenoids [ˈædɪnɔɪdz] *npl* vegetaciones *fpl* (adenoideas).

adequate [ˈædɪkwɪt] *a* (*enough*) suficiente; (*satisfactory*) adecuado,-a.

adequately *adv* suficientemente.

adhesive [ədˈhiːsɪv] **1** *a* adhesivo,-a. **2** *n* adhesivo *m*.

adjective [ˈædʒɪktɪv] adjetivo *m*.

adjust [əˈdʒʌst] **1** *vt* (*machine etc*) ajustar; (*methods*) variar. **2** *vi* (*person*) adaptarse (**to** a).

adjustable *a* ajustable.

adjustment (*by person*) adaptación *f*; (*change*) modificación *f*.

administer [ədˈmɪnɪstəʳ] *vt* (*country*) gobernar; (*justice*) administrar.

admini'stration (*of country*) gobierno *m*; (*of justice*) administración *f*.

ad'ministrative *a* administrativo,-a.

admiral [ˈædmərəl] almirante *m*.

admi'ration admiración *f*.

admire [ədˈmaɪəʳ] *vt* admirar.

admission [ədˈmɪʃən] (*to school etc*) ingreso *m*; (*price*) entrada *f*; (*of fact*) reconocimiento *m*.

admit [ədˈmɪt] *vt* (*person*) dejar entrar; (*crime, guilt*) confesar.

admittance (*entry*) entrada *f*.

adolescent [ædəˈlesənt] adolescente *mf*.

adopt [ə'dɒpt] *vt* adoptar.

adopted *a* **a. child** hijo,-a *mf* adoptivo,-a.

adoption adopción *f*.

adorable *a* adorable.

adore [ə'dɔ:ʳ] *vt* adorar.

adult ['ædʌlt] **1** *n* (*person*) adulto,-a *mf*. **2** *a* (*film, education*) para adultos.

advance [əd'vɑ:ns] **1** *n* (*movement*) avance *m*; (*progress*) progreso *m*; **in a.** de antemano. **2** *a* (*before time*) adelantado,-a; **a. payment** pago *m* por adelantado. **3** *vt* (*troops*) avanzar; (*time, date*) adelantar; (*idea*) proponer; (*loan*) prestar. **4** *vi* (*move forward, make progress*) avanzar.

advanced [əd'vɑ:nst] *a* (*developed*) avanzado,-a; (*student*) adelantado, -a; (*course*) superior; **A. level** ≈ COU *m*.

advantage [əd'vɑ:ntɪdʒ] ventaja *f*; **to take a. of sb** abusar de algn; **to take a. of sth** aprovechar algo.

adventure [əd'ventʃəʳ] aventura *f*.

adventurous *a* (*character*) aventurero,-a; (*bold*) atrevido, -a.

adverb ['ædvɜːb] adverbio *m*.

advert ['ædvɜːt] anuncio *m*.

advertise ['ædvətaɪz] **1** *vt* anunciar. **2** *vi* hacer publicidad; (*in newspaper*) poner un anuncio; **to a. for sth/sb** buscar algo/a algn mediante un anuncio.

advertisement [əd'vɜːtɪsmənt] anuncio *m*; **advertisements** publicidad *f sing*.

advice [əd'vaɪs] consejos *mpl*; **a piece of a.** un consejo.

advisable *a* aconsejable.

advise [əd'vaɪz] *vt* aconsejar; (*on business etc*) asesorar.

● **advise against** *vt* desaconsejar.

adviser consejero,-a *mf*; (*in business etc*) asesor,-a *mf*.

aerial ['eərɪəl] antena *f*.

aerobics [eə'rəʊbɪks] aerobic *m*.

aeroplane ['eərəpleɪn] avión *m*.

aerosol ['eərəsɒl] aerosol *m*.

affair [ə'feəʳ] (*matter*) asunto *m*; **business affairs** negocios *mpl*; **love a.** aventura *f* amorosa.

affect [ə'fekt] *vt* (*person, health*) afectar; (*prices, future*) influir en.

affection afecto *m*.

affectionate [ə'fekʃənɪt] *a* cariñoso,-a.

affluent ['æflʊənt] *a* (*society*) opulento,-a; (*person*) rico,-a.

afford [ə'fɔːd] *vt* (*be able to buy*) permitirse el lujo de.

affordable *a* (*price etc*) asequible.

afloat [ə'fləʊt] *adv* **to keep a.** mantenerse a flote.

afraid [əˈfreɪd] *a* **to be a.** tener miedo (*of sb* a algn; *of sth* de algo); **I'm a. of it** me da miedo; **I'm a. not/so** me temo que no/sí.

African [ˈæfrɪkən] *a & n* africano,-a (*mf*).

after [ˈɑːftəʳ] **1** *adv* después; **the day a.** el día siguiente. **2** *prep* (*later*) después de; (*behind*) detrás de; *US* **it's half a. five** son las cinco y media; **the day a. tomorrow** pasado mañana; **a. you!** ¡pase usted!; **they asked a. you** preguntaron por ti; **what's he a.?** ¿qué pretende?; **he takes a. his uncle** se parece a su tío. **3** *conj* después (de) que; **a. it happened** después de que ocurrió.

after-effects *npl* consecuencias *fpl*; (*of drug*) efectos *mpl* secundarios.

after'noon tarde *f*; **good a.!** ¡buenas tardes!; **in the a.** por la tarde.

after-sales service servicio *m* posventa.

aftershave (lotion) loción *f* para después del afeitado.

afterwards [ˈɑːftəwədz] *adv* después.

again [əˈgen] *adv* otra vez; **a. and a.** repetidas veces; **to do sth a.** volver a hacer algo; **never a.!** ¡nunca más!; **now and a.** de vez en cuando.

against [əˈgenst] *prep* contra; **a. the law** ilegal.

age [eɪdʒ] **1** *n* edad *f*; *fam* (*long time*) eternidad *f*; **she's 18 years of a.** tiene 18 años; **under a.** menor de edad; **old a.** vejez *f*; **the Iron A.** la Edad del Hierro. **2** *vti* envejecer.

aged[1] [ˈeɪdʒd] *a* de *or* a la edad de.

aged[2] [ˈeɪdʒɪd] *npl* **the a.** los ancianos.

agency [ˈeɪdʒənsɪ] agencia *f*.

agenda [əˈdʒendə] orden *m* del día.

agent [ˈeɪdʒənt] agente *mf*; (*representative*) representante *mf*.

aggravate [ˈægrəveɪt] *vt* (*worsen*) agravar; (*annoy*) molestar.

aggression agresión *f*.

aggressive [əˈgresɪv] *a* agresivo,-a.

agile [ˈædʒaɪl] *a* ágil.

agitated [ˈædʒɪteɪtɪd] *a* inquieto.

ago [əˈgəʊ] *adv* **a week a.** hace una semana; **how long a.?** ¿hace cuánto tiempo?

agony [ˈægənɪ] dolor *m* muy fuerte; (*mental*) angustia *f*.

agree [əˈgriː] *vi* (*be in agreement*) estar de acuerdo; (*reach agreement*) ponerse de acuerdo; **to a. to do sth** consentir en hacer algo; **onions don't a. with me** la cebolla no me sienta bien.

● **agree (up)on** *vt* (*decide*) ponerse de acuerdo en.

agreeable *a* (*pleasant*) agradable; (*person*) simpático,-a; (*in agreement*) de acuerdo.

agreed *a* (*time, place*) acordado.

agreement (*arrangement*) acuerdo *m*; (*contract etc*) contrato *m*.

agri'cultural *a* agrícola.

agriculture ['ægrɪkʌltʃər] agricultura *f*.

ahead [ə'hed] *adv* delante; (*early*) antes; **go a.!** ¡adelante!; **to be a.** (*in race etc*) llevar la ventaja; **to look a.** pensar en el futuro.

aid [eɪd] **1** *n* ayuda *f*; (*rescue*) auxilio *m*; **in a.** of a beneficio de. **2** *vt* ayudar.

Aids [eɪdz] SIDA *m*.

aim [eɪm] **1** *n* (*with weapon*) puntería *f*; (*objective*) propósito *m*. **2** *vti* (*gun*) apuntar (**at a**, hacia).

● **aim at** *vt* (*target*) apuntar a.

● **aim to** *vt* **to a. to do sth** tener la intención de hacer algo.

air [eər] **1** *n* aire *m*; **to travel by a.** viajar en avión; **to be on the a.** (*programme*) estar emitiendo. **2** *vt* (*bed, clothes*) airear; (*room*) ventilar.

air-conditioned *a* climatizado,-a.

air conditioning aire *m* acondicionado.

aircraft *inv* avión *m*.

aircraft carrier portaviones *m inv*.

air fare precio *m* del billete de avión.

air force fuerzas *fpl* aéreas.

air freshener ambientador *m*.

air hostess azafata *f*.

air letter carta *f* aérea.

airline línea *f* aérea.

airline ticket billete *m* de avión.

airmail correo *m* aéreo; **by a.** por avión.

airplane *US* avión *m*.

airport aeropuerto *m*.

air raid ataque *m* aéreo.

airsickness mareos *mpl* (del avión).

air terminal terminal *f* aérea.

airtight *a* hermético,-a.

air traffic control control *m* de tráfico aéreo.

air traffic controller controlador *m* aéreo.

aisle [aɪl] (*in church*) nave *f*; (*in theatre*) pasillo *m*.

ajar [ə'dʒɑːr] *a* & *adv* entreabierto,-a.

alarm [ə'lɑːm] **1** *n* alarma *f*; (*fear*) inquietud *f*. **2** *vt* alarmar.

alarm clock despertador *m*.

album ['ælbəm] álbum *m*.

alcohol ['ælkəhɒl] alcohol *m*.

alco'holic *a* & *n* alcohólico,-a (*mf*).

alert [ə'lɜːt] **1** *a* alerta; (*lively*) despabilado,-a. **2** *n* alerta *m*.

A-level ['eɪlevəl] *Br Educ abbr of* **Advanced level** ≈ Curso *m* de Orientación Universitaria, CKU *m*.

algebra ['ældʒɪbrə] álgebra *f.*

Algerian [æl'dʒɪərɪən] *a & n* argelino,-a (*mf*).

alibi ['ælɪbaɪ] coartada *f.*

alien ['eɪlɪən] *a & n* extranjero,-a (*mf*); (*from space*) extraterrestre *mf.*

alight [ə'laɪt] *a* (*on fire*) ardiendo,-a.

alike [ə'laɪk] **1** *a* (*similar*) parecidos,-as; (*the same*) iguales. **2** *adv* (*in the same way*) de la misma manera, igualmente.

alive [ə'laɪv] *a* vivo,-a; *fig* (*teeming*) lleno,-a (**with** de).

all [ɔːl] **1** *a* todo,-a, todos,-as; **a. year** (durante) todo el año; **a. kinds of things** todo tipo de cosas; **at a. times** siempre; **a. six of us were there** los seis estábamos allí. **2** *pron* todo,-a, todos,-as; **after a.** al fin y al cabo; **a. who saw it** todos los que lo vieron; **it's a. you can do** es lo único que puedes hacer; **I don't like it at a.** no me gusta en absoluto; **most of a., above a.** sobre todo; **once and for a.** de una vez para siempre; **thanks – not at a.** gracias – de nada; **a. in a.** en conjunto; **that's a.** ya está; **the score was one a.** empataron a uno; **it's still 3 a.** siguen empatados a tres. **3** *adv* **a. by myself** completamente solo,-a; **a. at once** (*suddenly*) de repente; (*altogether*) de una vez; **a. the better** tanto mejor; **a. the same** de todos modos; **if it's a. the same to you** si no te importa. **4** *n* **to give one's a.** darse por completo.

allergic [ə'lɜːdʒɪk] *a* alérgico,-a (**to** a).

alley ['ælɪ] callejón *m.*

alleyway callejón *m.*

alliance [ə'laɪəns] alianza *f.*

alligator ['ælɪgeɪtəʳ] caimán *m.*

all-in *a* (*price*) todo incluido; **a. wrestling** lucha *f* libre.

allocate ['æləkeɪt] *vt* destinar (**to** para).

allotment [ə'lɒtmənt] (*land*) parcela *f.*

all-out *a* (*effort*) supremo,-a; (*attack*) concentrado,-a.

allow [ə'laʊ] *vt* (*permit*) permitir; (*a request*) acceder a; (*allot*) (*time*) dejar; (*money*) destinar; **you're not allowed to do that** no puedes hacer eso; **I wasn't allowed to go** no me dejaron ir.

● **allow for** *vt* tener en cuenta.

allowance (*payment*) subsidio *m*; (*discount*) descuento *m*; **to make allowances for sb** disculpar a algn; **travel a.** dietas *fpl* de viaje.

all-purpose *a* (*tool*) multiuso, de uso universal.

all right 1 *a* (*okay*) bien; **thank you very much – that's a.** muchas gracias – de nada. **2** *adv* (*well*) bien; (*definitely*) sin duda; (*okay*) de acuerdo.

all-round *a* (*athlete etc*) completo,-a.

ally ['ælaɪ] aliado,-a *mf.*

almond ['ɑːmənd] almendra *f.*

almost ['ɔːlməʊst] *adv* casi.

alone [ə'ləʊn] **1** *a* solo,-a; **let a.** ni mucho menos; **leave it a.!** toques!; **leave me a.** déjame en paz. **2** *adv* solamente.

along [ə'lɒŋ] **1** *adv* **come a.!** ¡anda, ven!; **a. with** junto con. **2** *prep* (*the length of*) a lo largo de; **to walk a. the street** andar por la calle.

along'side 1 *adv* de costado. **2** *prep* al lado de.

aloud [ə'laʊd] *adv* en voz alta.

alphabet ['ælfəbet] alfabeto *m*.

alpha'betical *a* alfabético,-a.

alpha'betically *adv* por orden alfabético.

Alps ['ælps] *npl* **the A.** los Alpes.

already [ɔːl'redɪ] *adv* ya.

alright [ɔːl'raɪt] *a & adv* = **all right.**

Alsatian [æl'seɪʃən] pastor *m* alemán.

also ['ɔːlsəʊ] *adv* también.

altar ['ɔːltəʳ] altar *m*.

alter ['ɔːltəʳ] **1** *vt* (*plan*) cambiar; (*law, draft etc*) modificar. **2** *vi* cambiar(se).

alte'ration (*to plan*) cambio *m*; (*to law etc*) modificación *f*; (*to time-table*) revisión *f*.

alternate [ɔːl'tɜːnɪt] **1** *a* alterno,-a; **on a. days** cada dos días. **2** ['ɔːltəneɪt] *vt* alternar; **a alternates with b** a alterna con b.

alternately *adv* **a. hot and cold** ahora caliente, ahora frío.

alternative [ɔːl'tɜːnətɪv] **1** *a* alternativo,-a. **2** *n* alternativa *f*; **I have no a.** no tengo más remedio.

alternatively *adv* o bien.

although [ɔːl'ðəʊ] *conj* aunque.

altogether [ɔːltə'geðəʳ] *adv* (*in total*) en total; (*completely*) completamente.

aluminium [æljʊ'mɪnɪəm], *US* **aluminum** [ə'luːmɪnəm] aluminio *m*.

always ['ɔːlweɪz] *adv* siempre.

am [æm] *1st person sing pres of* **be.**

a.m. [eɪ'em] *abbr of* **ante meridiem** de la mañana; **2 a.m.** las dos de la mañana.

amateur ['æmətəʳ] **1** *n* aficionado,-a *mf*. **2** *a* aficionado,-a; (*pejorative*) chapucero,-a.

amaze [ə'meɪz] *vt* asombrar; **to be amazed at sth** quedar pasmado,-a de algo.

amazing *a* asombroso,-a.

ambassador [æm'bæsədəʳ] embajador,-a *mf*.

amber ['æmbəʳ] *a* (*traffic light*) amarillo,-a.

ambition [æm'bɪʃən] ambición *f*.

ambitious *a* ambicioso,-a.

ambulance ['æmbjʊləns] ambulancia *f*; **a. man** ambulanciero *m*.

American [ə'merɪkən] *a* & *n* americano,-a (*mf*); (*of USA*) norteamericano,-a (*mf*), estadounidense (*mf*).

ammunition [æmjʊ'nɪʃən] municiones *fpl*.

among(st) [ə'mʌŋ(st)] *prep* entre.

amorous ['æmərəs] *a* (*person*) ligón,-ona; (*feelings, relationship*) amoroso.

amount [ə'maʊnt] cantidad *f*; (*of money*) suma *f*; (*of bill*) importe *m*.
* **amount to** *vt* ascender a; (*be equivalent to*) equivaler a.

ample ['æmpəl] *a* (*enough*) bastante; (*more than enough*) abundante; (*large*) amplio,-a.

amplifier ['æmplɪfaɪə'] amplificador *m*.

amputate ['æmpjʊteɪt] *vt* amputar.

amuse [ə'mju:z] *vt* divertir.

amusement diversión *f*.

amusement arcade salón *m* de juegos.

amusing *a* divertido,-a.

an [æn, *unstressed* ən] *indef art see* **a.**

anaesthetic [ænɪs'θetɪk] anestesia *f*.

analyse ['ænəlaɪz] *vt* analizar.

analysis [ə'nælɪsɪs] (*pl* **analyses** [ə'nælɪsi:z]) análisis *m inv*.

anarchy ['ænəkɪ] anarquía *f*.

anatomy [ə'nætəmɪ] anatomía *f*.

ancestor ['ænsestə'] antepasado *m*.

anchor ['æŋkə'] **1** *n* ancla *f*. **2** *vt* anclar; *fig* (*fix securely*) sujetar.

anchovy ['æntʃəvɪ] anchoa *f*.

ancient ['eɪnʃənt] *a* antiguo,-a.

and [ænd, *unstressed* ən(d)] *conj* y; (*before stressed i-, hi-*) e; **a hundred a. one** ciento uno; **a. so on** etcétera; **come a. see us** ven a vernos; **she cried a. cried** no paró de llorar; **try a. help me** trata de ayudarme; **wait a. see** espera a ver; **worse a. worse** cada vez peor.

anesthetic [ænɪs'θetɪk] *US* anestesia *f*.

angel ['eɪndʒəl] ángel *m*.

anger ['æŋgə'] cólera *f*.

angle ['æŋgəl] ángulo *m*; (*point of view*) punto *m* de vista.

angler ['æŋglə'] pescador,-a *mf* de caña.

angling pesca *f* con caña.

angrily *adv* furiosamente.

angry ['æŋgrɪ] *a* enfadado,-a; **to get a.** enfadarse.

animal ['ænɪməl] *a* & *n* animal (*m*).

ankle ['æŋkəl] tobillo *m*; **a. socks** calcetines *mpl* cortos.

annexe, US annex ['æneks] (*building*) (edificio *m*) anexo *m*.

anniversary [ænɪˈvɜːsərɪ] aniversario *m*.

announce [əˈnaʊns] *vt* anunciar; (*news*) comunicar.

announcement anuncio *m*; (*news*) comunicación *f*; (*statement*) declaración *f*.

announcer (*on TV*) locutor,-a *mf*.

annoy [əˈnɔɪ] *vt* molestar; **to get annoyed** molestarse.

annoying *a* molesto,-a.

annual [ˈænjʊəl] **1** *a* anual. **2** *n* (*book*) anuario *m*.

annually *adv* anualmente.

anonymous [əˈnɒnɪməs] *a* anónimo,-a.

anorak [ˈænəræk] anorak *m*.

another [əˈnʌðəʳ] **1** *a* otro,-a; **a. one** otro,-a; **a. 15** otros quince. **2** *pron* otro,-a; **to love one a.** quererse el uno al otro.

answer [ˈɑːnsəʳ] **1** *n* (*to letter etc*) contestación *f*; (*to question*) respuesta *f*; (*to problem*) solución *f*; **there's no a.** (*on telephone*) no contestan; (*at door*) no abren. **2** *vt* contestar a; (*problem*) resolver; (*door*) abrir; (*phone*) contestar. **3** *vi* contestar.

● **answer back** *vi* replicar; **don't a. back!** ¡no repliques!

● **answer for** *vt* responder de; **he's got a lot to a. for** es responsable de muchas cosas.

● **answer to** *vt* (*name*) responder a; (*description*) corresponder a.

answering machine contestador *m* automático.

ant [ænt] hormiga *f*.

Antarctic [æntˈɑːktɪk] **1** *a* antártico,-a; **A. Ocean** océano *m* Antártico. **2** *n* **the A.** La Antártica.

antelope [ˈæntɪləʊp] antílope *m*.

antenna [ænˈtenə] (*pl* **antennae** [ænˈteniː]) antena *f*.

anthem [ˈænθəm] **national a.** himno *m* nacional.

anthology [ænˈθɒlədʒɪ] antología *f*.

antibiotic [æntɪbaɪˈɒtɪk] *a & n* antibiótico,-a (*m*).

antibody anticuerpo *m*.

anticipate [ænˈtɪsɪpeɪt] *vt* (*expect*) esperar; (*problems*) anticipar.

antici'pation (*excitement*) ilusión *f*.

anti'clockwise *adv* en sentido contrario a las agujas del reloj.

antics [ˈæntɪks] *npl* payasadas *fpl*; (*naughtiness*) travesuras *fpl*.

antifreeze anticongelante *m*.

antihistamine [æntɪˈhɪstəmɪn] *n* antihistamínico *m*.

antique [ænˈtiːk] **1** *a* antiguo,-a. **2** *n* antiguedad *f*.

antique dealer anticuario,-a *mf*.

antique shop tienda *f* de antiguedades.

antiseptic [æntɪˈseptɪk] *a & n* antiséptico,-a (*m*).

anxiety [æŋˈzaɪɪtɪ] (*concern*) inquietud *f*; (*worry*) preocupación *f*;

(eagerness) ansia *f*.

anxious ['æŋkʃəs] *a (concerned)* inquieto,-a; *(worried)* preocupado,-a; *(fearful)* angustiado,-a; *(eager)* ansioso,-a.

anxiously *adv (to wait)* con impaciencia.

any ['enɪ] **1** *a (in questions, conditionals)* algún,-una; **are there a. seats left?** ¿quedan plazas?; **is there a. water left?** ¿queda agua?; **if you see a. blouses you like** se ves algunos blusas que te gusten. ∥ *(in negative clauses)* ningún,-una; **there aren't a. others** no hay otros. ∥ *(no matter which)* cualquier,-a; *(every)* todo,-a; **a. doctor will say the same** cualquier médico te dirá lo mismo; **at a. moment** en cualquier momento; **in a. case** de todas formas. **2** *pron (in questions, conditionals)* alguno,-a; **do they have a.?** ¿tienen alguno?; **I need some paper, have you a.?** necesito papel, ¿tienes?; **if you see a., let me know** si ves alguno,-a, dímelo. ∥ *(in negative clauses)* ninguno,-a; **I don't want a.** no quiero ninguno,-a. ∥ *(no matter which)* cualquiera; **a. of them will do** cualquiera vale. **3** *adv* **is there a. more?** ¿hay más?; **not a. more/longer** ya no; **is that a. better?** ¿está mejor así?

anybody *pron (in questions, conditionals)* alguien; *(in negative clauses)* nadie; *(no matter who)* cualquiera; **bring a. you like** trae a quien quieras.

anyhow *adv (in spite of that)* de todas formas; *(changing the subject)* bueno; *(carelessly)* de cualquier forma.

anyone *pron* = **anybody**.

anyplace *adv US* = **anywhere**.

anything *pron (in questions, conditionals)* algo, alguna cosa; *(in negative clauses)* nada; *(no matter what)* cualquier cosa; **a. but that** cualquier cosa menos eso; **a. else?** ¿algo más?; **hardly a.** casi nada; **to run/work like a.** correr/trabajar a más no poder.

anyway *adv* = **anyhow**.

anywhere *adv (in questions, conditionals) (position)* en alguna parte; *(movement)* a alguna parte; **could it be a. else?** ¿podría estar en otro sitio? ∥ *(in negative clauses) (position)* en ninguna parte; *(movement)* a ninguna parte. ∥ *(no matter where)* en cualquier parte; **go a. you like** ve a donde quieras.

apart [ə'pɑːt] *adv* **you should keep them a.** debes matenerlos aparte; **to fall a.** deshacerse; **to take sth a.** desmontar algo; **with his feet a.** con los pies separados; **a. from** aparte de.

apartment [ə'pɑːtmənt] *US (flat)* piso *m*; **a. block** bloque *m* de pisos.

apartment house casa *f* de pisos.

ape [eɪp] mono *m*.

aperitif [ə'perɪtiːf] aperitivo *m*.

apologetic [əpɒlə'dʒetɪk] *a* **he was very a.** pidió mil perdones.

apologize [ə'pɒlədʒaɪz] *vi* disculparse *(for* por).

apology [ə'pɒlədʒɪ] disculpa *f*.

apostrophe [ə'pɒstrəfɪ] apóstrofo *m*.

appal, *US* **appall** [ə'pɔːl] *vt* horrorizar.

appalling *a* (*horrifying*) horroroso,-a; (*very bad*) fatal.

apparatus [æpə'reɪtəs] aparato *m*; (*equipment*) equipo *m*.

apparent [ə'pærənt] *a* (*obvious*) evidente; (*seeming*) aparente; **to become a.** ponerse de manifiesto.

apparently *adv* (*seemingly*) por lo visto.

appeal [ə'piːl] 1 *n* (*request*) solicitud *f*; (*plea*) súplica *f*; (*interest*) interés *m*; (*in law*) apelación *f*. 2 *vi* (*plead*) rogar (**to** a); **to a. for help** solicitar ayuda; **it doesn't a. to me** no me dice nada.

appear [ə'pɪə'] *vi* (*become visible*) aparecer; (*publicly*) presentarse; (*seem*) parecer; **so it appears** según parece.

appearance (*becoming visible*) aparición *f*; (*publicly*) presentación *f*; (*of book etc*) publicación *f*; (*look*) aspecto *m*; **to all appearances** al parecer.

appendicitis [əpendɪ'saɪtɪs] apendicitis *f*.

appendix [ə'pendɪks] (*pl* **appendices** [ə'pendɪsiːz]) apéndice *m*.

appetite ['æpɪtaɪt] apetito *m*; (*sexual*) deseo *m*; **he's lost his a. for this sort of job** se le han quitado los ganas de un trabajo de este tipo.

appetizing *a* apetitoso.

applaud [ə'plɔːd] *vti* aplaudir.

applause [ə'plɔːz] aplausos *mpl*.

apple ['æpəl] manzana *f*; **a. pie** tarta *f* manzana; **a. tree** manzano *m*.

appliance [ə'plaɪəns] dispositivo *m*.

applicant ['æplɪkənt] (*for post*) candidato,-a *mf*.

application (*of cream*) aplicación *f*; (*for post etc*) solicitud *f*; **a. form** solicitud *f*.

apply [ə'plaɪ] 1 *vt* aplicar; (*brake*) echar; (*law*) recurrir a; (*force*) usar; **to a. oneself to sth** dedicarse a algo. 2 *vi* (*for job*) presentar una solicitud.

● **apply for** *vt* (*post, information*) solicitar.

appoint [ə'pɔɪnt] *vt* (*person*) nombrar.

appointment (*to post*) nombramiento *m*; (*meeting*) cita *f*.

appreciate [ə'priːʃeɪt] 1 *vt* (*be thankful for*) agradecer; (*understand*) entender; (*value*) apreciar. 2 *vi* (*increase in value*) apreciarse.

appreci'ation (*of help, advice*) agradecimiento *m*; (*of difficulty*) comprensión *f*; (*increase in value*) apreciación *f*.

apprentice [ə'prentɪs] aprendiz,-a *mf*.

apprenticeship aprendizaje *m*.

approach [ə'prəʊtʃ] 1 *n* (*coming near*) acercamiento *m*; (*to town*) acceso *m*; (*to problem*) enfoque *m*. 2 *vt* (*come near to*) acercarse a; (*problem*) abordar. 3 *vi* acercarse.

appropriate [ə'prəʊprɪt] *a* (*suitable*) apropiado,-a; (*convenient*) oportuno,-a.

appropriately *adv* adecuadamente.

approval aprobación *f*; **on a.** sin compromiso de compra.

approve [ə'pruːv] *vt* aprobar.

● **approve of** *vt* aprobar.

approximate [ə'prɒksɪmɪt] *a* aproximado,-a.

approximately *adv* aproximadamente.

apricot ['eɪprɪkɒt] albaricoque *m*.

April ['eɪprəl] abril *m*; **A. Fools' Day** día *m* uno de abril, ≈ día de los Inocentes (28 de diciembre).

apron ['eɪprən] delantal *m*.

apt [æpt] *a* (*suitable*) apropiado,-a; (*description*) exacto,-a; **to be a. to do sth** (*liable*) tener tendencia a hacer algo.

aptitude ['æptɪtjuːd] capacidad *f*.

aquarium [ə'kweərɪəm] acuario *m*.

Arab ['ærəb] *a & n* árabe (*mf*).

Arabian [ə'reɪbɪən] *a* árabe.

Arabic **1** *a* árabe; **A. numerals** numeración arábiga. **2** *n* (*language*) árabe *m*.

arc [ɑːk] arco *m*.

arcade [ɑː'keɪd] arcada *f*; **shopping a.** galerías *fpl* (comerciales).

arch [ɑːtʃ] **1** *n* (*of bridge etc*) arco *m*; (*roof*) bóveda *f*. **2** *vt* (*back*) arquear.

archer ['ɑːtʃəʳ] arquero,-a *mf*.

archery tiro *m* con arco.

architect ['ɑːkɪtekt] arquitecto,-a *mf*.

architecture arquitectura *f*.

arctic ['ɑːktɪk] **the A.** el Ártico.

are [ɑːʳ] *2nd person sing pres, 1st, 2nd, 3rd person pl pres of* **be.**

area ['eərɪə] zona *f*; (*of surface*) superficie *f*.

area code prefijo *m* local.

Argentinian [ɑːdʒən'tɪnɪən] *a & n* argentino,-a (*mf*).

argue ['ɑːgjuː] **1** *vi* (*quarrel*) discutir; (*reason*) argumentar. **2** *vt* discutir; (*point of view*) mantener; **to a. that ...** sostener que ...

argument (*quarrel*) discusión *f*, disputa *f*; (*reason*) argumento *m* (**for** a favor de; **against** en contra de).

arise* [ə'raɪz] *vi* (*get up*) levantarse; (*problem, need*) surgir.

arithmetic [ə'rɪθmətɪk] aritmética *f*.

arm [ɑːm] **1** *n* brazo *m*; (*of garment*) manga *f*; **arms** (*weapons*) armas *fpl*. **2** *vt* armar.

armband brazalete *m*; (*for swimming*) manguito *m*.

armchair sillón *m*.

armour, *US* **armor** ['ɑːməʳ] (*of tank etc*) blindaje *m*; (**suit of**) **a.**

armadura *f*.
armoured car, *US* **armored car** coche *m* blindado.
armpit axila *f*.
army ['ɑːmɪ] ejército *m*.
around [ə'raʊnd] **1** *adv* alrededor; **all a.** por todos lados. **2** *prep* alrededor de; (*approximately*) aproximadamente; **a. the corner** a la vuelta de la esquina; **a. here** por aquí.
arrange [ə'reɪndʒ] **1** *vt* (*order*) ordenar; (*hair, flowers*) arreglar; (*music*) adaptar; (*plan*) organizar; (*agree on*) quedar en; **to a. a time** fijar una hora. **2** *vi* **I shall a. for him to be there** lo arreglaré para que pueda asistir.
arrangement (*display*) colocación *f*; (*of music*) adaptación *f*; (*agreement*) acuerdo *m*; **arrangements** (*plans*) planes *mpl*.
arrears [ə'rɪəz] *npl* atrasos *mpl*; **to be paid in a.** cobrar con retraso; **salaries are paid monthly in a.** los salarios se pagan mensualmente con un mes de retraso.
arrest [ə'rest] **1** *n* detención *f*; **to be under a.** estar detenido,-a. **2** *vt* (*criminal*) detener.
arrival llegada *f*.
arrive [ə'raɪv] *vi* llegar (**at, in** a).
arrow ['ærəʊ] flecha *f*.
art [ɑːt] arte *m*; (*drawing*) dibujo *m*; **arts** (*branch of knowledge*) letras *fpl*.
artery ['ɑːtərɪ] arteria *f*.
arthritis [ɑː'θraɪtɪs] artritis *f*.
article ['ɑːtɪkəl] artículo *m*.
articulate [ɑː'tɪkjʊleɪt] *vti* articular; (*words*) pronunciar.
artificial [ɑːtɪ'fɪʃəl] *a* artificial.
artist ['ɑːtɪst] artista *mf*; (*painter*) pintor,-a *mf*.
ar'tistic *a* artístico,-a.
as [æz, *unstressed* əz] *adv & conj* (*comparison*) **as … as …** tan … como …; **as far as** hasta; **as far as I'm concerned** por lo que a mí respecta; **as many as** tantos,-as como; **as much as** tanto,-a como; **as opposed to** a diferencia de; **as little as £5** tan sólo cinco libras; **as soon as they arrive** en cuanto lleguen; **I'll stay as long as I can** me quedaré todo el tiempo que pueda; **just as big as** igual de grande; **three times as fast** tres veces más rápido; **the same as** igual que. ‖ (*manner*) como; **as you like** como quieras; **leave it as it is** déjalo tal como está; **do as I say** haz lo que yo te digo; **it serves as a table** sirve de mesa; **she was dressed as a gypsy** iba vestida de gitana; **to act as if** actuar como si (+ *subjunctive*). ‖ (*time*) mientras; **as a child** de niño,-a; **as I was eating** mientras comía; **as we were leaving we saw Pat** al salir vimos a Pat; **as from, as of** a partir de. ‖ (*because*) como, ya que; **as it is getting late** ya que se está haciendo tarde. ‖ (*and so*) igual que; **as I do** igual que yo; **as well** también.

‖ (*concerning*) **as for my brother** en cuanto a mi hermano.

asap [eɪeseɪˈpiː] *abbr* (*as soon as possible*) lo antes posible.

ash[1] [æʃ] (*tree*) fresno *m*.

ash[2] ceniza *f*.

ashamed [əˈʃeɪmd] *a* avergonzado,-a; **you ought to be a. of yourself!** ¿no te da vergüenza?

ashcan *US* cubo *m* de la basura.

ashore [əˈʃɔː'] *adv* en tierra; **to go a.** desembarcar.

ashtray cenicero *m*.

Ash Wednesday miércoles *m inv* de ceniza.

Asian [ˈeɪʃən] *a & n* asiático,-a (*mf*).

aside [əˈsaɪd] **1** *adv* aparte; **to stand a.** apartarse. **2** *prep* **a. from** (*apart from*) aparte de; (*as well as*) además de. **3** *n* aparte *m*.

ask [ɑːsk] **1** *vt* preguntar; (*request*) pedir; (*invite*) invitar; **to a. sb a question** preguntar algo a algn; **to a. sb how to do sth** preguntar a algn cómo se hace algo. **2** *vi* (*inquire*) preguntar; (*request*) pedir.

● **ask after** *vt* preguntar por.

● **ask for** *vt* (*help*) pedir; (*person*) preguntar por; **to a. sb for sth** pedir algo a algn.

asleep [əˈsliːp] *a* dormido,-a; **to fall a.** quedarse dormido,-a.

asparagus [əˈspærəgəs] *inv* espárragos *mpl*.

aspect [ˈæspekt] aspecto *m*.

aspirin [ˈæsprɪn] aspirina *f*.

assault [əˈsɔːlt] **1** *n* ataque *m* (**on** a); (*crime*) agresión *f*. **2** *vt* atacar; (*sexually*) violar.

assemble [əˈsembəl] **1** *vt* (*people*) reunir; (*furniture*) montar. **2** *vi* (*people*) reunirse.

assembly asamblea *f*; (*of machinery etc*) montaje *m*; **morning a.** servicio *m* matinal.

assess [əˈses] *vt* (*estimate value*) valorar; (*damages, price*) calcular; (*effect*) evaluar.

asset [ˈæset] ventaja *f*; **to be an a.** (*person*) ser de gran valor; **assets** activo *m*.

assign [əˈsaɪn] *vt* asignar.

assignment (*task*) tarea *f*.

assist [əˈsɪst] *vti* ayudar.

assistance ayuda *f*.

assistant ayudante *mf*; **a. manager** subdirector,-a *mf*; **shop a.** dependiente,-a *mf*.

associate[1] [əˈsəʊʃɪeɪt] **1** *vt* (*ideas*) relacionar. **2** *vi* **to a. with** tratar con.

associate[2] [əˈsəʊʃɪt] (*colleague*) colega *mf*; (*partner*) socio,-a *mf*; (*accomplice*) cómplice *mf*.

association asociación f; (*company*) sociedad f.

assorted [ə'sɔːtid] a surtido,-a.

assortment surtido m.

assume [ə'sjuːm] vt (*suppose*) suponer; (*power*) asumir; (*attitude, name*) adoptar.

assurance (*guarantee*) garantía f; (*confidence*) confianza f; (*insurance*) seguro m.

assure [ə'ʃʊəˈ] vt asegurar.

asterisk ['æstərisk] asterisco m.

asthma ['æsmə] asma f.

asth'matic a & n asmático,-a (mf).

astonish [ə'stɒniʃ] vt asombrar.

astonishing a asombroso,-a.

astray [ə'strei] adv to go a. extraviarse; *fig* equivocarse.

astrology [ə'strɒlədʒi] astrología f.

astronaut ['æstrənɔːt] astronauta mf.

astronomy [ə'strɒnəmi] astronomía f.

at [æt] prep (*position*) en, a; **at school/work** en el colegio/trabajo; **at the window** a la ventana; **at the top** en lo alto. ‖ (*direction*) a; **to look at sth/sb** mirar algo/a algn; **to shout at sb** gritarle a algn. ‖ (*time*) a; **at Easter/ Christmas** en Semana Santa/Navidad; **at six o'clock** a las seis. ‖ **at best/ worst** en el mejor/peor de los casos; **not at all** en absoluto; (*don't mention it*) de nada. ‖ (*rate*) a; **at 100 pesetas each** a 100 pesetas la unidad; **two at a time** de dos en dos.

athlete ['æθliːt] atleta mf.

athletic [æθ'letik] a atlético,-a; (*sporty*) deportista.

athletics npl atletismo m sing.

Atlantic [ət'læntik] **the A. (Ocean)** el (océano) Atlántico.

atlas ['ætləs] atlas m.

atmosphere ['ætməsfiəˈ] (*air*) atmósfera f; (*ambience*) ambiente m.

atom ['ætəm] átomo m; **a. bomb** bomba f atómica.

a'tomic a atómico,-a.

attach [ə'tætʃ] vt (*stick*) pegar; (*document*) adjuntar; **to be attached to** (*be fond of*) tener cariño a.

attaché [ə'tæʃei] agregado,-a mf; **a. case** maletín m.

attack [ə'tæk] **1** n ataque m. **2** vt (*assault*) atacar; (*problem*) abordar.

attacker agresor,-a mf.

attempt [ə'tempt] **1** n intento m; **at the second a.** a la segunda. **2** vt intentar.

attend [ə'tend] **1** vt (*school*) frecuentar; (*meeting*) asistir a. **2** vi (*at meeting*) asistir.

● **attend to** vt (*business*) ocuparse de; (*in shop*) atender a.

attendance asistencia *f*.

attendant (*in museum*) guía *mf*; (*in car park*) vigilante,-a *mf*.

attention [ə'tenʃən] atención *f*; **for the a. of** a la atención de.

attentive *a* (*listener*) atento,-a; (*helpful*) solícito,-a.

attic ['ætɪk] ático *m*.

attitude ['ætɪtjuːd] actitud *f*; (*position of body*) postura *f*.

attorney [ə'tɜːnɪ] *US* (*lawyer*) abogado,-a *mf*; **A. General** ≈ Ministro, -a *mf* de Justicia; **district a.** fiscal *mf*.

attract [ə'trækt] *vt* atraer; **to a. attention** llamar la atención.

attraction (*attractive thing*) atractivo *m*; (*charm*) encanto *m*.

attractive *a* (*person*) guapo,-a; (*idea, proposition*) atrayente.

aubergine ['əʊbəʒiːn] berenjena *f*.

auction ['ɔːkʃən] **1** *n* subasta *f*. **2** *vt* subastar.

auctio'neer subastador,-a *mf*.

audible ['ɔːdɪbəl] *a* audible.

audience ['ɔːdɪəns] (*spectators*) público *m*; (*at concert, conference*) auditorio *m*; (*television*) telespectadores *mpl*; (*meeting*) audiencia *f*.

audio ['ɔːdɪəʊ] *a* de sonido.

audio-visual [ɔːdɪəʊ'vɪzjʊəl] *a* audiovisual.

August ['ɔːgəst] agosto *m*.

aunt [ɑːnt] (*also fam* **auntie, aunty** ['ɑːntɪ]) tía *f*.

au pair [əʊ'peəʳ] **a. (girl)** au pair *f*.

Australian [ɒ'streɪlɪən] *a & n* australiano,-a (*mf*).

Austrian ['ɒstrɪən] *a & n* austríaco,-a (*mf*).

author ['ɔːθəʳ] autor,-a *mf*.

authority [ɔː'θɒrɪtɪ] autoridad *f*; **local a.** ayuntamiento *m*.

authorize ['ɔːθəraɪz] *vt* autorizar; (*payment etc*) aprobar.

autobiography [ɔːtəʊbaɪ'ɒgrəfɪ] autobiografía *f*.

autograph ['ɔːtəgrɑːf] **1** *n* autógrafo *m*. **2** *vt* (*book, photo*) dedicar.

automatic [ɔːtə'mætɪk] **1** *a* automático,-a. **2** *n* (*car*) coche *m* automático.

automatically *adv* automáticamente.

automobile ['ɔːtəməbiːl] *US* automóvil *m*, *Am* carro *m*.

autumn ['ɔːtəm] otoño *m*.

auxiliary [ɔːg'zɪljərɪ] *a* auxiliar.

available [ə'veɪləbəl] *a* (*thing*) disponible; (*person*) libre.

avalanche ['ævəlɑːnʃ] avalancha *f*.

avenue ['ævɪnjuː] avenida *f*; *fig* vía *f*.

average ['ævərɪdʒ] **1** *n* promedio *m*; **on a.** por término medio. **2** *a* medio,-a; (*middling*) regular.

aviation [eɪvɪ'eɪʃən] aviación *f*.

avocado [ævə'kɑːdəʊ] (*also* **avocado pear**) aguacate *m*.

avoid [ə'vɔɪd] *vt* evitar; **to a. doing sth** evitar hacer algo.
awake [ə'weɪk] **1** *a* despierto,-a. **2** *vi** despertarse.
award [ə'wɔːd] **1** *n* (*prize*) premio *m*; (*medal*) condecoración *f*; (*grant*) beca *f*. **2** *vt* (*prize*) otorgar; (*medal*) dar; (*damages*) adjudicar.
aware [ə'weəʳ] *a* (*informed*) enterado,-a; **not that I'm a.** of que yo sepa no; **to become a. of sth** darse cuenta de algo.
away [ə'weɪ] *adv* **far a.** lejos; **go a.!** ¡lárgate!; **it's 3 miles a.** está a 3 millas (de distancia); **keep a. from the fire!** ¡no te acerques al fuego!; **right a.** en seguida; **to be a.** (*absent*) estar ausente; **to go a.** irse; **to play a.** (*in sport*) jugar fuera; **to turn a.** volver la çara; **to chatter/work a.** hablar/trabajar sin parar.
awful ['ɔːfʊl] *a* espantoso,-a; *fam* **an a. lot of work** muchísimo trabajo.
awfully *adv fam* terriblemente.
awkward ['ɔːkwəd] *a* (*clumsy*) torpe; (*difficult*) pesado,-a; (*moment*) inoportuno,-a.
awning ['ɔːnɪŋ] (*on shop*) marquesina *f*.
axe, *US* **ax** [æks] **1** *n* hacha *f*. **2** *vt* (*jobs*) suprimir; (*cut back*) reducir; (*plan*) cancelar.
axle ['æksəl] eje *m*.

B

BA [biːˈeɪ] *abbr of* **Bachelor of Arts.**
baby [ˈbeɪbɪ] bebé *m*; (*young child*) niño,-a *mf*.
baby carriage *US* cochecito *m* de niño.
baby-sit *vi* hacer de canguro.
baby-sitter canguro *mf*.
bachelor [ˈbætʃələ] soltero *m*; **B. of Arts/Science** licenciado,-a *mf* en Filosofía y Letras/Ciencias.
back [bæk] **1** *n* (*of person*) espalda *f*; (*of chair*) respaldo *m*; (*of hand*) dorso *m*; (*of house, car*) parte *f* de atrás; (*of stage, cupboard*) fondo *m*; **b. to front** al revés. **2** *a* trasero,-a; **b. door** puerta *f* de atrás; **b. seat** asiento *m* de detrás; **b. wheel** rueda *f* trasera; **b. number** número *m* atrasado. **3** *adv* (*at the rear*) atrás; (*towards the rear*) hacia atrás. **4** *vt* (*support*) apoyar; (*financially*) financiar; (*bet on*) apostar por.
● **back out** *vi* (*withdraw*) volverse atrás.
● **back up** *vt* (*support*) apoyar a.
backache dolor *m* de espalda.
back'fire *vi* (*car*) petardear.
background fondo *m*; (*origin*) origen *m*; (*past*) pasado *m*; (*education*) formación *f*; (*circumstances*) antecedentes *mpl*; **b. music** hilo *m* musical.
backing (*support*) apoyo *m*; (*financial*) respaldo *m* financiero.
backlog to have a b. of work tener un montón de trabajo atrasado.
backside *fam* trasero *m*.
backstage *adv* entre bastidores.
backup (*of disk*) backup *m*.
backward [ˈbækwəd] **1** *a* (*movement*) hacia atrás; (*child, country*) retrasado,-a. **2** *adv* (hacia) atrás.
backwards *adv* hacia atrás; **to walk b.** andar de espaldas.
back'yard patio *m* trasero; *US* jardín *m* trasero.
bacon [ˈbeɪkən] tocino *m*, beicon *m*.
bad [bæd] *a* malo,-a; (*decayed*) podrido,-a; (*accident*) grave; (*headache*) fuerte; (*ill*) enfermo,-a.
badge [bædʒ] insignia *f*; (*metal disc*) chapa *f*.
badger [ˈbædʒə] tejón *m*.
badly *adv* mal; (*seriously*) gravemente; (*very much*) mucho; **we need it b.** nos hace mucha falta; **to be b. off** (*financially*) andar mal de dinero.
bad-mannered *a* maleducado.
badminton [ˈbædmɪntən] bádminton *m*.
bad-'tempered *a* **to be b.** (*temperament*) tener mal genio; (*temporarily*) estar de mal humor.
baffle [ˈbæfəl] *vt* desconcertar.

bag [bæg] (*plastic, paper, shopping*) bolsa *f*; (*handbag*) bolso *m*; *fam* **bags of** montones de; **bags** (*under eyes*) ojeras *fpl*.

baggage ['bægɪdʒ] equipaje *m*.

baggy ['bægɪ] *a* holgado,-a; **b. trousers** pantalones *mpl* anchos.

bagpipes *npl* gaita *f sing*.

bail [beɪl] fianza *f*; **on b.** bajo fianza.

bait [beɪt] cebo *m*.

bake [beɪk] *vt* cocer al horno.

baked ['beɪkt] *a* al horno; **b. potato** patata *f* asada.

baked beans alubias *fpl* cocidas en salsa de tomate.

baker panadero,-a *mf*.

bakery panadería *f*.

balance ['bæləns] **1** *n* (*equilibrium*) equilibrio *m*; (*financial*) saldo *m*; (*remainder*) resto *m*. **2** *vt* poner en equilibrio (**on** en); (*budget*) equilibrar. **3** *vi* guardar el equilibrio.

balance sheet balance *m*.

balcony ['bælkənɪ] balcón *m*.

bald [bɔːld] *a* calvo,-a.

baldness calvicie *f*.

Balkans ['bɔːlkənz] *npl* **the Balkans** los Balcanes.

ball¹ [bɔːl] (*in cricket, tennis etc*) pelota *f*; (*football*) balón *m*; (*in billiards, golf etc*) bola *f*; (*of wool*) ovillo *m*; **to be on the b.** *fam* ser un espabilado.

ball² (*dance*) baile *m*.

ballerina [bælə'riːnəʳ] bailarina *f*.

ballet ['bæleɪ] ballet *m*.

balloon [bə'luːn] globo *m*.

ballot ['bælət] votación *f*.

ballpoint (pen) bolígrafo *m*.

ballroom salón *m* de baile.

ban [bæn] **1** *n* prohibición *f*. **2** *vt* (*prohibit*) prohibir; (*exclude*) excluir.

banana [bə'nɑːnə] plátano *m*, *Am* banana *f*.

band [bænd] (*strip*) tira *f*; (*stripe*) raya *f*; (*group*) grupo *m*; (*of musicians*) banda *f*.

bandage ['bændɪdʒ] **1** *n* venda *f*. **2** *vt* vendar.

Band-Aid(R) ['bændeɪd], *US* tirita(R) *f*.

bang [bæŋ] **1** *n* (*blow*) golpe *m*; (*noise*) ruido *m*; (*explosion*) estallido *m*; (*of gun*) estampido *m*. **2** *vt* golpear; **to b. sth shut** cerrar algo de golpe. **3** *vi* golpear; **to b. shut** cerrarse de golpe.

● **bang down** *vt* (*lid*) golpear con fuerza.

● **bang into** *vt* golpearse contra.

banger *fam* **old b.** (*car*) tartana *f*.

bangle ['bæŋgəl] brazalete *m*.

banister(s) ['bænɪstə'(z)] pasamanos *m inv*.

bank¹ [bæŋk] (*for money*) banco *m*.

bank² (*of river*) ribera *f*, orilla *f*.

● **bank on** *vt* contar con.

bank account cuenta *f* bancaria.

bank card tarjeta *f* bancaria.

banker banquero,-a *mf*.

bank holiday fiesta *f* nacional.

banking banca *f*.

banknote billete *m* de banco.

bankrupt ['bæŋkrʌpt] *a* en quiebra; **to go b.** quebrar.

bankruptcy bancarrota *f*.

banner ['bænə'] (*in demonstration*) pancarta *f*.

bar [ba:'] **1** *n* (*of gold*) barra *f*; (*of chocolate*) tableta *f*; (*of cage*) barrote *m*; (*pub*) bar *m*; (*counter*) barra *f*; (*of soap*) pastilla *f*. **2** *vt* (*door*) atrancar; (*road*) cortar; (*exclude*) excluir (**from** de); (*prohibit*) prohibir.

barbecue ['ba:bɪkju:] barbacoa *f*.

barbed [ba:bd] *a* **b. wire** alambre *m* de púas.

barber ['ba:bə'] barbero,-a *mf*; **b.'s (shop)** barbería *f*.

bare [beə'] *a* desnudo,-a; (*head*) descubierto,-a; (*foot*) descalzo,-a; (*room*) sin muebles; **with his b. hands** sólo con las manos.

barefoot *a & adv* descalzo,-a.

barely *adv* apenas.

bargain ['ba:gɪn] **1** *n* (*deal*) negocio *m*; (*cheap purchase*) ganga *f*; **b. price** precio *m* de oferta. **2** *vi* negociar.

● **bargain for** *vt* esperar; **I hadn't bargained for this** no contaba con esto.

barge [ba:dʒ] *n* gabarra *f*.

● **barge in** *vi* (*go in*) entrar sin permiso.

● **barge into** *vt* (*room*) irrumpir en; (*person*) tropezar con.

bark¹ [ba:k] *vi* (*dog*) ladrar.

bark² (*of tree*) corteza *f*.

barking ladridos *mpl*.

barley ['ba:lɪ] cebada *f*.

barmaid camarera *f*.

barman camarero *m*.

barmy ['ba:mɪ] *a* chalado,-a.

barn [ba:n] granero *m*.

barometer [bə'rɒmɪtə'] barómetro *m*.

barracks ['bærəks] *npl* cuartel *m sing*.

barrage ['bæra:dʒ] (*dam*) presa *f*.

barrel ['bærəl] (*of wine*) tonel *m*; (*of beer, oil*) barril *m*; (*of firearm*) cañón *m*.

barren ['bærən] *a* estéril; (*land*) yermo,-a.
barrette [bə'ret] *US* pasador *m* (del pelo).
barricade [bærɪ'keɪd] **1** *n* barricada *f.* **2** *vt* cerrar con barricadas.
barrier ['bærɪəʳ] barrera *f.*
barrister ['bærɪstəʳ] *Br* abogado,-a *mf* (*capacitado,-a para ejercer ante tribunales superiores*).
bartender *US* camarero *m.*
base [beɪs] **1** *n* base *f;* (*foot*) pie *m;* (*of column*) basa *f.* **2** *vt* basar (**on** en).
baseball béisbol *m.*
basement ['beɪsmənt] sótano *m.*
bash [bæʃ] **1** *n* (*heavy blow*) golpetazo *m;* (*dent*) bollo *m.* **2** *vt* golpear.
● **bash up** *vt* **to b. sb up** darle a algn una paliza.
basic ['beɪsɪk] **1** *a* básico,-a; **b. pay** sueldo *m* base. **2** *npl* **basics** lo fundamental.
basically *adv* fundamentalmente.
basin ['beɪsən] (*washbowl*) palangana *f;* (*for washing up*) barreño *m;* (*in bathroom*) lavabo *m.*
basis ['beɪsɪs] (*pl* **bases** ['beɪsi:z]) base *f;* **on the b. of** en base a.
bask [bɑ:sk] *vi* (*in sunlight*) tostarse.
basket ['bɑ:skɪt] (*big*) cesta *f;* (*small*) cesto *m.*
bat[1] [bæt] (*in cricket, baseball*) bate *m;* (*table tennis*) pala *f;* **to do sth off one's own b.** hacer algo por cuenta propia.
bat[2] (*animal*) murciélago *m.*
bat[3] *vt* **without batting an eyelid** sin pestañear.
batch [bætʃ] (*of bread*) hornada *f;* (*of goods*) lote *m.*
bath [bɑ:θ] **1** *n* baño *m;* (*tub*) bañera *f;* **to have a b.** bañarse. **2** *vt* bañar.
bathe [beɪð] *vi* bañarse.
bathing ['beɪðɪŋ] baño *m.*
bathing costume traje *m* de baño.
bathing trunks *npl* bañador *m.*
bathrobe albornoz *m.*
bathroom cuarto *m* de baño.
bathtub bañera *f.*
batter ['bætəʳ] **1** *n* pasta para rebozar. **2** *vt* (*baby*) maltratar.
● **batter down** *vt* (*door*) derribar.
● **battered** *a* (*car*) desvencijado,-a.
battery ['bætərɪ] (*for torch, radio*) pila *f;* (*for car*) batería *f.*
battle ['bætəl] **1** *n* batalla *f;* *fig* lucha *f.* **2** *vi* luchar.
battleship acorazado *m.*
baud baudio *m.*
bawl [bɔ:l] *vi* gritar.
bay [beɪ] bahía *f;* (*large*) golfo *m.*

BC [bi:'si:] *abbr of* **before Christ** a.C.

be* [bi:] **1** *vi* (*permanent state*) ser; **he is very tall** es muy alto; **Madrid is the capital** Madrid es la capital; **sugar is sweet** el azúcar es dulce. ▌ (*temporary state, location*) estar; **how are you?** ¿cómo estás?; **this soup is cold** esta sopa está fría. ▌ (*cost*) **a return ticket is £24** un billete de ida y vuelta cuesta 24 libras; **how much is it?** ¿cuánto es? ▌ (*weather*) **it's foggy** hay niebla; **it's cold/hot** hace frío/calor. ▌ (*time, date*) ser; **it's one o'clock** es la una; **it's four o'clock** son las cuatro; **it's the 11th/Tuesday today** hoy es 11/martes. ▌ **to be cold/afraid/hungry** tener frío/miedo/hambre; **she is thirty (years old)** tiene treinta años. **2** *v aux* estar; **he is writing a letter** está escribiendo una carta; **she was singing** cantaba; **they are leaving next week** se van la semana que viene; **we have been waiting for a long time** hace mucho que estamos esperando. ▌ (*passive*) ser; **he was murdered** fue asesinado. ▌ (*obligation*) **I am to see him this afternoon** debo verle esta tarde. ▌ **there is, there are** hay; **there was, there were** había; **there will be** habrá; **there would be** habría; **there have been a lot of complaints** ha habido muchas quejas; **there were ten of us** éramos diez. ▌ (*in tag questions*) ¿verdad?, ¿no?; **it's lovely, isn't it?** ¿es bonito, no?; **you're happy, aren't you?** ¿estás contento, verdad?

beach [bi:tʃ] playa *f.*

beacon ['bi:kən] baliza *f*; (*lighthouse*) faro *m.*

bead [bi:d] (*of necklace etc*) cuenta *f*; (*of liquid*) gota *f.*

beak [bi:k] (*of bird*) pico *m.*

beam [bi:m] (*in building*) viga *f*; (*of light*) rayo *m.*

beaming *a* (*smiling*) radiante.

bean [bi:n] alubia *f*, judía *f*; *Am* frijol *m*; **broad b.** haba *f*; **coffee b.** grano *m* de café; **green** *or* **runner b.** judía *f* verde.

bear*¹ [beəʳ] **1** *vt* (*carry*) llevar; (*endure*) soportar; **to b. in mind** tener presente. **2** *vi* **to b. left** girar a la izquierda.

● **bear out** *vt* confirmar.

bear² (*animal*) oso *m.*

bearable *a* soportable.

beard [bɪəd] barba *f.*

bearded *a* barbudo,-a.

bearing ['beərɪŋ] (*relevance*) relación *f*; **to have a b. on** estar relaciona-do,-a con; **to get one's bearings** orientarse.

beast [bi:st] bestia *f.*

beastly *a fam* asqueroso,-a.

beat* [bi:t] **1** *vt* (*hit*) pegar; (*drum*) tocar; (*in cooking*) batir; (*defeat*) vencer. **2** *vi* (*heart*) latir. **3** *n* (*of heart*) latido *m*; (*of policeman*) ronda *f.*

● **beat down** *vi* (*sun*) caer a plomo.

● **beat off** *vt* rechazar.

● **beat up** *vt* dar una paliza a.

beating (*thrashing*) paliza *f*; (*defeat*) derrota *f*.

beautiful ['bjuːtɪfʊl] *a* hermoso,-a, bello,-a.

beauty ['bjuːtɪ] belleza *f*, hermosura *f*.

beauty spot (*on face*) lunar *m*; (*place*) lugar *m* pintoresco.

beaver ['biːvəʳ] castor *m*.

because [bɪ'kɒz] **1** *conj* porque. **2** *prep* **b. of** a causa de.

become* [bɪ'kʌm] *vi* (*doctor, priest*) hacerse; (*mayor, officer*) llegar a ser; (*angry, sad*) ponerse; **what has b. of him?** ¿qué ha sido de él?

bed [bed] cama *f*; **to get out of b.** levantarse de la cama; **to go to b.** acostarse; *Br* **b. and breakfast** (*service*) cama *f* y desayuno *m*; (*sign*) 'pensión'.

bedclothes *npl*, **bedding** ropa *f* de cama.

bedroom dormitorio *m*.

bedside b. table mesilla *f* de noche.

bedsit, bed'sitter estudio *m*.

bedtime hora *f* de acostarse.

bee [biː] abeja *f*.

beech [biːtʃ] haya *f*.

beef [biːf] carne *f* de vaca, *Am* carne *f* de res.

beefburger hamburguesa *f*.

been [biːn] *pp of* **be**.

beer [bɪəʳ] cerveza *f*; **a glass of b.** una caña.

beet [biːt] remolacha *f*; *US* **red b.** remolacha *f*.

beetle ['biːtəl] escarabajo *m*.

beetroot remolacha *f*.

before [bɪ'fɔːʳ] **1** *conj* (*earlier than*) antes de que (+ *subjunctive*), antes de (+ *infinitive*); **b. she goes** antes de que se vaya; **b. leaving** antes de salir. **2** *prep* (*place*) delante de; (*in the presence of*) ante; (*order, time*) antes de. **3** *adv* (*time*) antes; (*place*) (por) delante; **I have met him b.** ya lo conozco; **the night b.** la noche anterior.

beg [beg] **1** *vt* (*money etc*) pedir; (*beseech*) rogar. **2** *vi* (*solicit*) mendigar; **to b. for money** pedir limosna.

beggar mendigo,-a *mf*.

begin* [bɪ'gɪn] *vti* empezar, comenzar; **to b. doing** *or* **to do sth** empezar a hacer algo; **to b. with ...** para empezar ...

beginner principiante *mf*.

beginning principio *m*, comienzo *m*; **at the b. of May** a principios de mayo.

begrudge [bɪ'grʌdʒ] *vt* dar de mala gana; (*envy*) envidiar; **to b. sb sth** envidiarle algo a algn.

behalf [bɪ'hɑːf] nombre *m*; **on b. of,** *US* **in b. of** de parte de.

behave [bɪ'heɪv] *vi* (*person*) (com)portarse; **b. yourself!** ¡pórtate bien!

behaviour, *US* **behavior** [bɪ'heɪvjəʳ] comportamiento *m*.

behind [bɪ'haɪnd] **1** *prep* detrás de. **2** *adv* (*in the rear*) detrás, atrás; **I've left my umbrella b.** se me ha olvidado el paraguas; **to be b. with one's payments** estar atrasado,-a en los pagos. **3** *n fam* (*bottom*) trasero *m*.

beige [beɪʒ] *a & n* beige (*m*).

belch [beltʃ] **1** *vi* eructar. **2** *n* eructo *m*.

Belgian ['beldʒən] *a & n* belga (*mf*).

belief [bɪ'li:f] creencia *f*; (*opinion*) opinión *f*; (*faith*) fe *f*; (*confidence*) confianza *f* (**in** en).

believable *a* creíble.

believe [bɪ'li:v] *vti* creer; **I b. so** creo que sí; **to b.in sb/sth** creer en algn/ algo.

believer (*religious*) creyente *mf*.

belittle [bɪ'lɪtəl] *vt* (*person*) restar importancia a.

bell [bel] (*of church*) campana *f*; (*small*) campanilla *f*; (*of school, door, bicycle etc*) timbre *m*; (*on animal*) cencerro *m*.

bellboy *US* botones *m inv*.

belly ['belɪ] (*of person*) barriga *f*.

bellyache *fam* dolor *m* de vientre.

belong [bɪ'lɒŋ] *vi* pertenecer (**to** a); (*be a member*) ser socio,-a (**to** de).

belongings *npl* efectos *mpl* personales.

below [bɪ'ləʊ] **1** *prep* debajo de. **2** *adv* abajo.

belt [belt] cinturón *m*; (*in machine*) correa *f*; (*area*) zona *f*.

● **belt along** *vi fam* ir a todo gas.

bench [bentʃ] (*seat*) banco *m*.

bend [bend] **1** *vt** doblar; (*back*) encorvar; (*head*) inclinar. **2** *vi** doblarse; (*road*) torcerse; **to b. (over)** inclinarse. **3** *n* (*in river, road*) curva *f*; (*in pipe*) recodo *m*.

● **bend down** *vi* inclinarse.

beneath [bɪ'ni:θ] **1** *prep* (*below*) bajo, debajo de. **2** *adv* debajo.

beneficial [benɪ'fɪʃəl] *a* (*doing good*) benéfico,-a; (*advantageous*) beneficioso,-a.

benefit ['benɪfɪt] **1** *vt* beneficiar. **2** *vi* sacar provecho (**from** *or* **by** de). **3** *n* (*advantage*) beneficio *m*; (*allowance*) subsidio *m*; **I did it for your b.** lo hice por tu bien.

bent [bent] *a* (*curved*) curvado,-a; **to be b. on doing sth** (*determined*) estar empeñado,-a en hacer algo.

bereavement [bɪ'ri:vmənt] duelo *m*.

berk [bɜːk] *fam* imbécil *mf*.

berry ['berɪ] baya *f*.

berserk [bə'zɜːk] *a* **to go b.** volverse loco,-a.

berth [bɜːθ] (*bed*) litera *f*.

beside [bɪ'saɪd] *prep* (*next to*) al lado de, junto a; (*compared with*) comparado con; **that's b. the point** eso no viene al caso.

besides 1 *prep* (*in addition to*) además de; (*except*) excepto. **2** *adv* además.

best [best] **1** *a* mejor; **the b. thing would be to phone them** lo mejor sería llamarles; **the b. part of a year** casi un año. **2** *adv* mejor; **as b. I can** lo mejor que pueda. **3** *n* lo mejor; **to do one's b.** hacer todo lo posible; **to make the b. of sth** sacar el mejor partido de algo.

best man ≈ padrino *m* de boda.

best-'seller best-seller *m*.

bet [bet] **1** *n* apuesta *f*. **2** *vti** apostar (**on** a).

betray [bɪ'treɪ] *vt* traicionar.

betrayal traición *f*.

better ['betə'] **1** *a* mejor; **that's b.!** ¡eso es!; **to get b.** mejorar; (*healthier*) mejor; **b. off** (*richer*) más rico,-a; **the b. part of the day** la mayor parte del día. **2** *adv* mejor; **we had b. leave** más vale que nos vayamos. **3** *vt* (*improve*) mejorar; (*surpass*) superar.

betting apuestas *fpl*.

between [bɪ'twiːn] **1** *prep* entre; **b. you and me** entre nosotros; **closed b. 1 and 3** cerrado de 1 a 3. **2** *adv* en, medio; **in b.** (*position*) en medio; (*time*) mientras (*tanto*).

beware [bɪ'weə'] *vi* tener cuidado (**of** con); **b.!** ¡cuidado!

bewilder [bɪ'wɪldə'] *vt* desconcertar.

beyond [bɪ'jɒnd] **1** *prep* más allá de; **it is b. me why ...** no comprendo por qué ...; **this task is b. me** no puedo con esta tarea. **2** *adv* más allá.

bias ['baɪəs] (*tendency*) tendencia *f* (**towards** hacia); (*prejudice*) prejuicio *m*.

bias(s)ed *a* parcial; **to be b. against sth/sb** tener prejuicio en contra de algo/algn.

bib [bɪb] (*for baby*) babero *m*.

Bible ['baɪbəl] Biblia *f*.

bicycle ['baɪsɪkəl] bicicleta *f*.

bid [bɪd] **1** *vti** (*at auction*) pujar (**for** por). **2** *n* (*offer*) oferta *f*; (*at auction*) puja *f*.

big [bɪg] *a* grande (gran *before sing noun*); **a b. clock** un reloj grande; **a b. surprise** una gran sorpresa; **my b. brother** mi hermano mayor; *fam* **b. deal!** ¿y qué?

bighead *fam* engreído,-a *mf*.

bike [baɪk] (*bicycle*) bici *f*; (*motorcycle*) moto *f*.

bikini [bɪ'kiːnɪ] bikini *m*.

bile [baɪl] bilis *f*.

bilingual [baɪ'lɪŋgwəl] *a* bilingüe.

bill [bɪl] *n* (*for gas etc*) factura *f*; (*in restaurant*) cuenta *f*; (*in parliament*) proyecto *m* de ley; *US* (*banknote*) billete *m* de banco.

billboard *US* cartelera *f*.

billfold *US* billetero *m*.

billiards ['bɪljədz] billar *m*.

billion ['bɪljən] (*thousand million*) mil millones *mpl*.

bin [bɪn] (*for storage*) cajón *m*; (**rubbish**) **b.** cubo *m* de la basura.

bind* [baɪnd] *vt* (*tie up*) atar; (*book*) encuadernar.

binder (*file*) carpeta *f*.

bingo ['bɪŋgəʊ] bingo *m*.

binoculars [bɪ'nɒkjʊləz] *npl* prismáticos *mpl*.

bio'logical *a* biológico,-a.

biology [baɪ'ɒlədʒɪ] biología *f*.

birch [bɜːtʃ] (*tree*) abedul *m*.

bird [bɜːd] (*small*) pájaro *m*; (*large*) ave *f*.

bird's-eye view vista *f* de pájaro.

Biro(R) ['baɪrəʊ] bolígrafo *m*.

birth [bɜːθ] nacimiento *m*; **to give b. to a child** dar a luz a un niño.

birth certificate partida *f* de nacimiento.

birthday cumpleaños *m inv*.

biscuit ['bɪskɪt] galleta *f*.

bishop ['bɪʃəp] obispo *m*; (*chess*) alfil *m*.

bit [bɪt] (*small piece*) trozo *m*; (*small quantity*) poco *m*; **a b. of sugar** un poco de azúcar; **b. by b.** poco a poco; **a b.** (*slightly*) un poco.

bite [baɪt] **1** *n* (*act*) mordisco *m*; (*wound*) mordedura *f*; (*mouthful, snack*) bocado *m*; (*insect*) **b.** picadura *f*. **2** *vti** morder; (*insect*) picar; **to b. one's nails** morderse las uñas.

bitter ['bɪtə'] **1** *a* amargo,-a; (*weather*) glacial; (*wind*) cortante; (*person*) amargado,-a; (*struggle*) enconado,-a; (*hatred*) implacable. **2** *n* (*beer*) cerveza *f* amarga.

bitterness amargura *f*; (*of weather*) crudeza *f*; (*of person*) rencor *m*.

bizarre [bɪ'zɑː'] *a* (*odd*) extraño,-a; (*eccentric*) estrafalario,-a.

black [blæk] **1** *a* (*colour*) negro,-a; *fig* **b. and blue** amoratado,-a. **2** *n* (*colour*) negro *m*; (*person*) negro,-a *mf*.

• **black out** *vi* (*faint*) desmayarse.

blackberry zarzamora *f*.

blackbird mirlo *m*.

blackboard pizarra *f*, encerado *m*.

black'currant grosella *f* negra.

black eye ojo *m* amoratado.

blacklist lista *f* negra.

blackmail 1 n chantaje m. **2** vt chantajear.
blackmailer chantajista mf.
blackout (of lights) apagón m; (fainting) pérdida f de conocimiento.
bladder ['blædə^r] vejiga f.
blade [bleɪd] (of grass) brizna f; (of knife etc) hoja f.
blame [bleɪm] **1** n culpa f. **2** vt echar la culpa a; **he is to b.** él tiene la culpa.
blameless a (person) inocente; (conduct) intachable.
bland [blænd] a (food) soso,-a.
blank [blæŋk] **1** a (without writing) en blanco; **b. cheque** cheque m en blanco. **2** n (space) espacio m en blanco.
blanket ['blæŋkɪt] manta f.
blare [bleə^r] vi resonar.
● **blare out** vt pregonar.
blast [blɑːst] **1** n (of wind) ráfaga f; (of horn etc) toque m; (explosion) explosión f; (shock wave) onda f de choque. **2** vt fam **b. (it)!** ¡maldito sea!
blasted a maldito,-a.
blast-off despegue m.
blaze [bleɪz] **1** n (burst of flame) llamarada f; (fierce fire) incendio m; (of sun) resplandor m. **2** vi (fire) arder; (sun etc) brillar.
blazer ['bleɪzə^r] chaqueta f deportiva.
bleach [bliːtʃ] (household) lejía f.
bleak [bliːk] a (countryside) desolado,-a.
bleed* [bliːd] vti sangrar.
bleep [bliːp] **1** n pitido m. **2** vi pitar.
bleeper (busca)personas m inv.
blemish ['blemɪʃ] (flaw) defecto m; (on fruit) maca f; fig **without b.** sin tacha.
blend [blend] **1** n mezcla f. **2** vt (mix) mezclar; (match) armonizar. **3** vi (mix) mezclarse.
blender (for food) licuadora f.
bless [bles] vt bendecir; **b. you!** (after sneeze) ¡Jesús!
blessing bendición f; (advantage) ventaja f.
blew [bluː] pt of **blow.**
blind [blaɪnd] **1** a ciego,-a; **a b. man** un ciego; **a b. woman** una ciega. **2** n (on window) persiana f; pl **the b.** los ciegos.
blindfold 1 n venda f. **2** vt vendar los ojos a.
blindly adv a ciegas; (love) ciegamente.
blindness ceguera f.
blink [blɪŋk] vi (eyes) pestañear; (lights) parpadear.
bliss [blɪs] felicidad f.
blister ['blɪstə^r] (on skin) ampolla f.

blizzard ['blɪzəd] ventisca *f*.

blob [blɒb] (*drop*) gota *f*; (*spot*) mancha *f*.

block [blɒk] **1** *n* bloque *m*; (*of wood*) taco *m*; (*group of buildings*) manzana *f*; **a b. of flats** un bloque de pisos. **2** *vt* (*obstruct*) obstruir.

● **block up** *vt* bloquear; **to get blocked up** (*pipe*) obstruirse.

blockage bloqueo *m*.

bloke [bləʊk] *fam* tío *m*, tipo *m*.

blond [blɒnd] *a & n* rubio (*m*).

blonde [blɒnd] *a & n* rubia (*f*).

blood [blʌd] sangre *f*; **b. donor** donante *mf* de sangre; **b. group** grupo *m* sanguíneo; **b. pressure** tensión *f* arterial; **high/low b. pressure** hipertensión *f*/hipotensión *f*.

bloodshed derramamiento *m* de sangre.

bloodshot *a* inyectado,-a de sangre.

bloody 1 *a* (*battle*) sangriento,-a; (*bloodstained*) manchado,-a de sangre; *fam* (*damned*) condenado,-a. **2** *adv fam* **it's b. difficult** ¡puñetas, qué difícil!

bloom [bluːm] **1** *n* (*flower*) flor *f*; **in full b.** en flor. **2** *vi* (*blossom*) florecer.

blossom ['blɒsəm] **1** *n* (*flower*) flor *f*. **2** *vi* florecer.

blot [blɒt] (*of ink*) borrón *m*.

blotchy ['blɒtʃɪ] *a* (*skin*) enrojecido,-a; (*paint*) cubierto,-a de manchas.

blotting-paper papel *m* secante.

blouse [blaʊz] blusa *f*.

blow¹ [bləʊ] golpe *m*.

blow² **1** *vi* (*wind*) soplar. **2** *vt* (*trumpet etc*) tocar; (*smoke*) echar; (*of wind*) llevarse; **to b. one's nose** sonarse la nariz.

● **blow away** *vt* **the wind blew it away** el viento se lo llevó.

● **blow down** *vt* derribar.

● **blow off 1** *vt* (*remove*) quitar. **2** *vi* (*hat*) salir volando.

● **blow out 1** *vt* apagar. **2** *vi* apagarse.

● **blow up 1** *vt* (*building*) volar; (*inflate*) inflar. **2** *vi* (*explode*) explotar.

blow-dry 1 *vt* marcar. **2** *n* marcado *m*.

blowtorch soplete *m*.

blowy *a fam* ventoso.

blue [bluː] **1** *a* azul; **b. jeans** vaqueros *mpl*, tejanos *mpl*. **2** *n* azul *m*.

blueberry ['bluːbərɪ] arándano *m*.

bluff [blʌf] **1** *n* (*deception*) farol *m*. **2** *vi* tirarse un farol.

blunder ['blʌndə'] **1** *n* metedura *f* de pata, *fam* patinazo *m*. **2** *vi* meter la pata.

blunt [blʌnt] *a* (*knife*) embotado,-a; (*pencil*) despuntado,-a; (*frank*) directo,-a; (*statement*) tajante.

blur [blɜːʳ] **1** *n* **he was just a b.** apenas se le veía. **2** *vt* (*shape*) desdibujar;

(*memory*) enturbiar.

blurred *a* borroso,-a.

blush [blʌʃ] *vi* ruborizarse.

blustery ['blʌstəri] *a* borrascoso,-a.

board [bɔːd] **1** *n* (*plank*) tabla *f*; (*meals*) pensión *f*; **full b.** pensión completa; **b. and lodging** casa *f* y comida; **b. of directors** consejo *m* de administración; **on b.** a bordo. **2** *vt* (*ship, plane etc*) embarcarse en.

boarder (*in boarding house*) huésped *mf*; (*at school*) interno,-a *mf*.

boarding (*embarkation*) embarque *m*.

boarding card *or* **pass** tarjeta *f* de embarque.

boarding house pensión *f*.

boarding school internado *m*.

boast [bəʊst] *vi* jactarse (**about** de).

boat [bəʊt] barco *m*; (*small*) barca *f*; (*large*) buque *m*.

bobby ['bɒbi] *fam* (*policeman*) poli *m*.

bodily *a* físico,-a.

body ['bɒdi] cuerpo *m*; (*corpse*) cadáver *m*; (*organization*) organismo *m*.

bodyguard guardaespaldas *mf inv*.

bodywork carrocería *f*.

bogus ['bəʊgəs] *a* falso,-a.

boil¹ [bɔil] **1** *n* **to come to the b.** empezar a hervir. **2** *vt* (*water, egg*) hervir; (*food*) cocer. **3** *vi* hervir.

● **boil over** *vi* (*milk*) salirse.

boil² (*on skin*) furúnculo *m*.

boiled *a* **b. egg** huevo *m* pasado por agua.

boiler caldera *f*.

boiling *a* (*water*) hirviente; **it's b. hot** (*food*) quema; (*weather*) hace un calor agobiante.

bold [bəʊld] *a* (*courageous*) valiente; (*dress, proposition etc*) audaz.

boldness audacia *f*.

Bolivian [bə'liviən] *a & n* boliviano,-a (*mf*).

bolt [bəʊlt] **1** *n* (*on door*) cerrojo *m*; (*small*) pestillo *m*; (*with nut*) tornillo *m*. **2** *vt* (*lock*) cerrar con cerrojo; (*food*) engullir. **3** *vi* (*person*) largarse; (*horse*) desbocarse.

bomb [bɒm] **1** *n* bomba *f*. **2** *vt* (*city etc*) bombardear; (*by terrorists*) volar.

bomber bombardero *m*.

bombing bombardeo *m*.

bond [bɒnd] (*link*) vínculo *m*; (*financial*) bono *m*.

bone [bəʊn] hueso *m*; (*in fish*) espina *f*.

bonfire ['bɒnfaiə'] hoguera *f*.

bonnet ['bɒnit] (*child's*) gorro *f*; (*of car*) capó *m*.

bonus ['bəʊnəs] plus *m*; (*on wages*) prima *f*; (*on shares*) dividendo *m* extraordinario.

bony ['bəʊnɪ] *a* (*person*) huesudo,-a; (*fish*) lleno,-a de espinas.

boo [buː] **1** *interj* ¡bu! **2** *vt* abuchear.

booby trap ['buːbɪtræp] trampa *f*; (*bomb etc*) trampa *f* explosiva.

book [bʊk] **1** *n* libro *m*; (*of stamps*) carpeta *f*; (*in commerce*) **books** cuentas *fpl*. **2** *vt* (*reserve*) reservar.

bookcase estantería *f*.

booked up *a* completo.

booking (*reservation*) reserva *f*.

booking office taquilla *f*.

bookkeeper contable *mf*.

bookkeeping contabilidad *f*.

booklet (*pamphlet*) folleto *m*.

bookmaker corredor,-a *mf* de apuestas.

bookseller librero,-a *mf*.

bookshelf estantería *f*.

bookshop librería *f*.

bookstore *US* librería *f*.

boom [buːm] (*noise*) estampido *m*; (*sudden prosperity*) auge *m*.

boost [buːst] **1** *n* estímulo *m*. **2** *vt* (*increase*) aumentar; (*tourism, exports*) fomentar; **to b. sb's confidence** subirle la moral a algn.

boot [buːt] *n* bota *f*; (*short*) botín *m*; (*of car*) maletero *m*; *fam* **she got the b.** la echaron (del trabajo).

● **boot out** *vt fam* echar a patadas.

booth [buːð] (*in language lab etc*) cabina *f*; **telephone b.** cabina *f* telefónica.

booze [buːz] *fam* **1** *n* priva *f*. **2** *vi* privar.

border ['bɔːdə'] *n* borde *m*; (*frontier*) frontera *f*.

● **border on** *vi* (*country*) lindar con.

borderline *a* (*case etc*) dudoso,-a.

bore [bɔː'] **1** *vt* aburrir. **2** *n* (*person*) pesado,-a *mf*; (*thing*) lata *f*; **what a b.!** ¡qué rollo!

boredom aburrimiento *m*.

boring *a* aburrido,-a, pesado,-a.

born [bɔːn] **to be b.** nacer; **I was b. in 1969** nací en 1969.

borrow ['bɒrəʊ] *vt* pedir prestado; **can I b. your pen?** ¿me dejas tu bolígrafo?

boss [bɒs] *n* (*head*) jefe,-a *mf*; (*factory owner etc*) patrón,-ona *mf*.

● **boss about** *or* **around** *vt* mangonear a.

bossy *a* mandón,-ona.

botch [bɒtʃ] *vt* chapucear; **a botched job** una chapuza.

both [bəʊθ] **1** *a* ambos,-as, los/las dos; **b. men are teachers** ambos so...
profesores; **hold it with b. hands** sujétalo con las dos manos. **2** *pron* **b. (of them)** ambos,-as, los/las dos; **b. of you** vosotros dos. **3** *adv* a la vez; **b. England and Spain are in Europe** tanto Inglaterra como España están en Europa.

bother ['bɒðə'] **1** *vt* (*disturb*) molestar; (*be a nuisance to*) dar la lata a; (*worry*) preocupar; **I can't be bothered** no tengo ganas; **he didn't b. shaving** no se molestó en afeitarse. **2** *vi* **don't b.** no te molestes **3** *n* (*disturbance*) molestia *f*; (*nuisance*) lata *f*; (*trouble*) problemas *mpl*. **4** *interj* ¡maldito sea!

bottle ['bɒtəl] botella *f*; (*of perfume, ink*) frasco *m*; **baby's b.** biberón *m*.

bottle opener abrebotellas *m inv*.

bottom ['bɒtəm] **1** *a* (*lowest*) más bajo,-a. **2** *n* parte *f* inferior; (*of sea, garden, street, box, bottle*) fondo *m*; (*of page, hill*) pie *m*; (*buttocks*) trasero *m*; **to be (at) the b. of the class** ser el último/la última de la clase.

boulder ['bəʊldə'] canto *m* rodado.

bounce [baʊns] **1** *vi* (*ball*) rebotar; (*cheque*) ser rechazado (por el banco). **2** *vt* (*ball*) botar.

bound¹ [baʊnd] *a* **he's b. to know it** seguro que lo sabe; **it's b. to happen** sucederá con toda seguridad; **it was b. to fail** estaba destinado al fracaso.

bound² *a* **to be b. for** dirigirse a.

boundary ['baʊndərɪ] límite *m*.

bounds *npl* **the river is out of b.** está prohibido bajar al río.

bouquet [bu:'keɪ] (*of flowers*) ramillete *m*.

boutique [bu:'ti:k] boutique *f*.

bow¹ [baʊ] **1** *vi* hacer una reverencia. **2** *n* (*with head, body*) reverencia *f*.

bow² [bəʊ] (*for violin, arrows*) arco *m*; (*knot*) lazo *m*.

bowels ['baʊəlz] *npl* entrañas *fpl*.

bowl¹ [bəʊl] (*dish*) cuenco *m*; (*for soup*) tazón *m*; (*for washing clothes, dishes*) barreño *m*.

bowl² *vi* (*in cricket*) lanzar la pelota.

bowler (*hat*) bombín *m*.

bowling (*game*) bolos *mpl*.

bowling alley bolera *f*.

bowls *npl* bolos *mpl*.

bow tie pajarita *f*.

box¹ [bɒks] caja *f*; (*large*) cajón *m*.

box² **1** *vi* boxear. **2** *vt* (*hit*) pegar.

• **box in** *vt* (*enclose*) aprisionar.

boxer boxeador *m*; (*dog*) bóxer *m*.

boxing boxeo *m*; **b. ring** cuadrilátero *m*.

Boxing Day *Br* el día de San Esteban (26 de diciembre).

...e taquilla *f*.

...*hild*) chico *m*; (*youth*) joven *m*.

...ɔɪkɒt] **1** *n* boicot *m*. **2** *vt* boicotear.

...**nd** novio *m*; (*live-in*) compañero *m*.

bra [brɑ:] sostén *m*.

bracelet ['breɪslɪt] pulsera *f*.

braces [breɪsɪz] *Br* tirantes *mpl*.

bracket ['brækɪt] (*round*) paréntesis *m*; (*square*) corchete *m*.

brag [bræg] *vi* jactarse (**about** de).

bragging fanfarronería *f*.

braid [breɪd] **1** *vt* trenzar. **2** *n esp US* trenza *f*.

brain [breɪn] cerebro *m*; **brains** inteligencia *f*; **to have brains** ser inteligente.

brainwash *vt* lavar el cerebro a.

brainy *a fam* inteligente.

brake [breɪk] **1** *n* freno *m*. **2** *vi* frenar.

brake light luz *f* de freno.

branch [brɑ:ntʃ] **1** *n* (*of tree*) rama *f*; (*of road*) bifurcación *f*; **b. (office)** sucursal *f*. **2** *vi* (*road*) bifurcarse.

● **branch off** *vi* desviarse.

● **branch out** *vi* diversificarse.

brand [brænd] marca *f*; **b. name** marca *f* de fábrica.

brand-new *a* flamante.

brandy ['brændɪ] brandy *m*.

brass [brɑ:s] latón *m*.

brave [breɪv] *a* valiente.

bravery valentía *f*.

brawl [brɔ:l] reyerta *f*.

brawny ['brɔːnɪ] *a* fornido,-a.

Brazilian [brə'zɪlɪən] *a & n* brasileño,-a (*mf*).

bread [bred] pan *m*; **b. and butter** pan con mantequilla.

breadbin, *US* **breadbox** panera *f*.

breadcrumb miga *f* de pan; **breadcrumbs** pan *m sing* rallado.

breadth [bredθ] (*width*) anchura *f*; (*extent*) amplitud *f*.

breadwinner cabeza *mf* de familia.

break [breɪk] **1** *vt** romper; (*fail to keep*) faltar a; (*destroy*) destrozar; (*financially*) arruinar; (*journey*) interrumpir; (*record*) batir; **to b. a leg** romperse la pierna; **to b. the law** violar la ley; **she broke the news to him** le comunicó la noticia. **2** *vi** romperse; (*storm*) estallar; (*story*) divulgarse. **3** *n* (*fracture*) rotura *f*; (*crack*) grieta *f*; (*opening*) abertura *f*; (*in a relationship*) ruptura *f*; (*pause*) pausa *f*; (*at school*) recreo *m*; *fam* (*chance*) oportunidad *f*; **to take a b.** descansar un rato; (*holiday*) tomar

unos días libres; **a lucky b.** un golpe de suerte.
- **break away** *vi* (*become separate*) desprenderse (**from** de).
- **break down 1** *vt* (*door*) derribar; (*resistance*) acabar con. **2** *vi* (*in car*) tener una avería; (*weep*) ponerse a llorar.
- **break in** *vi* (*burglar*) entrar a la fuerza.
- **break into** *vt* (*house*) allanar; (*safe*) forzar.
- **break loose** *vi* escaparse.
- **break off 1** *vt* (*relations*) romper. **2** *vi* (*become detached*) desprenderse; (*talks*) interrumpirse; (*stop*) pararse.
- **break out** *vi* (*prisoners*) escaparse; (*war etc*) estallar.
- **break up 1** *vt* (*object*) romper; (*car*) desguazar; (*crowd*) disolver. **2** *vi* romperse; (*crowd*) disolverse; (*meeting*) levantarse; (*relationship*) fracasar; (*couple*) separarse; (*at end of term*) terminar.

breakdown avería *f*; (*in communications*) ruptura *f*; (**nervous**) **b.** crisis *f* nerviosa.
breakfast ['brekfəst] desayuno *m*; **to have b.** desayunar.
break-in robo *m* (con allanamiento de morada).
breakthrough avance *m*.
breakup (*in marriage*) separación *f*.
breast [brest] (*chest*) pecho *m*; (*of chicken etc*) pechuga *f*.
breast-feed *vt* dar el pecho a.
breaststroke braza *f*.
breath [breθ] aliento *m*; **out of b.** sin aliento.
Breathalyzer(R) ['breθəlaɪzəʳ] *Br* alcoholímetro *m*.
breathe [briːð] *vti* respirar.
- **breathe in** *vi* aspirar.
- **breathe out** *vi* espirar.
breathing ['briːðɪŋ] respiración *f*; **b. space** respiro *m*.
breathtaking ['breθteɪkɪŋ] *a* impresionante.
breed [briːd] **1** *n* (*of animal*) raza *f*. **2** *vt** (*animals*) criar. **3** *vi** (*animals*) reproducirse.
breeder (*person*) criador,-a *mf*.
breeze [briːz] brisa *f*.
breezy *a* (*weather*) ventoso,-a.
brew [bruː] **1** *vt* (*beer*) elaborar; (*hot drink*) preparar. **2** *vi* (*tea*) reposar; **a storm is brewing** se prepara una tormenta; **something's brewing** algo se está cociendo.
brewery cervecería *f*.
bribe [braɪb] **1** *vt* sobornar. **2** *n* soborno *m*.
brick [brɪk] ladrillo *m*.
bricklayer albañil *m*.
bride [braɪd] novia *f*; **the b. and groom** los novios.

bridegroom novio *m*.

bridesmaid dama *f* de honor.

bridge [brɪdʒ] puente *m*.

brief [briːf] **1** *a* (*short*) breve; (*concise*) conciso,-a. **2** *n* **briefs** (*for men*) calzoncillos *mpl*; (*for women*) bragas *fpl*. **3** *vt* (*inform*) informar; (*instruct*) dar instrucciones a.

briefcase cartera *f*.

briefing (*meeting*) reunión *f* informativa.

briefly *adv* brevemente.

bright [braɪt] *a* (*light, sun, eyes*) brillante; (*colour*) vivo,-a; (*day*) claro,-a; (*cheerful*) alegre; (*clever*) listo,-a.

brighten *vi* (*prospects*) mejorar; (*face*) iluminarse.

● **brighten up 1** *vt* (*room etc*) hacer más alegre. **2** *vi* (*weather*) despejarse; (*person*) animarse.

brightly *adv* brillantemente.

brightness (*of sun*) resplandor *m*; (*of colour*) viveza *f*.

brilliance (*of light*) brillo *m*; (*of colour*) viveza *f*; (*of person*) brillantez *f*.

brilliant ['brɪljənt] *a* brillante; (*idea*) genial; (*very good*) estupendo,-a.

bring* [brɪŋ] *vt* traer; (*take to a different position*) llevar; (*cause*) provocar; **could you b. that book?** ¿podrías traerme el libro?

● **bring about** *vt* provocar.

● **bring along** *vt* traer.

● **bring back** *vt* (*return*) devolver; (*reintroduce*) volver a introducir; (*make one remember*) traer a la memoria.

● **bring down** *vt* (*from upstairs*) bajar (algo); (*government*) derribar; (*reduce*) rebajar.

● **bring forward** *vt* (*meeting etc*) adelantar.

● **bring in** *vt* (*yield*) dar; (*show in*) hacer entrar; (*law etc*) introducir.

● **bring out** *vt* (*publish*) publicar; (*emphasize*) recalcar.

● **bring round** *vt* (*revive*) hacer volver en sí; (*persuade*) convencer.

● **bring to** *vt* reanimar.

● **bring together** *vt* (*reconcile*) reconciliar.

● **bring up** *vt* (*educate*) educar; (*subject*) plantear; (*vomit up*) vomitar.

brink [brɪŋk] (*edge*) borde *m*.

brisk [brɪsk] *a* enérgico,-a; (*pace*) rápido,-a; (*trade*) activo,-a.

briskly *adv* (*to walk*) rápidamente.

bristle ['brɪsəl] cerda *f*.

British ['brɪtɪʃ] **1** *a* británico,-a; **the B. Isles** las Islas Británicas. **2** *npl* **the B.** los británicos.

Briton británico,-a *mf*.

brittle ['brɪtəl] *a* quebradizo,-a.

broad [brɔːd] *a* (*road, river*) ancho,-a; (*not detailed*) general; **in b.**

daylight a plena luz del día.
broadcast 1 *n* emisión *f*. **2** *vt** emitir.
broccoli ['brɒkəlɪ] brécol *m*.
brochure ['brəʊʃəʳ] folleto *m*.
broke [brəʊk] *a* **to be (flat) b.** estar sin blanca.
broken *a* roto,-a; (*machinery*) averiado,-a; (*leg*) fracturado,-a; **a b. home** una familia deshecha.
broken-down *a* (*machine*) averiado,-a.
bronchitis [brɒŋ'kaɪtɪs] bronquitis *f*.
bronze [brɒnz] bronce *m*.
brooch [brəʊtʃ] broche *m*.
brood [bru:d] **1** *n* (*of birds*) cría *f*. **2** *vi* (*ponder*) rumiar; **to b. over a problem** darle vueltas a un problema.
broody *a* (*pensive*) pensativo,-a; (*moody*) melancólico,-a; *fam* (*woman*) con ganas de tener hijos.
brook [brʊk] arroyo *m*.
broom [bru:m] escoba *f*; (*plant*) retama *f*.
broomstick palo *m* de escoba.
brother ['brʌðəʳ] hermano *m*; **brothers and sisters** hermanos.
brother-in-law cuñado *m*.
brought [brɔ:t] *pt & pp of* **bring**.
brown [braʊn] **1** *a* marrón; (*hair*) castaño,-a; (*tanned*) moreno,-a. **2** *n* marrón *m*.
browse [braʊz] *vi* (*person in shop*) mirar; (*through book*) hojear.
bruise [bru:z] **1** *n* morado *m*, cardenal *m*. **2** *vt* contusionar.
bruised *a* amoratado,-a.
brunch [brʌntʃ] combinación *f* de desayuno y almuerzo.
brunette [bru:'net] *a & n* morena (*f*).
brush [brʌʃ] **1** *n* (*for hair, teeth*) cepillo *m*; (*artist's*) pincel *m*; (*for house-painting*) brocha *f*. **2** *vt* cepillar; **to b. one's hair/teeth** cepillarse el pelo/los dientes.
● **brush aside** *vt* dejar de lado.
● **brush off** *vt* ignorar.
● **brush up (on)** *vt* revisar.
brutal *a* brutal, cruel.
brutality brutalidad *f*.
brute [bru:t] (*animal*) bruto *m*; (*person*) bestia *f*.
BSc [bi:es'si:] *abbr of* **Bachelor of Science**.
bubble ['bʌbəl] burbuja *f*.
● **bubble over** *vi* rebosar.
buck [bʌk] *US fam* dólar *m*.
bucket ['bʌkɪt] cubo *m*.

buckle ['bʌkəl] **1** *n* hebilla *f.* **2** *vt* abrochar (con hebilla). **3** *vi* (*wall, metal*) combarse.

buck up 1 *vt* **b. your ideas up!** ¡espabílate! **2** *vi* (*cheer up*) animarse.

bud [bʌd] **1** *n* (*shoot*) brote *m;* (*flower*) capullo *m.* **2** *vi* brotar.

Buddhist ['bʊdɪst] *a & n* budista *(mf).*

budge [bʌdʒ] *vi* (*move*) moverse.

budgerigar ['bʌdʒərɪgɑ:ʳ] periquito *m.*

budget ['bʌdʒɪt] **1** *n* presupuesto *m;* **the B.** (*of the state*) los presupuestos del Estado. **2** *vi* hacer un presupuesto (**for** para).

buffalo ['bʌfələʊ] (*pl* **buffaloes**) búfalo *m.*

buffet ['bʊfeɪ] (*snack bar*) bar *m;* (*at railway station*) cantina *f;* (*self-service meal*) bufet *m* libre.

buffet car coche *m* restaurante.

bug [bʌg] **1** *n* (*insect*) bicho *m;* (*microbe*) microbio *m;* **I've got a b.** tengo alguna infección; (*hidden microphone*) micrófono *m* oculto; (*in computer program*) error *m.* **2** *vt fam* (*annoy*) fastidiar.

buggy ['bʌgɪ] (*baby's pushchair*) cochecito *m* de niño.

bugle ['bju:gəl] bugle *m.*

build [bɪld] **1** *vt** construir. **2** *n* (*physique*) físico *m.*

builder constructor,-a *mf;* (*contractor*) contratista *mf.*

building edificio *m.*

building society sociedad *f* hipotecaria.

built-in [bɪlt'ɪn] *a* (*cupboard*) empotrado,-a; (*incorporated*) incorporado,-a.

built-up [bɪlt'ʌp] *a* urbanizado,-a.

bulb [bʌlb] (*of plant*) bulbo *m;* (*lightbulb*) bombilla *f.*

Bulgarian [bʌl'geərɪən] *a & n* búlgaro,-a *(mf).*

bulge [bʌldʒ] **1** *n* protuberancia *f;* (*in pocket*) bulto *m.* **2** *vi* (*swell*) hincharse; (*be full*) estar repleto,-a.

bulging *a* abultado,-a; (*eye*) saltón.

bulk [bʌlk] (*mass*) masa *f,* volumen *m;* (*greater part*) mayor parte *f.*

bulky *a* voluminoso,-a.

bull [bʊl] toro *m.*

bulldog buldog *m.*

bulldozer ['bʊldəʊzəʳ] bulldozer *m.*

bullet ['bʊlɪt] bala *f.*

bulletin ['bʊlɪtɪn] boletín *m.*

bullet-proof *a* a prueba de balas; **b. vest** chaleco *m* antibalas.

bullfight corrida *f* de toros.

bullfighter torero,-a *mf.*

bullfighting los toros *mpl;* (*art*) tauromaquia *f.*

bullring plaza *f* de toros.

bully ['bʊlɪ] **1** *n* matón *m*. **2** *vt* intimidar.

bum¹ [bʌm] *fam* (*bottom*) culo *m*.

bum² *US fam* (*tramp*) vagabundo *m*; (*idler*) holgazán,-ana *mf*.

● **bum around** *vi fam* vaguear.

bumblebee ['bʌmbəlbiː] abejorro *m*.

bump [bʌmp] **1** *n* (*swelling*) chichón *m*; (*on road*) bache *m*; (*blow*) golpe *m*; (*jolt*) sacudida *f*. **2** *vt* golpear; **to b. one's head** darse un golpe en la cabeza.

● **bump into** *vt* (*meet*) tropezar con.

bumper (*on vehicle*) parachoques *m inv*.

bumpy *a* (*road*) con muchos baches.

bun [bʌn] (*bread*) panecillo *m*; (*sweet*) magdalena *f*.

bunch [bʌntʃ] (*of keys*) manojo *m*; (*of flowers*) ramo *m*; (*of grapes*) racimo *m*; (*of people*) grupo *m*.

bundle ['bʌndəl] **1** *n* (*of clothes*) bulto *m*; (*of papers*) fajo *m*. **2** *vt* (*make bundle of*) liar; (*push*) empujar.

bungalow ['bʌŋgələʊ] bungalow *m*.

bung up [bʌŋ] *vt* atascar.

bunk [bʌŋk] (*bed*) litera *f*.

bunny ['bʌnɪ] *fam* **b. (rabbit)** conejito *m*.

buoy [bɔɪ] boya *f*.

burden ['bɜːdən] **1** *n* carga *f*. **2** *vt* cargar (**with** con).

bureaucracy [bjʊə'rɒkrəsɪ] burocracia *f*.

burger ['bɜːgə'] *fam* hamburguesa *f*.

burglar ['bɜːglə'] ladrón,-ona *mf*.

burglar alarm alarma *f* antirrobo.

burglarize *vt US* robar.

burglary robo *m* en una casa.

burgle *vt* robar.

burial ['berɪəl] entierro *m*.

burn [bɜːn] **1** *n* quemadura *f*. **2** *vt** quemar. **3** *vi** (*fire*) arder; (*building, food*) quemarse; (*ointment etc*) escocer.

● **burn down 1** *vt* incendiar. **2** *vi* incendiarse.

burner (*on cooker*) quemador *m*.

burning *a* (*on fire*) ardiendo,-a en llamas.

burp [bɜːp] **1** *n* eructo *m*. **2** *vi* eructar.

burst [bɜːst] **1** *n* (*explosion*) estallido *m*; (*of tyre*) reventón *m*; **b. of laughter** carcajada *f*. **2** *vt** (*balloon*) reventar. **3** *vi** reventarse; (*shell*) estallar.

● **burst into** *vi* **to b. into laughter/tears** echarse a reír/llorar; **to b. into a room** irrumpir en una habitación.

● **burst out** *vi* **to b. out laughing** echarse a reír.

bursting *a* **the bar was b. with people** el bar estaba atestado de gente.

bury ['berɪ] *vt* enterrar; (*hide*) ocultar; **to be buried in thought** estar absorto en pensamientos.

bus [bʌs] (*pl* **buses**, *US* **busses**) autobús *m*.

bus shelter marquesina *f* (de autobús).

bus station estación *f* de autobuses.

bush [bʊʃ] (*shrub*) arbusto *m*.

bushy *a* espeso,-a.

business ['bɪznɪs] (*commerce*) negocios *mpl*; (*firm*) empresa *f*; (*matter*) asunto *m*; **on b.** de negocios; **b. hours** horas *fpl* de oficina; **b. trip** viaje *m* de negocios; **it's no b. of mine** no es asunto mío; **mind your own b.** no te metas en donde no te llaman.

businessman hombre *m* de negocios.

businesswoman mujer *f* de negocios.

bus stop parada *f* de autobús.

bust¹ [bʌst] **1** (*of woman*) pecho *m*; (*sculpture*) busto *m*.

bust² *a fam* **to go b.** quebrar.

bustle ['bʌsəl] (*activity, noise*) bullicio *m*.

● **bustle about** *vi* ir y venir.

bustling *a* bullicioso,-a.

busy ['bɪzɪ] *a* ocupado,-a; (*life*) ajetreado,-a; (*street*) concurrido,-a; (*telephone*) ocupado,-a; **b. signal** señal *f* de comunicando.

busybody entrometido,-a *mf*.

but [bʌt] **1** *conj* pero; (*after negative*) sino; **not two b. three** no dos sino tres. **2** *adv* **had we b. known** de haberlo sabido; **we can b. try** al menos podemos intentarlo; **b. for her we would have drowned** si no hubiera sido por ella, nos habríamos ahogado. **3** *prep* menos; **everyone b. her** todos menos ella.

butcher ['bʊtʃəʳ] carnicero,-a *mf*; **b.'s (shop)** carnicería *f*.

butler ['bʌtləʳ] mayordomo *m*.

butt [bʌt] (*of cigarette*) colilla *f*; *US fam* (*bottom*) culo *m*.

butter ['bʌtəʳ] **1** *n* mantequilla *f*. **2** *vt* untar con mantequilla.

buttercup botón *m* de oro.

butterfly mariposa *f*.

buttock ['bʌtək] nalga *f*; **buttocks** nalgas *fpl*.

button ['bʌtən] **1** *n* botón *m*. **2** *vt* **to b. (up) one's jacket** abotonarse la chaqueta.

buttonhole ojal *m*.

buy [baɪ] **1** *n* **a good b.** una ganga. **2** *vt** comprar; **she bought that car from a neighbour** compró ese coche a un vecino.

buyer comprador,-a *mf*.

buzz [bʌz] **1** *n* (*of bee*) zumbido *m*; (*of conversation*) rumor *m*. **2** *vi* zumbar.

● **buzz off** *vi fam* largarse.

by [baɪ] **1** *prep* (*indicating agent*) por; **composed by Bach** compuesto,-a por Bach; **a film by Almodóvar** una película de Almodóvar. ▌ (*via*) por; **he left by the back door** salió por la puerta trasera. ▌ (*manner*) por; **by car/train** en coche/tren; **by credit card** con tarjeta de crédito; **by chance** por casualidad; **by oneself** solo,-a; **you can obtain a ticket by filling in the coupon** puede conseguir una entrada rellenando el cupón. ▌ (*amount*) por; **little by little** poco a poco; **they are sold by the dozen** se venden por docenas; **to be paid by the hour** cobrar por horas; **he won by a foot** ganó por un pie. ▌ (*beside*) al lado de, junto a; **side by side** juntos. ▌ (*past*) **to walk by a building** pasar por delante de un edificio. ▌ (*time*) para; **by now** ya; **by then** para entonces; **we have to be there by nine** tenemos que estar allí para las nueve; **by the time we arrive** (para) cuando lleguemos. ▌ (*during*) de; **by day/night** de día/noche. ▌ (*according to*) según; **is that O.K by you?** ¿te viene bien? **2** *adv* **to go by** (*past*) pasar; **she just walked by** pasó de largo; **by and by** con el tiempo; **by and large** en conjunto.

bye(-bye) [ˈbaɪ(baɪ)] ¡adiós!, ¡hasta luego!

by-election elección *f* parcial.

bypass 1 *n* (*road*) carretera *f* de circunvalación. **2** *vt* evitar.

bystander mirón,-ona *mf*.

C

cab [kæb] taxi *m*.

cabbage ['kæbɪdʒ] col *f*.

cabin ['kæbɪn] (*hut*) choza *f*; (*on ship*) camarote *m*.

cabinet ['kæbɪnɪt] (*furniture*) armario *m*; (*glass-fronted*) vitrina *f*; (*in government*) gabinete *m*.

cabinet meeting consejo *m* de ministros.

cable ['keɪbəl] cable *m*.

cable car teleférico *m*.

cable TV televisión *f* por cable.

cactus ['kæktəs] (*pl* **cacti** ['kæktaɪ]) cactus *m*.

café ['kæfeɪ], **cafeteria** [kæfɪ'tɪərɪə] cafetería *f*, bar *m*.

caffeine ['kæfiːn] cafeína *f*.

cage [keɪdʒ] jaula *f*.

cake [keɪk] pastel *m*.

calculate ['kælkjʊleɪt] *vt* calcular.

calcu'lation cálculo *m*.

calculator calculadora *f*.

calendar ['kælɪndə'] calendario *m*.

calf [kɑːf] (*pl* **calves** [kɑːvz]) (*of cattle*) becerro,-a *mf*, ternero,-a *mf*; (*part of leg*) pantorilla *f*.

call [kɔːl] **1** *vt* llamar; (*meeting etc*) convocar; **what's he called?** ¿cómo se llama? **2** *vi* llamar; **to c. at sb's (house)** pasar por casa de algn. **3** *n* llamada *f*; (*visit*) visita *f*; **(phone) c.** llamada *f*.

● **call back** *vti* (*phone again*) llamar otra vez.

● **call by** *vi* (*visit*) **why don't you c. by?** ¿por qué no te pasas por casa?

● **call in 1** *vt* (*doctor*) llamar; (*visit*) ir a ver. **2** *vi* entrar.

● **call on** *vt* visitar; **to c. on sb for support** recurrir a algn en busca de apoyo.

● **call out 1** *vt* (*shout*) gritar; (*doctor*) hacer venir. **2** *vi* gritar.

● **call up** *vi* llamar (por teléfono).

call box cabina *f* telefónica.

calm [kɑːm] **1** *a* (*weather, sea*) en calma; (*relaxed*) tranquilo,-a; **keep c.!** ¡tranquilo,-a! **2** *n* (*of weather, sea*) calma *f*. **3** *vt* calmar.

● **calm down** *vi* calmarse.

calmly *adv* con calma, tranquilamente.

calorie ['kælərɪ] caloría *f*.

camcorder ['kæmkɔːdə'] videocámara *f*.

came [keɪm] *pt of* **come**.

camel ['kæməl] camello,-a *mf*.

camera ['kæmərə] cámara *f*.

camp [kæmp] **1** *n* campamento *m*. **2** *vi* **to go camping** ir de camping.

campaign [kæm'peɪn] campaña *f*.

camp bed cama *f* plegable.

camper (*person*) campista *mf*; (*vehicle*) caravana *f*.

campfire fogata *f*.

camp(ing) site camping *m*.

can[1] [kæn] *v aux* (*pt* **could**) poder; (*know how to*) saber; **I'll phone you as soon as I c.** te llamaré en cuanto pueda; **she can't do it** no puede hacerlo; **I cannot understand why** no entiendo por qué; **he could have come** podría haber venido; **c. you ski?** ¿sabes esquiar?; **she could have forgotten** puede (ser) que lo haya olvidado; **they can't be very poor** no deben ser muy pobres; **what c. it be?** ¿qué será?

can[2] (*tin*) lata *f*.

Canadian [kə'neɪdɪən] *a & n* canadiense (*mf*).

canal [kə'næl] canal *m*.

canary [kə'neərɪ] canario *m*.

cancel ['kænsəl] *vt* (*train, booking*) cancelar; (*contract*) anular; (*permission*) retirar.

cance'llation cancelación *f*; (*of contract*) anulación *f*.

cancer ['kænsə'] cáncer *m*.

candid ['kændɪd] *a* franco,-a.

candidate ['kændɪdeɪt] candidato,-a *mf*; (*in state exam*) opositor,-a *mf*.

candle ['kændəl] vela *f*; (*in church*) cirio *m*.

candlestick palmatoria *f*; (*in church*) cirial *m*.

candy ['kændɪ] *US* caramelo *m*.

cane [keɪn] **1** *n* (*walking stick*) bastón *m*; (*for punishment*) palmeta *f*. **2** *vt* castigar con la palmeta.

cannabis ['kænəbɪs] canabis *m*.

canned [kænd] *a* enlatado,-a; **c. foods** conservas *fpl*.

cannibal ['kænɪbəl] *a & n* caníbal (*mf*).

canoe [kə'nu:] canoa *f*; (*for sport*) piragua *f*.

canoeing piragüismo *m*.

can-opener abrelatas *m*.

canopy ['kænəpɪ] (*awning*) toldo *m*.

canteen [kæn'ti:n] (*restaurant*) cantina *f*.

canvas ['kænvəs] lona *f*; (*painting*) lienzo *m*.

canyon ['kænjən] cañón *m*.

cap [kæp] gorro *m*; (*soldier's*) gorra *f*; (*of pen*) capuchón *m*; (*of bottle*) chapa *f*.

capa'bility habilidad *f*.

capable ['keɪpəbəl] *a* (*skilful*) hábil; (*able*) capaz (**of** de).

capacity [kə'pæsɪtɪ] capacidad *f*; (*position*) puesto *m*; **in her c. as**

manageress en calidad de gerente.

cape [keɪp] (*garment*) capa *f*.

capital ['kæpɪtəl] (*town*) capital *f*; (*money*) capital *m*; (*letter*) mayúscula *f*.

capsize [kæp'saɪz] **1** *vt* hacer zozobrar. **2** *vi* zozobrar.

capsule ['kæpsju:l] cápsula *f*.

captain ['kæptɪn] capitán *m*.

capture ['kæptʃəʳ] *vt* capturar; (*of troops*) (*town*) tomar.

car [kɑːʳ] coche *m*, *Am* carro *m*; **by c.** en coche.

caramel ['kærəmel] azúcar *m* quemado; (*sweet*) caramelo *m*.

caravan ['kærəvæn] (*vehicle*) caravana *f*.

carbon ['kɑːbən] carbono *m*; **c. copy** copia *f* al papel carbón.

carburettor [kɑːbjʊ'retəʳ], *US* **carburetor** ['kɑːbəreɪtəʳ] carburador *m*.

card [kɑːd] tarjeta *f*; (*of cardboard*) cartulina *f*; (*in file*) ficha *f*.

cardboard ['kɑːdbɔːd] cartón *m*.

cardigan ['kɑːdɪɡən] rebeca *f*.

cardinal ['kɑːdɪnəl] **1** *n* cardenal *m*. **2** *a* **c. numbers** números *mpl* cardinales.

care [keəʳ] **1** *vi* (*be concerned*) preocuparse (**about** por); **I don't c.** no me importa; **who cares?** ¿qué más da? **2** *n* (*attention, protection*) cuidado *m*; (*worry*) preocupación *f*; **to take c. of** cuidar; (*business*) ocuparse de; **take c.** (*be careful*) ten cuidado; (*as farewell*) ¡cuidate!; **to take care not to do sth** guardarse de hacer algo.

• **care about** *vt* (*something*) preocuparse de; (*somebody*) tener cariño a.

• **care for** *vt* (*look after*) cuidar; **I don't c. for that sort of thing** no me hace gracia una cosa así; **would you c. for a coffee?** ¿te apetece un café?

career [kə'rɪəʳ] carrera *f*.

carefree *a* despreocupado,-a.

careful *a* cuidadoso,-a; (*cautious*) prudente; **to be c.** tener cuidado; **be c.!** ¡ojo!

carefully *adv* (*painstakingly*) cuidadosamente; (*cautiously*) con cuidado.

careless *a* descuidado,-a; (*about clothes*) desaliñado,-a; (*driving*) negligente.

caretaker (*in school etc*) bedel,-a *mf*; (*in block of flats*) portero,-a *mf*.

car ferry transbordador *m* para coches.

cargo ['kɑːɡəʊ] (*pl* **cargoes** *or* **cargos**) carga *f*.

caring ['keərɪŋ] *a* solícito,-a.

carnation [kɑː'neɪʃən] clavel *m*.

carnival ['kɑːnɪvəl] carnaval *m*.

carol ['kærəl] villancico *m*.

carp [kɑːp] (*fish*) carpa *f*.

car park parking *m*, aparcamiento *m*.

carpenter [ˈkɑːpɪntəˈ] carpintero,-a *mf*.

carpentry carpintería *f*.

carpet [ˈkɑːpɪt] alfombra *f*; (*fitted*) moqueta *f*.

carpeting (**wall to wall**) c. *US* moqueta *f*.

carpet sweeper barredora *f* eléctrica.

carriage [ˈkærɪdʒ] (*horse-drawn*) carruaje *m*; (*on train*) vagón *m*, coche *m*.

carriageway *Br* calzada *f*.

carrier bag [ˈkærɪəbæg] bolsa *f* de plástico.

carrot [ˈkærət] zanahoria *f*.

carry [ˈkærɪ] **1** *vt* llevar; (*goods*) transportar; (*stock*) tener; (*responsibility, penalty*) conllevar; (*disease*) ser portador,-a de. **2** *vi* (*sound*) oírse.

● **carry away** *vt* llevarse; **to get carried away** entusiasmarse.

● **carry off** *vt* (*prize*) llevarse; **to c. it off** salir airoso,-a.

● **carry on 1** *vt* continuar; (*conversation*) mantener. **2** *vi* continuar; **c. on!** ¡adelante!

● **carry out** *vt* (*plan*) llevar a cabo; (*order*) cumplir; (*repairs*) hacer.

● **carry through** *vt* (*plan*) completar.

carryall bolsa *f*.

cart [kɑːt] **1** *n* (*horse-drawn*) carro *m*; (*handcart*) carretilla *f*. **2** *vt* acarrear.

● **cart around** *vt* *fam* llevar y traer.

carton [ˈkɑːtən] (*of cream etc*) paquete *m*.

cartoon [kɑːˈtuːn] (*strip*) tira *f* cómica; (*animated*) dibujos *mpl* animados.

cartridge [ˈkɑːtrɪdʒ] cartucho *m*; (*for pen*) recambio *m*.

carve [kɑːv] *vt* (*wood*) tallar; (*stone, metal*) esculpir; (*meat*) trinchar.

car wash túnel *m* or tren *m* de lavado.

case[1] [keɪs] (*instance, medical*) caso *m*; (*legal*) causa *f*; **in any c.** en cualquier caso; **just in c.** por si acaso.

case[2] (*suitcase*) maleta *f*; (*small*) estuche *m*; (*soft*) funda *f*.

cash [kæʃ] **1** *n* dinero *m* efectivo; **to pay c.** pagar al contado or en efectivo. **2** *vt* (*cheque*) cobrar.

cash desk caja *f*.

cashier [kæˈʃɪəˈ] cajero,-a *mf*.

cash price precio *m* al contado.

cash register caja *f* registradora.

casino [kəˈsiːnəʊ] casino *m*.

casserole [ˈkæsərəʊl] (*container*) cacerola *f*; (*food*) guisado *m*.

cassette [kæˈset] casete *f*.

cassette player cassette *m*.

cassette recorder casete *m*.

cast [kɑːst] **1** *vt** (*net, fishing line*) echar; (*light*) proyectar; (*glance*) lanzar; (*vote*) emitir; **to c. suspicion on sb** levantar sospechas sobre algn; (*play, film*) hacer el reparto de. **2** *n* (*plaster*) **c.** escayola *f*; (*of play*) reparto *m*.

caster sugar azúcar *f* molida muy fina.

castle [ˈkɑːsəl] castillo *m*; (*in chess*) torre *f*.

castor [ˈkɑːstəʳ] ruedecilla *f*.

casual [ˈkæʒʊəl] *a* informal; (*worker*) eventual; (*clothes*) (de) sport; (*unimportant*) casual.

casualty (*injured*) herido,-a *mf*; **casualties** víctimas *fpl*; **c. (department)** urgencias *fpl*.

cat [kæt] gato,-a *mf*.

catalogue, *US* **catalog** [ˈkætəlɒg] catálogo *m*.

catapult [ˈkætəpʌlt] tirachinas *m inv*.

catastrophe [kəˈtæstrəfɪ] catástrofe *f*.

catch [kætʃ] **1** *vt** (*thief, bus etc*) coger, *Am* agarrar; (*fish*) pescar; (*mouse etc*) atrapar; (*surprise*) sorprender; (*hear*) entender; **to c. fire** (*log*) prenderse; (*building*) incendiarse; **to c. one's breath** (*recover*) recuperar el aliento. **2** *vi** (*sleeve etc*) engancharse (**on** en); (*fire*) encenderse. **3** *n* (*of ball*) parada *f*; (*of fish*) presa *f*; (*on door*) pestillo *m*; (*drawback*) pega *f*.

● **catch on** *vi* (*become popular*) ganar popularidad; (*understand*) caer en la cuenta.

● **catch out** *vt* **to c. sb out** pillar a algn cometiendo una falta.

● **catch up** *vi* **to c. up (with) sb** (*reach*) alcanzar a algn; (*with news*) ponerse al corriente (**on** de); **to c. up with work** ponerse al día de trabajo.

catching *a* (*disease*) contagioso,-a.

category [ˈkætɪgərɪ] categoría *f*.

cater for [ˈkeɪtəʳ] *vt* (*wedding etc*) proveer comida para; (*taste*) atender a.

caterpillar [ˈkætəpɪləʳ] oruga *f*.

cathedral [kəˈθiːdrəl] catedral *f*.

Catholic [ˈkæθəlɪk] *a & n* católico,-a (*mf*).

cauliflower [ˈkɒlɪflaʊəʳ] coliflor *f*.

cause [kɔːz] **1** *n* (*of event etc*) causa *f*; (*reason*) motivo *m*. **2** *vt* provocar; **to c. sb to do sth** hacer que algn haga algo.

caution [ˈkɔːʃən] *n* (*care*) cautela *f*; (*warning*) aviso *m*.

cautious *a* cauteloso,-a.

cautiously *adv* con precaución.

cave [keɪv] cueva *f*.

● **cave in** *vi* (*roof etc*) derrumbarse.

cavity ['kævɪtɪ] (*hole*) cavidad *f*.

CD [siːˈdiː] *abbr of* **compact disc** CD *m*.

cease [siːs] **1** *vt* to c. doing *or* to do sth dejar de hacer algo. **2** *vi* cesar.

cease-fire alto *m* el fuego.

ceiling ['siːlɪŋ] techo *m*.

celebrate ['selɪbreɪt] **1** *vt* celebrar. **2** *vi* divertirse.

cele'bration celebración *f*.

celebrity [sɪ'lebrɪtɪ] celebridad *f*.

celery ['selərɪ] apio *m*.

cell [sel] (*in prison*) celda *f*; (*in organism*) célula *f*.

cellar ['selər] sótano *m*; (*for wine*) bodega *f*.

cellophane ['seləfeɪn] celofán *m*.

cement [sɪ'ment] **1** *n* cemento *m*. **2** *vt* (*fix with cement*) unir con cemento.

cement mixer hormigonera *f*.

cemetery ['semɪtrɪ] cementerio *m*.

cent [sent] centavo *m*, céntimo *m*.

centigrade ['sentɪgreɪd] *a* centígrado,-a.

centimetre, *US* **centimeter** ['sentɪmiːtər] centímetro *m*.

centipede ['sentɪpiːd] ciempiés *m inv*.

central *a* central.

Central American *a & n* centroamericano,-a (*mf*).

centre, *US* **center** ['sentər] centro *m*.

century ['sentʃərɪ] siglo *m*.

ceramic [sɪ'ræmɪk] *a* de cerámica.

cereal ['sɪərɪəl] cereal *m*.

ceremony ['serɪmənɪ] ceremonia *f*.

certain ['sɜːtən] **1** *a* (*sure*) seguro,-a; (*true*) cierto,-a; to make c. of sth asegurarse de algo; to a c. extent hasta cierto punto. **2** *adv* for c. a ciencia cierta.

certainly *adv* desde luego; c. not de ninguna manera.

certainty certeza *f*; (*assurance*) seguridad *f*.

certificate [səˈtɪfɪkɪt] certificado *m*; (*from college*) diploma *m*.

certify ['sɜːtɪfaɪ] *vt* certificar.

chain [tʃeɪn] **1** *n* cadena *f*; (*of events*) serie *f*; c. of mountains cordillera *f*. **2** *vt* to c. (up) encadenar.

chain store (*tienda*) *f* sucursal.

chair [tʃeər] *n* silla *f*; (*with arms*) sillón *m*; (*of meeting*) presidente *mf*.

chair lift telesilla *m*.

chairman presidente *m*.

chalet ['ʃæleɪ] chalet *m*, chalé *m*.

chalk [tʃɔːk] (*for writing*) tiza *f*.

challenge ['tʃælɪndʒ] **1** vt desafiar; (authority etc) poner a prueba; (statement) poner en duda; **to c. sb to do sth** retar a algn a que haga algo. **2** n desafío m.

challenging a (idea) desafiante; (task) que presenta un desafío.

chamber ['tʃeɪmbəʳ] **C. of Commerce** Cámara f de Comercio.

champagne [ʃæm'peɪn] (French) champán m; (from Catalonia) cava m.

champion ['tʃæmpɪən] campeón,-ona mf.

championship campeonato m.

chance [tʃɑːns] **1** n (fortune) azar m; (opportunity) oportunidad f; **by c.** por casualidad; **to take a c.** arriesgarse; **(the) chances are that ...** lo más probable es que ... **2** vt arriesgar.

chandelier [ʃændɪ'lɪəʳ] araña f (de luces).

change [tʃeɪndʒ] **1** vt cambiar; **to c. gear** cambiar de marcha; **to c. one's mind/the subject** cambiar de opinión/de tema; **to c. trains** hacer trasbordo; **to get changed** cambiarse de ropa. **2** vi cambiar(se); **I think he's changed** le veo cambiado. **3** n cambio m; (money after purchase) vuelta f; **for a c.** para variar; **c. of scene** cambio de aires; **small c.** suelto m.
● **change over** vi cambiarse.

changeable a (weather) variable; (person) inconstante.

changeover conversión f.

changing room vestuario m.

channel ['tʃænəl] canal m; (administrative) vía f; **the English C.** el Canal de la Mancha.

chant [tʃɑːnt] **1** n (of demonstrators) slogan m. **2** vti (demonstrators) corear.

chaos ['keɪɒs] caos m.

cha'otic a caótico,-a.

chap [tʃæp] tío m.

chapel ['tʃæpəl] capilla f.

chapped [tʃæpt] a agrietado,-a.

chapter ['tʃæptəʳ] capítulo m.

char [tʃɑːʳ] vt carbonizar.

character ['kærɪktəʳ] carácter m; (in play) personaje m; (person) tipo m.

characte'ristic 1 n característica f. **2** a característico,-a.

charge [tʃɑːdʒ] **1** vt cobrar; (the enemy) cargar contra; (battery) cargar; **to c. sb with a crime** acusar a algn de un crimen. **2** vi (battery, troops) cargar; **to c. about** andar a lo loco. **3** n (cost) precio m; (in court) acusación f; **bank charges** comisión f; **free of c.** gratis; **service c.** servicio m; **to be in c. of** estar a cargo de; **to take c. of** hacerse cargo de.

charity ['tʃærɪtɪ] (organization) institución f benéfica.

charm [tʃɑːm] **1** n (quality) encanto m; **lucky c.** amuleto m. **2** vt encantar.

charming *a* encantador,-a.

chart [tʃɑːt] (*giving information*) tabla *f*; (*graph*) gráfico *m*; (*map*) carta *f* de navegación; (*of hit records*) **the charts** la lista de éxitos.

chartered accountant *Br* contable *mf* diplomado,-a.

charter flight vuelo *m* chárter.

chase [tʃeɪs] *vt* perseguir; (*hunt*) cazar.

● **chase after** *vt* (*someone*) correr detrás de; (*something*) andar tras.

● **chase away** *or* **off** *vt* ahuyentar.

chasm ['kæzəm] sima *f*; *fig* abismo *m*.

chassis ['ʃæsɪ] chasis *m inv*.

chat [tʃæt] **1** *n* charla *f*. **2** *vi* charlar.

● **chat up** *vt* (intentar) ligar con.

chatter ['tʃætəʳ] **1** *vi* (*person*) parlotear; (*teeth*) castañetear. **2** *n* (*of person*) parloteo *m*; (*of teeth*) castañeteo *m*.

chatterbox parlanchín,-ina *mf*.

chatty *a* hablador,-a.

chauffeur ['ʃəʊfəʳ] chófer *m*.

cheap [tʃiːp] **1** *a* barato,-a; (*fare*) económico,-a; (*contemptible*) bajo,-a. **2** *adv* barato.

cheaply *adv* en plan económico.

cheat [tʃiːt] **1** *vt* engañar; **to c. sb out of sth** estafar algo a algn. **2** *vi* (*at games*) hacer trampa; (*in exam etc*) copiar(se). **3** *n* (*trickster*) tramposo, -a.

check [tʃek] **1** *vt* verificar; (*facts*) comprobar; (*tickets*) controlar; (*tyres, oil*) revisar; (*stop*) detener; (*in chess*) dar jaque a. **2** *vi* comprobar. **3** *n* (*of documents etc*) revisión *f*; (*of facts*) comprobación *f*; (*in chess*) jaque *m*; (*in restaurant etc*) cuenta *f*; *US* (*cheque*) cheque *m*.

● **check in** *vi* (*at airport*) facturar; (*at hotel*) registrarse (**at** en).

● **check off** *vt* (*names on list etc*) tachar.

● **check on** *vt* verificar.

● **check out 1** *vi* (*of hotel*) dejar el hotel. **2** *vt* (*facts*) verificar.

● **check up** *vi* **to c. up on sth** comprobar algo.

checkbook *US* talonario *m* de cheques.

checkers [tʃekəz] *US* (*game*) damas *fpl*.

check-in c. desk (*at airport*) mostrador *m* de facturación.

checkmate jaque mate *m*.

checkout (*counter*) caja *f*.

checkroom *US* guardarropa *f*; (*for luggage*) consigna *f*.

checkup (*medical*) chequeo *m*.

cheddar [tʃedəʳ] queso *m* cheddar.

cheek [tʃiːk] mejilla *f*; (*nerve*) cara *f*; **what c.!** ¡vaya jeta!

cheeky *a* fresco,-a.

cheer [tʃɪə^r] **1** vi aclamar. **2** vt (applaud) aclamar. **3** n viva m; **cheers**
aplausos mpl; **cheers!** (before drinking) ¡salud!; fam (thank you) gracias.
• **cheer up 1** vi animarse. **2** vt **to c. sb up** animar a algn.
cheerful a alegre.
cheering ovación f.
cheerio [tʃɪərɪˈəʊ] interj Br ¡hasta luego!
cheese [tʃiːz] queso m.
cheeseburger hamburguesa f de queso.
cheesecake tarta f de queso.
chef [ʃef] chef m.
chemical 1 n sustancia f química. **2** a químico,-a.
chemist [ˈkemɪst] farmacéutico,-a mf; (scientist) químico,-a mf; Br **c.'s
(shop)** farmacia f.
chemistry química f.
cheque [tʃek] cheque m.
chequebook talonario m (de cheques).
cherry [ˈtʃerɪ] cereza f.
cherry brandy licor m de cerezas.
chess [tʃes] ajedrez m.
chessboard tablero m de ajedrez.
chest [tʃest] pecho m; (for linen) arca f; (for valuables) cofre m; **c. of
drawers** cómoda f.
chestnut [ˈtʃesnʌt] (nut) castaña f.
chew [tʃuː] vt masticar.
chewing gum chicle m.
chick [tʃɪk] pollito m.
chicken [ˈtʃɪkɪn] n pollo m; fam (coward) gallina m.
• **chicken out** vi rajarse (por miedo).
chickenpox varicela f.
chickpea garbanzo m.
chicory [ˈtʃɪkərɪ] achicoria f.
chief [tʃiːf] **1** n jefe m. **2** a principal.
chiefly adv (above all) sobre todo; (mainly) principalmente.
chilblain [ˈtʃɪlbleɪn] sabañón m.
child [tʃaɪld] (pl **children** [ˈtʃɪldrən]) niño,-a mf; (son) hijo m; (daughter)
hija f.
child care (for working parents) servicio m de guardería.
childhood infancia f, niñez f.
childish a pueril.
child minder persona f que cuida niños en su propia casa.
Chilean [ˈtʃɪlɪən] adj & n chileno,-a (mf).
chill [tʃɪl] **1** n (illness) resfriado m; (coldness) fresco m. **2** vt (meat)

refrigerar; (*wine*) enfriar.
chilled *a* (*wine*) frío,-a.
chil(l)i ['tʃɪlɪ] chile *m.*
chilly ['tʃɪlɪ] *a* frío,-a.
chime [tʃaɪm] *vi* sonar.
chimney ['tʃɪmnɪ] chimenea *f.*
chimneypot cañón *m.*
chimpanzee [tʃɪmpæn'zi:] chimpancé *m.*
chin [tʃɪn] barbilla *f.*
china ['tʃaɪnə] loza *f;* **bone c.** porcelana *f.*
Chinese [tʃaɪ'ni:z] **1** *a* chino,-a. **2** *n* (*person*) chino,-a *mf;* (*language*) chino *m.*
chip [tʃɪp] **1** *n* (*in cup*) mella *f;* (*microchip*) chip *m;* (*in gambling*) ficha *f;* **chips** patatas *fpl* fritas. **2** *vt* (*china, glass*) mellar.
chipboard madera *f* aglomerada.
chiropodist [kɪ'rɒpədɪst] pedicuro,-a *mf.*
chisel ['tʃɪzəl] cincel *m.*
chives [tʃaɪvz] *npl* cebolleta *f sing.*
choc-ice ['tʃɒkaɪs] (*ice cream*) helado *m* cubierto de chocolate.
chock-a-block [tʃɒkə'blɒk], **chock-full** [tʃɒk'fʊl] *a* hasta los topes.
chocolate ['tʃɒkəlɪt] **1** *n* chocolate *m;* **chocolates** bombones *mpl.* **2** *a* de chocolate.
choice [tʃɔɪs] elección *f;* **a wide c.** un gran surtido; **there's no c.** no hay más remedio.
choir ['kwaɪəʳ] coro *m.*
choke [tʃəʊk] **1** *vt* (*person*) ahogar; (*obstruct*) obstruir. **2** *vi* ahogarse.
cholesterol [kə'lestərɒl] colesterol *m.*
choose* [tʃu:z] **1** *vt* elegir; (*decide on*) optar por. **2** *vi* elegir.
choos(e)y *a* exigente.
chop [tʃɒp] **1** *vt* (*wood*) cortar; (*tree*) talar; (*food*) cortar a pedacitos. **2** *n* (*of lamb, pork etc*) chuleta *f.*
● **chop down** *vt* (*tree*) talar.
● **chop off** *vt* (*branch, finger etc*) cortar.
● **chop up** *vt* cortar en pedazos.
chopper *fam* (*helicopter*) helicóptero *m.*
chopsticks *npl* palillos *mpl.*
chord [kɔːd] (*musical*) acorde *m.*
chore [tʃɔːʳ] tarea *f.*
chorus ['kɔːrəs] coro *m;* (*in a song*) estribillo *m.*
christen ['krɪsən] *vt* bautizar.
christening bautizo *m.*
Christian ['krɪstʃən] *n & a* cristiano,-a (*mf*).

Christian name nombre *m* de pila.

Christmas ['krɪsməs] Navidad *f*; **merry C.** feliz Navidad; **C. Day** día *m* de Navidad; **C. Eve** Nochebuena *f*.

chrome [krəʊm] cromo *m*.

chrysanthemum [krɪ'sænθəməm] crisantemo *m*.

chubby ['tʃʌbɪ] *a* rellenito,-a.

chuck [tʃʌk] *vt fam* tirar.

chum [tʃʌm] compañero,-a *mf*.

chunk [tʃʌŋk] pedazo *m*.

church [tʃɜ:tʃ] iglesia *f*.

chute [ʃu:t] (*for refuse*) conducto *m*; (*slide*) tobogán *m*.

cider ['saɪdəʳ] sidra *f*.

cigar [sɪ'gɑ:ʳ] puro *m*.

cigarette [sɪgə'ret] cigarrillo *m*.

cigarette end colilla *f*.

cigarette lighter mechero *m*.

cine camera ['sɪnɪkæmərə] cámara *f* cinematográfica.

cinema ['sɪnɪmə] cine *m*.

cinnamon ['sɪnəmən] canela *f*.

circle ['sɜ:kəl] **1** *n* círculo *m*; (*of people*) corro *m*; **in business circles** en el mundo de los negocios. **2** *vt* (*move round*) dar la vuelta a. **3** *vi* dar vueltas.

circuit ['sɜ:kɪt] circuito *m*.

circular ['sɜ:kjʊləʳ] *a & n* circular (*f*).

circulate ['sɜ:kjʊleɪt] **1** *vt* (*news*) hacer circular. **2** *vi* circular.

circu'lation (*of blood*) circulación *f*; (*of newspaper*) tirada *f*.

circumference [sə'kʌmfərəns] circunferencia *f*.

circumstance ['sɜ:kəmstəns] circunstancia *f*; **under no circumstances** en ningún caso.

circus ['sɜ:kəs] circo *m*.

citizen ['sɪtɪzən] ciudadano,-a *mf*.

city ['sɪtɪ] ciudad *f*.

city centre centro *m* urbano.

city hall ayuntamiento *m*.

civil ['sɪvəl] *a* civil; (*polite*) educado,-a; **c. rights** derechos *mpl* civiles.

ci'vilian [sɪ'vɪljən] *a & n* civil (*mf*).

civilization [sɪvɪlaɪ'zeɪʃən] civilización *f*.

civil servant funcionario,-a *mf*.

civil service administración *f* pública.

claim [kleɪm] **1** *vt* (*benefits, rights*) reclamar; (*assert*) afirmar. **2** *n* (*demand*) reclamación *f*; (*right*) derecho *m*; (*assertion*) pretensión *f*; **to put in a c.** pedir una indemnización.

clam [klæm] almeja *f*.

clamp [klæmp] **wheel c.** cepo *m*.

clap [klæp] *vi* aplaudir.

clapping aplausos *mpl*.

clarinet [klærɪ'net] clarinete *m*.

clash [klæʃ] **1** *vi* (*disagree*) estar en desacuerdo; (*colours*) desentonar; (*dates*) coincidir. **2** *n* (*sound*) sonido *m*; (*fight*) choque *m*; (*conflict*) conflicto *m*.

clasp [klɑːsp] **1** *n* (*on belt*) cierre *m*; (*on necklace*) broche *m*. **2** *vt* (*object*) agarrar.

class [klɑːs] **1** *n* clase *f*; **second c. ticket** billete *m* de segunda (clase). **2** *vt* clasificar.

classic ['klæsɪk] **1** *a* clásico,-a. **2** *n* (*author*) autor *m* clásico; (*work*) obra *f* clásica.

classical *a* clásico,-a.

classmate compañero,-a *mf* de clase.

classroom aula *f*.

clause [klɔːz] oración *f*.

claw [klɔː] (*of bird, lion*) garra *f*; (*of cat*) uña *f*; (*of crab*) pinza *f*.

clay [kleɪ] arcilla *f*.

clean [kliːn] **1** *a* limpio,-a; (*unmarked, pure*) sin defecto. **2** *adv* por completo; **it went c. through the middle** pasó justo por el medio. **3** *vt* (*room*) limpiar; **to c. one's teeth** lavarse los dientes.

cleaner limpiador,-a *mf*.

cleaning limpieza *f*.

cleaning woman señora *f* de la limpieza.

cleanly *adv* (*to break, cut*) limpiamente.

cleansing ['klenzɪŋ] **c. lotion** leche *f* limpiadora.

clear [klɪəʳ] **1** *a* claro,-a; (*road, day*) despejado,-a; (*obvious*) claro,-a; (*majority*) absoluto; (*profit*) neto; **to make sth c.** aclarar algo. **2** *adv* **stand c.!** ¡apártese!; **to stay c. of** evitar. **3** *vt* (*room*) vaciar; (*authorize*) autorizar; (*hurdle*) salvar; **to c. one's throat** aclararse la garganta; **to c. the table** quitar la mesa; **to c. sb of a charge** exculpar a algn de un delito. **4** *vi* (*sky*) despejarse.

● **clear away** *vt* quitar.

● **clear off** *vi fam* largarse.

● **clear out** *vt* (*room*) limpiar a fondo; (*cupboard*) vaciar.

● **clear up** **1** *vt* (*tidy*) recoger; (*arrange*) ordenar; (*mystery*) resolver. **2** *vi* (*weather*) despejarse.

clearance (*of area*) despeje *m*.

clearance sale liquidación *f* (de existencias).

clear-cut *a* claro,-a.

clearly *adv* claramente; (*at start of sentence*) evidentemente.

clearway carretera *f* donde está prohibido parar.

clementine ['klemɔntaɪn] clementina *f*.

clench [klentʃ] *vt* (*teeth, fist*) apretar.

clerical ['klerɪkɔl] *a* (*of an office*) de oficina.

clerk [klɑːk] (*office worker*) oficinista *mf*; (*civil servant*) funcionario,-a *mf*; *US* (*in shop*) dependiente,-a *mf*.

clever ['klevɔʳ] *a* (*person*) inteligente; (*argument*) ingenioso,-a; **to be c. at sth** tener aptitud para algo.

click [klɪk] (*sound*) clic *m*.

client ['klaɪɔnt] cliente *mf*.

cliff [klɪf] acantilado *m*.

climate ['klaɪmɪt] clima *m*.

climax ['klaɪmæks] (*peak*) punto *m* culminante.

climb [klaɪm] **1** *vt* (*ladder*) subir por; (*mountain*) escalar; (*tree*) trepar a. **2** *vi* (*plants*) trepar.

● **climb down** *vi* bajar.

climber alpinista *mf*, *Am* andinista *mf*.

cling* [klɪŋ] *vi* (*hang on*) agarrarse (**to** a); (*clothes*) ajustarse; **to c. together** unirse.

clingfilm plástico *m* doméstico.

clinic ['klɪnɪk] (*in state hospital*) ambulatorio *m*; (*specialized*) clínica *f*.

clip[1] [klɪp] *vt* (*cut*) cortar; (*ticket*) picar.

clip[2] *n* (*for hair*) pasador *m*; (*for paper*) sujetapapeles *m inv*; (*brooch*) clip *m*.

● **clip on** *vt* (*brooch*) prender (**to** a); (*documents*) sujetar (**to** a).

clippers *npl* (*for hair*) maquinilla *f* para rapar; (*for nails*) cortauñas *m inv*; (*for hedge*) tijeras *fpl* de podar.

clipping (*newspaper*) recorte *m*.

cloak [klɔʊk] (*garment*) capa *f*.

cloakroom guardarropa *m*; (*toilets*) servicios *mpl*.

clock [klɒk] reloj *m*; **to be open round the c.** estar abierto las 24 horas (del día).

clockwise *a & adv* en el sentido de las agujas del reloj.

close[1] ['klɔʊs] **1** *a* (*in space, time*) cercano,-a; (*contact*) directo,-a; **c. to** cerca de; (*relationship*) estrecho,-a; (*friend*) íntimo,-a; (*weather*) bochornoso,-a; **c. together** juntos. **2** *adv* cerca; **they live c. by** *or* **c. at hand** viven cerca.

close[2] ['klɔʊz] **1** *vt* cerrar; (*bring to a close*) concluir; (*meeting*) levantar. **2** *vi* (*shut*) cerrar(se). **3** *n* fin *m*, final *m*.

● **close down** *vti* (*business*) cerrar para siempre.

● **close in** *vi* **to c. in on sb** rodear a algn.

● **close up** 1 *vtr* cerrar del todo. 2 *vi* cerrarse; (*ranks*) apretarse.

closely ['kləʊslɪ] *adv* (*listen*) con atención; **c. contested/connected** muy reñido,-a/relacionado,-a; **to follow (events) c.** seguir de cerca (los acontecimientos).

closet ['klɒzɪt] *US* armario *m*.

closing time hora *f* de cierre.

clot [klɒt] 1 *n* (*of blood*) coágulo *m*. 2 *vi* coagularse.

cloth [klɒθ] paño *m*; (*rag*) trapo *m*; (*tablecloth*) mantel *m*.

clothes [kləʊðz] *npl* ropa *f sing*.

clothes brush cepillo *m* de la ropa.

clothes hanger percha *f*.

clothes line tendedero *m*.

clothes peg pinza *f*.

clothes shop tienda *f* de ropa.

clothing ['kləʊðɪŋ] ropa *f*.

cloud [klaʊd] *n* nube *f*.

● **cloud over** *vi* nublarse.

cloudy *a* (*sky*) nublado,-a.

clove [kləʊv] (*of garlic*) diente *f*.

clown [klaʊn] payaso *m*.

club [klʌb] (*society*) club *m*; (*for golf*) palo *m*; (*in cards*) trébol *m*.

clue [kluː] (*sign*) indicio *m*; (*to mystery*) pista *f*; (*in crossword*) clave *f*; *fam* **I haven't a c.** no tengo (ni) idea.

clumsy ['klʌmzɪ] *a* torpe; (*awkward*) tosco,-a.

clutch [klʌtʃ] 1 *vt* agarrar. 2 *n* (*in vehicle*) embrague *m*.

clutter ['klʌtə'] *vt* **to c. (up)** llenar de cosas.

Co *Com abbr of* **Company** C., Cª, Cía.

coach [kəʊtʃ] 1 *n* autocar *m*; (*carriage*) carruaje *m*; (*of train*) coche *m*, vagón *m*. 2 *vt* (*student*) dar clases particulares a; (*team*) entrenar.

coal [kəʊl] carbón *m*.

coal mine mina *f* de carbón.

coarse [kɔːs] *a* (*material*) basto,-a; (*language*) grosero,-a.

coast [kəʊst] costa *f*.

coat [kəʊt] 1 *n* (*overcoat*) abrigo *m*; (*short*) chaquetón *m*; (*of animal*) pelo *m*; (*of paint*) capa *f*. 2 *vt* cubrir (**with** de); (*with liquid*) bañar (**with** en).

coat hanger percha *f*.

coating capa *f*.

cob [kɒb] mazorca *f*.

cobbled ['kɒbəld] *a* adoquinado,-a.

cobweb telaraña *f*.

cocaine [kə'keɪn] cocaína *f*.

cock [kɒk] (*bird*) gallo *m*.

cockle ['kɒkəl] berberecho *m*.

cockpit cabina *f* del piloto.

cockroach ['kɒkrəʊtʃ] cucaracha *f*.

cocktail cóctel *m*.

cocoa ['kəʊkəʊ] cacao *m*.

coconut ['kəʊkənʌt] coco *m*.

cod [kɒd] bacalao *m*.

code [kəʊd] código *m*; (*symbol*) clave *f*; (*for telephone*) prefijo *m*.

cod-liver oil aceite *m* de hígado de bacalao.

co-ed [kəʊ'ed] **1** *a* mixto,-a. **2** *n* colegio *m* mixto.

coffee ['kɒfɪ] café *m*.

coffee bar cafetería *f*.

coffee break pausa *f* para el café.

coffeepot cafetera *f*.

coffee table mesita *f* de café.

coffin ['kɒfɪn] ataúd *m*.

cognac ['kɒnjæk] coñac *m*.

coil [kɔɪl] **1** *vt* to c. (**up**) enrollar. **2** *n* (*loop*) vuelta *f*; (*of rope*) rollo *m*.

coin [kɔɪn] moneda *f*.

coincide [kəʊɪn'saɪd] *vi* coincidir (**with** con).

coincidence [kəʊ'ɪnsɪdəns] coincidencia *f*.

Coke^(R) [kəʊk] (*abbr of* **Coca-Cola**^(R)) coca-cola *f*.

colander ['kɒləndə'] colador *m*.

cold [kəʊld] **1** *a* frío,-a; **I'm c.** tengo frío; **it's c.** (*weather*) hace frío. **2** *n* frío *m*; (*illness*) resfriado *m*; **to catch a c.** resfriarse, acatarrarse; **to have a c.** estar resfriado,-a.

coldness frialdad *f*.

coleslaw ['kəʊlslɔː] ensalada *f* de col.

collaborate [kə'læbəreɪt] *vi* colaborar (**with** con).

collabo'ration colaboración *f*.

collapse [kə'læps] **1** *vi* (*fall down*) derrumbarse; (*cave in*) hundirse. **2** *n* (*falling down*) derrumbamiento *m*; (*caving in*) hundimiento *m*.

collar ['kɒlə'] *n* (*of garment*) cuello *m*; (*for dog*) collar *m*.

collarbone clavícula *f*.

colleague ['kɒliːg] colega *mf*.

collect [kə'lekt] **1** *vt* (*gather*) recoger; (*stamps etc*) coleccionar; (*taxes*) recaudar. **2** *vi* (*for charity*) hacer una colecta (**for** para). **3** *adv* **to call c.** llamar a cobro revertido.

collection (*of mail*) recogida *f*; (*of money*) colecta *f*; (*of stamps*) colección *f*; (*of taxes*) recaudación *f*.

collector (*of stamps*) coleccionista *mf*.

college ['kɒlɪdʒ] ≈ centro *m* de enseñanza superior, ≈ politécnico *m*;

C. of Further Education Escuela *f* de Formación Profesional; **to go to c.** seguir estudios superiores.

collide [kə'laɪd] *vi* chocar.

collision [kə'lɪʒən] choque *m*.

colloquial [kə'ləʊkwɪəl] *a* coloquial.

cologne [kə'ləʊn] (agua *f* de) colonia *f*.

Colombian [kə'lɒmbɪən] *a & n* colombiano,-a (*mf*).

colon ['kəʊlən] (*punctuation*) dos puntos *mpl*.

colonel ['kɜːnəl] coronel *m*.

colony ['kɒlənɪ] colonia *f*.

colour, *US* **color** ['kʌlə^r] **1** *n* color *m*; **c. film/television** película *f*/ televisión *f* en color. **2** *vt* colorear.

coloured *a* (*person, pencil*) de color; (*photograph*) en color.

colourful *a* (*with colour*) lleno,-a de color; (*person*) pintoresco,-a.

column ['kɒləm] columna *f*.

coma ['kəʊmə] coma *m*; **to go into a c.** entrar en coma.

comb [kəʊm] **1** *n* peine *m*. **2** *vt* **to c. one's hair** peinarse.

combination [kɒmbɪ'neɪʃən] combinación *f*.

combine [kəm'baɪn] **1** *vt* combinar. **2** *vi* combinarse; (*companies*) asociarse.

come* [kʌm] *vi* venir; (*arrive*) llegar; (*happen*) suceder; **to c. apart/ undone** desatarse/ soltarse; **that's what comes of being too impatient** es lo que pasa por ser demasiado impaciente.

● **come about** *vi* ocurrir, suceder.

● **come across** *vt* (*thing*) encontrar por casualidad; **to c. across sb** tropezar con algn.

● **come along** *vi* (*arrive*) venir; (*make progress*) progresar; **c. along!** ¡venga!

● **come away** *vi* (*leave*) salir; (*part*) desprenderse (**from** de).

● **come back** *vi* (*return*) volver.

● **come by** (*acquire*) *vt* adquirir.

● **come down** *vi* bajar; (*rain*) caer.

● **come forward** *vi* (*advance*) avanzar; (*volunteer*) ofrecerse.

● **come in** *vi* (*enter*) entrar; (*arrive*) (*train*) llegar; (*tide*) subir.

● **come into** *vt* (*enter*) entrar en; (*inherit*) heredar.

● **come off 1** *vt* (*fall from*) caerse de. **2** *vi* (*button*) caerse; (*succeed*) salir bien.

● **come on** *vi* (*make progress*) progresar; **c. on!** (*hurry*) ¡venga!

● **come out** *vi* salir (**of** de); (*book*) aparecer; (*stain*) quitarse; **to c. out (on strike)** declararse en huelga.

● **come over 1** *vi* venir. **2** *vt* **what's c. over you?** ¿qué te pasa?

● **come round 1** *vt* (*corner*) dar la vuelta a. **2** *vi* (*visit*) venir; (*regain* *consciousness*) volver en sí.

● **come through** *vt* (*cross*) cruzar; (*illness*) recuperarse de; (*accident*) sobrevivir a.

● **come to 1** *vi* (*regain consciousness*) volver en sí. **2** *vt* (*amount to*) ascender a; (*arrive at*) llegar a.

● **come up** *vi* (*rise*) subir; (*sun*) salir; (*approach*) acercarse (**to** a); (*difficulty, question*) surgir.

● **come up against** *vt* (*problems etc*) encontrarse con.

● **come upon** *vt see* **come across**.

● **come up to** *vt* (*equal*) igualar.

● **come up with** *vt* (*solution etc*) encontrar.

comedian [kə'mi:dɪən] cómico *m*.

comedy ['kɒmɪdɪ] comedia *f*.

comfort ['kʌmfət] **1** *n* comodidad *f*; (*consolation*) consuelo *m*. **2** *vt* consolar.

comfortable *a* cómodo,-a; (*temperature*) agradable.

comforter *US* edredón *m*.

comic ['kɒmɪk] **1** *a* cómico,-a. **2** *n* tebeo *m*, comic *m*.

comic strip tira *f* cómica.

coming ['kʌmɪŋ] **comings and goings** idas y venidas *fpl*.

comma ['kɒmə] coma *f*.

command [kə'mɑ:nd] **1** *vt* mandar. **2** *n* (*order*) orden *f*; (*authority*) mando *m*; (*of language*) dominio *m*.

commemorate [kə'meməreɪt] *vt* conmemorar.

commence [kə'mens] *vti* comenzar.

comment ['kɒment] *n* comentario *m*.

● **comment on** *vt* (*event etc*) comentar.

commentary comentario *m*.

commentator ['kɒmənteɪtəʳ] comentarista *mf*.

commerce ['kɒmɜːs] comercio *m*.

co'mmercial *a* comercial.

commission [kə'mɪʃən] comisión *f*.

commit [kə'mɪt] *vt* (*crime*) cometer; **to c. suicide** suicidarse.

commitment compromiso *m*.

committee [kə'mɪtɪ] comisión *f*, comité *m*.

commodity [kə'mɒdɪtɪ] artículo *m*.

common ['kɒmən] *a* común; (*ordinary*) corriente.

commonly *adv* (*generally*) en general.

Common Market Mercado *m* Común.

commonplace *a* corriente.

common room (*for teachers*) sala *f* de profesores; (*for students*) sala *f* de estudiantes.

common sense sentido *m* común.

commotion [kə'məʊʃən] alboroto *m*.

communal [kɒmjuːnəl] *a* (*bathroom etc*) comunitario,-a.

communicate [kə'mjuːnɪkeɪt] **1** *vi* comunicarse (**with** con). **2** *vt* comunicar.

communi'cation comunicación *f*.

communion [kə'mjuːnjən] comunión *f*.

community [kə'mjuːnɪtɪ] comunidad *f*; (*people*) colectividad *f*.

community centre centro *m* social.

commute [kə'mjuːt] *vi* viajar diariamente al lugar de trabajo.

commuter persona *f* que viaja diariamente al lugar de trabajo.

commuting desplazarse diariamente al lugar de trabajo.

compact [kəm'pækt] **1** *a* compacto,-a; (*style*) conciso,-a. **2** ['kɒmpækt] *n* (*for powder*) polvera *f*.

compact disc disco *m* compacto.

companion [kəm'pænjən] compañero,-a *mf*.

company ['kʌmpənɪ] compañía *f*; (*business*) empresa *f*; **to keep sb c.** hacer compañía algn.

comparative [kəm'pærətɪv] **1** *a* comparativo,-a; (*relative*) relativo,-a. **2** *n* (*in grammar*) comparativo *m*.

comparatively *adv* relativamente.

compare [kəm'peəʳ] **1** *vt* comparar (**to, with** con); (**as**) **compared with** en comparación con. **2** *vi* compararse.

comparison [kəm'pærɪsən] comparación *f*.

compartment [kəm'pɑːtmənt] (*on train*) departamento *m*.

compass ['kʌmpəs] brújula *f*; (**pair of**) **compasses** compás *m*.

compatible [kəm'pætəbəl] *a* compatible.

compel [kəm'pel] *vt* (*oblige*) obligar; **to c. sb to do sth** obligar a algn a hacer algo.

compensate ['kɒmpenseɪt] *vti* compensar; **to c. sb for sth** indemnizar a algn de algo.

compen'sation (*for loss*) indemnización *f*.

compere ['kɒmpeəʳ] animador,-a *mf*.

compete [kəm'piːt] *vi* competir.

competent ['kɒmpɪtənt] *a* competente.

competition [kɒmpɪ'tɪʃən] competencia *f*; (*contest*) concurso *m*.

compe'titive [kəm'petɪtɪv] *a* competitivo,-a.

compe'titor competidor,-a *mf*.

compile [kəm'paɪl] *vt* compilar.

complain [kəm'pleɪn] *vi* quejarse (**of, about** de).

complaint queja *f*; (*formal*) reclamación *f*; (*illness*) enfermedad *f*.

complete [kəm'pliːt] **1** *a* (*entire*) completo,-a; (*absolute*) total. **2** *vt* completar; (*form*) rellenar.

completely *adv* completamente, por completo.

complex ['kɒmpleks] **1** *a* complejo,-a. **2** *n* complejo *m*.

complexion [kəm'plekʃən] tez *f*; *fig* aspecto *m*.

complicate ['kɒmplɪkeɪt] *vt* complicar.

complicated *a* complicado,-a.

compli'cation complicación *f*.

compliment ['kɒmplɪmənt] cumplido *m*.

comply [kəm'plaɪ] *vi* obedecer; **to c. with** (*order*) cumplir con.

compose [kəm'pəʊz] *vti* componer; **to be composed of** componerse de; **to c. oneself** calmarse.

composed *a* (*calm*) sereno,-a.

composer compositor,-a *mf*.

compo'sition (*essay*) redacción *f*.

compound ['kɒmpaʊnd] compuesto *m*.

comprehensive [kɒmprɪ'hensɪv] *a* completo,-a; (*insurance*) a todo riesgo; **c. school** escuela *f* secundaria.

comprise [kəm'praɪz] *vt* (*include*) comprender; (*consist of*) constar de; (*constitute*) constituir.

compromise ['kɒmprəmaɪz] acuerdo *m*.

compulsive [kəm'pʌlsɪv] *a* compulsivo,-a.

compulsory [kəm'pʌlsərɪ] *a* obligatorio,-a.

computer [kəm'pjuːtəʳ] ordenador *m*.

computerized *a* informatizado,-a.

computer programmer programador,-a *mf* de ordenadores.

computer science informática *f*.

con [kɒn] *vt fam* estafar.

conceal [kən'siːl] *vt* ocultar; (*emotions*) disimular.

conceited [kən'siːtɪd] *a* presuntuoso,-a.

conceivable [kən'siːvəbəl] *a* concebible.

concentrate ['kɒnsəntreɪt] **1** *vt* concentrar. **2** *vi* **to c. on sth** concentrarse en algo.

concen'tration concentración *f*.

concern [kən'sɜːn] **1** *vt* concernir; (*worry*) preocupar. **2** *n* (*worry*) preocupación *f*; (*business*) negocio *m*.

concerned *a* (*worried*) preocupado,-a (**about** por).

concerning *prep* con respecto a.

concert ['kɒnsɜːt] concierto *m*.

concise [kən'saɪs] *a* conciso,-a.

conclude [kən'kluːd] *vti* concluir.

conclusion conclusión *f*.

concrete ['kɒnkriːt] **1** *n* hormigón *m*. **2** *a* (*made of concrete*) de hormigón; (*definite*) concreto,-a.

condemn [kən'dem] *vt* condenar.

condensation [kɒnden'seɪʃən] condensación *f.*

condition [kən'dɪʃən] condición *f*; **on c. that** ... a condición de que ...

conditioner acondicionador *m.*

condominium [kɒndə'mɪnɪəm] *US* (*building*) condominio *m.*

condom ['kɒndəm] preservativo *m.*

conduct ['kɒndʌkt] **1** *n* (*behaviour*) conducta *f.* **2** [kən'dʌkt] *vt* (*lead*) guiar; (*business, orchestra*) dirigir.

conducted tour visita *f* acompañada.

conductor (*on bus*) cobrador *m*; *US* (*on train*) revisor,-a *mf*; (*of orchestra*) director,-a *mf.*

cone [kəʊn] cono *m*; **ice-cream c.** cucurucho *m.*

conference ['kɒnfərəns] congreso *m.*

confess [kən'fes] *vti* confesar; (*to priest*) confesarse.

confession confesión *f.*

confetti [kən'feti] confeti *m.*

confidence ['kɒnfɪdəns] confianza *f*; **in c.** en confianza.

confident *a* seguro,-a.

confi'dential *a* (*secret*) confidencial; (*entrusted*) de confianza.

confidently *adv* con seguridad.

confine [kən'faɪn] *vt* limitar.

confirm [kən'fɜːm] *vt* confirmar.

confir'mation confirmación *f.*

confirmed *a* empedernido,-a.

confiscate ['kɒnfɪskeɪt] *vt* confiscar.

conflict ['kɒnflɪkt] **1** *n* conflicto *m.* **2** [kən'flɪkt] *vi* chocar (**with** con).

conflicting *a* contradictorio,-a.

conform [kən'fɔːm] *vi* conformarse; **to c. to** *or* **with** (*customs*) amoldarse a; (*rules*) someterse a.

confront [kən'frʌnt] *vt* hacer frente a.

confuse [kən'fjuːz] *vt* (*person*) despistar; (*thing*) confundir (**with** con); **to get confused** confundirse.

confused *a* (*person*) confundido,-a; (*mind, ideas*) confuso,-a.

confusing *a* confuso,-a.

confusion confusión *f.*

congested [kən'dʒestɪd] *a* (*street*) repleto,-a de gente.

congestion congestión *f.*

congratulate [kən'grætjʊleɪt] *vt* felicitar.

congratu'lations *npl* felicitaciones *fpl*; **c.!** ¡enhorabuena!

congregate ['kɒŋgrɪgeɪt] *vi* congregarse.

congress ['kɒŋgres] congreso *m.*

Congressman congresista *m.*

conjugate ['kɒndʒʊgeɪt] *vt* conjugar.

conjugation conjugación *f.*

conjunction [kən'dʒʌŋkʃən] conjunción *f.*

conjurer ['kʌndʒərəʳ] prestidigitador,-a *mf.*

conjuring trick juego *m* de manos.

con man estafador *m.*

connect [kə'nekt] **1** *vt* unir; (*wires*) empalmar; (*install*) instalar; (*electricity*) conectar; (*on phone*) poner. **2** *vi* (*train, flight*) enlazar (**with** con).

connected *a* unido,-a; (*events*) relacionado,-a.

connection conexión *f*; (*installation*) instalación *f*; (*rail, flight*) enlace *m*; (*of ideas*) relación *f*; (*person*) contacto *m*; **in c. with** (*regarding*) con respecto a.

conquer ['kɒŋkəʳ] *vt* (*enemy, bad habit*) vencer; (*country*) conquistar.

conscience ['kɒnʃəns] conciencia *f.*

conscientious [kɒnʃɪ'enʃəs] *a* concienzudo,-a.

conscious ['kɒnʃəs] *a* (*aware*) consciente; (*choice etc*) deliberado,-a.

consent [kən'sent] **1** *n* consentimiento *m.* **2** *vi* consentir (**to** en).

consequence ['kɒnsɪkwəns] consecuencia *f.*

consequently *adv* por consiguiente.

conser'vation conservación *f.*

Conservative [kən'sɜːvətɪv] *a & n* conservador,-a (*mf*).

conservatory [kən'sɜːvətrɪ] (*greenhouse*) invernadero *m.*

conserve [kən'sɜːv] **1** *vt* conservar. **2** ['kɒnsɜːv] *n* conserva *f.*

consider [kən'sɪdəʳ] *vt* (*ponder on, regard*) considerar; (*keep in mind*) tener en cuenta; **to c. doing sth** pensar hacer algo.

considerable *a* considerable.

considerate [kən'sɪdərɪt] *a* considerado,-a.

conside'ration consideración *f.*

considering *prep* teniendo en cuenta.

consignment [kən'saɪnmənt] envío *m.*

consist [kən'sɪst] *vi* **to c. of** consistir en.

consistent [kən'sɪstənt] *a* consecuente; **c. with** de acuerdo con.

conso'lation consuelo *m*; **c. prize** premio *m* de consolación.

console[1] [kən'səʊl] *vt* consolar.

console[2] ['kɒnsəʊl] consola *f.*

consonant ['kɒnsənənt] consonante *f.*

conspicuous [kən'spɪkjʊəs] *a* (*striking*) llamativo,-a; (*easily seen*) visible.

constable ['kʌnstəbəl] policía *m.*

constant ['kɒnstənt] *a* constante; (*continuous*) incesante; (*loyal*) fiel.

constantly *adv* constantemente.

constipated ['kɒnstɪpeɪtɪd] *a* estreñido,-a.

constitution [kɒnstɪ'tjuːʃən] constitución *f*.

construct [kən'strʌkt] *vt* construir.

construction construcción *f*.

consul ['kɒnsəl] cónsul *mf*.

consulate consulado *m*.

consult [kən'sʌlt] *vti* consultar (**about** sobre).

consultancy (firm) empresa *f* de asesores.

consultant (*doctor*) especialista *mf*; (*in business*) asesor,-a *mf*.

consul'tation consulta *f*.

consume [kən'sjuːm] *vt* consumir.

consumer consumidor,-a *mf*.

consumption [kən'sʌmpʃən] consumo *m*.

contact ['kɒntækt] **1** *n* contacto *m*. **2** *vt* ponerse en contacto con.

contact lenses lentes *fpl* de contacto.

contagious [kən'teɪdʒəs] *a* contagioso,-a.

contain [kən'teɪn] *vt* contener.

container (*box, package*) recipiente *m*; (*for shipping*) contenedor *m*.

contemporary [kən'tempərɪ] *a & n* contemporáneo,-a (*mf*).

contempt [kən'tempt] desprecio *m*.

contend [kən'tend] *vi* competir; **there are many problems to c. with** se han planteado muchos problemas.

content[1] ['kɒntent] contenido *m*; **table of contents** índice *m* de materias.

content[2] [kən'tent] *a* contento,-a.

con'tented *a* satisfecho,-a.

contest ['kɒntest] prueba *f*.

con'testant concursante *mf*.

context ['kɒntekst] contexto *m*.

continent ['kɒntɪnənt] continente *m*; **(on) the C.** (en) Europa.

conti'nental *a* continental; (*European*) **C.** europeo,-a.

continual *a* continuo,-a, constante.

continually *adv* continuamente.

continuously *adv* continuamente.

continue [kən'tɪnjuː] *vti* continuar, seguir; **to c. to do sth** seguir *or* continuar haciendo algo.

continuous *a* continuo,-a.

contraceptive [kɒntrə'septɪv] *a & n* anticonceptivo (*mf*).

contract ['kɒntrækt] contrato *m*.

contradict [kɒntrə'dɪkt] *vt* contradecir.

contradiction contradicción *f*.

contrary ['kɒntrərɪ] **1** *n* **on the c.** todo lo contrario. **2** *adv* **c. to** en contra de.

contrast ['kɒntrɑːst] contraste *m*.

contrasting *a* opuesto,-a.

contribute [kən'trɪbjuːt] **1** *vt* (*money*) contribuir; (*ideas, information*) aportar. **2** *vi* contribuir; (*in discussion*) participar; (*to publication*) colaborar (**to** en).

contri'bution (*of money*) contribución *f*; (*to publication*) colaboración *f*.

contrive [kən'traɪv] *vi* **to c. to do sth** buscar la forma de hacer algo.

contrived *a* artificial.

control [kən'trəʊl] **1** *vt* controlar; (*person, animal*) dominar; (*vehicle*) manejar; **to c. one's temper** controlarse. **2** *n* (*power*) control *m*; (*authority*) autoridad *f*; (*in car, plane*) (*device*) mando *m*; (*on TV*) botón *m* de control; **out of c.** fuera de control; **to be in c.** estar al mando; **to be under c.** (*situation*) estar bajo control; **to go out of c.** descontrolarse; **to lose c.** perder los estribos.

control tower torre *f* de control.

convalesce [kɒnvə'les] *vi* convalecer.

convalescence convalecencia *f*.

convalescent home clínica *f* de reposo.

convenience [kən'viːnɪəns] comodidad *f*; *Br* **public conveniences** aseos *mpl* públicos.

convenience food comida *f* precocinada.

convenient *a* (*arrangement*) conveniente; (*time*) oportuno,-a; (*place*) bien situado,-a.

convent ['kɒnvənt] convento *m*.

conver'sation conversación *f*.

converse [kən'vɜːs] *vi* conversar.

convert [kən'vɜːt] *vt* convertir (**into** en).

con'vertible 1 *a* convertible. **2** *n* (*car*) descapotable *m*.

convey [kən'veɪ] *vt* (*carry*) transportar; (*sound*) transmitir; (*idea*) comunicar.

conveyor belt cinta *f* transportadora.

convict [kən'vɪkt] *vt* declarar culpable a.

con'viction (*belief*) creencia *f*, convicción *f*; (*for crime*) condena *f*.

convince [kən'vɪns] *vt* convencer.

convincing *a* convincente.

convoy ['kɒnvɔɪ] convoy *m*.

cook [kʊk] **1** *vt* cocinar, guisar; (*dinner*) preparar. **2** *vi* (*person*) cocinar, guisar; (*food*) cocerse. **3** *n* cocinero,-a *mf*.

cookbook libro *m* de cocina.

cooker cocina *f*.

cookery cocina *f*.

cookery book libro *m* de cocina.

cookie *US* galleta *f*.

cooking cocina *f*.

cooking apple manzana *f* ácida para cocinar.

cool [ku:l] **1** *a* fresco,-a; (*calm*) tranquilo,-a; (*reserved*) frío,-a; **it's c.** (*weather*) hace fresquito. **2** *n* (*coolness*) fresco *m*; **to lose one's c.** perder la calma. **3** *vt* (*air*) refrescar; (*drink*) enfriar.

● **cool down** *or* **off** *vi* (*something hot*) enfriarse; *fig* calmarse; (*feelings*) enfriarse.

cooler (*for food*) nevera *f* portátil.

coolness (*calmness*) calma *f*; (*composure*) aplomo *m*.

co-operate [kəʊˈɒpəreɪt] *vi* cooperar.

co-ope'ration cooperación *f*.

coop up [ku:p] *vt* encerrar.

cop [kɒp] *fam* (*policeman*) poli *m*.

cope [kəʊp] *vi* arreglárselas; **to c. with** (*person, work*) poder con; (*problem*) hacer frente a.

copper [ˈkɒpəʳ] (*metal*) cobre *m*.

copy [ˈkɒpɪ] **1** *n* copia *f*; (*of book*) ejemplar *m*. **2** *vti* copiar.

● **copy out/down** *vt* (*letter etc*) pasar a limpio.

cord [kɔ:d] (*string*) cuerda *f*; (*electrical*) cordón *m*.

cordial [ˈkɔ:dɪəl] (*drink*) licor *m*.

cordon off [ˈkɔ:dən] *vt* acordonar.

corduroy [ˈkɔ:dərɔɪ] pana *f*.

core [kɔ:ʳ] (*of fruit*) corazón *m*.

cork [kɔ:k] corcho *m*.

corkscrew sacacorchos *m inv*.

corn[1] [kɔ:n] (*maize*) maíz *m*; (*grain*) granos *mpl*; (*seed*) cereal *m*.

corn[2] (*on foot*) callo *m*.

corned beef carne *f* acecinada.

corner [ˈkɔ:nəʳ] **1** *n* (*of street*) esquina *f*; (*bend in road*) curva *f*; (*of room*) rincón *m*; (*in football*) **c. (kick)** córner *m*. **2** *vt* (*enemy*) arrinconar; (*market*) acaparar.

cornet [ˈkɔ:nɪt] (*for ice cream*) cucurucho *m*.

cornflakes *npl* copos *mpl* de maíz, cornflakes *mpl*.

corny [ˈkɔ:nɪ] *a* gastado,-a.

corporal [ˈkɔ:pərəl] cabo *m*.

corpse [kɔ:ps] cadáver *m*.

correct [kəˈrekt] **1** *vt* (*mistake*) corregir; (*child*) reprender. **2** *a* correcto, -a; (*behaviour*) formal.

correction corrección *f*.

correctly *adv* correctamente.

correspond [kɒrɪ'spɒnd] *vi* corresponder; (*by letter*) escribirse; **to c. to** equivaler a.

correspondence correspondencia *f*; **c. course** curso *m* por correspondencia.

corresponding *a* (*matching*) correspondiente.

corridor ['kɒrɪdɔ:ʳ] pasillo *m*.

corrugated ['kɒrʊgeɪtəd] *a* **c. iron** hierro *m* ondulado.

corrupt [kə'rʌpt] *a* (*person*) corrupto,-a; (*actions*) deshonesto,-a.

cosmetic [kɒz'metɪk] cosmético *m*.

cosmonaut ['kɒzmənɔ:t] cosmonauta *mf*.

cost [kɒst] **1** *n* (*price*) precio *m*; coste *m*; **at all costs** a toda costa. **2** *vti** costar, valer; **how much does it c.?** ¿cuánto cuesta?

Costa Rican [kɒstə'ri:kən] *a & n* costarricense (*mf*).

costly *a* costoso,-a.

costume ['kɒstju:m] traje *m*; **swimming c.** bañador *m*; **c. jewellery** bisutería *f*.

cosy ['kəʊzɪ] *a* (*atmosphere*) acogedor,-a; (*bed*) calentito,-a.

cot [kɒt] cuna *f*.

cottage ['kɒtɪdʒ] casa *f* de campo.

cottage cheese requesón *m*.

cotton ['kɒtən] algodón *m*; (*thread*) hilo *m*.

cotton wool algodón *m* hidrófilo.

couch [kaʊtʃ] sofá *m*.

couchette [ku:'ʃet] litera *f*.

cough [kɒf] **1** *vi* toser. **2** *n* tos *f*.

● **cough up** *vt fam* **to c. up the money** soltar la pasta.

cough mixture jarabe *m* para la tos.

could [kʊd] *v aux of* **can**[1].

council ['kaʊnsəl] (*body*) consejo *m*; **town c.** consejo *m* municipal.

council house ≈ vivienda *f* de protección oficial.

councillor, *US* **councilor** concejal *mf*.

count[1] [kaʊnt] **1** *vt* contar. **2** *vi* contar; **that doesn't c.** eso no vale.

● **count in** *vt* incluir a, contar con.

● **count on** *vt* contar con.

● **count out** *vt* (*banknotes*) contar uno por uno.

count[2] (*nobleman*) conde *m*.

countdown cuenta *f* atrás.

counter ['kaʊntəʳ] (*in shop*) mostrador *m*; (*in bank*) ventanilla *f*; (*in board games*) ficha *f*.

counter- *prefix* contra-.

counterattack contraataque *m*.

counter clockwise *a & adv US* en sentido inverso a las agujas del

reloj.
counterfoil (*of cheque*) matriz *f*.
country ['kʌntrɪ] (*state*) país *m*; (*rural area*) campo *m*; **native c.** patria *f*.
countryside (*area*) campo *m*; (*scenery*) paisaje *m*.
county ['kaʊntɪ] condado *m*.
couple ['kʌpəl] (*of people*) pareja *f*; (*of things*) par *m*; **a married c.** un matrimonio; **a c. of times** un par de veces.
coupon ['kuːpɒn] cupón *m*.
courage ['kʌrɪdʒ] valor *m*.
courageous [kə'reɪdʒəs] *a* valiente.
courgette [kʊə'ʒet] calabacín *m*.
courier ['kʊərɪəʳ] (*messenger*) mensajero,-a *mf*; (*guide*) guía *mf* turístico,-a.
course [kɔːs] (*of river*) curso *m*; (*of ship, plane*) rumbo *m*; (*series*) ciclo *m*; (*for golf*) campo *m*; (*of meal*) plato *m*; (*degree*) carrera *f*; (*in single subject*) curso *m*; (*short course*) cursillo *m*; **in the c. of construction** en vías de construcción; **a c. of treatment** un tratamiento; **of c.** claro, por supuesto; **of c. not!** ¡claro que no!
court [kɔːt] (*of law*) tribunal *m*; (*royal*) corte *f*; (*for sport*) pista *f*, cancha *f*.
courteous ['kɜːtɪəs] *a* cortés.
courtroom sala *f* de justicia.
courtyard patio *m*.
cousin ['kʌzən] primo,-a *mf*.
cover ['kʌvəʳ] **1** *vt* cubrir (**with** de); (*with lid*) tapar; (*hide*) disimular; (*protect*) abrigar; (*include*) abarcar. **2** *n* cubierta *f*; (*lid, of book*) tapa *f*; (*on bed*) manta *f*; (*of chair etc*) funda *f*; (*of magazine*) portada *f*; (*in restaurant*) cubierto *m*; **full c.** (*in insurance*) cobertura *f* completa; **to take c.** refugiarse.
● **cover over** *vt* (*floor etc*) recubrir.
● **cover up 1** *vt* cubrir; (*crime*) encubrir. **2** *vi* (*person*) abrigarse; **to c. up for sb** encubrir a algn.
coveralls *npl US* mono *m sing*.
cover charge (*in restaurant*) precio *m* del cubierto.
covering 1 *n* cubierta *f*. **2** *a* (*letter*) explicatorio,-a.
cow [kaʊ] vaca *f*.
coward ['kaʊəd] cobarde *mf*.
cowardice cobardía *f*.
cowardly *a* cobarde.
cowboy vaquero *m*.
cozy ['kəʊzɪ] *a US see* **cosy**.
crab [kræb] cangrejo *m*.

crack [kræk] **1** *vt* (*cup*) partir; (*nut*) cascar; (*whip*) hacer restallar; (*joke*) contar. **2** *vi* (*glass*) partirse; (*wall*) agrietarse; *fam* **to get cracking on sth** ponerse a hacer algo. **3** *n* (*in cup*) raja *f*; (*in wall, ground*) grieta *f*; (*of whip*) restallido *m*; (*of gun*) detonación *f*; *fam* (*drug*) crack *m*.

● **crack up** *vi* (*go mad*) desquiciarse; (*with laughter*) partirse de risa.

cracker (*biscuit*) galleta *f* seca; (*firework*) petardo *m*.

crackpot *fam* chiflado,-a.

cradle ['kreɪdəl] (*baby's*) cuna *f*.

craft [krɑːft] (*occupation*) oficio *m*; (*art*) arte *m*; (*skill*) destreza *f*.

craftsman artesano *m*.

crafty *a* astuto,-a.

cram [kræm] **1** *vt* atiborrar; **crammed with** atestado-a de. **2** *vi* (*for exam*) empollar.

cramp [kræmp] (*in leg etc*) calambre *m*.

cramped [kræmpt] *a* atestado,-a.

crane [kreɪn] (*device*) grúa *f*.

crash [kræʃ] **1** *vt* **to c. one's car** tener un accidente con el coche. **2** *vi* (*car, plane*) estrellarse; (*collide*) chocar; **to c. into** estrellarse contra. **3** *n* (*noise*) estrépito *m*; (*collision*) choque *m*; (*of market*) quiebra *f*; **car/plane c.** accidente *m* de coche/avión.

crash course curso *m* intensivo.

crash helmet casco *m* protector.

crash-land *vi* hacer un aterrizaje forzoso.

crash landing aterrizaje *m* forzoso.

crate [kreɪt] caja *f* (para embalaje).

craving ['kreɪvɪŋ] ansia *f*.

crawl [krɔːl] **1** *vi* (*baby*) gatear; (*vehicle*) avanzar lentamente. **2** *n* (*swimming*) crol *m*.

crayon ['kreɪɒn] cera *f*.

craze [kreɪz] manía *f*; (*fashion*) moda *f*.

crazy ['kreɪzɪ] *a* loco,-a.

creak [kriːk] *vi* (*hinge*) chirriar.

cream [kriːm] (*of milk*) nata *f*; **c. coloured** color crema.

cream cheese queso *m* crema.

creamy *a* cremoso,-a.

crease [kriːs] **1** *n* (*wrinkle*) arruga *f*; (*on trousers*) raya *f*. **2** *vt* (*clothes*) arrugar. **3** *vi* arrugarse.

create [kriː'eɪt] *vt* crear.

creation creación *f*.

creative *a* (*person*) creativo,-a.

creature ['kriːtʃər] (*animal*) criatura *f*.

crèche [kreʃ] guardería *f*.

credible ['kredɪbəl] *a* creíble.

credit ['kredɪt] **1** *n* (*financial*) crédito *m;* (*merit*) honor *m;* or
to be a c. to hacer honor a. **2** *vt* to c. sb's account abonar en cuenta a

credit card tarjeta *f* de crédito.

credit facilities facilidades *fpl* de pago.

creditworthy *a* solvente.

creek [kri:k] cala *f;* US riachuelo *m.*

creep* [kri:p] *vi* (*insect*) arrastrarse; (*cat*) deslizarse; (*person*) arrastrarse.

creepy *a fam* espeluznante.

cremate [krɪ'meɪt] *vt* incinerar.

crematorium [kremə'tɔ:rɪəm] crematorio *m.*

crepe paper [kreɪppeɪpə'] papel *m* crespón.

cress [kres] berro *m.*

crest [krest] (*of cock, wave*) cresta *f;* (*of hill*) cima *f.*

crew [kru:] (*of plane, yacht*) tripulación *f.*

crib [krɪb] **1** *n* (*for baby*) cuna *f.* **2** *vt* (*copy*) copiar.

cricket[1] ['krɪkɪt] (*insect*) grillo *m.*

cricket[2] (*game*) cricket *m.*

crime [kraɪm] delincuencia *f;* (*offence*) delito *m.*

criminal ['krɪmɪnəl] *a & n* criminal (*mf*).

cripple ['krɪpəl] lisiado,-a *mf.*

crisis ['kraɪsɪs] (*pl* **crises** ['kraɪsi:z]) crisis *f inv.*

crisp [krɪsp] **1** *a* crujiente; (*lettuce*) fresco,-a. **2** *n Br* (**potato**) **c.** patata *f*
frita.

critic ['krɪtɪk] crítico,-a *mf.*

critical *a* crítico,-a.

critically *adv* **c. ill** gravemente enfermo,-a.

criticism crítica *f.*

criticize *vt* criticar.

crochet ['krəʊʃeɪ] ganchillo *m.*

crockery ['krɒkərɪ] loza *f.*

crocodile ['krɒkədaɪl] cocodrilo *m.*

crocus ['krəʊkəs] crocus *m.*

crook [krʊk] *fam* caco *m.*

crooked ['krʊkɪd] *a* (*stick, picture*) torcido,-a; (*path*) tortuoso,-a.

crop [krɒp] cultivo *m;* (*harvest*) cosecha *f.*

● **crop up** *vi* surgir.

croquet ['krəʊkeɪ] croquet.

cross [krɒs] **1** *n* cruz *f;* (*of breeds*) cruce *m;* **c. section** sección *f*
transversal. **2** *vt* cruzar. **3** *vi* cruzar; (*roads*) cruzarse. **4** *a* (*angry*)
enfadado,-a.

● **cross off** *or* **out** *vt* tachar.

● **cross over** vi cruzar.

cross-country race cros m.

cross-eyed a bizco,-a.

crossing pedestrian c. paso m de peatones; **sea c.** travesía f.

cross-'reference referencia f.

crossroads cruce m; (fig) encrucijada f.

crosswalk US paso m de peatones.

crossword (puzzle) crucigrama m.

crouch [kraʊʃ] vi **to c. (down)** agacharse.

crow [krəʊ] cuervo m.

crowbar palanca f.

crowd [kraʊd] **1** n muchedumbre f; (gang) pandilla f; **the c.** el vulgo; **there was such a c. there** había tantísima gente allí. **2** vi **to c. in/out** entrar/salir en tropel.

● **crowd round** vt apiñarse alrededor de.

crowded a lleno,-a, atestado,-a.

crown [kraʊn] corona f.

crucial ['kru:ʃəl] a decisivo,-a.

crude [kru:d] a (manners, style) grosero,-a.

cruel [kru:əl] a cruel (**to** con).

cruelty crueldad f (**to** hacia).

cruet ['kru:ɪt] **c. set** vinagreras fpl.

cruise [kru:z] **1** vi (ship) hacer un crucero; (car) viajar a velocidad constante; (plane) viajar a velocidad de crucero. **2** n (on ship) crucero m.

crumb [krʌm] miga f.

crumble ['krʌmbəl] **1** vt desmigar. **2** vi (wall) desmoronarse; (bread) desmigajarse.

crumbly a que se desmigaja.

crummy ['krʌmɪ] a fam chungo,-a.

crumpet ['krʌmpɪt] crepe m grueso para tostar.

crumple ['krʌmpəl] vt (clothes) arrugar.

crunch [krʌntʃ] vt (food) mascar.

crunchy a crujiente.

crush [krʌʃ] **1** vt aplastar; (wrinkle) arrugar; (grind) moler. **2** n (of people) gentío m.

crust [krʌst] corteza f.

crutch [krʌtʃ] (for walking) muleta f.

cry [kraɪ] **1** vi gritar; (weep) llorar. **2** n grito m; (weep) llanto m.

● **cry off** vi rajarse.

● **cry out** vi gritar; **to c. out for sth** pedir algo a gritos.

● **cry over** vt llorar por.

crystal ['krɪstəl] cristal m.

cub [kʌb] (*junior scout*) niño *m* explorador.
Cuban ['kjuːbən] *a & n* cubano,-a (*mf*).
cube [kjuːb] cubo *m*; (*of sugar*) terrón *m*.
cubic ['kjuːbɪk] *a* cúbico,-a.
cubicle ['kjuːbɪkəl] cubículo *m*; (*at swimming pool*) caseta *f*.
cuckoo ['kʊkuː] cuco *m*.
cucumber ['kjuːkʌmbəʳ] pepino *m*.
cuddle ['kʌdəl] **1** *vt* abrazar. **2** *vi* abrazarse.
● **cuddle up to** *vt* acurrucarse contra.
cuddly toy muñeco *m* de peluche.
cue [kjuː] (*in play*) pie *m*.
cuff [kʌf] (*of sleeve*) puño *m*; US (*of trousers*) dobladillo *m*.
cufflinks *npl* gemelos *mpl*.
cul-de-sac ['kʌldəsæk] callejón *m* sin salida.
culprit ['kʌlprɪt] culpable *mf*.
cultivate ['kʌltɪveɪt] *vt* cultivar.
cultivated *a* (*person*) culto,-a.
cultural *a* cultural.
culture ['kʌltʃəʳ] cultura *f*.
cultured *a* (*person*) culto,-a.
cumbersome ['kʌmbəsəm] *a* (*bulky*) voluminoso,-a.
cunning ['kʌnɪŋ] **1** *a* astuto,-a. **2** *n* astucia *f*.
cup [kʌp] taza *f*; (*trophy*) copa *f*.
cupboard ['kʌbəd] armario *m*; (*on wall*) alacena *f*.
curable *a* curable.
curb [kɜːb] (*kerb*) bordillo *m*.
cure [kjʊəʳ] **1** *vt* curar. **2** *n* (*remedy*) cura *f*, remedio *m*.
curi'osity curiosidad *f*.
curious ['kjʊərɪəs] *a* (*inquisitive*) curioso,-a; (*odd*) extraño,-a.
curl [kɜːl] **1** *vt* (*hair*) rizar. **2** *vi* rizarse. **3** *n* (*of hair*) rizo *m*.
● **curl up** *vi* (*cat etc*) enroscarse; (*person*) hacerse un ovillo.
curly *a* rizado,-a.
currant ['kʌrənt] pasa *f* (de Corinto).
currency ['kʌrənsɪ] moneda *f*; **foreign c.** divisas *fpl*.
current ['kʌrənt] *a* actual; (*opinion*) general; (*year*) en curso.
current account cuenta *f* corriente.
current affairs actualidad *f sing* (política).
currently *adv* actualmente.
curriculum [kəˈrɪkjʊləm] (*pl* **curricula** [kəˈrɪkjʊlə]) plan *m* de estudios; **c. vitae** currículum *m* (vitae).
curry ['kʌrɪ] curry *m*.
curse [kɜːs] *vi* blasfemar.

cursor ['kɜːsəʳ] cursor *m*.
curtain ['kɜːtən] cortina *f*.
curts(e)y ['kɜːtsɪ] **1** *n* reverencia *f*. **2** *vi* hacer una reverencia (**to** a).
curve [kɜːv] **1** *n* curva *f*. **2** *vi* (*road, river*) describir una curva.
cushion ['kʊʃən] cojín *m*; (*large*) almohadón *m*.
custard ['kʌstəd] natillas *fpl*.
custom ['kʌstəm] (*habit*) costumbre *f*; (*in shop, business etc*) clientela *f*.
customer cliente *mf*.
customs *n sing or pl* aduana *f*.
customs duty derechos *mpl* de aduana.
customs officer agente *mf* de aduana.
cut [kʌt] **1** *vt** cortar; (*stone*) tallar; (*reduce*) reducir; (*divide up*) dividir (**into** en). **2** *vi** cortar. **3** *n* corte *m*; (*in skin*) cortadura *f*; (*wound*) herida *f*; (*with knife*) cuchillada *f*; (*of meat*) clase *f* de carne; (*reduction*) reducción *f*.
● **cut away** (*remove*) cortar.
● **cut back** *vt* (*expenses*) reducir; (*production*) disminuir.
● **cut down** *vt* (*tree*) talar.
● **cut down on** *vt* reducir.
● **cut off** *vt* (*water etc*) cortar; (*place*) aislar; (*heir*) excluir.
● **cut out 1** *vt* (*from newspaper*) recortar; (*delete*) suprimir; (*person*) **to be c. out for sth** estar hecho,-a para algo; *fam* **c. it out!** ¡basta ya! **2** *vi* (*engine*) calarse.
● **cut up** *vt* cortar en pedazos.
cutback reducción *f* (**in** de).
cute [kjuːt] *a* mono,-a, lindo,-a.
cutlery ['kʌtlərɪ] cubiertos *mpl*.
cutlet ['kʌtlɪt] chuleta *f*.
cut-'price *a* (*article*) a precio rebajado.
cutting (*from newspaper*) recorte *m*.
CV, cv [siː'viː] *abbr of* **curriculum vitae.**
cycle ['saɪkəl] **1** *n* ciclo *m*; (*bicycle*) bicicleta *f*; (*motorcycle*) moto *f*. **2** *vi* ir en bicicleta.
cycle path/track carril *m* de bicicletas.
cycling ciclismo *m*.
cyclist ciclista *mf*.
cylinder ['sɪlɪndəʳ] cilindro *m*; (*for gas*) bombona *f*.
cymbal ['sɪmbəl] platillo *m*.
Czech [tʃek] **1** *a* checo,-a. **2** *n* (*person*) checo,-a (*mf*); (*language*) checo *m*.

D

dab [dæb] *vt* (*apply*) aplicar; (*touch lightly*) tocar ligeramente.

dad [dæd], **daddy** ['dædɪ] *fam* papá *m*, papi *m*.

daffodil ['dæfədɪl] narciso *m*.

daft [dɑːft] *a Br fam* chalado,-a; (*idea*) tonto,-a.

daily ['deɪlɪ] **1** *a* diario,-a. **2** *adv* diariamente. **3** *n* (*newspaper*) diario *m*; *Br* (*cleaning lady*) asistenta *f*.

dairy ['deərɪ] lechería *f*; **d. farming** industria *f* lechera; **d. produce** productos *mpl* lácteos.

daisy ['deɪzɪ] margarita *f*.

dam [dæm] (*barrier*) dique *m*; (*lake*) presa *f*.

damage ['dæmɪdʒ] **1** *n* daño *m*; (*to health, reputation*) perjuicio *m*. **2** *vt* (*harm*) dañar; (*spoil*) estropear.

damn [dæm] *fam* **1** *interj* **d. (it)!** ¡maldito,-a sea! **2** *n* **I don't give a d.** me importa un bledo. **3** *a* maldito,-a. **4** *adv* (*very*) muy, sumamente.

damp [dæmp] **1** *a* húmedo,-a; (*wet*) mojado,-a. **2** *n* humedad *f*.

dampen *vt* humedecer.

dampness humedad *f*.

dance [dɑːns] **1** *n* baile *m*; (*classical, tribal*) danza *f*. **2** *vti* bailar.

dance hall salón *m* de baile.

dancer (*by profession*) bailarín,-ina *mf*; **she's a good d.** baila muy bien.

dandelion ['dændɪlaɪən] diente *m* de león.

dandruff ['dændrəf] caspa *f*.

Dane [deɪn] danés,-esa *mf*.

danger ['deɪndʒəʳ] (*peril*) peligro *m*; (*risk*) riesgo *m*; (*of war etc*) amenaza *f*; **out of d.** fuera de peligro.

dangerous *a* peligroso,-a; (*risky*) arriesgado,-a; (*harmful*) nocivo,-a; (*illness*) grave.

dangerously *adv* peligrosamente.

Danish ['deɪnɪʃ] **1** *a* danés,-esa. **2** *n* (*language*) danés *m*.

dare [deəʳ] **1** *vi* atreverse, osar. **2** *vt* (*challenge*) desafiar; **to d. to do sth** atreverse a hacer algo

daring *a* osado,-a.

dark [dɑːk] **1** *a* (*unlit, colour*) oscuro,-a; (*hair, complexion*) moreno,-a; (*eyes, future*) negro,-a. **2** *n* (*darkness*) oscuridad *f*.

dark-haired *a* moreno,-a.

darkness oscuridad *f*.

dark-skinned *a* de piel oscura.

darling ['dɑːlɪŋ] *a & n* querido,-a (*mf*).

dart [dɑːt] (*missile*) dardo *m*; **darts** *sing* (*game*) dardos *mpl*.

dartboard diana *f*.

dash [dæʃ] **1** n (*hyphen*) guión m. **2** vi (*rush*) correr.

● **dash off** vi salir corriendo.

dashboard salpicadero m.

data ['deɪtə] npl datos mpl.

database base m de datos.

data processing (*act*) proceso m de datos; (*science*) informática f.

date[1] [deɪt] n fecha f; (*social event*) compromiso m; (*with girl, boy*) cita f; (*person dated*) ligue m; **what's the d. today?** ¿qué día es hoy?; **out of d.** (*ideas*) anticuado,-a; (*expression*) desusado,-a; (*invalid*) caducado,-a; **to be up to d.** estar al día.

● **date back to, date from** vt datar de; (*origins etc*) remontarse a.

date[2] (*fruit*) dátil m.

daughter ['dɔːtəʳ] hija f.

daughter-in-law nuera f.

dawdle ['dɔːdəl] vi (*walking*) andar despacio; (*waste time*) perder el tiempo.

dawn [dɔːn] amanecer m.

day [deɪ] día m; **(on) the next** or **following d.** el or al día siguiente; **the d. after tomorrow** pasado mañana; **the d. before yesterday** anteayer.

daylight luz f del día.

day return (ticket) billete m de ida y vuelta para el mismo día.

daytime día m.

dead [ded] **1** a muerto,-a; **he was shot d.** le mataron a tiros. **2** adv fam (*tired, easy*) muy.

dead end (*street*) callejón m sin salida.

deadline (*date*) fecha f tope; (*time*) hora f tope.

deaf [def] **1** a sordo,-a; **d. mute** sordomudo,-a mf. **2** npl **the d.** los sordos.

deafness sordera f.

deal [diːl] (*in business, politics*) trato m; (*amount*) cantidad f; (*at cards*) reparto m; **business d.** contrato m; **to do a d. with sb** (*transaction*) cerrar un trato con algn; (*agreement*) pactar algo con algn; **it's a d.!** ¡trato hecho!; **a good d. (of sth)** una gran parte (de algo); **a good d. slower** mucho más despacio.

● **deal* in** vt (*goods*) comerciar en; (*drugs*) traficar con.

● **deal* out** vt repartir.

● **deal* with** vt (*firm, person*) tratar con; (*subject, problem*) abordar; (*book etc*) tratar de.

dealer (*in goods*) comerciante mf; (*in drugs*) traficante mf.

dealings npl (*relations*) trato m sing; (*in business*) negocios mpl.

dear [dɪəʳ] **1** a (*loved*) querido,-a; (*expensive*) caro,-a; (*in letter*) **D. Andrew** Querido Andrew; **D. Madam** Estimada señora; **D. Sir(s)** Muy señor(es) mío(s). **2** n querido,-a mf; **my d.** mi vida. **3** interj **oh d.!, d. me!** (*surprise*) ¡vaya por Dios!; (*disappointment*) ¡qué pena!

death [deθ] muerte *f*.

death certificate certificado *m* de defunción.

debate [dɪ'beɪt] **1** *n* debate *m*. **2** *vti* discutir.

debit ['debɪt] **1** *n* débito *m*. **2** *vt* **to d. sb's account** cargar una suma en la cuenta de algn.

debt [det] deuda *f*.

decade ['dekeɪd] década *f*, decenio *m*.

decaffeinated [dɪ'kæfɪneɪtɪd] *a* descafeinado,-a.

decay [dɪ'keɪ] (*of food, body*) descomposición *f*; (*of teeth*) caries *f inv*; (*of buildings*) desmoronamiento *m*.

deceive [dɪ'siːv] *vt* (*mislead*) engañar; (*lie to*) mentir.

December [dɪ'sembəʳ] diciembre *m*.

decent ['diːsənt] *a* (*person*) honrado,-a; (*kind*) simpático,-a.

decide [dɪ'saɪd] **1** *vt* decidir; **to d. to do sth** decidir hacer algo. **2** *vi* (*reach decision*) decidirse.

● **decide on** *vt* (*choose*) optar por.

decimal ['desɪməl] **1** *a* decimal; **d. point** coma *f* (de fracción decimal). **2** *n* decimal *m*.

decision [dɪ'sɪʒən] decisión *f*.

decisive [dɪ'saɪsɪv] *a* (*resolute*) decidido,-a,; (*conclusive*) decisivo,-a.

deck [dek] (*of ship*) cubierta *f*.

deckchair tumbona *f*.

declare [dɪ'kleəʳ] *vt* declarar; (*winner, innocence*) proclamar.

decline [dɪ'klaɪn] *vi* (*decrease*) disminuir; (*amount*) bajar; (*business*) decaer; (*deteriorate*) deteriorarse; (*health*) empeorar.

decorate ['dekəreɪt] *vt* (*adorn*) decorar (**with** con); (*paint*) pintar; (*wallpaper*) empapelar.

deco'ration (*decor*) decoración *f*.

decorative *a* decorativo,-a.

decorator decorador,-a *mf*; (*painter*) pintor,-a *mf*; (*paperhanger*) empapelador,-a *mf*.

decrease ['diːkriːs] **1** *n* disminución *f*; (*in speed, size, price*) reducción *f*. **2** [dɪ'kriːs] *vi* disminuir; (*price, temperature*) bajar; (*speed, size*) reducirse. **3** *vt* disminuir; (*price, temperature*) bajar.

dedicated ['dedɪkeɪtɪd] *a* ardiente.

deduct [dɪ'dʌkt] *vt* descontar (**from** de).

deduction (*conclusion*) conclusión *f*; (*subtraction*) descuento *m*.

deed [diːd] (*act*) acto *m*; (*legal document*) escritura *f*.

deep [diːp] *a* profundo,-a; (*breath, sigh*) hondo,-a; (*voice*) bajo,-a; **it's ten metres d.** tiene diez metros de profundidad.

deep-'freeze 1 *n* congelador *m*. **2** *vt* congelar.

deer [dɪəʳ] *n inv* ciervo *m*.

defeat [dɪˈfiːt] **1** vt derrotar. **2** n (of army, team) derrota f.

defect [ˈdiːfekt] defecto m.

de'fective a (faulty) defectuoso,-a.

defence [dɪˈfens] defensa f.

defend [dɪˈfend] vt defender.

defendant acusado,-a mf.

defiant [dɪˈfaɪənt] a (behaviour) desafiante; (person) insolente.

deficiency falta f, carencia f.

deficient [dɪˈfɪʃənt] a deficiente; **to be d. in sth** carecer de algo.

deficit [ˈdefɪsɪt] déficit m.

define [dɪˈfaɪn] vt definir; (duties, powers) delimitar.

definite [ˈdefɪnɪt] a (clear) claro,-a; (progress) notable; (date, place) determinado,-a.

definitely adv sin duda.

definition [defɪˈnɪʃən] definición f.

deformed [dɪˈfɔːmd] a deforme.

defrost [diːˈfrɒst] vt (freezer, food) descongelar.

defy [dɪˈfaɪ] vt desafiar; (law, order) contravenir.

degenerate [dɪˈdʒenəreɪt] vi degenerar (**into** en).

degree [dɪˈɡriː] grado m; (qualification) título m; **to some d.** hasta cierto punto; **to have a d. in science** ser licenciado en ciencias.

de-icer anticongelante m.

dejected [dɪˈdʒektɪd] a deprimido,-a.

delay [dɪˈleɪ] **1** vt (flight, train) retrasar; (person) entretener; (postpone) aplazar. **2** n retraso m.

delegate [ˈdelɪɡɪt] **1** n delegado,-a mf. **2** [ˈdelɪɡeɪt] vt delegar (**to** en); **to d. sb to do sth** encargar a algn que haga algo.

dele'gation delegación f.

delete [dɪˈliːt] vt suprimir; (cross out) tachar.

deliberate [dɪˈlɪbərɪt] a (intentional) deliberado,-a.

deliberately adv (intentionally) a propósito; (unhurriedly) pausadamente.

delicacy (food) manjar m (exquisito).

delicate [ˈdelɪkɪt] a delicado,-a; (handiwork) fino,-a; (instrument) sensible; (flavour) fino,-a.

delicatessen delicatessen m.

delicious [dɪˈlɪʃəs] a delicioso,-a.

delight [dɪˈlaɪt] **1** n (pleasure) placer m; (source of pleasure) encanto m; **he took d. in it** le encantó. **2** vt encantar.

delighted a encantado,-a.

delightful a (person) encantador,-a; (view) muy agradable; (meal, weather) delicioso,-a.

delinquent [dɪ'lɪŋkwənt] *a & n* delincuente (*mf*).

deliver [dɪ'lɪvə'] *vt* (*goods, letters*) repartir; (*parcel, manuscript etc*) entregar; (*speech, verdict*) pronunciar.

delivery (*of goods*) reparto *m*; (*of parcel, manuscript etc*) entrega *f*; (*of baby*) parto *m*.

delude [dɪ'lu:d] *vt* engañar; **don't d. yourself** no te hagas ilusiones.

de luxe [də'lʌks] *a* de lujo *inv*.

demand [dɪ'mɑ:nd] **1** *n* (*request*) petición *f*; (*for pay rise, rights*) reclamación *f*; (*need*) necesidad *f*; (*claim*) exigencia *f*; (*economic*) demanda *f*; **to be in d.** ser solicitado,-a. **2** *vt* exigir; (*rights*) reclamar; **to d. that ...** insistir en que ... (+ *subjunctive*).

demanding *a* (*hard to please*) exigente; (*job*) agotador,-a.

demerara (sugar) azúcar *m* moreno.

democracy [dɪ'mɒkrəsɪ] democracia *f*.

demo'cratic *a* democrático,-a.

demolish [dɪ'mɒlɪʃ] *vt* (*building*) derribar.

demo'lition demolición *f*.

demonstrate ['demənstreɪt] **1** *vt* demostrar. **2** *vi* (*politically*) manifestarse.

demonstration (*proof*) demostración *f*; (*explanation*) explicación *f*; (*political*) manifestación *f*.

de'monstrative *a* franco,-a.

demonstrator manifestante *mf*.

demoralize [dɪ'mɒrəlaɪz] *vt* desmoralizar.

den [den] (*of animal*) guarida *f*; (*study*) estudio *m*.

denial [dɪ'naɪəl] (*of charge*) desmentido *m*; (*of rights*) denegación *f*.

denim ['denɪm] dril *m*; **denims** tejanos *mpl*, vaqueros *mpl*.

denounce [dɪ'naʊns] *vt* denunciar.

dent [dent] **1** *n* abolladura *f*. **2** *vt* abollar.

dental ['dentəl] *a* dental.

dentist ['dentɪst] dentista *mf*.

dentures ['dentʃəz] *npl* dentadura *f* postiza.

deny [dɪ'naɪ] *vt* (*repudiate, refuse*) negar; (*rumour, report*) desmentir; (*charge*) rechazar; **to d. sb sth** negarle a algn.

deodorant [di:'əʊdərənt] desodorante *m*.

depart [dɪ'pɑ:t] *vi* marcharse, irse; (*from subject*) desviarse (**from** de).

department [dɪ'pɑ:tmənt] sección *f*; (*in university*) departamento *m*; (*in government*) ministerio *m*.

department store grandes almacenes *mpl* .

departure partida *f*; (*of plane, train*) salida *f*.

depend [dɪ'pend] **1** *vi* (*rely*) fiarse (**on, upon** de). **2** *v impers* (*be determined by*) depender (**on** de); **it depends on the weather** según el tiempo que haga; **that depends** según.

dependable *a* (*person*) fiable.

dependant, US dependent dependiente *mf*.

depict [dɪ'pɪkt] *vt* (*in painting*) representar; (*describe*) describir.

deplorable *a* lamentable.

deplore [dɪ'plɔːʳ] *vt* deplorar.

deposit [dɪ'pɒzɪt] **1** *n* (*in bank, on rented car*) depósito *m*; (*in river, test tube*) sedimento *m*; (*in wine*) poso *m*; (*on purchase*) señal *f*; (*on house*) entrada *f*. **2** *vt* depositar; (*into account*) ingresar.

deposit account cuenta *f* de ahorros.

depot ['depəʊ] almacén *m*; (*bus garage*) cochera *f* (de autobuses).

depress [dɪ'pres] *vt* (*discourage*) deprimir.

depressed [dɪ'prest] *a* (*person*) deprimido,-a; **to get d.** deprimirse.

depression depresión *f*.

deprive [dɪ'praɪv] *vt* privar (**of** de).

deprived *a* necesitado,-a.

depth [depθ] profundidad *f*; (*of emotion*) intensidad *f*.

deputy ['depjʊtɪ] (*substitute*) suplente *mf*; **d. head** subdirector,-a *mf*.

derailment descarrilamiento *m*.

derelict ['derɪlɪkt] *a* abandonado,-a.

derive [dɪ'raɪv] *vt* sacar.

descend [dɪ'send] **1** *vi* descender; **to d. from** (*be related to*) descender de. **2** *vt* (*stairs*) bajar.

● **descend upon** *vt* (*area*) invadir.

descendant descendiente *mf*.

descent descenso *m*.

describe [dɪ'skraɪb] *vt* describir.

description [dɪ'skrɪpʃən] descripción *f*; (*type*) clase *f*.

desert[1] ['dezət] desierto *m*.

desert[2] [dɪ'zɜːt] *vt* (*place, family*) abandonar.

deserve [dɪ'zɜːv] *vt* (*rest, punishment*) merecer; (*prize, praise*) ser digno,-a de.

design [dɪ'zaɪn] **1** *n* diseño *m*; (*of building etc*) plano *m*; (*of room*) disposición *f*; (*pattern*) dibujo *m*. **2** *vt* diseñar.

designer diseñador,-a *mf*; **d. jeans** pantalones *mpl* de marca.

designer clothes ropa *f* de marca.

desirable *a* deseable; (*asset, offer*) atractivo,-a.

desire [dɪ'zaɪəʳ] **1** *n* deseo *m*; **I haven't the slightest d. to go** no me apetece nada ir. **2** *vt* desear.

desk [desk] (*in school*) pupitre *m*; (*in office*) escritorio *m*; **(reception) d.** recepción *f*.

desk clerk *US* recepcionista *mf*.

desktop computer ordenador *m* de sobremesa.
despair [dɪ'speəʳ] **1** *n* desesperación *f*. **2** *vi* desesperar(se) (**of** de).
despatch [dɪ'spætʃ] *n & vt see* **dispatch.**
desperate ['despərɪt] *a (person, situation, action)* desesperado,-a; *(need)* apremiante; **to be d. for sth** necesitar algo con urgencia.
desperately *adv (need)* urgentemente; *(bad, busy)* terriblemente.
despicable [dɪ'spɪkəbəl] *a* despreciable; *(behaviour)* indigno,-a.
despise [dɪ'spaɪz] *vt* despreciar.
despite [dɪ'spaɪt] *prep* a pesar de.
dessert [dɪ'zɜːt] postre *m*.
dessertspoon cuchara *f* de postre.
destination [destɪ'neɪʃən] destino *m*.
destitute ['destɪtjuːt] *a* indigente.
destroy [dɪ'strɔɪ] *vt* destruir; *(vehicle, old furniture)* destrozar.
destruction [dɪ'strʌkʃən] destrucción *f*.
destructive [dɪ'strʌktɪv] *a (gale etc)* destructor,-a.
detach [dɪ'tætʃ] *vt (remove)* separar.
detachable *a* separable (**from** de).
detached *a (separated)* separado,-a.
detached house casa *f* independiente.
detail ['diːteɪl] detalle *m*, pormenor *m*.
detailed *a* detallado,-a.
detain [dɪ'teɪn] *vt (police etc)* detener; *(delay)* retener.
detect [dɪ'tekt] *vt (error, movement)* advertir; *(difference)* notar; *(smell, sound)* percibir; *(discover)* descubrir.
detective detective *mf*; **d. story** novela *f* policíaca.
detector aparato *m* detector.
detention [dɪ'tenʃən] *(of suspect etc)* detención *f*.
deter [dɪ'tɜːʳ] *vt (dissuade)* disuadir (**from** de); **to d. sb from doing sth** impedir a algn hacer algo.
detergent [dɪ'tɜːdʒənt] detergente *m*.
deteriorate [dɪ'tɪərɪəreɪt] *vi* deteriorarse.
deterio'ration empeoramiento *m*; *(of substance, friendship)* deterioro *m*.
determi'nation *(resolution)* resolución *f*.
determine [dɪ'tɜːmɪn] *vt* determinar.
determined *a (person)* decidido,-a; *(effort)* enérgico,-a.
deterrent [dɪ'terənt] fuerza *f* disuasoria.
detour ['diːtʊəʳ] desvío *m*.
develop [dɪ'veləp] **1** *vt* desarrollar; *(trade)* fomentar; *(plan)* elaborar; *(illness, habit)* contraer; *(interest)* mostrar; *(natural resources)* aprovechar; *(build on) (site)* urbanizar. **2** *vi (body, industry)* desarrollarse;

(system) perfeccionarse; *(interest)* crecer.

● **develop into** *vt* transformarse en.

development desarrollo *m*; *(of trade)* fomento *m*; *(of skill)* perfección *f*; *(of character)* formación *f*; *(advance)* avance *m*; *(exploitation)* explotación *f*; *(of land, site)* urbanización *f*; **there are no new developments** no hay ninguna novedad.

deviate ['di:vɪeɪt] *vi* desviarse **(from** de).

device [dɪ'vaɪs] aparato *m*; *(mechanism)* mecanismo *m*.

devil ['devəl] diablo *m*, demonio *m*; *fam* **where the d. did you put it?** ¿dónde demonios lo pusiste?

devise [dɪ'vaɪz] *vt* idear.

devote [dɪ'vəʊt] *vt* dedicar.

devoted *a* dedicado,-a **(to** a).

devotion devoción *f*; *(to cause)* dedicación *f*.

dew [dju:] rocío *m*.

diabetes [daɪə'bi:tɪs] diabetes *f*.

diabetic [daɪə'betɪk] *a & n* diabético,-a *(mf)*.

diagnosis [daɪəg'nəʊsɪs] *(pl* **diagnoses** [daɪəg'nəʊsi:z]) diagnóstico *m*.

diagonal [daɪ'ægənəl] *a & n* diagonal *(f)*.

diagonally *adv* en diagonal, diagonalmente.

diagram ['daɪəgræm] diagrama *m*; *(of process, system)* esquema *m*; *(of workings)* gráfico *m*.

dial ['daɪəl] **1** *n (of clock)* esfera *f*; *(on machine)* botón *m* selector; *(on radio)* dial *m*. **2** *vti* marcar.

dialling code prefijo *m*.

dialling tone señal *f* de marcar.

dialect [daɪə'lekt] dialecto *m*.

dialogue, *US* **dialog** ['daɪəlɒg] diálogo *m*.

diameter [daɪ'æmɪtə'] diámetro *m*.

diamond ['daɪəmənd] diamante *m*; *(shape)* rombo *m*.

diaper ['daɪəpə'] *US* pañal *m*.

diarrhoea, *US* **diarrhea** [daɪə'rɪə] diarrea *f*.

diary ['daɪərɪ] diario *m*; *(for appointments)* agenda *f*.

dice [daɪs] **1** *n* dado *m*. **2** *vt (food)* cortar en cuadritos.

dictate [dɪk'teɪt] **1** *vt (letter, order)* dictar. **2** *vi (order about)* dar órdenes.

dictation dictado *m*.

dictionary ['dɪkʃənərɪ] diccionario *m*.

did [dɪd] *pt of* do.

die [daɪ] *vi* morir(se); **to be dying for sth/to do sth** morirse por algo/de ganas de hacer algo.

● **die away** *vi* desvanecerse.

● **die down** *vi* (*wind*) amainar; (*noise, excitement*) disminuir.

● **die out** *vi* extinguirse.

diesel ['di:zəl] (*oil*) gasoil *m*; **d. engine** motor *m* diesel.

diet ['daɪət] **1** *n* (*normal food*) dieta *f*; (*selected food*) régimen *m*. **2** *vi* estar a régimen.

differ ['dɪfəʳ] *vi* (*be unlike*) ser distinto,-a; (*disagree*) discrepar.

difference diferencia *f*; (*disagreement*) desacuerdo *m*; **it makes no d. (to me)** (me) da igual; **what d. does it make?** ¿qué más da?

different *a* distinto,-a.

differently *adv* de otra manera.

difficult ['dɪfɪkəlt] *a* difícil.

difficulty dificultad *f*; (*problem*) problema *m*.

dig* [dɪg] **1** *vt* (*earth*) cavar; (*tunnel*) excavar; (*hole*) hacer. **2** *vi* cavar.

● **dig out** *vt fig* (*find*) sacar; (*information*) descubrir.

● **dig up** *vt* (*weeds*) arrancar; (*buried object*) desenterrar.

digest [dɪ'dʒest] *vt* (*food*) digerir; (*facts*) asimilar.

digestion digestión *f*.

digger excavadora *f*.

digit ['dɪdʒɪt] (*number*) dígito *m*.

digital *a* digital.

dilapidated [dɪ'læpɪdeɪtɪd] *a* en mal estado.

dilute [daɪ'lu:t] *vt* diluir; (*wine, milk*) aguar.

dim [dɪm] **1** *a* (*light*) tenue; (*room*) oscuro,-a; (*outline*) borroso,-a; (*memory*) vago,-a; *fam* (*stupid*) torpe. **2** *vt* (*light*) bajar.

dime [daɪm] *US* moneda *f* de diez centavos.

dimension [daɪ'menʃən] dimensión *f*.

din [dɪn] estrépito *m*.

dine [daɪn] *vi* (*formal use*) cenar.

diner (*person*) comensal *mf*; *US* (*restaurant*) restaurante *m* barato.

dinghy ['dɪŋɪ] bote *m*; (**rubber**) **d.** bote *m* neumático.

dingy ['dɪndʒɪ] *a* (*street, house*) oscuro,-a; (*dirty*) sucio,-a; (*colour*) desteñido,-a.

dining car ['daɪnɪŋkɑːʳ] vagón *m* restaurante.

dining room comedor *m*.

dinner ['dɪnəʳ] (*at midday*) comida *f*; (*in evening*) cena *f*.

dinner jacket smoking *m*.

dinner party cena *f*.

dinner service vajilla *f*.

dinosaur ['daɪnəsɔːʳ] dinosaurio *m*.

dip [dɪp] **1** *n* (*bathe*) chapuzón *m*; (*of road*) pendiente *f*. **2** *vt* poner; *Br* **to d. one's lights** poner luces de cruce. **3** *vi* (*road*) bajar.

● **dip into** *vt* (*savings*) echar mano de.

diphthong ['dɪfθɒŋ] diptongo *m*.

diploma [dɪ'pləʊmə] diploma *m*.

dipped headlights (*of vehicle*) luces *mpl* de cruce.

direct [dɪ'rekt] **1** *a* directo,-a. **2** *adv* directamente. **3** *vt* dirigir; **can you d. me to a bank?** ¿me puede indicar dónde hay un banco?

direction dirección *f*; **directions** (*to place*) señas *fpl*; **directions for use** modo *m* de empleo.

directly 1 *adv* (*above etc*) justo; (*speak*) directamente; (*at once*) en seguida. **2** *conj* en cuanto.

director director,-a *mf*.

directory (*for telephone*) guía *f* telefónica.

directory enquiries (servicio *m* de) información *f*.

dirt [dɜːt] suciedad *f*.

dirt-cheap *adv & a fam* tirado,-a.

dirty 1 *a* sucio,-a; (*joke*) verde; (*mind*) pervertido,-a; **d. word** palabrota *f*; **to get sth d.** ensuciar algo. **2** *vt* ensuciar.

disa'bility discapacidad *f*.

disabled [dɪ'seɪbəld] **1** *a* minusválido,-a. **2** *npl* **the d.** los minusválidos *mpl*.

disadvantage desventaja *f*; (*obstacle*) inconveniente *m*.

disagree *vi* (*differ*) no estar de acuerdo (**with** con); (*quarrel*) reñir (**about** por); **garlic disagrees with me** el ajo no me sienta bien.

disagreeable *a* desagradable.

disagreement desacuerdo *m*; (*argument*) riña *f*.

disappear *vi* desaparecer.

disappearance desaparición *f*.

disappoint [dɪsə'pɔɪnt] *vt* decepcionar.

disappointing *a* decepcionante.

disappointment decepción *f*.

disapproval desaprobación *f*.

disapprove *vi* **to d. of** desaprobar.

disarm 1 *vt* desarmar. **2** *vi* desarmarse.

disaster [dɪ'zɑːstə^r] desastre *m*.

disastrous *a* desastroso,-a.

disc [dɪsk] disco *m*; (*for computer*) disquete *m*.

discard [dɪs'kɑːd] *vt* (*old things*) deshacerse de; (*plan*) descartar.

discharge [dɪs'tʃɑːdʒ] *vt* (*prisoner*) soltar; (*patient*) dar de alta; (*soldier*) licenciar; (*dismiss*) despedir.

discontinued *a* (*article*) que no se fabrica más.

discipline ['dɪsɪplɪn] **1** *n* disciplina *f*. **2** *vt* (*child*) castigar; (*worker*) sancionar.

disc jockey disc-jockey *mf*, pinchadiscos *mf inv*.

disclose [dɪs'kləʊz] *vt* revelar.

disco ['dɪskəʊ] discoteca *f.*

discomfort (*pain*) malestar *m.*

disconnect *vt* desconectar (**from** de); (*gas, electricity*) cortar.

discontented *a* descontento,-a.

discotheque ['dɪskətek] discoteca *f.*

discount ['dɪskaʊnt] descuento *m.*

discourage *vt* (*dishearten*) desanimar; (*advances*) rechazar.

discover *vt* descubrir; (*missing person, object*) encontrar.

discovery descubrimiento *m.*

discreet [dɪ'skriːt] *a* discreto,-a.

discriminate [dɪ'skrɪmɪneɪt] *vi* discriminar (**between** entre); **to d. against sth/sb** discriminar algo/a algn.

discrimi'nation (*bias*) discriminación *f.*

discuss [dɪ'skʌs] *vt* discutir; (*in writing*) tratar de.

discussion discusión *f.*

disease [dɪ'ziːz] enfermedad *f.*

disembark *vti* desembarcar.

disfigured [dɪs'fɪgəd] *a* desfigurado,-a.

disgrace 1 *n* desgracia *f.* **2** *vt* deshonrar.

disgraceful *a* vergonzoso,-a.

disguise [dɪs'gaɪz] **1** *n* disfraz *m;* **in d.** disfrazado,-a. **2** *vt* (*person*) disfrazar (**as** de).

disgust [dɪs'gʌst] **1** *n* repugnancia *f,* asco *m.* **2** *vt* (*revolt*) dar asco a.

disgusted *a* indignado.

disgusting *a* repugnante; (*behaviour, state of affairs*) intolerable.

dish [dɪʃ] (*for serving*) fuente *f;* (*course*) plato *m;* **to wash** or **do the dishes** fregar los platos.

● **dish up** *vt* (*meal*) servir.

dishcloth trapo *m* de fregar.

dishevelled, US **disheveled** [dɪ'ʃevəld] *a* (*hair*) despeinado,-a; (*appearance*) desaliñado,-a.

dishonest *a* (*person*) poco honrado,-a; (*means*) fraudulento,-a.

dishwasher lavaplatos *m inv.*

disillusioned *a* desilusionado,-a.

disincentive freno *m.*

disinfect *vt* desinfectar.

disinfectant desinfectante *m.*

disk [dɪsk] disco *m;* (*for computer*) disquete *m.*

disk drive unidad *f* de disquete, disquetera *f.*

dislike 1 *n* antipatía *f* (**for, of** a, hacia). **2** *vt* tener antipatía hacia.

dislocate ['dɪsləkeɪt] *vt* (*joint*) dislocar.

dismal ['dızməl] *a* (*prospect*) sombrío,-a; (*place, weather*) deprimente; (*person*) triste.

dismantle [dıs'mæntəl] *vt* desmontar.

dismay [dıs'meı] **1** *n* consternación *f*. **2** *vt* consternar.

dismiss [dıs'mıs] *vt* (*employee*) despedir.

dismissal (*of employee*) despido *m*.

disobedience desobediencia *f*.

disobedient *a* desobediente.

disobey *vt* desobedecer; (*law*) violar.

disorder (*untidiness*) desorden *m*; (*riot*) disturbio *m*; (*illness*) trastorno *m*.

disorganized *a* desorganizado,-a.

dispatch [dı'spætʃ] *vt* (*mail*) enviar; (*goods*) expedir.

dispel [dı'spel] *vt* disipar.

dispenser [dıs'pensə^r] (*device*) máquina *f* expendedora; **cash d.** cajero *m* automático.

disperse [dı'spɜːs] **1** *vt* dispersar. **2** *vi* dispersarse.

display [dı'spleı] **1** *n* (*exhibition*) exposición *f*; (*on computer screen*) visualización *f*. **2** *vt* mostrar; (*goods*) exponer; (*on computer screen*) visualizar; (*feelings*) manifestar.

displeased *a* contrariado,-a.

disposable *a* (*throwaway*) desechable.

disposal at my d. a mi disposición.

dispose [dı'spəʊz] *vi* **to d. of** (*rubbish*) tirar; (*unwanted object*) deshacerse de.

dispute ['dıspjuːt] **1** *n* (*disagreement*) discusión *f*; (*quarrel*) disputa *f*; **industrial d.** conflicto *m* laboral. **2** [dı'spjuːt] *vt* refutar.

disqualify *vt* (*team*) descalificar; (*make ineligible*) incapacitar.

disregard *vt* (*ignore*) ignorar.

disrupt [dıs'rʌpt] *vt* (*meeting, traffic*) interrumpir; (*order*) trastornar; (*schedule etc*) desbaratar.

disruption (*of meeting, traffic*) interrupción *f*; (*of schedule etc*) desbaratamiento *m*.

dissatis'faction descontento *m*.

dissatis'fied *a* descontento,-a.

dissolve [dı'zɒlv] **1** *vt* disolver. **2** *vi* disolverse.

dissuade [dı'sweıd] *vt* disuadir (**from** de).

distance ['dıstəns] distancia *f*; **in the d.** a lo lejos.

distant *a* (*place, time*) lejano,-a; (*look*) distraído,-a; (*aloof*) distante.

distaste aversión *f*.

distasteful *a* desagradable.

distinct [dı'stıŋkt] *a* (*different*) diferente; (*smell, change*) marcado,-a;

(*idea, intention*) claro,-a; **as d. from** a diferencia de.

distinction (*difference*) diferencia *f*; (*excellence*) distinción *f*; (*in exam*) sobresaliente *m*.

distinctive *a* distintivo,-a.

distinctly *adv* (*clearly*) claramente; (*definitely*) sensiblemente.

distinguish [dɪˈstɪŋgwɪʃ] *vt* distinguir.

distinguished *a* distinguido,-a.

distort [dɪˈstɔːt] *vt* (*misrepresent*) deformar.

distract [dɪˈstrækt] *vt* distraer.

distraction (*interruption*) distracción *f*; **to drive sb to d.** volver loco a algn.

distress [dɪˈstres] (*mental*) angustia *f*; (*physical*) dolor *m*.

distressing *a* penoso,-a.

distribute [dɪˈstrɪbjuːt] *vt* distribuir.

distri'bution distribución *f*.

distributor distribuidor,-a *mf*; (*in car engine*) delco *m*.

district [ˈdɪstrɪkt] (*of country*) región *f*; (*of town*) barrio *m*; *US* **d. attorney** fiscal *mf*.

distrust *vt* desconfiar de.

disturb [dɪˈstɜːb] *vt* (*inconvenience*) molestar; (*silence*) romper; (*sleep*) interrumpir; (*worry*) perturbar; (*papers*) desordenar.

disturbance (*commotion*) disturbio *m*.

disturbing *a* inquietante.

ditch [dɪtʃ] zanja *f*; (*at roadside*) cuneta *f*; (*for irrigation*) acequia *f*.

ditto [ˈdɪtəʊ] ídem.

divan [dɪˈvæn] diván *m*.

dive [daɪv] **1** *n* (*into water*) zambullida *f*; (*of diver*) buceo *m*; (*of plane*) picado *m*; (*in sport*) salto *m*. **2** *vi** zambullirse; (*diver*) bucear; (*plane*) bajar en picado; (*in sport*) saltar; **he dived for the phone** se precipitó hacia el teléfono.

diver (*person*) buceador,-a *mf*; (*professional*) buzo *m*; (*from diving board*) saltador,-a *mf*.

diversion (*distraction*) distracción *f*; *Br* (*detour*) desvío *m*.

divert [daɪˈvɜːt] *vt* desviar.

divide [dɪˈvaɪd] **1** *vt* dividir. **2** *vi* (*road, stream*) bifurcarse.

● **divide off** *vt* separar.

● **divide up** *vt* (*share out*) repartir.

diving submarinismo *m*; (*sport*) salto *m* de trampolín.

diving board trampolín *m*.

division [dɪˈvɪʒən] división *f*; (*sharing*) reparto *m*; (*of organization*) sección *f*.

divorce [dɪˈvɔːs] **1** *n* divorcio *m*. **2** *vt* **she divorced him** se divorció de él.

divorced [dɪ'vɔːst] divorciado,-a; **to get d.** divorciarse.

DIY [diːaɪ'waɪ] *Br abbr of* **do-it-yourself** bricolaje *m*.

dizziness vértigo *m*.

dizzy ['dɪzɪ] *a* (*person*) (*unwell*) mareado,-a.

DJ ['diːdʒeɪ] *abbr of* **disc jockey.**

do[1]* [duː] **1** *v aux* (*in negatives and questions*) (*not translated in Spanish*) **do you drive?** ¿tienes carnet de conducir?; **don't you want to come?** ¿no quieres venir?; **he doesn't smoke** no fuma. ‖ (*emphatic*) (*not translated in Spanish*) **do come with us!** ¡ánimo, vente con nosotros!; **I do like your bag** me encanta tu bolso. ‖ (*substituting main verb*) (*not translated in Spanish*) **I don't believe him – neither do I** no le creo – yo tampoco; **I'll go if you do** si vas tú, voy yo; **I think it's dear, but he doesn't** a mí me parece caro pero a él no; **who went? – I did** ¿quién asistió? – yo. ‖ (*in question tags*) **he refused, didn't he?** dijo que no, ¿verdad?; **I don't like it, do you?** a mí no me gusta, ¿y a ti? **2** *vt* hacer; (*task*) realizar; (*duty*) cumplir con; (*distance*) recorrer; **he doesn't smoke** no fuma; **what can I do for you?** ¿en qué puedo servirle?; **what do you do (for a living)?** ¿a qué te dedicas?; **he's done it!** ¡lo ha conseguido!; **we were doing eighty** íbamos a ochenta. **3** *vi* (*act*) hacer; **do as I tell you** haz lo que te digo; **how are you doing?** ¿qué tal?; **to do well** (*person*) tener éxito; (*business*) ir bien; **five pounds will do** con cinco libras será suficiente; **that will do!** ¡basta ya!; **this cushion will do as a pillow** este cojín servirá de almohada.

do[2] *Br fam* (*party*) fiesta *f*; (*event*) ceremonia *f*.

● **do away with** *vt* (*abolish*) abolir; (*discard*) deshacerse de.

● **do for** *vt* (*destroy, ruin*) arruinar; **I'm done for if I don't finish this** estoy perdido,-a si no acabo esto.

● **do in** *vt* **I'm done in** (*exhausted*) estoy hecho,-a polvo.

● **do over** *vt US* (*repeat*) repetir.

● **do out** *vt* (*clean*) limpiar a fondo.

● **do up** *vt* (*wrap*) envolver; (*belt etc*) abrochar; (*laces*) atar; (*dress up*) arreglar; (*redecorate*) renovar.

● **do with** *vt* **I could do with a rest** (*need*) un descanso no me vendría nada mal; **to have** *or* **be to do with** (*concern*) tener que ver con.

● **do without** *vt* pasar sin, prescindir de.

dock [dɒk] **1** *n* **the docks** el muelle. **2** *vi* (*ship*) atracar.

docker estibador *m*.

dockyard astillero *m*.

doctor ['dɒktəʳ] médico,-a *mf*; (*academic*) doctor,-a *mf*.

doctorate doctorado *m*.

document ['dɒkjʊmənt] documento *m*.

docu'mentary *a* & *n* documental (*m*).

dodge [dɒdʒ] *vt* (*blow*) esquivar; (*pursuer*) despistar; (*tax*) evadir.

dodgem ['dɒdʒəm] coche *m* de choque.

does [dʌz] *3rd person sing pres of* **do.**

dog [dɒg] perro,-a *mf.*

doggy bag (*in restaurant*) *US* bolsita *f* para llevarse los restos de la comida.

doghouse *US* perrera *f*; *fam* **to be in the d.** estar en desgracia.

doing ['duɪŋ] **it was none of my d.** yo no tuve nada que ver.

do-it-yourself bricolaje *m.*

dole [dəʊl] *Br* **the d.** el paro; **to be** *or* **go on the d.** estar en el paro.

doll [dɒl] (*toy*) muñeca *f.*

dollar ['dɒləʳ] dólar *m.*

doll's house, *US* **dollhouse** casa *f* de muñecas.

dolphin ['dɒlfɪn] delfín *m.*

dome [dəʊm] cúpula *f.*

domestic [də'mestɪk] *a* (*appliance, pet*) doméstico,-a; (*flight, news*) nacional; (*trade, policy*) interior.

dominant ['dɒmɪnənt] *a* dominante.

dominate ['dɒmɪneɪt] *vti* dominar.

Dominican [də'mɪnɪkən] *a & n* dominicano,-a (*mf*).

domino ['dɒmɪnəʊ] (*pl* **dominoes**) (*piece*) ficha *f* de dominó; **dominoes** (*game*) dominó *m sing.*

donate [dəʊ'neɪt] *vt* donar.

donation donativo *m.*

done [dʌn] *a* (*finished*) terminado,-a; (*meat*) hecho,-a; (*vegetables*) cocido,-a.

donkey ['dɒŋkɪ] burro,-a *mf.*

door [dɔːʳ] puerta *f.*

doorbell timbre *m* (de la puerta).

doorknob pomo *m.*

door knocker picaporte *m.*

doorman portero *m.*

doormat felpudo *m.*

doorstep peldaño *m.*

doorway entrada *f.*

dope [dəʊp] *fam* (*drug*) chocolate *m.*

dormitory ['dɔːmɪtərɪ] (*in school*) dormitorio *m*; *US* (*in university*) colegio *m* mayor.

dosage ['dəʊsɪdʒ] (*amount*) dosis *f inv.*

dose [dəʊs] dosis *f inv.*

dot [dɒt] punto *m.*

dotted line línea *f* de puntos.

double ['dʌbəl] **1** *a* doble. **2** *adv* doble; **folded d.** doblado,-a por la mitad; **it's d. the price** cuesta dos veces más. **3** *n* **to earn d.** ganar el doble.

● **double back** *vi* **to d. back on one's tracks** volver sobre sus pasos.

● **double up** *vi* (*bend*) doblarse.

double bed cama *f* de matrimonio.

double-'breasted *a* cruzado,-a.

double-'decker *Br* **d. (bus)** autobús *m* de dos pisos.

double glazing doble acristalamiento *m*.

doubt [daʊt] **1** *n* duda *f*; **no d.** sin duda; **to be in d. about sth** dudar algo. **2** *vt* dudar.

doubtful *a* **I'm a bit d. about it** no me convence del todo; **it's d. whether** ... no se sabe seguro si ...

dough [dəʊ] (*for bread*) masa *f*; (*for pastries*) pasta *f*; *fam* (*money*) pasta *f*.

doughnut rosquilla *f*, dónut$^{(R)}$ *m*.

dove [dʌv] paloma *f*.

down [daʊn] **1** *adv* (*to or at lower level*) abajo; (*to floor*) al suelo; (*to ground*) a tierra; **to go d.** (*price, person*) bajar; **d. there** allí abajo; **to be d. with a cold** estar resfriado,-a; **to feel d.** estar deprimido,-a. **2** *prep* (*along*) por; **to go d. the road** bajar la calle.

down-and-out vagabundo,-a *mf*.

down'hill *adv* **to go d.** ir cuesta abajo.

down payment entrada *f*, fianza *f*.

downpour chaparrón *m*.

downright 1 *a* (*liar, rogue*) declarado,-a; (*lie*) manifesto,-a. **2** *adv* (*totally*) completamente.

downstairs 1 *adv* abajo; (*to ground floor*) a la planta baja; **to go d.** bajar la escalera. **2** *a* (*on ground floor*) de la planta baja.

downtown *adv* en el centro (de la ciudad).

downward(s) ['daʊnwəd(z)] *adv* hacia abajo.

doze [dəʊz] **1** *vi* dormitar. **2** *n* cabezada *f*; **to have a d.** echar una cabezada.

● **doze off** *vi* quedarse dormido,-a.

dozen ['dʌzən] docena *f*; **half a d./a d. eggs** media docena/una docena de huevos.

Dr *abbr of* **Doctor** Doctor,-a *mf*, Dr., Dra.

drab [dræb] *a* (*dreary*) gris; (*colour*) pardo,-a.

drag [dræg] **1** *vt* (*pull*) arrastrar. **2** *vi* (*trail*) arrastrarse; (*person*) rezagarse.

● **drag on** *vi* (*war, strike*) hacerse interminable.

● **drag out** *vt* (*speech etc*) alargar.

● **drag along** *vt* arrastrar.

dragon ['drægən] dragón *m*.

drain [dreɪn] **1** n (*for water*) desagüe m; (*grating*) sumidero m. **2** vt (*marsh etc*) avenar; (*reservoir*) desecar. **3** vi to d. (**away**) (*liquid*) irse.

draining board escurridero m.

drainpipe tubo m de desagüe.

drama ['drɑːmə] (*play*) obra f de teatro; (*subject*) teatro m; (*tense situation*) drama m.

dramatic [drə'mætɪk] a (*change*) impresionante; (*moment*) emocionante; (*of the theatre*) dramático,-a.

dramatically adv (*to change*) de forma espectacular.

drapes [dreɪps] npl US cortinas fpl.

drastic ['dræstɪk] a (*severe*) drástico,-a; (*change*) radical.

drastically adv radicalmente.

draught [drɑːft] (*of cold air*) corriente f (de aire); **d. (beer)** cerveza f de barril; Br **draughts** (*game*) damas fpl.

draughtboard Br tablero m de damas.

draughty a **this room is very d.** en esta habitación hay mucha corriente.

draw [drɔː] **1** vt* (*picture*) dibujar; (*line*) trazar; (*curtains*) (*open*) descorrer; (*close*) correr; (*attract*) atraer; (*attention*) llamar. **2** vi* (*sketch*) dibujar; **they drew two all** empataron a dos. **3** n (*score*) empate m.

● **draw in** vi (*days*) acortarse.

● **draw near (to)** vt acercarse (a).

● **draw on** vt (*savings*) recurrir a; (*experience*) aprovecharse de.

● **draw out** vt (*withdraw*) sacar.

● **draw up** vt (*contract*) preparar; (*plan*) esbozar.

drawback inconveniente m.

drawer cajón m.

drawing dibujo m.

drawing pin chincheta f.

drawing room sala f de estar.

dread [dred] **1** vt temer. **2** n temor m.

dreadful a (*shocking*) espantoso,-a; (*awful*) fatal.

dreadfully adv (*horribly*) terriblemente; (*very*) muy.

dream [driːm] **1** n sueño m; (*marvel*) maravilla f. **2** vti* soñar (**of, about** con).

● **dream up** vt (*excuse*) inventarse; (*plan*) idear.

dreary ['drɪərɪ] a (*gloomy*) triste; (*boring*) aburrido,-a.

drench [drentʃ] vt empapar.

dress [dres] **1** n (*frock*) vestido m; (*clothing*) ropa f. **2** vt (*person*) vestir; (*wound*) vendar; **he was dressed in a grey suit** llevaba (puesto) un traje gris. **3** vi vestirse.

● **dress up** vi (*in disguise*) disfrazarse (**as** de); (*in best clothes*) vestirse elegante.

dresser *US* (*in bedroom*) tocador *m*.
dressing (*bandage*) vendaje *m*; **(salad) d.** aliño *m*.
dressing gown bata *f*.
dressing table tocador *m*.
dressmaker modista *mf*.
drew [dru:] *pt of* **draw**.
dribble ['drɪbəl] **1** *vi* (*baby*) babear; (*liquid*) gotear. **2** *vt* (*ball*) driblar.
dried [draɪd] *a* (*fruit*) seco,-a; (*milk*) en polvo.
drier ['draɪər] *see* **dryer**.
drift [drɪft] *vi* (*boat*) ir a la deriva; (*person*) ir sin rumbo, vagar; **they drifted away** se marcharon poco a poco.
drill [drɪl] **1** *n* (*handtool*) taladro *m*; **dentist's d.** fresa *f*; **pneumatic d.** martillo *m* neumático. **2** *vt* (*wood etc*) taladrar.
drink [drɪŋk] **1** *vti** beber; **to have sth to d.** tomarse algo; **to d. to sth/sb** brindar por algo/algn. **2** *n* bebida *f*; (*alcoholic*) copa *f*.
● **drink up 1** *vt* beberse todo. **2** *vi* **d. up!** ¡bébelo todo!
drinkable *a* potable; (*not unpleasant*) agradable.
drinking water agua *f* potable.
drip [drɪp] **1** *n* goteo *m*; *fam* (*person*) necio,-a *mf*. **2** *vi* gotear; **he was dripping with sweat** el sudor le caía a gotas.
drip-dry *a* que no necesita planchado.
drive [draɪv] **1** *vt* (*vehicle*) conducir, *Am* manejar; (*person*) llevar; (*stake*) hincar; (*nail*) clavar; (*compel*) forzar; **to d. sb mad** volver loco,-a a algn. **2** *vi** (*in car*) conducir, *Am* manejar. **3** *n* (*approach to house*) camino *m* de entrada; (*energy*) energía *f*; **to go for a d.** dar una vuelta en coche; **left-hand d.** conducción *f* por la izquierda.
● **drive along** *vti* (*in car*) conducir.
● **drive back 1** *vt* (*enemy*) rechazar; (*passenger*) llevar de vuelta a. **2** *vi* volver en coche.
● **drive in** *vt* (*nail*) clavar.
● **drive off** *vi* salir (en coche).
● **drive on** *vi* (*after stopping*) continuar.
● **drive out** *vt* expulsar.
● **drive up** *vi* llegar en coche.
drivel ['drɪvəl] tonterías *mpl*.
driver (*of car, bus*) conductor,-a *mf*; (*of train*) maquinista *mf*; (*of lorry*) camionero,-a *mf*.
driver's license *US* carnet *m* de conducir.
driving lesson clase *f* de conducir.
driving licence carnet *m* de conducir.
driving school autoescuela *f*.
driving test examen *m* de conducir.

drizzle ['drɪzəl] **1** n llovizna f. **2** vi lloviznar.

droop [dru:p] vi (flower) marchitarse.

drop [drɒp] **1** n (liquid) gota f; (descent) desnivel m; (in price) bajada f; (in temperature) descenso m. **2** vt (let fall) dejar caer; (lower) bajar; (reduce) disminuir; (abandon) (subject, charge etc) abandonar. **3** vi (object) caerse; (voice, price, temperature) bajar; (speed) disminuir.

● **drop behind** vi quedarse atrás.

● **drop in** or **round** vi (visit) pasarse (**at** por).

● **drop off 1** vi (fall asleep) quedarse dormido,-a. **2** vt (deliver) dejar en casa (de algn).

● **drop out** vi (of college) dejar los estudios; (of society) marginarse; (of competition) retirarse.

drought [draʊt] sequía f.

drown [draʊn] **1** vt ahogar; (place) inundar. **2** vi ahogarse; **he drowned** murió ahogado.

drowsy ['draʊzɪ] a soñoliento,-a; **to feel d.** tener sueño.

drug [drʌg] **1** n (medicine) medicamento m; (narcotic) droga f; **to be on drugs** drogarse. **2** vt (person) drogar; (food, drink) adulterar con drogas.

drug addict drogadicto,-a mf.

druggist US farmacéutico,-a mf.

drugstore US establecimiento m donde se compran medicamentos, periódicos etc.

drum [drʌm] tambor m; (container) bidón m; **to play the drums** tocar la batería.

drummer (in band) tambor mf; (in pop group) batería mf.

drunk [drʌŋk] **1** a borracho,-a; **to get d.** emborracharse. **2** n borracho,-a mf.

drunkard borracho,-a mf.

drunken a (driver) borracho,-a; **d. driving** conducir en estado ebrio.

dry [draɪ] **1** a seco,-a. **2** vt secar. **3** vi **to d. (off)** secarse.

● **dry up 1** vt secar. **2** vi secarse.

dry-'clean vt lavar en seco.

dry-cleaner (shop) tintorería f.

dryer secadora f.

dual ['dju:əl] a doble.

dual carriageway autovía f.

dub [dʌb] vt (subtitle) doblar (**into** a).

dubious ['dju:bɪəs] a (morals etc) dudoso,-a; (doubting) indeciso,-a.

duchess ['dʌtʃɪs] duquesa f.

duck¹ [dʌk] pato,-a mf; (as food) pato m.

duck² vi (bow down) agacharse. **2** vt (evade) esquivar.

due [dju:] **1** a (expected) esperado,-a; (money) pagadero,-a; **the train is d.**

(to arrive) at ten el tren debe llegar a las diez; **in d. course** a su debido tiempo; **to be d. to** deberse a. **2** *adv* (*north etc*) derecho hacia.

duel ['dju:əl] duelo *m*.

duffel coat ['dʌfəlkəʊt] trenca *f*.

duke [dju:k] duque *m*.

dull [dʌl] *a* (*boring*) pesado,-a; (*place*) sin interés; (*light*) apagado,-a; (*weather*) gris; (*sound, ache*) sordo,-a.

dumb [dʌm] *a* mudo,-a; (*stupid*) tonto,-a.

dummy ['dʌmɪ] (*in shop window*) maniquí *m*; *Br* (*for baby*) chupete *m*.

dump [dʌmp] **1** *n* (*tip*) vertedero *m*; *fam* (*place*) lugar *m* de mala muerte; (*town*) poblacho *m*; (*dwelling*) tugurio *m*. **2** *vt* (*rubbish*) verter.

dump truck volquete *m*.

dungarees [dʌŋgə'ri:z] *npl* mono *m sing*.

duplex ['dju:pleks] *US* casa *f* adosada; **d. apartment** dúplex *m inv*.

duplicate ['dju:plɪkɪt] duplicado *m*; **in d.** por duplicado.

durable ['djʊərəbəl] *a* duradero,-a.

duration [djʊ'reɪʃən] duración *f*.

during ['djʊərɪŋ] *prep* durante.

dusk [dʌsk] crepúsculo *m*; **at d.** al anochecer.

dust [dʌst] **1** *n* polvo *m*. **2** *vt* (*furniture*) quitar el polvo a.

dustbin *Br* cubo *m* de la basura.

duster (*for housework*) trapo *m* (del polvo).

dustman *Br* basurero *m*.

dusty *a* polvoriento,-a.

Dutch [dʌtʃ] **1** *a* holandés,-esa. **2** *n* (*language*) holandés *m*; **the D.** los holandeses *mpl*.

Dutchman holandés *m*.

Dutchwoman holandesa *f*.

duty ['dju:tɪ] deber *m*; (*task*) función *f*; (*tax*) impuesto *m*; **to be on d.** estar de servicio; (*doctor, soldier*) estar de guardia; **d. chemist** farmacia *f* de guardia; **customs d.** derechos *mpl* de aduana.

duty-'free *a* libre de impuestos.

duvet ['du:veɪ] edredón *m*.

dwarf [dwɔ:f] (*pl* **dwarves** [dwɔ:vz]) enano,-a *mf*.

dye [daɪ] **1** *n* tinte *m*. **2** *vt* teñir; **to d. one's hair black** teñirse el pelo de negro.

dynamic [daɪ'næmɪk] *a* dinámico,-a.

dynamite ['daɪnəmaɪt] dinamita *f*.

dynamo ['daɪnəməʊ] dínamo *f*.

dyslexic [dɪs'leksɪk] *a* disléxico,-a.

E

each [i:tʃ] **1** *a* cada,-s; **e. day/month** todos los días/meses. **2** *pron* cada uno,-a; **we bought one e.** nos compramos uno cada uno; **e. other** el uno al otro; **they hate e. other** se odian.

eager ['i:gəʳ] *a* (*anxious*) impaciente (**to** por); (*keen*) deseoso,-a.

eagerly *adv* (*anxiously*) con impaciencia; (*keenly*) con ilusión.

eagerness impaciencia *f* (**to do** por hacer); (*keeness*) afán *m*.

eagle ['i:gəl] águila *f*.

ear [ɪəʳ] oreja *f*; (*inner ear*) oído *m*; (*of corn*) espiga *f*.

earache dolor *m* de oídos.

early ['ɜ:lɪ] **1** *a* (*before usual time*) temprano,-a; **to have an e. night** acostarse pronto; **you're e.!** ¡qué pronto has venido! ‖ (*at first stage, period*) **in her e. forties** a los cuarenta y pocos; **in e. July** a principios de julio. ‖ (*in the near future*) **an e. reply** una respuesta pronta. **2** *adv* (*before the expected time*) temprano; **to leave e.** irse pronto; **e. on** al principio; **earlier on** antes; **five minutes e.** con cinco minutos de adelanto; **as e. as possible** tan pronto como sea posible; **to book e.** reservar con tiempo; **at the earliest** cuanto antes.

earn [ɜ:n] *vt* ganarse; (*money*) ganar; **to e. one's living** ganarse la vida.

earnings *npl* ingresos *mpl*.

earphones *npl* auriculares *mpl*, cascos *mpl*.

earplug tapón *m* para los oídos.

earring pendiente *m*.

earth ['ɜ:θ] *n* tierra *f*; (*electric*) toma *f* de tierra; **to be down to e.** ser práctico; *fam* **where/why on e. ....?** ¿pero dónde/por qué demonios ...?

earthquake terremoto *m*.

ease [i:z] **1** *n* (*lack of difficulty*) facilidad *f*; (*affluence*) comodidad *f*; (*freedom from discomfort*) tranquilidad *f*; **at e.** relajado,-a. **2** *vt* (*pain*) aliviar; (*move gently*) deslizar con cuidado.

● **ease off** *or* **up** *vi* (*decrease*) disminuir; (*slow down*) ir más despacio.

easel ['i:zəl] caballete *m*.

easily *adv* fácilmente; **e. the best** con mucho el mejor.

east [i:st] **1** *n* este *m*. **2** *a* del este, oriental. **3** *adv* al este.

eastbound *a* (con) dirección este.

Easter ['i:stəʳ] Semana Santa *f*; **E. Sunday** Domingo *m* de Resurrección.

eastern *a* oriental, del este.

eastward(s) ['i:stwəd(z)] *adv* hacia el este.

easy ['i:zɪ] **1** *a* fácil; (*comfortable*) cómodo,-a; *fam* **I'm e.!** me da lo mismo; **e. chair** butacón *m*. **2** *adv* **go e. on the wine** no te pases con el vino; **to take things e.** tomarse las cosas con calma; **take it e.!** ¡tranquilo!

easy-going *a* (*calm*) tranquilo,-a; (*lax*) despreocupado,-a; (*unde-*

manding) poco exigente.

eat* [iːt] *vt* comer.

○ **eat away** *vt* desgastar; (*metal*) corroer.

● **eat out** *vi* comer fuera.

● **eat up** *vt* (*meal*) terminar; (*petrol*) consumir; (*miles*) tragar.

eau de Cologne [əʊdəkə'ləʊn] colonia *f*.

EC [iː'siː] *abbr* (*European Community*) CE.

eccentric [ɪk'sentrɪk] *a & n* excéntrico,-a (*mf*).

echo ['ekəʊ] **1** *n* (*pl* **echoes**) eco *m*. **2** *vt* (*repeat*) repetir. **3** *vi* resonar.

eco'nomic *a* económico,-a; (*profitable*) rentable.

eco'nomical *a* económico,-a.

economize *vi* economizar (**on** en).

economy [ɪ'kɒnəmɪ] (*national*) economía *f*; (*saving*) ahorro *m*; **e. class** (clase *f*) turista *f*.

edge [edʒ] **1** *n* borde *m*; (*of knife*) filo *m*; (*of water*) orilla *f*; **on the e. of town** en las afueras de la ciudad; **to have the e. on sb** llevar ventaja a algn; **to be on e.** tener los nervios de punta. **2** *vi* **to e. closer** acercarse lentamente; **to e. forward** avanzar poco a poco.

edible ['edɪbəl] *a* comestible.

edit ['edɪt] *vt* editar; (*proofs*) corregir; (*newspaper*) ser redactor,-a de; (*film, TV programme*) montar; (*cut*) cortar.

● **edit out** *vt* suprimir.

edition [ɪ'dɪʃən] edición *f*.

editor (*of book*) editor,-a *mf*; (*of newspaper*) redactor,-a *mf*; (*of film, TV programme*) montador,-a *mf*.

edi'torial 1 *a* **e. staff** redacción *f*. **2** *n* editorial *m*.

educate ['edjʊkeɪt] *vt* educar.

educated *a* culto,-a.

edu'cation (*schooling*) enseñanza *f*; (*training*) formación *f*; (*studies*) estudios *mpl*; (*culture*) cultura *f*.

edu'cational *a* educativo,-a.

EEC [iːiː'siː] *abbr* (*European Economic Community*) CEE.

eel [iːl] anguila *f*.

effect [ɪ'fekt] efecto *m*; (*impression*) impresión *f*; **in e.** efectivamente; **to come into e.** entrar en vigor; **to have an e. on** afectar a; **to no e.** sin resultado alguno; **effects** (*possessions*) efectos *mpl*.

effective *a* (*successful*) eficaz; (*impressive*) impresionante.

effectively *adv* (*successfully*) eficazmente; (*in fact*) en efecto.

efficiency (*of person*) eficacia *f*; (*of machine*) rendimiento *m*.

efficient [ɪ'fɪʃənt] *a* eficaz; (*person*) eficiente; (*machine*) de buen rendimiento.

efficiently *adv* eficazmente; **to work e.** tener buen rendimiento.

effort ['efət] esfuerzo *m*; (*attempt*) intento *m*; **to make an e.** hacer un esfuerzo.

eg [iː'dʒiː] *abbr* p. ej.

egg [eg] **1** *n* huevo *m*. **2** *vt* **to e. sb on (to do sth)** empujar a algn (a hacer algo).

egg cup huevera *f*.

eggplant berenjena *f*.

egg timer reloj *m* de arena.

egg white clara *f* de huevo.

Egyptian [ɪ'dʒɪpʃən] *a & n* egipcio,-a (*mf*) .

eiderdown ['aɪdədaʊn] edredón *m*.

eight [eɪt] *a & n* ocho (*m*).

eighteen *a & n* dieciocho (*m*) *inv*.

eighth *a & n* octavo,-a (*mf*).

eighty *a & n* ochenta (*m*) *inv*.

either ['aɪðəʳ] **1** *pron* (*affirmative*) cualquiera; (*negative*) ninguno, ninguna, ni el uno ni el otro, ni la una ni la otra; **e. of them** cualquiera de los dos; **I don't want e. of them** no quiero ninguno de los dos. **2** *a* (*both*) cada, los dos, las dos; **on e. side** en ambos lados. **3** *conj* o; **e. ... or ... o ... o ...;** **e. Friday or Saturday** o (bien) el viernes o el sábado. **4** *adv* (*after negative*) tampoco; **I don't want to do it e.** yo tampoco quiero hacerlo.

elastic [ɪ'læstɪk] **1** *a* elástico,-a; *fig* flexible; **e. band** goma elástica. **2** *n* elástico *m*.

elbow ['elbəʊ] **1** *n* codo *m*. **2** *vt* **to e. sb** dar un codazo a algn.

elder ['eldəʳ] *a* mayor.

elderly 1 *a* anciano,-a. **2** *npl* **the e.** los ancianos.

eldest 1 *a* mayor. **2** *n* el/la mayor.

elect [ɪ'lekt] *vt* elegir.

election 1 *n* elección *f*; **general e.** elecciones *fpl* generales. **2** *a* electoral.

electric [ɪ'lektrɪk] *a* eléctrico,-a; *fig* electrizante.

electrical *a* eléctrico,-a.

electric blanket manta *f* eléctrica.

electric chair silla *f* eléctrica.

elec'trician electricista *mf*.

elec'tricity electricidad *f*; **e. bill** recibo *m* de la luz.

electric shock electrochoque *m*.

electrocute [ɪ'lektrəkjuːt] *vt* electrocutar.

electronic [ɪlek'trɒnɪk] *a* electrónico,-a.

electronics electrónica *f*.

elegance elegancia *f*.

elegant ['elɪgənt] *a* elegante.

elegantly *adv* con elegancia.
element ['elɪmənt] elemento *m*; (*electrical*) resistencia *f*.
elementary *a* (*not developed*) rudimentario,-a; (*easy*) fácil; **e. school** escuela *f* primaria.
elephant ['elɪfənt] elefante *m*.
elevator ['elɪveɪtə'] *US* ascensor *m*.
eleven [ɪ'levən] *a & n* once (*m*) inv.
eleventh *a & n* undécimo,-a (*mf*).
eligible ['elɪdʒəbəl] *a* apto,-a; **he isn't e. to vote** no tiene derecho al voto.
eliminate [ɪ'lɪmɪneɪt] *vt* eliminar.
else [els] *adv* **anything e.?** ¿algo más?; **everything e.** todo lo demás; **no-one e.** nadie más; **someone e.** otro,-a; **something e.** otra cosa; **somewhere e.** en otra parte; **what e.?** ¿qué más?; **where e.?** ¿en qué otro sitio?; **or e.** si no.
elsewhere *adv* en otra parte.
elude [ɪ'lu:d] *vt* (*avoid*) esquivar; **his name eludes me** no consigo acordarme de su nombre.
embark [em'bɑːk] *vi* embarcar(se); **to e. upon sth** emprender algo.
embarrass [ɪm'bærəs] *vt* avergonzar.
embarrassing *a* embarazoso,-a; (*situation*) violento,-a.
embarrassment vergüenza *f*.
embassy ['embəsɪ] embajada *f*.
emblem ['embləm] emblema *m*.
embrace [ɪm'breɪs] **1** *vt* abrazar; (*include*) abarcar. **2** *vi* abrazarse. **3** *n* abrazo *m*.
embroider [ɪm'brɔɪdə'] *vt* bordar; (*story, truth*) adornar.
embroidery bordado *m*.
emerald ['emərəld] esmeralda *f*.
emerge [ɪ'mɜːdʒ] *vi* salir; (*problem*) surgir; **it emerged that ...** resultó que ...
emergency [ɪ'mɜːdʒənsɪ] emergencia *f*; (*medical*) urgencia *f*; **in an e.** en caso de emergencia; **e. exit** salida *f* de emergencia; **e. landing** aterrizaje *m* forzoso; **state of e.** estado *m* de excepción.
emigrate ['emɪgreɪt] *vi* emigrar.
emotion [ɪ'məʊʃən] emoción *f*.
emotional *a* emocional; (*moving*) conmovedor,-a.
emperor ['empərə'] emperador *m*.
emphasis ['emfəsɪs] énfasis *m*; **to place e. on sth** hacer hincapié en algo.
emphasize *vt* subrayar.
empire ['empaɪə'] imperio *m*.
employ [ɪm'plɔɪ] *vt* emplear; (*time*) ocupar.
employee [emplɔɪ'iː] empleado,-a *mf*.
employer empresario,-a *mf*.

employment [ɪm'plɔɪmənt] empleo *m*.

employment agency agencia *f* de colocaciones.

empty ['emptɪ] **1** *a* vacío,-a; **e. promises** promesas *fpl* vanas. **2** *vt* vaciar. **3** *vi* vaciarse. **4** *npl* **empties** envases *mpl*.

empty-handed *adv* con las manos vacías.

emulsion [ɪ'mʌlʃən] **e. (paint)** pintura *f* mate.

enable [ɪn'eɪbəl] *vt* **to e. sb to do sth** permitir a algn hacer algo.

enamel [ɪ'næməl] esmalte *m*.

enchanting [ɪn'tʃɑːntɪŋ] *a* encantador,-a.

enclose [ɪn'kləʊz] *vt* (*surround*) rodear; (*fence in*) cercar; (*in envelope*) adjuntar; **please find enclosed** le enviamos adjunto.

enclosure (*fenced area*) cercado *m*; (*in envelope*) documento *m* adjunto.

encounter [ɪn'kaʊntəʳ] **1** *n* encuentro *m*. **2** *vt* encontrarse con; (*problems*) tropezar con.

encourage [ɪn'kʌrɪdʒ] *vt* (*urge*) animar; (*help to develop*) fomentar.

encouragement estímulo *m*.

encyclop(a)edia [ensaɪkləʊ'piːdɪə] enciclopedia *f*.

end [end] **1** *n* (*of stick*) punta *f*; (*of street*) final *m*; (*conclusion*) fin *m*, final *m*; (*aim*) objetivo *m*; **in the e.** al final; **for hours on e.** hora tras hora; **to put an e. to** acabar con; **it makes my hair stand on e.** me pone el pelo de punta. **2** *vt* acabar, terminar. **3** *vi* acabarse, terminarse.

● **end up** *vi* terminar; **to e. up doing sth** terminar por hacer algo.

endanger [ɪn'deɪndʒəʳ] *vt* poner en peligro.

ending final *m*.

endive ['endaɪv] endibia *f*; *US* escarola *f*.

endless *a* interminable.

endorse [ɪn'dɔːs] *vt* (*cheque etc*) endosar; (*approve*) aprobar; (*support*) apoyar.

endorsement (*on cheque etc*) endoso *m*; (*approval*) aprobación *f*.

endurance resistencia *f*.

endure [ɪn'djʊəʳ] **1** *vt* (*bear*) aguantar. **2** *vi* perdurar.

enemy ['enəmɪ] *a & n* enemigo,-a (*mf*).

ener'getic *a* enérgico,-a.

energy ['enədʒɪ] **1** *n* energía *f*. **2** *a* energético,-a.

enforce [ɪn'fɔːs] *vt* (*law*) hacer cumplir.

engaged [ɪn'geɪdʒd] *a* (*betrothed*) prometido,-a; (*busy*) ocupado,-a; **to get e.** prometerse; **it's e.** (*phone*) está comunicando.

engagement (*to marry*) noviazgo *m*; (*appointment*) cita *f*.

engagement ring anillo *m* de compromiso.

engine ['endʒɪn] motor *m*; (*of train*) locomotora *f*.

engine driver maquinista *mf*.

engineer [endʒɪ'nɪəʳ] ingeniero,-a *mf*; *US* (*on train*) maquinista *mf*.

engineering ingeniería *f*.

English ['ɪŋglɪʃ] **1** *a* inglés,-esa. **2** *n* (*language*) inglés *m*; **the E.** los ingleses *mpl*.

Englishman inglés *m*.

English-speaking *a* de habla inglesa.

Englishwoman inglesa *f*.

engrave [ɪn'greɪv] *vt* grabar.

engraving grabado *m*.

enjoy [ɪn'dʒɔɪ] *vt* disfrutar; **to e. oneself** pasarlo bien; **he enjoys swimming** le gusta nadar.

enjoyable *a* agradable.

enjoyment disfrute *m*.

enlarge [ɪn'lɑːdʒ] *vt* ampliar.

enlighten [ɪn'laɪtən] *vt* iluminar.

enormous [ɪ'nɔːməs] *a* enorme.

enormously *adv* enormemente; **I enjoyed myself e.** lo pasé genial.

enough [ɪ'nʌf] **1** *a* bastante, suficiente; **e. books** bastantes libros; **have we got e. petrol?** ¿tenemos suficiente gasolina? **2** *adv* bastante; **sure e.** en efecto. **3** *n* lo suficiente; **e. to live on** lo suficiente para vivir; **it isn't e.** no basta; **I've had e.!** ¡estoy harto!

enquire [ɪn'kwaɪəʳ] *vi* preguntar.

enquiry (*question*) pregunta *f*; (*investigation*) investigación *f*; **enquiries** información *f*.

enrol, *US* **enroll** [ɪn'rəʊl] **1** *vt* matricular. **2** *vi* matricularse.

enrolment matrícula *f*.

ensure [ɪn'ʃʊəʳ] *vt* asegurar.

entail [ɪn'teɪl] *vt* suponer.

enter ['entəʳ] **1** *vt* (*go into*) entrar en; (*data into computer*) introducir; (*join*) ingresar en; **to e. one's name for a course** matricularse en un curso. **2** *vi* entrar.

• **enter into** *vt* (*agreement*) firmar; (*negotiations*) iniciar.

enterprise empresa *f*; **free e.** libre empresa.

enterprising ['entəpraɪzɪŋ] *a* emprendedor,-a.

entertain [entə'teɪn] **1** *vt* (*amuse*) divertir; (*consider*) considerar. **2** *vi* (*have guests*) tener invitados.

entertainer artista *mf*.

entertaining *a* divertido,-a.

entertainment diversión *f*; (*show*) espectáculo *m*.

enthusiasm [ɪn'θjuːzɪæzəm] entusiasmo *m*.

enthusiast entusiasta *mf*.

enthusi'astic *a* entusiasta; (*praise*) caluroso,-a; **to be e. about sth** entusiasmarse por algo.

enthusiastically *adv* con entusiasmo.

entire [ɪn'taɪəʳ] *a* todo,-a; **the e. family** toda la familia.

entirely *adv* (*completely*) totalmente; (*solely*) exclusivamente.

entitle [ɪn'taɪtəl] *vt* (*permit*) dar derecho a; **to be entitled to** tener derecho a.

entrance ['entrəns] entrada *f*; (*admission*) ingreso *m*; **e. examination** examen *m* de ingreso.

entrant ['entrənt] (*in competition*) participante *mf*.

entry ['entrɪ] (*entrance*) entrada *f*; **no e.** dirección prohibida.

entry form hoja *f* de inscripción.

envelope ['envələʊp] sobre *m*.

envious ['envɪəs] *a* envidioso,-a; **to feel e.** tener envidia.

environment [ɪn'vaɪərənmənt] entorno *m*; (*natural*) medio ambiente *m*.

environ'mental *a* medio ambiental.

envy ['envɪ] **1** *n* envidia *f*. **2** *vt* **to e. sb sth** envidiar algo a algn.

epidemic [epɪ'demɪk] epidemia *f*.

episode ['epɪsəʊd] episodio *m*.

equal ['iːkwəl] **1** *a* igual; **to be e. to the occasion** estar a la altura de las circunstancias. **2** *n* igual *mf*; **to treat sb as an e.** tratar a algn de igual a igual. **3** *vt* equivaler a.

e'quality igualdad *f*.

equalize *vi* (*in sport*) empatar.

equally *adv* igualmente; **e. pretty** igual de bonito; **to share sth e.** dividir algo en partes iguales.

equation [ɪ'kweɪʒən] ecuación *f*.

equator [ɪ'kweɪtəʳ] ecuador *m*.

equip [ɪ'kwɪp] *vt* (*supply*) equipar; (*person*) proveer.

equipment (*materials*) equipo *m*.

equivalent [ɪ'kwɪvələnt] *a* & *n* equivalente (*m*).

erase [ɪ'reɪz] *vt* borrar.

eraser goma *f* de borrar.

erect [ɪ'rekt] **1** *a* (*upright*) erguido,-a. **2** *vt* (*monument*) eregir.

errand ['erənd] recado *m*.

erratic [ɪ'rætɪk] *a* (*performance, behaviour*) irregular; (*weather*) muy variable; (*person*) caprichoso,-a.

error ['erəʳ] error *m*.

escalator ['eskəleɪtəʳ] escalera *f* mecánica.

escape [ɪs'keɪp] **1** *n* fuga *f*; (*of gas*) escape *m*. **2** *vi* escaparse. **3** *vt* (*avoid*) evitar; **the name escapes me** se me escapa el nombre.

escort ['eskɔːt] **1** *n* (*bodyguard etc*) escolta *f*. **2** [ɪs'kɔːt] *vt* (*protect*) escoltar.

Eskimo ['eskɪməʊ] *a & n* esquimal (*mf*).

especially *adv* especialmente.

espresso [e'spresəʊ] café *m* exprés.

essay ['eseɪ] (*at school*) redacción *f*.

essential [ɪ'senʃəl] *a* esencial.

essentially *adv* esencialmente.

establish [ɪ'stæblɪʃ] *vt* (*found*) establecer; (*business*) montar; **to e. the truth** demostrar la verdad.

establishment establecimiento *m*; **the E.** el sistema.

estate [ɪ'steɪt] (*land*) finca *f*; (*property*) bienes *mpl*; (*inheritance*) herencia *f*; (**housing**) **e.** urbanización *f*.

estate agent agente *mf* inmobiliario,-a.

estate car coche *m* modelo familiar.

estimate ['estɪmɪt] **1** *n* (*calculation*) cálculo *m*; (*likely cost of work*) presupuesto *m*. **2** ['estɪmeɪt] *vt* calcular.

etiquette ['etɪket] etiqueta *f*.

Euro- ['jʊərəʊ] *prefix* Euro-.

European [jʊərə'pɪən] *a & n* europeo,-a (*mf*); **E. Economic Community** Comunidad *f* Económica Europea.

evacuate [ɪ'vækjʊeɪt] *vt* evacuar.

evade [ɪ'veɪd] *vt* evadir.

evaluate [ɪ'væljʊeɪt] *vt* evaluar.

evaporate [ɪ'væpəreɪt] *vi* evaporarse.

eve [iːv] víspera *f*; **on the e. of** en vísperas de.

even ['iːvən] **1** *a* (*smooth*) liso,-a; (*regular*) uniforme; (*equally balanced*) igual; (*number*) par; (*in football match etc*) **to be e.** ir empatados,-as; **to get e. with sb** desquitarse con algn. **2** *adv* aun; **e. now** incluso ahora; **e. the children knew** hasta los niños lo sabían; **e. as** mientras; **e. if** incluso si; **e. though** aunque. ‖ (*with negative*) ni siquiera; **she can't e. write her name** ni siquiera sabe escribir su nombre. ‖ (*before comparative*) aun, todavía; **e. worse** aun peor.

evening ['iːvnɪŋ] (*early*) tarde *f*; (*late*) noche *f*; **in the e.** por la tarde; **tomorrow e.** mañana por la tarde.

evening class clase *f* nocturna.

evenly *adv* (*uniformly*) de modo uniforme; (*fairly*) equitativamente.

event [ɪ'vent] (*happening*) suceso *m*; (*in sport*) prueba *f*; **at all events** en todo caso; **in the e. of fire** en caso de incendio.

eventual [ɪ'ventʃʊəl] *a* (*ultimate*) final; (*resulting*) consiguiente.

eventually *adv* finalmente.

ever ['evəʳ] *adv* (*always*) siempre; **for e.** para siempre; **stronger than e.** más fuerte que nunca; **have you e. been there?** ¿has estado allí alguna vez?; **how e. did you manage it?** ¿cómo diablos lo conseguiste?; *fam* **e. so**

... muy ...; **thank you e. so much** muchísimas gracias.

every ['evrɪ] *a* (*each*) cada; (*all*) todos,-as; **e. now and then** de vez en cuando; **e. day** todos los días; **e. other day** cada dos días; **e. one of you** todos,-as vosotros,-as; **e. citizen** todo ciudadano.

everybody *pron* todo el mundo, todos,-as; **e. who** ... todos los que ...

everyday *a* de todos los días; **an e. occurrence** un suceso cotidiano.

everyone *pron* = **everybody.**

everyplace *adv* US en todos sitios.

everything *pron* todo; **he eats e.** come de todo; **e. I have** todo lo que tengo.

everywhere *adv* por *or* en todas partes; **e. I go** por todas partes adonde voy.

evidence *n* (*proof*) evidencia *f*; (*in court case*) testimonio *m*; (*sign*) indicio *m*; **to give e.** prestar declaración.

evident ['evɪdənt] *a* evidente.

evidently *adv* evidentemente.

evil ['iːvəl] **1** *a* (*wicked*) malvado,-a; (*harmful*) nocivo,-a. **2** *n* mal *m*.

ewe [juː] oveja *f*.

ex [eks] her **e.** su ex marido; his **e.** su ex mujer.

ex- *prefix* ex-; **ex-minister** ex ministro *m*.

exact [ɪg'zækt] *a* exacto,-a; **this e. spot** ese mismo lugar.

exactly *adv* exactamente; **e.!** ¡exacto!

exaggerate [ɪg'zædʒəreɪt] *vti* exagerar.

exagge'ration exageración *f*.

exam [ɪg'zæm] examen *m*.

exami'nation examen *m*; (*medical*) reconocimiento *m*; **to sit an e.** hacer un examen.

examine [ɪg'zæmɪn] *vt* examinar; (*customs*) registrar; (*medically*) reconocer a.

examiner examinador,-a *mf*.

example [ɪg'zaːmpəl] ejemplo *m*; **for e.** por ejemplo.

exceed [ek'siːd] *vt* exceder.

exceedingly *adv* extremadamente.

excel [ɪk'sel] *vi* sobresalir.

excellent ['eksələnt] *a* excelente.

except [ɪk'sept] *prep* excepto; **e. for the little ones** excepto los pequeños; **e. that** ... salvo que ...

exception excepción *f*; **with the e. of** a excepción de; **to take e. to sth** ofenderse por algo.

exceptional *a* excepcional.

exceptionally *adv* excepcionalmente.

excerpt [ek'sɜːpt] extracto *m*.

excess [ɪk'ses] **1** *n* exceso *m*. **2** *a* ['ekses] excedente; **e. baggage** exceso *m* de equipaje; **e. fare** suplemento *m*.

ex'cessive *a* excesivo,-a.

ex'cessively *adv* excesivamente, en exceso.

exchange [ɪks'tʃeɪndʒ] **1** *n* cambio *m*; **(telephone) e. central** *f* telefónica; **in e. for** a cambio de. **2** *vt* intercambiar; **to e. blows** golpearse.

exchange rate tipo *m* de cambio.

excite [ɪk'saɪt] *vt* (*enthuse*) entusiasmar; (*arouse*) provocar; **to get excited** entusiasmarse.

excited *a* ilusionado,-a.

excitement (*emotion*) emoción *f*.

exciting *a* emocionante.

exclaim [ɪk'skleɪm] *vi* exclamar.

excla'mation exclamación *f*.

excla'mation mark *or US* **point** signo *m* de admiración.

exclude [ɪk'sklu:d] *vt* excluir; (*from club*) no admitir.

exclusive [ɪk'sklu:sɪv] **1** *a* exclusivo,-a; (*select*) selecto,-a. **2** *n* (*in newspaper*) exclusiva *f*.

exclusively *adv* exclusivamente.

excursion [ɪk'skɜ:ʃən] excursión *f*.

excuse [ɪk'skju:z] **1** *vt* disculpar; (*exempt*) dispensar; (*justify*) justificar; **e. me!** con permiso. **2** [ɪk'skju:s] *n* excusa *f*; **to make excuses** dar excusas.

ex-directory *a* que no se encuentra en la guía telefónica.

execute ['eksɪkju:t] *vt* (*order*) cumplir; (*task*) realizar; (*person*) ejecutar.

exe'cution (*of order*) cumplimiento *m*; (*of task*) realización *f*; (*of person*) ejecución *f*.

executive [ɪg'zekjʊtɪv] *a & n* ejecutivo,-a (*mf*).

exempt [ɪg'zempt] **1** *vt* eximir (**from** de). **2** *a* exento,-a; **e. from tax** libre de impuesto.

exemption exención *f*.

exercise ['eksəsaɪz] **1** *n* ejercicio *m*. **2** *vt* (*rights, duties*) ejercer. **3** *vi* hacer ejercicio.

exercise book cuaderno *m*.

exert [ɪg'zɜ:t] *vt* (*influence*) ejercer; **to e. oneself** esforzarse.

exertion esfuerzo *m*.

exhaust [ɪg'zɔ:st] **1** *vt* agotar. **2** *n* (*gas*) gases *mpl* de combustión; **e. pipe** tubo *m* de escape.

exhausting *a* agotador,-a.

exhibit [ɪg'zɪbɪt] **1** *n* objeto *m* expuesto. **2** *vt* exponer; (*manifest*) mostrar.

exhi'bition exposición *f*.

exhibitor expositor,-a *mf*.

exist [ɪg'zɪst] *vi* existir; (*stay alive*) subsistir.

existence existencia *f*.

existing *a* actual.

exit ['eksɪt] salida *f*.

exorbitant [ɪg'zɔːbɪtənt] *a* exorbitante.

expand [ɪk'spænd] **1** *vt* ampliar. **2** *vi* (*grow*) ampliarse; (*metal*) dilatarse.
• **expand on** *vt* ampliar.

expanse [ɪk'spæns] extensión *f*.

expansion (*in size*) expansión *f*; (*of gas, metal*) dilatación *f*.

expansion slot ranura *f* de expansión.

expect [ɪk'spekt] **1** *vt* (*anticipate*) esperar; (*suppose*) suponer; **to e. sth from sb/sth** esperar algo de algn/algo; **to e. to do sth** contar con hacer algo; **she's expecting a baby** está esperando un niño. **2** *vi* **to be expecting** estar embarazada.

expec'tation esperanza *f*; **contrary to e.** contrariamente a lo que se esperaba.

expedition [ekspɪ'dɪʃən] expedición *f*.

expel [ɪk'spel] *vt* expulsar.

expenditure [ɪk'spendɪtʃəʳ] desembolso *m*.

expense [ɪk'spens] gasto *m*; **to spare no e.** no escatimar gastos; *fig* **at the e. of** a costa de.

expensive *a* caro,-a.

experience [ɪk'spɪərɪəns] **1** *n* experiencia *f*. **2** *vt* (*sensation*) experimentar; (*difficulty, loss*) sufrir.

experienced [ɪk'spɪərɪənst] *a* experimentado,-a.

experiment [ɪk'sperɪmənt] **1** *n* experimento *m*. **2** *vi* experimentar (**on, with** con).

expert ['ekspɜːt] *a & n* experto,-a (*mf*).

expertise [ekspɜː'tiːz] pericia *f*.

expire [ɪk'spaɪəʳ] *vi* (*come to an end*) terminar; (*policy, contract*) vencer; (*ticket*) caducar.

expired *a* (*ticket*) caducado,-a.

expiry vencimiento *m*.

expiry date fecha *f* de caducidad.

explain [ɪk'spleɪn] *vt* explicar; (*clarify*) aclarar; **to e. oneself** justificarse.
• **explain away** *vt* justificar.

explanation [eksplə'neɪʃən] explicación *f*; (*clarification*) aclaración *f*.

explode [ɪk'spləʊd] **1** *vt* hacer explotar. **2** *vi* (*bomb*) explotar; **to e. with anger** montar en cólera.

exploit ['eksplɔɪt] **1** *n* hazaña *f*. **2** [ek'splɔɪt] *vt* explotar.

exploration exploración *f*.

explore [ɪk'splɔːʳ] *vt* explorar.

explorer explorador,-a *mf*.

explosion [ɪk'spləʊʒən] explosión *f*.

explosive 1 *a* explosivo,-a. **2** *n* explosivo *m*.

export [ɪk'spɔːt] **1** *vt* exportar. **2** ['ekspɔːt] *n* exportación *f*.

expose [ɪk'spəʊz] *vt* (*uncover*) exponer; (*secret*) revelar; (*plot*) descubrir.

express [ɪk'spres] **1** *a* (*explicit*) expreso,-a; *Br* (*letter*) urgente. **2** *n* (*train*) expreso *m*. **3** *vt* expresar.

expression expresión *f*.

expressway *US* autopista *f*.

extend [ɪk'stend] **1** *vt* (*enlarge*) ampliar; (*lengthen*) alargar; (*prolong*) prolongar; (*increase*) aumentar. **2** *vi* (*stretch*) extenderse; (*last*) prolongarse.

extension extensión *f*; (*of time*) prórroga *f*; (*of building*) anexo *m*.

extensive *a* extenso,-a.

extensively *adv* extensamente; (*frequently*) con frecuencia.

extent [ɪk'stent] (*area*) extensión *f*; **to some e.** hasta cierto punto; **to a large e.** en gran parte; **to such an e.** hasta tal punto.

exterior [ɪk'stɪərɪərˈ] *a & n* exterior (*m*).

external [ek'stɜːnəl] *a* externo,-a.

extinguisher [ɪk'stɪŋgwɪʃərˈ] extintor *m*.

extra ['ekstrə] **1** *a* extra; (*spare*) de sobra. **2** *adv* extra; **e. fine** extra fino. **3** *n* (*additional charge*) suplemento *m*; (*in film*) extra *mf*.

extract ['ekstrækt] **1** *n* extracto *m*. **2** [ɪk'strækt] *vt* (*tooth, information*) extraer.

extracurricular [ekstrəkə'rɪkjʊlərˈ] *a* extracurricular.

extraordinary [ɪk'strɔːdənərɪ] *a* extraordinario,-a; (*strange*) raro,-a.

extravagant [ɪk'strævɪgənt] *a* (*wasteful*) derrochador,-a; (*excessive*) exagerado,-a.

extreme [ɪk'striːm] **1** *a* extremo,-a; **an e. case** un caso excepcional. **2** *n* extremo *m*; **in the e.** en sumo grado.

extremely *adv* extremadamente; **I'm e. sorry** lo siento de veras.

eye [aɪ] *n* ojo *m*; **I couldn't believe my eyes** no podía creerlo; **not to take one's eyes off sb/sth** no quitar la vista de encima a algn/algo; **to catch sb's e.** llamar la atención a algn; **to turn a blind e.** hacer la vista gorda (**to** a); **with an e. to** con miras a; **to keep an e. on sb/sth** vigilar a algn/algo.

eyebrow ceja *f*.

eyeglasses *npl US* gafas *fpl*.

eyelash pestaña *f*.

eyelid párpado *m*.

eyeliner lápiz *m* de ojos.

eyeshadow sombra *f* de ojos.

eyesight vista *f*.

F

fabulous ['fæbjʊləs] *a* fabuloso,-a.

face [feɪs] **1** *n* cara *f*; (*surface*) superficie *f*; **f. to f.** cara a cara; **she slammed the door in my f.** me dió con la puerta en las narices; **in the f. of danger** ante el peligro; **to pull faces** hacer muecas; **f. down/up** boca abajo/ arriba; **to save f.** salvar las apariencias. **2** *vt* (*look onto*) dar a; (*be opposite*) estar enfrente de; (*problem*) hacer frente a; **to f. up to** hacer cara a; (*tolerate*) aguantar. **3** *vi* **to f. on to** dar a; **to f. towards** mirar hacia.

face cloth paño *m*.

facility [fə'sɪlɪtɪ] (*ease*) facilidad *f*; **facilities** (*means*) facilidades *fpl*; (*rooms, equipment*) instalaciones *fpl*.

fact [fækt] hecho *m*; (*reality*) realidad *f*; **as a matter of f.** de hecho; **in f.** en realidad.

factor ['fæktə'] factor *m*.

factory ['fæktərɪ] fábrica *f*.

fade [feɪd] *vi* (*colour*) desteñirse; (*flower*) marchitarse; (*light*) apagarse.

● **fade away** *vi* desvanecerse.

● **fade in/out** *vt* fundir.

fag [fæg] *Br fam* (*cigarette*) pitillo *m*; *US fam* (*homosexual*) marica *m*.

fail [feɪl] **1** *n* (*at school*) suspenso *m*; **without f.** sin falta. **2** *vt* (*exam*) suspender; **to f. to do sth** (*be unable*) no poder hacer algo; (*neglect*) dejar de hacer algo. **3** *vi* (*show, film*) fracasar; (*brakes*) fallar; (*at school*) suspender; (*health*) deteriorarse.

failed *a* (*attempt, poet*) fracasado,-a.

failing 1 *n* (*shortcoming*) defecto *m*; (*weakness*) punto *m* débil. **2** *prep* a falta de.

failure fracaso *m*; (*at school*) suspenso *m*; (*person*) fracasado,-a *mf*; (*breakdown*) avería *f*; **power f.** apagón *m*; **heart f.** paro *m* cardíaco; **her f. to answer** el hecho de que no contestara.

faint [feɪnt] **1** *a* (*sound*) débil; (*colour*) pálido,-a; (*outline*) borroso,-a; (*recollection*) vago,-a; (*giddy*) mareado,-a; **I haven't the faintest idea** no tengo la más mínima idea. **2** *n* desmayo *m*. **3** *vi* desmayarse.

faintly *adv* (*with little strength*) débilmente; (*unclear*) vagamente.

fair[1] [feə'] **1** *a* (*impartial*) imparcial; (*just*) justo,-a; (*hair*) rubio,-a; (*weather*) bueno,-a; **it's not f.** no hay derecho; **f. enough!** ¡vale!; **a f. number** un buen número. **2** *adv* **to play f.** jugar limpio.

fair[2] feria *f*; **trade f.** feria *f* de muestras.

fair-haired *a* rubio,-a.

fairly *adv* (*justly*) justamente; (*moderately*) bastante.

fair play juego *m* limpio.

fair-sized *a* bastante grande.

fairy ['feərɪ] hada f; **f. tale** cuento m de hadas.
faith [feɪθ] fe f; (trust) confianza f.
faithful a fiel.
faithfully adv **yours f.** (in letter) le saluda atentamente.
fake [feɪk] **1** a falso,-a. **2** n (object) falsificación f; (person) impostor,-a mf. **3** vt (forge) falsificar; (feign) fingir.
fall [fɔːl] **1** n caída f; (decrease) baja f; US otoño m; **falls** (waterfall) cascada f; **Niagara Falls** las cataratas del Niágara. **2** vi* caer, caerse; (temperature, prices) bajar; **night was falling** anochecía; **to f. asleep** dormirse; **to f. ill** caer enfermo,-a; **to f. in love** enamorarse.
● **fall apart** vi (of machine) deshacerse.
● **fall back on** vt (as last resort) recurrir a.
● **fall behind** vi (in race) quedarse atrás; **to f. behind with one's work** retrasarse en el trabajo.
● **fall down** vi (picture etc) caerse; (building) derrumbarse.
● **fall for** vt (person) enamorarse de; (trick) dejarse engañar por.
● **fall in** vi (roof) desplomarse.
● **fall off** vi (drop off) caer; (part) desprenderse; (diminish) disminuir.
● **fall out** vi (hair) caerse; (quarrel) pelearse.
● **fall over** vi caerse.
● **fall through** vi (plan) fracasar.
false [fɔːls] a falso,-a; **f. teeth** dentadura f postiza; **f. alarm** falsa alarma f.
fame [feɪm] fama f.
familiar [fə'mɪlɪə'] a (common) conocido,-a; **his face is f.** su cara me suena; **to be on f. terms with sb** (know well) tener confianza con algn.
famili'arity familiaridad f (with con); (intimacy) confianza f.
familiarize vt (make acquainted) familiarizar (with con); **to become familiarized with sth** familiarizarse con algo.
family ['fæmɪlɪ] familia f; **f. doctor** médico m de cabecera; **f. planning** planificación f familiar; **f. tree** árbol m genealógico.
famous ['feɪməs] a famoso,-a (for por).
fan [fæn] (held in hand) abanico m; (electric) ventilador m; (person) aficionado,-a mf; (of pop star etc) fan mf; **football f.** hincha mf.
fancy ['fænsɪ] **1** a de fantasía; **f. goods** artículos mpl de fantasía. **2** n (whim) capricho m; **to take a f. to sth** encapricharse con algo; **what takes your f.?** ¿qué se le antoja? **3** vt (imagine) imaginarse; (like, want) apetecer; fam **f. that!** ¡fíjate!; **do you f. a drink?** ¿te apetece una copa?
fancy dress disfraz m; **f. dress ball** baile m de disfraces.
fan heater estufa f de aire.
fantastic [fæn'tæstɪk] a fantástico,-a.
far [fɑː'] **1** a (distant) lejano,-a; **at the f. end** en el otro extremo. **2** adv

(*distant*) lejos; **f. off** a lo lejos; **farther back** más atrás; **how f. is it to Cardiff?** ¿cuánto hay de aquí a Cardiff?; **as f. as I can** en lo que puedo; **as f. as I know** que yo sepa; **as f. as possible** en lo posible; **f. from complaining, he seemed pleased** lejos de quejarse, parecía contento; **in so f. as . . .** en la medida en que . . .; **to go too f.** pasarse de la raya; **f. into the night** hasta muy entrada la noche; **so f.** (*in time*) hasta ahora; **by f.** con mucho; **f. cleverer** mucho más listo,-a; **f. too much** demasiado.

faraway *a* lejano,-a.

farce [fɑːs] farsa *f*.

fare [feəʳ] (*ticket price*) tarifa *f*, precio *m* del billete; (*for boat*) pasaje *m*; (*passenger*) pasajero,-a *mf*.

farewell [feəˈwel] **1** *interj* (*old use*) ¡adiós! **2** *n* despedida *f*.

far-'fetched *a* rebuscado,-a.

farm [fɑːm] **1** *n* granja *f*, *Am* hacienda *f*. **2** *vt* cultivar.

● **farm out** *vt* encargar fuera.

farmer granjero,-a *mf*, *Am* hacendado,-a *mf*.

farmhouse granja *f*, *Am* hacienda *f*.

farming 1 *n* (*agriculture*) agricultura *f*; (*of land*) cultivo *m*. **2** *a* agrícola.

farmyard corral *m*.

far-off *a* lejano,-a.

farther [ˈfɑːðəʳ] *adv* más lejos.

farthest 1 *a* más lejano,-a. **2** *adv* más lejos.

fascinate [ˈfæsɪneɪt] *vt* fascinar.

fasci'nation fascinación *f*.

fashion [ˈfæʃən] **1** *n* (*manner*) manera *f*; (*latest style*) moda *f*; **to go/be out of f.** pasar/no estar de moda; **f. parade** desfile *m* de modelos.

fashion show pase *m* de modelos.

fast [fɑːst] **1** *a* (*quick*) rápido,-a; (*clock*) adelantado,-a. **2** *adv* rápidamente, deprisa; **how f.?** ¿a qué velocidad?; **f. asleep** profundamente dormido,-a.

fasten [ˈfɑːsən] *vt* (*attach*) sujetar; (*fix*) fijar; (*belt*) abrochar; (*bag*) asegurar; (*shoe laces*) atar.

fastener cierre *m*.

fat [fæt] **1** *a* gordo,-a; (*thick*) grueso,-a; (*meat*) poco magra. **2** *n* grasa *f*; **cooking f.** manteca *f* de cerdo.

fatal [ˈfeɪtəl] *a* (*accident, illness*) mortal; (*ill-fated*) funesto,-a.

fatally *adv* **f. wounded** mortalmente herido,-a.

fate [feɪt] destino *m*.

father [ˈfɑːðəʳ] padre *m*; **my f. and mother** mis padres.

Father Christmas Papá *m* Noel.

father-in-law suegro *m*.

fatigue [fəˈtiːg] fatiga *f*.

fattening ['fætənɪŋ] *a* que engorda.

fatty ['fætɪ] *a* (*food*) graso,-a.

faucet ['fɔːsɪt] *US* grifo *m*.

fault [fɔːlt] (*defect*) defecto *m*; (*in merchandise*) desperfecto *m*; (*blame*) culpa *f*; **to find f. with** poner reparos a; **to be at f.** tener la culpa.

faulty *a* defectuoso,-a.

favour, *US* **favor** ['feɪvəʳ] **1** *n* favor *m*; **in f. of** a favor de; **to ask sb a f.** pedirle un favor a algn. **2** *vt* (*treat favourably*) favorecer; (*approve*) estar a favor de.

favourable *a* favorable.

favourite *a* & *n* favorito,-a (*mf*).

fax [fæks] **1** *n* fax *m*. **2** *vt* (*document*) mandar por fax; **to f. sb** mandar un fax a algn.

fear [fɪəʳ] **1** *n* miedo *m*; **for f. of** por temor a. **2** *vt* temer; **I f. it's too late** me temo que ya es tarde.

fearless *a* intrépido,-a.

feast [fiːst] banquete *m*.

feat [fiːt] hazaña *f*.

feather ['feðəʳ] pluma *f*; **f. duster** plumero *m*.

feature ['fiːtʃəʳ] **1** *n* (*of face*) facción *f*; (*characteristic*) característica *f*; **f. film** largometraje *m*. **2** *vi* figurar.

February ['febrʊərɪ] febrero *m*.

fed up [fed'ʌp] *a fam* harto,-a (**with** de).

fee [fiː] (*of lawyer, doctor*) honorarios *mpl*; (*at university*) **fees** tasas *fpl*.

feeble ['fiːbəl] *a* débil.

feed* [fiːd] **1** *vt* (*give food to*) dar de comer a; **to f. a baby** (*breast-feed*) amamantar a un bebé; (*with bottle*) dar el biberón a un bebé. **2** *vi* comer; (*cows, sheep*) pacer.

feedback feedback *m*; *fig* reacción *f*.

feel [fiːl] **1** *vi** (*have emotion, sensation*) sentirse; (*have opinion*) opinar; **how do you f.?** ¿qué tal te encuentras?; **I f. bad about it** me da pena; **to f. happy** sentirse feliz; **to f. cold/sleepy** tener frío/sueño; **to f. up to sth** sentirse con ánimos para hacer algo; **I feel that ...** me parece que ...; **it feels like summer** parece verano; **I f. sure that ...** estoy seguro,-a de que ...; **I f. like an ice cream** me apetece un helado; **to f. like doing sth** tener ganas de hacer algo. **2** *vt** (*touch*) tocar; (*sense*) sentir; (*the cold*) notar; **she feels a failure** se siente inútil. **3** *n* (*touch, sensation*) tacto *m*.

● **feel for** *vt* (*have sympathy for*) compadecer.

● **feel up to** *vt* tener ánimos para.

feeling (*emotion*) sentimiento *m*; (*physical*) sensación *f*; (*opinion*) opinión *f*; **I had the f. that ...** (*impression*) tuve la impresión de que ...; **to express one's feelings** expresar sus opiniones.

feet [fi:t] *npl see* **foot.**

fell [fel] *pt of* **fall.**

fellow ['feləʊ] **1** *n* (*chap*) tipo *m*, tío *m*. **2 f. citizen** conciudadano,-a *mf*; **f. countryman/countrywoman** compatriota *mf*.

felt¹ [felt] *pt & pp of* **feel.**

felt² fieltro *m*.

felt-tip(ped) pen rotulador *m*.

female ['fi:meɪl] **1** *a* femenino,-a; (*animal*) hembra. **2** *n* (*animal*) hembra *f*; (*woman*) mujer *f*; (*girl*) chica *f*.

feminine ['femɪnɪn] *a* femenino,-a.

fence [fens] **1** *n* cerca *f*. **2** *vi* (*in sport*) practicar la esgrima.

● **fence in** *vt* meter en un cercado.

fencing ['fensɪŋ] (*sport*) esgrima *f*.

fend [fend] *vi* **to f. for oneself** valerse por sí mismo.

● **fend off** *vt* (*blow*) parar; (*attack*) rechazar.

fender *US* (*on car*) parachoques *m inv*.

fern [fɜːn] helecho *m*.

ferocious [fəˈrəʊʃəs] *a* feroz.

ferry ['ferɪ] **1** *n* (*small*) barca *f* de pasaje; (*large, for cars*) ferry *m*. **2** *vt* transportar.

fertile ['fɜːtaɪl] *a* fértil.

fertilizer ['fɜːtɪlaɪzə'] abono *m*.

festival festival *m*.

festive ['festɪv] *a* festivo,-a; **the f. season** las fiestas de Navidad.

fe'stivity the festivities las fiestas.

fetch [fetʃ] *vt* (*go for*) ir a buscar; (*bring*) traer; **how much did it f.?** (*sell for*) ¿por cuánto se vendió?

fete [feɪt] fiesta *f*.

fever ['fi:və'] fiebre *f*.

feverish *a* febril.

few [fju:] **1** *a* (*not many*) pocos,-as; **as f. as** solamente; **a f.** unos,-as, algunos,-as; **in the next f. days** dentro de unos días; **she has fewer books than I thought** tiene menos libros de lo que pensaba; **quite a f.** un buen número. **2** *pron* (*not many*) pocos,-as; **there are too f.** no hay suficientes; **a f.** (*some*) algunos,-as; **who has the fewest?** ¿quién tiene menos?

fiancé [fɪˈɒnseɪ] prometido *m*.

fiancée prometida *f*.

fibre, *US* **fiber** ['faɪbə'] fibra *f*.

fiction ['fɪkʃən] ficción *f*.

fiddle ['fɪdəl] *fam* **1** *n* (*musical instrument*) violín *m*; (*shady deal*) trampa *f*. **2** *vt* estafar; (*accounts*) falsificar.

● **fiddle about** *vi* juguetear (**with** con).

fidget ['fɪdʒɪt] *vi* moverse; **stop fidgeting!** ¡estáte quieto!; **to f. with sth** jugar con algo.

field [fiːld] **1** *n* campo *m*; (*oilfield, coalfield etc*) yacimiento *m*. **2** *vt* (*in sport*) (*ball*) parar y devolver; (*team*) presentar

field trip viaje *m* de estudios.

field work trabajo *m* de campo.

fierce [fɪəs] *a* (*animal*) feroz; (*argument*) acalorado,-a; (*heat, competition*) intenso,-a.

fifteen [fɪf'tiːn] *a & n* quince *m inv*.

fifteenth *a & n* decimoquinto,-a (*mf*).

fifth [fɪfθ] *a & n* quinto,-a (*mf*).

fiftieth *adj & n* quincuagésimo,-a (*mf*).

fifty ['fɪftɪ] **1** *a* cincuenta *inv*; **a f.-f. chance** una probabilidad del cincuenta por ciento; **to go f.-f.** ir a medias. **2** *n* cincuenta *m inv*.

fig [fɪg] (*fruit*) higo *m*.

fight [faɪt] **1** *vt** combatir; (*bull*) lidiar. **2** *vi** pelear(se); (*quarrel*) reñir; *fig* (*struggle*) luchar (**for/against** por/contra). **3** *n* pelea *f*; (*boxing*) combate *m*; (*quarrel*) riña *f*; *fig* (*struggle*) lucha *f*.

● **fight back 1** *vt* (*tears*) contener. **2** *vi* (*recover ground*) resistir.

● **fight off** *vt* (*attack*) rechazar.

● **fight out** *vt* discutir.

fighter (*person*) combatiente *mf*; (*boxing*) púgil *m*; *fig* luchador,-a *mf*; **f. (plane)** (avión *m* de) caza *m*.

figure¹ ['fɪgəʳ] **1** *n* (*numeral*) cifra *f*; (*form, outline*) forma *f*; (*shape, statue, character*) figura *f*; **she has a good f.** tiene buen tipo; **f. of speech** figura retórica. **2** *vt US fam* imaginarse. **3** *vi* (*appear*) figurar; *US fam* **that figures** eso tiene sentido.

figure² *vt* (*guess*) imaginar.

● **figure on** *vt* **to f. on doing sth** esperar hacer algo.

● **figure out** *vt* comprender; **I can't f. it out** no me lo explico.

file [faɪl] **1** *n* (*tool*) lima *f*; (*folder*) carpeta *f*; (*archive*) archivo *m*; (*of computer*) fichero *m*; (*line*) fila *m*; **on f.** archivado,-a; **in single f.** en fila india. **2** *vt* (*smooth*) limar; (*put away*) archivar. **3** *vi* **to f. past** desfilar.

● **file away** *vt* (*put away*) archivar; (*in card-index*) clasificar.

● **file down** *vt* limar.

● **file in/out** *vi* entra/salir en fila.

filing clasificación *f*.

filing cabinet archivador *m*; (*for cards*) fichero *m*.

fill [fɪl] **1** *vt* (*space, time*) llenar (**with** de); (*post, requirements*) cubrir. **2** *vi* llenarse (**with** de).

● **fill in 1** *vt* (*space, form*) rellenar; (*time*) pasar; (*inform*) *fam* poner al corriente (**on** de). **2** *vi* **to f. in for sb** sustituir a algn.

● **fill out** vt US (form) rellenar.

● **fill up 1** vt llenar hasta arriba; **f. her up!** ¡llénelo! **2** vi llenarse.

fillet ['fɪlɪt] filete m; **f. steak** filete m.

filling 1 a que llena mucho. **2** n (stuffing) relleno m; (in tooth) empaste m.

filling station Br gasolinera f.

film [fɪlm] **1** n película f. **2** vt filmar. **3** vi rodar.

film star estrella f de cine.

filter ['fɪltəʳ] **1** n filtro m; **f. lane** carril m de acceso. **2** vt filtrar. **3** vi (traffic) **to f. to the right** girar a la derecha.

filth [fɪlθ] (dirt) porquería f; fig porquerías fpl.

filthy a (dirty) asqueroso,-a; (obscene) obsceno,-a.

fin [fɪn] (of fish) aleta f.

final ['faɪnəl] **1** a último,-a; (definitive) definitivo,-a. **2** n (sport) final f.

finalize vt ultimar; (date) fijar.

finally adv finalmente.

finance ['faɪnæns] **1** n finanzas fpl; **finances** fondos mpl. **2** vt financiar.

fi'nancial a financiero,-a.

find [faɪnd] **1** vt* (locate, think) encontrar; (discover) descubrir; **it has been found that …** se ha comprobado que …; **I found it impossible to get away** me resultó imposible irme. **2** n hallazgo m.

● **find out** vt (enquire) averiguar; (discover) descubrir. **2** vi **to f. out about sth** informarse sobre algo; (discover) enterarse de algo.

fine¹ [faɪn] **1** n (sum of money) multa f. **2** vt multar.

fine² **1** a (delicate etc) fino,-a; (excellent) excelente; (weather) bueno; **it was f.** hacía buen tiempo. **2** adv muy bien. **3** interj ¡vale!

finger ['fɪŋgəʳ] dedo m (de la mano); **to keep one's fingers crossed** esperar que todo salga bien.

fingernail uña f.

fingerprint huella f dactilar.

fingertip punta f or yema f del dedo.

finish ['fɪnɪʃ] **1** n fin m; (of race) llegada f. **2** vt (complete) acabar, terminar; (use up) agotar; **to f. doing sth** terminar de hacer algo. **3** vi acabar, terminar.

● **finish off** vt (complete) terminar completamente; (kill) rematar.

● **finish up 1** vt acabar; **to f. up doing sth** acabar haciendo algo. **2** vi **to f. up in jail** ir a parar a la cárcel.

Finn [fɪn] finlandés,-esa mf.

Finnish 1 a finlandés,-esa. **2** n (language) finlandés m.

fir [fɜː] abeto m.

fire ['faɪəʳ] **1** n fuego m; (accident etc) incendio m; (heater) estufa f; (gunfire) fuego m; **to open f.** abrir fuego. **2** vt (gun) disparar (at a); (dismiss) despedir. **3** vi (shoot) disparar (at sobre).

fire alarm alarma *f* de incendios.

fire brigade (cuerpo *m* de) bomberos *mpl*.

firecracker petardo *m*.

fire exit salida *f* de emergencia.

fire extinguisher extintor *m*

fireman bombero *m*.

fireplace chimenea *f*; (*hearth*) hogar *m*.

firewood leña *f*.

fireworks *npl* fuegos *mpl* artificiales.

firm [fɜ:m] **1** *a* firme. **2** *n* empresa *f*.

first [fɜ:st] **1** *a* primero,-a; (*before masculine singular noun*) primer; **for the f. time** por primera vez; **in the f. place** en primer lugar. **2** *adv* (*before anything else*) primero; **f. and foremost** ante todo; **at f.** al principio. **3** *n* **the f.** el primero, la primera; **the f. of April** el uno *or* el primero de abril; **from the (very) f.** desde el principio.

firstly *adv* en primer lugar.

first aid primeros auxilios.

first-class 1 *a* de primera clase. **2** *adv* **to travel f.** viajar en primera.

fish [fɪʃ] **1** *n* (*pl* **fish**) pez *m*; (*as food*) pescado *m*. **2** *vi* pescar.

fisherman pescador *m*.

fishfinger palito *m* de pescado.

fishing pesca *f*; **to go f.** ir de pesca.

fishing rod caña *f* de pescar.

fishmonger ['fɪʃmʌŋgəʳ] *Br* pescadero,-a *mf*.

fish shop pescadería *f*.

fist [fɪst] puño *m*.

fit¹ [fɪt] **1** *vt* (*clothes*) ir bien a; (*slot*) encajar; (*install*) colocar; **that suit doesn't f. you** ese traje no te entalla; **a car fitted with a radio** un coche provisto de radio; **she doesn't f. the description** no responde a la descripción. **2** *vi* (*be of right size*) caber; (*be suitable*) encajar; (*facts etc*) cuadrar. **3** *a* (*suitable*) apto,-a (**for** para); (*healthy*) en (plena) forma; **are you f. to drive?** ¿estás en condiciones de conducir?; **to keep f.** mantenerse en forma. **4** *n* **to be a good f.** encajar bien.

fit² (*attack*) ataque *m*; *fig* arrebato *m*; **by fits and starts** a trompicones.

● **fit in 1** *vi* (*tally*) cuadrar (**with** con); **he didn't f. in with his colleagues** no encajó con sus compañeros de trabajo. **2** *vt* (*find time for*) encontrar un hueco para.

● **fit on 1** *vt* **to f. sth on to sth** poner algo en algo. **2** *vi* ir.

● **fit out** *vt* equipar.

fitness (*health*) (buen) estado *m* físico.

fitted *a* empotrado,-a; **f. carpet** moqueta *f*.

fitting room probador *m*.

fittings *npl* accesorios *mpl*; **light f.** apliques *mpl* eléctricos.
five [faɪv] *a & n* cinco (*m*) *inv*; **f. hundred** quinientos,-as.
fiver *fam* billete *m* de cinco libras/dólares.
fix [fɪks] **1** *n* **to be in a f.** estar en un apuro. **2** *vt* (*fasten*) fijar; (*date, price*) fijar; (*repair*) arreglar; *US* (*food, drink*) preparar; **he'll f. it with the boss** (*arrange*) se las arreglará con el jefe.
● **fix on** *vt* (*lid etc*) encajar.
● **fix up** *vt* (*arrange*) arreglar; **to f. sb up with sth** proveer a algn de algo.
fizzy ['fɪzɪ] *a* (*water*) con gas.
flag [flæg] **1** *n* bandera *f*; (*on ship*) pabellón *m*. **2** *vi* (*interest*) decaer; (*conversation*) languidecer.
flake [fleɪk] **1** *n* (*of snow*) copo *m*; (*of skin, soap*) escama *f*. **2** *vi* (*paint*) desconcharse.
flame [fleɪm] llama *f*; **to go up in flames** incendiarse.
flammable ['flæməbəl] *a* inflamable.
flan [flæn] tarta *f* rellena; **fruit f.** tarta *f* de fruta.
flannel ['flænəl] (*material*) franela *f*; *Br* (*face cloth*) toallita *f*.
flap [flæp] **1** *vt* (*wings, arms*) batir. **2** *vi* (*wings*) aletear; (*flag*) ondear. **3** *n* (*of envelope, pocket*) solapa *f*; **to get into a f.** ponerse nervioso,-a.
flare [fleər] **1** *n* (*distress signal*) bengala *f*. **2** *vi* (*fire*) llamear; (*trouble*) estallar.
flash [flæʃ] **1** *n* (*of light*) destello *m*; (*of lightning*) relámpago *m*; (*for camera*) flash *m*. **2** *vt* (*torch*) dirigir; **he flashed his card** enseñó rápidamente su carnet. **3** *vi* (*sudden light*) destellar; (*shine*) brillar; **a car flashed past** un coche pasó como un rayo.
flashlight *US* linterna *f*.
flask [flɑ:sk] frasco *m*; (**thermos**) **f.** termo *m*.
flat [flæt] **1** *a* (*surface*) llano,-a; (*beer*) sin gas; (*battery*) descargado,-a; (*tyre*) desinflado,-a; (*dull*) soso,-a; (*in music*) **B f.** si *m* bemol. **2** *adv* **to fall f. on one's face** caerse de bruces; **to go f. out** ir a todo gas. **3** *n* (*apartment*) piso *m*; (*flat tyre*) pinchazo *m*.
flatly *adv* rotundamente.
flatten *vt* (*make level*) allanar; (*crush*) aplastar.
flatter ['flætər] *vt* halagar; (*clothes, portrait*) favorecer.
flavour, *US* **flavor** ['fleɪvər] **1** *n* sabor *m*. **2** *vt* (*food*) sazonar (**with** con).
flavouring, *US* **flavoring** condimento *m*; **artificial f.** aroma *m* artificial.
flaw [flɔ:] (*failing*) defecto *m*; (*fault*) desperfecto *m*.
flea [fli:] pulga *f*.
flea market rastro *m*.
flee* [fli:] **1** *vt* huir. **2** *vi* huir (**from** de).
fleet [fli:t] flota *f*.

Flemish ['flemɪʃ] **1** *a* flamenco,-a. **2** *n* (*language*) flamenco *m*.

flesh [fleʃ] carne *f*; (*of fruit*) pulpa *f*; **in** *the* **f.** en persona.

flex [fleks] **1** *n Br* (*cable*) cable *m*. **2** *vt* (*muscles*) flexionar.

flexible ['fleksɪbəl] *a* flexible.

flick [flɪk] **1** *n* (*of finger*) capirotazo *m*. **2** *vt* (*finger*) dar un capirotazo a.

● **flick off** *vt* (*piece of fluff*) quitar con un golpe del dedo.

● **flick through** *vt* hojear.

flies [flaɪz] *npl* (*on trousers*) bragueta *f*.

flight [flaɪt] vuelo *m*; (*escape*) huida *f*; (*of stairs*) tramo *m*; **to take f.** darse a la fuga.

flimsy ['flɪmzɪ] *a* (*cloth*) ligero,-a; (*structure*) poco sólido,-a; (*excuse*) poco convincente.

fling* [flɪŋ] *vt* arrojar.

flint [flɪnt] (*in lighter*) piedra *f* de mechero.

flip-flop ['flɪpflɒp] (*footwear*) chancleta *f*.

flip through *vt* ['flɪpθruː] (*book*) hojear.

float [fləʊt] **1** *n* flotador *m*; (*in procession*) carroza *f*. **2** *vi* flotar.

flock [flɒk] **1** *n* rebaño *m*; (*of birds*) bandada *f*. **2** *vi* acudir en masa.

flood [flʌd] **1** *n* inundación *f*; (*of river*) riada *f*. **2** *vt* inundar. **3** *vi* (*river*) desbordarse.

floodlight foco *m*.

floor [flɔːʳ] (*of room*) suelo *m*; (*storey*) piso *m*; **first f.** *Br* primer piso *m*, *US* planta *f* baja; **ground f.** planta *f* baja.

floorboard tabla *f* (del suelo).

flop [flɒp] **1** *n* (*failure*) fracaso *m*. **2** *vi* fracasar.

floppy *a* flojo,-a.

floppy disk disquete *m*, disco *m* flexible.

florist ['flɒrɪst] florista *mf*; **f.'s** floristería *f*.

flour ['flaʊəʳ] harina *f*.

flow [fləʊ] **1** *n* flujo *m*; (*of traffic*) circulación *f*; (*of people*, *goods*) movimiento *m*. **2** *vi* (*blood*, *river*) fluir; (*traffic*) circular.

flow chart organigrama *m*.

flower ['flaʊəʳ] **1** *n* flor *f*. **2** *vi* florecer.

flower bed arriate *m*.

flower shop floristería *f*.

flu [fluː] gripe *f*.

fluent ['fluːənt] *a* (*eloquent*) fluido,-a; **he speaks f. German** habla el alemán con soltura.

fluently *adv* (*to speak*) con soltura.

fluff [flʌf] (*down*) pelusa *f*.

fluid ['fluːɪd] líquido *m*.

flunk [flʌŋk] *vt US fam* catear.

fluorescent [fluə'resənt] *a* fluorescente.

flush [flʌʃ] **1** *a* f. with (*level*) a ras de. **2** *n* (*blush*) rubor *m*. **3** *vt* to f. the lavatory tirar de la cadena. **4** *vi* (*blush*) ruborizarse.

flute [fluːt] flauta *f*.

flutter ['flʌtər] *vi* (*leaves, birds*) revolotear; (*flag*) ondear.

fly[1] [flaɪ] **1** *vt* (*plane*) pilotar. **2** *vi* (*bird, plane*) volar; (*go by plane*) ir en avión; (*flag*) ondear.

● **fly over** *vt* (*country etc*) sobrevolar.

fly[2] (*insect*) mosca *f*; f. spray spray *m* matamoscas.

fly[3] (*on trousers*) bragueta *f*.

flying 1 *a* (*soaring*) volante; (*rapid*) rápido,-a. **2** *n* (*action*) vuelo *m*; (*aviation*) aviación *f*.

flying saucer platillo *m* volante.

flyover paso *m* elevado.

foam [fəʊm] espuma *f*; f. rubber goma *f* espuma.

focus ['fəʊkəs] **1** *vt* centrar (on en). **2** *vi* to f. on sth enfocar algo; *fig* centrarse en algo. **3** *n* foco *m*.

fog [fɒg] niebla *f*; (*at sea*) bruma *f*.

foggy *a* it is f. hay niebla.

foil [fɔɪl] **1** *n* aluminium f. papel *m* de aluminio. **2** *vt* (*plot*) frustrar.

fold [fəʊld] **1** *n* (*crease*) pliegue *m*. **2** *vt* doblar; to f. one's arms cruzar los brazos. **3** *vi* to f. (up) (*chair etc*) plegarse.

● **fold away** *vt* plegar.

folder carpeta *f*.

folding *a* (*chair etc*) plegable.

folk [fəʊk] *npl* (*people*) gente *f*.

folk music música *f* folk.

follow ['fɒləʊ] **1** *vt* seguir; (*understand*) comprender. **2** *vi* (*come after*) seguir; (*result*) resultar; (*understand*) entender; that doesn't f. eso no es lógico.

● **follow around** *vt* to f. sb around seguir a algn por todas partes.

● **follow on** *vi* (*come after*) venir detrás.

● **follow up** *vt* (*idea*) llevar a cabo; (*clue*) investigar.

follower seguidor,-a *mf*.

following 1 *a* siguiente. **2** *n* seguidores *mpl*.

fond [fɒnd] *a* to be f. of sb tenerle mucho cariño a algn; to be f. of doing sth ser aficionado,-a a hacer algo.

font [fɒnt] (*of characters*) fuente *f*.

food [fuːd] comida *f*.

food poisoning intoxicación *f* alimenticia.

fool [fuːl] **1** *n* tonto,-a *mf*; to play the f. hacer el tonto. **2** *vt* (*deceive*) engañar. **3** *vi* (*joke*) bromear.

● **fool about** or **around** vi hacer el tonto.

foolish a (silly) tonto,-a; (unwise) estúpido,-a.

foolishly adv estúpidamente.

foot [fʊt] **1** n (pl **feet** [fi:t]) pie m; (of animal) pata f; **on f.** a pie; **to put one's f. in it** meter la pata. **2** vt **to f. the bill** (pay) pagar la cuenta.

football (soccer) fútbol m; (ball) balón m; **f. match** partido m de fútbol.

footballer futbolista mf.

footbridge puente m para peatones.

footpath sendero m.

footprint pisada f.

footstep paso m.

for [fɔː^r] prep (purpose) para; **what's this f.?** ¿para qué sirve esto?; **f. sale** en venta. ▌ (because of, on behalf of) por; **famous f. its cuisine** famoso,-a por su cocina; **will you do it f. me?** ¿lo harás por mí? ▌ (instead of) por; **can you go f. me?** puede ir por mí? ▌ (during) por, durante; **I was ill f. a month** estuve enfermo,-a durante un mes; **I've been here f. three months** hace tres meses que estoy aquí. ▌ (distance) por; **I walked f. ten kilometres** caminé diez kilómetros. ▌ (at a point in time) para; **I can do it f. next Monday** puedo hacerlo para el lunes que viene; **f. the last time** por última vez. ▌ (in exchange for) por; **I got the car f. five hundred pounds** conseguí el coche por quinientas libras. ▌ (in favour of) a favor de; **are you f. or against?** ¿estás a favor o en contra? ▌ (towards) hacia, por; **affection f. sb** cariño hacia algn. ▌ **it's time f. you to go** es hora de que os marchéis.

forbid* [fə'bɪd] vt prohibir; **to f. sb to do sth** prohibirle a algn hacer algo.

force [fɔːs] **1** n fuerza f; **to come into f.** entrar en vigor; **the (armed) forces** las fuerzas armadas. **2** vt forzar; **to f. sb to do sth** forzar a algn a hacer algo.

forecast ['fɔːkɑːst] **1** n pronóstico m, previsión f. **2** vt* pronosticar.

forehead ['fɒrɪd] frente f.

foreign ['fɒrɪn] a extranjero,-a; (trade, policy) exterior.

foreigner extranjero,-a mf.

foreman ['fɔːmən] capataz m.

foremost ['fɔːməʊst] a principal; **first and f.** ante todo.

forerunner ['fɔːrʌnə^r] precursor,-a mf.

foresee* [fɔː'siː] vt prever.

forest ['fɒrɪst] bosque m.

forever [fə'revə^r] adv (constantly) siempre; (for good) para siempre.

forge [fɔːdʒ] vt (counterfeit) falsificar; (metal) forjar.

● **forge ahead** vi hacer grandes progresos.

forgery ['fɔːdʒərɪ] falsificación f.

forget* [fə'get] **1** vt olvidar; **I forgot to close the window** se me olvidó cerrar la ventana. **2** *vi* olvidarse.

● **forget about** *vt* olvidar.

forgetful *a* olvidadizo,-a.

forgive* [fə'gɪv] *vt* perdonar; **to f. sb for sth** perdonarle algo a algn.

fork [fɔːk] **1** *n* (*cutlery*) tenedor *m*; (*farming*) horca *f*; (*in road*) bifurcación *f*. **2** *vi* (*roads*) bifurcarse.

● **fork out** *vt fam* (*money*) soltar.

form [fɔːm] **1** *n* forma *f*; (*type*) clase *f*; (*document*) formulario *m*; (*at school*) clase *f*; **on/on top/off f.** en/en plena/en baja forma. **2** *vt* formar. **3** *vi* formarse.

formal ['fɔːməl] *a* (*official*) oficial; (*party, dress*) de etiqueta; (*person*) formalista.

for'mality formalidad *f*.

formally *adv* oficialmente.

format *a* formato *m*.

for'mation formación *f*.

former *a* (*time*) anterior; (*one-time*) antiguo,-a; (*first*) aquél, aquélla; **the f. champion** el excampeón.

formerly *adv* antiguamente.

formula ['fɔːmjʊlə] fórmula *f*.

fort [fɔːt] fortaleza *f*.

fortieth ['fɔːtɪɪθ] *adj & n* cuadragésimo,-a (*mf*).

fortnight ['fɔːtnaɪt] *Br* quincena *f*.

fortress ['fɔːtrɪs] fortaleza *f*.

fortunate ['fɔːtʃənɪt] *a* afortunado,-a; **it was f. that he came** fue una suerte que viniera.

fortunately *adv* afortunadamente.

fortune ['fɔːtʃən] (*luck, fate*) suerte *f*; (*money*) fortuna *f*.

forty ['fɔːtɪ] *a & n* cuarenta (*m*) *inv*.

forward ['fɔːwəd] **1** *adv* (*also* **forwards**) (*direction and movement*) hacia adelante; **from this day f.** de ahora en adelante. **2** *a* (*person*) fresco,-a. **3** *n* (*in football*) delantero,-a *mf*. **4** *vt* (*send on*) remitir; (*goods*) expedir.

foul [faʊl] **1** *a* (*smell*) fétido,-a; (*taste*) asqueroso,-a; (*language*) grosero, -a. **2** *n* (*in football etc*) falta *f*.

found¹ [faʊnd] *pt & pp of* **find.**

found² *vt* (*establish*) fundar.

fountain ['faʊntɪn] fuente *f*.

fountain pen pluma estilográfica.

four [fɔːʳ] *a & n* cuatro (*m*) *inv*; **on all fours** a gatas.

fourteen [fɔː'tiːn] *a & n* catorce (*m*) *inv*.

fourth *a & n* cuarto,-a (*mf*).

fowl [faʊl] aves *fpl* de corral.

fox [fɒks] zorro,-a *mf*.

foyer ['fɔɪeɪ] vestíbulo *m*.

fraction ['frækʃən] fracción *f*.

fracture ['fræktʃəʳ] **1** *n* fractura *f*. **2** *vt* fracturar.

fragile ['frædʒaɪl] *a* frágil.

fragment ['frægmənt] fragmento *m*.

fragrance ['freɪgrəns] fragancia *f*.

frail [freɪl] *a* frágil.

frame [freɪm] **1** *n* (*of window, door, picture*) marco *m*; (*of machine*) armazón *m*; **f. of mind** estado *m* de ánimo. **2** *vt* (*picture*) enmarcar; (*question*) formular; (*innocent person*) incriminar.

framework within the f. of ... dentro del marco de ...

franc [fræŋk] franco *m*.

frank [fræŋk] *a* franco,-a.

frankly *adv* francamente.

frankness franqueza *f*.

frantic ['fræntɪk] *a* (*anxious*) desesperado,-a; (*hectic*) frenético,-a.

frantically *adv* desesperadamente.

fraud [frɔːd] fraude *m*; (*person*) impostor,-a *mf*.

fray [freɪ] *vi* (*cloth*) deshilacharse.

freckle ['frekəl] peca *f*.

freckled *a* pecoso,-a.

free [friː] **1** *a* libre; **f. (of charge)** gratuito,-a; (*generous*) generoso,-a. **2** *adv* **(for) f.** gratis. **3** *vt* (*liberate*) poner en libertad.

freedom libertad *f*.

Freefone^(R) teléfono *m* gratuito.

free-range *a* *Br* de granja.

freeway *US* autopista *f*.

freeze* [friːz] **1** *vt* congelar. **2** *vi* (*liquid*) helarse; (*food*) congelarse.

● **freeze up** *or* **over** *vi* helarse.

freezer congelador *m*.

freezing *a* glacial; **above/below f. point** sobre/bajo cero.

French [frentʃ] **1** *a* francés,-esa. **2** *n* (*language*) francés *m*; *pl* **the F.** los franceses.

French fries *npl* patatas *fpl* fritas.

Frenchman francés *m*.

Frenchwoman francesa *f*.

frequent ['friːkwənt] *a* frecuente.

frequently *adv* frecuentemente.

fresh [freʃ] *a* fresco,-a; (*new*) nuevo,-a; **in the f. air** al aire libre.

freshen up *vi* asearse.

fret [fret] *vi* preocuparse (**about** por).

Friday ['fraɪdɪ] viernes *m*.

fridge [frɪdʒ] nevera *f*, frigorífico *m*.

fried [fraɪd] *a* frito,-a.

friend [frend] amigo,-a *mf*; **a f. of mine** un,-a amigo,-a mío,-a.

friendly *a* (*person*) simpático,-a; (*atmosphere*) acogedor,-a.

friendship amistad *f*.

fright [fraɪt] (*fear*) miedo *m*; (*shock*) susto *m*; **to get a f.** pegarse un susto.

frighten *vt* asustar.

● **frighten away** or **off** *vt* ahuyentar.

frightened *a* asustado,-a; **to be f. of sb** tenerle miedo a algn.

frightening ['fraɪtənɪŋ] *a* espantoso,-a.

frill [frɪl] (*dress*) volante *m*.

fringe [frɪndʒ] (*of hair*) flequillo *m*.

frock [frɒk] vestido *m*.

frog [frɒg] rana *f*.

from [frɒm, *unstressed* frəm] *prep* (*time*) desde, a partir de; **f. the eighth to the seventeenth** desde el ocho hasta el diecisiete; **f. time to time** de vez en cuando. ▌ (*price, number*) desde, de; **dresses f. five pounds** vestidos desde cinco libras. ▌ (*origin*) de; **he's f. Malaga** es de Málaga; **the train f. Bilbao** el tren procedente de Bilbao ▌ (*distance*) de; **the town is four miles f. the coast** el pueblo está a cuatro millas de la costa. ▌ (*remove, subtract*) a; **he took the book f. the child** le quitó el libro al niño. ▌ (*according to*) según, por; **f. what the author said** según lo que dijo el autor. ▌ (*position*) desde, de; **f. here** desde aquí.

front [frʌnt] **1** *n* parte *f* delantera; (*of building*) fachada *f*; (*military, political, of weather*) frente *m*; **in f. (of)** delante (de). **2** *a* delantero,-a.

front door puerta *f* principal.

frost [frɒst] *n* (*covering*) escarcha *f*; (*freezing*) helada *f*.

frostbite congelación *f*.

frosty *a fig* glacial; **it will be a f. night tonight** esta noche habrá helada.

froth [frɒθ] espuma *f*.

frown [fraʊn] *vi* fruncir el ceño.

● **frown upon** *vt* desaprobar.

frozen ['frəʊzən] *a* (*liquid, feet etc*) helado,-a; (*food*) congelado,-a.

fruit [fru:t] fruta *f*; **fruits** (*rewards*) frutos *mpl*.

fruit salad macedonia *f* de frutas

frustrated [frʌ'streɪtɪd] *a* frustrado,-a.

frustrating *a* frustrante.

fry [fraɪ] *vt* freír.

frying pan, *US* **fry-pan** sartén *f*.

fuel ['fjʊəl] combustible *m*; (*for engines*) carburante *m*.

fugitive ['fju:dʒɪtɪv] fugitivo,-a *mf*.

fulfil, US **fulfill** [fʊlˈfɪl] vt (*task, ambition*) realizar; (*promise*) cumplir; (*wishes*) satisfacer.

fulfilling a que llena.

full [fʊl] **1** a lleno,-a (**of** de); (*complete*) completo,-a; **I'm f. (up)** no puedo más. **2** n **in f.** en su totalidad.

full board pensión f completa.

full-scale a (*model*) de tamaño natural.

full stop punto m.

full-time 1 a de jornada completa. **2** adv **to work f.** trabajar aa jornada completa.

fully adv completamente.

fumes [fjuːmz] npl humo m.

fun [fʌn] (*amusement*) diversión f; **in** or **for f.** en broma; **to have f.** pasarlo bien; **to make f. of sb** reírse de algn.

function [ˈfʌŋkʃən] **1** n función f; (*ceremony*) acto m; (*party*) recepción f. **2** vi funcionar.

fund [fʌnd] **1** n fondo m; **funds** fondos mpl. **2** vt (*finance*) financiar.

funeral [ˈfjuːnərəl] funeral m.

funfair Br parque m de atracciones.

funnel [ˈfʌnəl] (*for liquids*) embudo m; (*of ship*) chimenea f.

funny [ˈfʌnɪ] a (*peculiar*) raro,-a; (*amusing*) divertido,-a; (*ill*) mal; **I found it very f.** me hizo mucha gracia.

fur [fɜːʳ] (*of living animal*) pelo m; (*of dead animal*) piel f.

furious [ˈfjʊərɪəs] a (*angry*) furioso,-a.

furnish [ˈfɜːnɪʃ] vt (*house*) amueblar.

furniture [ˈfɜːnɪtʃəʳ] muebles mpl; **a piece of f.** un mueble.

further [ˈfɜːðəʳ] **1** a (*new*) nuevo,-a; (*additional*) otro,-a. **2** adv más lejos; (*more*) más; **f. back** más atrás.

further education estudios mpl superiores.

furthermore adv además.

furthest a más lejano,-a.

fury [ˈfjʊərɪ] furia f.

fuse [fjuːz] **1** n fusible m; (*of bomb*) mecha f. **2** vi **the lights fused** se fundieron los plomos.

fuss [fʌs] **1** n (*commotion*) jaleo m; **to kick up a f.** armar un escándalo; **to make a f. of** (*pay attention to*) mimar a. **2** vi preocuparse (**about** por).

● **fuss over** vt consentir a.

fussy a (*nitpicking*) quisquilloso,-a; (*thorough*) exigente.

future [ˈfjuːtʃəʳ] **1** n futuro m; **in the near f.** en un futuro próximo. **2** a futuro,-a.

fuzzy [ˈfʌzɪ] a (*hair*) muy rizado,-a; (*blurred*) borroso,-a.

G

gadget ['gædʒɪt] aparato *m*.

Gaelic ['geɪlɪk] **1** *a* gaélico,-a. **2** *n* (*language*) gaélico *m*.

gag [gæg] **1** *n* mordaza *f*; (*joke*) chiste *m*. **2** *vt* amordazar.

gaiety ['geɪətɪ] regocijo *m*.

gaily ['geɪlɪ] *adv* alegremente.

gain [geɪn] **1** *n* ganancia *f*; (*increase*) aumento *m*. **2** *vt* (*obtain*) ganar; (*increase*) aumentar; **to g. weight** aumentar de peso.

● **gain on** *vt* ganar terreno a.

gala ['gɑːlə] gala *f*.

galaxy ['gæləksɪ] galaxia *f*.

gale [geɪl] vendaval *m*.

gallant ['gælənt] *a* (*chivalrous*) galante.

gallery ['gælərɪ] galería *f*.

gallivant ['gælɪvænt] *vi fam* callejear.

gallon ['gælən] galón *m*.

gallop ['gæləp] **1** *n* galope *m*. **2** *vi* galopar.

gamble ['gæmbəl] **1** *n* (*risk*) riesgo *m*; (*bet*) apuesta *f*. **2** *vi* (*bet*) jugar; (*take a risk*) arriesgarse.

● **gamble away** *vt* (*lose*) perder en el juego.

gambler jugador,-a *mf*.

gambling juego *m*.

game [geɪm] juego *m*; (*match*) partido *m*; (*of bridge*) partida *f*; **games** *Br* (*at school*) educación *f* física.

gammon ['gæmən] *Br* jamón *m* ahumado *or* curado.

gang [gæŋ] (*of criminals*) banda *f*; (*of youths*) pandilla *f*.

● **gang up** *vi* confabularse (**on** contra).

gangster gángster *m*.

gangway pasarela *f*.

gaol [dʒeɪl] *n* & *vt Br see* **jail.**

gap [gæp] hueco *m*; (*blank space*) blanco *m*; (*in time*) intervalo *m*; (*gulf*) diferencia *f*; (*deficiency*) laguna *f*.

gape [geɪp] *vi* (*person*) mirar boquiabierto,-a.

garage ['gærɑːʒ] garaje *m*; (*for repairs*) taller *m* mecánico; (*filling station*) gasolinera *f*.

garbage ['gɑːbɪdʒ] *US* basura *f*; **g. can** cubo *m* de la basura.

garden ['gɑːdən] jardín *m*.

gardener jardinero,-a *mf*.

gardening jardinería *f*.

gargle ['gɑːgəl] *vi* hacer gárgaras.

garland ['gɑːlənd] guirnalda *f*.

garlic ['gɑːlɪk] ajo *m*.

garment ['gɑːmənt] prenda *f*.

gas [gæs] **1** *n* gas *m*; *US* gasolina *f*; **g. cooker** cocina *f* de gas; **g. fire** estufa *f* de gas. **2** *vt* (*asphyxiate*) asfixiar con gas.

gash [gæʃ] **1** *n* herida *f* profunda. **2** *vt* **he gashed his forehead** se hizo una herida en la frente.

gasoline ['gæsəliːn] *US* gasolina *f*.

gasp [gɑːsp] **1** *n* (*cry*) grito *m* sordo; (*breath*) bocanada *f*. **2** *vi* (*in surprise*) quedar boquiabierto,-a; (*breathe*) jadear.

gas station gasolinera *f*.

gassy ['gæsɪ] *a* gaseoso,-a.

gasworks fábrica *f* de gas.

gate [geɪt] puerta *f*; (*at football ground*) entrada *f*.

gatecrash *vti* colarse.

gather ['gæðər] **1** *vt* (*collect*) juntar; (*pick up*) recoger; (*bring together*) reunir; (*understand*) suponer; **to g. speed** ir ganando velocidad; **I g. that ... I** tengo entendido que ... **2** *vi* (*come together*) reunirse.

● **gather round** *vi* agruparse.

gathering reunión *f*.

gaudy ['gɔːdɪ] *a* chillón,-ona.

gauge [geɪdʒ] **1** *n* (*of railway*) ancho *m* de vía; (*calibrator*) indicador *m*. **2** *vt* (*judge*) juzgar.

gaunt [gɔːnt] *a* (*lean*) demacrado,-a; (*desolate*) lúgubre.

gauze [gɔːz] gasa *f*.

gave [geɪv] *pt of* **give**.

gay [geɪ] *a* (*homosexual*) gay; (*happy*) alegre.

gaze [geɪz] **1** *n* mirada *f* fija. **2** *vi* mirar fijamente.

● **gaze at** *vt* mirar fijamente.

GB [dʒiː'biː] *abbr of* **Great Britain.**

GCE [dʒiːsiː'iː] *abbr of* **General Certificate of Education (A-Level),** ≈ COU *m*.

GCSE [dʒiːsiːes'iː] *abbr of* **General Certificate of Secondary Education** ≈ BUP *m*.

gear [gɪər] **1** *n* (*equipment*) equipo *m*; (*belongings*) bártulos *mpl*; (*clothing*) ropa *f*; (*in car etc*) marcha *f*. **2** *vt* adaptar (**to** a).

gearbox caja *f* de cambios.

geese [giːs] *npl see* **goose.**

gel [dʒel] gel *m*; (*for hair*) gomina *f*.

gem [dʒem] piedra *f* preciosa.

gen [dʒen] *fam* **to get the g. on sth** informarse sobre algo.

gender ['dʒendər] género *m*.

general ['dʒenərəl] **1** *a* general; **in g.** en general; **the g. public** el público.

2 n (*in army*) general m.
generally adv generalmente.
generation [dʒenə'reɪʃən] generación f.
generation gap abismo m or conflicto m generacional.
generator ['dʒenəreɪtəʳ] generador m.
gene'rosity generosidad f.
generous ['dʒenərəs] a generoso,-a; (*plentiful*) copioso,-a.
generously adv generosamente.
genius ['dʒiːnɪəs] (*person*) genio m; (*gift*) don m.
gentle ['dʒentəl] a dulce; (*breeze*) suave.
gentleman caballero m.
gentleness (*mildness*) ternura f; (*kindness*) amabilidad f.
gently con cuidado.
gents [dʒents] npl servicio m de caballeros.
genuine ['dʒenjʊɪn] a auténtico,-a; (*sincere*) sincero,-a.
genuinely adv auténticamente.
geo'graphic(al) a geográfico,-a.
geography [dʒɪ'ɒgrəfɪ] geografía f.
geo'metric(al) a geométrico,-a.
geometry [dʒɪ'ɒmɪtrɪ] geometría f.
germ [dʒɜːm] microbio m.
German ['dʒɜːmən] **1** a alemán,-ana; **G. measles** rubeola f. **2** n alemán,
-ana mf; (*language*) alemán m.
German shepherd (*dog*) pastor m alemán.
gesture ['dʒestʃəʳ] gesto m.
get* [get] **1** vt (*obtain*) obtener, conseguir; (*earn*) ganar; (*fetch*) (*something*) traer; (*somebody*) ir a por; (*receive*) recibir; (*bus, train, thief etc*) coger, Am agarrar; (*understand*) entender; (*on phone*) **g. me** Mr Brown póngame con el Sr. Brown; **can I g. you something to eat?** ¿quieres comer algo?; **g. him to call me** dile que me llame; **to g. one's hair cut** cortarse el pelo; **to g. sb to do sth** (*ask*) pedir a algn que haga algo. **2** vi (*become*) ponerse; **to g. late** hacerse tarde; **to g. dressed** vestirse; **to g. married** casarse; **to g. to** (*come to*) llegar a; **to g. to know sb** llegar a conocer a algn.

● **get about** or **around** vi (*person*) salir; (*news*) difundirse.
● **get across** vt (*idea etc*) hacer comprender.
● **get along** vi (*manage*) arreglárselas; (*two people*) llevarse bien.
● **get at** vt (*reach*) alcanzar; (*criticize*) criticar.
● **get away** vi escaparse.
● **get back 1** vi (*return*) volver; **g. back!** (*move backwards*) ¡atrás! **2** vt (*recover*) recuperar.
● **get by** vi (*manage*) arreglárselas; **she can g. by in French** sabe

defenderse en francés.
- **get down 1** *vt* (*depress*) deprimir. **2** *vi* (*descend*) bajar.
- **get in 1** *vi* (*arrive*) llegar; (*politician*) ser elegido,-a. **2** *vt* (*buy*) comprar; (*collect*) recoger.
- **get off 1** *vt* (*bus etc*) bajarse de; (*remove*) quitarse. **2** *vi* bajarse; (*escape*) escaparse; **to g. off lightly** salir bien librado,-a.
- **get on 1** *vt* (*board*) subir a. **2** *vi* (*board*) subirse; (*make progress*) hacer progresos; **how are you getting on?** ¿cómo te van las cosas?; **to g. on (well with sb)** llevarse bien (con algn); (*continue*) **to g. on with sth** seguir con algo.
- **get on to** *vt* (*find*) (*person*) localizar; (*find out*) descubrir; (*continue*) pasar a.
- **get out 1** *vt* (*object*) sacar. **2** *vi* (*of room etc*) salir (**of** de); (*of train*) bajar (**of** de); (*news*) difundirse; (*secret*) hacerse público.
- **get over** *vt* (*illness*) recuperarse de; (*difficulty*) vencer; (*convey*) hacer comprender.
- **get round** *vt* (*problem*) salvar; (*difficulty*) vencer.
- **get round to** *vi* **if I g. round to it** si tengo tiempo; **I'll g. round to it later** encontraré tiempo para hacerlo más tarde.
- **get through 1** *vi* (*message*) llegar; (*on phone*) **to g. through to sb** conseguir comunicar con algn. **2** *vt* (*consume*) consumir; **to g. through a lot of work** trabajar mucho.
- **get together** *vi* (*people*) reunirse.
- **get up 1** *vi* (*rise*) levantarse. **2** *vt* (*wake up*) despertar.
- **get up to** *vi* hacer; **to g. up to mischief** hacer de las suyas.
get-together reunión *f*.
ghastly ['gɑːstlɪ] *a* espantoso,-a.
gherkin ['gɜːkɪn] pepinillo *m*.
ghetto ['getəʊ] gueto *m*.
ghost [gəʊst] fantasma *m*.
giant ['dʒaɪənt] *a & n* gigante (*m*).
giddy ['gɪdɪ] *a* mareado,-a; **it makes me g.** me da vértigo; **to feel g.** sentirse mareado,-a.
gift [gɪft] regalo *m*; (*talent*) don *m*.
gifted *a* dotado,-a.
gigantic [dʒaɪˈgæntɪk] *a* gigantesco,-a.
giggle ['gɪgəl] *vi* reírse tontamente.
gimmick ['gɪmɪk] truco *m*; (*in advertising*) reclamo *m*.
gin [dʒɪn] ginebra *f*; **g. and tonic** gin tonic *m*.
ginger ['dʒɪndʒəʳ] *a* (*hair*) pelirrojo,-a.
giraffe [dʒɪˈrɑːf] jirafa *f*.
girl [gɜːl] chica *f*; (*child*) niña *f*; (*daughter*) hija *f*.

girlfriend novia *f*; (*female friend*) amiga *f*.

give* [gɪv] *vt* dar; **to g. sb sth as a present** regalar algo a algn; **to g. sb to understand that ...** dar a entender a algn que ...

● **give away** *vt* (*present*) regalar; (*disclose*) revelar.

● **give back** *vt* devolver.

● **give in 1** *vi* (*admit defeat*) darse por vencido,-a; (*surrender*) rendirse. **2** *vt* (*hand in*) entregar.

● **give off** *vt* (*smell etc*) despedir.

● **give out** *vt* repartir.

● **give up** *vt* (*idea*) abandonar; **to g. up smoking** dejar de fumar; **to g. oneself up** entregarse.

glad [glæd] *a* contento,-a; **to be g.** alegrarse.

gladly *adv* con mucho gusto.

glamorous *a* atractivo,-a.

glamour ['glæmə'] atractivo *m*; (*charm*) encanto *m*.

glance [glɑ:ns] **1** *n* vistazo *m*. **2** *vi* echar un vistazo (**at** a).

gland [glænd] glándula *f*.

glaring ['gleərɪŋ] *a* (*light*) deslumbrante; (*obvious*) evidente.

glass [glɑ:s] (*material*) vidrio *m*; (*drinking vessel*) vaso *m*; **pane of g.** cristal *m*; **wine g.** copa *f* (para vino); **glasses** (*spectacles*) gafas *fpl*.

glee [gli:] gozo *m*.

glide [glaɪd] *vi* (*plane*) planear.

gliding vuelo *m* sin motor.

glimmer ['glɪmə'] *fig* (*trace*) destello *m*.

glimpse [glɪmps] **1** *n* atisbo *m*. **2** *vt* atisbar.

glittering ['glɪtərɪŋ] *a* reluciente.

globe [gləʊb] globo *m*.

gloom [glu:m] (*obscurity*) penumbra *f*; (*melancholy*) melancolía *f*.

gloomy ['glu:mɪ] *a* (*dismal*) deprimente; (*despondent*) pesimista; (*sad*) triste.

glorified *a* **a g. boarding house** una pensión con pretensiones.

glorious *a* (*momentous*) glorioso,-a; (*splendid*) espléndido,-a.

glory ['glɔ:rɪ] gloria *f*; (*splendour*) esplendor *m*.

gloss [glɒs] (*sheen*) brillo *m*; **g. (paint)** pintura *f* brillante.

glossy *a* lustroso,-a; **g. magazine** revista *f* de lujo.

glove [glʌv] guante *m*; **g. compartment** guantera *f*.

glow [gləʊ] **1** *n* brillo *m*. **2** *vi* brillar.

glue [glu:] **1** *n* pegamento *m*. **2** *vt* pegar (**to** a).

glum [glʌm] *a* alicaído,-a.

glutton ['glʌtən] glotón,-ona *mf*.

gnat [næt] mosquito *m*.

gnaw [nɔ:] *vti* (*chew*) roer.

go* [gəʊ] **1** *vi* ir; *(depart)* irse, marcharse; *(bus)* salir; *(disappear)* desaparecer; *(function)* funcionar; *(become)* quedarse, volverse; *(fit)* caber; *(time)* pasar; **how's it going?** qué tal (te van las cosas)?; **to get or be going** marcharse; **to be going to** *(in the future)* ir a; *(on the point of)* estar a punto de; **there are only two weeks to go** sólo quedan dos semanas; **to let sth go** soltar algo. **2** *n* *(try)* intento *m*; *(turn)* turno *m*; **to have a go at sth** probar suerte con algo; **it's your go** te toca a ti; **to have a go at sb** criticar a algn.

● **go about 1** *vt* *(task)* emprender; **how do you go about it?** ¿cómo hay que hacerlo? **2** *vi* *(rumour)* correr.

● **go after** *vt* *(pursue)* andar tras.

● **go against** *vt* *(oppose)* ir en contra de.

● **go ahead** *vi* *(proceed)* proceder; **we'll go on ahead** iremos delante.

● **go along** *vt* *(street)* pasar por.

● **go along with** *vt* *(agree)* estar de acuerdo con; *(accompany)* acompañar.

● **go away** *vi* marcharse.

● **go back** *vi* *(return)* volver.

● **go back on** *vt* **to go back on one's word** faltar a su palabra.

● **go back to** *vt* volver a; *(date from)* datar de.

● **go by** *vi* pasar.

● **go down** *vi* *(descend)* bajar; *(sun)* ponerse; *(ship)* hundirse; *(diminish)* disminuir; *(temperature)* bajar.

● **go down with** *vt* *(contract)* coger.

● **go for** *vt* *(fetch)* ir por; *(attack)* atacar.

● **go in** *vi* entrar.

● **go in for** *vt* *(exam)* presentarse a; *(hobby)* dedicarse a.

● **go into** *vt* *(enter)* entrar en; *(matter)* investigar.

● **go off** *vi* *(leave)* irse, marcharse; *(bomb)* explotar; *(gun)* dispararse; *(alarm)* sonar; *(food)* pasarse.

● **go on** *vi* *(continue)* seguir, continuar; *(happen)* pasar; *(light)* encenderse; **to go on talking** seguir hablando.

● **go out** *vi* *(leave)* salir; *(fire, light)* apagarse.

● **go over** *vt* *(cross)* atravesar; *(revise)* repasar.

● **go over to** *vt* *(switch to)* pasar a; **to go over to the enemy** pasarse al enemigo.

● **go round** *vi* *(revolve)* dar vueltas; **to go round to sb's house** pasar por casa de algn.

● **go through** *vt* *(endure)* sufrir; *(examine)* examinar; *(search)* registrar; *(spend)* gastar.

● **go under** *vi* *(ship)* hundirse; *(business)* fracasar.

● **go up** *vi* subir.

- **go without** *vt* pasarse sin.
go-ahead to give sb the g. dar luz verde a algn.
goal [gəʊl] gol *m*; (*aim, objective*) meta *f*.
goalkeeper portero,-a *mf*.
goat [gəʊt] (*male*) macho cabrío *m*; (*female*) cabra *f*.
god [gɒd] dios *m*.
goddaughter ahijada *f*.
godfather padrino *m*.
godmother madrina *f*.
godsend to be a g. venir como agua de mayo.
godson ahijado *m*.
goggles ['gɒgəlz] *npl* (*for diving*) gafas *fpl* de bucear; (*protective*) gafas *fpl* protectoras.
going *a* (*price*) corriente.
goings-on *npl* tejemanejes *mpl*.
gold [gəʊld] **1** *n* oro *m*. **2** *a* de oro; (*colour*) dorado,-a.
golden *a* de oro; (*colour*) dorado,-a.
goldfish pez *m* de colores.
gold-plated *a* chapado,-a en oro.
golf [gɒlf] golf *m*.
golfer golfista *mf*.
gone [gɒn] *pp of* go.
good [gʊd] **1** *a* (*before noun*) buen,-a; (*after noun*) bueno,-a; (*kind*) amable; (*generous*) generoso,-a; (*morally correct*) correcto,-a; **g. afternoon, g. evening** buenas tardes; **g. morning** buenos días; **g. night** buenas noches; **to have a g. time** pasarlo bien; **be g.!** ¡pórtate bien!; **he's g. at languages** tiene facilidad para los idiomas; **he's in a g. mood** está de buen humor. **2** *n* bien *m*; **for your own g.** para tu propio bien; **it's no g. waiting** no sirve de nada esperar. **3** *adv* **she's gone for g.** se ha ido para siempre. **4** *interj* **g.!** ¡muy bien!
goodbye [gʊd'baɪ] *interj* ¡adiós!
good-looking *a* guapo,-a.
goods *npl* (*possessions*) bienes *mpl*; (*commercial*) mercancías *fpl*.
goodwill buena voluntad *f*.
goose [guːs] (*pl* **geese** [giːs]) ganso *m*, oca *f*.
gooseberry ['gʊzbərɪ] grosella *f* espinosa.
gooseflesh, goosepimples *npl* carne *f* de gallina.
gorge [gɔːdʒ] desfiladero *m*.
gorgeous ['gɔːdʒəs] *a* magnífico,-a; (*person*) atractivo,-a.
gorilla [gə'rɪlə] gorila *m*.
gospel ['gɒspəl] **the G.** el Evangelio.
gossip ['gɒsɪp] (*rumour*) cotilleo *m*; (*person*) chismoso,-a *mf*.

got [gɒt] *pt* & *pp of* **get.**

gotten ['gɒtən] *pp US of* **get.**

gourmet ['guəmeɪ] gourmet *mf.*

govern ['gʌvən] *vt* gobernar; (*determine*) dcterminar.

government gobierno *m.*

governor (*ruler*) gobernador,-a *mf;* (*of school*) administrador,-a *mf.*

gown [gaun] (*dress*) vestido *m* largo; (*of lawyer, professor*) toga *f.*

GP [dʒiː'piː] *abbr of* **general practioner** médico *m* de cabecera.

grab [græb] *vt* agarrar; **to g. hold of sb** agarrarse a algn.

grace [greɪs] gracia *f;* (*elegance*) elegancia *f.*

graceful *a* elegante; (*movement*) garboso,-a.

grade [greɪd] **1** *n* (*rank*) categoría *f;* (*in army*) rango *m;* (*mark*) nota *f; US* (*class*) clase *f.* **2** *vt* clasificar.

gradual ['grædjuəl] *a* gradual.

gradually *adv* poco a poco.

graduate ['grædjuɪt] **1** *n* licenciado,-a *mf.* **2** *vi* ['grædjueɪt] (*from university*) licenciarse (**in** en).

graduation ceremony ceremonia *f* de entrega de los títulos.

graffiti [græ'fiːtiː] *npl* grafiti *mpl.*

graft [grɑːft] **1** *n* injerto *m.* **2** *vt* injertar (**on to** en).

grain [greɪn] (*cereals*) cereales *mpl;* (*particle*) grano *m.*

gram [græm] gramo *m.*

grammar ['græmə^r] gramática *f.*

grammar school ≈ instituto *m* de Bachillerato.

gra'mmatical *a* gramatical.

grand [grænd] *a* (*splendid*) grandioso,-a; (*impressive*) impresionante.

grandchild nieto,-a *mf.*

granddad *fam* abuelo *m.*

granddaughter nieta *f.*

grandfather abuelo *m.*

grandma *fam* abuelita *f.*

grandmother abuela *f.*

grandparents *npl* abuelos *mpl.*

grandson nieto *m.*

granny ['grænɪ] *fam* abuelita *f.*

grant [grɑːnt] **1** *vt* (*give*) conceder; (*accept*) admitir; **to take for granted** dar por sentado. **2** *n* (*for study*) beca *f;* (*subsidy*) subvención *f.*

grape [greɪp] uva *f;* **g. juice** mosto *m.*

grapefruit pomelo *m.*

graph [grɑːf] gráfica *f.*

graphics ['græfɪks] *npl* gráficos *mpl.*

grasp [grɑːsp] **1** *vt* agarrar; (*understand*) comprender. **2** *n* (grip) agarrón *m*; (*understanding*) comprensión *f*.

grass [grɑːs] hierba *f*; (*lawn*) césped *m*.

grasshopper saltamontes *m inv*.

grate [greɪt] **1** *vt* (*food*) rallar. **2** *vi* chirriar. **3** *n* (*in fireplace*) rejilla *f*.

grateful *a* agradecido,-a; **to be g. for** agradecer.

grater rallador *m*.

gratifying ['grætɪfaɪŋ] *a* grato,-a.

gratitude ['grætɪtjuːd] agradecimiento *m*.

grave[1] [greɪv] tumba *f*.

grave[2] *a* (*situation*) grave.

gravel ['grævəl] gravilla *f*.

graveyard cementerio *m*.

gravity ['grævɪtɪ] gravedad *f*.

gravy ['greɪvɪ] salsa *f*.

gray [greɪ] *a* & *n US see* **grey**.

graze [greɪz] **1** *vt* (*scratch*) rasguñar; (*brush against*) rozar. **2** *vi* (*cattle*) pacer. **3** *n* rasguño *m*.

grease [griːs] **1** *n* grasa *f*. **2** *vt* engrasar.

greaseproof paper papel *m* graso.

greasy *a* (*hair, food*) graso,-a.

great [greɪt] *a* grande; (*before sing noun*) gran; *fam* (*excellent*) estupendo,-a; **a g. many** muchos,-as; **to have a g. time** pasarlo en grande.

great-grandfather bisabuelo *m*.

great-grandmother bisabuela *f*.

greatly *adv* (*with adjective*) muy; (*with verb*) mucho.

greed [griːd], **greediness** (*for food*) gula *f*; (*for money*) codicia *f*.

greedy *a* (*for food*) glotón,-ona; (*for money*) codicioso,-a (**for** de).

Greek [griːk] **1** *a* griego,-a. **2** *n* (*person*) griego,-a *mf*; (*language*) griego *m*.

green [griːn] **1** *n* (*colour*) verde *m*; (*for golf*) campo *m*; **greens** verduras *fpl*. **2** *a* verde.

greengrocer *Br* verdulero,-a *mf*.

greenhouse invernadero *m*; **g. effect** efecto *m* invernadero.

greet [griːt] *vt* saludar.

greeting saludo *m*.

grenade [grɪ'neɪd] granada *f*.

grey [greɪ] *a* (*colour*) gris; (*hair*) cano,-a; (*sky*) nublado,-a.

greyhound galgo *m*.

grief [griːf] dolor *m*.

grieve [griːv] *vi* **to g. for sb** llorar la muerte de algn.

grill [grɪl] **1** *vt* (*food*) asar a la parrilla. **2** *n* parrilla *f*; (*dish*) parrillada *f*.

grim [grɪm] *a* (*landscape*) lúgubre; (*manner*) severo,-a; (*unpleasant*) desagradable.

grime [graɪm] mugre f.

grimy ['graɪmɪ] a mugriento,-a.

grin [grɪn] **1** vi sonreír abiertamente. **2** n sonrisa abierta.

grind* [graɪnd] vt moler; **to g. one's teeth** hacer rechinar los dientes.

grip [grɪp] **1** n (hold) agarrón m; (handle) asidero m. **2** vt agarrar; **to be gripped by fear** ser presa del miedo.

gripping a (film, story) apasionante.

groan [grəʊn] **1** n gemido m. **2** vi gemir.

grocer ['grəʊsəʳ] tendero,-a mf.

grocery (shop) tienda f de ultramarinos; **g. store** supermercado m.

groin [grɔɪn] ingle f.

groom [gruːm] (bridegroom) novio m.

groove [gruːv] (furrow etc) ranura f; (of record) surco m.

grope [grəʊp] vi **to g. for sth** buscar algo a tientas.

● **grope about** vi andar a tientas; (looking for sth) buscar a tientas.

gross [grəʊs] a grosero,-a; (not net) bruto,-a.

grossly adv enormemente.

gross national product producto m nacional bruto.

ground¹ [graʊnd] suelo m; (terrain) terreno m; **football g.** campo m de fútbol; **grounds** (gardens) jardines mpl; (reason) motivo m sing.

ground² a (coffee) molido,-a; US (meat) picado,-a.

ground floor planta f baja.

groundwork trabajo m preparatorio.

group [gruːp] grupo m.

grow* [grəʊ] **1** vt (cultivate) cultivar; **to g. a beard** dejarse (crecer) la barba. **2** vi crecer; (increase) aumentar; (become) volverse.

● **grow into** vi convertirse en.

● **grow out of** vt (phase etc) superar; **he's grown out of his shirt** se le ha quedado pequeña la camisa.

● **grow up** vi crecer.

growl [graʊl] **1** vi gruñir. **2** n gruñido m.

grown [grəʊn] a crecido,-a.

grown-up a & n adulto,-a (mf) ; **the grown-ups** los mayores.

growth [grəʊθ] crecimiento m; (increase) aumento m; (development) desarrollo m; (diseased part) bulto m.

grub [grʌb] fam (food) comida f.

grubby ['grʌbɪ] a sucio,-a.

grudge [grʌdʒ] **1** n rencor m; **to bear sb a g.** guardar rencor a algn. **2** vt **he grudges me my success** me envidia el éxito.

gruelling, US grueling ['gruːəlɪŋ] a penoso,-a.

gruesome ['gruːsəm] a espantoso,-a.

grumble ['grʌmbəl] *vi* refunfuñar.

grumpy ['grʌmpɪ] *a* gruñón,-ona.

grunt [grʌnt] **1** *vi* gruñir. **2** *n* gruñido *m*.

guarantee [gærən'tiː] **1** *n* garantía *f*. **2** *vt* garantizar; (*assure*) asegurar.

guard [gɑːd] **1** *vt* (*protect*) proteger; (*keep watch over*) vigilar; (*control*) guardar. **2** *n* (*sentry*) guardia *mf*; *Br* (*on train*) jefe *m* de tren; **to be on one's g.** estar en guardia; **to stand g.** montar la guardia.

Guatemalan [gwɑːtə'mɑːlən] *adj* & *n* guatemalteco,-a (*mf*).

guess [ges] **1** *vti* adivinar; *US fam* suponer. **2** *n* conjetura *f*; (*estimate*) cálculo *m*; **to have** *or* **make a g.** intentar adivinar.

guesswork conjetura *f*.

guest [gest] invitado,-a *mf*; (*in hotel*) cliente,-a *mf*, huésped,-a *mf*.

guesthouse casa *f* de huéspedes.

guidance orientación *f*.

guide [gaɪd] **1** *vt* guiar. **2** *n* (*person*) guía *mf*; (*guidebook*) guía *f*.

guideline pauta *f*.

guilt [gɪlt] culpabilidad *f*.

guilty *a* culpable (**of** de).

guinea pig ['gɪnɪpɪg] conejillo *m* de Indias.

guitar [gɪ'tɑːʳ] guitarra *f*.

guitarist guitarrista *mf*.

gulf [gʌlf] golfo *m*; *fig* abismo *m*.

gull [gʌl] gaviota *f*.

gulp [gʌlp] trago *m*.

gum[1] [gʌm] **1** *n* goma *f*. **2** *vt* pegar con goma.

gum[2] (*around teeth*) encía *f*.

gun [gʌn] (*handgun*) pistola *f*; (*rifle*) fusil *m*; (*cannon*) cañón *m*.

● **gun down** *vt* matar a tiros.

gunfire tiros *mpl*.

gunman pistolero *m*.

gunpoint at g. a punta de pistola.

gunpowder pólvora *f*.

gunshot tiro *m*.

gush [gʌʃ] *vi* brotar.

gust [gʌst] (*of wind*) ráfaga *f*.

guts [gʌts] *npl* (*entrails*) tripas *fpl*.

gutter ['gʌtəʳ] (*in street*) cuneta *f*; (*on roof*) canalón *m*.

guy [gaɪ] *fam* tipo *m*, tío *m*.

gym [dʒɪm] (*gymnasium*) gimnasio *m*; (*gymnastics*) gimnasia *f*.

gynaecologist, *US* **gynecologist** [gaɪnɪ'kɒlədʒɪst] ginecólogo,-a *mf*.

H

habit [ˈhæbɪt] costumbre *f*; **to be in the h. of doing sth** soler hacer algo; **to get into the h. of doing sth** acostumbrarse a hacer algo.

hack [hæk] **1** *n* (*cut*) corte *m*; (*with an axe*) hachazo *m*. **2** *vt* (*with knife, axe*) cortar.

had [hæd] *pt* & *pp of* **have**.

haddock [ˈhædək] abadejo *m*.

haemorrhage [ˈhemərɪdʒ] hemorragia *f*.

hag [hæg] bruja *f*.

haggle [ˈhægəl] *vi* regatear.

hail [heɪl] **1** *n* granizo *m*; **a h. of bullets** una lluvia de balas. **2** *vi* granizar.

hailstone granizo *m*.

hair [heəʳ] pelo *m*; (*on arm, leg*) vello *m*; **to have long h.** tener el pelo largo.

hairbrush cepillo *m* (para el pelo).

haircut corte *m* de pelo; **to have a h.** cortarse el pelo.

hairdo *fam* peinado *m*.

hairdresser peluquero,-a *mf*; **h.'s (shop)** peluquería *f*.

hairdryer, hairdrier secador *m* (de pelo).

hairgrip horquilla *f*.

hairpin bend curva *f* muy cerrada.

hair-raising *a* espeluznante.

hairspray laca *f* (para el pelo).

hairstyle peinado *m*.

hairy *a* (*with hair*) peludo,-a; *fam* (*frightening*) espeluznante.

half [hɑːf] **1** *n* (*pl* **halve**) mitad *f*; (*period in match*) tiempo *m*; **he's four and a h.** tiene cuatro años y medio; **to cut in h.** cortar por la mitad. **2** *a* medio,-a; **h. a dozen/an hour** media docena/hora; **h. fare** media tarifa *f*. **3** *adv* a medias; **h. asleep** medio dormido,-a. **h. past one** la una y media.

half board media pensión *f*.

half-hour media hora *f*.

half term (*holiday*) vacación *f* a mitad de trimestre.

half-time descanso *m*.

halfway *adv* a medio camino.

halibut [ˈhælɪbət] mero *m*.

hall [hɔːl] (*lobby*) vestíbulo *m*; (*building*) sala *f*; **h. of residence** colegio *m* mayor.

hallstand percha *f*.

hallo [həˈləʊ] *interj* = **hello**.

Hallowe('e)en [hæləʊˈiːn] víspera *f* de Todos los Santos.

hallway vestíbulo *m*.

halt [hɔːlt] alto *m*; **to call a h. to sth** poner fin a algo.

halve [hɑːv] *vt* reducir a la mitad.

ham [hæm] jamón *m*.

hamburger ['hæmbɜːgəʳ] hamburguesa *f*.

hammer ['hæməʳ] **1** *n* martillo *m*. **2** *vt* (*nail*) clavar; *fig* **to h. home** insistir sobre. **3** *vi* dar golpes.

hammering *fam* (*defeat*) paliza *f*.

hammock ['hæmək] hamaca *f*.

hamper¹ ['hæmpəʳ] cesta *f*.

hamper² *vt* dificultar.

hamster ['hæmstəʳ] hámster *m*.

hand [hænd] **1** *n* mano *f*; (*worker*) trabajador,-a *mf*; (*of clock*) aguja *f*; **by h. a mano**; (*close*) **at h. a mano**; **on the one/other h.** por una/otra parte; **to get out of h.** descontrolarse; **to be on h.** estar a mano; **to have a h. in** intervenir en; **to give sb a h.** echarle una mano a algn; **to give sb a big h.** (*applause*) dedicar a algn una gran ovación. **2** *vt* (*give*) dar.

● **hand back** *vt* devolver.

● **hand in** *vt* (*homework*) entregar.

● **hand out** *vt* repartir.

● **hand over** *vt* entregar.

handbag bolso *m*.

handbook manual *m*.

handbrake freno *m* de mano.

handcuff **1** *vt* esposar. **2** *npl* **handcuffs** esposas *fpl*.

handful puñado *m*.

hand grenade granada *f* de mano.

handicap ['hændɪkæp] **1** *n* (*physical*) minusvalía *f*; (*in sport*) hándicap *m*. **2** *vt* impedir.

handicapped *a* (*physically*) minusválido,-a; (*mentally*) retrasado,-a; *fig* desfavorecido,-a.

handkerchief ['hæŋkətʃiːf] pañuelo *m*.

handle ['hændəl] **1** *n* (*of knife*) mango *m*; (*of cup*) asa *f*; (*of door*) pomo *m*; (*of drawer*) tirador *m*. **2** *vt* manejar; (*problem*) encargarse de; (*people*) tratar; **'h. with care'** 'frágil'.

handlebars *npl* manillar *m*.

hand luggage equipaje *m* de mano.

handmade *a* hecho,-a a mano.

handout (*leaflet*) folleto *m*; (*charity*) limosna *f*.

handrail pasamanos *m sing inv*.

handshake apretón *m* de manos.

handsome ['hænsəm] *a* (*person*) guapo,-a; (*substantial*) considerable.

handwriting letra *f*.

handy ['hændɪ] *a* (*useful*) útil; (*nearby*) a mano; (*dexterous*) diestro,-a.

handyman manitas *m inv*.

hang* [hæŋ] **1** *vt* colgar; (*head*) bajar. **2** *vi* colgar (**from** de); (*in air*) flotar; (*criminal*) ser ahorcado,-a; **to h. oneself** ahorcarse.

● **hang about** *vi fam* perder el tiempo; (*wait*) esperar.

● **hang around 1** *vi fam* no hacer nada; (*wait*) esperar. **2** *vt* (*bar etc*) frequentar.

● **hang on** *vi* agarrarse; (*wait*) esperar; **to h. on to sth** (*keep*) guardar.

● **hang out 1** *vt* (*washing*) tender. **2** *vi* **his tongue was hanging out** le colgaba la lengua.

● **hang up** *vt* (*picture, telephone*) colgar.

hangar ['hæŋəʳ] hangar *m*.

hanger percha *f*.

hang-glider ala *f* delta.

hangover resaca *f*.

hang-up *fam* (*complex*) complejo *m*.

happen ['hæpən] *vi* suceder, ocurrir; **if you h. to see my friend** si por casualidad ves a mi amigo.

happening acontecimiento *m*.

happily *adv* (*with pleasure*) felizmente; (*fortunately*) afortunadamente.

happiness felicidad *f*.

happy ['hæpɪ] *a* feliz; **h. birthday!** ¡feliz cumpleaños!

harass ['hærəs] *vt* acosar.

harbour, US harbor ['hɑːbəʳ] **1** *n* puerto *m*. **2** *vt* (*criminal*) encubrir; (*doubts*) abrigar.

hard [hɑːd] **1** *a* duro,-a; (*solid*) sólido,-a; (*difficult*) difícil; (*harsh*) severo,-a; (*strict*) estricto,-a; **h. of hearing** duro,-a de oído; **to be h. up** estar sin blanca; **to take a h. line** tomar medidas severas; **h. drugs** droga *f* dura; **a h. worker** un trabajador concienzudo; **h. luck!** ¡mala suerte!; **h. evidence** pruebas definitivas; **h. currency** divisa *f* fuerte. **2** *adv* (*forcibly*) fuerte; (*with application*) mucho; **to be h. done by** ser tratado,-a injustamente.

hard-boiled *a* duro,-a.

hard-core *a* irreductible.

hard disk disco *m* duro.

harden 1 *vt* endurecer. **2** *vi* endurecerse.

hardly *adv* apenas; **h. anyone/ever** casi nadie/nunca; **he had h. begun when ...** apenas había comenzado cuando ...

hardness dureza *f*; (*difficulty*) dificultad *f*.

hardship privación *f*.

hardware ['hɑːdweəʳ] (*goods*) ferretería *f*; (*computer equipment*) hardware *m*; **h. shop** ferretería *f*.

hardwearing *a* duradero,-a.

hardworking *a* muy trabajador,-a.
hare [heə^r] liebre *f.*
harm [hɑːm] **1** *n* daño *m.* **2** *vt* hacer daño a.
harmful *a* perjudicial (**to** para).
harmless *a* inofensivo,-a.
harmonica [hɑːˈmɒnɪkə] armónica *f.*
harmonious *a* armonioso,-a.
harmony [ˈhɑːmənɪ] armonía *f.*
harness [ˈhɑːnɪs] **1** *n* (*for horse*) arreos *mpl.* **2** *vt* (*horse*) enjaezar.
harp [hɑːp] arpa *f.*
• **harp on** *vi fam* hablar sin parar; **to h. on about sth** hablar sin parar sobre algo.
harsh [hɑːʃ] *a* severo,-a; (*voice*) áspero,-a; (*sound*) discordante.
harshly *adv* duramente.
harshness dureza *f;* (*discordancy*) discordancia *f.*
harvest [ˈhɑːvɪst] **1** *n* cosecha *f;* (*of grapes*) vendimia *f.* **2** *vt* cosechar, recoger.
has [hæz] *3rd person sing pres of* **have.**
hassle [ˈhæsəl] *fam* **1** *n* (*nuisance*) rollo *m;* (*problem*) lío *m;* (*wrangle*) bronca *f.* **2** *vt* fastidiar.
haste [heɪst] prisa *f.*
hasten *vi* apresurarse.
hastily *adv* (*quickly*) de prisa.
hasty *a* apresurado,-a; (*rash*) precipitado,-a.
hat [hæt] sombrero *m.*
hatch[1] [hætʃ] escotilla *f;* **serving h.** ventanilla *f.*
hatch[2] **1** *vt* (*egg*) empollar. **2** *vi* (*bird*) salir del huevo.
hatchback coche *m* de 3/5 puertas.
hate [heɪt] **1** *n* odio *m.* **2** *vt* odiar.
hateful *a* odioso,-a.
hatred odio *m.*
haul [hɔːl] **1** *n* (*journey*) trayecto *m.* **2** *vt* tirar; (*drag*) arrastrar.
haunted [ˈhɔːntɪd] *a* embrujado,-a.
have* [hæv] **1** *vt* tener; (*party, meeting*) hacer; **h. you got a car?** ¿tienes coche?; **to h. a holiday** tomarse unas vacaciones; **to h. a cigarette** fumarse un cigarrillo; **to h. breakfast/lunch/tea/dinner** desayunar/comer/merendar/cenar; **to h. a bath/shave** bañarse/afeitarse; **what will you h.?** ¿qué quieres tomar?; **can I h. your pen a moment?** (*borrow*) ¿me dejas tu bolígrafo un momento? ∥ **to h. to** (*obligation*) tener que, deber; **I h. to go now** tengo que irme ya ∥ (*make happen*) hacer; **I'll h. someone come round** haré que venga alguien. **2** *v aux* (*compound*) haber; **yes I h.!** ¡que sí!; **you haven't seen my book, h. you?** no has visto mi libro, ¿verdad?; **he's**

been to France, hasn't he? ha estado en Francia, ¿verdad?

● **have on** vt (wear) vestir; fam **to h. sb on** tomarle el pelo a algn.

● **have out** vt **to h. it out with sb** ajustar cuentas con algn.

● **have over** vt (invite) recibir.

havoc ['hævək] **to play h. with** hacer estragos en.

hawk [hɔ:k] halcón m.

hay [heɪ] heno m.

hay fever fiebre f del heno.

haystack almiar m.

hazard ['hæzəd] peligro m.

haze [heɪz] (mist) neblina f.

hazelnut ['heɪzəlnʌt] avellana f.

hazy a nebuloso,-a.

he [hi:] pers pron él; **he who** el que.

head [hed] **1** n cabeza f; (mind) mente f; (of company) director,-a mf; (of coin) cara f; **to be h. over heels in love** estar locamente enamorado,-a; **to keep one's h.** mantener la calma; **to lose one's h.** perder la cabeza; **heads or tails** cara o cruz. **2** a principal; **h. office** sede f. **3** vt (list etc) encabezar.

● **head for** vt dirigirse hacia.

headache dolor m de cabeza; fig quebradero m de cabeza.

heading título m; (of letter) membrete m.

headlight faro m.

headline titular m.

headmaster director m.

headmistress directora f.

headphones npl auriculares mpl.

headquarters npl oficina f central; (military) cuartel m general.

head teacher director,-a mf.

head waiter jefe m de comedor.

headway **to make h.** avanzar.

heal [hi:l] **1** vi cicatrizar. **2** vt curar.

health [helθ] salud f; fig prosperidad f; **to be in good/bad h.** estar bien/ mal de salud; **h. foods** alimentos mpl naturales; **h. service** ≈ Insalud m.

healthy a sano,-a; (good for health) saludable.

heap [hi:p] **1** n montón m. **2** vt amontonar; (praises) colmar de; **to h. praises on sb** colmar a algn de elogios.

hear [hɪəʳ] vt oír; (listen to) escuchar; (find out) enterarse de; (evidence) oír; **I won't h. of it!** ¡ni hablar!; **to h. from sb** tener noticias de algn.

hearing oído m; (legal) audiencia f.

hearing aid audífono m.

hearse [hɜ:s] coche m fúnebre.

heart [hɑ:t] corazón m; **hearts** corazones; **at h.** en el fondo; **to lose h.**

desanimarse.

heart attack infarto m (de miocardio).

heartbeat latido m del corazón.

heart-breaking a desgarrador,-a.

heartening a alentador,-a.

hearty a (*person*) francote; (*meal*) abundante; **to have a h. appetite** ser de buen comer.

heat [hi:t] **1** n calor m; (*in sport*) eliminatoria f. **2** vt calentar.

● **heat up** vi (*warm up*) calentarse.

heater calentador m.

heath [hi:θ] (*land*) brezal m.

heather ['heðəʳ] brezo m.

heating calefacción f.

heatwave ola f de calor.

heave [hi:v] vt (*lift*) levantar; (*haul*) tirar; (*push*) empujar; (*throw*) arrojar.

heaven ['hevən] cielo m; **for heaven's sake!** ¡por Dios!

heavily adv **it rained h.** llovió mucho; **to sleep h.** dormir profundamente.

heavy ['hevɪ] **1** a pesado,-a; (*rain, meal*) fuerte; (*traffic*) denso,-a; (*loss*) grande; **is it h.?** ¿pesa mucho?; **a h. drinker/smoker** un,-a bebedor,-a/ fumador,-a empedernido,-a.

Hebrew ['hi:bru:] a hebreo,-a mf; (*language*) hebreo m.

hectic ['hektɪk] a agitado,-a.

hedge [hedʒ] **1** n seto m. **2** vt **to h. one's bets** cubrirse.

hedgehog erizo m.

heel [hi:l] talón m; (*of shoe*) tacón m.

heel bar reparación f de calzado.

hefty ['heftɪ] a (*person*) fornido,-a; (*package*) pesado,-a.

height [haɪt] altura f; (*of person*) estatura f; **what h. are you?** ¿cuánto mides?

heir [eəʳ] heredero m.

heiress heredera f.

held [held] pt & pp of **hold.**

helicopter ['helɪkɒptəʳ] helicóptero m.

hell [hel] infierno m; *fam* **what the h. are you doing?** ¿qué diablos estás haciendo?; *fam* **go to h.!** ¡vete a hacer puñetas!; *fam* **a h. of a party** una fiesta estupenda; *fam* **she's had a h. of a day** ha tenido un día fatal; *fam* **h.!** ¡demonios!

hello [he'ləʊ] interj ¡hola!; (*on phone*) ¡diga!; (*showing surprise*) ¡hala!

helm [helm] timón m.

helmet ['helmɪt] casco m.

help [help] **1** n ayuda f; **h.!** ¡socorro!; (**daily**) **h.** asistenta f. **2** vt ayudar;

can I h. you? (in shop) ¿qué desea?; **h. yourself!** (to food etc) ¡sírvete!; **I couldn't h. laughing** no pude evitar reírme; **I can't h. it** no lo puedo remediar.

● **help out** vt **to h. sb out** echarle una mano a algn.

helper ayudante,-a mf.

helpful a (person) amable; (thing) útil.

helping ración f.

helpless a (defenceless) desamparado,-a; (powerless) impotente.

hem [hem] dobladillo m.

● **hem in** vt cercar, rodear.

hemorrhage ['hemərɪdʒ] US hemorragia f.

hen [hen] gallina f.

hepatitis [hepə'taɪtɪs] hepatitis f.

her [hɜːʳ] 1 poss a (one thing) su; (more than one) sus; (to distinguish male from female) de ella; **are they h. books or his?** ¿los libros son de ella o de él? 2 object pron (direct object) la; **I saw h. recently** la vi hace poco. ‖ (indirect object) le; (with other third person pronouns) se; **he gave h. money** le dio dinero; **they handed it to h.** se lo entregaron. ‖ (after prep) ella; **for h.** para ella. ‖ (emphatic) ella; **look, it's h.!** ¡mira, es ella!

herb [hɜːb] hierba f; **herb tea** infusión f.

herd [hɜːd] (of cattle) manada f; (of goats) rebaño m.

here [hɪəʳ] 1 adv aquí; **h.!** ¡presente!; **h. you are!** ¡toma! 2 interj **look h., you can't do that!** ¡oiga, que no se permite hacer eso!

hermit ['hɜːmɪt] ermitaño,-a mf.

hero ['hɪərəʊ] (pl **heroes**) héroe m; (in novel) protagonista m.

he'roic a heroico,-a.

heroin ['herəʊɪn] heroína f.

heroine ['herəʊɪn] heroína f; (in novel) protagonista f.

herring ['herɪŋ] arenque m.

hers [hɜːz] poss pron (attribute) (one thing) suyo,-a; (more than one) suyos,-as; (to distinguish male from female) de ella; **they are h. not his** son de ella, no de él. ‖ (one thing) el suyo, la suya; (more than one) los suyos, las suyas.

herself pers pron (reflexive) se; **she dressed h.** se vistió. ‖ (alone) ella misma; **she was by h.** estaba sola. ‖ (emphatic) **she told me so h.** eso me dijo ella.

hesitant a vacilante.

hesitate ['hezɪteɪt] vi vacilar.

hesitation indecisión f.

het up ['hetʌp] a nervioso,-a.

hey [heɪ] interj ¡oye!, ¡oiga!

hi [haɪ] interj ¡hola!

hiccup [ˈhɪkʌp] hipo *m*; (*minor problem*) problemilla *m*; **to have hiccups** tener hipo.

hide¹ [haɪd] **1** *vt* (*conceal*) esconder; (*obscure*) ocultar. **2** *vi* esconderse, ocultarse.

hide² (*skin*) piel *f*.

hide-and-'seek escondite *m*.

hideous [ˈhɪdɪəs] *a* (*horrific*) horroroso,-a; (*extremely ugly*) espantoso, -a.

hideously *adv* horrorosamente.

hide-out escondrijo *m*.

hiding [ˈhaɪdɪŋ] **a good h.** una buena paliza.

hiding place escondite *m*.

hi-fi [ˈhaɪfaɪ] hifi *m*.

high [haɪ] **1** *a* alto,-a; (*price*) elevado,-a; (*drugged*) colocado,-a; **how h. is that wall?** ¿qué altura tiene esa pared?; **it's three feet h.** tiene tres pies de alto; **to be in h. spirits** estar de buen humor; **h. wind** viento *m* fuerte; **to have a h. opinion of sb** tener muy buena opinión de algn. **2** *adv* alto; **to fly h.** volar a gran altura.

high-class *a* de alta categoría.

High Court Tribunal *m* Supremo.

high density *a* de alta densidad.

higher *a* superior; **h. education** enseñanza *f* superior.

highlands *npl* tierras *fpl* altas.

highlight 1 *n* (*in hair*) reflejo *m*; (*of event*) atracción *f* principal. **2** *vt* hacer resaltar; (*with highlighter*) subrayar con marcador.

highlighter marcador *m*.

highly *adv* (*very*) sumamente; **to speak h. of sb** hablar muy bien de algn.

high-pitched *a* estridente.

high-rise *a* **h. building** rascacielos *m inv*.

high school instituto *m* de enseñanza media.

high-speed *a & adv* **h. lens** objetivo *m* ultrarrápido; **h. train** tren *m* de alta velocidad.

high street calle *f* mayor.

highway *US* autopista *f*; *Br* **H. Code** código *m* de la circulación.

hijack [ˈhaɪdʒæk] **1** *vt* secuestrar. **2** *n* secuestro *m*.

hijacker secuestrador,-a *mf*; (*of planes*) pirata *mf* del aire.

hijacking secuestro *m*.

hike [haɪk] **1** *n* (*walk*) excursión *f*. **2** *vi* ir de excursión.

hiker excursionista *mf*.

hilarious [hɪˈleərɪəs] *a* graciosísimo,-a.

hill [hɪl] colina *f*; (*slope*) cuesta *f*.

hillside ladera *f*.

hilly *a* accidentado,-a.

him [hɪm] *object pron* (*direct object*) lo, le; **hit h.!** ¡pégale!; **she loves h.** lo quiere. ‖ (*indirect object*) le; (*with other third person pronouns*) se; **give h. the money** dale el dinero; **give it to h.** dáselo. ‖ (*after prep*) él; **it's not like h. to say that** no es propio de él decir eso. ‖ (*emphatic*) él; **it's h.** es él.

himself *pers pron* (*reflexive*) se; **he hurt h.** se hizo daño. ‖ (*alone*) por sí mismo; **by h.** solo. ‖ (*emphatic*) él mismo. **he told me so h.** me lo dijo él mismo.

hinder ['hɪndə'] *vt* dificultar.

Hindu ['hɪnduː] *a & n* hindú (*mf*).

hinge [hɪndʒ] bisagra *f.*

● **hinge on** *vt* depender de.

hint [hɪnt] **1** *n* indirecta *f*; (*clue*) pista *f*; (*advice*) consejo *m*. **2** *vi* lanzar indirectas. **3** *vt* (*imply*) insinuar.

● **hint at** *vt* aludir a.

hip [hɪp] cadera *f.*

hippopotamus [hɪpə'pɒtəməs] hipopótamo *m.*

hire ['haɪə'] **1** *n* **bicycles for h.** se alquilan bicicletas. **2** *vt* (*rent*) alquilar; (*employ*) contratar.

● **hire out** *vt* (*car*) alquilar.

hire purchase *Br* compra *f* a plazos.

his [hɪz] **1** *poss a* (*one thing*) su; (*more than one*) sus; (*to distinguish male from female*) de él; **he washed h. face** se lavó la cara; **is it h. dog or hers?** ¿el perro es de él o de ella? **2** *poss pron* (*attribute*) (*one thing*) suyo,-a; (*more than one*) suyos,-as; (*to distinguish male from female*) de él. ‖ (*one thing*) el suyo, la suya; (*more than one*) los suyos, las suyas.

Hispanic [hɪ'spænɪk] **1** *a* hispánico,-a. **2** *n* hispano,-a *mf.*

hiss [hɪs] **1** *n* siseo *m*; (*in theatre*) silbido *m*. **2** *vti* silbar.

historic [hɪ'stɒrɪk] *a* histórico,-a.

historical *a* histórico,-a.

history ['hɪstərɪ] historia *f.*

hit [hɪt] **1** *n* (*blow*) golpe *m*; (*success*) éxito *m*. **2** *vt** (*strike*) pegar; (*affect*) afectar; **he was h. in the leg** le dieron en la pierna; **the car h. the kerb** el coche chocó contra el bordillo.

● **hit back** *vi* (*reply to criticism*) replicar.

● **hit out** *vi* **to h. out at sb** atacar a algn.

● **hit (up)on** *vt* dar con; **we h. on the idea of ...** se nos ocurrió la idea de ...

hit-and-run driver conductor *m* que atropella a algn y no para.

hitch [hɪtʃ] **1** *n* dificultad *f*. **2** *vi* (*hitch-hike*) hacer autostop.

hitchhike *vi* hacer autostop.

hitchhiker autostopista *mf.*

hitchhiking autostop *m*.

hive [haɪv] colmena *f*.

hoard [hɔːd] **1** *n* (*provisions*) reservas *fpl*; (*money etc*) tesoro *m*. **2** *vt* (*objects*) acumular; (*money*) atesorar.

hoarding (*billboard*) valla *f* publicitaria.

hoarse [hɔːs] *a* ronco,-a; **to be h.** tener la voz ronca.

hoax [həʊks] (*joke*) broma *f* pesada; (*trick*) engaño *m*.

hobby ['hɒbɪ] pasatiempo *m*.

hobo ['həʊbəʊ] *US* vagabundo,-a *mf*.

hockey ['hɒkɪ] hockey *m*.

hold* [həʊld] **1** *vt* (*keep in hand*) tener (en la mano); (*grip*) agarrar; (*opinion*) sostener; (*contain*) dar cabida a; (*meeting*) celebrar; (*reserve: ticket*) guardar; (*at police station etc*) detener; (*office*) ocupar; **to h. sb's hand** cogerle la mano a algn; **the jug holds a litre** en la jarra cabe un litro; **to h. one's breath** contener la respiración; **to h. sb hostage** retener a algn como rehén; **to h. the line** no colgar. **2** *vi* (*rope*) aguantar; (*offer*) ser válido,-a. **3** *n* (*in ship*) bodega *f*; (*control*) control *m*; **to get h. of** (*grip*) coger; (*get in touch with*) localizar.

● **hold back** *vt* (*crowd*) contener; (*feelings*) reprimir; (*truth*) ocultar; (*suspect*) retener; (*store*) guardar.

● **hold down** *vt* (*control*) dominar; (*job*) desempeñar.

● **hold on** *vi* (*keep a firm grasp*) agarrarse bien; (*wait*) esperar; **h. on!** (*on phone*) ¡no cuelgue!

● **hold out 1** *vt* (*hand*) tender. **2** *vi* (*last*) (*things*) durar; (*person*) resistir.

● **hold up** *vt* (*support*) apuntalar; (*rob*) (*train*) asaltar; (*bank*) atracar; (*delay*) retrasar; **we were held up for half an hour** sufrimos media hora de retraso.

holdall bolsa *f* de viaje.

holder (*receptacle*) recipiente *m*; (*owner*) poseedor,-a *mf*; (*bearer*) portador,-a *mf*; (*of passport*) titular *mf*.

hold-up (*robbery*) atraco *m*; (*delay*) retraso *m*; (*in traffic*) atasco *m*.

hole [həʊl] agujero *m*; (*large, in golf*) hoyo *m*.

holiday ['hɒlɪdeɪ] (*one day*) día *m* de fiesta *f*; (*several days*) vacaciones *fpl*; **to be/go on h.** estar/ir de vacaciones.

holiday-maker turista *mf*; (*in summer*) veraneante *mf*.

hollow ['hɒləʊ] **1** *a* hueco,-a; (*cheeks, eyes*) hundido,-a. **2** *n* hueco *m*.

holy ['həʊlɪ] *a* sagrado,-a; (*blessed*) bendito,-a.

Holy Ghost Espíritu *m* Santo.

home [həʊm] **1** *n* casa *f*, hogar *m*; (*institution*) asilo *m*; (*country*) patria *f*; **at h.** en casa; **make yourself at h.!** ¡estás en tu casa!; **old people's h.** asilo *m* de ancianos; **to play at h.** jugar en casa. **2** *a* (*domestic*) del hogar; (*political*) interior; (*native*) natal; **h. affairs** asuntos *mpl* interiores. **3** *adv* en casa; **to go h.** irse a casa; **to leave h.** irse de casa.

home computer ordenador *m* doméstico.

home help asistenta *f*.

homeless 1 *a* sin hogar. **2** *npl* **the h.** los sin hogar.

home-made *a* casero,-a.

Home Office *Br* Ministerio *m* del Interior.

homesick *a* **to be h.** tener morriña.

home town ciudad *f* natal.

homework deberes *mpl*.

homosexual [həʊməʊˈseksjʊəl] *a & n* homosexual (*mf*).

Honduran [hɒnˈdjʊərən] *adj & n* hondureño,-a (*mf*).

honest [ˈɒnɪst] *a* honrado,-a; (*sincere*) sincero,-a; (*fair*) justo,-a.

honestly *adv* honradamente; **h.?** ¿de verdad?

honesty honradez *f*.

honey [ˈhʌnɪ] miel *f*; *fam* (*endearment*) cariño *m*.

honeymoon luna *f* de miel.

honk [hɒŋk] *vi* (*person in car*) tocar la bocina.

honour, *US* **honor** [ˈɒnəʳ] **1** *n* honor *m*. **2** *vt* (*respect*) honrar; (*obligation*) cumplir.

honourable, *US* **honorable** *a* (*person*) honrado,-a; (*actions*) honroso,-a.

hood [hʊd] (*of garment*) capucha *f*; (*of car*) capota *f*; *US* (*bonnet*) capó *m*.

hoof [huːf] (*pl* **hoofs** *or* **hooves** [huːvz]) (*of horse*) casco *m*; (*of cow, sheep*) pezuña *f*.

hook [hʊk] gancho *m*; (*for fishing*) anzuelo *m*; **to take the phone off the h.** descolgar el teléfono.

● **hook up** *vti* conectar (**with** con).

hooked [hʊkt] *a* (*nose*) aguileño,-a; (*addicted*) enganchado,-a (**on** a); **to get h.** engancharse.

hook(e)y [ˈhʊkɪ] *US* **to play h.** hacer novillos.

hooligan [ˈhuːlɪgən] gamberro,-a *mf*.

hoop [huːp] aro *m*.

hoot [huːt] **1** *n* (*owl*) grito *m*; (*of car horn*) bocinazo *m*; **hoots of laughter** carcajadas *fpl*. **2** *vi* (*owl*) ulular; (*car*) dar un bocinazo; (*train*) silbar; (*siren*) pitar.

hooter (*of car*) bocina *f*; (*siren*) sirena *f*.

Hoover[R] [ˈhuːvəʳ] **1** *n* aspiradora *f*. **2** *vt* **to h.** pasar la aspiradora a.

hop [hɒp] **1** *vi* saltar; **to h. on one leg** andar a la pata coja. **2** *n* (*small jump*) brinco *m*.

hope [həʊp] **1** *n* esperanza *f*; (*false*) ilusión *f*; **to have little h. of doing sth** tener pocas posibilidades de hacer algo. **2** *vti* esperar; **I h. so/not** espero que sí/no.

● **hope for** *vt* esperar.

hopeful *a* (*confident*) optimista; (*promising*) prometedor,-a.

hopefully *adv* **h. she won't come** esperemos que no venga.

hopeless *a* desesperado,-a; **to be h. at sports** ser negado,-a para los deportes.

hopelessly *adv* desesperadamente; **h. lost** completamente perdido,-a.

hops *npl* lúpulo *m*.

hopscotch infernáculo *m*.

horizon [hə'raɪzən] horizonte *m*.

horizontal [hɒrɪ'zɒntəl] *a* horizontal.

horn [hɔːn] cuerno *m*; (*on car*) bocina *f*.

horrible ['hɒrəbəl] *a* horrible.

horribly *adv* horriblemente.

horrific [hə'rɪfɪk] *a* horrendo,-a.

horrify ['hɒrɪfaɪ] *vt* horrorizar.

horror ['hɒrəʳ] horror *m*; **a little h.** un diablillo.

horror film película *f* de terror.

horse [hɔːs] caballo *m*.

horseback on h. a caballo.

horse race carrera *f* de caballos.

horseshoe herradura *f*.

hose [həʊz] (*pipe*) manguera *f*.

hosepipe manguera *f*.

hospitable ['hɒspɪtəbəl] *a* hospitalario,-a.

hospital ['hɒspɪtəl] hospital *m*.

hospi'tality hospitalidad *f*.

hospitalize *vt* hospitalizar.

host [həʊst] **1** *n* (*at home*) anfitrión *m*; (*on TV*) presentador *m*. **2** *vt* (*TV show etc*) presentar.

hostage ['hɒstɪdʒ] rehén *m*; **to take sb h.** tomar a algn como rehén.

hostel ['hɒstəl] hostal *m*.

hostess ['həʊstɪs] (*at home etc*) anfitriona *f*; (*on TV*) presentadora *f*; **(air) h.** azafata *f*.

hostile ['hɒstaɪl] *a* hostil.

ho'stility hostilidad *f*.

hot [hɒt] *a* caliente; (*weather*) caluroso,-a; (*spicy*) picante; (*temper*) fuerte; **it's very h.** hace mucho calor; **to feel h.** tener calor; **it's not so h.** (*not very good*) no es nada del otro mundo.

hot dog perrito *m* caliente.

hotel [həʊ'tel] hotel *m*.

hot-water bottle bolsa *f* de agua caliente.

hound [haʊnd] **1** *n* perro *m* de caza. **2** *vt* acosar.

hour ['aʊə'] hora *f*; **60 miles an h.** 60 millas por hora; **by the h.** por horas.

hourly 1 *a* cada hora. **2** *adv* por horas.

house [haʊs] **1** *n* casa *f*; (*in theatre*) sala *f*; **at my h.** en mi casa. **2** [haʊz] *vt* alojar; (*store*) guardar.

household hogar *m*; **h. products** productos *mpl* domésticos.

housekeeping administración *f* doméstica.

house-warming party fiesta *f* que se da al estrenar casa.

housewife ama *f* de casa.

housework trabajo *m* doméstico.

housing ['haʊzɪŋ] vivienda *f*.

housing estate urbanización *f*.

hovel ['hɒvəl] casucha *f*.

hover ['hɒvə'] *vi* (*bird*) cernerse; (*helicopter*) permanecer inmóvil (en el aire).

hovercraft aerodeslizador *m*.

how [haʊ] *adv* ¿cómo?; **h. are you?** ¿cómo estás?; **h. do you do?** mucho gusto; **h. funny!** ¡qué divertido!; **h. about ...?** ¿y si ...?; **h. about a stroll?** ¿qué te parece un paseo?; **h. old is she?** ¿cuántos años tiene?; **h. tall are you?** ¿cuánto mides?; **h. many?** ¿cuántos,-as?; **h. much?** ¿cuánto,-a?

however *adv* no obstante, sin embargo; **h. difficult it may be** por difícil que sea; **h. much** por mucho que (+ *subjunctive*).

howl [haʊl] **1** *n* aullido *m*. **2** *vi* aullar.

HP [eɪtʃ'piː] *Br abbr of* **hire purchase.**

HQ [eɪtʃ'kjuː] *abbr of* **headquarters.**

hubcap ['hʌbkæp] tapacubos *m inv*.

huddle ['hʌdəl] **1** *n* grupo *m*. **2** *vi* **to h. (up** *or* **together)** acurrucarse.

hug [hʌg] **1** *vt* abrazar. **2** *n* abrazo *m*.

huge [hjuːdʒ] *a* enorme.

hull [hʌl] casco *m*.

hullo [hʌ'ləʊ] *interj* = **hello.**

hum [hʌm] **1** *vt* (*tune*) tararear. **2** *vi* (*bees, engine*) zumbar. **3** *n* (*of bees*) zumbido *m*.

human ['hjuːmən] **1** *a* humano,-a; **h. race** raza *f* humana. **2** *n* ser humano.

human being ser *m* humano.

hu'manity humanidad *f*; **the humanities** las humanidades.

humble ['hʌmbəl] *a* humilde.

humid ['hjuːmɪd] *a* húmedo,-a.

hu'midity humedad *f*.

humiliate [hjuː'mɪlɪeɪt] *vt* humillar.

humili'ation humillación *f*.

humorous *a* (*person, story*) gracioso,-a; (*writer*) humorístico,-a.

humour, *US* **humor** ['hju:mə'] humor *m.*

hump [hʌmp] (*on back*) joroba *f*; (*small hill*) montículo *m.*

hunch [hʌntʃ] (*idea*) corazonada *f.*

hundred ['hʌndrəd] **1** *n* cien *m*, ciento *m*; (*rough number*) centenar *m*; **a h. and twenty-five** ciento veinticinco; **five h.** quinientos. **2** *a* cien; **a h. people** cien personas; **a h. per cent** cien por cien; **two h. chairs** doscientas sillas.

hundredth *a & n* centésimo,-a (*m*).

Hungarian [hʌŋ'geərɪən] *adj & n* húngaro,-a (*mf*).

hunger ['hʌŋgə'] hambre *m*; **h. strike** huelga *f* de hambre.

hungry *a* **to be h.** tener hambre.

hunt [hʌnt] **1** *vt* cazar. **2** *vi* (*for game*) cazar; (*search*) buscar. **3** *n* caza *f*; (*search*) búsqueda *f.*

● **hunt down** *vt* perseguir.

hunter cazador,-a *mf.*

hunting caza *f*; (*expedition*) cacería *f.*

hurdle ['hɜːdəl] (*in sport*) valla *f*; *fig* obstáculo *m.*

hurl [hɜːl] *vt* lanzar.

hurrah [hʊ'rɑː] **hurray** [hʊ'reɪ] *interj* ¡hurra!; **h. for John!** ¡viva John!

hurricane ['hʌrɪkən] huracán *m.*

hurry ['hʌrɪ] **1** *vi* darse prisa. **2** *vt* meter prisa a. **3** *n* **to be in a h.** tener prisa.

● **hurry up** *vi* (*go faster*) darse prisa.

hurt* [hɜːt] **1** *vt* hacer daño a; (*wound*) herir; (*mentally*) ofender. **2** *vi* doler; **my arm hurts** me duele el brazo. **3** *a* (*physically*) herido,-a; (*mentally*) dolido,-a.

husband ['hʌzbənd] marido *m*, esposo *m.*

hush [hʌʃ] **1** *n* silencio *m.* **2** *interj* ¡silencio!

hustle ['hʌsəl] **1** *vt* (*jostle*) empujar; (*hurry along*) meter prisa a. **2** *n* **h. and bustle** ajetreo *m.*

hut [hʌt] cabaña *f*; (*shed*) cobertizo *m.*

hygiene ['haɪdʒiːn] higiene *f.*

hy'gienic *a* higiénico,-a.

hymn [hɪm] himno *m*; **h. book** cantoral *m.*

hypermarket ['haɪpəmɑːkɪt] hipermercado *m.*

hyphen ['haɪfən] guión *m.*

hyphenated *a* (*word*) (escrito,-a) con guión.

hypocrisy [hɪ'pɒkrəsɪ] hipocresía *f.*

'hypocrite hipócrita *mf.*

hysterical [hɪ'sterɪkəl] *a* histérico,-a.

hysterically *adv* (*to cry*) histéricamente.

I

I [aɪ] *pers pron* yo.

ice [aɪs] hielo *m*.

● **ice up** *vi* (*pond etc*) helarse; (*windscreen*) cubrirse de hielo.

iceberg ['aɪsbɜːg] iceberg *m*.

ice-cold *a* helado,-a.

ice cream helado *m*.

ice cube cubito *m* de hielo.

ice lolly polo *m*.

ice-skating patinaje *m* sobre hielo.

icicle ['aɪsɪkəl] carámbano *m*.

icing alcorza *f*.

icing sugar azúcar *m* glas.

icon ['aɪkɒn] icono *m*.

icy ['aɪsɪ] *a* (*road etc*) helado,-a; (*smile*) glacial.

ID [aɪ'diː] **ID card** documento *m* nacional de identidad, DNI *m*.

idea [aɪ'dɪə] idea *f*.

ideal [aɪ'dɪəl] *a & n* ideal (*m*).

ideally *adv* (*if possible*) de ser posible.

identical [aɪ'dentɪkəl] *a* idéntico,-a.

identifi'cation identificación *f*; (*papers*) documentación *f*.

identify [aɪ'dentɪfaɪ] **1** *vt* identificar. **2** *vi* identificarse (**with** con).

identity identidad *f*.

idiom ['ɪdɪəm] modismo *m*.

idiot ['ɪdɪət] idiota *mf*.

idi'otic *a* idiota.

idle ['aɪdəl] *a* holgazán,-ana; (*not working*) (*person*) desempleado,-a.

idol ['aɪdəl] ídolo *m*.

idolize *vt* idolatrar.

i.e. *abbr* a saber.

if [ɪf] *conj* si; **if I were rich** si fuera rico,-a; **if I were you** yo en tu lugar.

igloo ['ɪgluː] iglú *m*.

ignorance ['ɪgnərəns] ignorancia *f*.

ignorant *a* ignorante (**of** de).

ignore [ɪg'nɔːr] *vt* (*warning, remark*) no hacer caso de; (*behaviour, fact*) pasar por alto.

ill [ɪl] **1** *a* enfermo,-a; (*bad*) malo,-a. **2** *n* mal *m*.

illegal [ɪ'liːgəl] *a* ilegal.

illegible [ɪ'ledʒɪbəl] *a* ilegible.

illiterate [ɪ'lɪtərɪt] *a* analfabeto,-a.

illness enfermedad *f*.

ill-'treat *vt* maltratar.

illusion [ı'luːʒən] ilusión *f*.

illustrate ['ıləstreıt] *vt* ilustrar.

illu'stration ilustración *f*.

image ['ımıdʒ] imagen *f*.

imaginary [ı'mædzınərı] *a* imaginario,-a.

imagi'nation imaginación *f*.

imagine [ı'mædʒın] *vt* imaginarse; (*think*) suponer.

imitate ['ımıteıt] *vt* imitar.

imi'tation 1 *n* imitación *f*. **2** *a* de imitación.

immaculate [ı'mækjʊlıt] *a* impecable.

immature *a* inmaduro,-a.

immediate [ı'miːdıət] *a* inmediato,-a.

immediately 1 *adv* inmediatamente. **2** *conj* (*as soon as*) en cuanto.

immense [ı'mens] *a* inmenso,-a.

immensely *adv* sumamente.

immigrant ['ımıgrənt] *a & n* inmigrante (*mf*).

immi'gration inmigración *f*.

immortal *a* inmortal.

immune [ı'mjuːn] *a* inmune.

'immunize *vt* inmunizar (**against** contra).

impact ['ımpækt] impacto *m*; (*crash*) choque *m*.

impatience impaciencia *f*.

impatient *a* impaciente.

impatiently *adv* con impaciencia.

imperative [ım'perətıv] (*form of verb*) imperativo *m*.

impersonate [ım'pɜːsəneıt] *vt* hacerse pasar por; (*famous people*) imitar.

impersonator (*on TV etc*) imitador,-a *mf*.

impertinent [ım'pɜːtınənt] *a* impertinente.

impetus ['ımpıtəs] ímpetu *m*; *fig* impulso *m*.

implement ['ımplımənt] **1** *n* (*tool*) herramienta *f*. **2** ['ımplıment] *vt* (*decision, plan*) llevar a cabo.

implication [ımplı'keıʃən] implicación *f*; (*consequence*) consecuencia *f*.

imply [ım'plaı] *vt* (*hint*) dar a entender.

impolite *a* maleducado,-a.

import ['ımpɔːt] **1** *n* importación *f*. **2** [ım'pɔːt] *vt* importar.

importance importancia *f*; **of little i.** de poca monta.

important [ım'pɔːtənt] *a* importante; **it's not i.** no importa.

im'porter importador,-a *mf*.

impose [ım'pəʊz] **1** *vt* imponer (**on, upon** a). **2** *vi* **to i. on** *or* **upon** (*take advantage of*) abusar de.

imposing *a* imponente.

impo'sition would it be an i. if ...? ¿le molestaría si ...?

impossi'bility imposibilidad *f*.

impossible *a* imposible.

impostor [ɪmˈpɒstəʳ] impostor,-a *mf*.

impractical *a* poco práctico,-a.

impress [ɪmˈpres] *vt* impresionar.

impression impresión *f*; **to be under the i. that** ... tener la impresión de que ...

impressive *a* impresionante.

imprison [ɪmˈprɪzən] *vt* encarcelar.

improbable *a* improbable.

improper *a* (*indecent*) indecente.

improve [ɪmˈpruːv] **1** *vt* mejorar. **2** *vi* mejorarse.

● **improve on** *vt* superar.

improvement mejora *f*.

improvise [ˈɪmprəvaɪz] *vti* improvisar.

impudent [ˈɪmpjʊdənt] *a* insolente.

impulse [ˈɪmpʌls] impulso *m*.

im'pulsive *a* irreflexivo,-a.

im'pulsively *adv* de forma impulsiva.

impurity [ɪmˈpjʊərɪtɪ] impureza *f*.

in [ɪn] **1** *prep* (*place*) en; **in prison** en la cárcel; **in the distance** a lo lejos; **she arrived in Paris** llegó a París. ▌ (*time*) (*during*) en, durante; **in May/1945** en mayo/1945; **in spring** en primavera; **in the daytime** durante el día; **in the morning** por la mañana. ▌ (*time*) (*within*) dentro de. ▌ (*time*) (*after*) al cabo de. ▌ (*manner*) en; **in a loud/quiet voice** en voz alta/baja; **in French** en francés; **dressed in blue** vestido,-a de azul; **in uniform** de uniforme. ▌ (*ratio, numbers*) de; **one in six** uno de cada seis; **two metres in length** dos metros de largo. ▌ (*after superlative*) de; **the smallest car in the world** el coche más pequeño del mundo. **2** *adv* **to be in** (*at home*) estar (en casa); (*in fashion*) estar de moda; **the bus is in** el autobús ha llegado.

inability incapacidad *f*.

inaccessible *a* inaccesible.

inaccuracy (*error*) inexactitud *f*.

inaccurate *a* incorrecto,-a.

inadequacy (*lack*) insuficiencia *f*; (*inability*) incompetencia *f*.

inadequate *a* (*lacking*) insuficiente; (*unsuitable*) inadecuado,-a.

inappropriate *a* (*behaviour*) poco apropiado,-a.

inaugurate [ɪnˈɔːgjʊreɪt] *vt* (*building*) inaugurar.

inaugu'ration (*of building*) inauguración *f*.

Inc, inc *US abbr of* **Incorporated** ≈ S.A.

incapable *a* incapaz (**of doing sth** de hacer algo).

incense [ɪn'sens] *vt* enfurecer.

incentive [ɪn'sentɪv] incentivo *m*.

inch [ɪntʃ] pulgada *f* (*approx* 2,54 cm).

incident ['ɪnsɪdənt] incidente *m*.

inci'dentally *adv* a propósito.

incite [ɪn'saɪt] *vt* incitar; **to i. sb to do sth** incitar a algn a hacer algo.

incitement incitación *f*.

incli'nation deseo *m*; **my i. is to stay** yo prefiero quedarme.

incline [ɪn'klaɪn] **1** *vt* **she's inclined to be aggressive** tiende a ser agresiva. **2** *vi* (*slope*) inclinarse.

include [ɪn'kluːd] *vt* incluir (**in** en); (*in price*) comprender (**in** en).

including *prep* incluso, inclusive.

inclusive [ɪn'kluːsɪv] *a* inclusivo,-a; **the rent is i. of bills** el alquiler incluye las facturas.

income ['ɪnkʌm] ingresos *mpl*; (*from investment*) réditos *mpl*.

income tax impuesto *m* sobre la renta.

incompatible *a* incompatible (**with** con).

incompetent *a* incompetente.

incomplete *a* incompleto,-a.

inconceivable *a* inconcebible.

inconsiderate *a* desconsiderado,-a.

inconsistency inconsecuencia *f*.

inconsistent *a* inconsecuente; **your evidence is i. with the facts** su testimonio no concuerda con los hechos.

inconspicuous *a* que pasa desapercibido,-a.

inconvenience 1 *n* molestia *f*; (*disadvantage*) inconvenientes *mpl*; **the i. of living out here** los inconvenientes de vivir aquí. **2** *vt* molestar.

inconvenient *a* molesto,-a; (*time*) inoportuno,-a.

incorporate [ɪn'kɔːpəreɪt] *vt* (*include*) incluir; (*contain*) contener.

incorrect *a* incorrecto,-a.

increase ['ɪnkriːs] **1** *n* aumento *m*; (*in number*) incremento; (*in price etc*) subida *f*. **2** [ɪn'kriːs] *vt* aumentar; (*price etc*) subir. **3** *vi* aumentar.

increasing *a* creciente.

increasingly *adv* cada vez más.

incredible *a* increíble.

incredibly *adv* increíblemente.

incubator ['ɪnkjʊbeɪtə] incubadora *f*.

incur [ɪn'kɜːʳ] *vt* (*blame*) incurrir en; (*debt*) contraer; (*loss*) sufrir.

incurable [ɪn'kjʊərəbəl] *a* incurable.

indecent *a* indecente.

indecisive *a* indeciso,-a.

indeed [ɪn'diːd] *adv* (*in fact*) efectivamente; **it's very hard i.** es verdaderamente difícil; **thank you very much i.** muchísimas gracias.

indefinite *a* indefinido,-a.

indefinitely *adv* indefinidamente.

independence independencia *f.*

independent *a* independiente; **to become i.** independizarse.

independently *adv* independientemente.

index ['ɪndeks] **1** *n* (*in book*) índice *m*; (*in library*) catálogo *m.* **2** *vt* catalogar.

index card ficha *f.*

index finger dedo *m* índice.

index-linked *a* sujeto,-a al aumento de la inflación.

Indian ['ɪndɪən] *a & n* (*of America*) indio,-a (*mf*) ; (*of India*) hindú (*mf*).

indicate ['ɪndɪkeɪt] **1** *vt* indicar. **2** *vi* (*driving*) poner el intermitente.

indi'cation indicio *m.*

indicator indicador *m*; (*on car*) intermitente *m.*

indifference indiferencia *f.*

indifferent *a* (*uninterested*) indiferente; (*mediocre*) regular.

indigestion indigestión *f*; **to have i.** tener un empacho.

indignant [ɪn'dɪgnənt] *a* indignado,-a; **to get i. about sth** indignarse por algo.

indirect *a* indirecto,-a.

indirectly *adv* indirectamente.

indiscreet *a* indiscreto,-a.

indiscriminate [ɪndɪ'skrɪmɪnɪt] *a* indiscriminado,-a.

indiscriminately *adv* (*at random*) sin criterio.

indistinguishable *a* indistinguible.

individual [ɪndɪ'vɪdjʊəl] **1** *a* (*separate*) individual; (*for one*) particular; (*characteristic*) particular. **2** *n* (*person*) individuo *m.*

individually *adv* individualmente.

indoor ['ɪndɔːʳ] *a* (*plant*) interior; **i. pool** piscina cubierta.

in'doors *adv* (*inside*) dentro (de casa).

induce [ɪn'djuːs] *vt* (*persuade*) inducir; (*cause*) producir.

indulge [ɪn'dʌldʒ] *vt* (*child*) consentir; (*person*) complacer.

indulgent *a* indulgente.

industrial [ɪn'dʌstrɪəl] *a* industrial; (*accident*) laboral; *Br* **i. dispute** conflicto *m* laboral; **i. estate** polígono *m* industrial.

industry ['ɪndəstrɪ] industria *f.*

inedible *a* incomible.

ineffective *a* ineficaz.

inefficiency ineficacia *f*; (*of person*) incompetencia *f.*

inefficient *a* ineficaz; (*person*) inepto,-a.

inept [ɪnˈept] *a* (*person*) inepto,-a; (*remark*) estúpido,-a.

inequality desigualdad *f*.

inevitable [ɪnˈevɪtəbəl] *a* inevitable.

inevitably *adv* inevitablemente.

inexcusable [ɪnɪkˈskjuːzəbəl] *a* inexcusable.

inexpensive *a* económico,-a.

inexperienced *a* inexperto,-a.

inexplicable [ɪnɪkˈsplɪkəbəl] *a* inexplicable.

infallible [ɪnˈfæləbəl] *a* infalible.

infamous [ˈɪnfəməs] *a* infame.

infancy infancia *f*.

infant [ˈɪnfənt] niño,-a *mf*.

infantry [ˈɪnfəntrɪ] infantería *f*.

infatuated [ɪnˈfætjʊeɪtɪd] *a* encaprichado,-a (**with** con.)

infatu'ation encaprichamiento *m*.

infect [ɪnˈfekt] *vt* infectar.

infection infección *f*.

infectious *a* (*disease*) infeccioso,-a; *fig* contagioso,-a.

inferior [ɪnˈfɪərɪəʳ] *a* inferior (**to** a).

inferi'ority inferioridad *f*.

infest [ɪnˈfest] *vt* infestar (**with** de).

infinite [ˈɪnfɪnɪt] *a* infinito,-a.

infinitely *adv* infinitamente.

infinitive [ɪnˈfɪnɪtɪv] infinitivo *m*.

infinity [ɪnˈfɪnɪtɪ] infinidad *f*.

infirm [ɪnˈfɜːm] *a* (*ailing*) enfermizo,-a; (*weak*) débil.

inflamed [ɪnˈfleɪmd] *a* inflamado,-a; **to become i.** inflamarse.

infla'mmation inflamación *f*.

inflate [ɪnˈfleɪt] *vt* inflar.

inflation inflación *f*.

inflexible *a* inflexible.

inflict [ɪnˈflɪkt] *vt* (*damage*) causar (**on** a); (*defeat*) infligir (**on** a).

influence [ˈɪnflʊəns] **1** *n* influencia *f*; **to be under the i.** llevar una copa de más; (*formally*) estar en estado de embriaguez. **2** *vt* influir en.

influ'ential *a* influyente.

influenza [ɪnflʊˈenzə] gripe *f*.

influx [ˈɪnflʌks] afluencia *f*.

info [ˈɪnfəʊ] *fam* información *f*.

inform [ɪnˈfɔːm] *vt* informar (**of, about** de, sobre).

informal [ɪnˈfɔːməl] *a* (*occasion, behaviour*) informal; (*language, treatment*) familiar; (*unofficial*) no oficial.

informally *adv* (*to speak, behave*) de manera informal.

information [ɪnfəˈmeɪʃən] información *f*; **a piece of i.** un dato.

information technology informática *f*.

informative *a* informativo,-a.

infuriate [ɪnˈfjʊərɪeɪt] *vt* poner furioso,-a.

infuriating *a* exasperante.

ingenious [ɪnˈdʒiːnɪəs] *a* ingenioso,-a.

ingratitude ingratitud *f*.

ingredient [ɪnˈgriːdɪənt] ingrediente *m*.

inhabit [ɪnˈhæbɪt] *vt* vivir en, ocupar.

inhabitant habitante *mf*.

inhale [ɪnˈheɪl] *vt* (*gas*) inhalar; (*air*) aspirar.

inherit [ɪnˈherɪt] *vt* heredar (**from** de).

inheritance herencia *f*.

inhibit [ɪnˈhɪbɪt] *vt* (*freedom*) limitar; (*person*) cohibir; **to be inhibited** (*person*) sentirse cohibido,-a.

inhiˈbition cohibición *f*.

inhospitable *a* inhospitalario,-a.

inhuman *a* inhumano,-a.

initial [ɪˈnɪʃəl] **1** *a* inicial. **2** *n* **initials** (*of name*) iniciales *fpl*; (*abbreviation*) siglas *fpl*.

initially *adv* al principio.

inject [ɪnˈdʒekt] *vt* (*drug etc*) inyectar.

injection inyección *f*.

injure [ˈɪndʒəʳ] *vt* herir; **to i. oneself** hacerse daño.

injured 1 *a* herido,-a. **2** *npl* **the i.** los heridos.

injury [ˈɪndʒərɪ] herida *f*.

injustice injusticia *f*.

ink [ɪŋk] tinta *f*.

inkjet printer impresora *f* injección.

inkling [ˈɪŋklɪŋ] (*idea*) idea *f*.

inland [ˈɪnlənd] **1** *a* (del) interior. **2** [ɪnˈlænd] *adv* (*travel*) tierra adentro.

Inland Revenue *Br* Hacienda *f*.

in-laws [ˈɪnlɔːz] *npl* familia *f* política.

inmate [ˈɪnmeɪt] (*of prison*) preso,-a *mf*.

inn [ɪn] (*with lodging*) posada *f*.

inner [ˈɪnəʳ] *a* interior; **i. city** casco *m* urbano.

innocence inocencia *f*.

innocent [ˈɪnəsənt] *a & n* inocente (*mf*).

inoculate [ɪˈnɒkʊleɪt] *vt* inocular.

inocuˈlation inoculación *f*.

input [ˈɪnpʊt] (*of data*) input *m*, entrada *f*.

inquire [ɪnˈkwaɪəʳ] **1** vt preguntar. **2** vi preguntar (**about** por); (find out) informarse (**about** de).

● **inquire into** vt investigar.

inquiry pregunta f; (investigation) investigación f; '**inquiries**' 'información'.

inquisitive [ɪnˈkwɪzɪtɪv] a curioso,-a; (questioning) preguntón,-ona.

insane a loco,-a.

insanity locura f.

inscription [ɪnˈskrɪpʃən] (on stone, coin) inscripción f; (in book, on photo) dedicatoria f.

insect [ˈɪnsekt] insecto m; **i. bite** picadura f.

in'secticide [ɪnˈsektɪsaɪd] insecticida m.

insecure a inseguro,-a.

insensitive a insensible.

insensi'tivity insensibilidad f.

insert [ɪnˈsɜːt] vt introducir.

inside [ɪnˈsaɪd] **1** n interior m; **on the i.** por dentro; **to turn sth i. out** volver algo al revés. **2** [ˈɪnsaɪd] a interior; **i. lane** carril m interior. **3** [ɪnˈsaɪd] adv (be) dentro, adentro; (run etc) (hacia) adentro. **4** prep (place) dentro de.

insight [ˈɪnsaɪt] (quality) perspicacia f.

insignificant a insignificante.

insincere a poco sincero,-a.

insist [ɪnˈsɪst] **1** vi insistir (**on** en). **2** vt **to i. that ...** insistir en que ...

insistence insistencia f.

insistent a insistente.

insolence insolencia f.

insolent [ˈɪnsələnt] a insolente.

insomnia [ɪnˈsɒmnɪə] insomnio m.

inspect [ɪnˈspekt] vt inspeccionar.

inspection inspección f.

inspector inspector,-a mf; (on bus, train) revisor,-a mf.

inspi'ration inspiración f.

inspire [ɪnˈspaɪəʳ] vt inspirar; **to i. respect in sb** infundir respeto a algn.

install, US **instal** [ɪnˈstɔːl] vt instalar.

instalment, US **installment** (of payment) plazo m; (of novel, programme) entrega f.

instance [ˈɪnstəns] caso m; **for i.** por ejemplo.

instant [ˈɪnstənt] **1** n (moment) instante m. **2** a inmediato,-a; (coffee, meal) instantáneo,-a.

instantly adv inmediatamente.

instead [ɪnˈsted] **1** adv en cambio. **2** prep **i. of** en vez de.

instinct ['ɪnstɪŋkt] instinto *m*.

in'stinctive *a* instintivo,-a.

in'stinctively *adv* instintivamente.

institution [ɪnstɪ'tjuːʃən] institución *f*.

instruct [ɪn'strʌkt] *vt* instruir; (*order*) mandar.

instruction instructions instrucciones *fpl*; **'instructions for use'** 'modo de empleo'.

instructive *a* instructivo,-a.

instructor instructor,-a *mf*; (*of driving*) profesor,-a *mf*.

instrument ['ɪnstrəmənt] instrumento *m*.

insufficient *a* insuficiente.

insulate ['ɪnsjʊleɪt] *vt* aislar (**against, from** de).

insu'lation aislamiento *m*.

insult 1 *n* ['ɪnsʌlt] insulto *m*. **2** [ɪn'sʌlt] *vt* insultar.

insurance seguro *m*; **i. company** compañía *f* de seguros.

insure [ɪn'ʃʊəʳ] *vt* asegurar (**against** contra).

intact [ɪn'tækt] *a* intacto,-a.

intellect ['ɪntɪlekt] intelecto *m*.

inte'llectual *a & n* intelectual (*mf*).

intelligence inteligencia *f*.

intelligent [ɪn'telɪdʒənt] *a* inteligente.

intelligible [ɪn'telɪdʒəbəl] *a* inteligible.

intend [ɪn'tend] *vt* (*mean*) tener la intención de.

intense [ɪn'tens] *a* intenso,-a.

intensely *adv* (*extremely*) sumamente.

intensify *vt* intensificar.

intensity intensidad *f*.

intensive *a* intensivo,-a; **i. care unit** unidad *f* de vigilancia intensiva.

intent [ɪn'tent] *a* **to be i. on doing sth** estar resuelto,-a a hacer algo.

intention intención *f*.

intentional *a* deliberado,-a.

intentionally *adv* a propósito.

intercept [ɪntə'sept] *vt* interceptar.

interchange ['ɪntətʃeɪndʒ] (*on motorway*) cruce *m*.

inter'changeable *a* intercambiable.

intercom ['ɪntəkɒm] (*at entrance*) portero automático.

interconnected [ɪntəkə'nektɪd] *a* (*facts etc*) interrelacionado,-a.

interest ['ɪntrɪst] **1** *n* interés *m*; **i. rate** tipo *m* de interés. **2** *vt* interesar; **to be interested in** interesarse en; **I'm not interested** no me interesa.

interesting *a* interesante.

interfere [ɪntə'fɪəʳ] *vi* (*meddle*) entrometerse (**in** en).

interference (*meddling*) intromisión *f*; (*on radio etc*) interferencia *f*.

interior [ɪn'tɪərɪəʳ] **1** *a* interior. **2** *n* interior *m*.

interlude ['ɪntəluːd] (*at cinema, in theatre*) intermedio *m*; (*in music*) interludio *m*.

intermediary [ɪntə'miːdɪərɪ] intermediario,-a *mf*.

intermediate [ɪntə'miːdɪɪt] *a* intermedio,-a.

intern ['ɪntɜːn] US (*doctor*) interno,-a *mf*.

internal [ɪn'tɜːnəl] *a* interior; (*dispute, injury*) interno,-a.

Internal Revenue US Hacienda *f*.

international [ɪntə'næʃənəl] *a* internacional.

interpret [ɪn'tɜːprɪt] *vt* interpretar.

interpreter intérprete *mf*.

interrogate [ɪn'terəgeɪt] *vt* interrogar.

interro'gation interrogatorio *m*.

interrupt [ɪntə'rʌpt] *vti* interrumpir.

interruption interrupción *f*.

intersect [ɪntə'sekt] **1** *vt* cruzar. **2** *vi* cruzarse.

intersection (*crossroads*) cruce *m*.

interval ['ɪntəvəl] (*of time, space*) intervalo *m*; Br (*in concert etc*) descanso *m*.

intervene [ɪntə'viːn] *vi* (*person*) intervenir (**in** en); (*event*) sobrevenir.

intervention [ɪntə'venʃən] intervención *f*.

interview ['ɪntəvjuː] **1** *n* entrevista *f*. **2** *vt* entrevistar.

interviewer entrevistador,-a *mf*.

intimate ['ɪntɪmɪt] *a* íntimo,-a.

intimidate [ɪn'tɪmɪdeɪt] *vt* intimidar.

into ['ɪntuː, *unstressed* 'ɪntə] *prep* (*motion*) en, a; **to get i. a car** subir a un coche; **to go i. a house** entrar en una casa; **to change pounds i. pesetas** cambiar libras en *or* por pesetas; **to translate sth i. French** traducir algo al francés; *fam* **to be i. sth** ser aficionado,-a a algo.

intolerable [ɪn'tɒlərəbəl] *a* intolerable.

intoxicate [ɪn'tɒksɪkeɪt] *vt* embriagar.

intoxicated *a* borracho,-a.

intransitive *a* intransitivo,-a.

intricate ['ɪntrɪkɪt] *a* intrincado,-a.

introduce [ɪntrə'djuːs] *vt* (*person, programme*) presentar (**to** a); (*bring in*) introducir (**into, to** en).

introduction (*of person, programme*) presentación *f*; (*in book, bringing in*) introducción *f*.

intrude [ɪn'truːd] *vi* entrometerse (**into, on** en); (*disturb*) molestar.

intruder intruso,-a *mf*.

intrusion intrusión *f*.

intuition [ɪntjʊ'ɪʃən] intuición *f*.

inundate ['ɪnʌndeɪt] *vt* inundar (**with** de); **I was inundated with offers** me llovieron las ofertas.

invade [ɪn'veɪd] *vt* invadir.

invader invasor,-a *mf*.

invalid[1] ['ɪnvəlɪd] (*disabled person*) minusválido,-a *mf*; (*sick person*) enfermo,-a *mf*.

invalid[2] [ɪn'vælɪd] *a* nulo,-a.

invaluable *a* inestimable.

invariably [ɪn'veərɪəblɪ] *adv* (*always*) invariablemente.

invent [ɪn'vent] *vt* inventar.

invention invento *m*.

inventor inventor,-a *mf*.

inventory ['ɪnvəntərɪ] inventario *m*.

inverted [ɪn'vɜːtɪd] *a* (**in**) **i. commas** (entre) comillas *fpl*.

invest [ɪn'vest] *vt* invertir (**in** en).

investigate [ɪn'vestɪgeɪt] *vt* (*crime, subject*) investigar; (*cause, possibility*) estudiar.

investi'gation (*of crime*) investigación *f*; (*of cause*) examen *m*.

investigator investigador,-a *mf*.

investor inversor,-a *mf*.

invigorating [ɪn'vɪgəreɪtɪŋ] *a* vigorizante.

invisible *a* invisible.

invi'tation invitación *f*.

invite [ɪn'vaɪt] *vt* invitar (**to** a); (*comments etc*) solicitar; (*criticism*) provocar.

inviting *a* (*attractive*) atractivo,-a; (*food*) apetitoso,-a.

invoice ['ɪnvɔɪs] **1** *n* factura *f*. **2** *vt* facturar.

involve [ɪn'vɒlv] *vt* (*entail*) suponer; (*concern*) implicar (**in** en); **to be involved in an accident** sufrir un accidente.

involved *a* (*complicated*) complicado,-a; (*romantically*) enredado,-a.

involvement (*participation*) participación *f*; (*in crime*) implicación *f*; **emotional i.** relación *f* sentimental.

inwards ['ɪnwədz] *adv* hacia dentro.

IQ [aɪ'kjuː] coeficiente *m* intelectual, CI *m*.

Iranian [ɪ'reɪnɪən] *a & n* iraní (*mf*).

Iraqi [ɪ'rɑːkɪ] *a & n* iraquí (*mf*).

iris ['aɪrɪs] (*of eye*) iris *m inv*; (*plant*) lirio *m*.

Irish ['aɪrɪʃ] **1** *a* irlandés,-esa. **2** *npl* **the I.** los irlandeses.

Irishman irlandés *m*.

Irishwoman irlandesa *f*.

iron ['aɪən] **1** *n* hierro *m*; (*for clothes*) plancha *f*; **the i. and steel industry** la industria siderúrgica. **2** *vt* (*clothes*) planchar.

ironic(al) [aɪ'rɒnɪk(əl)] *a* irónico,-a.
ironing to do the i. planchar.
ironing board tabla *f* de planchar.
ironmonger ['aɪənmʌŋgə'] *Br* ferretero,-a *mf*; **i.'s (shop)** ferretería *f*.
irony ['aɪrənɪ] ironía *f*.
irrational *a* irracional.
irregular *a* irregular.
irrelevance irrelevancia *f*.
irrelevant *a* no pertinente.
irresistible [ɪrɪ'zɪstəbəl] *a* irresistible.
irrespective *a* i. of sin tener en cuenta.
irrigate ['ɪrɪgeɪt] *vt* regar.
irritable *a* irritable.
irritate ['ɪrɪteɪt] *vt* (*annoy*) fastidiar.
irritating *a* irritante.
irri'tation (*annoyance*) fastidio *m*; (*ill humour*) mal humor *m*.
is [ɪz] *3rd person sing pres of* **be**.
Islamic [ɪz'læmɪk] *a* islámico,-a.
island ['aɪlənd] isla *f*.
isolate ['aɪsəleɪt] *vt* aislar (**from** de).
isolated *a* aislado,-a.
iso'lation aislamiento *m*.
issue ['ɪʃuː] **1** *n* (*matter*) cuestión *f*; (*of journal etc*) ejemplar *m*. **2** *vt*
  (*book*) publicar; (*banknotes etc*) emitir; (*passport*) expedir; (*supplies*)
  repartir; (*order, instructions*) dar.
it [ɪt] *pers pron* (*subject*) él, ella (*often omitted*); **it's here** está aquí.
  ▮ (*direct object*) lo, la; **I don't believe it** no me lo creo. ▮ (*indirect
  object*) le; **give it a kick** dale una patada. ▮ (*after prep*) él, ella, ello;
  we'll talk about it later ya hablaremos de ello. ▮ (*impersonal*) **it's late** es
  tarde; **it's me** soy yo; **it's raining** está lloviendo; **who is it?** ¿quién es?
Italian [ɪ'tæljən] **1** *a* italiano,-a. **2** *n* (*person*) italiano,-a *mf*; (*language*)
  italiano *m*.
italic [ɪ'tælɪk] *a* in italics en cursiva.
itch [ɪtʃ] **1** *n* picor *m*. **2** *vi* (*skin*) picar.
itchy *a* que pica.
item ['aɪtəm] (*in list*) artículo *m*; (*in collection*) pieza *f*; (*on agenda*) asunto
  m; **i. of clothing** prenda *f* de vestir; **news i.** noticia *f*.
its [ɪts] *poss a* (*one thing*) su; (*more than one*) sus.
it'self *pers pron* ▮ (*reflexive*) se; **the cat scratched i.** el gato se rascó.
  ▮ (*emphatic*) él *or* ella mismo,-a.
ivory ['aɪvərɪ] marfil *m*.
ivy ['aɪvɪ] hiedra *f*.

J

jab [dʒæb] **1** *n* pinchazo *m*; (*poke*) golpe *m* seco. **2** *vt* pinchar.

jack [dʒæk] (*for car*) gato *m*; (*cards*) sota *f*.

jacket ['dʒækɪt] chaqueta *f*; (*of suit*) americana *f*; **j. potatoes** patatas *fpl* al horno.

jacuzzi [dʒə'kuːzɪ] jacuzzi *m*.

jagged ['dʒægɪd] *a* dentado,-a.

jail [dʒeɪl] **1** *n* cárcel *f*. **2** *vt* encarcelar.

jam¹ [dʒæm] mermelada *f*.

jam² **1** *n* (*blockage*) atasco *m*. **2** *vt* (*cram*) meter a la fuerza; (*block*) atascar. **3** *vi* (*door*) atrancarse; (*brakes*) agarrotarse.

● **jam into** *vt* (*crowd*) apretarse en; **to j. sth into sth** meter algo a la fuerza en algo.

jam jar pote *m* de mermelada.

jam-packed *a fam* (*with people*) atestado,-a; (*with things*) atiborrado, -a.

January ['dʒænjʊərɪ] enero *m*.

Japanese [dʒæpə'niːz] **1** *a* japonés,-esa. **2** *n* (*person*) japonés,-esa *mf*; (*language*) japonés *m*.

jar [dʒɑːʳ] (*glass*) tarro *m*; (*earthenware*) tinaja *f*.

jaundice ['dʒɔːndɪs] ictericia *f*.

javelin ['dʒævəlɪn] jabalina *f*.

jaw [dʒɔː] mandíbula *f*.

jazz [dʒæz] jazz *m*.

jealous ['dʒeləs] *a* celoso,-a; (*envious*) envidioso,-a; **to be j. of** tener celos de.

jealousy celos *mpl*; (*envy*) envidia *f*.

jeans [dʒiːnz] *npl* vaqueros *mpl*, tejanos *mpl*.

jeep [dʒiːp] jeep *m*.

jeer [dʒɪəʳ] **1** *n* (*boo*) abucheo *m*. **2** *vi* (*boo*) abuchear; (*mock*) burlarse.

jeering *a* burlón,-ona.

jelly ['dʒelɪ] gelatina *f*.

jeopardize *vt* poner en peligro; (*agreement etc*) comprometer.

jerk [dʒɜːk] **1** *n* (*jolt*) sacudida *f*; *fam* (*idiot*) imbécil *mf*. **2** *vt* (*shake*) sacudir.

jersey ['dʒɜːzɪ] jersey *m*.

jet [dʒet] reactor *m*; **j. engine** reactor *m*.

jet lag desfase *m* horario.

jet-lagged *a* que sufre los efectos del desfase horario.

jetty ['dʒetɪ] muelle *m*.

Jew [dʒuː] judío,-a *mf*.

jewel ['dʒu:əl] joya *f*; (*in watch*) rubí *m*.

jeweller, *US* **jeweler** joyero,-a *mf*.

jewellery, *US* **jewelry** joyas *fpl*.

Jewish *a* judío,-a.

jigsaw ['dʒɪgsɔ:] (*puzzle*) rompecabezas *m inv*.

jingle ['dʒɪŋgəl] *vi* tintinear.

jitters ['dʒɪtəz] *npl* **to get the j.** tener canguelo.

job [dʒɒb] trabajo *m*; (*task*) tarea *f*; (*occupation*) (puesto *m* de) trabajo *m*; **we had a j. to ...** nos costó (trabajo) ...; **it's a good j. that ...** menos mal que ...

job centre oficina *f* de empleo.

jobless *a* parado,-a.

jockey ['dʒɒkɪ] jinete *m*.

jog [dʒɒg] **1** *n* trote *m*. **2** *vt* empujar; (*memory*) refrescar. **3** *vi* (*run*) hacer footing.

john [dʒɒn] *US fam* meódromo *m*.

join [dʒɔɪn] **1** *vt* juntar; (*road*) empalmar con; (*river*) desembocar en; (*meet*) reunirse con; (*group*) unirse a; (*institution*) entrar en; (*army*) alistarse a; (*party*) afiliarse a; (*club*) hacerse socio,-a de. **2** *vi* unirse; (*roads*) empalmar; (*rivers*) confluir; (*become a member*) afiliarse; (*club*) hacerse socio,-a. **3** *n* juntura *f*.

● **join in 1** *vi* participar. **2** *vt* participar en.

● **join up 1** *vt* juntar. **2** *vi* (*roads*) unirse; (*join army*) alistarse.

joint [dʒɔɪnt] **1** *n* articulación *f*; (*of meat*) corte *m* de carne para asar; (*once roasted*) asado *m*. **2** *a* colectivo,-a; **j. (bank) account** cuenta *f* conjunta.

joke [dʒəʊk] **1** *n* chiste *m*; (*prank*) broma *f*. **2** *vi* estar de broma.

joker bromista *mf*; (*in cards*) comodín *m*.

jolly [dʒɒlɪ] **1** *a* alegre. **2** *adv fam* **she played j. well** jugó muy bien.

jolt [dʒəʊlt] **1** *n* sacudida *f*. **2** *vi* moverse a sacudidas. **3** *vt* sacudir.

jostle ['dʒɒsəl] **1** *vt* dar empujones a. **2** *vi* dar empujones.

● **jot down** [dʒɒt] *vt* apuntar.

journalist ['dʒɜ:nəlɪst] periodista *mf*.

journey ['dʒɜ:nɪ] viaje *m*; (*distance*) trayecto *m*.

joy [dʒɔɪ] alegría *f*.

joyful *a* alegre.

joystick palanca *f* de mando; (*of video game*) joystick *m*.

judge [dʒʌdʒ] **1** *n* juez *mf*, jueza *f*. **2** *vt* juzgar; (*estimate*) considerar; (*assess*) valorar. **3** *vi* juzgar.

judg(e)ment sentencia *f*; (*opinion*) opinión *f*.

judo ['dʒu:dəʊ] judo *m*.

jug [dʒʌg] *Br* jarra *f*; **milk j.** jarra de leche.

juggle ['dʒʌgəl] *vi* hacer juegos malabares (**with** con).

juggler malabarista *mf*.

juice [dʒuːs] jugo *m*; (*of citrus fruits*) zumo *m*.

juicy *a* jugoso,-a.

July [dʒuːˈlaɪ] julio *m*.

jumble ['dʒʌmbəl] **1** *n* revoltijo *m*. **2** *vt* revolver.

jumble sale mercadillo *m* de caridad.

jumbo ['dʒʌmbəʊ] *a* gigante.

jumbo jet jumbo *m*.

jump [dʒʌmp] **1** *n* salto *m*; (*sudden increase*) subida repentina *f*. **2** *vi* saltar; (*start*) sobresaltarse; (*increase*) aumentar de golpe. **3** *vt* saltar; *Br* **to j. the queue** colarse.

◊ **jump in** *or* **on 1** *vt* (*train etc*) subirse a. **2** *vi* subir.

jumper *Br* (*sweater*) jersey *m*.

jumpy *a fam* nervioso,-a.

junction ['dʒʌŋkʃən] (*of roads*) cruce *m*.

June [dʒuːn] junio *m*.

jungle ['dʒʌŋgəl] jungla *f*.

junior ['dʒuːnjəˈ] **1** *a* (*lower in rank*) subalterno,-a; (*younger*) menor; **j. team** equipo juvenil. **2** *n* (*of lower rank*) subalterno,-a *mf*; (*younger person*) menor *mf*.

junior high school *US* = instituto *m* de enseñanza secundaria.

junior school escuela *f* de EGB (Enseñanza General Básica).

junk [dʒʌŋk] trastos *mpl*.

junk shop tienda *f* de segunda mano.

jury ['dʒʊərɪ] jurado *m*.

just [dʒʌst] **1** *a* (*fair*) justo,-á. **2** *adv* (*at this very moment*) ahora mismo, en este momento; (*only*) solamente; (*barely*) por poco; (*exactly*) exactamente; **he had j. arrived** acababa de llegar; **he was j. leaving when Rosa arrived** estaba a punto de salir cuando llegó Rosa; **j. as I came in** justo cuando entré; **I only j. caught the bus** cogí el autobús por los pelos; **j. about** casi; **j. as fast as** tan rápido como.

justice ['dʒʌstɪs] justicia *f*.

justify ['dʒʌstɪfaɪ] *vt* justificar.

jut out [dʒʌt] *vi* sobresalir.

K

kangaroo [kæŋgə'ru:] canguro *m*.

karate [kə'rɑːtɪ] kárate *m*.

kebab [kə'bæb] pincho moruno *m*.

keen [ki:n] *a* (*eager*) entusiasta; (*intense*) profundo,-a; (*mind, senses*) agudo,-a.

keep [ki:p] **1** *n* to earn one's k. ganarse el pan. **2** *vt** mantener; (*letters, memories, silence, secret*) guardar; (*retain possession of*) quedarse con; (*hold back*) entretener; (*in prison*) detener; (*promise*) cumplir; (*diary, accounts*) llevar; **to k. sb waiting** hacer esperar a algn; **to k. doing sth** no dejar de hacer algo; **it keeps on breaking** siempre se está rompiendo. **2** *vi* **the rain kept on** la lluvia siguió/continuó; **he just kept on** (*talking, complaining*) siguió machacando; **k. straight on** sigue todo derecho.
- **keep away 1** *vt* mantener a distancia. **2** *vi* mantenerse a distancia.
- **keep back 1** *vt* (*information*) callar; (*money etc*) retener. **2** *vi* (*crowd*) mantenerse atrás.
- **keep down** *vt* to k. prices down mantener los precios bajos.
- **keep off** *vt* k. off the grass prohibido pisar la hierba.
- **keep on 1** *vt* (*clothes etc*) no quitarse; (*continue to employ*) no despedir a; **it keeps on breaking** siempre se está rompiendo. **2** *vi* **the rain kept on** la lluvia siguió/continuó; **he just kept on** (*talking, complaining*) siguió machacando; **k. straight on** sigue todo derecho.
- **keep out 1** *vt* no dejar pasar. **2** *vi* k. out! ¡no entres!
- **keep to** *vt* to k. to the left circular por la izquierda.
- **keep up 1** *vt* mantener. **2** *vi* (*in race etc*) no rezagarse.
- **keep up with** *vt* to k. up with sb (*in a race*) mantenerse a la altura de algn; **to k. up with the times** estar al día.

keeper guarda *m*, guardesa *f*.

kennel ['kenəl] caseta *f* para perros.

Kenyan ['kenjən] *a & n* keniano,-a (*mf*).

kept [kept] *pt & pp of* **keep.**

kerb [kɜ:b] bordillo *m*.

kerosene ['kerəsi:n] *US* queroseno *m*.

ketchup ['ketʃəp] ketchup *m*.

kettle ['ketəl] hervidor *m*.

key [ki:] **1** *n* (*for lock*) llave *f*; (*of piano, typewriter*) tecla *f*. **2** *a* clave.

keyboard teclado *m*.

key ring llavero *m*.

kick [kɪk] **1** *n* (*from person*) puntapié *m*. **2** *vi* (*animal*) cocear; (*person*) dar patadas. **3** *vt* dar un puntapié a.
- **kick down** *or* **in** *vt* (*door etc*) derribar a patadas.
- **kick out** *vt* echar a patadas.

kick-off saque *m* inicial.

kid¹ [kɪd] *fam* (*child*) niño,-a *mf*; **the kids** los críos.

kid² **1** *vt* tomar el pelo a. **2** *vi* tomar el pelo.

kidnap ['kɪdnæp] *vt* secuestrar.

kidnapper secuestrador,-a *mf*.

kidney riñón *m*.

kill [kɪl] *vt* matar.

killer asesino,-a *mf*.

kilo ['ki:ləʊ] kilo *m*.

kilogram(me) ['kɪləʊgræm] kilogramo *m*.

kilometre, *US* **kilometer** [kɪ'lɒmɪtəʳ] kilómetro *m*.

kind¹ [kaɪnd] **1** *n* clase *f*; **what k. of?** ¿qué tipo de? **2** *adv fam* **k. of** en cierta manera.

kind² *a* amable.

kindergarten ['kɪndəgɑːtən] jardín *m* de infancia.

kindness amabilidad *f*.

king [kɪŋ] rey *m*.

kingdom reino *m*.

kiosk ['ki:ɒsk] quiosco *m*.

kiss [kɪs] **1** *n* beso *m*. **2** *vt* besar. **3** *vi* besarse.

kit [kɪt] (*gear*) equipo *m*; (*clothing*) ropa *f*; (*toy model*) maqueta *f*.

kitchen ['kɪtʃɪn] cocina *f*.

kite [kaɪt] (*toy*) cometa *f*.

kitten ['kɪtən] gatito,-a *mf*.

knack [næk] **to get the k. of doing sth** cogerle el truquillo a algo.

knee [ni:] rodilla *f*.

kneel* [ni:l] *vi* **to k. (down)** arrodillarse.

knew [nju:] *pt of* **know**.

knickers ['nɪkəz] *npl* bragas *fpl*.

knife [naɪf] (*pl* **knives** [naɪvz]) cuchillo *m*.

knight [naɪt] caballero *m*; (*in chess*) caballo *m*.

knit [nɪt] **1** *vt* tejer; (*join*) juntar; **to k. one's brow** fruncir el ceño. **2** *vi* hacer punto; (*bone*) soldarse.

knitting punto *m*.

knitting machine máquina *f* de hacer punto.

knitting needle aguja *f* de hacer punto.

knob [nɒb] (*of stick*) puño *m*; (*of drawer*) tirador *m*; (*button*) botón *m*.

knock [nɒk] **1** *n* golpe *m*; **there was a k. at the door** llamaron a la puerta. **2** *vt* golpear. **3** *vi* chocar (**against, into** contra); (*at door*) llamar (**at** a).

● **knock down** *vt* (*demolish*) derribar; (*car*) atropellar.

● **knock off** *vt* tirar.

● **knock out** *vt* (*make unconscious*) dejar sin conocimiento; (*in boxing*)

derrotar por K.O.
● **knock over** vt volcar; (car) atropellar.
knocker (on door) aldaba f.
knot [nɒt] **1** n nudo m. **2** vt anudar.
know* [nəʊ] **1** vt saber; (be acquainted with) conocer; **she knows how to ski** sabe esquiar; **we got to k. each other at the party** nos conocimos en la fiesta. **2** vi saber; **to let sb k.** avisar a algn.
know-how conocimiento m práctico.
knowledge ['nɒlɪdz] conocimiento m; (learning) conocimientos mpl.
known a conocido,-a.
knuckle ['nʌkəl] nudillo m.
Koran [kɔː'rɑːn] Corán m.
Korean [kə'riːən] a & n coreano,-a (mf).

L

lab [læb] *fam* laboratorio *m*.
label ['leɪbəl] **1** *n* etiqueta *f*. **2** *vt* poner etiqueta a.
laboratory [lə'bɒrətərɪ, *US* 'læbrətɔ:rɪ] laboratorio *m*.
labour, *US* **labor** ['leɪbə'] **1** *n* (*work*) trabajo *m*; (*workforce*) mano *f* de obra; **L. (Party)** el Partido Laborista, los laboristas; **to be in l.** estar de parto. **2** *a* (*market etc*) laboral. **3** *vi* (*work*) trabajar (duro).
labor union *US* sindicato *m*.
labourer peón *m*; **farm l.** peón *m* agrícola.
lace [leɪs] *n* (*fabric*) encaje *m*; **laces** cordones *mpl*; **to do up one's laces** atarse los cordones.
lack [læk] **1** *n* falta *f*. **2** *vt* carecer de. **3** *vi* carecer (**in** de).
lad [læd] chaval *m*.
ladder ['lædə'] escalera *f* (de mano).
ladle ['leɪdəl] cucharón *m*.
lady ['leɪdɪ] señora *f*; **'Ladies'** (*WC*) 'Señoras'.
ladybird, *US* **ladybug** mariquita *f*.
lager ['lɑ:gə'] cerveza *f* (rubia).
lake [leɪk] lago *m*.
lamb [læm] cordero *m*; (*meat*) carne *f* de cordero.
lame [leɪm] *a* cojo,-a.
lamp [læmp] lámpara *f*.
lamppost farola *f*.
lampshade pantalla *f*.
land [lænd] **1** *n* tierra *f*; (*country*) país *m*; (*property*) tierras *fpl*; **piece of l.** terreno *m*; **by l.** por tierra. **2** *vt* (*plane*) hacer aterrizar. **3** *vi* (*plane*) aterrizar; (*passengers*) desembarcar.
landing (*of staircase*) rellano *m*; (*of plane*) aterrizaje *m*.
landlady (*of flat*) propietaria *f*; (*of boarding house*) patrona *f*; (*of pub*) dueña *f*.
landlord (*of flat*) propietario *m*; (*of pub*) dueño *m*.
landscape ['lændskeɪp] paisaje *m*.
landslide desprendimiento *m* de tierras.
lane [leɪn] (*in country*) camino *m*; (*in town*) callejón *m*; (*of motorway*) carril *m*.
language ['læŋgwɪdʒ] idioma *m*, lengua *f*.
language laboratory laboratorio *m* de idiomas.
lantern ['læntən] farol *m*.
lap[1] [læp] (*knees*) rodillas *fpl*.
lap[2] (*circuit*) vuelta *f*.
lapel [lə'pel] solapa *f*.

larder ['lɑːdə^r] despensa f.

large [lɑːdʒ] a grande; (amount) importante; **by and l.** por lo general.

largely adv (mainly) en gran parte; (chiefly) principalmente.

lark¹ [lɑːk] (bird) alondra f.

lark² (joke) broma f.

laser ['leɪzə^r] láser m; **l. printer** impresora f láser.

last [lɑːst] **1** a (final, most recent) último,-a; (past) pasado,-a; (previous) anterior; **l. but one** penúltimo,-a; **l. month** el mes pasado; **l. night** anoche. **2** adv (on final occasion) por última vez; (at the end) en último lugar; (in race etc) último; **at (long) l.** por fin. **3** n el último, la última. **4** vi (time) durar; (hold out) aguantar.

lastly adv por último.

latch [lætʃ] pestillo m.

late [leɪt] **1** a (not on time) tardío,-a; (hour) avanzado,-a; (far on in time) tarde; **to be five minutes l.** llegar con cinco minutos de retraso; **in the l. afternoon** a última hora de la tarde. **2** adv tarde; **l. at night** a altas horas de la noche.

latecomer rezagado,-a mf.

lately adv últimamente.

Latin ['lætɪn] **1** a latino,-a; **L. America** América Latina, Latinoamérica f; **L. American** latinoamericano,-a (mf). **2** n latino,-a (mf); (language) latín m.

latter ['lætə^r] **1** a (last) último,-a; (second of two) segundo,-a. **2** pron éste,-a.

laugh [lɑːf] **1** n risa f. **2** vi reír, reírse.

● **laugh about** vt to l. about sb/sth reírse de algn/algo.

● **laugh at** vt to l. at sb/sth reírse de algn/algo.

laughter ['lɑːftə^r] risa f.

launch [lɔːntʃ] **1** n (vessel) lancha f; (of product) lanzamiento m. **2** vt (rocket, new product) lanzar; (ship) botar; (film, play) estrenar.

launderette [lɔːndə'ret], US **Laundromat**^(R) ['lɔːndrəmæt] lavandería f automática.

laundry ['lɔːndrɪ] (place) lavandería f; (dirty clothes) ropa f sucia; **to do the l.** lavar la ropa.

lavatory ['lævətərɪ] retrete m; (room) baño m; **public l.** servicios mpl.

law [lɔː] ley f; (as subject) derecho m.

law court tribunal m de justicia.

lawn [lɔːn] césped m.

lawnmower ['lɔːnməʊə^r] cortacésped m.

lawsuit pleito m.

lawyer ['lɔːjə^r] abogado,-a mf.

lay* [leɪ] vt (place) poner; (cable, trap) tender; (foundations) echar; (table,

eggs) poner; (*set down*) asentar.
● **lay down** *vt* (*put down*) poner.
● **lay off** *vt* (*dismiss*) despedir.
● **lay on** *vt* (*provide*) provecr de; (*food*) preparar.
● **lay out** *vt* (*open out*) extender; (*arrange*) disponer; (*ideas*) exponer; (*spend*) gastar.
layabout vago,-a *mf*.
lay-by área *f* de descanso.
layer ['leɪə'] capa *f*.
layout (*arrangement*) disposición *f*; (*presentation*) presentación *f*.
lazy ['leɪzɪ] *a* vago,-a.
lead[1] [led] (*metal*) plomo *m*; (*in pencil*) mina *f*.
lead[2] [liːd] **1** *n* (*front position*) delantera *f*; (*advantage*) ventaja *f*; (*leash*) correa *f*; (*electric cable*) cable *m;* **to be in the l.** ir en cabeza; **to take the l.** (*in race*) tomar la delantera; (*score*) adelantarse. **2** *vt** (*conduct*) conducir; (*be the leader of*) dirigir; (*life*) llevar; **to l. sb to think sth** hacer a algn pensar algo. **3** *vi** (*road*) llevar (**to** a); (*in race*) llevar la delantera.
● **lead away** *vt* llevar.
● **lead to** *vt* (*result in*) dar lugar a
leader jefe,-a *mf*; (*political*) líder *mf*.
leading *a* (*main*) principal.
leaf [liːf] (*pl* **leaves** [liːvz]) hoja *f*.
leaflet folleto *m*.
leak [liːk] **1** *n* (*of gas, liquid*) escape *m*; (*of information*) filtración *f*. **2** *vi* (*gas, liquid*) escaparse. **3** *vt* (*information*) filtrar.
lean* [liːn] **1** *vi* inclinarse; (*thing*) estar inclinado; **to l. on/against** apoyarse en/contra. **2** *vt* apoyar (**on** en).
● **lean forward** *vi* inclinarse hacia delante.
● **lean over** *vi* inclinarse.
leap [liːp] **1** *n* (*jump*) salto *m*. **2** *vi** saltar.
leap year año *m* bisiesto.
learn* [lɜːn] **1** *vt* aprender; (*find out about*) enterarse de; **to l. (how) to ski** aprender a esquiar. **2** *vi* aprender; **to l. about** *or* **of** (*find out*) enterarse de.
learner (*beginner*) principiante *mf*.
learning (*knowledge*) conocimientos *mpl*; (*erudition*) saber *m*.
leash [liːʃ] correa *f*.
least [liːst] **1** *a* menor. **2** *adv* menos. **3** *n* lo menos; **at l.** por lo menos.
leather ['leðə'] **1** *n* (*fine*) piel *f*; (*heavy*) cuero *m*. **2** *a* de piel.
leave[1]* [liːv] **1** *vt* dejar; (*go away from*) abandonar; (*go out of*) salir de; **I have two biscuits left** me quedan dos galletas. **2** *vi* (*go away*) irse, marcharse; (*go out*) salir; **the train leaves in five minutes** el tren sale

dentro de cinco minutos.
- **leave behind** *vt* dejar atrás.
- **leave on** *vt* (*clothes*) dejar puesto,-a; (*lights, radio*) dejar encendido,-a.
- **leave out** *vt* (*omit*) omitir.

leave² (*time off*) vacaciones *fpl*.

lecture ['lektʃə'] **1** *n* conferencia *f*; (*at university*) clase *f*; **to give a l.** dar una conferencia (**on** sobre). **2** *vi* (*at university*) dar clases.

lecturer conferenciante *mf*; (*at university*) profesor,-a *mf*.

leek [li:k] puerro *m*.

left¹ [left] **1** *a* izquierdo,-a. **2** *adv* a la izquierda. **3** *n* izquierda *f*; **on the l.** a mano izquierda.

left² *pt & pp* of **leave¹**.

left-hand *a* **on the l. side** a mano izquierda.

left-'handed *a* zurdo,-a.

left-luggage *Br* **l. office** consigna *f*.

leftovers *npl* sobras *fpl*.

leg [leg] pierna *f*; (*of animal, table*) pata *f*.

legal ['li:gəl] *a* legal; (*permitted by law*) lícito,-a; (*relating to the law*) jurídico,-a.

legend ['ledʒənd] leyenda *f*.

legible ['ledʒəbəl] *a* legible.

leisure ['leʒə', *US* 'li:ʒə'] ocio *m*; (*free time*) tiempo *m* libre; **l. activities** pasatiempos *mpl*.

lemon ['lemən] limón *m*; **l. juice** zumo *m* de limón; **l. tea** té *m* con limón.

lemonade [lemə'neɪd] gaseosa *f*.

lend* [lend] *vt* prestar.

length [leŋθ] largo *m*; (*duration*) duración *f*; (*section of string etc*) trozo *m*.

lengthen 1 *vt* alargar; (*lifetime*) prolongar. **2** *vi* alargarse; (*lifetime*) prolongarse.

lenient ['li:nɪənt] *a* indulgente.

lens [lenz] (*of spectacles*) lente *f*; (*of camera*) objetivo *m*.

lentil ['lentɪl] lenteja *f*.

leopard ['lepəd] leopardo *m*.

leotard ['li:ətɑ:d] mallas *fpl*.

less [les] menos; **l. and l.** cada vez menos; **a year l. two days** un año menos dos días.

lesson ['lesən] clase *f*; (*in book*) lección *f*.

let* [let] **1** *vt* dejar; (*rent out*) alquilar; **to l. sb do sth** dejar a algn hacer algo; **to l. go of sth** soltar algo; **to l. sb know** avisar a algn. **2** *v aux* **l. him wait** que espere; **l.'s go!** ¡vamos!, ¡vámonos!

● **let down** vt (lower) bajar; (fail) defraudar.
● **let in** vt (admit) dejar entrar.
● **let off** vt (bomb) hacer explotar; (fireworks) hacer estallar; **to l. sb off** (pardon) perdonar.
● **let out** vt (release) soltar; (news) divulgar; (secret) revelar; (cry) soltar.
● **let up** vi (cease) cesar.
letdown decepción f.
letter ['letəʳ] (of alphabet) letra f; (written message) carta f.
letter box buzón m.
lettuce ['letɪs] lechuga f.
level ['levəl] **1** a (flat) llano,-a; (even) nivelado,-a; **to be l. with** estar a nivel de. **2** n nivel m; **to be on a l. with** estar al mismo nivel que.
level crossing paso m a nivel.
lever ['liːvəʳ] palanca f.
liable ['laɪəbəl] a **the river is l. to freeze** el río tiene tendencia a helarse.
liar ['laɪəʳ] mentiroso,-a mf.
liberty ['lɪbətɪ] libertad f; **to be at l. to say sth** ser libre de decir algo.
librarian [laɪ'breərɪən] bibliotecario,-a mf.
library ['laɪbrərɪ] biblioteca f.
Libyan ['lɪbɪən] a & n libio,-a (mf).
lice [laɪs] npl see **louse**.
licence ['laɪsəns] (permit) permiso m; **l. number** (of car) matrícula f.
lick [lɪk] vt lamer.
licorice ['lɪkərɪs] US regaliz m.
lid [lɪd] (cover) tapa f; (of eye) párpado m.
lie¹ [laɪ] **1** vi mentir. **2** n mentira f.
lie²* vi (act) acostarse; (state) estar acostado,-a.
● **lie about** or **around** vi (person) estar tumbado,-a; (things) estar tirado,-a.
● **lie down** vi acostarse.
life [laɪf] (pl lives [laɪvz]) vida f; **to come to l.** cobrar vida.
life belt cinturón m salvavidas.
lifeboat (on ship) bote m salvavidas; (on shore) lancha f de socorro.
lifeguard socorrista mf.
life insurance seguro m de vida.
life jacket chaleco m salvavidas.
lifetime vida f; **in his l.** durante su vida.
lift [lɪft] **1** vt levantar; (head etc) alzar; (pick up) coger. **2** n Br (elevator) ascensor m; **to give sb a l.** llevar a algn en coche.
● **lift down** vt bajar.
● **lift out** vt (take out) sacar.
● **lift up** vt levantar.

light¹ [laɪt] **1** n luz f; (lamp) lámpara f; (headlight) faro m; **to set l. to sth** prender fuego a algo; **have you got a l.?** ¿tiene fuego? **2** vt* (illuminate) iluminar; (ignite) encender. **3** a claro,-a; (hair) rubio,-a.

● **light up 1** vt iluminar. **2** vi iluminarse; (light cigarette) encender un cigarrillo.

light² **1** a ligero,-a; (rain) fino,-a. **2** adv **to travel l.** ir ligero,-a de equipaje.

light bulb bombilla f.

lighter (cigarette) l. mechero m.

lighthouse faro m.

lighting (act) iluminación f.

lightning ['laɪtnɪŋ] (flash) relámpago m; (which hits the earth) rayo m.

like¹ [laɪk] **1** prep (similar to) parecido,-a a; (the same as) igual que; **l. that** así; **what's he l.?** ¿cómo es?; **to feel l.** tener ganas de. **2** a parecido,-a; (equal) igual.

like² **1** vt do you l. chocolate? ¿te gusta el chocolate?; **he likes dancing** le gusta bailar; **I would l. a coffee** quisiera un café; **would you l. to go now?** ¿quieres que nos vayamos ya? **2** vi querer; **as you l.** como quieras.

likeable a simpático,-a.

likelihood ['laɪklɪhʊd] probabilidad f.

likely **1** a probable; **he's l. to cause trouble** es probable que cause problemas. **2** adv probablemente; **not l.!** ¡ni hablar!

likewise adv (also) asimismo.

liking ['laɪkɪŋ] (for thing) afición f; (for person) simpatía f; (for friend) cariño m.

lily ['lɪlɪ] lirio m.

limb [lɪm] miembro m.

lime [laɪm] (fruit) lima f; (tree) limero m.

limit ['lɪmɪt] **1** n límite m; (maximum) máximo m; (minimum) mínimo m. **2** vt (restrict) limitar (to a).

limousine ['lɪməziːn] limusina f.

limp [lɪmp] **1** vi cojear. **2** n cojera f.

line¹ [laɪn] línea f; (straight) raya f; (of writing) renglón m; (of poetry) verso m; (row) fila f; (of trees) hilera f; US (queue) cola f; (rope) cuerda f; (telephone) línea f; (of railway) vía f.

line² vt (clothes) forrar.

● **line up 1** vt (arrange in rows) poner en fila; **he has something lined up for this evening** tiene algo organizado para esta noche. **2** vi (people) ponerse en fila; (in queue) hacer cola.

linen ['lɪnɪn] (sheets etc) ropa f blanca.

liner ['laɪnəʳ] transatlántico m.

lining ['laɪnɪŋ] forro m.

link [lɪŋk] **1** n (of chain) eslabón m; (connection) conexión f. **2** vt unir.
● **link up** vi unirse; (meet) encontrarse.

lino ['laɪnəʊ] linóleo m.

lion ['laɪən] león m.

lip [lɪp] labio m.

lipstick lápiz m de labios.

liqueur [lɪ'kjʊəʳ] licor m.

liquid ['lɪkwɪd] a & n líquido,-a (m).

liquor ['lɪkəʳ] US bebidas fpl alcohólicas.

liquorice ['lɪkərɪs] regaliz m.

list [lɪst] **1** n lista f; (catalogue) catálogo m. **2** vt (make a list of) hacer una lista de; (put on a list) poner en una lista.

listen ['lɪsən] vi escuchar; (pay attention) prestar atención.
● **listen out** vi estar atento,-a (for a).

listener oyente mf.

liter ['liːtəʳ] US litro m.

literary ['lɪtərərɪ] a literario,-a.

literature ['lɪtərɪtʃəʳ] literatura f; (documentation) folleto m informativo.

litre ['liːtəʳ] litro m.

litter ['lɪtəʳ] (rubbish) basura f; (papers) papeles mpl; (offspring) camada f.

litter bin papelera f.

little ['lɪtəl] **1** a pequeño,-a; **a l. dog** un perrito; **a l. house** una casita. **2** pron poco m; **save me a l.** guárdame un poco; **a l. cheese** un poco de queso. **3** adv poco; **l. by l.** poco a poco; **as l. as possible** lo menos posible; **l. milk/money** poca leche/poco dinero.

live¹ [lɪv] vti vivir; **to l. an interesting life** llevar una vida interesante.

live² [laɪv] a (TV etc) en directo; (wire) con corriente.
● **live off** or **on** vt vivir de.
● **live through** vt vivir (durante).
● **live together** vi vivir juntos.
● **live up to** vt **to l. up to expectations** estar a la altura de lo que se esperaba.
● **live with** vt vivir con.

lively ['laɪvlɪ] a (person) vivo,-a; (place) animado,-a.

liver ['lɪvəʳ] hígado m.

living ['lɪvɪŋ] **1** a vivo,-a. **2** n vida f; **to earn** or **make one's l.** ganarse la vida.

living room sala f de estar.

lizard ['lɪzəd] (large) lagarto m; (small) lagartija f.

load [ləʊd] **1** n (cargo) carga f; (weight) peso m; fam **loads (of)** montones de; *fam* **that's a l. of rubbish!** ¡no son más que tonterías! **2** *vt* cargar.

● **load up** *vti* cargar.

loaf [ləʊf] (*pl* **loaves**) pan *m*.

loan [ləʊn] **1** *n* (*to individual*) préstamo *m*; (*to company etc*) empréstito *m*; **on l.** prestado,-a. **2** *vt* prestar.

lobby ['lɒbɪ] (*hall*) vestíbulo *m*.

lobster ['lɒbstə] langosta *f*.

local ['ləʊkəl] *a* local; (*person*) del pueblo.

local area network red *f* local.

locally *adv* en *or* de la localidad.

locate [ləʊ'keɪt] *vt* (*situate*) ubicar; (*find*) localizar.

location ubicación *f*.

lock[1] [lɒk] **1** *n* (*on door etc*) cerradura *f*; (*bolt*) cerrojo *m*; (*padlock*) candado *m*; (*on canal*) esclusa *f*. **2** *vt* cerrar con llave *or* cerrojo *or* candado.

lock[2] (*of hair*) mechón *m*.

● **lock in** *vt* (*person*) encerrar a.

● **lock out** *vt* (*person*) cerrar la puerta a.

● **lock up** *vt* (*house*) cerrar; (*in jail*) meter en la cárcel.

locker (*cupboard*) armario *m* ropero.

locket ['lɒkɪt] medallón *m*.

lodger huésped,-a *mf*.

lodging ['lɒdʒɪŋ] alojamiento *m*; **l. house** casa *f* de huéspedes.

loft [lɒft] desván *m*.

log [lɒg] (*wood*) tronco *m*; (*for fire*) leño *m*.

logical ['lɒdʒɪkəl] *a* lógico,-a.

lollipop ['lɒlɪpɒp], **lolly** ['lɒlɪ] chupachup[R] *m*; **ice(d) l.** polo *m*.

loneliness soledad *f*.

lonely ['ləʊnlɪ] *a* (*person*) solo,-a; (*place*) solitario,-a.

long[1] [lɒŋ] **1** *a* (*size*) largo,-a; (*time*) mucho,-a; **it's three metres l.** tiene tres metros de largo; **it's a l. way** está lejos; **at l. last** por fin; **how l. is the film?** ¿cuánto tiempo dura la película? **2** *adv* mucho tiempo; **as l. as the exhibition lasts** mientras dure la exposición; **as l. as** *or* **so l. as you don't mind** con tal de que no te importe; **before l.** dentro de poco; **how l. have you been here?** ¿cuánto tiempo llevas aquí?

long-distance *a* de larga distancia; **l. call** conferencia interurbana.

long-term *a* a largo plazo.

loo [luː] *fam* wáter *m*.

look [lʊk] **1** *n* (*glance*) mirada *f*; (*appearance*) aspecto *m*; **to take a l. at** echar un vistazo a. **2** *vi* mirar; (*seem*) parecer; **he looks well** tiene buena cara; **she looks like her father** se parece a su padre.

● **look after** *vt* ocuparse de.

- **look at** *vt* mirar.
- **look for** *vt* buscar.
- **look forward to** *vt* esperar con ilusión; **I l. forward to hearing from you** (*in letter*) espero noticias suyas.
- **look into** *vt* investigar.
- **look onto** *vt* dar a.
- **look out** *vi* **the bedroom looks out onto the garden** el dormitorio da al jardín; **l. out!** ¡cuidado!, ¡ojo!
- **look over** *vt* (*examine*) revisar; (*place*) inspeccionar.
- **look round 1** *vi* mirar alrededor; (*turn head*) volver la cabeza. **2** *vt* (*house, shop*) ver.
- **look up 1** *vi* (*glance upwards*) alzar la vista. **2** *vt* (*look for*) buscar.

lookout (*person*) centinela *mf*; (*place*) mirador *m*; **to be on the l. for** estar al acecho de.

loose [luːs] **1** *a* (*not secure*) flojo,-a; (*papers, hair, clothes*) suelto,-a; (*baggy*) holgado,-a; (*not packaged*) a granel; **to set sb l.** soltar a algn; **l. change** suelto *m*. **2** *n* **to be on the l.** (*prisoner*) andar suelto.

loosen *vt* aflojar; (*belt*) desabrochar.

lord [lɔːd] señor *m*; (*British peer*) lord *m*; **the House of Lords** la Cámara de los Lores.

lorry ['lɒrɪ] *Br* camión *m*; **l. load** carga *f*.

lorry driver camionero,-a *mf*.

lose* [luːz] *vti* perder; **to l. to sb** perder contra algn.

loser perdedor,-a *mf*.

loss [lɒs] pérdida *f*.

lost [lɒst] *a* perdido,-a; **to get l.** perderse; **get l.!** *fam* ¡vete a la porra!

lost property office, *US* **lost and found department** oficina *f* de objetos perdidos.

lot [lɒt] **a l. of** (*much*) mucho,-a; (*many*) muchos,-as; **he feels a l. better** se encuentra mucho mejor; **lots of** montones de; **what a l. of bottles!** ¡qué cantidad de botellas!

lotion ['ləʊʃən] loción *f*.

lottery ['lɒtərɪ] lotería *f*.

loud [laʊd] **1** *a* (*voice*) alto,-a; (*noise*) fuerte; (*protests, party*) ruidoso,-a. **2** *adv* **to read/think out l.** leer/pensar en voz alta.

loudly *adv* (*to speak etc*) en voz alta.

loudspeaker altavoz *m*.

lounge [laʊndʒ] *Br* salón *m*.

lousy ['laʊzɪ] *a fam* fatal; **a l. trick** una cochinada.

love [lʌv] **1** *n* amor *m*; **to be in l. with sb** estar enamorado,-a de algn; **to make l.** hacer el amor. **2** *vt* (*person*) querer; (*sport etc*) ser muy aficionado,-a a; **he loves cooking** le encanta cocinar.

lovely *a* (*charming*) encantador,-a; (*beautiful*) precioso,-a; (*delicious*) riquísimo,-a.

lover (*enthusiast*) aficionado,-a *mf*.

loving *a* cariñoso,-a.

low [ləʊ] **1** *a* bajo,-a; (*poor*) pobre; (*reprehensible*) malo,-a; **to feel l.** sentirse deprimido,-a. **2** *adv* bajo.

lower 1 *a* inferior. **2** *vt* bajar; (*reduce*) reducir; (*price*) rebajar.

low-fat *a* (*milk*) desnatado,-a; (*food*) light *inv*.

loyal ['lɔɪəl] *a* leal.

lozenge ['lɒzɪndʒ] pastilla *f*.

LP [el'pi:] LP *m*, elepé *m*.

luck [lʌk] suerte *f*; **bad l.!** ¡mala suerte!; **good l.!** ¡(buena) suerte!

luckily *adv* afortunadamente.

lucky *a* (*person*) afortunado,-a; (*charm*) de la suerte; **that was l.** ha sido una suerte.

ludicrous ['lu:dɪkrəs] *a* ridículo,-a.

luggage ['lʌgɪdʒ] equipaje *m*.

lukewarm ['lu:kwɔ:m] *a* (*water etc*) tibio,-a.

lullaby ['lʌləbaɪ] nana *f*.

luminous ['lu:mɪnəs] *a* luminoso,-a.

lump [lʌmp] (*of coal etc*) trozo *m*; (*of sugar, earth*) terrón *m*; (*swelling*) bulto *m*.

lump sum suma *f* global.

lunatic ['lu:nətɪk] *a & n* loco,-a (*mf*).

lunch [lʌntʃ] comida *f*, almuerzo *m*; **l. hour** hora *f* de comer.

luncheon voucher vale *m* de comida.

lung [lʌŋ] pulmón *m*.

luxurious [lʌg'zjʊərɪəs] *a* lujoso,-a.

luxury ['lʌkʃərɪ] lujo *m*.

M

mac [mæk] (*raincoat*) impermeable *m*.

mac(c)aroni [mækə'rəʊnɪ] macarrones *mpl*.

machine [mə'ʃiːn] máquina *f*.

machinery (*machines*) maquinaria *f*; (*workings of machine*) mecanismo *m*.

mackerel ['mækrəl] *inv* caballa *f*.

mac(k)intosh ['mækɪntoʃ] impermeable *m*.

mad [mæd] *a* loco,-a; **to be m. about sth/sb** estar loco,-a por algo/algn; **to be m. at sb** estar enfadado,-a con algn.

madam ['mædəm] señora *f*.

made [meɪd] *pt & pp of* **make.**

madman loco *m*.

madness locura *f*.

magazine [mægə'ziːn] (*periodical*) revista *f*.

maggot ['mægət] gusano *m*.

magic ['mædʒɪk] **1** *n* magia *f*. **2** *a* mágico,-a; **m. wand** varita *f* mágica.

magical *a* mágico,-a.

ma'gician (*wizard*) mago,-a *mf*; (*conjuror*) prestidigitador,-a *mf*.

magistrate ['mædʒɪstreɪt] juez,-a *mf* de paz.

magnet ['mægnɪt] imán *m*.

magnificent [mæg'nɪfɪsənt] *a* magnífico,-a.

magnifying glass ['mægnɪfaɪɪŋglɑːs] lupa *f*.

mahogany [mə'hɒgənɪ] caoba *f*.

maid [meɪd] criada *f*.

mail [meɪl] **1** *n* correo *m*; **2** *vt* (*post*) echar (al buzón).

mailbox *US* buzón *m*.

mailman *US* cartero *m*.

main [meɪn] **1** *a* (*problem, door etc*) principal; (*square, mast, sail*) mayor; (*office*) central; **the m. thing is to keep calm** lo esencial es mantener la calma; **m. road** carretera *f* principal. **2** *n* (*pipe, wire*) conducto *m* principal; **the mains** (*water or gas system*) la conducción; (*electrical*) la red (eléctrica).

mainly *adv* principalmente; (*for the most part*) en su mayoría.

maintain [meɪn'teɪn] *vt* (*road, machine*) conservar en buen estado; **to m. that** sostener que.

maisonette [meɪzə'net] dúplex *m*.

maître d' [metrə'diː] *US* jefe *mf* de sala.

maize [meɪz] maíz *m*.

majesty ['mædʒɪstɪ] majestad *f*.

major ['meɪdʒə'] **1** *a* principal; (*contribution, operation*) importante. **2** *n* *(officer)* comandante *m*.

majorette majorette *f*.

majority [məˈdʒɒrɪtɪ] mayoría *f*.

make* [meɪk] **1** *vt* hacer; *(manufacture)* fabricar; *(clothes, curtains)* confeccionar; *(meal)* preparar; *(decision)* tomar; *(earn)* ganar; **to be made of** ser de; **to m. sb do sth** obligar a algn a hacer algo; **to m. do with sth** arreglárselas con algo; **I don't know what to m. of it** no sé qué pensar de eso; **we've made it!** *(succeeded)* ¡lo hemos conseguido! **2** *n* *(brand)* marca *f*.

● **make for** *vt* *(move towards)* dirigirse hacia.

● **make out 1** *vt* *(list, receipt)* hacer; *(cheque)* extender; *(perceive)* distinguir; *(understand)* entender; *(claim)* pretender. **2** *vi* **how did you m. out?** ¿qué tal te fue?

● **make up** *vt* *(parcel, list)* hacer; *(assemble)* montar; *(invent)* inventar; *(apply cosmetics to)* maquillar; *(one's face)* maquillarse; *(loss)* compensar; **to m. it up (with sb)** hacer las paces (con algn).

● **make up for** *vt* *(loss, damage)* compensar por; *(lost time, mistake)* recuperar.

maker fabricante *mf*.

make-up *(cosmetics)* maquillaje *m*.

malaria [məˈleərɪə] malaria *f*.

male [meɪl] **1** *a* *(animal, plant)* macho; *(person)* varón; *(sex)* masculino. **2** *n* *(person)* varón *m*; *(animal, plant)* macho *m*.

malice [ˈmælɪs] *(wickedness)* malicia *f*.

malicious *a* *(wicked)* malévolo,-a.

mall [mɔːl] *(shopping)* centro *m* comercial.

mammal [ˈmæməl] mamífero *m*.

man [mæn] *(pl* **men**) hombre *m*; **old m.** viejo *m*; **young m.** joven *m*; *(humanity)* el hombre; *(human being)* ser *m* humano.

manage [ˈmænɪdʒ] **1** *vt* *(company, household)* llevar; *(money, affairs, person)* manejar; *(achieve)* conseguir; **to m. to do sth** lograr hacer algo. **2** *vi* *(cope physically)* poder; *(financially)* arreglárselas.

management dirección *f*.

manager *(of company, bank)* director,-a *mf*; *(of department)* jefe,-a *mf*.

manageress *(of shop, restaurant)* encargada *f*; *(of company)* directora *f*.

managing director director,-a *mf* gerente.

mane [meɪn] *(of horse)* crin *f*; *(of lion)* melena *f*.

maneuver [məˈnuːvəʳ] *n & vt US* = **manoeuvre**.

maniac [ˈmeɪnɪæk] maníaco,-a *mf*; *fam* loco,-a *mf*.

man-made *a* *(lake)* artificial; *(fibres, fabric)* sintético,-a.

manner [ˈmænəʳ] *(way, method)* manera *f*, modo *m*; *(way of behaving)* forma *f* de ser; **(good) manners** buenos modales *mpl*; **bad manners** falta *f* *sing* de educación.

manoeuvre [mə'nuːvəʳ] **1** *n* maniobra *f*. **2** *vt* maniobrar; *(person)* manejar. **3** *vi* maniobrar.

mantelpiece ['mæntəlpiːs] *(shelf)* repisa *f* de chimenea; *(fireplace)* chimenea *f*.

manual ['mænjʊəl] *a* & *n* manual (*m*).

manufacture [mænjʊ'fæktʃəʳ] **1** *vt* fabricar. **2** *n* fabricación *f*.

manufacturer fabricante *mf*.

manure [mə'njʊəʳ] estiércol *m*.

many ['menɪ] **1** *a* muchos,-as; **a great m.** muchísimos,-as; **as m. ... as ...** tantos,-as ... como ...; **how m. days?** ¿cuántos días?; **not m. books** pocos libros; **so m. flowers!** ¡cuántas flores!; **too m.** demasiados,-as. **2** *pron* muchos,-as.

map [mæp] *(of country)* mapa *m*; *(of town, bus)* plano *m*.

marathon ['mærəθən] maratón *m or f*.

marble ['mɑːbəl] *(stone)* mármol *m*; *(glass ball)* canica *f*.

March [mɑːtʃ] marzo *m*.

march 1 *n* marcha *f*. **2** *vi* marchar.

mare [meəʳ] yegua *f*.

margarine [mɑːdʒə'riːn] margarina *f*.

margin ['mɑːdʒɪn] margen *m*.

mark¹ [mɑːk] **1** *n* *(trace)* huella *f*; *(stain)* mancha *f*; *(symbol)* signo *m*; *(sign, token)* señal *f*; *(in exam etc)* nota *f*. **2** *vt* *(make mark on)* marcar; *(stain)* manchar; *(exam)* corregir.

● **mark out** *vt* *(area)* delimitar.

marker *(pen)* rotulador *m*.

market ['mɑːkɪt] mercado *m*.

marketing marketing *m*.

marmalade ['mɑːməleɪd] mermelada *f* (de cítricos).

marriage ['mærɪdʒ] *(state)* matrimonio *m*; *(wedding)* boda *f*.

married ['mærɪd] *a* casado,-a.

marrow ['mærəʊ] *(bone)* **m.** médula *f*; *(vegetable)* calabacín *m*.

marry ['mærɪ] *vt* casarse con; *(priest)* casar; **to get married** casarse.

marsh [mɑːʃ] pantano *m*; **salt m.** marisma *f*.

Martian ['mɑːʃən] *n* & *a* marciano,-a (*mf*).

marvellous, *US* **marvelous** ['mɑːvələs] *a* maravilloso,-a.

marzipan ['mɑːzɪpæn] mazapán *m*.

mascara [mæ'skɑːrə] rímel *m*.

mascot ['mæskət] mascota *f*.

masculine ['mæskjʊlɪn] *a* masculino,-a.

mashed potatoes [mæʃd] *npl* puré *m* de patatas.

mask [mɑːsk] máscara f.

mass¹ [mæs] (in church) misa f; **to say m.** decir misa.

mass² 1 n masa f; (large quantity) montón m; (of people) multitud f. 2 a masivo,-a.

massacre ['mæsəkəʳ] 1 n masacre f. 2 vt masacrar.

massage ['mæsɑːʒ] 1 n masaje m. 2 vt dar masaje a.

masseur [mæ'sɜːʳ] masajista m.

masseuse [mæ'sɜːz] masajista f.

massive ['mæsɪv] a enorme.

mast [mɑːst] mástil m; (radio etc) torre f.

master ['mɑːstəʳ] 1 n (of dog, servant) amo m; (of household) señor m; (teacher) profesor m; **m.'s degree** ≈ máster m. 2 vt (person, situation) dominar; (subject, skill) llegar a dominar.

masterpiece obra f maestra.

mat [mæt] (rug) alfombrilla f; (doormat) felpudo m; (rush mat) estera f.

match¹ [mætʃ] cerilla f.

match² 1 n (sport) partido m. 2 vt (be in harmony with) armonizar con; (colours, clothes) hacer juego con; **they are well matched** (teams) van iguales; (couple) hacen buena pareja. 3 vi (harmonize) hacer juego.

● **match up to** vt estar a la altura de.

matchbox caja f de cerillas.

matching a a juego.

matchstick cerilla f.

mate [meɪt] (at school) compañero,-a mf; (at work) colega mf; (friend) amigo,-a mf.

material [mə'tɪərɪəl] (substance) materia f; (cloth) tejido m; **materials** (ingredients, equipment) materiales mpl.

maternal [mə'tɜːnəl] a maternal; (uncle etc) materno,-a.

maternity [mə'tɜːnɪtɪ] maternidad f.

maternity hospital maternidad f.

math [mæθ] US matemáticas fpl.

mathematical a matemático,-a.

mathematics [mæθə'mætɪks] matemáticas fpl.

maths [mæθs] matemáticas fpl.

matinée ['mætɪneɪ] (cinema) sesión f de tarde; (theatre) función f de tarde.

matt [mæt] a mate.

matter ['mætəʳ] 1 n (affair, question) asunto m; (problem) problema m; (substance) materia f; **what's the m.?** ¿qué pasa?. 2 vi importar; **it doesn't m.** no importa, da igual.

mattress ['mætrɪs] colchón m.

mature [mə'tʃʊəʳ] a maduro,-a.

maximum ['mæksɪməm] **1** *n* máximo *m*. **2** *a* máximo,-a.

may [meɪ] *v aux* (*pt* **might**) (*possibility, probability*) poder, ser posible; **he m.** *or* **might come** puede que venga; **you m.** *or* **might as well stay** más vale que te quedes. ‖ (*permission*) poder; **m. I?** ¿me permite?; **you m. smoke** pueden fumar. ‖ (*wish*) ojalá (+ *subjunctive*); **m. you always be happy!** ¡ojalá seas siempre feliz!

May mayo *m*; **M. Day** el Primero *or* el Uno de Mayo.

maybe *adv* quizá(s), tal vez.

mayonnaise [meɪə'neɪz] mayonesa *f*.

mayor [meəʳ] (*man*) alcalde *m*; (*woman*) alcaldesa *f*.

mayoress alcaldesa *f*.

maze [meɪz] laberinto *m*.

me [miː] *pron* (*as object*) me; **he gave it to me** me lo dio; **listen to me** escúchame; **she knows me** me conoce. ‖ (*after prep*) mí; **it's for me** es para mí; **with me** conmigo. ‖ (*emphatic*) yo; **it's me** soy yo; **what about me?** ¿y yo, qué?

meadow ['medəʊ] prado *m*.

meal [miːl] (*food*) comida *f*.

mean[1] * [miːn] *vt* (*signify*) querer decir; (*intend*) pensar; (*wish*) querer; **what do you m. by that?** ¿qué quieres decir con eso?; **I m. it** (te) lo digo en serio; **she was meant to arrive on the 7th** tenía que *or* debía llegar el día 7; **they m. well** tienen buenas intenciones; **I didn't m. to do it** lo hice sin querer.

mean[2] *a* (*miserly*) tacaño,-a; (*unkind*) malo,-a; (*bad-tempered*) malhumorado,-a.

meaning sentido *m*.

meaningless *a* sin sentido.

meanness (*miserliness*) tacañería *f*; (*nastiness*) maldad *f*.

means [miːnz] *sing or pl* (*method*) medio *m*; *pl* (*resources, wealth*) recursos *mpl* (económicos); **by m. of** por medio de, mediante; **by all m.!** ¡por supuesto!; **by no m.** de ninguna manera.

meantime in the m. mientras tanto.

meanwhile *adv* mientras tanto.

measles ['miːzəlz] sarampión *m*.

measure ['meʒəʳ] **1** *n* medida *f*; (*ruler*) regla *f*. **2** *vt* (*object, area*) medir.
● **measure up** *vi* to **m. up to sth** estar a la altura de algo.

measurement medida *f*.

meat [miːt] carne *f*.

mechanic [mɪ'kænɪk] mecánico,-a *mf*.

mechanical *a* mecánico,-a.

mechanism mecanismo *m*.

medal ['medəl] medalla *f*.

medallist, *US* **medalist** medalla *mf*; **to be a gold m.** ser medalla de oro.

media ['mi:dɪə] *npl* medios *mpl* de comunicación.

medical ['medɪkəl] *a* (*treatment*) médico,-a; (*book*) de medicina.

medication medicación *f*.

medicine ['medɪsɪn] (*science*) medicina *f*; (*drug etc*) medicamento *m*.

medicine cabinet botiquín *m*.

medieval [medɪ'i:vəl] *a* medieval.

Mediterranean [medɪtə'reɪnɪən] 1 *a* mediterráneo,-a. 2 *n* the M. el Mediterráneo.

medium ['mi:dɪəm] *a* (*average*) mediano,-a.

medium-sized *a* de tamaño mediano.

meet* [mi:t] 1 *vt* (*by chance*) encontrar; (*by arrangement*) reunirse con; (*pass in street etc*) toparse con; (*get to know*) conocer; (*await arrival of*) esperar; (*collect*) ir a buscar; **pleased to m. you!** ¡mucho gusto! 2 *vi* (*by chance*) encontrarse; (*by arrangement*) reunirse; (*formal meeting*) entrevistarse; (*get to know each other*) conocerse.

• **meet with** *vt* (*difficulty*) tropezar con; (*loss*) sufrir; (*success*) tener; (*person*) reunirse con.

meeting (*prearranged*) cita *f*; (*formal*) entrevista *f*; (*of committee etc*) reunión *f*; (*of assembly*) sesión *f*.

melody ['melədɪ] melodía *f*.

melon ['melən] melón *m*.

melt [melt] 1 *vt* (*metal*) fundir. 2 *vi* (*snow*) derretirse; (*metal*) fundirse.

member ['membə'] miembro *mf*; (*of a society*) socio,-a *mf*; (*of party, union*) afiliado,-a *mf*; **M. of Parliament (MP)** diputado,-a *mf*.

memo ['meməʊ] (*official*) memorándum *m*; (*personal*) apunte *m*.

memory ['memərɪ] memoria *f*; (*recollection*) recuerdo *m*.

men [men] *npl see* **man**.

mend [mend] *vt* reparar; (*clothes*) remendar; (*socks etc*) zurcir.

mental ['mentəl] *a* mental; **m. home, m. hospital** hospital *m* psiquiátrico; **m. illness** enfermedad *f* mental.

mentally *adv* **to be m. handicapped** ser un,-a disminuido,-a psíquico,-a.

mention ['menʃən] 1 *n* mención *f*. 2 *vt* mencionar; **don't m. it!** ¡de nada!

menu ['menju:] (*à la carte*) carta *f*; (*fixed meal*) menú *m*; **today's m.** menú del día; (*computer*) menú *m*.

mercy ['mɜ:sɪ] misericordia *f*; **at the m. of** a la merced de.

mere [mɪə'] *a* mero,-a.

merely *adv* simplemente.

merge [mɜ:dʒ] *vi* unirse; (*roads*) converger; (*companies*) fusionarse.

merger (*of companies*) fusión *f*.

merry ['merɪ] *a* alegre; (*tipsy*) achispado,-a; **m. Christmas!** ¡felices

Navidades!

merry-go-round tiovivo *m*.

mesh [meʃ] malla *f*.

mess [mes] (*confusion*) confusión *f*; (*disorder*) desorden *m*; (*mix-up*) lío *m*; (*dirt*) suciedad *f*.

● **mess about, mess around 1** *vt* fastidiar. **2** *vi* (*act the fool*) hacer el tonto.

● **mess about with** *vt* (*fiddle with*) manosear.

● **mess up** *vt* (*make untidy*) desordenar; (*dirty*) ensuciar; (*spoil*) estropear.

message ['mesɪdʒ] recado *m*.

messenger ['mesɪndʒəʳ] mensajero,-a *mf*.

messy *a* (*untidy*) desordenado,-a; (*dirty*) sucio,-a.

metal ['metəl] **1** *n* metal *m*. **2** *a* metálico,-a.

meter[1] ['miːtəʳ] contador *m*.

meter[2] *US* metro *m*.

method ['meθəd] método *m*.

me'thodical *a* metódico,-a.

metre ['miːtəʳ] metro *m*.

metric ['metrɪk] *a* métrico,-a.

Mexican ['meksɪkən] *a & n* mejicano,-a (*mf*) , mexicano,-a (*mf*).

miaow [miːˈaʊ] maullido *m*.

mice [maɪs] *npl see* **mouse.**

microchip ['maɪkrəʊtʃɪp] microchip *m*.

microphone ['maɪkrəfəʊn] micrófono *m*.

microscope ['maɪkrəskəʊp] microscopio *m*.

microwave (oven) ['maɪkrəʊweɪv] (horno *m*) microondas *m inv*.

mid [mɪd] *a* (**in**) **m. afternoon** a media tarde; (**in**) **m. April** a mediados de abril.

midair *a* (*collision, explosion*) en el aire.

midday mediodía *m*.

middle ['mɪdəl] **1** *a* de en medio; **the M. Ages** la Edad Media. **2** *n* medio *m*; (*waist*) cintura *f*; **in the m. of** en medio de; **in the m. of winter** en pleno invierno.

middle-'aged *a* de mediana edad.

middle-'class *a* de clase media.

midnight medianoche *f*.

midst [mɪdst] **in the m. of** en medio de.

midwife comadrona *f*.

might [maɪt] *v aux see* **may.**

mild [maɪld] *a* (*person, character*) apacible; (*climate*) templado,-a; (*punishment*) leve; (*tobacco, taste*) suave.

mile [maɪl] milla *f*; *fam* **miles better** muchísimo mejor.

mileage ['maɪlɪdʒ] kilometraje *m*.

military ['mɪlɪtərɪ] *a* militar.

milk [mɪlk] leche *f*.

milk chocolate chocolate *m* con leche.

milkman lechero *m*.

milk shake batido *m*.

mill [mɪl] (*grinder*) molino *m*; (*for coffee*) molinillo *m*; (*factory*) fábrica *f*.

millimetre, *US* **millimeter** ['mɪlɪmiːtəʳ] milímetro *m*.

million ['mɪljən] millón *m*.

millionaire millonario,-a *mf*.

mime [maɪm] *vt* imitar.

mimic ['mɪmɪk] *vt* imitar.

mince(meat) ['mɪns(miːt)] carne *f* picada.

mincer ['mɪnsəʳ] picadora *f* de carne.

mind [maɪnd] **1** *n* (*intellect*) mente *f*; (*brain*) cabeza *f*; **what kind of car do you have in m.?** ¿en qué clase de coche estás pensando?; **to be in two minds** estar indeciso,-a; **to my m.** a mi parecer. **2** *vt* (*child*) cuidar; (*house*) vigilar; (*be careful of*) tener cuidado con; (*object to*) tener inconveniente en; **m. the step!** ¡ojo con el escalón!; **I wouldn't m. a cup of coffee** me vendría bien un café; **never m.** no importa. **3** *vi* (*object*) **do you m. if I open the window?** ¿le importa que abra la ventana?

minder (*for child*) niñera *f*; (*babysitter*) canguro *mf*.

mine[1] [maɪn] *poss pron* (el) mío, (la) mía, (los) míos, (las) mías; **a friend of m.** un amigo mío; **these gloves are m.** estos guantes son míos; **which is m.?** ¿cuál es el mío?

mine[2] (*for coal etc*) mina *f*.

miner minero,-a *mf*.

mineral ['mɪnərəl] *a* mineral.

mineral water agua *f* mineral.

mini- ['mɪnɪ] *prefix* mini-.

miniature ['mɪnɪtʃəʳ] **1** *n* miniatura *f*. **2** *a* (en) miniatura.

minibus ['mɪnɪbʌs] microbús *m*.

minicab microtaxi *m*.

minimum ['mɪnɪməm] *a* mínimo,-a.

minister ['mɪnɪstəʳ] ministro,-a *mf*; (*of church*) pastor,-a *mf*.

ministry (*political*) ministerio *m*; (*in church*) sacerdocio *m*.

minor ['maɪnəʳ] *a* (*lesser*) menor; (*unimportant*) sin importancia.

minority [maɪˈnɒrɪtɪ] minoría *f*.

mint [mɪnt] (*herb*) menta *f*; (*sweet*) pastilla *f* de menta.

minus ['maɪnəs] *prep* **5 m. 3** 5 menos 3; **m. 10 degrees** 10 grados bajo cero.

minute[1] ['mɪnɪt] minuto *m*; **just a m.** (espera) un momento.

minute[2] [maɪ'njuːt] *a* (*tiny*) diminuto,-a.

miracle ['mɪrəkəl] milagro *m*.

mi'raculous *a* milagroso,-a.

mirror ['mɪrə'] espejo *m*; **rear-view m.** retrovisor *m*.

misbehave [mɪsbɪ'heɪv] *vi* portarse mal.

miscellaneous [mɪsɪ'leɪnɪəs] *a* variado,-a.

mischief ['mɪstʃɪf] (*naughtiness*) travesura *f*; (*evil*) malicia *f*; **to get up to m.** hacer travesuras.

mischievous *a* (*naughty*) travieso,-a; (*playful*) juguetón,-ona; (*wicked*) malicioso,-a.

miser ['maɪzə'] avaro,-a *mf*.

miserable ['mɪzərəbəl] *a* (*sad*) triste; (*wretched*) miserable.

miserly ['maɪzəlɪ] *a* tacaño,-a.

misery ['mɪzərɪ] (*sadness*) tristeza *f*; (*wretchedness*) desgracia *f*; (*suffering*) sufrimiento *m*; (*poverty*) miseria *f*.

misfortune [mɪs'fɔːtʃən] desgracia *f*.

mishap ['mɪshæp] contratiempo *m*.

mislay* [mɪs'leɪ] *vt* extraviar.

mislead* [mɪs'liːd] *vt* despistar; (*deliberately*) engañar.

misleading *a* (*erroneous*) erróneo,-a; (*deliberately*) engañoso,-a.

miss[1] [mɪs] señorita *f*.

miss[2] **1** *vt* (*train etc*) perder; (*opportunity*) dejar pasar; (*regret absence of*) echar de menos; **you have missed the point** no has captado la idea. **2** *vi* (*throw etc*) fallar; (*shot*) errar; **is anything missing?** ¿falta algo?

● **miss out 1** *vt* (*omit*) saltarse; **2** *vi* **don't worry, you're not missing out** no te preocupes, que no te pierdes nada.

● **miss out on** *vt* perderse.

missile ['mɪsaɪl, *US* 'mɪsəl] misil *m*; (*object thrown*) proyectil *m*.

missing *a* (*lost*) perdido,-a; (*disappeared*) desaparecido,-a; (*absent*) ausente; **m. person** desaparecido,-a *mf*; **three cups are m.** faltan tres tazas.

mission ['mɪʃən] misión *f*.

mist [mɪst] (*fog*) niebla *f*; (*thin*) neblina *f*; (*at sea*) bruma *f*.

mistake [mɪ'steɪk] **1** *n* error *m*; **by m.** por equivocación; (*unintentionally*) sin querer; **to make a m.** cometer un error. **2** *vt** (*meaning*) malentender; **to m.** Jack **for Bill** confundir a Jack con Bill.

mistaken *a* erróneo,-a; **you are m.** estás equivocado,-a.

mistakenly *adv* por error.

mistress ['mɪstrɪs] (*of house*) ama *f*; (*primary school*) maestra *f*; (*secondary school*) profesora *f*; (*lover*) amante *f*.

mistrust [mɪs'trʌst] **1** *n* recelo *m*. **2** *vt* desconfiar de.

misty ['mɪstɪ] *a* (*day*) de niebla; (*window etc*) empañado,-a.

misunderstand* [mɪsʌndə'stænd] *vti* malentender.

misunderstanding malentendido *m*; (*disagreement*) desavenencia *f*.

mitten ['mɪtən] manopla *f*.

mix [mɪks] **1** *vt* mezclar. **2** *vi* (*blend*) mezclarse (**with** con).

● **mix up** *vt* (*ingredients*) mezclar bien; (*confuse*) confundir (**with** con); (*papers*) revolver.

mixed [mɪkst] *a* (*assorted*) surtido,-a; (*varied*) variado,-a; (*school*) mixto,-a.

mixer (*for food*) batidora *f*.

mixture mezcla *f*.

mix-up confusión *f*.

moan [məʊn] *vi* (*groan*) gemir; (*complain*) quejarse (**about** de).

mob [mɒb] **1** *n* multitud *f*. **2** *vt* acosar.

mobile ['məʊbaɪl] *a* móvil.

mobile phone teléfono *m* móvil.

model ['mɒdəl] **1** *n* modelo *mf*; (**scale**) **m.** maqueta *f*. **2** *a* (*railway*) en miniatura.

modem ['məʊdem] módem *m*.

moderate ['mɒdərɪt] *a* moderado,-a; (*reasonable*) razonable; (*average*) regular; (*ability*) mediocre.

mode'ration moderación *f*.

modern ['mɒdən] *a* moderno,-a; **m. languages** lenguas *fpl* modernas.

modernize *vt* modernizar.

modest ['mɒdɪst] *a* modesto,-a; (*chaste*) púdico,-a; (*price*) módico,-a; (*success*) discreto,-a.

modesty (*humility*) modestia *f*; (*chastity*) pudor *m*.

modifi'cation modificación *f*.

modify ['mɒdɪfaɪ] *vt* modificar.

moist [mɔɪst] *a* húmedo,-a.

moisture humedad *f*.

mold [məʊld] *US* = **mould.**

mole¹ [məʊl] (*beauty spot*) lunar *m*.

mole² (*animal*) topo *m*.

mom [mɒm] *US fam* mamá *f*.

moment ['məʊmənt] momento *m*.

Monday ['mʌndɪ] lunes *m*.

money ['mʌnɪ] dinero *m*.

money order giro *m* postal.

monitor ['mɒnɪtə'] (*of computer*) monitor *m*.

monk [mʌŋk] monje *m*.

monkey ['mʌŋkɪ] mono *m*.

monopolize [mə'nɒpəlaɪz] *vt* (*attention etc*) acaparar.

monotonous *a* monótono,-a.

monotony [mə'nɒtənɪ] monotonía *f*.

monster ['mɒnstə^r] monstruo *m*.

month [mʌnθ] mes *m*.

monthly 1 *a* mensual. **2** *adv* mensualmente.

monument ['mɒnjʊmənt] monumento *m*.

moo [mu:] *vi* mugir.

mood [mu:d] humor *m*; **to be in a good/bad m.** estar de buen/mal humor; **to be in the m. for (doing) sth** estar de humor para (hacer) algo.

moody *a* (*changeable*) de humor variable; (*bad-tempered*) malhumorado,-a.

moon [mu:n] luna *f*.

moonlight luz *f* de la luna.

moor [mʊə^r] (*heath*) páramo *m*.

mop [mɒp] (*for floor*) fregona *f*.

● **mop up** *vt* (*liquids*) limpiar.

moped ['məʊped] ciclomotor *m*.

moral ['mɒrəl] **1** *a* moral. **2** *n* moraleja *f*; **morals** moral *f sing*, moralidad *f sing*.

morale [mə'rɑːl] moral *f*.

more [mɔː^r] **1** *a* más; **and what is m.** y lo que es más; **is there any m. tea?** ¿queda más té?; **I've no m. money** no me queda más dinero. **2** *pron* más; **how many m.?** ¿cuántos más?; **I need some m.** necesito más; **many/much m.** muchos,-as/mucho más; **m. than a hundred** más de cien. **3** *adv* más; **I won't do it any m.** no lo volveré a hacer; **m. and m. difficult** cada vez más difícil; **m. or less** más o menos; **she doesn't live here any m.** ya no vive aquí.

mo'reover *adv* además.

morning ['mɔːnɪŋ] mañana *f*; (*before dawn*) madrugada *f*; **in the m.** por la mañana; **on Monday mornings** los lunes por la mañana; **tomorrow m.** mañana por la mañana.

Moroccan [mə'rɒkən] *a & n* marroquí (*mf*).

mortal ['mɔːtəl] *a & n* mortal (*mf*).

mortgage ['mɔːgɪdʒ] hipoteca *f*.

Moslem ['mɒzləm] *a & n* musulmán,-ana (*mf*).

mosque [mɒsk] mezquita *f*.

mosquito [mɒs'kiːtəʊ] (*pl* mosquitoes) mosquito *m*.

moss [mɒs] musgo *m*.

most [məʊst] **1** *a* (*greatest in quantity etc*) más; (*the majority of*) la mayor parte de; **this house suffered (the) m. damage** esta casa fue la más afectada; **who made (the) m. mistakes?** ¿quién cometió más errores?; **m. of the time** la mayor parte del tiempo; **m. people** la mayoría de la gente. **2** *pron* (*greatest part*) la mayor parte; (*greatest number*) lo máximo; (*the majority of people*) la mayoría; **at the (very) m.** como máximo. **3** *adv* más; **the m. intelligent student** el estudiante más inteligente; **what I like m.** lo que más me gusta; **m. of all** sobre todo.

mostly *adv* (*chiefly*) en su mayor parte; (*generally*) generalmente; (*usually*) normalmente.

motel [məʊ'tel] motel *m*.

moth [mɒθ] mariposa *f* nocturna; **clothes m.** polilla *f*.

mother ['mʌðə'] madre *f*; **M.'s Day** Día *m* de la Madre.

mother-in-law suegra *f*.

motion ['məʊʃən] **1** *n* (*movement*) movimiento *m*; (*gesture*) ademán *m*. **2** *vi* **to m. (to) sb to do sth** hacer señas a algn para que haga algo.

motivated *a* motivado,-a.

motive ['məʊtɪv] (*reason*) motivo *m*.

motor ['məʊtə'] (*engine*) motor *m*.

motorbike moto(cicleta) *f*.

motorboat (lancha) motora *f*.

motorcar automóvil *m*.

motorcycle motocicleta *f*.

motorcyclist motociclista *mf*.

motorist automovilista *mf*.

motorway *Br* autopista *f*.

mould[1] [məʊld] (*fungus*) moho *m*.

mould[2] **1** *n* (*shape*) molde *m*. **2** *vt* moldear; (*clay*) modelar.

mouldy *a* mohoso,-a; **to go m.** enmohecerse.

mount [maʊnt] **1** *n* (*horse*) montura *f*; (*for photograph*) marco *m*. **2** *vt* (*horse*) subirse *or* montar a; (*photograph*) enmarcar. **3** *vi* (*go up*) subir; (*get on horse, bike*) montar.

● **mount up** *vi* (*increase*) subir; (*accumulate*) acumularse.

mountain ['maʊntɪn] montaña *f*; **m. bike** bicicleta *f* de montaña.

mountai'neer alpinista *mf*, *Am* andinista *mf*.

mountai'neering alpinismo *m*, *Am* andinismo *m*.

mountainous *a* montañoso,-a.

mourn [mɔːn] *vti* **to m. (for) sb** llorar la muerte de algn.

mourning luto *m*; **in m.** de luto.

mouse [maʊs] (*pl* **mice**) ratón *m*.

mousse [muːs] (*dessert*) mousse *f*.

moustache [məˈstɑːʃ] bigote(s) *m*(*pl*).

mouth [maʊθ] (*pl* **mouths** [maʊðz]) boca *f*; (*of river*) desembocadura *f*.

mouth organ armónica *f*.

mouthwash enjuague *m* bucal.

move [muːv] **1** *n* (*movement*) movimiento *m*; (*in game*) jugada *f*; (*turn*) turno *m*; (*course of action*) medida *f*; (*to new home*) mudanza *f*. **2** *vt* mover; (*transfer*) trasladar; (*affect emotionally*) conmover; **to m. house** mudarse (de casa); **to m. job** cambiar de trabajo. **3** *vi* (*change position*) moverse; (*change house*) mudarse (de casa); (*change post*) trasladarse; (*leave*) marcharse; (*in game*) hacer una jugada.

● **move about, move around 1** *vt* cambiar de sitio. **2** *vi* (*be restless*) ir y venir.

● **move along 1** *vt* (*move forward*) hacer avanzar. **2** *vi* (*move forward*) avanzar.

● **move away** *vi* (*move aside*) apartarse; (*change house*) mudarse (de casa).

● **move back 1** *vt* (*to original place*) volver a. **2** *vi* (*withdraw*) retirarse; (*to original place*) volver.

● **move forward** *vti* avanzar.

● **move in** *vi* (*into new home*) instalarse.

● **move off** *vi* (*go away*) marcharse; (*train*) salir; (*car, train*) arrancar.

● **move on** *vi* (*go forward*) avanzar; (*time*) transcurrir.

● **move out** *vi* (*leave house*) mudarse.

● **move over** *vi* correrse.

● **move up** *vi* (*go up*) subir; (*move along*) correrse.

movement movimiento *m*; (*gesture*) ademán *m*; (*trend*) corriente *f*; (*of goods, capital*) circulación *f*.

movie ['mu:vɪ] película *f*.

moving ['mu:vɪŋ] *a* (*that moves*) móvil; (*car etc*) en marcha; (*touching*) conmovedor,-a.

mow* [məʊ] *vt* (*lawn*) cortar.

mower cortacésped *m & f*.

MP [em'pi:] *abbr of* **Member of Parliament** diputado,-a *mf*.

Mr ['mɪstəʳ] *abbr of* **mister** señor *m*, Sr.

Mrs ['mɪsɪs] *abbr* señora *f*, Sra.

Ms [məz] *abbr* señora *f*, Sra, señorita *f*, Srta.

MSc [emes'si:] *abbr of* **Master of Science** Licenciado,-a en Ciencias *mf*.

much [mʌtʃ] **1** *a* mucho,-a; **as m. ... as** tanto,-a ... como; **how m. chocolate?** ¿cuánto chocolate?; **so m.** tanto,-a. **2** *adv* mucho; **as m. as** tanto como; **as m. as possible** todo lo posible; **how m.?** ¿cuánto?; **how m. is it?** ¿cuánto es?; **m. better** mucho mejor; **m. more** mucho más; **too m.** demasiado. **3** *pron* mucho; **I thought as m.** lo suponía; **m. of the town was destroyed** gran parte de la ciudad quedó destruida.

mud [mʌd] barro *m*.

muddle ['mʌdəl] **1** *n* desorden *m*; (*mix-up*) embrollo *m*; **to get into a m.** hacerse un lío. **2** *vt* **to m. (up)** confundir.

muddy *a* fangoso,-a; (*hands*) cubierto,-a de barro; (*liquid*) turbio,-a.

muesli ['mju:zlɪ] muesli *m*.

mug[1] [mʌg] (*large cup*) tazón *m*; (*beer tankard*) jarra *f*.

mug[2] *vt* (*assault*) asaltar.

mugger asaltante *mf*.

mule [mju:l] mulo,-a *mf*.

multiple ['mʌltɪpəl] **1** *a* múltiple. **2** *n* múltiplo *m*.

multipli'cation multiplicación *f*.

multiply ['mʌltɪplaɪ] *vt* multiplicar (**by** por).

mum [mʌm] *fam* mamá *f*.

mumble ['mʌmbəl] **1** *vt* decir entre dientes. **2** *vi* hablar entre dientes.

mummy ['mʌmɪ] *fam* mami *f*.

mumps [mʌmps] paperas *fpl*.

murder ['mɜ:dəʳ] **1** *n* asesinato *m*. **2** *vt* asesinar.

murderer asesino *m*.

murmur ['mɜ:məʳ] *vti* murmurar.

muscle ['mʌsəl] músculo *m*.

muscular *a* (*person*) musculoso,-a.

museum [mju:'zɪəm] museo *m*.

mushroom ['mʌʃru:m] seta *f*; (*food*) champiñón *m*.

music ['mju:zɪk] música *f*.

musical **1** *a* musical; **to be m.** estar dotado,-a para la música. **2** *n* musical *m*.

musician [mju:'zɪʃən] músico,-a *mf*.

Muslim ['mʊzlɪm] *a & n* musulmán,-ana (*mf*).

mussel ['mʌsəl] mejillón *m*.

must [mʌst] *v aux* (*obligation*) deber, tener que; **you m.** **arrive on time** tienes que *or* debes llegar a la hora. ‖ (*probability*) deber (de); **he m. be ill** debe (de) estar enfermo.

mustache [mə'stɑ:ʃ] *US* bigote *m*.

mustard ['mʌstəd] mostaza *f*.

musty ['mʌstɪ] *a* que huele a cerrado *or* a humedad.

mutter ['mʌtəʳ] *vti* murmurar.

mutton ['mʌtən] (carne *f* de) cordero *m*.

mutual ['mju:tʃʊəl] *a* mutuo,-a; (*shared*) común.

muzzle ['mʌzəl] (*for animal*) bozal *m*.

my [maɪ] *poss* mi; **I washed my hair** me lavé el pelo; **my cousins** mis primos; **my father** mi padre; **one of my friends** un amigo mío.

myself *pers pron* (*emphatic*) yo mismo,-a; **my husband and m.** mi marido y yo. ‖ (*reflexive*) me; **I hurt m.** me hice daño. ‖ (*after prep*) mí (mismo, -a).

mysterious [mɪ'stɪərɪəs] *a* misterioso,-a.

mystery ['mɪstərɪ] misterio *m*.

N

nail [neɪl] **1** n (*of finger, toe*) uña f; (*metal*) clavo m. **2** vt clavar.
● **nail down** vt clavar.
nailfile lima f de uñas.
nail polish, nail varnish esmalte m or laca f de uñas.
naïve [naɪˈiːv] a ingenuo,-a.
naked [ˈneɪkɪd] a desnudo,-a.
name [neɪm] **1** n nombre m; (*surname*) apellido m; (*reputation*) reputación f; **what's your n.?** ¿cómo te llamas? **2** vt llamar; (*appoint*) nombrar.
nanny [ˈnænɪ] niñera f.
nap [næp] (*sleep*) siesta f; **to have a n.** echar la or una siesta.
napkin [ˈnæpkɪn] **(table) n.** servilleta f.
nappy [ˈnæpɪ] pañal m.
narrow [ˈnærəʊ] **1** a (*passage, road etc*) estrecho,-a. **2** vi estrecharse.
● **narrow down** vt reducir.
narrowly adv (*closely*) de cerca; (*by a small margin*) por poco.
nastily adv (*to behave*) antipáticamente.
nasty [ˈnɑːstɪ] a (*unpleasant*) desagradable; (*unfriendly*) antipático,-a; (*malicious*) mal intencionado,-a.
nation [ˈneɪʃən] nación f.
national [ˈnæʃnəl] a nacional.
natio'nality nacionalidad f.
native [ˈneɪtɪv] **1** a (*place*) natal; **n. language** lengua f materna. **2** n nativo,-a mf.
natural [ˈnætʃərəl] a natural; (*normal*) normal; (*born*) nato,-a.
naturally adv (*of course*) naturalmente; (*by nature*) por naturaleza; (*in a relaxed manner*) con naturalidad.
nature [ˈneɪtʃəʳ] naturaleza f; **n. study** historia f natural.
naughty [ˈnɔːtɪ] a (*child*) travieso,-a.
nauseous [ˈnɔːzɪəs] a **to feel n.** tener ganas de vomitar.
naval [ˈneɪvəl] a naval; **n. officer** oficial mf de marina.
navel [ˈneɪvəl] ombligo m.
navigate [ˈnævɪgeɪt] **1** vt (*river*) navegar por; (*ship*) gobernar. **2** vi navegar.
navigation navegación f.
navy [ˈneɪvɪ] marina f; **n. blue** azul m marino.
near [nɪəʳ] **1** a (*space*) cercano,-a; (*time*) próximo,-a; **in the n. future** en un futuro próximo; **it was a n. thing** poco faltó. **2** adv (*space*) cerca; **that's n. enough** ya vale. **3** prep cerca de; **n. the end of the film** hacia el final de la película.
nearby 1 a cercano,-a. **2** adv cerca.

nearly *adv* casi; **very n.** casi, casi; **we haven't n. enough** no alcanza ni con mucho.

neat [ni:t] *a* (*room, habits etc*) ordenado,-a; (*appearance*) pulcro,-a.

neatly *adv* (*carefully*) cuidadosamente; (*cleverly*) hábilmente.

nece'ssarily *adv* necesariamente.

necessary ['nesɪsərɪ] *a* necesario,-a; **to do what is n.** hacer lo que haga falta; **if n.** si es preciso.

necessity [nɪ'sesɪtɪ] necesidad *f*; (*article*) requisito *m* indispensable.

neck [nek] cuello *m*; (*of animal*) pescuezo *m*.

necklace ['neklɪs] coloar *m*.

nectarine ['nektəri:n] nectarina *f*.

need [ni:d] **1** *n* necesidad *f*; (*poverty*) indigencia *f*; **if n. be** si fuera necesario; **there's no n. for you to do that** no hace falta que hagas eso. **2** *vt* necesitar; (*require*) requerir; **I n. to see him** tengo que verle. **3** *v aux* tener que, deber; **n. he go?** ¿tiene que ir?; **you needn't wait** no hace falta que esperes.

needle ['ni:dəl] aguja *f*.

needlessly *adv* innecesariamente.

needlework (*sewing*) costura *f*; (*embroidery*) bordado *m*.

negative ['negətɪv] **1** *a* negativo,-a. **2** *n* (*in grammar*) negación *f*; (*photo*) negativo *m*.

neglect [nɪ'glekt] *vt* (*not look after*) descuidar; **to n. to do sth** (*omit to do*) no hacer algo.

neglected *a* (*appearance*) desarreglado,-a; (*garden*) descuidado,-a; **to feel n.** sentirse desatendido,-a.

negligence ['neglɪdʒəns] negligencia *f*.

negligent *a* negligente.

negotiate [nɪ'gəʊʃɪeɪt] *vti* negociar.

negoti'ation negociación *f*.

neigh [neɪ] *vi* relinchar.

neighbour, *US* **neighbor** ['neɪbəʳ] vecino,-a *mf*.

neighbourhood, *US* **neighborhood** (*district*) barrio *m*; (*people*) vecindario *m*.

neighbouring, *US* **neighboring** *a* vecino,-a.

neither ['naɪðəʳ] **1** *a & pron* ninguno de los dos, ninguna de las dos. **2** *adv & conj* ni; **n. ... nor** nor ni ... ni; **it's n. here nor there** no viene al caso; **she was not there and n. was her sister** ella no estaba, ni su hermana tampoco.

neon ['ni:ɒn] neón *m*; **n. light** luz *f* de neón.

nephew ['nefju:] sobrino *m*.

nerve [nɜ:v] nervio *m*; (*courage*) valor *m*; (*cheek*) descaro *m*; **to get on sb's nerves** poner los nervios de punta a algn.

nervous *a* (*apprehensive*) nervioso,-a; (*afraid*) miedoso,-a; (*timid*) tímido,-a; **to be n.** tener miedo.

nest [nest] nido *m*.

net [net] red *f*.

net² *a* neto,-a.

netting (*wire*) alambrada *f*.

nettle ['netəl] ortiga *f*.

network red *f*.

neutral ['nju:trəl] **1** *a* neutro,-a. **2** *n* (*gear*) punto *m* muerto.

never ['nevəʳ] *adv* nunca, jamás; **he n. complains** no se queja nunca; **n. again** nunca (ja)más.

never-'ending *a* interminable.

neverthe'less *adv* sin embargo, no obstante.

new [nju:] *a* nuevo,-a.

newborn *a* recién nacido,-a.

newcomer recién llegado,-a *mf*; (*to job etc*) nuevo,-a *mf*.

newly *adv* recién.

news [nju:z] noticias *fpl*; **a piece of n.** una noticia.

newsagent vendedor,-a *mf* de periódicos.

news bulletin boletín *m* informativo.

newsflash noticia *f* de última hora.

newsletter hoja *f* informativa.

newspaper periódico *m*.

next [nekst] **1** *a* (*in position*) de al lado; (*in time*) próximo,-a; (*in order*) siguiente, próximo,-a; **the n. day** el día siguiente; **n. Friday** el viernes que viene. **2** *adv* después; (*next time*) la próxima vez; **what shall we do n.?** ¿qué hacemos ahora? **3** *prep* **n. to** al lado de.

next door *a & adv* de al lado; **our n. neighbour** el vecino *or* la vecina de al lado.

NHS [enetʃ'es] *Br abbr of* **National Health Service** ≈ Seguridad *f* Social, SS *f*.

nib [nɪb] plumilla *f*.

nibble ['nɪbəl] *vti* mordisquear.

nice [naɪs] *a* (*person*) simpático,-a; (*thing*) agradable; (*nice-looking*) bonito,-a, *Am* lindo,-a; **n. and cool** fresquito,-a; **to smell/taste n.** oler/saber bien.

nicely *adv* muy bien.

nickel ['nɪkəl] *US* moneda *f* de cinco centavos.

nickname ['nɪkneɪm] apodo *m*.

niece [ni:s] sobrina *f*.

night [naɪt] noche *f*; **at twelve o'clock at n.** a las doce de la noche; **last n.** anoche; **to have a n. out** salir por la noche.

nightclub sala *f* de fiestas; (*disco*) discoteca *f*.

nightdress camisón *m*.

nightgown camisón *m*.

nightingale ['naɪtɪŋgeɪl] ruiseñor *m*.

nightmare pesadilla *f*.

night-time noche *f*; **at n.** por la noche.

night watchman vigilante *m* nocturno.

nil [nɪl] nada *f*; (*in sport*) cero *m*.

nine [naɪn] *a & n* nueve (*m*) *inv*; **n. hundred** novecientos,-as.

nine'teen *a & n* diecinueve (*m*) *inv*.

ninety *a & n* noventa (*m*) *inv*.

ninth [naɪnθ] *a & n* noveno,-a (*mf*).

nip [nɪp] *vt* (*pinch*) pellizcar; (*bite*) morder.

● **nip in/out** *vi fam* entrar/salir un momento.

● **nip round** *vi fam* **to n. round to sb's** pasarse a ver a algn.

nipple ['nɪpəl] (*female*) pezón *m*; (*male*) tetilla *f*.

nitrogen ['naɪtrədʒən] nitrógeno *m*.

no [nəʊ] **1** *adv* no; **no longer** ya no; **no less than** no menos de. **2** *a* ninguno,-a; **she has no children** no tiene hijos; **I have no idea** no tengo (ni) idea; **no sensible person** ninguna persona razonable; **'no parking'** 'prohibido aparcar'; **no way!** ¡ni hablar!

noble ['nəʊbəl] *a* noble.

nobody ['nəʊbədɪ] *pron* nadie; **there was n. there** no había nadie; **n. else** nadie más.

nod [nɒd] **1** *n* (*in agreement*) señal *f* de asentimiento. **2** *vi* (*in agreement*) asentir con la cabeza. **3** *vt* **to n. one's head** inclinar la cabeza.

● **nod off** *vi* dormirse.

noise [nɔɪz] ruido *m*; **to make a n.** hacer ruido.

noisily *adv* ruidosamente.

noisy *a* ruidóso,-a.

nominate ['nɒmɪneɪt] *vt* (*appoint*) nombrar.

non- [nɒn] *prefix* no.

none [nʌn] *pron* ninguno,-a; **n. at all** nada en absoluto.

nonethe'less *adv* no obstante, sin embargo.

non-ex'istent *a* inexistente.

non-'fiction literatura *f* no novelesca.

nonsense ['nɒnsəns] tonterías *fpl*; **that's n.** eso es absurdo.

non'smoker no fumador,-a *mf*.

non'stick *a* antiadherente.

non'stop **1** *a* continuo; (*train*) directo,-a. **2** *adv* sin parar.

noodles ['nuːdəlz] *npl* fideos *mpl*.

noon [nuːn] mediodía *m*; **at n.** a mediodía.

nor [nɔːʳ] *conj* ni, ni … tampoco; **neither … n.** ni … ni; **neither you n. I** ni tú ni yo; **n. do I** (ni) yo tampoco.

normal ['nɔːməl] *a* normal.

normally *adv* normalmente.

north [nɔːθ] **1** *n* norte *m*. **2** *adv* hacia el norte. **3** *a* del norte; **n. wind** viento del norte.

northbound *a* (con) dirección norte.

northeast nor(d)este *m*.

northern *a* del norte.

northerner norteño,-a *mf*.

northward ['nɔːθwəd] *a & adv* hacia el norte.

northwest noroeste *m*.

Norwegian [nɔːˈwiːdʒən] **1** *a* noruego,-a. **2** *n* (*person*) noruego,-a *mf*; (*language*) noruego *m*.

nose [nəʊz] nariz *f*; **her n. is bleeding** le está sangrando la nariz.

nosebleed hemorragia *f* nasal.

nostril ['nɒstrɪl] orificio *m* nasal.

nosy ['nəʊzɪ] *a* entrometido,-a.

not [nɒt] *adv* no; **he's n. in today** hoy no está; **n. at all** en absoluto; **thank you – n. at all** gracias – no hay de qué; **n. one (of them) said thank you** nadie me dio las gracias.

note [nəʊt] **1** *n* (*in music, written*) nota *f*; (*money*) billete *m* (de banco); **to take n. of** (*notice*) prestar atención a; **to take notes** (*at lecture*) tomar apuntes. **2** *vt* (*write down*) anotar; (*notice*) darse cuenta de.

notebook cuaderno *m*.

notepad bloc *m* de notas.

notepaper papel *m* de carta.

nothing ['nʌθɪŋ] **1** *n* nada; **I saw n.** no vi nada; **for n.** (*free*) gratis; **it's n. to do with you** no tiene nada que ver contigo; **n. else** nada más; **n. much** poca cosa. **2** *adv* **she looks n. like her sister** no se parece en nada a su hermana.

notice ['nəʊtɪs] **1** *n* (*warning*) aviso *m*; (*attention*) atención *f*; (*in newspaper etc*) anuncio *m*; (*sign*) aviso *m*; **he gave a month's n.** presentó la dimisión con un mes de antelación; **at short n.** con poca antelación; **until further n.** hasta nuevo aviso; **to take n. of sth** prestar atención a algo. **2** *vt* darse cuenta de.

noticeable *a* obvio, evidente.

noticeboard tablón *m* de anuncios.

notifi'cation aviso *m*.

notify ['nəʊtɪfaɪ] *vt* avisar.

notion ['nəʊʃən] idea *f*.

nought [nɔːt] cero *m*.

noun [naʊn] sustantivo *m*.
nourishing ['nʌrɪʃɪŋ] *a* nutritivo,-a.
novel[1] ['nɒvəl] novela *f*.
novel[2] *a* original.
novelist novelista *mf*.
November [nəʊ'vembər] noviembre *m*.
now [naʊ] **1** *adv* ahora; (*at present, these days*) actualmente; **just n., right n.** ahora mismo; **from n. on** de ahora en adelante; **n. and then, n. and again** de vez en cuando; **n. (then)** ahora bien; **n., n.!** ¡de eso nada! **2** *conj* **n. (that)** ahora que.
nowadays *adv* hoy (en) día.
nowhere ['nəʊweər] *adv* en ninguna parte; **it's n. near ready** no está preparado, ni mucho menos.
nozzle ['nɒzəl] boquilla *f*.
nuclear ['nju:klɪər] *a* nuclear.
nude [nju:d] *a* desnudo,-a; **in the n.** al desnudo.
nudge [nʌdʒ] **1** *vt* dar un codazo a. **2** *n* codazo *m*.
nuisance ['nju:səns] pesadez *f*; (*person*) pesado,-a *mf*; **what a n.!** ¡qué lata!
numb [nʌm] *a* (*without feeling*) entumecido,-a.
number ['nʌmbər] **1** *n* número *m*; **have you got my (phone) n.?** ¿tienes mi (número de) teléfono?; **a n. of people** varias personas. **2** *vt* (*put a number on*) numerar.
numberplate matrícula *f*.
numeral ['nju:mərəl] número *m*.
numerous ['nju:mərəs] *a* numeroso,-a.
nun [nʌn] monja *f*.
nurse [nɜ:s] **1** *n* enfermera *f*; (*male*) enfermero *m*. **2** *vt* (*look after*) cuidar.
nursery ['nɜ:sərɪ] guardería *f*; (*in house*) cuarto *m* de los niños; (*garden centre*) vivero *m*.
nursery rhyme canción *f* infantil.
nursery school jardín *m* de infancia.
nut [nʌt] (*fruit*) fruto *m* seco; (*for bolt*) tuerca *f*.
nutcracker cascanueces *m inv*.
nylon ['naɪlɒn] **1** *n* nailon *m*; **nylons** medias *fpl* de nailon. **2** *a* de nailon.

O

oak [əʊk] roble *m*.

OAP [əʊeɪ'pi:] *Br abbr of* **old-age pensioner**.

oar [ɔ:'] remo *m*.

oats [əʊts] avena *f*.

obedience obediencia *f*.

obedient [ə'bi:dɪənt] *a* obediente.

obey [ə'beɪ] *vt* obedecer; (*law*) cumplir.

object¹ ['ɒbdʒɪkt] (*thing*) objeto *m*; (*aim, purpose*) objetivo *m*; (*in grammar*) complemento *m*.

object² [əb'dʒekt] *vi* oponerse (**to** a); **do you o. to my smoking?** ¿le molesta que fume?

objection [əb'dʒekʃən] objeción *f*.

objective [əb'dʒektɪv] objetivo *m*.

obligation [ɒblɪ'geɪʃən] obligación *f*.

oblige [ə'blaɪdʒ] *vt* (*compel*) obligar; (*do a favour for*) hacer un favor a; **I'm obliged to do it** me veo obligado,-a a hacerlo.

obliging *a* solícito,-a.

oblique [ə'bli:k] *a* oblicuo,-a, inclinado,-a.

obscene [əb'si:n] *a* obsceno,-a.

observant *a* observador,-a.

obser'vation observación *f*; (*surveillance*) vigilancia *f*.

observe [əb'sɜ:v] *vt* observar; (*on surveillance*) vigilar; (*remark*) advertir.

obstacle ['ɒbstəkəl] obstáculo *m*.

obstinate ['ɒbstɪnɪt] *a* (*person*) obstinado,-a.

obstruct [əb'strʌkt] *vt* obstruir; (*pipe etc*) atascar; (*view*) tapar; (*hinder*) estorbar; (*progress*) dificultar.

obtain [əb'teɪn] *vt* obtener.

obvious ['ɒbvɪəs] *a* obvio,-a, evidente.

obviously *adv* evidentemente; **o.!** ¡claro!

occasion [ə'keɪʒən] ocasión *f*; (*event*) acontecimiento *m*.

occasional *a* eventual.

occasionally *adv* de vez en cuando.

occupant ocupante *mf*; (*tenant*) inquilino,-a *mf*.

occu'pation (*job, profession*) profesión *f*; (*task*) trabajo *m*.

occupy ['ɒkjʊpaɪ] *vt* (*live in*) habitar en; **to o. one's time in doing sth** dedicar su tiempo a hacer algo; **to keep oneself occupied** mantenerse ocupado,-a.

occur [ə'kɜ:'] *vi* (*event*) suceder; (*change*) producirse; (*be found*) encontrarse; **it occurred to me that ...** se me ocurrió que ...

occurrence acontecimiento *m*.

ocean ['əʊʃən] océano *m*.

o'clock [ə'klɒk] *adv* (*it's*) one o'c. (es) la una; (*it's*) two o'c. (son) las dos.

October [ɒk'təʊbəʳ] octubre *m*.

octopus ['ɒktəpəs] pulpo *m*.

odd [ɒd] **1** *a* (*strange*) raro,-a; (*occasional*) esporádico,-a; (*extra*) adicional; (*not even*) impar; (*unpaired*) desparejado,-a; **the o. customer** algún que otro cliente; **o. job** trabajillo *m*; **to be the o. man out** estar de más; **an o. sock** un calcetín suelto. **2** *adv* y pico; **twenty o. people** veinte y pico *o* y tantas personas.

oddly *adv* extrañamente.

odds [ɒdz] *npl* (*chances*) probabilidades *fpl*; (*in betting*) puntos *mpl* de ventaja; **the o. are that ...** lo más probable es que ... (+ *subjunctive*); **at o. with sb** reñido,-a con algn; **o. and ends** (*small things*) cositas *fpl*.

odour, US odor ['əʊdəʳ] olor *m*; (*fragrance*) perfume *m*.

of [ɒv, *unstressed* əv] *prep* de; **a friend of mine** un amigo mío; **there are four of us** somos cuatro; **two of them** dos de ellos; **that's very kind of you** es usted muy amable.

off [ɒf] **1** *prep* de; **she fell o. her horse** se cayó del caballo; **a house o. the road** una casa apartada de la carretera; **I'm o. wine** he perdido el gusto al vino. **2** *adv* (*absent*) fuera; **I have a day o.** tengo un día libre; **to be o. sick** estar de baja por enfermedad. ‖ **his arrival is three days o.** faltan tres días para su llegada; **six miles o.** a seis millas. ‖ **I'm o. to London** me voy a Londres; **she ran o.** se fue corriendo. ‖ **ten per cent o.** un descuento del diez por ciento. ‖ **with his shoes o.** descalzo. ‖ **on and o.** de vez en cuando. **3** *a* **to be o.** (*meat, fish*) estar pasado,-a; (*milk*) estar agrio,-a; (*gas etc*) estar apagado,-a; (*water*) estar cortado,-a; (*cancelled*) estar cancelado,-a; **on the o. chance** por si acaso; **the o. season** la temporada baja; **you're better o. like that** así estás mejor.

off-'colour, US off-'color *a* Br (*ill*) indispuesto,-a.

offence, US offense [ə'fens] delito *m*; (*insult*) ofensa *f*; **to take o. at sth** ofenderse por algo.

offend [ə'fend] *vt* ofender.

offensive *a* (*insulting*) ofensivo,-a; (*repulsive*) repugnante.

offer ['ɒfəʳ] **1** *vt* ofrecer; (*propose*) proponer; (*provide*) proporcionar; **to o. to do a job** ofrecerse para hacer un trabajo. **2** *n* oferta *f*; (*proposal*) propuesta *f*; **on o.** de oferta.

off'hand 1 *a* (*abrupt*) brusco,-a. **2** *adv* de improviso.

office ['ɒfɪs] (*room*) despacho *m*; (*building*) oficina *f*; (*position*) cargo *m*.

officer ['ɒfɪsəʳ] oficial *mf*; (**police**) **o.** agente *mf* de policía.

official [ə'fɪʃəl] **1** *a* oficial. **2** *n* funcionario,-a *mf*.

officially *adv* oficialmente.

off-licence *Br* tienda *f* de bebidas alcohólicas.

often ['ɒfən] *adv* a menudo; **every so o.** de vez en cuando.

oh [əʊ] *interj* ¡oh!

oil [ɔɪl] **1** *n* aceite *m*; (*crude*) petróleo *m*. **2** *vt* engrasar.

oilcan aceitera *f*.

oil change cambio *m* de aceite.

ointment ['ɔɪntmənt] pomada *f*.

OK, okay [əʊ'keɪ] **1** *interj* ¡vale! **2** *a* bien; **is it OK if ...?** ¿está bien si ...?

old [əʊld] *a* viejo,-a; (*previous*) antiguo,-a; **an o. man** un anciano; **o. age** vejez *f*; **how o. are you?** ¿cuántos años tienes?; **she's five years o.** tiene cinco años.

old-'fashioned *a* (*outdated*) a la antigua; (*unfashionable*) anticuado,-a.

olive ['ɒlɪv] (*tree*) olivo *m*; (*fruit*) aceituna *f*, oliva *f*.

Olympic [ə'lɪmpɪk] *a* olímpico,-a; **O. Games** Juegos *mpl* Olímpicos.

omelette, US omelet ['ɒmlɪt] tortilla *f*; **Spanish o.** tortilla española *or* de patatas.

on [ɒn] **1** *prep* (*position*) sobre, encima de, en; **it's on the table** está encima de *or* sobre la mesa; **on page four** en la página cuatro; **a town on the coast** un pueblo en la costa; **on the right** a la derecha; **on the way** en el camino. ▌ (*time*) **on April 3rd** el tres de abril; **on a sunny day** un día de sol; **on Monday** el lunes; **on the following day** al día siguiente; **on his arrival** a su llegada; **on time** a tiempo. ▌ (*means*) **on the radio** en la radio; **to play sth on the piano** tocar algo al piano; **on TV** en la tele; **on the phone** al teléfono; **on foot** a pie; **on the train/plane** en tren/avión. ▌ (*about*) **a lecture on numismatics** una conferencia sobre numismática. **2** *a* **to be on** (*TV, radio, light*) estar encendido,-a; (*engine*) estar en marcha; (*tablecloth*) estar puesto; **she had a coat on** llevaba un abrigo puesto; **that film was on last week** pusieron esa película la semana pasada. **3** *adv* **have you anything on tonight?** ¿tienes algún plan para esta noche?; **he talks on and on** habla sin parar; **to work on** seguir trabajando.

once [wʌns] **1** *adv* (*one time*) una vez; (*formerly*) en otro tiempo; **o. a week** una vez por semana; **o. in a while** de vez en cuando; **o. more** una vez más; **at o.** en seguida; **don't speak all at o.** no habléis todos a la vez. **2** *conj* una vez que.

one [wʌn] **1** *a* un, una; **he'll come back o. day** un día volverá. **2** *dem pron* **any o.** cualquiera; **that o.** ése, ésa; (*distant*) aquél, aquélla; **the blue ones** los azules, las azules; **the o. on the table** el *or* la que está encima de la mesa; **the ones that, the ones who** los *or* las que; **this o.** éste, ésta. **3** *indef pron* uno,-a *mf*; **give me o.** dame uno; **o. by o.** uno tras otro; **o. never knows** nunca se sabe; **to cut o.'s finger** cortarse el dedo; **o. another** el uno al otro; **they love o. another** se quieren. **4** *n* (*digit*) uno *m*; **a hundred and o.** ciento uno.

one'self *pron* uno,-a mismo,-a *mf*; (*reflexive*) sí mismo,-a *mf*; **to talk to o.** hablar para sí; **by o.** solo,-a.

one-way *a* (*ticket*) de ida; (*street*) de dirección única.

onion ['ʌnjən] cebolla *f*.

onlooker ['ɒnlʊkəʳ] espectador,-a *mf*.

only ['əʊnlɪ] **1** *adv* solamente, sólo; **he has o. just left** acaba de marcharse hace un momento; **o. yesterday** ayer mismo. **2** *a* único,-a. **3** *conj* pero.

onto ['ɒntʊ] *prep see* **on**.

onward(s) ['ɒnwəd(z)] *adv* en adelante; **from this time o.** de ahora en adelante.

opaque [əʊ'peɪk] *a* opaco,-a.

open ['əʊpən] **1** *a* abierto,-a; **wide o.** abierto de par en par; **in the o. air** al aire libre; **o. ticket** billete abierto. **2** *vt* abrir; (*exhibition etc*) inaugurar; (*negotiations, conversation*) entablar. **3** *vi* abrirse. **4** *n* **in the o.** al aire libre; *fig* **to bring into the o.** hacer público.

● **open out 1** *vt* desplegar. (*flowers*) abrirse; (*view*) extenderse.

● **open up 1** *vt* (*market etc*) abrir; (*possibilities*) crear. **2** *vi* abrirse.

opening (*act*) apertura *f*; (*beginning*) comienzo *m*; (*aperture*) abertura *f*; (*gap*) brecha *f*; (*in market*) oportunidad *f*.

openly *adv* abiertamente.

openness (*frankness*) franqueza *f*.

opera ['ɒpərə] ópera *f*.

operate ['ɒpəreɪt] **1** *vi* (*function*) funcionar; (*act*) actuar; (*surgeon*) operar. **2** *vt* (*switch on*) accionar; (*control*) manejar; (*business*) dirigir.

operating system sistema *m* operativo.

ope'ration (*of machine*) funcionamiento *m*; (*surgical*) operación *f*.

operator (*of machine*) operario,-a *mf*; (*telephone*) operador,-a *mf*.

opinion [ə'pɪnjən] opinión *f*; **in my o.** en mi opinión.

opponent [ə'pəʊnənt] adversario,-a *mf*.

opportunity [ɒpə'tjuːnɪtɪ] oportunidad *f*; (*prospect*) perspectiva *f*.

oppose [ə'pəʊz] *vt* oponerse a.

opposed *a* opuesto,-a; **to be o. to sth** estar en contra de algo.

opposing *a* adversario,-a.

opposite ['ɒpəzɪt] **1** *a* (*facing*) de enfrente; (*page*) contiguo,-a; (*contrary*) contrario,-a; **in the o. direction** en dirección contraria. **2** *n* lo contrario *m*; **quite the o.!** ¡al contrario! **3** *prep* enfrente de. **4** *adv* enfrente.

oppo'sition oposición *f*; **in o.** to en contra de.

opt [ɒpt] *vi* **to o. for** optar por; **to o. to do sth** optar por hacer algo.

optician [ɒp'tɪʃən] óptico,-a *mf*.

optimist ['ɒptɪmɪst] optimista *mf*.

opti'mistic *a* optimista.

option ['ɒpʃən] opción *f*; **I have no o.** no tengo más remedio.

optional ['ɒpʃənəl] *a* optativo,-a.

or [ɔːʳ] *conj* o; (*before a word beginning with a stressed o or* ho) u; (*with negative*) ni; **he can't read or write** no sabe leer ni escribir.

oral ['ɔːrəl] **1** *a* oral. **2** *n* examen *m* oral.

orange ['ɒrɪndʒ] **1** *n* naranja *f*. **2** *a* de color naranja.

orangeade naranjada *f*.

orange juice zumo *m* de naranja.

orbit ['ɔːbɪt] órbita *f*.

orchard ['ɔːtʃəd] huerto *m*.

orchestra ['ɔːkɪstrə] orquesta *f*.

ordeal [ɔːˈdiːl] mala experiencia.

order ['ɔːdəʳ] **1** *n* (*sequence, command*) orden *m*; (*commission*) pedido *m*; **to put in o.** ordenar; **is your passport in o.?** ¿tienes el pasaporte en regla?; **'out of o.'** 'averiado'; **to be on o.** estar pedido; **in o. that** para que (+ *subjunctive*), a fin de que (+ *subjunctive*); **in o. to** parà (+ *infinitive*), a fin de (+ *infinitive*). **2** *vt* (*command*) ordenar; (*goods*) encargar; **to o. sb to do sth** mandar a algn hacer algo; **to o. a dish** pedir un plato.

ordinary ['ɔːdənrɪ] **1** *a* normal; (*average*) corriente. **2** *n* **out of the o.** fuera de lo común.

ore [ɔːʳ] mineral *m*.

organ ['ɔːgən] órgano *m*.

organic [ɔːˈgænɪk] *a* orgánico,-a.

organi'zation organización *f*.

organize ['ɔːgənaɪz] *vt* organizar.

organizer organizador,-a *mf*.

Oriental [ɔːrɪˈentəl] *a & n* oriental (*mf*).

origin ['ɒrɪdʒɪn] origen *m*.

o'riginal **1** *a* original; (*first*) primero,-a; (*novel*) original. **2** *n* original *m*.

originality [ərɪdʒɪˈnælɪtɪ] originalidad *f*.

originally *adv* (*at first*) en un principio.

ornament ['ɔːnəmənt] adorno *m*.

orphan ['ɔːfən] huérfano,-a *mf*.

orphanage orfanato *m*.

ostrich ['ɒstrɪtʃ] avestruz *f*.

other ['ʌðəʳ] **1** *a* otro,-a; **the o. one** el otro, la otra. **2** *pron* otro,-a *mf*; **many others** otros muchos; **the others** los otros, los demás; **we see each o. quite often** nos vemos con bastante frecuencia.

otherwise *adv* (*if not*) si no; (*differently*) de otra manera; (*in other respects*) por lo demás.

ought [ɔːt] *v aux* deber; **I thought I o. to tell you** creí que debía decírtelo; **she o. to do it** debería hacerlo; **you o. to see the exhibition** deberías ver la exposición. ▌ (*expectation*) **he o. to pass the exam** seguramente aprobará

el examen; **that o. to do** con eso bastará.
ounce [aʊns] onza *f*.
our [aʊəʳ] *poss a* nuestro,-a.
ours *poss pron* (el) nuestro, (la) nuestra, (los) nuestros, (las) nuestras; **a friend of o.** un amigo nuestro.
our'selves *pers pron pl* (*reflexive*) nos; (*emphatic*) nosotros mismos, nosotras mismas; **by o.** a solas.
out [aʊt] **1** *adv* (*outside, away*) fuera; **o. there** ahí fuera; **to go o.** salir. **2** *prep* **o. of** (*place*) fuera de; (*cause, motive*) por; (*made from*) de; (*short of, without*) sin; **move o. of the way!** ¡quítate de en medio!; **he jumped o. the window** saltó por la ventana; **o. of danger** fuera de peligro; **forty o. of fifty** cuarenta de cada cincuenta. **3** *a* **to be o.** (*unfashionable*) estar pasado,-a de moda; (*not lit*) estar apagado,-a; (*eliminated from game*) quedar eliminado; **the sun is o.** ha salido el sol; **she's o.** (*not in*) ha salido.
outbreak (*of war*) comienzo *m*; (*of disease*) epidemia *f*; (*of violence*) ola *f*.
outburst (*of anger*) arrebato *m*.
outcome resultado *m*.
outdated *a* anticuado,-a.
outdo* *vt* exceder; **to o. sb** superar a algn.
outdoor *a* al aire libre; (*clothes*) de calle.
outdoors *adv* al aire libre.
outer *a* exterior.
outer space espacio *m* sideral.
outfit (*kit, equipment*) equipo *m*; (*set of clothes*) conjunto *m*.
outing excursión *f*.
outlet (*for goods*) mercado *m*.
outline (*draft*) bosquejo *m*; (*outer line*) contorno *m*; (*silhouette*) perfil *m*; (*sketch*) boceto *m*.
outlook (*point of view*) punto *m* de vista; (*prospect*) perspectiva *f*.
outnumber *vt* exceder en número.
out-of-doors *adv* al aire libre.
output producción *f*; (*of machine*) rendimiento *m*.
outrage **1** *n* ultraje *m*; **it's an o.!** ¡es un escándalo! **2** *vt* **to be outraged by sth** indignarse por algo.
outrageous *a* (*behaviour*) escandaloso,-a; (*clothes*) extravagante.
outright *adv* (*completely*) por completo; (*directly*) directamente.
outside [aʊt'saɪd] **1** *prep* fuera de; (*beyond*) más allá de; (*other than*) aparte de. **2** ['aʊtsaɪd] *a* (*exterior*) exterior, externo,-a. **3** [aʊt'saɪd] *adv* (a)fuera. **4** *n* exterior *m*; **on the o.** por fuera.
outskirts *npl* afueras *fpl*.

outstanding a (*exceptional*) destacado,-a; (*unpaid, unresolved*) pendiente.

outward ['aʊtwəd] a (*appearance*) externo,-a; **the o. journey** el viaje de ida.

outward(s) adv hacia (a)fuera.

oval ['əʊvəl] **1** a ovalado,-a. **2** n óvalo m.

oven ['ʌvən] horno m.

over ['əʊvə^r] **1** prep (*above*) encima de; (*across*) al otro lado de; (*during*) durante; (*more than*) más de; **the bridge o. the river** el puente que cruza el río; **all o. Spain** por toda España; **it's all o. the carpet** está por toda la alfombra; **o. the phone** por teléfono; **men o. twenty-five** hombres mayores de veinticinco años. **2** adv (*more*) más; (*again*) otra vez; (*in excess*) de más; **o. there** allá; **all o.** por todas partes; **o. and o. (again)** una y otra vez; **there are still some o.** todaría quedan algunos. **3** a (*finished*) acabado,-a; **it's (all) o.** se acabó; **the danger is o.** ha pasado el peligro.

overall ['əʊvərɔːl] **1** a total. **2** [əʊvər'ɔːl] adv (*on the whole*) en conjunto. **3** ['əʊvərɔːl] n Br guardapolvo m; **overalls** mono m sing.

overboard adv por la borda.

over'charge vt (*charge too much*) cobrar de más.

overcoat abrigo m.

over'come* vt (*conquer*) vencer; (*overwhelm*) abrumar; (*surmount*) superar.

over'do* vt (*carry too far*) exagerar; (*in cooking*) cocer or asar demasiado.

overdraft crédito m al descubierto.

over'due a (*rent, train etc*) atrasado,-a.

overeat vi comer en exceso.

overexcited a sobreexcitado,-a.

over'flow vi (*river*) desbordarse; (*cup etc*) derramarse.

over'head a (por) encima de la cabeza.

over'hear vt oír por casualidad.

over'heat vi recalentarse.

over'joyed a rebosante de alegría.

over'lap vi superponerse.

over'leaf adv al dorso.

over'load vt sobrecargar.

over'look vt (*fail to notice*) pasar por alto; (*ignore*) no hacer caso de; (*have a view of*) tener vista a.

overnight 1 adv por la noche; **we stayed there o.** pasamos la noche allí. **2** ['əʊvənaɪt] a (*journey*) de noche.

overpass ['əʊvəpɑːs] (*bridge*) US paso m elevado.

overrated a sobrestimado,-a.

overseas [əʊvəˈsiːz] **1** *adv* en ultramar; **to live o.** vivir en el extranjero. **2** [ˈəʊvəsiːz] *a* de ultramar; (*visitor*) extranjero,-a; (*trade*) exterior.

oversight descuido *m*.

over'sleep *vi* quedarse dormido,-a.

overspend *vi* gastar demasiado.

over'take* *vt Br* adelantar.

overtime horas *fpl* extra.

over'turn *vti* volcar.

over'weight *a* **to be o.** ser gordo,-a.

over'whelm [əʊvəˈwelm] *vt* (*defeat*) aplastar; (*overpower*) abrumar.

over'whelming *a* (*desire*) irresistible.

over'work *vi* trabajar demasiado.

owe [əʊ] *vt* deber.

owing *a* **o. to** debido a.

owl [aʊl] búho *m*.

own [əʊn] **1** *a* propio,-a; **it's his o. fault** es culpa suya. **2** *pron* **my o., your o., his o.** *etc* lo mío, lo tuyo, lo suyo *etc;* **to get one's o. back** tomarse la revancha; **on one's o.** (*without help*) uno,-a mismo,-a; (*alone*) solo,-a. **3** *vt* poseer.

● **own up** *vi* **to o. up (to)** confesar.

owner propietario,-a *mf*.

oxygen [ˈɒksɪdʒən] oxígeno *m*.

oyster [ˈɔɪstəˈ] ostra *f*.

P

pace [peɪs] (*step*) paso *m*; (*speed*) ritmo *m*.

Pacific [pə'sɪfɪk] **the P. (Ocean)** el (océano) Pacífico.

pacifier ['pæsɪfaɪə'] US (*of baby*) chupete *m*.

pack [pæk] **1** *n* paquete *m*; (*rucksack*) mochila *f*; Br (*of cards*) baraja *f*; (*of hounds*) jauría *f*. **2** *vt* (*goods*) embalar; (*in suitcase*) poner; (*fill*) atestar; (*press down*) (*snow*) apretar; **to p. one's bags** hacer las maletas; *fig* marcharse. **3** *vi* (*baggage*) hacer las maletas.

● **pack away** *vt* (*tidy away*) guardar.

● **pack up** *fam* **1** *vt* (*give up*) dejar. **2** *vi* (*stop working*) terminar; (*machine etc*) estropearse.

package ['pækɪdʒ] (*parcel, software*) paquete *m*.

package tour viaje *m* todo incluido.

packaging embalaje *m*.

packed [pækt] *a* (*place*) atestado,-a.

packed lunch almuerzo *m* (para tomar fuera).

packet ['pækɪt] paquete *m*.

packing embalaje *m*.

pad [pæd] **1** *n* almohadilla *f*; (*of paper*) bloc *m*. **2** *vt* (*chair*) rellenar.

padded *a* (*cell*) acolchado,-a.

paddle[1] ['pædəl] (*oar*) pala *f*.

paddle[2] *vi* chapotear.

paddling pool piscina *f* para niños.

padlock candado *m*.

page[1] [peɪdʒ] página *f*.

page[2] (*at club etc*) botones *m inv*.

pain [peɪn] dolor *m*; (*grief*) sufrimiento *m*; **to take pains over sth** esmerarse en algo.

painful *a* doloroso,-a.

painkiller analgésico *m*.

paint [peɪnt] **1** *n* pintura *f*. **2** *vt* pintar; **to p. sth white** pintar algo de blanco.

paintbrush pincel *m*; (*for walls*) brocha *f*.

painter pintor,-a *mf*.

painting cuadro *m*; (*activity*) pintura *f*.

paint stripper quitapinturas *mpl inv*.

pair [peə'] (*of gloves, shoes*) par *m*; (*of people, cards*) pareja *f*.

pajamas [pə'dʒæməz] *npl* US pijama *m*.

Pakistani [pɑːkɪ'stɑːnɪ] *a & n* paquistaní (*mf*).

pal [pæl] *fam* amigo,-a *mf*.

palace ['pælɪs] palacio *m*.

palate ['pælɪt] paladar *m.*
pale [peɪl] *a* (*skin*) pálido,-a; (*colour*) claro,-a.
Palestinian [pælɪ'stɪnɪən] *a & n* palestino,-a (*mf*).
palette ['pælɪt] paleta *f.*
palm [pɑːm] (*of hand*) palma *f;* (*tree*) palmera *f;* **p. leaf** palma *f.*
pamphlet ['pæmflɪt] folleto *m.*
pan [pæn] (*saucepan*) cazuela *f.*
pancake crepe *f.*
pane [peɪn] cristal *m,* vidrio *m.*
panel ['pænəl] (*of wall*) panel *m;* (*of instruments*) tablero *m;* (*jury*) jurado *m.*
panic ['pænɪk] pánico *m;* **to get into a p.** ponerse histérico,-a.
pant [pænt] *vi* jadear.
panties ['pæntɪz] *npl* bragas *fpl.*
pantomime ['pæntəmaɪm] (*play*) función *f* musical navideña.
pantry ['pæntrɪ] despensa *f.*
pants [pænts] *npl* (*underpants*) (*ladies'*) bragas *fpl;* (*men's*) calzoncillos *mpl;* US (*trousers*) pantalón *m.*
pantyhose ['pæntɪhəʊz] US panties *mpl.*
paper ['peɪpəʳ] papel *m;* (*newspaper*) periódico *m;* (*exam*) examen *m;* (*essay*) trabajo *m* (escrito).
paperback libro *m* en rústica.
paperclip clip *m.*
paper knife cortapapeles *mpl inv.*
parachute ['pærəʃuːt] paracaídas *m inv.*
parade [pə'reɪd] desfile *m.*
paradise ['pærədaɪs] paraíso *m.*
paraffin ['pærəfɪn] parafina *f.*
paragraph ['pærəgrɑːf] párrafo *m.*
Paraguayan [pærə'gwaɪən] *a & n* paraguayo,-a (*mf*).
parallel ['pærəlel] *a* paralelo,-a (**to, with** a).
paralyse, US **paralyze** ['pærəlaɪz] *vt* paralizar.
parasite ['pærəsaɪt] parásito *m.*
parasol ['pærəsɒl] sombrilla *f.*
parcel ['pɑːsəl] paquete *m.*
pardon ['pɑːdən] **1** *n* perdón *m;* **I beg your p.** (Vd.) perdone; **(I beg your) p.?** ¿cómo (dice)? **2** *vt* perdonar; **p. me!** ¡Vd. perdone!
parents ['peərənts] *npl* padres *mpl.*
parish ['pærɪʃ] parroquia *f.*
park [pɑːk] **1** *n* parque *m.* **2** *vt* (*car*) aparcar, *Am* parquear.
parking aparcamiento *m;* **'no p.'** 'prohibido aparcar'.
parking light luz *f* de estacionamiento.

parking lot *US* aparcamiento *m*.
parking meter parquímetro *m*.
parking space aparcamiento *m*.
parking ticket multa *f* aparcamiento.
parliament ['pɑːləmənt] parlamento *m*.
parrot ['pærət] loro *m*.
parsley ['pɑːslɪ] perejil *m*.
parsnip ['pɑːsnɪp] chirivía *f*.
part [pɑːt] **1** *n* parte *f*; (*piece*) trozo *m*; (*of machine, engine*) pieza *f*; (*in play etc*) papel *m*; **for the most p.** en la mayor parte; **to take p. in sth** participar en algo; **in these parts** por estos lugares. **2** (*partly*) en parte. **3** *vi* separarse; (*say goodbye*) despedirse.
● **part with** *vi* separarse de.
partial ['pɑːʃəl] *a* parcial; **to be p. to sth** ser aficionado,-a a algo.
participant participante *mf*.
participate [pɑːˈtɪsɪpeɪt] *vi* participar (**in** en).
partici'pation participación *f*.
participle [pɑːˈtɪsɪpəl] participio *m*.
particular [pəˈtɪkjələ'] **1** *a* (*special*) particular; (*fussy*) exigente; **in this p. case** en este caso concreto. **2** *npl* **particulars** pormenores *mpl*; **to take down sb's particulars** tomar nota de los datos personales de algn.
particularly *adv* particularmente.
parting (*in hair*) raya *f*.
partition [pɑːˈtɪʃən] (*wall*) tabique *m*.
partly *adv* en parte.
partner ['pɑːtnə'] compañero,-a *mf*; (*in dancing, tennis*) pareja *f*; (*in business*) socio,-a *mf*.
partnership (*in business*) sociedad *f*.
partridge ['pɑːtrɪdʒ] perdiz *f*.
part-'time 1 *a* (*work etc*) de media jornada. **2** *adv* a tiempo parcial.
party ['pɑːtɪ] (*celebration*) fiesta *f*; (*group*) grupo *m*; (*political*) partido *m*.
pass [pɑːs] **1** *n* (*of mountain*) desfiladero *m*; (*permit*) permiso *m*; (*in football etc*) pase *m*. **2** *vt* pasar; (*overtake*) adelantar; (*exam, law*) aprobar. **3** *vi* pasar; (*car*) adelantar; (*people*) cruzarse; (*in football etc*) hacer un pase; (*in exam*) aprobar; **we passed on the stairs** nos cruzamos en la escalera.
● **pass away** *vi* pasar a mejor vida.
● **pass by 1** *vt* pasar de largo por. **2** *vi* pasar cerca; **if you're ever passing by** si alguna vez pasas por aquí.
● **pass off 1** *vt* **to p. oneself off as sth** hacerse pasar por algo. **2** *vi* (*happen*) transcurrir.
● **pass on** *vt* (*hand on*) transmitir. **2** *vi* (*die*) pasar a mejor vida.

- **pass out** vi (faint) desmayarse.
- **pass over** vt (disregard) pasar por alto.
- **pass round** vt (cakes etc) pasar (de uno a otro).
- **pass through** vi estar de paso.
- **pass up** vt (opportunity) renunciar a; (offer) rechazar.

passable a (road) transitable; (acceptable) pasable.

passage ['pæsɪdʒ] (hallway) pasillo m; (in music, text) pasaje m.

passageway (interior) pasillo m; (exterior) pasaje m.

passbook libreta f de banco.

passenger ['pæsɪndʒəʳ] pasajero,-a mf.

passer-'by transeúnte mf.

passion ['pæʃən] pasión f.

passionate a apasionado,-a.

passive ['pæsɪv] a pasivo,-a.

pass mark (in exam) aprobado m.

passport pasaporte m.

past [pɑːst] **1** n pasado m; **in the p.** antiguamente. **2** a pasado,-a; (former) anterior; **in the p. weeks** en las últimas semanas. **3** adv por delante; **to run p.** pasar corriendo. **4** prep (beyond) más allá de; (more than) más de; **it's five p. ten** son las diez y cinco.

pasta ['pæstə] pasta f.

paste [peɪst] **1** n pasta f; (glue) engrudo m. **2** vt (stick) pegar.

pasteurized ['pæstjəraɪzd] a pasteurizado,-a.

pastille ['pæstɪl] pastilla f.

pastime ['pɑːstaɪm] pasatiempo m.

pastry ['peɪstrɪ] (dough) pasta f; (cake) pastel m.

pasture ['pɑːstʃəʳ] pasto m.

pat [pæt] vt acariciar.

patch [pætʃ] (of material) parche m; (of colour) mancha f; **to go through a bad p.** pasar por una mala racha.

- **patch up** vt (garment) poner un parche en; **to p. up a quarrel** hacer las paces (**with** con).

path [pɑːθ] sendero m; (route) camino m.

pathetic [pə'θetɪk] a (hopeless) malísimo,-a.

pathway sendero m.

patience paciencia f; **to lose one's p. with sb** perder la paciencia con algn.

patient ['peɪʃənt] **1** a paciente. **2** n paciente mf.

patiently adv con paciencia.

patio ['pætɪəʊ] patio m.

patriotic [pætrɪ'ɒtɪk] a (person) patriota; (speech, act) patriótico,-a.

patrol [pə'trəʊl] **1** n patrulla f. **2** vt patrullar por.

pattern ['pætən] (*in sewing*) patrón; (*design*) dibujo *m*.

pause [pɔ:z] **1** *n* pausa *f*; (*in conversation*) silencio *m*. **2** *vi* hacer una pausa.

paved [peɪvd] *a* pavimentado,-a.

pavement ['peɪvmənt] acera *f*; *US* (*road surface*) calzada *f*.

pavilion [pə'vɪljən] pabellón *m*.

paving stone losa *f*.

paw [pɔ:] (*foot*) pata *f*; (*of cat*) garra *f*.

pawn [pɔ:n] (*in chess*) peón *m*.

pay [peɪ] **1** *n* (*wages*) paga *f*. **2** *vt** pagar; (*attention*) prestar; (*visit*) hacer; (*be profitable for*) compensar; **to be** *or* **get paid** cobrar; **to p. sb a compliment** halagar a algn. **3** *vi* pagar; (*be profitable*) ser rentable; **to p. for sth** pagar (por) algo.

● **pay back** *vt* reembolsar.

● **pay in** *vt* (*money*) ingresar.

● **pay off** *vt* (*debt*) liquidar.

● **pay out** *vt* (*spend*) gastar (**on** en).

● **pay up 1** *vt* (*bill*) liquidar, saldar. **2** *vi* pagar.

payable *a* pagadero,-a.

pay cheque, *US* **paycheck** sueldo *m*.

payment pago *m*.

payphone teléfono *m* público.

pay slip nómina *f*.

pea [pi:] guisante *m*.

peace [pi:s] paz *f*; (*calm*) tranquilidad *f*; **at** *or* **in p.** en paz; **p. and quiet** tranquilidad.

peaceful *a* (*non-violent*) pacífico,-a; (*calm*) tranquilo,-a.

peach [pi:tʃ] melocotón *m*.

peacock ['pi:kɒk] pavo *m* real.

peak [pi:k] (*of mountain*) pico *m*; (*summit*) cima *f*; **p. hours** horas *fpl* punta.

peaky ['pi:kɪ] *a fam* (*ill*) pálido,-a.

peanut ['pi:nʌt] cacahuete *m*.

pear [peəʳ] pera *f*.

pearl [pɜ:l] perla *f*.

pebble ['pebəl] guijarro *m*; (*small*) china *f*.

pecan [pɪ'kæn] (*nut*) pacana *f*.

peck [pek] *vt* picotear.

peckish ['pekɪʃ] *a* **to feel p.** empezar a tener hambre.

peculiar [pɪ'kju:lɪəʳ] *a* (*odd*) extraño,-a; (*particular*) característico,-a.

peculi'arity (*characteristic*) característica *f*.

pedal ['pedəl] **1** *n* pedal *m*. **2** *vi* pedalear.

pedestrian [pɪ'destrɪən] peatón,-ona *mf*.

pedestrian crossing paso *m* de peatones.

peek [piːk] **1** *n* ojeada *f*. **2** *vi* to p. at sth mirar algo a hurtadillas.

peel [piːl] **1** *n* piel *f*; (*of orange, lemon*) cáscara *f*. **2** *vt* (*fruit*) pelar. **3** *vi* (*paint*) desconcharse; (*skin*) pelarse.

● **peel off** *vt* (*skin of fruit*) pelar; (*clothes*) quitarse.

peeler potato p. pelapatatas *m inv*.

peep [piːp] **1** *n* (*glance*) ojeada *f*; (*furtive look*) mirada furtiva. **2** *vi* to p. at sth echar una ojeada a algo.

peer [pɪəʳ] *vi* mirar detenidamente.

peg [peg] clavija *f*; (*for coat, hat*) colgador *m*.

pen¹ [pen] pluma *f*.

pen² (*for animals*) corral *m*.

penalty ['penəltɪ] (*punishment*) pena *f*; (*in sport*) castigo *m*; (*in football*) penalti *m*.

pence [pens] *npl see* **penny**.

pencil ['pensəl] lápiz *m*.

pencil case estuche *m* de lápices.

pencil sharpener sacapuntas *m inv*.

pendulum ['pendjʊləm] péndulo *m*.

penetrate ['penɪtreɪt] *vt* (*break through, grasp*) penetrar; (*forest, territory*) adentrarse en.

penfriend amigo,-a *mf* por carta.

penguin ['pengwɪn] pingüino *m*.

penicillin [penɪ'sɪlɪn] penicilina *f*.

peninsula [pɪ'nɪnsjʊlə] península *f*.

penknife navaja *f*.

penniless *a* sin dinero.

penny ['penɪ] (*pl* pennies; (*value*) pence [pens] penique *m*.

pension ['penʃən] pensión *f*; retirement p. jubilación *f*.

pensioner jubilado,-a *mf*.

people ['piːpəl] *npl* gente *f sing*; (*individuals*) personas *fpl*; (*nation*) pueblo *m*; old p.'s home asilo *m* de ancianos; p. say that ... se dice que ...

pepper ['pepəʳ] (*spice*) pimienta *f*; (*fruit*) pimiento *m*.

peppermint hierbabuena *f*; (*sweet*) pastilla *f* de menta.

per [pɜːʳ] *prep* por; 5 times p. week 5 veces a la semana; p. cent por ciento; p. day/annum al or por día/año; p. capita or person per cápita.

percentage [pə'sentɪdʒ] porcentaje *m*.

perch [pɜːtʃ] **1** *n* (*for bird*) percha *f*. **2** *vi* (*bird*) posarse (on en).

percolator ['pɜːkəleɪtəʳ] cafetera *f* de filtro.

perfect ['pɜːfɪkt] **1** *a* perfecto,-a; p. tense tiempo perfecto. **2** [pə'fekt] *vt* perfeccionar.

perfectly *adv* perfectamente; (*absolutely*) completamente.
per'fection perfección *f.*
perform [pəˈfɔːm] **1** *vt* (*task*) realizar; (*piece of music*) interpretar; (*play*) representar. **2** *vi* (*machine*) funcionar; (*musician*) tocar; (*actor*) actuar.
performance (*of task*) realización *f*; (*of piece of music*) interpretación *f*; (*of play*) representación *f*; (*in sport*) actuación *f*; (*of machine etc*) rendimiento *m.*
performer (*singer*) intérprete *mf*; (*actor*) actor *m*, actriz *f.*
perfume [ˈpɜːfjuːm] perfume *m.*
perhaps [pəˈhæps] *adv* tal vez, quizá(s).
peril [ˈperil] (*danger*) peligro *m.*
period [ˈpɪərɪəd] período *m*; (*stage*) etapa *f*; (*at school*) clase *f*; (*full stop*) punto *m*; (*menstruation*) regla *f.*
peri'odical revista *f.*
peripheral [pəˈrɪfərəl] periférico *m.*
perk [pɜːk] extra *m.*
● **perk up** *vi* animarse.
perm [pɜːm] **1** *n* permanente *f.* **2** *vt* **to have one's hair permed** hacerse la permanente.
permanent [ˈpɜːmənənt] *a* permanente; (*address, job*) fijo,-a.
permanently *adv* permanentemente.
per'mission permiso *m.*
permit [ˈpɜːmɪt] **1** *n* permiso *m.* **2** [pəˈmɪt] *vt* **to p. sb to do sth** permitir a algn hacer algo.
perpendicular [pɜːpənˈdɪkjʊləʳ] *a* perpendicular.
persecute [ˈpɜːsɪkjuːt] *vt* perseguir.
perse'cution persecución *f.*
perseverance perseverancia *f.*
persevere [pɜːsɪˈvɪəʳ] *vi* perseverar.
persist [pəˈsɪst] *vi* empeñarse (**in** en).
persistent *a* (*person*) perseverante; (*continual*) constante.
person [ˈpɜːsən] persona *f*; **in p.** en persona.
personal [ˈpɜːsənəl] *a* (*private*) personal; (*friend*) íntimo,-a; *pej* (*comment etc*) indiscreto,-a; **he will make a p. appearance** estará aquí en persona.
personality personalidad *f.*
personally *adv* (*for my part*) personalmente; (*in person*) en persona.
personnel [pɜːsəˈnel] personal *m.*
persuade [pəˈsweɪd] *vt* persuadir; **to p. sb to do sth** persuadir a algn para que haga algo.
persuasion persuasión *f.*
Peruvian [pəˈruːvɪən] *a & n* peruano,-a (*mf*).

pessimist ['pesɪmɪst] pesimista *mf*.
pessi'mistic *a* pesimista.
pest [pest] (*animal, insect*) plaga *f*; *fam* (*person*) pelma *mf*; (*thing*) lata *f*.
pester ['pestəʳ] *vt* molestar.
pet [pet] **1** *n* animal *m* doméstico. **2** *a* (*favourite*) preferido,-a.
petal ['petəl] pétalo *m*.
petition [pɪ'tɪʃən] petición *f*.
petrol ['petrəl] gasolina *f*.
petroleum [pə'trəʊlɪəm] petróleo *m*.
petrol station gasolinera *f*.
petrol tank depósito *m* de gasolina.
petticoat ['petɪkəʊt] enaguas *fpl*.
petty ['petɪ] *a* (*trivial*) insignificante; (*small-minded*) mezquino,-a.
petty cash dinero *m* para gastos pequeños.
pharmacist farmacéutico,-a *mf*.
pharmacy ['fɑːməsɪ] farmacia *f*.
phase [feɪz] **1** *n* fase *f*. **2** *vt* **to p. sth in/out** introducir/retirar algo progresivamente.
PhD [piːeɪtʃ'diː] Doctor,-a *mf* en Filosofía.
pheasant ['fezənt] faisán *m*.
phenomenal [fɪ'nɒmɪnəl] *a* fenomenal.
phenomenon [fɪ'nɒmɪnən] (*pl* **phenomena** [fɪ'nɒmɪnə] fenómeno *m*.
philosopher filósofo,-a *mf*.
philo'sophical *a* filosófico,-a.
philosophy [fɪ'lɒsəfɪ] filosofía *f*.
phlegm [flem] flema *f*.
phone [fəʊn] **1** *n* teléfono *m*. **2** *vt* llamar por teléfono a.
• **phone back** *vti* (volver a) llamar por teléfono.
• **phone up** *vt* llamar por teléfono.
phone book guía *f* telefónica.
phone booth *or* **box** cabina *f* telefónica.
phonecall llamada *f* (telefónica).
phonecard tarjeta *f* telefónica.
phone number número *m* de teléfono.
phonetic [fə'netɪk] *a* fonético,-a.
photo ['fəʊtəʊ] foto *f*.
photocopier fotocopiadora *f*.
photocopy 1 *n* fotocopia *f*. **2** *vt* fotocopiar.
photograph 1 *n* fotografía *f*. **2** *vt* fotografiar.
photographer fotógrafo,-a *mf*.
photography fotografía *f*.
phrase [freɪz] frase *f*.

phrasebook libro *m* de frases.
physical ['fɪzɪkəl] *a* físico,-a.
physically *adv* físicamente; **p. handicapped** minusválido,-a.
physics física *f*.
'pianist pianista *mf*.
piano [pɪ'ænəʊ] piano *m*.
pick [pɪk] **1** *n* (*tool*) pico *m*; **take your p.** (*choice*) elige el que quieras. **2** *vt* (*choose*) escoger; (*team*) seleccionar; (*flowers, fruit*) coger; (*lock*) forzar. **to p. one's nose** hurgarse la nariz.
● **pick on** *vt* (*persecute*) meterse con.
● **pick out** *vt* (*choose*) elegir; (*identify*) identificar.
● **pick up 1** *vt* (*object on floor*) recoger; (*telephone*) descolgar; (*collect*) recoger; (*shopping, person*) buscar; (*acquire*) conseguir; (*learn*) aprender; **to p. up speed** ganar velocidad. **2** *vi* (*improve*) mejorarse.
pickaxe, *US* **pickax** piqueta *f*.
pickle ['pɪkəl] *vt* (*food*) conservar en adobo *or* escabeche; **pickled onions** cebollas *fpl* en vinagre.
pickpocket carterista *mf*.
picnic ['pɪknɪk] comida *f* de campo, picnic *m*.
picture ['pɪktʃəʳ] **1** *n* (*painting*) cuadro *m*; (*drawing*) dibujo *m*; (*portrait*) retrato *m*; (*photo*) foto *f*; (*on TV*) imagen *f*; (*at cinema*) película *f*; **to go to the pictures** ir al cine. **2** *vt* (*imagine*) imaginarse.
picture frame marco *m*.
picturesque [pɪktʃə'resk] *a* pintoresco,-a.
pie [paɪ] (*fruit*) tarta *f*; (*big*) (*small*) pastel *m*; (*meat etc*) empanada *f*; (*pasty*) empanadilla *f*.
piece [piːs] pedazo *m*; (*of paper*) trozo *m*; (*part*) pieza *f*; (*coin*) moneda *f*; **a p. of news** una noticia; **to break sth into pieces** hacer algo pedazos.
pier [pɪəʳ] embarcadero *m*, muelle *m*.
pierce [pɪəs] *vt* perforar.
piercing *a* (*sound etc*) penetrante.
pig [pɪg] cerdo *m*.
pigeon ['pɪdʒɪn] paloma *f*.
pigeonhole casilla *f*.
piggyback to give sb a p. llevar a algn a cuestas.
pigtail trenza *f*.
pilchard ['pɪltʃəd] sardina *f*.
pile [paɪl] **1** *n* montón *m*. **2** *vt* amontonar.
● **pile up 1** *vt* (*things*) amontonar; (*riches, debts*) acumular. **2** *vi* amontonarse.
piles *sing* (*illness*) hemorroides *fpl*.
pile-up choque *m* en cadena.

pill [pɪl] píldora *f*; **to be on the p.** estar tomando la píldora (anticonceptiva).

pillar ['pɪlə'] pilar *m*, columna *f*.

pillar box buzón *m*.

pillow ['pɪləʊ] almohada *f*.

pillowcase funda *f* de almohada.

pilot ['paɪlət] piloto *m*.

pimple ['pɪmpəl] espinilla *f*.

pin [pɪn] **1** *n* alfiler *m*. **2** *vt* (*onto board*) clavar con chinchetas.

pin up *vt* clavar con chinchetas.

pinafore ['pɪnəfɔ:'] (*apron*) delantal *m*.

'pinball flipper *m*.

pincers ['pɪnsəz] *npl* (*tool*) tenazas *fpl*.

pinch [pɪntʃ] **1** *n* (*nip*) pellizco *m*; **a p. of salt** una pizca de sal. **2** *vt* pellizcar; *fam* (*steal*) birlar.

pincushion acerico *m*.

pine [paɪn] (*tree*) pino *m*.

pineapple piña *f*.

pink [pɪŋk] *a* rosa *inv*.

pinkie ['pɪŋkɪ] *US* dedo *m* meñique.

pint [paɪnt] pinta *f* (*Br = 0.57 litre, Am = 0.47 liter*); **a p. of beer** una cerveza.

pip [pɪp] (*seed*) pepita *f*.

pipe [paɪp] tubería *f*; (*for smoking*) pipa *f*.

pirate ['paɪrɪt] pirata *m*.

pistachio [pɪs'tɑ:ʃɪəʊ] pistacho *m*.

pistol ['pɪstəl] pistola *f*.

pit [pɪt] hoyo *m*; (*large*) hoya *f*; (*coal mine*) mina *f* de carbón.

pitch [pɪtʃ] **1** *vt* (*throw*) lanzar; (*tent*) armar. **2** *n* (*for sport*) campo *m*; (*throw*) lanzamiento *m*.

pitch-'black, pitch-'dark *a* negro,-a como boca de lobo.

pity ['pɪtɪ] **1** *n* (*compassion*) compasión *f*; (*shame*) lástima *f*; **what a p.!** ¡qué pena! **2** *vt* compadecerse de.

pizza ['pi:tsə] pizza *f*.

placard ['plækɑ:d] pancarta *f*.

place [pleɪs] **1** *n* sitio *m*, lugar *m*; (*seat*) sitio *m*; (*on bus*) asiento *m*; (*position on scale*) posición *f*; (*house*) casa *f*; (*building*) lugar *m*; **to take p.** tener lugar; **to take sb's p.** sustituir a algn; **in the first p.** en primer lugar; **we're going to his p.** vamos a su casa. **2** *vt* poner, colocar; (*face, person*) recordar.

place mat tapete *m* individual.

place setting cubierto *m*.

plague peste *f*.

plaice [pleɪs] *inv* (*fish*) platija *f*.

plain ['pleɪn] **1** *a* (*clear*) claro,-a; (*simple*) sencillo,-a; (*unattractive*) poco atractivo,-a; **the p. truth** la verdad lisa y llana. **2** *n* (*land*) llanura *f*.

plainly *adv* claramente; (*simply*) sencillamente; **to speak p.** hablar con franqueza.

plait [plæt] **1** *n* trenza *f*. **2** *vt* trenzar.

plan [plæn] plan *m*. **2** *vt* (*for future*) planear; (*economy*) planificar; (*intend*) pensar; **to p. on doing sth** tener la intención de hacer algo.

plan for *vt* (*disaster*) prevenirse contra.

plane[1] [pleɪn] avión *m*.

plane[2] (*tool*) cepillo *m*.

plane[3] **p. (tree)** plátano *m*.

planet ['plænɪt] planeta *m*.

plank [plæŋk] tabla *f*.

plant[1] [plɑːnt] **1** *n* planta *f*. **2** *vt* (*flowers*) plantar; (*bomb*) colocar.

plant[2] (*factory*) planta *f* (industrial).

plaster ['plɑːstəʳ] yeso *m*; (*for broken limb*) escayola *f*; Br **sticking p.** esparadrapo *m*.

plaster cast (*for broken arm*) escayola *f*.

plastic ['plæstɪk] **1** *n* plástico *m*. **2** *a* (*cup, bag*) de plástico.

Plasticine(R) ['plæstɪsiːn] plastilina *f*.

plastic surgery cirugía *f* plástica.

plate [pleɪt] plato *m*; (*sheet*) placa *f*.

platform ['plætfɔːm] plataforma *f*; (*at meeting*) tribuna *f*; (*at station*) andén *m*.

play [pleɪ] **1** *vt* (*game*) jugar a; (*team*) jugar contra; (*instrument, tune*) tocar; (*part*) hacer (el papel) de; **to p. a record** poner un disco; *fig* **to p. a part in sth** participar en algo. **2** *vi* jugar (**with** con). **3** *n* obra *f* de teatro.

• **play back** *vt* (*tape*) volver a poner.

• **play down** *vt* quitar importancia a.

player jugador,-a *mf*; (*in play*) (*man*) actor *m*; (*woman*) actriz *f*.

playground (*in school*) patio *m* de recreo; (*recreation ground*) parque *m* infantil.

playgroup jardín *m* de infancia.

playing card carta *f*.

playing field campo *m* de deportes.

playpen corralito *m* or parque *m* (de niños).

playschool jardín *m* de infancia.

playtime recreo *m*.

pleasant ['plezənt] *a* agradable.

pleasantly *adv* agradablemente.

please [pli:z] **1** *adv* por favor; **'p. do not smoke'** 'se ruega no fumar'. **2** *vt* (*give pleasure to*) complacer. **3** *vi* do as you p. haz lo que quieras.

pleased *a* (*happy*) contento,-a; (*satisfied*) satisfecho,-a; **p. to meet you!** ¡encantado,-a!.

pleasing *a* (*pleasant*) agradable.

pleasure ['pleʒə^r] placer *m*; **with p.** con mucho gusto.

pleat [pli:t] pliegue *m*.

pleated *a* plisado,-a.

plentiful *a* abundante.

plenty ['plentɪ] **p. of potatoes** muchas patatas; **p. of time** tiempo de sobra.

pliers ['plaɪəz] *npl* alicates *mpl*, tenazas *fpl*.

plimsolls ['plɪmsəlz] *npl* Br zapatos *mpl* de tenis.

plot¹ [plɒt] **1** *n* (*conspiracy*) complot *m*; (*story*) argumento *m*. **2** *vi* conspirar.

plot² (*ground*) terreno *m*; (*for building*) solar *m*.

plough [plaʊ] **1** *n* arado *m*. **2** *vt* arar.

plow [plaʊ] *US* = **plough**.

pluck [plʌk] *vt* (*flowers*) coger; (*chicken*) desplumar.

plug [plʌg] **1** *n* (*in bath etc*) tapón *m*; (*electric*) enchufe *m*; **2/3 pin p.** clavija bipolar/tripolar. **2** *vt* (*hole*) tapar.

● **plug in 1** *vt* enchufar. **2** *vi* enchufarse.

plum [plʌm] (*fruit*) ciruela *f*.

plumber ['plʌmə^r] fontanero,-a *mf*.

plumbing (*system*) fontanería *f*.

plump [plʌmp] *a* (*person*) rechoncho,-a; (*baby*) rellenito,-a.

plunge [plʌndʒ] **1** *vt* (*immerse*) sumergir; (*thrust*) arrojar. **2** *vi* (*dive*) zambullirse; (*fall*) caer.

plural ['plʊərəl] *a & n* plural (*m*); **in the p.** en plural.

plus [plʌs] *prep* más; **three p. four makes seven** tres más cuatro hacen siete.

p.m. [pi:'em] (*from midday to early evening*) de la tarde; (*at night*) de la noche.

pneumatic [njʊ'mætɪk] *a* neumático,-a.

pneumatic drill martillo *m* neumático.

PO Box [pi:'əʊbɒks] apartado *m* (de Correos).

poach [pəʊtʃ] *vt* (*egg*) escalfar.

pocket ['pɒkɪt] bolsillo *m*.

pocketbook *US* bolso *m*.

pocketful **a p. of** un bolsillo de.

pocket money dinero *m* de bolsillo.

poem ['pəʊɪm] poema *m*.

poet poeta *mf*.

po'etic *a* poético,-a.

poetry poesía *f*.

point [pɔɪnt] **1** *n* (*sharp end*) punta *f*; (*place*) punto *m*; (*score*) tanto *m*; (*moment*) **at that p.** en aquel momento; **to be on the p. of doing sth** estar a punto de hacer algo; **there's no p. in going** no merece la pena ir; **six p. three** seis coma tres; **up to a p.** hasta cierto punto; **power p.** toma *f* de corriente; **points** (*on railway*) agujas *fpl*. **2** *vt* (*way etc*) indicar; **to p. a gun at sb** apuntar a algn con una pistola. **3** *vi* **to p. at sth/sb** (*with finger*) señalar algo/a algn con el dedo.

● **point out** *vt* indicar; (*mention*) hacer resaltar.

pointed *a* (*sharp*) puntiagudo,-a.

pointless *a* sin sentido.

poison ['pɔɪzən] **1** *n* veneno *m*. **2** *vt* envenenar.

poisonous *a* (*plant, snake*) venenoso,-a; (*gas*) tóxico,-a.

poke [pəʊk] *vt* (*fire*) atizar; (*with finger*) dar con la punta del dedo a; (*with stick*) dar con la punta del bastón; **to p. one's head out** asomar la cabeza.

● **poke about,** *or* **around** *vi* fisgonear *or* hurgar en.

poker (*for fire*) atizador *m*.

polar ['pəʊlə°] *a* polar.

polar bear oso *m* polar.

Pole polaco,-a *mf*.

pole[1] [pəʊl] *n* palo *m*.

pole[2] (*north, south*) polo *m*.

police [pə'li:s] *npl* policía *f sing*.

police car coche *m* patrulla.

policeman policía *m*.

police station comisaría *f*.

policewoman (mujer *f*) policía *f*.

policy ['pɒlɪsɪ] política *f*; (*insurance*) póliza *f* (de seguros).

polio ['pəʊlɪəʊ] poliomielitis *f*.

polish ['pɒlɪʃ] **1** *vt* pulir; (*furniture*) encerar; (*shoes*) limpiar. **2** *n* (*for furniture*) cera *f*; (*for shoes*) betún *m*; (*for nails*) esmalte *m*.

● **polish off** *vt* (*food*) zamparse.

● **polish up** *vt fig* perfeccionar.

Polish ['pəʊlɪʃ] **1** *a* polaco,-a. **2** *n* (*language*) polaco *m*.

polite [pə'laɪt] *a* educado,-a.

politely *adv* educadamente.

politeness educación *f*.

po'litical [pə'lɪtɪkəl] *a* político,-a.

poli'tician político,-a *mf*.

politics ['pɒlɪtɪks] política *f*.

poll [pəʊl] votación *f*; (*survey*) encuesta *f*; **to go to the polls** acudir a las urnas.

pollen ['pɒlən] polen *m*.

polling station colegio *m* electoral.

pollute [pə'luːt] *vt* contaminar.

pollution contaminación *f*.

polo ['pəʊləʊ] **p. neck sweater** jersey *m* de cuello vuelto.

polyester [pɒlɪ'estəʳ] poliéster *m*.

polytechnic [pɒlɪ'teknɪk] politécnico *m*.

polythene ['pɒlɪθiːn] polietileno *m*.

pomegranate ['pɒmɪgrænɪt] granada *f*.

pond [pɒnd] estanque *m*.

pony ['pəʊnɪ] poney *m*.

ponytail cola *f* de caballo.

poodle ['puːdəl] caniche *m*.

pool [puːl] (*of water, oil etc*) charco *m*; **swimming p.** piscina *f*.

pooped [puːpt] *a fam* hecho,-a polvo.

poor [pʊəʳ] **1** *a* pobre; (*quality*) malo,-a. **2** *npl* **the p.** los pobres.

poorly 1 (*badly*) mal. **2** *a* (*ill*) enfermo,-a.

pop [pɒp] **1** *vt* (*burst*) hacer reventar. **2** *vi* (*burst*) reventar; *fam* **I'm just popping over to Ian's** voy un momento a casa de Ian. **3** *n* (*drink*) gaseosa *f*; *fam* (*father*) papá *m*; (*music*) música *f* pop.

● **pop in** *vi fam* entrar un momento.

popcorn palomitas *fpl*.

Pope [pəʊp] **the P.** el Papa.

poppy ['pɒpɪ] amapola *f*.

popsicle ['pɒpsɪkəl] (*ice lolly*) US polo *m*.

pop singer cantante *mf* pop.

popular ['pɒpjʊləʳ] *a* popular; (*fashionable*) de moda.

populated *a* **thinly p.** poco poblado.

population [pɒpjʊ'leɪʃən] población *f*.

porch [pɔːtʃ] (*of house*) porche *m*; US (*veranda*) terraza *f*.

pork [pɔːk] carne *f* de cerdo.

porridge ['pɒrɪdʒ] gachas *fpl* de avena.

port [pɔːt] (*harbour, of computer*) puerto *m*.

portable ['pɔːtəbəl] *a & n* portátil (*m*).

porter ['pɔːtəʳ] (*in hotel etc*) portero,-a *mf*.

porthole portilla *f*.

portion ['pɔːʃən] (*part, piece*) parte *f*; (*of food*) ración *f*.

portrait ['pɔːtrɪt] retrato *m*.

Portuguese [pɔːtjʊ'giːz] **1** *a* portugués,-esa. **2** *n* (*person*) portugués,-esa *mf*; (*language*) portugués *m*.

pose [pəʊz] **1** vt (problem) plantear; (threat) representar. **2** vi (for painting) posar; **to p. as** hacerse pasar por.

posh [pɒʃ] Br a elegante; (person) presumido,-a; (accent) de clase alta.

position [pə'zɪʃən] posición f; (location) situación f, (rank) rango m; **to be in a p. to do sth** estar en condiciones de hacer algo.

positive ['pɒzɪtɪv] a positivo,-a; (sign) favorable; (sure) seguro,-a.

possess [pə'zes] vt poseer.

possessions npl bienes mpl.

possessive a posesivo,-a.

possi'bility posibilidad f.

possible ['pɒsɪbəl] a posible; **as much as p.** todo lo posible; **as often as p.** cuanto más mejor; **as soon as p.** cuanto antes.

possibly adv posiblemente; (perhaps) quizás; **I can't p. come** no puedo venir de ninguna manera.

post¹ [pəʊst] (wooden) poste m.

post² (job) puesto m.

post³ Br **1** n (mail) correo m; **by p.** por correo. **2** vt (letter) echar al correo; **to p. sth to sb** mandar algo por correo a algn.

post up vt (notice) fijar.

postage franqueo m.

postage stamp sello m (de correos).

postal a postal.

postal order giro m postal.

postbox Br buzón m.

postcard (tarjeta f) postal f.

postcode Br código m postal.

poster ['pəʊstə'] póster m; (advertising) cartel m.

post'graduate posgraduado,-a mf.

postman cartero m.

postmark matasellos m inv.

post office oficina f de correos; **where is the p.?** ¿dónde está correos?

postpone [pə'spəʊn] vt aplazar.

postponement aplazamiento m.

pot [pɒt] (for cooking) olla f; (for flowers) maceta f.

potato [pə'teɪtəʊ] (pl potatoes) patata f.

potential [pə'tenʃəl] **1** a potencial. **2** n potencial m.

potter ['pɒtə'] alfarero,-a mf.

pottery (craft, place) alfarería f; (objects) cerámica f.

potty ['pɒtɪ] orinal m.

pouch [paʊtʃ] bolsa f pequeña; (of animal) bolsa f abdominal.

pouf(fe) [pu:f] (seat) puf m.

poultry ['pəʊltrɪ] (live) aves fpl de corral; (food) pollos mpl.

pounce [paʊns] *vi* **to p. on** abalanzarse encima de.

pound¹ [paʊnd] *(money, weight)* libra *f*.

pound² *(for dogs)* perrera *f*; *(for cars)* depósito *m* de coches.

pour [pɔːʳ] **1** *vt* verter; **to p. sb a drink** servirle una copa a algn. **2** *vi* **it's pouring with rain** está lloviendo a cántaros.

● **pour away** *vt* *(liquid)* vaciar.

● **pour in** *vi* *(water)* entrar a raudales; *(applications)* llegar sin parar.

● **pour out 1** *vt* verter. **2** *vi* *(liquid, people)* salir a raudales.

poverty ['pɒvətɪ] pobreza *f*.

powder ['paʊdəʳ] **1** *n* polvo *m*. **2** *vt* **to p. one's nose** empolvarse la cara.

powdered *a* *(milk)* en polvo.

power ['paʊəʳ] fuerza *f*; *(energy)* energía *f*; *(ability, authority)* poder *m*; *(nation)* potencia *f*; **to be in p.** estar en el poder.

powerful *a* *(influential)* poderoso,-a; *(engine, machine)* potente.

power point enchufe *m*.

power station central *f* eléctrica.

practical ['præktɪkəl] *a* práctico,-a.

practical joke broma *f* pesada.

practically *(almost)* casi.

practice ['præktɪs] **1** *n* *(exercise)* práctica *f*; *(in sport)* entrenamiento *m*; *(rehearsal)* ensayo *m*; *(habit)* costumbre *f*; *(way of doing sth)* práctica *f*; **to be out of p.** no estar en forma; **in p.** en la práctica. **2** *vti* US = **practise**.

practise 1 *vt* practicar; *(principle)* poner en práctica; *(profession)* ejercer. **2** *vi* practicar; *(in sport)* entrenar; *(rehearse)* ensayar; *(doctor)* practicar; *(lawyer)* ejercer.

praise [preɪz] **1** *n* alabanza *f*. **2** *vt* alabar.

pram [præm] *Br* cochecito *m* de niño.

prank [præŋk] travesura *f*; *(joke)* broma *f*.

prawn [prɔːn] gamba *f*.

pray [preɪ] *vi* rezar.

prayer [preəʳ] oración *f*.

precaution [prɪ'kɔːʃən] precaución *f*.

precede [prɪ'siːd] *vt* preceder.

preceding *a* precedente.

precious ['preʃəs] *a* precioso,-a.

precise [prɪ'saɪs] *a* preciso,-a; *(meticulous)* meticuloso,-a.

precocious [prɪ'kəʊʃəs] *a* precoz.

predecessor ['priːdɪsesəʳ] antecesor,-a *mf*.

predicament [prɪ'dɪkəmənt] apuro *m*, aprieto *m*.

predict [prɪ'dɪkt] *vt* predecir.

predictable *a* previsible.

prediction pronóstico *m*.

preface ['prefis] prefacio *m*.

prefer [prɪ'fɜːʳ] *vt* preferir; **I p. coffee to tea** prefiero el café al té.

preferable ['prefərəbəl] *a* preferible (**to** a).

'preferably *adv* preferentemente.

'preference preferencia *f*.

prefix ['priːfɪks] prefijo *m*.

pregnancy ['pregnənsɪ] embarazo *m*.

pregnant *a* embarazada.

prehistoric(al) [priːhɪ'stɒrɪk(əl)] *a* prehistórico,-a.

prejudice ['predʒʊdɪs] (*bias*) prejuicio *m*.

preliminary [prɪ'lɪmɪnərɪ] *a* preliminar.

premises ['premɪsɪz] *npl* local *m*; **on the p.** en el local.

premium ['priːmɪəm] prima *f*.

prepa'ration preparación *f*; (*plan*) preparativo *m*.

prepare [prɪ'peəʳ] **1** *vt* preparar; **to p. to do sth** prepararse para hacer algo. **2** *vi* prepararse (**for** para).

prepared *a* (*ready*) preparado,-a; **to be p. to do sth** (*willing*) estar dispuesto,-a a hacer algo.

preposition [prepə'zɪʃən] preposición *f*.

prescribe [prɪ'skraɪb] *vt* (*medicine*) recetar.

prescription (*medical*) receta *f*.

presence ['prezəns] presencia *f*; (*attendance*) asistencia *f*.

present[1] ['prezənt] **1** *a* (*in attendance*) presente; (*current*) actual; **p. tense** (tiempo *m*) presente *m*. **2** *n* (*time*) presente *m*; **at p.** actualmente.

present[2] [prɪ'zent] **1** *vt* (*opportunity*) ofrecer; (*problems*) plantear; (*prize*) entregar; (*introduce*) (*person, programme*) presentar; **to p. sb with sth** obsequiar a algn con algo. **2** ['prezənt] *n* (*gift*) regalo *m*.

presentation presentación *f*; **p. ceremony** ceremonia *f* de entrega.

presently *adv* (*soon*) dentro de poco; *US* ahora.

preser'vation conservación *f*.

preservative conservante *m*.

preserve [prɪ'zɜːv] **1** *vt* (*keep*) mantener. **2** *n* conserva *f*.

presidency presidencia *f*.

president ['prezɪdənt] presidente,-a *mf*.

presi'dential *a* presidencial.

press [pres] **1** *vt* apretar; (*button*) pulsar; (*iron*) planchar; (*urge*) presionar; **to p. sb to do sth** acosar a algn para que haga algo. **2** *vi* (*push*) apretar; **to p. (down) on sth** hacer presión sobre algo. **3** *n* (*newspapers*) prensa *f*.

● **press on** *vi* seguir adelante.

press conference rueda *f* de prensa.

pressure ['preʃəʳ] presión *f*; **to bring p. (to bear) on sb** ejercer presión sobre algn.

pressure cooker olla *f* a presión.

pressure gauge manómetro *m*.

presume [prɪ'zju:m] *vt* suponer.

pretend [prɪ'tend] *vti* fingir.

pretext ['pri:tekst] pretexto *m*; **on the p. of** so pretexto de.

pretty ['prɪtɪ] **1** *a* (*thing*) bonito,-a; (*person*) guapo,-a. **2** *adv* bastante; **p. much the same** más o menos lo mismo.

prevent [prɪ'vent] *vt* impedir; (*accident*) evitar; **to p. sb from doing sth** impedir a algn hacer algo.

prevention prevención *f*.

previous ['pri:vɪəs] *a* anterior.

previously *adv* previamente.

prey [preɪ] presa *f*; *fig* víctima *f*.

price [praɪs] precio *m*.

price list lista *f* de precios.

prick [prɪk] *vt* picar; **to p. one's finger** pincharse el dedo.

prickly ['prɪklɪ] *a* espinoso,-a; (*touchy*) enojadizo,-a.

pride [praɪd] **1** *n* orgullo *m*; (*arrogance*) soberbia *f*; **to take p. in sth** enorgullecerse de algo. **2** *vt* **to p. oneself on** enorgullecerse de.

priest [pri:st] sacerdote *m*, cura *m*.

primarily *adv* ante todo.

primary ['praɪmərɪ] *a* **p. education/school** enseñanza *f*/escuela *f* primaria.

Prime Minister [praɪm] primer,-a ministro,-a *mf*.

prime number número *m* primo.

primitive ['prɪmɪtɪv] *a* primitivo,-a.

primrose ['prɪmrəʊz] primavera *f*.

prince [prɪns] príncipe *m*; **P. Charming** Príncipe Azul.

prin'cess princesa *f*.

principal ['prɪnsɪpəl] **1** *a* principal. **2** *n* (*of college etc*) director,-a *mf*.

principle principio *m*; **on p.** por principio.

print [prɪnt] **1** *vt* (*publish*) publicar; (*write*) escribir con letra de imprenta; **printed matter** impresos *mpl*. **2** *n* letra *f*; (*of hand, foot*) huella *f*; (*of photo*) copia *f*; **out of p.** agotado,-a.

• **print out** *vt* imprimir.

printer (*person*) impresor,-a *mf*; (*machine*) impresora *f*.

printout impresión *f*.

prior ['praɪəʳ] *a* anterior; **without p. warning** sin previo aviso.

priority [praɪ'ɒrɪtɪ] prioridad *f*.

prison ['prɪzən] prisión *f*.

prisoner preso,-a *mf*; **to hold sb p.** detener a algn.

privacy ['prɪvəsɪ] intimidad *f*.

private 1 *a* privado,-a; (*individual*) particular; (*personal*) personal; (*letter*) confidencial. **2** *n* (*soldier*) soldado *m* raso.

privately *adv* en privado; (*personally*) personalmente.

prize [praɪz] premio *m*.

prize-giving distribución *f* de premios.

prizewinner premiado,-a *mf*.

probable ['prɒbəbəl] *a* probable.

probably *adv* probablemente.

problem ['prɒbləm] problema *m*.

proceed [prə'siːd] *vi* proseguir; **to p. to do sth** ponerse a hacer algo.

process ['prəʊses] **1** *n* proceso *m*; **in the p. of** en vías de. **2** *vt* procesar.

processed cheese queso *m* tratado.

procession [prə'sefən] *n* desfile *m*; (*religious*) procesión *f*.

processor procesador *m*.

produce [prə'djuːs] **1** *vt* producir; (*manufacture*) fabricar; (*give birth to*) dar a luz a; (*show*) enseñar; (*bring out*) sacar. **2** ['prɒdjuːs] *n* productos *mpl*.

pro'ducer productor,-a *mf*; (*manufacturer*) fabricante *mf*.

product ['prɒdʌkt] producto *m*.

production producción *f*; (*manufacture*) fabricación *f*.

production line cadena *f* de montaje.

profession [prə'fefən] profesión *f*.

professional 1 *a* profesional; (*polished*) de gran calidad. **2** *n* profesional *mf*.

professor [prə'fesə'] catedrático,-a *mf*.

profit ['prɒfɪt] **1** *n* beneficio *m*; **to make a p. on** sacar beneficios de. **2** *vi* **to p. from** aprovecharse de.

profitable *a* rentable; (*worthwhile*) provechoso,-a.

program ['prəʊgræm] **1** *n* programa *m*. **2** *vti* programar.

programme, US **program 1** *n* programa *m*; (*plan*) plan. *m*. **2** *vt* (*computer*) programar.

progress ['prəʊgres] **1** *n* progreso *m*; **to make p.** hacer progresos; **in p.** en curso. **2** [prəʊ'gres] *vi* avanzar; (*develop*) desarrollarse; (*medically*) mejorar.

prohibit [prə'hɪbɪt] *vt* prohibir; **to p. sb from doing sth** prohibir a algn hacer algo

project ['prɒdʒekt] proyecto *m*; (*at school*) trabajo *m*.

pro'jector proyector *m*.

prolong [prə'lɒŋ] *vt* prolongar.

promenade [prɒmə'nɑːd] (*at seaside*) paseo *m* marítimo.

prominent ['prɒmɪnənt] a (*important*) importante; (*famous*) eminente.

promise ['prɒmɪs] **1** n promesa f; **to show p.** ser prometedor,-a. **2** vti prometer.

promising a prometedor,-a.

promote [prə'məʊt] vt ascender; (*product*) promocionar.

promotion (*in rank*) ascenso m; (*of product*) promoción f.

prompt [prɒmpt] **1** a (*quick*) rápido,-a; (*punctual*) puntual. **2** adv **at 2 o'clock p.** a las 2 en punto.

prone [prəʊn] a **to be p. to do sth** ser propenso,-a a hacer algo.

pronoun ['prəʊnaʊn] pronombre m.

pronounce [prə'naʊns] vt pronunciar.

pronunci'ation pronunciación f.

proof [pru:f] prueba f.

propeller [prə'pelə'] hélice f.

proper ['prɒpə'] a adecuado,-a; (*real*) auténtico,-a; **p. noun** nombre propio.

properly (*suitably, correctly, decently*) correctamente.

property ['prɒpətɪ] (*possession*) propiedad f; **personal p.** bienes mpl.

proportion [prə'pɔ:ʃən] proporción f; (*part, quantity*) parte f.

proposal propuesta f; **p. of marriage** propuesta de matrimonio.

propose [prə'pəʊz] **1** vt proponer; (*suggest*) sugerir. **2** vi (*ask to marry*) declararse.

props [prɒps] npl (*in theatre*) accesorios mpl.

prose [prəʊz] prosa f; (*translation*) traducción f inversa.

prospect ['prɒspekt] (*outlook*) perspectiva f; (*hope*) esperanza f.

prosperous ['prɒspərəs] a próspero,-a.

protect [prə'tekt] vt **to p. sb from sth** proteger a algn de algo.

protection protección f.

protective a protector,-a.

protest ['prəʊtest] **1** n protesta f. **2** vi protestar.

Protestant ['prɒtɪstənt] a & n protestante (*mf*).

protester manifestante mf.

proud [praʊd] a orgulloso,-a; (*arrogant*) soberbio,-a.

proudly adv con orgullo; (*arrogantly*) con soberbia.

prove [pru:v] vt demostrar; **it proved to be disastrous** resultó ser desastroso,-a.

proverb ['prɒvɜ:b] refrán m, proverbio m.

provide [prə'vaɪd] vt proporcionar; (*supplies*) suministrar.

provided conj **p. (that)** con tal de que.

province ['prɒvɪns] provincia f.

pro'vincial a provincial; *pej* provinciano,-a.

provoke [prə'vəʊk] vt provocar.

prowl 222

prowl [praʊl] *vi* merodear; **to p. about** *or* **around** rondar.

prowler merodeador *m*.

prune¹ [pru:n] ciruela *f* pasa.

prune² *vt* (*roses etc*) podar.

psychiatrist [saɪˈkaɪətrɪst] psiquiatra *mf*.

psycho'logical *a* psicológico,-a.

psychologist [saɪˈkɒlədʒɪst] psicólogo,-a *mf*.

pub [pʌb] *n* bar *m*.

public [ˈpʌblɪk] **1** *a* público,-a; **p. holiday** fiesta *f* nacional. **2** *n* **the p.** el público; **in p.** en público.

publication [pʌblɪˈkeɪʃən] publicación *f*.

publicity [pʌˈblɪsɪtɪ] publicidad *f*.

publish [ˈpʌblɪʃ] *vt* publicar, editar.

publisher editor,-a *mf*.

publishing (*business*) industria *f* editorial.

pudding [ˈpʊdɪŋ] pudín *m*; (*dessert*) postre *m*.

puddle [ˈpʌdəl] charco *m*.

puff [pʌf] **1** *n* (*of smoke*) bocanada *f*. **2** *vi* (*person*) jadear; **to p. on one's pipe** chupar la pipa.

pull [pʊl] **1** *n* **to give sth a p.** (*tug*) dar un tirón a algo. **2** *vt* (*tug*) dar un tirón a; (*drag*) tirar de; **to p. a muscle** sufrir un tirón en un músculo; **to p. the trigger** apretar el gatillo; **to p. sth to pieces** hacer pedazos algo.

• **pull apart** *vt* desmontar.

• **pull down** *vt* (*building*) derribar.

• **pull in 1** *vt* (*crowds*) atraer. **2** *vi* **to p. in(to the station)** entrar en la estación.

• **pull out 1** *vt* (*withdraw*) retirar. **2** *vi* (*car*) **to p. out to overtake** salirse para adelantar.

• **pull over** *vi* hacerse a un lado.

• **pull through** *vi* reponerse.

• **pull up 1** *vt* (*uproot*) desarraigar; (*draw close*) acercar. **2** *vi* (*stop*) pararse.

pullover jersey *m*.

pulse [pʌls] (*in body*) pulso *m*.

pump [pʌmp] **1** *n* bomba *f*. **2** *vt* bombear.

• **pump up** *vt* (*tyre*) inflar.

pumpkin [ˈpʌmpkɪn] calabaza *f*.

punch¹ [pʌntʃ] **1** *n* (*for making holes*) perforadora *f*. **2** *vt* (*ticket*) picar.

punch² **1** *n* (*blow*) puñetazo *m*. **2** *vt* (*with fist*) dar un puñetazo a.

punctual [ˈpʌŋktjʊəl] *a* puntual.

punctuation [pʌŋktjʊˈeɪʃən] puntuación *f*.

puncture [ˈpʌŋktʃəʳ] **1** *n* pinchazo *m*. **2** *vt* (*tyre*) pinchar.

punish ['pʌnɪʃ] *vt* castigar.
punishment castigo *m*.
pupil[1] ['pjuːpəl] (*at school*) alumno,-a *mf*.
pupil[2] (*in eye*) pupila *f*.
puppet ['pʌpɪt] títere *m*.
puppy ['pʌpɪ] cachorro,-a *mf* (de perro).
purchase ['pɜːtʃɪs] **1** *n* compra *f*. **2** *vt* comprar.
purchasing power poder *m* adquisitivo.
pure [pjʊəʳ] *a* puro,-a.
purely *adv* simplemente.
purple ['pɜːpəl] *a* morado,-a.
purpose ['pɜːpəs] propósito *m*; **on p.** a propósito.
purposely *adv* adrede.
purse [pɜːs] *Br* monedero *m*; *US* (*bag*) bolso *m*.
pursue [pəˈsjuː] *vt* (*criminal*) perseguir; (*person*) seguir.
push [pʊʃ] **1** *n* empujón *m*; **to give sth a p.** dar un empujón a algn. **2** *vt* empujar; (*button*) pulsar; **to p. one's finger into a hole** meter el dedo en un agujero. **3** *vi* empujar.
• **push aside** *vt* (*object*) apartar.
• **push in** *vi* colarse.
• **push off** *vi fam* **p. off!** ¡lárgate!
• **push on** *vi* (*continue*) seguir adelante.
• **push through** *vt* (*crowd*) abrirse paso entre; (*law*) aceptar (a la fuerza).
pushchair *Br* sillita *f* (de ruedas).
pushed [pʊʃt] *a* **to be p. for time/money** estar justo,-a de tiempo/dinero.
puss [pʊs], **pussy** ['pʊsɪ] minino *m*.
put[*] [pʊt] *vt* poner; (*place*) colocar; (*insert*) meter; (*express*) expresar; (*invest*) (*money*) invertir; **to p. a stop to sth** poner término a algo; **to p. a question to sb** hacer una pregunta a algn.
• **put across** *vt* (*idea etc*) comunicar.
• **put aside** *vt* (*money*) ahorrar; (*time*) reservar.
• **put away** *vt* (*tidy away*) recoger; (*save money*) ahorrar.
• **put back** *vt* (*postpone*) aplazar.
• **put by** *vt* (*money*) ahorrar.
• **put down** *vt* (*set down*) dejar; (*criticize*) criticar; (*write down*) apuntar.
• **put forward** *vt* (*theory*) exponer; (*proposal*) hacer.
• **put in** *vt* (*install*) instalar; (*complaint, request*) presentar; (*time*) pasar.
• **put off** *vt* (*postpone*) aplazar; (*switch off*) (*radio, light*) apagar; **to p. sb off (doing) sth** (*dissuade*) disuadir a algn de (hacer) algo.
• **put on** *vt* (*clothes*) poner(se); (*switch on*) (*radio*) poner; (*light*) encen-

der; **to p. on weight** engordar.

- **put out** *vt* (*switch off, extinguish*) apagar; (*place outside*) sacar; (*extend*) (*arm*) extender; (*hand*) tender; (*annoy*) molestar; (*inconvenience*) incordiar.
- **put through** *vt* (*on telephone*) **p. me through to Pat, please** póngame con Pat, por favor.
- **put together** *vt* (*assemble*) montar.
- **put up** *vt* (*raise*) levantar; (*picture*) colocar; (*curtains*) colgar; (*tent*) armar; (*prices*) subir; (*accommodate*) alojar; **to p. up a fight** ofrecer resistencia.
- **put up with** *vt* aguantar.

putty ['pʌtɪ] masilla *f*.

puzzle ['pʌzəl] **1** *n* rompecabezas *m inv*; (*mystery*) misterio *m*. **2** *vt* dejar perplejo,-a.

puzzling *a* extraño,-a.

pyjamas [pə'dʒɑːməz] *npl* pijama *m*.

pylon ['paɪlən] torre *f* (de conducción eléctrica).

pyramid ['pɪrəmɪd] pirámide *f*.

Q

qualification [kwɒlɪfɪ'keɪʃən] (*diploma etc*) título *m*.

qualified *a* capacitado,-a; **q. teacher** profesor titulado.

qualify *vi* (*in competition*) quedar clasificado,-a; **to q. as** (*doctor etc*) sacar el título de.

quality ['kwɒlɪtɪ] (*excellence*) calidad *f*; (*attribute*) cualidad *f*.

quantity ['kwɒntɪtɪ] cantidad *f*.

quarrel ['kwɒrəl] **1** *n* (*argument*) riña *f*, pelea *f*. **2** *vi* (*argue*) reñir.

quarrelling, *US* **quarreling** disputas *fpl*.

quarry ['kwɒrɪ] cantera *f*.

quart [kwɔːt] cuarto *m* de galón (*Br* 1,13 litros; *US* 0,94 litros).

quarter cuarto *m*; *US Canada* (*coin*) cuarto *m* (de dólar); (*district*) barrio *m*; **it's a q. to three**, *US* **it's a q. of three** son las tres menos cuarto.

quartz [kwɔːts] cuarzo *m*; **q. watch** reloj *m* de cuarzo.

quay(side) ['kiː(saɪd)] muelle *m*.

queen [kwiːn] reina *f*.

queer [kwɪəʳ] *a* (*strange*) extraño,-a.

quench [kwentʃ] *vt* apagar.

query [kwɪərɪ] (*question*) pregunta *f*.

question ['kwestʃən] **1** *n* pregunta *f*; (*problem, issue*) asunto *m*; **to ask sb a q.** hacer una pregunta a algn; **out of the q.** imposible; **that's out of the q.** ¡ni hablar! **2** *vt* (*interrogate*) interrogar; (*query*) poner en duda.

question mark signo *m* de interrogación.

questionnaire cuestionario *m*.

queue [kjuː] *Br* **1** *n* cola *f*. **2** *vi* **to q. (up)** hacer cola.

quibble ['kwɪbəl] *vi* poner pegas (**with** a).

quiche [kiːʃ] quiche *f*.

quick [kwɪk] *a* (*fast*) rápido,-a; **be q.!** ¡date prisa!

quickly *adv* deprisa.

quiet ['kwaɪət] *a* (*silent*) silencioso,-a; (*calm, not crowded*) tranquilo,-a.

quietly *adv* (*silently*) silenciosamente; (*calmly*) tranquilamente; **he spoke q.** habló en voz baja.

quit*∗* [kwɪt] **1** *vt* (*leave*) dejar; **q. making that noise!** ¡deja de hacer ese ruido! **2** *vi* (*go*) irse; (*resign*) dimitir.

quite [kwaɪt] *adv* (*entirely*) totalmente; (*rather*) bastante; **q. a few** bastantes; **q. often** con bastante frecuencia; **q. (so)!** ¡exacto!

quiz [kwɪz] **q. show** concurso *m*.

quo'tation cita *f*; (*commercial*) cotización *f*.

quotation marks *npl* comillas *fpl*.

quote [kwəʊt] **1** *vt* (*cite*) citar; **to q. a price** dar un presupuesto. **2** *n* cita *f*; (*commercial*) presupuesto *m*.

R

rabbi ['ræbaɪ] rabino *m*.

rabbit ['ræbɪt] conejo,-a *mf*.

rabies ['reɪbiːz] rabia *f*.

race¹ [reɪs] **1** *n* (*in sport*) carrera *f*. **2** *vt* (*car, horse*) hacer correr; **I'll r. you!** ¡te echo una carrera! **3** *vi* (*go quickly*) correr.

race² (*people*) raza *f*.

racecourse *Br* hipódromo *m*.

racehorse caballo *m* de carreras.

racial ['reɪʃəl] *a* racial.

racing ['reɪsɪŋ] carreras *fpl*.

racing bike (*motorbike*) moto *f* de carreras; (*bicycle*) bicicleta *f* de carreras.

racing car coche *m* de carreras.

racing driver piloto *mf* de carreras.

racism ['reɪsɪzəm] racismo *m*.

racist *a & n* racista (*mf*).

rack [ræk] (*shelf*) estante *m*; (*for clothes*) percha *f*; **luggage r.** portaequipajes *m inv*; **roof r.** baca *f*.

racket¹ ['rækɪt] (*din*) jaleo *m*.

racket² (*for tennis etc*) raqueta *f*.

radar ['reɪdɑːʳ] radar *m*.

radiator ['reɪdɪeɪtəʳ] radiador *m*.

radio ['reɪdɪəʊ] radio *f*; **on the r.** en *or* por la radio; **r. station** emisora *f* (de radio).

radio'active *a* radiactivo,-a.

radish ['rædɪʃ] rábano *m*.

radius ['reɪdɪəs] radio *m*.

raffle ['ræfəl] rifa *f*.

raft [rɑːft] balsa *f*.

rag [ræg] *n* (*torn piece*) harapo *m*; (*for cleaning*) trapo *m*; **rags** (*clothes*) trapos *mpl*.

rage [reɪdʒ] **1** *n* (*fury*) cólera *f*. **2** *vi* (*person*) estar furioso,-a.

ragged ['rægɪd] *a* (*clothes*) hecho,-a jirones; (*person*) harapiento,-a.

raid [reɪd] **1** *n* (*by police*) redada *f*; (*robbery etc*) atraco *m*. **2** *vt* (*police*) hacer una redada en; (*rob*) asaltar.

rail [reɪl] barra *f*; (*railing*) barandilla *f*; (*on railway*) carril *m*; **by r.** (*send sth*) por ferrocarril; (*travel*) en tren.

railings *npl* verja *f*.

railroad *US* ferrocarril *m*.

railway *Br* ferrocarril *m*.

railway line vía *f* férrea.
railway station estación *f* de ferrocarril.
railway track vía *f* férrea.
rain [reɪn] **1** *n* lluvia *f*; **in the r.** bajo la lluvia. **2** *vi* llover; **it's raining** llueve.
rainbow arco *m* iris.
raincoat impermeable *m*.
rainy *a* lluvioso,-a.
raise [reɪz] **1** *n US* aumento *m* (de sueldo). **2** *vt* levantar; (*voice*) subir; (*increase*) aumentar; (*money, help*) reunir; (*issue, question*) plantear; (*crops, children*) criar.
raisin ['reɪzən] pasa *f*.
rake [reɪk] **1** *n* (*garden tool*) rastrillo *m*. **2** *vt* (*leaves*) rastrillar.
rally ['rælɪ] (*political*) mitin *m*.
• **rally round** *vi* (*help out*) echar una mano.
ram [ræm] **1** *n* (*sheep*) carnero *m*. **2** *vt* (*drive into place*) hincar; (*crash into*) chocar con.
ramble ['ræmbəl] (*walk*) caminata *f*.
ramp [ræmp] rampa *f*.
ran [ræn] *pt of* **run**.
ranch [rɑːntʃ] rancho *m*.
random ['rændəm] **1** *n* **at r.** al azar. **2** *a* fortuito,-a; **r. selection** selección *f* hecha al azar.
range [reɪndʒ] **1** *n* (*of mountains*) cordillera *f*; (*of products*) gama *f*; (*of missile*) alcance *m*; (*stove*) cocina *f* de carbón. **2** *vi* (*extend*) extenderse (**to** hasta); **prices r. from five to twenty pounds** los precios oscilan entre cinco y veinte libras.
rank [ræŋk] (*position in army*) graduación *f*; (*in society*) rango *m*; **(taxi) r.** parada *f* de taxis.
ransom ['rænsəm] rescate *m*.
rape [reɪp] **1** *n* violación *f*. **2** *vt* violar.
rapid ['ræpɪd] *a* rápido,-a.
rapidly *adv* rápidamente.
rapist ['reɪpɪst] violador,-a *mf*.
rare [reəʳ] *a* poco común; (*steak*) poco hecho,-a.
rarely *adv* raras veces.
rascal ['rɑːskəl] granuja *mf*.
rash[1] [ræʃ] (*on skin*) sarpullido *m*.
rash[2] *a* (*reckless*) impetuoso,-a; (*words, actions*) precipitado,-a.
rashly *adv* a la ligera.
raspberry ['rɑːzbərɪ] frambuesa *f*.
rat [ræt] rata *f*.
rate [reɪt] **1** *n* tasa *f*; **at any r.** (*anyway*) en cualquier caso; (*of interest*,

exchange) tipo *m*; **at the r. of** (*speed*) a la velocidad de; (*quantity*) a razón de. **2** *vt* (*estimate*) estimar; (*evaluate*) tasar; (*consider*) considerar.

rather ['rɑːðəʳ] *adv* (*quite*) más bien, bastante; (*more accurately*) mejor dicho; **r. than** (*instead of*) en vez de; (*more than*) más que; **she would r. stay here** prefiere quedarse aquí.

ratio ['reɪʃɪəʊ] razón *f*.

ration ['ræʃən] **1** *n* (*allowance*) ración *f*; **rations** víveres *mpl*. **2** *vt* racionar.

rational *a* racional.

rationing racionamiento *m*.

rattle ['rætəl] **1** *n* (*toy*) sonajero *m*; (*instrument*) carraca *f*. **2** *vt* (*keys etc*) hacer sonar. **3** *vi* sonar; (*metal*) repiquetear; (*glass*) tintinear; (*window, shelves*) vibrar.

ravenous ['rævənəs] *a* **I'm r.** tengo un hambre que no veo.

raw [rɔː] *a* (*uncooked*) crudo,-a; **r. material** materia prima; **r. flesh** carne viva.

ray [reɪ] rayo *m*.

razor ['reɪzəʳ] (*for shaving*) maquinilla *f* de afeitar.

razor blade hoja *f* de afeitar.

reach [riːtʃ] **1** *vt* (*arrive at*) llegar a; (*contact*) localizar. **2** *vi* alcanzar. **3** *n* (*range*) alcance *m*; **out of r.** fuera del alcance; **within r.** al alcance.

● **reach out** *vi* (*with hand*) extender la mano.

react [rɪ'ækt] *vi* reaccionar.

reaction reacción *f*.

reactor reactor *m*.

read* [riːd] *vt* leer; (*decipher*) descifrar.

● **read about** *vt* leer.

● **read out** *vt* leer en voz alta.

● **read up on** *vt* estudiar.

reader lector,-a *mf*; (*book*) libro *m* de lectura.

readily ['redɪlɪ] *adv* (*easily*) fácilmente; (*willingly*) de buena gana.

reading lectura *f*; *fig* interpretación *f*.

ready ['redɪ] *a* (*prepared*) listo,-a; (*willing*) dispuesto,-a; **r. to** (*about to*) a punto de; **r. cash** dinero *m* en efectivo.

ready-'cooked *a* precocinado,-a.

ready-'made *a* confeccionado,-a; (*food*) preparado,-a.

real [rɪəl] *a* verdadero,-a; (*genuine*) auténtico,-a.

real estate bienes *mpl* inmuebles.

real estate agent agente *m* inmobiliario.

rea'listic *a* realista.

reality [rɪ'ælɪtɪ] realidad *f*.

realize ['rɪəlaɪz] *vt* (*become aware of*) darse cuenta de; **don't you r.**

that ...? ¿no te das cuenta de que ...?

really adv (truly) verdaderamente; **r.?** ¿de veras?

rear[1] [rɪəʳ] **1** n (back part) parte f de atrás. **2** a trasero,-a; **r. entrance** puerta f de atrás.

rear[2] **1** vt (breed, raise) criar. **2** vi **to r. up** (horse) encabritarse.

rearrange vt (furniture) colocar de otra manera; (fix new date) fijar otra fecha para.

reason ['ri:zən] **1** n motivo m; **for no r.** sin razón. **2** vi (argue, work out) razonar.

reasonable a (fair) razonable; (sensible) sensato,-a.

reasonably adv (fairly, quite) bastante.

reasoning razonamiento m.

reassure vt (comfort) tranquilizar; (restore confidence of) dar confianza a.

reassuring a consolador,-a.

rebel ['rebəl] **1** a & n rebelde (mf). **2** [rɪ'bel] vi rebelarse (**against** contra).

rebellion [rɪ'beljən] rebelión f.

rebound ['ri:baʊnd] **1** n (of ball) rebote m. **2** [rɪ'baʊnd] vi (ball) rebotar.

rebuild vt reconstruir.

recall vt (remember) recordar.

receipt [rɪ'si:t] (paper) recibo m; **receipts** (takings) recaudación f sing.

receive [rɪ'si:v] vt recibir.

receiver (of phone) auricular m; (radio) receptor m.

recent ['ri:sənt] a reciente; **in r. years** en los últimos años.

recently adv recientemente.

reception [rɪ'sepʃən] (party, of TV pictures etc) recepción f; (welcome) acogida f; **r. (desk)** recepción f.

receptionist recepcionista mf.

recharge vt (battery) recargar.

recipe ['resɪpɪ] receta f.

recite [rɪ'saɪt] vti recitar.

reckless ['reklɪs] a (unwise) imprudente.

reckon ['rekən] vt (calculate) calcular; fam (think) creer.

● **reckon on** vt contar con.

● **reckon with** vt (take into account) contar con.

reclaim [rɪ'kleɪm] vt (recover) recuperar; (demand back) reclamar; (marshland etc) convertir.

recognize ['rekəgnaɪz] vt reconocer.

recollect [rekə'lekt] vt recordar.

recollection recuerdo m.

recommend [rekə'mend] vt recomendar.

recommendation recomendación f.

record ['rekɔːd] **1** n (of music etc) disco m; (in sport etc) récord m; (document) documento m; (case history) historial médico; **public records** archivos mpl. **2** [rɪ'kɔːd] vt (relate) hacer constar; (note down) apuntar; (record, voice) grabar.

recorder [re'kɔːdəʳ] (musical instrument) flauta f; **(tape)** r. magnetófono m; **(video)** r. vídeo m.

recording grabación f.

record player tocadiscos m inv.

recover [rɪ'kʌvəʳ] **1** vt (items, time) recuperar; (consciousness) recobrar. **2** vi (from illness etc) reponerse; (economy) recuperarse.

recruit [rɪ'kruːt] recluta m.

rectangle ['rektæŋgəl] rectángulo m.

rec'tangular a rectangular.

recycle [riː'saɪkəl] vt reciclar.

red [red] **1** a rojo,-a; r. light semáforo en rojo; r. wine vino tinto; to go r. ponerse colorado,-a; to have r. hair ser pelirrojo,-a. **2** n (colour) rojo m; to be in the r. estar en números rojos.

red-'handed a to catch sb r. coger a algn con las manos en la masa.

redhead pelirrojo,-a mf.

red-hot a al rojo vivo.

redirect vt (forward) remitir a la nueva dirección.

redo* [riː'duː] vt (exercise, house) rehacer.

reduce [rɪ'djuːs] vt reducir.

reduction [rɪ'dʌkʃən] (decrease) reducción f; (cut in price) descuento m.

redundancy despido m.

redundant [rɪ'dʌndənt] a to be made r. perder el empleo; to make sb r. despedir a algn.

reed [riːd] (plant) caña f.

reef [riːf] arrecife m.

reel [riːl] (spool) bobina f, carrete m.

refectory [rɪ'fektərɪ] refectorio m.

refer [rɪ'fɜːʳ] **1** vt to r. a matter to a tribunal remitir un asunto a un tribunal. **2** vi (allude) referirse (to a).

referee [refə'riː] **1** n árbitro,-a mf. **2** vt arbitrar.

reference ['refərəns] referencia f; (character report) informe m; with r. to referente a, con referencia a.

refill ['riːfɪl] **1** n (replacement) recambio m; (another drink) otra copa f. **2** [riː'fɪl] vt rellenar.

reflect [rɪ'flekt] **1** vt (light, attitude) reflejar; to be reflected reflejarse. **2** vi (think) reflexionar.

reflection (indication, mirror image) reflejo m.

reflex ['riːfleks] reflejo m.

reform 1 *n* reforma *f*. **2** *vt* reformar.
refrain [rɪ'freɪn] *vi* abstenerse (**from** de).
refresh *vt* refrescar.
refresher course cursillo *m* de reciclaje.
refreshing *a* refrescante.
refreshment refresco *m*.
refrigerator [rɪ'frɪdʒəreɪtə^r] nevera *f*.
refuge ['refjuːdʒ] refugio *m*; **to take r.** refugiarse.
refu'gee refugiado,-a *mf*.
refund ['riːfʌnd] **1** *n* reembolso *m*. **2** [riː'fʌnd] *vt* reembolsar.
refusal negativa *f*.
refuse [rɪ'fjuːz] **1** *vt* (*reject*) rechazar; **to r. sb sth** negar algo a algn; **to r. to do sth** negarse a hacer algo. **2** *vi* negarse.
regain [rɪ'geɪn] *vt* recuperar.
regard [rɪ'gɑːd] **1** *n* (*concern*) consideración *f*; **with r. to, as regards** (con) respecto a; **give him my regards** dale recuerdos de mi parte. **2** *vt* (*consider*) considerar.
regarding *prep* (con) respecto a.
regardless 1 *prep* **r. of** a pesar de; **r. of the outcome** pase lo que pase. **2** *adv* a toda costa.
regiment ['redʒɪmənt] regimiento *m*.
region ['riːdʒən] región *f*, zona *f*; **in the r. of** aproximadamente.
regional *a* regional.
register ['redʒɪstə^r] **1** *n* registro *m*. **2** *vt* (*record*) registrar; (*letter*) certificar. **3** *vi* (*enter one's name*) inscribirse; (*at univeristy*) matricularse.
regi'stration inscripción *f*; (*at university*) matrícula *f*; *Br* **r. number** matrícula *f*.
regret [rɪ'gret] **1** *n* (*remorse*) remordimiento *m*; (*sadness*) pesar *m*. **2** *vt* arrepentirse de, lamentar.
regular ['regjʊlə^r] **1** *a* regular; (*usual*) normal; (*frequent*) frecuente.
regularly *adv* con regularidad.
regulation [regjʊ'leɪʃən] **1** *n* (*control*) regulación *f*; (*rule*) regla *f*. **2** *a* reglamentario,-a.
rehearsal ensayo *m*.
rehearse [rɪ'hɜːs] *vti* ensayar.
reign [reɪn] **1** *n* reinado *m*. **2** *vi* reinar.
reins [reɪnz] (*for horse*) riendas *fpl*.
reindeer ['reɪndɪə^r] reno *m*.
reinforce [riːɪn'fɔːs] *vt* (*strengthen*) reforzar.
reinforcements *npl* refuerzos *mpl*.
reinstate [riːɪn'steɪt] *vt* (*to job*) reincorporar.
reject [rɪ'dʒekt] *vt* rechazar.

rejection rechazo *m*.
rejoice [rɪˈdʒɔɪs] *vi* regocijarse (**at, over** de).
relate [rɪˈleɪt] **1** *vt* (*connect*) relacionar; (*tell*) contar. **2** *vi* relacionarse (**to** con).
related *a* (*linked*) relacionado,-a (**to** con); **to be r. to sb** ser pariente de algn.
relation (*link*) relación *f*; (*family*) pariente,-a *mf*; **in** *or* **with r. to** (con) respecto a.
relationship (*link*) relación *f*; (*between people*) relaciones *fpl*.
relative [ˈrelətɪv] **1** *n* pariente,-a *mf*. **2** *a* relativo,-a.
relatively *adv* relativamente.
relax [rɪˈlæks] **1** *vi* relajarse; **r.!** ¡cálmate! **2** *vt* (*calm*) relajar; (*loosen*) aflojar.
relax'ation (*rest*) relajación *f*.
relaxed [rɪˈlækst] *a* relajado,-a.
release [rɪˈliːs] **1** *n* (*setting free*) liberación *f*; (*of product*) puesta *f* en venta; (*of film*) estreno *m*; (*press release*) comunicado *m*. **2** *vt* (*set free*) poner en libertad; (*let go*) soltar; (*product, record*) poner a la venta; (*film*) estrenar.
relevant [ˈreləvənt] *a* pertinente (**to** a); **it is not r.** no viene al caso.
reliable [rɪˈlaɪəbəl] *a* (*person*) de fiar; (*thing*) fiable.
relia'bility (*of person*) formalidad *f*; (*of thing*) fiabilidad *f*.
relief [rɪˈliːf] alivio *m*; (*aid*) auxilio *m*; (*in art, geography*) relieve *m*.
relieve [rɪˈliːv] *vt* aliviar; (*substitute*) relevar.
religion [rɪˈlɪdʒən] religión *f*.
religious *a* religioso,-a.
relish [ˈrelɪʃ] (*seasoning*) condimento *m*.
reload *vt* (*gun, camera*) recargar.
reluctance [rɪˈlʌktəns] desgana *f*.
reluctant *a* reacio,-a; **to be r. to do sth** estar poco dispuesto,-a a hacer algo.
reluctantly *adv* de mala gana.
rely on [rɪˈlaɪ] *vi* confiar en.
remain [rɪˈmeɪn] *vi* (*stay*) permanecer, quedarse; (*be left*) quedar.
remaining *a* restante.
remark [rɪˈmɑːk] **1** *n* comentario *m*. **2** *vt* comentar.
remarkable *a* (*extraordinary*) extraordinario,-a.
remarkably *adv* extraordinariamente.
remedial [rɪˈmiːdɪəl] *a* **r. classes** clases *fpl* para niños atrasados en los estudios.
remember [rɪˈmembəʳ] **1** *vt* (*recall*) acordarse de. **2** *vi* acordarse.
remind [rɪˈmaɪnd] *vt* recordar; **r. me to do it** recuérdame que lo haga.

reminder aviso *m*.

remorse [rɪ'mɔːs] remordimiento *m*.

remote [rɪ'məʊt] *a* (*far away*) remoto,-a; (*isolated*) aislado,-a.

remote control mando *m* a distancia.

removal (*moving house*) mudanza *f*; (*getting rid of*) eliminación *f*.

removal man hombre *m* de la mudanza.

removal van camión *m* de mudanzas.

remove [rɪ'muːv] *vt* quitar.

renew [rɪ'njuː] *vt* (*contract etc*) renovar; (*talks etc*) reanudar.

rent [rent] **1** *n* (*of building, car, TV*) alquiler *m*. **2** *vt* alquilar.

● **rent out** *vt* alquilar.

rental (*of house etc*) alquiler *m*.

reorganize *vt* reorganizar.

repair [rɪ'peəʳ] **1** *n* reparación *f*; **in good/bad r.** en buen/mal estado. **2** *vt* arreglar; (*car*) reparar; (*clothes*) remendar.

repairman técnico *m*.

repay *vt* devolver; (*debt*) liquidar.

repayment pago *m*.

repeat [rɪ'piːt] **1** *vt* repetir. **2** *n* (*repetition*) repetición *f*; (*on TV*) reposición *f*.

repeated *a* repetido,-a.

repeatedly *adv* repetidas veces.

repel [rɪ'pel] *vt* (*fight off*) repeler.

repetition [repɪ'tɪʃən] repetición *f*.

re'petitive [rɪ'petɪtɪv] *a* repetitivo,-a.

replace [rɪ'pleɪs] *vt* (*put back*) volver a poner en su sitio; (*substitute*) sustituir.

replacement (*person*) sustituto,-a *mf*; (*part*) pieza *f* de recambio.

replica ['replɪkə] réplica *f*.

reply [rɪ'plaɪ] **1** *n* respuesta *f*. **2** *vi* responder.

report [rɪ'pɔːt] **1** *n* informe *m*; (*piece of news*) noticia *f*; (*in newspaper, on TV etc*) reportaje *m*; (*rumour*) rumor *m*; *Br* **school r.** informe escolar. **2** *vt* (*tell police, authorities about*) denunciar; (*journalist*) hacer un reportaje sobre; **it is reported that ...** se dice que ... **3** *vi* (*committee etc*) hacer un informe; (*journalist*) hacer un reportaje; (*to work etc*) presentarse.

reported *a* **r. speech** estilo indirecto.

reportedly *adv* según se dice.

reporter periodista *mf*.

represent [reprɪ'zent] *vt* representar.

representative representante *mf*.

reptile ['reptaɪl] reptil *m*.

republic [rɪ'pʌblɪk] república *f*.

reputable ['repjʊtəbəl] *a* (*company etc*) acreditado,-a; (*person, products*) de toda confianza.

reputation [repjʊ'teɪʃən] reputación *f*.

request [rɪ'kwest] **1** *n* petición *f*. **2** *vt* pedir.

require [rɪ'kwaɪə'] *vt* (*need*) necesitar; (*demand*) exigir.

required *a* necesario,-a.

rescue ['reskjuː] **1** *n* rescate *m*. **2** *vt* rescatar.

research [rɪ'sɜːtʃ] **1** *n* investigación *f*. **2** *vti* investigar.

researcher investigador,-a *mf*.

resemblance semejanza *f*.

resemble [rɪ'zembəl] *vt* parecerse a.

reser'vation reserva *f*.

reserve [rɪ'zɜːv] **1** *n* reserva *f*; (*in sport*) suplente *mf*; **to keep sth in r.** guardar algo de reserva. **2** *vt* reservar.

reserved *a* reservado,-a.

residence ['rezɪdəns] (*home*) residencia *f*; (*address*) domicilio *m*.

resident *a & n* residente (*mf*).

resi'dential *a* residencial.

resign [rɪ'zaɪn] **1** *vt* **to r. oneself to sth** resignarse a algo. **2** *vi* dimitir.

resig'nation (*from a job*) dimisión *f*.

resist [rɪ'zɪst] *vt* (*not yield to*) resistir; (*oppose*) oponerse a; **I couldn't r. telling her** no pude resistir a la tentación de decírselo.

resistance resistencia *f*.

resit *vt* (*in exam*) volver a presentarse a.

resort [rɪ'zɔːt] (*recourse*) recurso *m*; (*place*) lugar *m* de vacaciones; **as a last r.** como último recurso; **tourist r.** centro *m* turístico.

● **resort to** *vt* recurrir a.

resource [rɪ'sɔːs] recurso *m*.

respect [rɪ'spekt] **1** *n* (*reference*) respeto *m*; **in that r.** a ese respecto; **with r. to** con referencia a. **2** *vt* respetar.

respectable *a* respetable; (*clothes*) decente.

respond [rɪ'spɒnd] *vi* responder (**to** a).

response (*reply*) respuesta *f*; (*reaction*) reacción *f*.

responsi'bility responsabilidad *f*.

responsible [rɪ'spɒnsəbəl] *a* responsable (**for** de).

rest[1] [rest] **1** *n* (*break*) descanso *m*; (*peace*) tranquilidad *f*. **2** *vt* (*lean*) apoyar. **3** *vi* descansar.

rest[2] **the r.** (*remainder*) el resto; **the r. of the day** el resto del día; **the r. of the girls** las demás chicas.

restaurant ['restərɒnt] restaurante *m*.

restful *a* relajante.

restless *a* inquieto,-a.

restore [rɪ'stɔːʳ] vt (give back) devolver; (repair) restaurar.

restrict [rɪ'strɪkt] vt restringir.

restricted a restringido,-a.

restricted area zona f de velocidad limitada.

restriction restricción f.

rest room US aseos mpl.

result [rɪ'zʌlt] resultado m; **as a r. of** como consecuencia de.

resume [rɪ'zjuːm] **1** vt (journey, work, conversation) reanudar; (control) reasumir. **2** vi recomenzar.

résumé ['rezjʊmeɪ] resumen m.

retail ['riːteɪl] **1** n **r. price** precio m de venta al público. **2** vt vender al por menor. **3** adv al por menor.

retailer detallista mf.

retain [rɪ'teɪn] vt conservar.

retire [rɪ'taɪəʳ] vi (stop working) jubilarse; (withdraw) retirarse; **to r. for the night** irse a la cama.

retired a jubilado,-a.

retirement jubilación f.

return 1 n (coming or going back) regreso m; (giving back) devolución f; (profit) beneficio m; **r. ticket** billete m de ida y vuelta. **2** vt (give back) devolver. **3** vi (come or go back) regresar.

returnable a (bottle) retornable.

reveal [rɪ'viːl] vt (make known) revelar; (show) dejar ver.

revenge [rɪ'vendʒ] venganza f; **to take r. on sb for sth** vengarse de algo en algn.

reverse [rɪ'vɜːs] **1** a inverso,-a. **2** n quite the r. todo lo contrario; **r. (gear)** marcha f atrás. **3** vt **to r. the charges** poner una conferencia a cobro revertido. **4** vi (in car) dar marcha atrás; **to r. in/out** entrar/salir marcha atrás.

review 1 n (in press) crítica f. **2** vt (book etc) hacer una crítica de.

revise [rɪ'vaɪz] vt (look over) revisar; (at school) repasar.

revision revisión f; (at school) repaso m.

revive [rɪ'vaɪv] **1** vt (sick person) reanimar. **2** vi (interest, hopes) renacer; (sick person) volver en sí.

revolt [rɪ'vəʊlt] rebelión f.

revolting a repugnante.

revolution [revə'luːʃən] revolución f.

revolutionary a & n revolucionario,-a (mf).

revolve [rɪ'vɒlv] vi girar; fig **to r. around** girar en torno a.

revolver revólver m.

revolving a giratorio,-a.

revolving door puerta f giratoria.

reward [rɪ'wɔ:d] **1** *n* recompensa *f*. **2** *vt* recompensar.

rewind* 1 *vt* (*tape*) rebobinar. **2** *vi* rebobinarse.

rheumatism ['ru:mətɪzəm] reúma *m*.

rhinoceros [raɪ'nɒsərəs] rinoceronte *m*.

rhubarb ['ru:ba:b] ruibarbo *m*.

rhyme [raɪm] **1** *n* rima *f*; (*poem*) poema *m*. **2** *vi* rimar.

rhythm ['rɪðəm] ritmo *m*.

rib [rɪb] costilla *f*.

ribbon ['rɪbən] cinta *f*; (*in hair etc*) lazo *m*.

rice [raɪs] arroz *m*.

rich [rɪtʃ] **1** *a* rico,-a. **2** *npl* **the r.** los ricos.

riches *npl* riquezas *fpl*.

rid [rɪd] *vt* **to get r. of sth** deshacerse de algo.

riddle ['rɪdəl] (*puzzle*) adivinanza *f*; (*mystery*) enigma *m*.

ride [raɪd] **1** *n* paseo *m*; **a short bus r.** un corto trayecto en autobús; **horse r.** paseo a caballo. **2** *vt** (*bicycle, horse*) montar en; **can you r. a bike?** ¿sabes montar en bici? **3** *vi** (*on horse*) montar a caballo; (*travel*) (*on bus, train etc*) viajar.

rider (*of horse*) (*man*) jinete *m*, (*woman*) amazona *f*; (*of bicycle*) ciclista *mf*; (*of motorbike*) motociclista *mf*.

ridiculous [rɪ'dɪkjʊləs] *a* ridículo,-a.

riding ['raɪdɪŋ] equitación *f*.

rifle ['raɪfəl] rifle *m*.

rig [rɪg] **(oil) r.** (*onshore*) torre *f* de perforación; (*offshore*) plataforma *f* petrolífera.

right [raɪt] **1** *a* (*not left*) derecho,-a; (*correct*) correcto,-a; (*suitable*) adecuado,-a; (*proper*) apropiado,-a; (*exact*) (*time*) exacto,-a; **all r.** de acuerdo; **r.?** ¿vale?; **that's r.** eso es; **isn't that r.?** ¿no es verdad?; **the r. word** la palabra justa; **to be r.** tener razón; **the r. time** (*appropriate time*) el momento oportuno; **r. angle** ángulo recto. **2** *n* (*right side*) derecha *f*; (*right hand*) mano *f* derecha; (*in politics*) **the R.** la derecha; (*lawful claim*) derecho *m*; **r. and wrong** el bien y el mal. **3** *adv* (*correctly*) bien; (*to the right*) a la derecha; **r. away** en seguida; **to turn r.** girar a la derecha; **go r. on** sigue recto; **r. at the top** en todo lo alto; **r. in the middle** justo en medio; **r. to the end** hasta el final.

right-hand *a* derecho,-a.

right-'handed *a* (*person*) que usa la mano derecha.

rightly *adv* debidamente; **and r. so** y con razón.

rigid ['rɪdʒɪd] *a* rígido,-a.

rim [rɪm] (*edge*) borde *m*.

rind [raɪnd] (*of fruit, cheese*) corteza *f*.

ring[1] [rɪŋ] **1** *n* (*of doorbell, alarm clock*) timbre *m*; (*of phone*) llamada *f*.

2 vt* (bell) tocar; (on phone) llamar por teléfono. **3** vi* (bell, phone etc) sonar.

ring² [rɪŋ] **1** n sortija f; (wedding ring) anillo m; (metal hoop) aro m; (circle) círculo m; (group of people) corro m; (in boxing) cuadrilátero m; (for bullfights) ruedo m. **2** vt (surround) rodear.

● **ring back 1** vt volver a llamar a. **2** vi volver a llamar.

● **ring off** vi (person on phone) colgar.

● **ring out** vi (bell etc) resonar.

● **ring up** vt (on phone) llamar por teléfono a.

● **ringing tone** (on phone) señal f de llamada.

ring road carretera f de circunvalación.

rinse [rɪns] vt aclarar; (the dishes) enjuagar.

● **rinse out** vt enjuagar.

riot ['raɪət] **1** n disturbio m; **r. police** policía f antidisturbios. **2** vi amotinarse.

rip [rɪp] **1** n (tear) rasgón m. **2** vt rasgar. **3** vi rasgarse.

● **rip off** vt fam **to r. sb off** timar a algn.

● **rip up** vt hacer pedacitos.

ripe [raɪp] a maduro,-a.

ripen vti madurar.

rip-off fam timo m.

rise [raɪz] **1** n (of slope, hill) cuesta f; (in prices, temperature) subida f; (of wages) aumento m; **to give r. to** ocasionar. **2** vi* (prices, temperature) subir; (wages) aumentar; (from bed) levantarse; (stand up) levantarse; (city, building) erguirse.

risk [rɪsk] **1** n riesgo m; **at r.** en peligro; **to take risks** arriesgarse. **2** vt arriesgar; **I'll r. it** correré el riesgo.

risky a arriesgado,-a.

rival ['raɪvəl] **1** a & n rival (mf). **2** vt rivalizar con.

river ['rɪvəʳ] río m.

road [rəʊd] carretera f; (street) calle f; (way) camino m; **r. accident** accidente m de tráfico; **r. safety** seguridad f vial.

roadside borde m de la carretera.

roadway calzada f.

roadworks npl obras fpl.

roam [rəʊm] **1** vt vagar por. **2** vi vagar.

roar [rɔːʳ] **1** n (of lion) rugido m; (of bull, sea, wind) bramido m. **2** vi (lion, crowd) rugir; (bull, sea, wind) bramar.

roast [rəʊst] **1** a (meat) asado,-a; **r. beef** rosbif m. **2** n asado m. **3** vt (meat) asar; (coffee, nuts) tostar. **4** vi asarse.

rob [rɒb] vt robar; (bank) atracar.

robber ladrón,-a mf; **bank r.** atracador,-a mf.

robbery robo *m*.

robe [rəʊb] (*ceremonial*) toga *f*; (*dressing gown*) bata *f*.

robin ['rɒbɪn] petirrojo *m*.

robot ['rəʊbɒt] robot *m*.

rock [rɒk] **1** *n* roca *f*; US (*stone*) piedra *f*; (*music*) música *f* rock. **2** *vt*
(*chair*) mecer; (*baby*) acunar; (*shake*) sacudir. **3** *vi* (*move to and fro*)
mecerse; (*shake*) vibrar.

rocket ['rɒkɪt] **1** *n* cohete *m*. **2** *vi* (*prices*) dispararse.

rocking-chair mecedora *f*.

rod [rɒd] (*of metal*) barra *f*; (*stick*) vara *f*; **fishing r.** caña *f* de pescar.

rogue [rəʊg] granuja *m*.

role, rôle [rəʊl] papel *m*; **to play a r.** desempeñar un papel.

roll [rəʊl] **1** *n* rollo *m*; (**bread**) **r.** bollo *m*; (*of drum*) redoble *m*. **2** *vt* hacer
rodar. **3** *vi* (*ball*) rodar; (*animal*) revolcarse.

● **roll by** *vi* (*years*) pasar.

● **roll down** *vt* (*blinds*) bajar; (*sleeves*) bajarse; (*hill*) bajar rodando.

● **roll over** *vi* dar una vuelta.

● **roll up** *vt* (*paper etc*) enrollar; (*blinds*) subir; **to r. up one's sleeves**
(ar)remangarse.

roller rodillo *m*; **rollers** (*for hair*) rulos *mpl*.

roller skate patín *m* de ruedas.

rolling pin rodillo *m* (de cocina).

rolling stock material *m* rodante.

Roman ['rəʊmən] *a & n* romano,-a (*mf*).

Roman Catholic *a & n* católico,-a (*mf*) (romano,-a).

romance [rəʊ'mæns] (*love affair*) aventura *f* amorosa.

romantic *a & n* romántico,-a (*mf*).

roof [ruːf] tejado *m*; (*of car*) techo *m*.

roof rack baca *f*.

room [ruːm] habitación *f*; (*space*) espacio *m*; **single r.** habitación
individual; **make r. for me** hazme sitio.

roommate compañero,-a *mf* de habitación.

roomy *a* amplio,-a.

root [ruːt] raíz *f*; **to take r.** echar raíces.

● **root for** *vt* **to r. for a team** animar a un equipo.

● **root out** *or* **up** *vt* arrancar de raíz.

rope [rəʊp] (*small*) cuerda *f*; (*big*) soga *f*.

● **rope off** *vt* acordonar.

rose [rəʊz] rosa *f*; **r. bush** rosal *m*.

rot [rɒt] *vi* pudrirse.

rota ['rəʊtə] *Br* lista *f*.

rotten ['rɒtən] *a* (*decayed*) podrido,-a; *fam* (*very bad*) malísimo,-a;

(*health*) enfermo,-a; **I feel r.** me encuentro fatal.

rough [rʌf] *a* (*surface, skin*) áspero,-a; (*terrain*) accidentado,-a; (*road*) desigual; (*sea*) agitado,-a; (*rude*) grosero,-a; (*violent*) violento,-a; (*approximate*) aproximado,-a; (*plan etc*) preliminar; **r. draft** borrador *m*; **r. sketch** esbozo *m*.

roughly *adv* (*crudely*) toscamente; (*not gently*) bruscamente; (*approximately*) aproximadamente.

round [raʊnd] **1** *a* redondo,-a. **2** *n* (*of drinks*) ronda *f*; (*at golf*) partido *m*; (*at cards*) partida *f*; (*in boxing*) round *m*; (*in a competition*) eliminatoria *f*; **rounds** (*doctor's*) visita *f sing*. **3** *adv* **all year r.** durante todo el año; **to invite sb r.** invitar a algn a casa. **4** *prep* (*place etc*) alrededor de; **r. here** por aquí; **r. the corner** a la vuelta de la esquina.

● **round on** *vt* (*attack*) atacar.

● **round up** *vt* (*cattle*) acorralar; (*people*) reunir.

roundabout 1 *n* (*merry-go-round*) tiovivo *m*; *Br* (*on road*) glorieta *f*. **2** *a* indirecto,-a.

round trip viaje *m* de ida y vuelta.

route [ru:t] ruta *f*; (*of bus*) línea *f*.

routine [ru:'ti:n] rutina *f*.

row¹ [rəʊ] fila *f*; **three times in a r.** tres veces seguidas.

row² [rəʊ] *vi* (*in a boat*) remar.

row³ [raʊ] **1** *n* (*quarrel*) bronca *f*; (*noise*) jaleo *m*. **2** *vi* pelearse.

rowboat *US* bote *m* de remos.

royal ['rɔɪəl] **1** *a* real. **2** *npl* **the Royals** los miembros de la Familia Real.

royalty (*royal persons*) miembro(s) *m(pl)* de la Familia Real; **royalties** derechos *mpl* de autor.

rub [rʌb] **1** *vt* frotar; (*hard*) restregar; (*massage*) friccionar. **2** *vi* rozar (**against** contra).

● **rub down** *vt* frotar; (*horse*) almohazar; (*surface*) raspar.

● **rub in** *vt* (*cream etc*) frotar con.

● **rub off** *vt* (*erase*) borrar.

● **rub out** *vt* borrar.

rubber ['rʌbə'] (*substance*) caucho *m*; (*eraser*) goma *f* (de borrar).

rubbish ['rʌbɪʃ] (*refuse*) basura *f*; *fam* (*worthless thing*) birria *f*; *fam* (*nonsense*) tonterías *fpl*.

rubbish bin cubo *m* de la basura.

rubbish dump vertedero *m*.

rubbishy *a fam* (*book, film*) sin valor.

rubble ['rʌbəl] escombros *mpl*.

ruby ['ru:bɪ] rubí *m*.

rucksack ['rʌksæk] mochila *f*.

rudder ['rʌdə'] timón *m*.

rude [ruːd] *a* (*impolite*) maleducado,-a; (*foul-mouthed*) grosero,-a.

rudeness (*impoliteness*) falta *f* de educación; (*offensiveness*) grosería *f*.

rug [rʌg] alfombra *f*.

rugby ['rʌgbɪ] rugby *m*.

ruin ['ruːɪn] **1** *n* ruina *f*; **in ruins** en ruinas. **2** *vt* arruinar; (*spoil*) estropear.

rule [ruːl] **1** *n* regla *f*; (*of monarch*) reinado *m*; **as a r.** por regla general. **2** *vti* (*govern*) gobernar; (*monarch*) reinar.

• **rule out** *vt* descartar.

ruler (*monarch*) soberano,-a *mf*; (*for measuring*) regla *f*.

rum [rʌm] ron *m*.

Rumanian [ruːˈmeɪnɪən] **1** *a* rumano,-a. **2** *n* (*person*) rumano,-a *mf*; (*language*) rumano *m*.

rumour, *US* **rumor** ['ruːməʳ] rumor *m*.

run [rʌn] **1** *n* (*act of running, in stocking*) carrera *f*; (*trip*) vuelta *f*; **on the r.** fugado,-a; **to go for a r.** hacer footing; (*in car*) dar un paseo; **in the long r.** a largo plazo; **ski r.** pista *f* de esquí. **2** *vt** correr; (*business*) llevar; (*company*) dirigir; (*organize*) organizar; **to r. a program** pasar un programa. **3** *vi** (*person, river*) correr; (*colour*) desteñirse; (*operate*) funcionar; (*film, play*) estar en cartel; **your nose is running** se te caen los mocos; **trains r. every two hours** hay trenes cada dos horas; **we're running low on milk** nos queda poca leche.

• **run across** *vt* (*meet*) tropezar con.

• **run away** *vi* fugarse.

• **run down** *vt* (*stairs*) bajar corriendo; (*knock down*) atropellar.

• **run in** *vi* entrar corriendo.

• **run into** *vt* (*room etc*) entrar corriendo en; (*people, problems*) tropezar con; (*crash into*) chocar contra.

• **run off** *vi* escaparse.

• **run out** *vi* (*exit*) salir corriendo; (*finish*) agotarse; (*contract*) vencer; **to r. out of** quedarse sin.

• **run over** *vt* (*knock down*) atropellar.

runaway *a* (*vehicle*) incontrolado,-a; (*inflation*) galopante; (*success*) clamoroso,-a.

rung [rʌŋ] (*of ladder*) peldaño *m*.

runner corredor,-a *mf*.

runner-'up subcampeón,-ona *mf*.

running 1 *n* atletismo *m*; (*management*) dirección *f*. **2** *a* **r. water** agua *f* corriente; **three weeks r.** tres semanas seguidas.

runny *a* (*nose*) que moquea.

runway pista *f* (de aterrizaje y despegue).

rush [rʌʃ] **1** *n* (*hurry*) prisa *f*; (*hustle and bustle*) ajetreo *m*; **there's no r.** no corre prisa. **2** *vt* (*go hastily*) hacer de prisa; **to r. sb to hospital** llevar a algn urgentemente al hospital. **3** *vi* (*go quickly*) precipitarse.

● **rush about** *vi* correr de un lado a otro.

● **rush off** *vi* irse corriendo.

rush hour hora *f* punta.

Russian ['rʌʃən] **1** *a* ruso,-a. **2** *n* (*person*) ruso,-a *mf*; (*language*) ruso *m*.

rust [rʌst] **1** *n* herrumbre *f*. **2** *vi* oxidarse.

rusty *a* oxidado,-a.

rye [raɪ] centeno *m*; **r. bread** pan *m* de centeno.

S

sack [sæk] **1** n (bag) saco m; **to get the s.** ser despedido,-a; **to give sb the s.** despedir a algn. **2** vt (employee) despedir a.

sacrifice ['sækrɪfaɪs] **1** n sacrificio m. **2** vt sacrificar.

sad [sæd] a triste.

sadden vt entristecer.

saddle ['sædəl] n (for horse) silla f (de montar); (of bicycle etc) sillín m.

sadly adv tristamente.

sadness tristeza f.

safe [seɪf] **1** a (unharmed) ileso,-a; (out of danger) a salvo; (not dangerous) inocuo,-a; (secure, sure) seguro,-a; **s. and sound** sano,-a y salvo,-a. **2** n (for money etc) caja f fuerte.

safely adv con toda seguridad; **to arrive s.** llegar sin accidentes.

safety seguridad f.

safety belt cinturón m de seguridad.

safety pin imperdible m.

sag [sæg] vi (roof) hundirse.

said [sed] **1** pt & pp of **say**. **2** a dicho,-a.

sail [seɪl] **1** n (canvas) vela f; (trip) paseo m en barco; **to set s.** zarpar. **2** vt (ship) gobernar. **3** vi ir en barco; (set sail) zarpar.

sailboard tabla f de windsurf.

sailboat US barco m de vela.

sailing navegación f; (yachting) vela f.

sailing boat barco m de vela.

sailor marinero m.

saint [seɪnt] n santo,-a mf; (before all masculine names except those beginning **Do** or **To**) San; (before feminine names) Santa.

sake [seɪk] n **for the s. of** por (el bien de); **for your own s.** por tu propio bien.

salad ['sæləd] ensalada f.

salad bowl ensaladera f.

salad dressing aliño m.

salary ['sælərɪ] salario m.

sale [seɪl] venta f; (at low prices) rebajas fpl; **for** or **on s.** en venta.

salesclerk dependiente,-a mf.

salesman vendedor m; (in shop) dependiente m; (commercial traveller) representante m.

saleswoman vendedora f; (in shop) dependienta f; (commercial traveller) representante f.

saliva [sə'laɪvə] saliva f.

salmon ['sæmən] salmón m.

salt [sɔːlt] **1** *n* sal *f*; **bath salts** sales de baño. **2** *vt* (*add salt to*) echar sal a.

saltcellar salero *m*.

salty *a* salado,-a.

same [seɪm] **1** *a* mismo,-a; **at the s. time** al mismo tiempo; **the two cars are the s.** los dos coches son iguales. **2** *pron* el mismo, la misma, lo mismo; **all the s., just the s.** aun así; **it's all the s. to me** (a mí) me da igual.

sample ['sɑːmpəl] **1** *n* muestra *f*. **2** *vt* (*wines*) catar; (*dish*) probar.

sand [sænd] arena *f*.

sandal ['sændəl] sandalia *f*.

sand castle castillo *m* de arena.

sandpaper papel *m* de lija.

sandwich ['sænwɪdʒ] (*roll*) bocadillo *m*; (*sliced bread*) sandwich *m*.

sandy *a* (*earth, beach*) arenoso,-a; (*hair*) rubio rojizo.

sanitary ['sænɪtərɪ] **s. towel**, *US* **s. napkin** compresa *f*.

Santa Claus [sæntə'klɔːz] Papá Noel *m*.

sardine [sɑːˈdiːn] sardina *f*.

sat [sæt] *pt & pp of* **sit**.

satchel ['sætʃəl] cartera *f* (de colegial).

satellite ['sætəlaɪt] satélite *m*; **s. dish** antena *f* parabólica.

satin ['sætɪn] satén *m*.

satisfaction [sætɪsˈfækʃən] satisfacción *f*.

satisfactory *a* satisfactorio,-a.

'satisfy *vt* satisfacer; (*fulfil*) cumplir con.

'satisfying *a* satisfactorio,-a.

satsuma [sætˈsuːmə] (*fruit*) mandarina *f*.

saturate ['sætʃəreɪt] *vt* saturar (**with** de).

Saturday ['sætədɪ] sábado *m*.

sauce [sɔːs] salsa *f*.

saucepan cacerola *f*; (*large*) olla *f*.

saucer ['sɔːsəʳ] platillo *m*.

Saudi Arabian [saʊdɪəˈreɪbɪən] *a & n* saudita (*mf*), saudí (*m*).

sauna ['sɔːnə] sauna *f*.

sausage ['sɒsɪdʒ] (*frankfurter etc*) salchicha *f*; (*cured*) salchichón *m*; (*spicy*) chorizo *m*.

save [seɪv] **1** *vt* (*rescue*) rescatar; (*put by, computer file*) guardar; (*money*) ahorrar; (*food*) almacenar; **it saved him a lot of trouble** le evitó muchos problemas. **2** *n* (*in football*) parada *f*.

savings ['seɪvɪŋz] *npl* ahorros *mpl*.

savings account cuenta *f* de ahorros.

savings bank caja *f* de ahorros.

saw[1] [sɔː] **1** *n* (*tool*) sierra *f*. **2** *vti** serrar.

• **saw off** *vt* serrar.

saw² *pt* **see.**

saxophone ['sæksəfəʊn] saxofón *m*.

say* [seɪ] *vt* decir; **it is said that ...** se dice que ...; **that is to s.** es decir; **what does the sign s.?** ¿qué ponc en el letrero?; **shall we s. Friday then ?** ¿quedamos el viernes, pues?

saying refrán *m*.

scab [skæb] (*on cut*) costra *f*.

scaffolding ['skæfəldɪŋ] andamio *m*.

scald [skɔːld] *vt* escaldar.

scale¹ [skeɪl] (*of fish, on skin*) escama *f*; (*in boiler*) incrustaciones *fpl*.

scale² escala *f*; (*extent*) alcance *m*.

scales *npl* (**pair of**) **s.** (*shop, kitchen*) balanza *f sing*; (*bathroom*) báscula *f sing*.

scan *vt* (*text, graphics*) escanear.

scandal ['skændəl] escándalo *m*; (*gossip*) chismes *mpl*.

Scandinavian [skændɪ'neɪvɪən] *a & n* escandinavo,-a (*mf*).

scanner ['skænəʳ] escáner *m*.

scar [skaːʳ] cicatriz *f*.

scarce [skeəs] *a* escaso,-a.

scarcely *adv* apenas.

scarcity escasez *f*.

scare [skeəʳ] *vt* asustar.

● **scare away** *or* **off** *vt* ahuyentar.

scarecrow espantapájaros *m inv*.

scarf [skaːf] (*pl* **scarfs** *or* **scarves** [skaːvz]) (*long, woollen*) bufanda *f*; (*square*) pañuelo *m*.

scarlet ['skaːlɪt] *a* **s. fever** escarlatina *f*.

scary *a* espantoso,-a; (*film*) de terror.

scatter ['skætəʳ] **1** *vt* (*papers etc*) esparcir; (*disperse*) dispersar. **2** *vi* dispersarse.

scene [siːn] (*in theatre etc*) escena *f*; (*place*) lugar *m*; **to make a s.** (*fuss*) montar un espectáculo.

scenery (*landscape*) paisaje *m*; (*in theatre*) decorado *m*.

scent [sent] (*smell*) olor *m*; (*perfume*) perfume *m*.

schedule ['ʃedjuːl, *US* 'skedjuːl] **1** *n* (*plan, agenda*) programa *m*; (*timetable*) horario *m*; **on s.** a la hora (prevista); **to be behind s.** llevar retraso. **2** *vt* (*plan*) programar.

scheduled *u* previsto,-a; **s. flight** vuelo *m* regular.

scheme [skiːm] (*plan*) plan *m*; (*project*) proyecto *m*; (*trick*) ardid *m*.

scholarship ['skɒləʃɪp] (*grant*) beca *f*.

school [skuːl] (*primary*) escuela *f*; (*secondary*) colegio *m*; *US* (*university*) universidad *f*; **s. year** año *m* escolar.

schoolboy alumno *m*.
schoolgirl alumna *f*.
schoolmate compañero,-a *mf* clase.
schoolteacher profesor,-a *mf*; (*primary school*) maestro,-a *mf*.
science ['saɪəns] ciencia *f*; (*school subject*) ciencias *fpl*.
science fiction ciencia-ficción *f*.
scientific *a* científico,-a.
scientist científico,-a *mf*.
scissors ['sɪzəz] *npl* tijeras *fpl*.
scold [skəʊld] *vt* regañar, reñir.
scone [skɒn] bollo *m*.
scoop [sku:p] (*in press*) exclusiva *f*.
scooter ['sku:təʳ] (*child's*) patinete *m*; (*adult's*) Vespa[R] *f*.
scope [skəʊp] (*range*) alcance *m*; (*freedom*) libertad *f*.
scorch [skɔːtʃ] *vt* (*burn*) quemar; (*singe*) chamuscar.
score [skɔːʳ] **1** (*in sport*) tanteo *m*; (*cards, golf*) puntuación *f*; (*result*) resultado *m*; (*twenty*) veintena *f*; (*music*) partitura *f*. **2** *vt* (*goal*) marcar; (*points*) conseguir. **3** *vi* (*in sport*) marcar un tanto; (*football*) marcar un gol; (*keep the score*) llevar el marcador.
scorn [skɔːn] desprecio *m*.
Scot [skɒt] escocés,-esa *mf*.
Scotch [skɒtʃ] **1** *a* S. tape[R] cinta *f* adhesiva, celo[R] *m*. **2** *n* (*whisky*) whisky *m* escocés.
Scots *a* escocés,-esa.
Scotsman escocés *m*.
Scotswoman escocesa *f*.
scoundrel ['skaʊndrəl] canalla *m*.
scout [skaʊt] **boy s.** boy *m* scout; (*talent*) **s.** cazatalentos *m inv*.
scramble ['skræmbl] *vt* scrambled eggs huevos *mpl* revueltos.
scrap¹ [skræp] **1** *n* (*small piece*) pedazo *m*; **scraps** (*of food*) sobras *fpl*. **2** *vt* (*discard*) desechar; (*idea*) descartar.
scrap² **1** *n* (*fight*) pelea *f*. **2** *vi* pelearse (**with** con).
scrapbook álbum *m* de recortes.
scrape [skreɪp] **1** *vt* (*paint, wood*) raspar; (*graze*) arañarse. **2** *vi* (*rub*) rozar. **3** *n* (*trouble*) lío *m*.
● **scrape through** *vti* (*exam*) aprobar por los pelos.
scrap metal chatarra *f*.
scrap paper papel *m* de borrador.
scratch [skrætʃ] **1** *n* (*on skin, paintwork*) arañazo *m*; **to be up to s.** dar la talla; **to start from s.** partir de cero. **2** *vt* (*with nail, claw*) arañar; (*paintwork*) rayar; (*to relieve itching*) rascarse.
scream [skriːm] **1** *n* chillido *m*. **2** *vt* (*insults etc*) gritar. **3** *vi* **to s. at sb**

chillar a algn.

screen [skriːn] (*movable partition*) biombo *m*; (*cinema, TV, computer*) pantalla *f*.

screw [skruː] **1** *n* tornillo *m*. **2** *vt* atornillar; **to s. sth down** *or* **in** *or* **on** fijar algo con tornillos.

screwdriver destornillador *m*.

scribble ['skrɪbəl] *vt* (*message etc*) garabatear.

script [skrɪpt] (*of film*) guión *m*; (*in exam*) examen *m*.

scrub [skrʌb] *vt* frotar.

scrubbing brush estregadera *f*.

scrum [skrʌm] (*in rugby*) melée *f*; **s. half** medio *m* melée.

scuba diving ['skuːbə] submarinismo *m*.

sculptor ['skʌlptə^r] escultor *m*.

sculpture escultura *f*.

sea [siː] mar *mf*; **by the s.** a orillas del mar; **out at s.** en alta mar; **to go by s.** ir en barco.

seafood mariscos *mpl*.

seafront paseo *m* marítimo.

seagull gaviota *f*.

seal[1] [siːl] (*animal*) foca *f*.

seal[2] **1** *n* (*official stamp*) sello *m*; (*airtight closure*) cierre *m* hermético. **2** *vt* (*with official stamp*) sellar; (*with wax*) lacrar; (*close*) cerrar.

● **seal off** *vt* (*area*) acordonar.

seam [siːm] (*in cloth*) costura *f*.

search [sɜːtʃ] **1** *vt* (*files etc*) buscar en; (*building, suitcase*) registrar; (*person*) cachear. **2** *vi* buscar; **to s. through** registrar. **3** *n* búsqueda *f*; (*of building etc*) registro *m*; (*of person*) cacheo *m*; **in s. of** en busca de.

seashell concha *f* marina.

seashore (*beach*) playa *f*.

seasick *a* **to get s.** marearse.

seasickness mareo *m*.

seaside playa *f*.

season[1] ['siːzən] (*of year*) estación *f*; (*for sport etc*) temporada *f*; **high/ low s.** temporada *f* alta/baja.

season[2] *vt* (*food*) sazonar.

seasoning condimento *m*.

season ticket abono *m*.

seat [siːt] **1** *n* asiento *m*; (*place*) plaza *f*; (*in cinema, theatre*) localidad *f*; (*in parliament*) escaño *m*; **to take a s.** sentarse. **2** *vt* (*guests etc*) sentar; (*accommodate*) tener cabida para.

seating asientos *mpl*.

seaweed ['siːwiːd] alga *f* (marina).

second¹ ['sekənd] **1** *a* segundo,-a; **every s. day** cada dos días. **2** *n* (*in series*) segundo,-a *mf*; (*gear*) segunda *f*; **the s. of October** el dos de octubre. **3** *adv* **to come s.** terminar en segundo lugar.

second² (*time*) segundo *m*.

secondary *a* secundario,-a.

second-'class 1 *a* de segunda clase. **2** *adv* **to travel s.** viajar en segunda.

second-'hand *a* & *adv* de segunda mano.

secondly *adv* en segundo lugar.

secret ['si:krɪt] *a* secreto,-a; **in s.** en secreto.

secretary ['sekrətrɪ] secretario,-a *mf*.

section ['sekʃən] sección *f*.

secure [sɪ'kjɔə'] **1** *a* seguro,-a; (*window, door*) bien cerrado,-a; (*ladder etc*) firme. **2** *vt* sujetar; (*window, door*) cerrar bien; (*obtain*) obtener.

securely *adv* (*firmly*) firmemente.

security seguridad *f*; (*financial guarantee*) fianza *f*.

sedation [sɪ'deɪʃən] sedación *f*.

'sedative *a* & *n* sedante (*m*).

see* [si:] *vti* ver; **let's s.** a ver; **s. you (later)/soon!** ¡hasta luego/pronto!; **to s. sb home** acompañar a algn a casa.

• **see about** *vt* (*deal with*) ocuparse de.

• **see off** *vt* (*say goodbye to*) despedirse de.

• **see out** *vt* (*show out*) acompañar hasta la puerta.

• **see to** *vt* (*deal with*) ocuparse de.

seed [si:d] semilla *f*; (*of fruit*) pepita *f*.

seeing *conj* **s. that** dado que.

seek* [si:k] **1** *vt* (*look for*) buscar; (*ask for*) solicitar. **2** *vi* buscar; **to s. to do sth** procurar hacer algo.

seem [si:m] *vi* parecer; **I s. to remember his name was Colin** creo recordar que su nombre era Colin; **it seems to me that** me parece que; **so it seems** eso parece.

seesaw balancín *m*.

segment ['segmənt] segmento *m*; (*of orange*) gajo *m*.

seize [si:z] *vt* (*grab*) agarrar; **to s. an opportunity** aprovechar una ocasión; **to s. power** hacerse con el poder.

seldom ['seldəm] *adv* rara vez, raramente.

select [sɪ'lekt] *vt* (*thing*) escoger; (*team*) seleccionar.

selection (*people or things chosen*) selección *f*; (*range*) surtido *m*.

self-assurance confianza *f* en uno mismo.

self-assured *a* seguro,-a de uno mismo,-a.

self-confidence confianza *f* en uno mismo,-a.

self-confident *a* seguro,-a de uno mismo,-a.

self-conscious *a* cohibido,-a.

self-control autocontrol *m*.

self-defence, *US* **self-defense** autodefensa *f*.

self-employed *a* (*worker*) autónomo,-a.

selfish ['selfɪʃ] *a* egoísta.

self-respect amor *m* propio.

self-service 1 *n* (*in shop etc*) autoservicio *m*. **2** *a* de autoservicio.

sell* [sel] **1** *vt* vender. **2** *vi* venderse.

• **sell out** *vi* **'sold out'** (*theatre*) 'agotadas las localidades'.

seller vendedor,-a *mf*.

sellotape[R] ['seləteɪp] celo[R] *m*, cinta *f* adhesiva.

semester [sɪ'mestə[r]] semestre *m*.

semi- ['semɪ] *prefix* semi-.

semicircle semicírculo *m*.

semi'colon punto y coma *m*.

semiconductor semiconductor *m*.

semide'tached casa *f* adosada.

semi'final [semɪ'faɪnəl] semifinal *f*.

semolina [semə'liːnə] sémola *f*.

senate ['senɪt] senado *m*.

senator senador,-a *mf*.

send* [send] **1** *vt* enviar; (*cause to become*) volver. **2** *vi* **to s. for sb** mandar llamar a algn.

• **send away 1** *vt* (*dismiss*) despedir. **2** *vi* **to s. away for sth** escribir pidiendo algo.

• **send back** *vt* (*goods etc*) devolver.

• **send in** *vt* (*application etc*) mandar; (*troops*) enviar.

• **send off** *vt* (*letter etc*) enviar; (*player*) expulsar.

• **send on** *vt* (*luggage*) (*ahead*) facturar.

• **send out** *vt* (*person*) echar; (*invitations*) enviar.

• **send up** *vt* hacer subir; (*make fun of*) burlarse de.

sender remitente *mf*.

senior ['siːnjə[r]] **1** *a* (*in age*) mayor; (*in rank*) superior; (*with longer service*) más antiguo,-a; **William Armstrong S.** William Armstrong padre. **2** *n Br* (*at school*) mayor *mf*; *US* (*at school*) estudiante *mf* del último curso; **she's three years my s.** (*in age*) me lleva tres años.

sensation [sen'seɪʃən] sensación *f*.

sensational *a* (*marvellous*) sensacional.

sense [sens] **1** *n* (*faculty*) sentido *m*; (*of word*) significado *m*; (*meaning*) sentido *m*; **s. of direction/humour** sentido *m* de la orientación/del humor; **common s.** sentido *m* común; **it doesn't make s.** no tiene sentido; **to come to one's senses** recobrar el juicio. **2** *vt* sentir.

senseless a (absurd) absurdo,-a.
sensible ['sensɪbəl] a (wise) sensato,-a; (choice) acertado,-a; (clothes, shoes) práctico,-a.
sensitive ['sensɪtɪv] a sensible; (touchy) susceptible; (skin) delicado,-a.
sentence ['sentəns] 1 n frase f; (legal) sentencia f; **life s.** cadena f perpetua. 2 vt (judge) condenar.
separate ['sepəreɪt] 1 vt separar (**from** de). 2 vi separarse. 3 ['sepərɪt] a separado,-a; (different) distinto,-a.
separately adv por separado.
September [sep'tembə'] se(p)tiembre m.
sequence ['si:kwəns] (order) orden m; (series) sucesión f.
sergeant ['sɑːdʒənt] sargento m; (of police) cabo m.
serial ['sɪərɪəl] (on TV etc) serial m; (soap opera) telenovela f.
series ['sɪəriːz] inv serie f.
serious ['sɪərɪəs] a serio,-a; (causing concern) grave; **I am s.** hablo en serio.
seriously adv (in earnest) en serio; (dangerously, severely) gravemente.
servant ['sɜːvənt] (domestic) criado,-a mf.
serve [sɜːv] vt servir; (customer) atender; **it serves him right** bien merecido lo tiene.
● **serve out, serve up** vt servir.
server (for computers) servidor m.
service ['sɜːvɪs] 1 n servicio m; (maintenance) mantenimiento m; **s. (charge) included** servicio incluido. 2 vt (car, machine) revisar.
service area área m de servicio.
service station estación f de servicio.
serviette [sɜːvɪ'et] Br servilleta f.
session ['seʃən] sesión f.
set[1]* [set] 1 vt (put, place) poner, colocar; (time, price) fijar; (record) establecer; (mechanism etc) ajustar; **to s. one's watch** poner el reloj en hora; **to s. the table** poner la mesa; **to s. sb free** poner en libertad a algn. 2 vi (sun, moon) ponerse; (jelly, jam) cuajar; **to s. to** (begin) ponerse a. 3 n (stage) (for film) plató m; (in theatre) escenario m; (scenery) decorado m; **shampoo and s.** lavado y marcado m. 4 a (task, idea) fijo,-a; (date, time) señalado,-a; (ready) listo,-a; **s. phrase** frase f hecha; **to be s. on doing sth** estar empeñado,-a en hacer algo.
● **set about** vt (begin) empezar.
● **set aside** vt (time, money) reservar.
● **set back** vt (delay) retrasar.
● **set down** vt (luggage etc) dejar (en el suelo).
● **set off 1** vi (depart) salir. 2 vt (bomb) hacer estallar; (burglar alarm) hacer sonar.

● **set out 1** *vi* (*depart*) salir; **to s. out for ...** partir hacia ...; **to s. out to do sth** proponerse hacer algo. **2** *vt* (*arrange*) disponer; (*present*) presentar.

● **set up 1** *vt* (*tent, stall*) montar; (*business etc*) establecer. **2** *vi* establecerse.

set² (*series*) serie *f*; (*of golf clubs, keys etc*) juego *m*; (*of tools*) estuche *m*; (*of people*) grupo *m*; (*in maths*) conjunto *m*; (*tennis*) set *m*; **TV s.** televisor *m*; **chess s.** juego *m* de ajedrez.

setback revés *m*, contratiempo *m*.

settee [se'ti:] sofá *m*.

setting (*background*) marco *m*.

settle ['setəl] **1** *vt* (*decide on*) acordar; (*date, price*) fijar; (*debt*) pagar; (*account*) saldar. **2** *vi* (*bird, insect*) posarse; (*put down roots*) afincarse; **to s. into an armchair** acomodarse en un sillón.

● **settle down** *vi* (*put down roots*) instalarse; (*marry*) casarse; (*child*) calmarse; (*situation*) normalizarse.

● **settle with** *vt* (*pay debt to*) ajustar cuentas con.

settlement (*agreement*) acuerdo *m*; (*colony*) asentamiento *m*..

settler colono *m*.

seven ['sevən] *a & n* siete (*m*) inv.

seven'teen *a & n* diecisiete (*m*).

seventh *a & n* séptimo,-a (*mf*).

seventieth *a & n* septuagésimo,-a (*mf*).

seventy *a & n* setenta (*m*) inv; **in the seventies** en los (años) setenta.

several ['sevərəl] **1** *a* varios,-as. **2** *pron* algunos,-as.

severe [sɪ'vɪəʳ] *a* severo,-a; (*climate, blow*) duro,-a; (*illness, loss*) grave.

se'verity severidad *f*.

sew* [səʊ] *vti* coser.

● **sew on** *vt* coser.

● **sew up** *vt* (*mend*) remendar.

sewer alcantarilla *f*.

sewing costura *f*.

sewing machine máquina *f* de coser.

sex [seks] sexo *m*; **s. education** educación *f* sexual; **to have s. with sb** tener relaciones sexuales con algn.

sexual *a* sexual.

sexy *a* sexi.

sh! [ʃ] *int* ¡chitón!, ¡chh!

shabby ['ʃæbɪ] *a* (*garment*) raído,-a; (*unkempt*) desaseado,-a.

shade [ʃeɪd] (*shadow*) sombra *f*; (*lampshade*) pantalla *f*; (*of colour*) matiz *m*; **in the s.** a la sombra.

shadow ['ʃædəʊ] sombra *f*.

shady *a* (*place*) a la sombra.

shake* [ʃeɪk] **1** *vt* sacudir; (*bottle*) agitar; **the news shook him** la noticia le conmocionó; **to s. hands with sb** estrechar la mano a algn; **to s. one's head** negar con la cabeza. **2** *vi* (*person, building*) temblar.

shall [ʃæl, *unstressed* ʃəl] *v aux* (*used to form future tense*) (*first person only*) **I s.** (*or* **I'll**) **buy it** lo compraré; **I s. not** (*or* **I shan't**) **say anything** no diré nada. ▌ (*used to form questions*) (*usually first person*) **s. I close the door ?** ¿cierro la puerta?; **s. we go?** ¿nos vamos?

shallow [ˈʃæləʊ] *a* poco profundo,-a.

shame [ʃeɪm] vergüenza *f*; (*pity*) pena; **what a s. !** ¡qué lástima!

shameful *a* vergonzoso,-a.

shampoo [ʃæmˈpuː] **1** *n* champú *m*. **2** *vt* (*one's hair*) lavarse.

shandy [ˈʃændɪ] *Br* clara *f*.

shan't [ʃɑːnt] = **shall not**.

shape [ʃeɪp] forma *f*; **to take s.** tomar forma; **in good/bad s.** (*condition*) en buen/mal estado; **to be in good s.** (*health*) estar en forma.

share [ˈʃeəʳ] **1** *n* (*portion*) parte *f*; (*financial*) acción *f*. **2** *vt* (*divide*) dividir; (*have in common*) compartir.

● **share in** *vt* participar en.

● **share out** *vt* repartir.

shareholder accionista *mf*.

shark [ʃɑːk] (*fish*) tiburón *m*.

sharp [ʃɑːp] **1** *a* (*razor, pencil, knife*) afilado,-a; (*needle*) puntiagudo,-a; (*bend*) cerrado,-a; (*pain, cry*) agudo,-a. **2** *adv* **at 2 o'clock s.** a las dos en punto.

sharpen *vt* (*knife*) afilar; (*pencil*) sacar punta a.

sharpener sacapuntas *m*.

sharply *adv* (*abruptly*) bruscamente.

shatter [ˈʃætəʳ] **1** *vt* hacer añicos. **2** *vi* hacerse añicos.

shave [ʃeɪv] **1** *n* afeitado *m*; **to have a s.** afeitarse. **2** *vt* (*person*) afeitar. **3** *vi* afeitarse.

shaver (electric) s. máquina *f* de afeitar.

shaving brush brocha *f* de afeitar.

shaving cream crema *f* de afeitar.

shawl [ʃɔːl] chal *m*.

she [ʃiː] *pers pron* ella.

shed¹ [ʃed] (*in garden*) cobertizo *m*; (*workmen's hut*) barraca *f*.

shed²* *vt* (*blood, tears*) derramar.

sheep [ʃiːp] *inv* oveja *f*.

sheepskin piel *f* de carnero.

sheet [ʃiːt] (*on bed*) sábana *f*; (*of paper*) hoja *f*; (*of tin, glass, plastic*) lámina *f*; (*of ice*) capa *f*.

shelf [ʃelf] (*pl* **shelves** [ʃelvz]) (*on bookcase*) estante *m*; **shelves** estantería *f*.

shell [ʃel] **1** *n* (*of egg, nut*) cáscara *f*; (*of tortoise etc*) caparazón *m*; (*of snail etc*) concha *f*; (*from gun*) obús *m*. **2** *vt* (*peas*) desvainar; (*with guns*) bombardear.

shellfish *inv* marisco *m*; mariscos *mpl*.

shelter ['ʃeltə^r] **1** *n* (*protection*) abrigo *m*; **to take s.** refugiarse (**from** de); **bus s.** marquesina *f*. **2** *vt* proteger. **3** *vi* refugiarse.

shelving estanterías *fpl*.

shepherd ['ʃepəd] pastor *m*.

sheriff ['ʃerɪf] sheriff *m*.

sherry ['ʃerɪ] jerez *m*.

shield [ʃiːld] **1** *n* escudo *m*; (*of policeman*) placa *f*. **2** *vt* proteger (**from** de).

shift [ʃɪft] **1** *n* (*change*) cambio *m*; (*period of work, group of workers*) turno *m*; *US* (**gear**) **s.** cambio *m* de velocidades. **2** *vt* (*change*) cambiar; (*move*) cambiar de sitio. **3** *vi* (*move*) mover; (*change place*) cambiar de sitio.

shin [ʃɪn] espinilla *f*.

shine* [ʃaɪn] **1** *vi* brillar. **2** *vt* (*lamp*) dirigir; (*pt & pp* **shined**) (*polish*) sacar brillo a; (*shoes*) limpiar. **3** *n* brillo *m*.

shiny *a* brillante.

ship [ʃɪp] barco *m*.

shipping barcos *mpl*.

shipwreck 1 *n* naufragio *m*. **2** *vt* **to be shipwrecked** naufragar.

shipyard astillero *m*.

shirt [ʃɜːt] camisa *f*.

shiver ['ʃɪvə^r] **1** *vi* (*with cold*) tiritar; (*with fear*) temblar. **2** *n* escalofrío *m*.

shock [ʃɒk] **1** *n* (*jolt*) choque *m*; (*scare*) susto *m*; (*in medical sense*) shock *m*. **2** *vt* (*scandalize*) escandalizar.

shock absorber amortiguador *m*.

shocking *a* (*causing horror*) espantoso,-a; (*disgraceful*) escandaloso,-a.

shoe [ʃuː] zapato *m*; **shoes** calzado *m sing*.

shoelace cordón *m* (de zapatos).

shoe polish betún *m*.

shoot [ʃuːt] **1** *n* (*on plant*) brote *m*; (*of vine*) sarmiento *m*. **2** *vt** (*fire on*) pegar un tiro a; (*wound*) herir (de bala); (*kill*) matar; (*execute*) fusilar; (*film*) rodar, filmar; (*with still camera*) fotografiar. **3** *vi** (*with gun*) disparar (**at sb** sobre, a algn).

● **shoot down** *vt* (*aircraft*) derribar.

● **shoot up** *vi* (*prices*) dispararse.

shooting 1 *n* (*shots*) tiros *mpl*; (*murder*) asesinato *m*; (*hunting*) caza *f*;

(of film) rodaje *m*. **2** *a (pain)* punzante.

shooting star estrella *f* fugaz.

shop [ʃɒp] **1** *n* tienda *f*; *(large store)* almacén *m*. **2** *vi* hacer compras; **to go shopping** ir de compras.

shop assistant dependiente,-a *mf*.

shopkeeper tendero,-a *mf*.

shopping *(purchases)* compras *fpl*.

shopping bag bolsa *f* de la compra.

shopping basket cesta *f* de la compra.

shopping centre centro *m* comercial.

shop window escaparate *m*.

shore [ʃɔːʳ] *(of sea, lake)* orilla *f*; *(coast)* costa *f*.

short [ʃɔːt] **1** *a* corto,-a; *(not tall)* bajo,-a; **in a s. while** dentro de un rato; **in the s. term** a corto plazo; **'Bob' is s. for 'Robert'** 'Bob' es el diminutivo de 'Robert'; **to be s. of food** andar escaso,-a de comida. **2** *adv* **to cut s.** *(holiday)* interrumpir; *(meeting)* suspender; **we're running s. of coffee** se nos está acabando el café.

shortage escasez *f*.

short cut atajo *m*.

shorten *vt (skirt, visit)* acortar.

shorthand typist taquimecanógrafo,-a *mf*.

shortly *adv (soon)* dentro de poco; **s. after** poco después.

shorts [ʃɔːts] *npl* **a pair of s.** un pantalón corto; *US (underpants)* unos calzoncillos *mpl*.

short-'sighted *a (person)* miope.

short-'term *a* a corto plazo.

shot¹ [ʃɒt] *(act, sound)* disparo *m*; *(football)* tiro *m* (a puerta); *(photography)* foto *f*; *(in film)* toma *f*.

shot² *pt & pp of* **shoot**.

shotgun escopeta *f*.

should [ʃʊd, *unstressed* ʃəd] *v aux (duty)* deber; **all employees s. wear helmets** todos los empleados deben llevar casco; **he s. have been an architect** debería haber sido arquitecto. ‖ *(probability)* deber de; **he s. have finished by now** ya debe de haber acabado. ‖ *(conditional use)* **if anything strange s. happen** si pasara algo raro; **I s. like to ask a question** quisiera hacer una pregunta.

shoulder ['ʃəʊldəʳ] hombro *m*; **hard s.** arcén *m*.

shoulder bag bolso *m* (de bandolera).

shout [ʃaʊt] **1** *n* grito *m*. **2** *vti* gritar; **to s. at sb** gritar a algn.

shouting gritos *mpl*.

shove [ʃʌv] **1** *n* empujón *m*. **2** *vt* empujar. **3** *vi* empujar; *(jostle)* dar empellones.

shovel ['ʃʌvəl] **1** n pala f. **2** vt mover con pala.

show [ʃəʊ] **1** vt* (ticket etc) mostrar; (painting etc) exponer; (film) poner; (latest plans etc) presentar; (teach) enseñar; (temperature, way etc) indicar; **to s. sb to the door** acompañar a algn hasta la puerta. **2** vi (be visible) notarse; **what's showing?** (at cinema) ¿qué ponen? **3** n (entertainment) espectáculo m; **on s.** expuesto,-a; **boat s.** salón m náutico; **motor s.** salón m del automóvil.

● **show off 1** vt (flaunt) hacer alarde de. **2** vi farolear.

● **show up 1** vt (embarrass) dejar en evidencia. **2** vi (arrive) aparecer.

shower ['ʃaʊəʳ] (rain) chaparrón m; (bath) ducha f; **to have a s.** ducharse.

showing (cinema performance) sesión f.

show-off farolero,-a mf.

shrimp [ʃrɪmp] camarón m.

shrink* [ʃrɪŋk] **1** vt encoger. **2** vi encoger(se).

shrub [ʃrʌb] arbusto m.

shrug [ʃrʌɡ] vt **to s. one's shoulders** encogerse de hombros.

shudder ['ʃʌdəʳ] vi (person) estremecerse.

shuffle ['ʃʌfəl] vt (cards) barajar.

shut [ʃʌt] **1** vt* cerrar. **2** vi* cerrarse. **3** a cerrado,-a.

● **shut down 1** vt (factory) cerrar. **2** vi (factory) cerrar.

● **shut off** vti (gas, water etc) cortar.

● **shut out** vt (lock out) dejar fuera a.

● **shut up 1** vt (close) cerrar; (imprison) encerrar. **2** vi (keep quiet) callarse.

shutter ['ʃʌtəʳ] (on window) postigo m.

shuttle ['ʃʌtəl] (plane) puente m aéreo; **(space) s.** transbordador m espacial.

shy [ʃaɪ] a (timid) tímido,-a; (reserved) reservado,-a.

shyness timidez f.

sick [sɪk] a (ill) enfermo,-a; fam (fed up) harto,-a; **s. leave** baja f por enfermedad; **to feel s.** (about to vomit) tener ganas de devolver; **to be s.** devolver.

sickness (illness) enfermedad f; (nausea) náuseas fpl.

side [saɪd] n lado m; (of coin etc) cara f; (of hill) ladera f; (edge) borde m; (of lake, river) orilla f; (team) equipo m; (in politics) partido m; **by the s. of** junto a; **by my s.** a mi lado; **s. by s.** juntos; **she's on our s.** está de nuestro lado; **to take sides with sb** ponerse de parte de algn.

sideboard aparador m.

sidelight piloto m.

sidewalk US acera f.

sideways adv de lado.

sieve [sɪv] colador m; (coarse) criba f.

sift [sɪft] *vt* tamizar.

sigh [saɪ] **1** *vi* suspirar. **2** *n* suspiro *m*.

sight [saɪt] *(faculty)* vista *f*; *(spectacle)* espectáculo *m*; **at first s.** a primera vista; **to catch s. of** divisar; **to lose s. of sth/sb** perder algo/a algn de vista; **within s.** a la vista.

sightseeing to go s. hacer turismo.

sign [saɪn] **1** *n (signal)* señal *f*; *(trace)* rastro *m*; *(notice)* anuncio *m*; *(board)* letrero *m*. **2** *vti (letter etc)* firmar.

● **sign on** *vi (worker)* firmar un contrato; *(unemployed person)* apuntarse al paro.

● **sign up** *vi (soldier)* alistarse; *(worker)* firmar un contrato.

signal ['sɪgnəl] **1** *n* señal *f*. **2** *vt (direction etc)* indicar.

signature ['sɪgnɪtʃəʳ] firma *f*.

significant [sɪg'nɪfɪkənt] *a (important)* importante.

significantly *adv (markedly)* sensiblemente.

signpost poste *m* indicador.

silence ['saɪləns] **1** *n* silencio *m*. **2** *vt* acallar.

silent *a* silencioso,-a; *(film)* mudo,-a; **to remain s.** guardar silencio.

silently *adv* silenciosamente.

silk [sɪlk] seda *f*.

sill [sɪl] *(of window)* alféizar *m*.

silly ['sɪlɪ] *a (stupid)* tonto,-a; *(ridiculous)* ridículo,-a.

silver ['sɪlvəʳ] **1** *n (metal)* plata *f*; *(tableware)* vajilla *f* de plata. **2** *a* de plata; **s. paper** papel *m* de plata.

silver-'plated *a* plateado,-a.

silverware vajilla *f* de plata.

similar ['sɪmɪləʳ] *a* semejante (**to** a); **to be s.** parecerse.

simi'larity semejanza *f*.

simple ['sɪmpəl] *a* sencillo,-a.

simplify *vt* simplificar.

simply *adv (only)* simplemente; *(just, merely)* meramente.

simultaneous [sɪməl'teɪnɪəs] *a* simultáneo,-a.

simultaneously *adv* simultáneamente.

sin [sɪn] pecado *m*.

since [sɪns] **1** *adv (ever)* **s.** desde entonces. **2** *prep* desde; **she has been living here s. 1975** vive aquí desde 1975. **3** *conj (time)* desde que; **how long is it s. you last saw him?** ¿cuánto tiempo hace (desde) que lo viste por última vez? ▮ *(because, as)* ya que.

sincere [sɪn'sɪəʳ] *a* sincero,-a.

sincerely *adv* sinceramente; **Yours s.** *(in letter)* (le saluda) atentamente.

sin'cerity sinceridad *f*.

sing* [sɪŋ] *vti* cantar.

singer cantante *mf*.

single ['sɪŋgəl] **1** *a* solo,-a; (*unmarried*) soltero,-a; **s. bed/room** cama *f*/habitación *f* individual. **2** *n Rail* billete *m* de ida; (*record*) single *m*.

● **single out** *vt* (*choose*) escoger.

singular ['sɪŋgjʊləʳ] **1** *a* (*noun form etc*) singular. **2** *n* singular *m*.

singularly *adv* excepcionalmente.

sinister ['sɪnɪstəʳ] *a* siniestro,-a.

sink¹ [sɪŋk] (*in kitchen*) fregadero *m*.

sink² *vi* (*ship*) hundirse.

● **sink in** *vi* (*penetrate*) penetrar; *fig* causar impresión.

sip [sɪp] *vt* beber a sorbos.

sir [sɜːʳ] señor *m*; (*title*) sir.

siren ['saɪərən] sirena *f*.

sister ['sɪstəʳ] hermana *f*.

sister-in-law cuñada *f*.

sit [sɪt] *vt* (*child etc*) sentar (**in, on** en); *Br* (*exam*) presentarse a. **2** *vi* (*action*) sentarse; (*be seated*) estar sentado,-a.

● **sit around** *vi* holgazanear.

● **sit down** *vi* sentarse.

● **sit up** *vi* incorporarse.

site [saɪt] (*area*) lugar *m*; **building s.** solar *m*; (*under construction*) obra *f*.

sitting room sala *f* de estar.

situated *a* **to be s.** estar situado,-a.

situ'ation [sɪtjʊ'eɪʃən] situación *f*.

six [sɪks] *a & n* seis (*m*) *inv*.

six'teen *a & n* dieciséis (*m*) *inv*.

sixth 1 *a* sexto,-a; **s. form** ≈ COU *m*; **s. former** ≈ estudiante *m* de COU. **2** *n* (*in series*) sexto,-a *mf*; (*fraction*) sexto *m*.

sixtieth *a & n* sexagésimo,-a (*mf*).

sixty *a & n* sesenta (*m*) *inv*.

size [saɪz] tamaño *m*; (*of garment*) talla *f*; (*of shoes*) número *m*; (*of person*) estatura *f*.

skate [skeɪt] **1** *n* patín *m*. **2** *vi* patinar.

skateboard monopatín *m*.

skater patinador,-a *mf*.

skating patinaje *m*.

skating rink pista *f* de patinaje.

skeleton ['skelɪtən] esqueleto *m*.

sketch [sketʃ] **1** *n* (*preliminary drawing*) bosquejo *m*; (*on TV etc*) sketch *m*. **2** *vt* (*preliminary drawing*) bosquejar.

skewer ['skjʊəʳ] pincho *m*, broqueta *f*.

ski [skiː] **1** n esquí m. **2** vi esquiar; **to go skiing** ir a esquiar.

skid [skɪd] **1** n patinazo m. **2** vi patinar.

skier esquiador,-a mf.

skiing esquí m.

skilful, US **skillful** a hábil.

ski lift telesquí m; (with seats) telesilla f.

skill [skɪl] (ability) habilidad f; (technique) técnica f.

skilled a (worker) cualificado,-a.

skimmed milk [skɪmd] leche f desnatada.

skin [skɪn] piel f; (of face) cutis m; (complexion) tez f; (of fruit) piel f.

skin-diving submarinismo m.

skinny ['skɪnɪ] a flaco,-a.

skip[1] [skɪp] **1** vi (jump) saltar, brincar; (with rope) saltar a la comba. **2** vt (omit) saltarse.

skip[2] (container) contenedor m.

skipping rope comba f.

skirt [skɜːt] falda f.

skittle ['skɪtəl] (pin) bolo m; **skittles** (game) (juego m de los) bolos mpl.

skull [skʌl] calavera f; (cranium) cráneo m.

sky [skaɪ] cielo m; **s. blue** azul m celeste.

skyscraper rascacielos m inv.

slack [slæk] a (not taut) flojo,-a; **business is s.** hay poco negocio.

slacken vt (rope) aflojar; (speed) reducir.

slacks npl pantalones mpl.

slam [slæm] **1** n (of door) portazo m. **2** vt (bang) cerrar de golpe; **to s. the door** dar un portazo. **3** vi cerrarse de golpe.

slang [slæŋ] jerga f popular.

slant [slɑːnt] **1** n inclinación f. **2** vi inclinarse.

slap [slæp] **1** n palmada f; (in face) bofetada f. **2** vt pegar con la mano; (hit in face) dar una bofetada a; **to s. sb on the back** dar a algn una palmada en la espalda.

slate [sleɪt] pizarra f.

slaughter ['slɔːtəʳ] **1** n (of animals) matanza f; (of people) carnicería f. **2** vt (animals) matar; (people) masacrar.

slave [sleɪv] esclavo,-a mf.

slavery esclavitud f.

sledge [sledʒ] Br trineo m.

sleep [sliːp] **1** n sueño m. **2** vi* dormir; **to go to s.** dormirse.

● **sleep in** vi Br (oversleep) quedarse dormido,-a.

sleeper (on train) (coach) coche-cama m; (berth) litera f.

sleeping bag saco m de dormir.

sleeping car coche-cama m.

sleeping pill somnífero *m*.

sleepy *a* **to be** *or* **feel s.** tener sueño.

sleet [sli:t] **1** *n* aguanieve *f*. **2** *vi* **it's sleeting** cae aguanieve.

sleeve [sli:v] (*of garment*) manga *f*; (*of record*) funda *f*.

sleigh [sleɪ] trineo *m*.

slept [slept] *pt* & *pp* of **sleep.**

slice [slaɪs] **1** *n* (*of bread*) rebanada *f*; (*of cake*) trozo *m*; (*of meat*) loncha *f*. **2** *vt* (*food*) cortar a rebanadas.

slide [slaɪd] **1** *n* (*in playground*) tobogán *m*; (*photographic*) diapositiva *f*; Br (*for hair*) pasador *m*; **s. projector** proyector *m* de diapositivas. **2** *vt** deslizar; (*furniture*) correr. **3** *vi** deslizarse; (*slip*) resbalar.

sliding *a* (*door, window*) corredizo,-a.

slight [slaɪt] *a* (*small*) pequeño,-a; (*trivial*) leve; **not in the slightest** en absoluto.

slightly *adv* (*a little*) ligeramente.

slim [slɪm] **1** *a* (*person*) delgado,-a; (*slender*) esbelto,-a. **2** *vi* adelgazar.

sling [slɪŋ] **1** *n* (*for arm*) cabestrillo *m*. **2** *vt** (*throw*) tirar.

slip [slɪp] **1** *n* (*mistake*) error *m*; (*moral*) desliz *m*; (*underskirt*) combinación *f*; (*of paper*) papelito *m*. **2** *vi* (*slide*) resbalar. **3** *vt* **to s. sth into sth** meter algo en algo; **to s. sth to sb** dar algo a algn con disimulo.

• **slip away** *vi* (*person*) escabullirse.

• **slip off** *vt* (*clothes*) quitarse rápidamente.

• **slip on** *vt* (*clothes*) ponerse rápidamente.

• **slip out** *vi* (*leave*) salir.

• **slip up** *vi* (*make a mistake*) equivocarse.

slipper ['slɪpə'] zapatilla *f*.

slippery *a* resbaladizo,-a.

slit [slɪt] (*opening*) hendidura *f*; (*cut*) raja *f*.

slogan ['sləʊgən] (e)slogan *m*, lema *m*.

slope [sləʊp] **1** *n* (*incline*) cuesta *f*; (*of mountain*) ladera *f*; (*of roof*) vertiente *f*. **2** *vi* inclinarse.

sloping *a* inclinado,-a.

slot [slɒt] (*for coin*) ranura *f*; (*opening*) rendija *f*.

slot machine (*for gambling*) (máquina *f*) tragaperras *f inv*; (*vending machine*) distribuidor *m* automático.

slow [sləʊ] **1** *a* lento,-a; (*clock*) atrasado,-a; (*stupid*) torpe; **in s. motion** a cámara lenta; **to be s. to do sth** tardar en hacer algo. **2** *adv* despacio.

• **slow down** *or* **up** *vi* ir más despacio; (*in car*) reducir la velocidad.

slowly *adv* despacio.

slug [slʌg] (*animal*) babosa *f*.

slums [slʌmz] barrios bajos *mpl*.

sly [slaɪ] *a* (*cunning*) astuto,-a.

smack [smæk] **1** n (slap) bofetada f. **2** vt (slap) dar una bofetada a; (hit) golpear.

small [smɔːl] a pequeño,-a; (in height) bajo,-a; **s. change** cambio m.

smallpox ['smɔːlpɒks] viruela f.

smart [smɑːt] a (elegant) elegante; (clever) listo,-a.

smash [smæʃ] vt (break) romper; (shatter) hacer pedazos. **3** vi (break) romperse; (shatter) hacerse pedazos.

● **smash into** vt (vehicle) estrellarse contra.

smashing a fam estupendo,-a.

smell [smel] **1** n (sense) olfato m; (odour) olor m. **2** vt* oler. **3** vi* oler (**of** a); (stink) apestar; **it smells good/like lavender** huele bien/a lavanda.

smile [smaɪl] **1** n sonrisa f. **2** vi sonreír.

smock [smɒk] (blouse) blusón m.

smoke [sməʊk] **1** n humo m. **2** vi fumar; (chimney etc) echar humo. **3** vt (tobacco) fumar; **to s. a pipe** fumar en pipa.

smoker (person) fumador,-a mf; (compartment) vagón m de fumadores.

smooth [smuːð] a (surface) liso,-a; (skin) suave; (beer, wine) suave; (flight) tranquilo,-a.

● **smooth out** vt (creases) alisar.

● **smooth over** vt **to s. things over** limar asperezas.

smoothly adv sobre ruedas.

smuggle ['smʌgəl] vt pasar de contrabando.

smuggler contrabandista mf.

smuggling contrabando m.

snack [snæk] bocado m.

snack bar cafetería f.

snail [sneɪl] caracol m.

snake [sneɪk] (big) serpiente f; (small) culebra f.

snap [snæp] **1** n (photo) (foto f) instantánea f. **2** vt (branch etc) partir (en dos). **3** vi (break) romperse.

● **snap off** vt (branch etc) arrancar.

snapshot ['snæpʃɒt] (foto f) instantánea f.

snatch [snætʃ] **1** vt (grab) arrebatar. **2** vi **to s. at** intentar agarrar.

sneakers ['sniːkəz] npl US zapatillas fpl de deporte.

sneer [snɪəʳ] vi **to s. at** hacer un gesto de desprecio a.

sneeze [sniːz] **1** n estornudo m. **2** vi estornudar.

sniff [snɪf] vt (flower etc) oler.

snip [snɪp] vt cortar a tijeretazos.

snooker ['snuːkəʳ] snooker m, billar m ruso.

snore [snɔːʳ] **1** n ronquido m. **2** vi roncar.

snoring ronquidos mpl.

snow [snəʊ] **1** n nieve f. **2** vi nevar; **it's snowing** está nevando.

snowball bola *f* de nieve.
snowdrift ventisquero *m*.
snowflake copo *m* de nieve.
snowman hombre *m* de nieve.
snowplough, *US* **snowplow** quitanieves *m inv*.
snowstorm nevada *f*.
so [səʊ] **1** *adv* (*to such an extent*) tanto; **he was so tired that ...** estaba tan cansado que ...; **so long!** ¡hasta luego! ▌ (*degree*) tanto; **we loved her so (much)** la queríamos tanto; **so many books** tantos libros. ▌ (*thus, in this way*) así; **and so on, and so forth** y así sucesivamente; **if so** en este caso; **I think/hope so** creo/espero que sí; ▌ (*also*) **I'm going to Spain – so am I** voy a España – yo también. **2** *conj* (*expresses result*) así que; **so you like England, do you?** ¿así que te gusta Inglaterra, no? ▌ (*expresses purpose*) para que; **I'll put the key here so (that) everyone can see it** pongo la llave aquí para que todos la vean.
soak [səʊk] **1** *vt* (*washing, food*) remojar. **2** *vi* (*washing, food*) estar en remojo.
● **soak up** *vt* absorber.
soaked through *a* (*person*) empapado,-a.
soaking *a* (*object*) empapado,-a; (*person*) calado,-a hasta los huesos.
soap [səʊp] jabón *m*.
soap flakes jabón *m* en escamas.
soap powder jabón *m* en polvo.
soapy *a* jabonoso,-a.
sob [spb] **1** *n* sollozo *m*. **2** *vi* sollozar.
sober ['səʊbə^r] *a* (*not drunk, moderate*) sobrio,-a.
soccer ['spkə^r] fútbol *m*.
social ['səʊʃəl] *a* social; **s. climber** arribista *mf*; **s. security** seguridad *f* social; **s. welfare** seguro *m* social; **s. work** asistencia *f* social; **s. worker** asistente,-a *mf* social.
socialist *a* & *n* socialista (*mf*).
society [sə'saɪətɪ] sociedad *f*.
sock [spk] calcetín *m*.
socket ['spkɪt] (*for electricity*) enchufe *m*.
soda ['səʊdə] **s. water** soda *f*; *US* (*fizzy drink*) gaseosa *f*.
sofa ['səʊfə] sofá *m*; **s. bed** sofá *m* cama.
soft [spft] *a* (*not hard*) blando,-am ; (*skin, colour, hair, light, music*) suave; (*drink*) no alcohólico,-a; **s. drinks** refrescos *mpl*.
softly *adv* (*gently*) suavemente; (*quietly*) silenciosamente.
software ['spftweə^r] software *m*; **s. package** paquete *m*.
soil [sɔɪl] (*earth*) tierra *f*.
soldier ['səʊldʒə^r] soldado *m*.

sole¹ [səʊl] (*of foot*) planta *f*; (*of shoe, sock*) suela *f*.

sole² (*fish*) lenguado *m*.

solemn ['sɒləm] *a* solemne.

solicitor [sə'lɪsɪtəʳ] abogado,-a *mf*.

solid ['sɒlɪd] **1** *a* (*not liquid*) sólido,-a; (*firm*) firme; (*not hollow, pure*) (*metal*) macizo,-a; (*reliable*) formal. **2** *n* sólido *m*.

solution [sə'lu:ʃən] solución *f*.

solve [sɒlv] *vt* resolver.

some [sʌm] **1** *a* (*with plural nouns*) unos,-as, algunos,-as; (*several*) varios,-as; (*a few*) unos,-as cuantos,-as; **there were s. roses** había unas rosas. ‖ (*with singular nouns*) algún, alguna; (*a little*) un poco de; **there's s. wine left** queda un poco de vino. ‖ (*certain*) cierto,-a; **to s. extent** hasta cierto punto. ‖ (*unspecified*) algún, alguna; **s. day** algún día; **s. other time** otro día. ‖ (*quite a lot of*) bastante; **it's s. distance away** queda bastante lejos. **2** *pron* algunos,-as, unos,-as. ‖ (*a few*) unos,-as cuantos,-as. ‖ (*a little*) un poco.

somebody *pron* alguien; **s. else** otro,-a.

somehow *adv* (*in some way*) de alguna forma; (*for some reason*) por alguna razón.

someone *pron & n* = **somebody.**

someplace *adv US* = **somewhere.**

somersault ['sʌməsɔ:lt] (*by acrobat etc*) voltereta *f*.

something *pron & n* algo; **is s. the matter?** ¿le pasa algo?; **s. else** otra cosa; **s. of the kind** algo por el estilo.

sometime *adv* algún día.

sometimes *adv* a veces.

somewhat *adv* un tanto.

somewhere *adv* (*in some place*) en alguna parte; (*to some place*) a alguna parte.

son [sʌn] hijo *m*.

song [sɒŋ] canción *f*; (*of bird*) canto *m*.

son-in-law yerno *m*.

soon [su:n] *adv* (*within a short time*) dentro de poco; (*quickly*) rápidamente; (*early*) pronto; **s. afterwards** poco después; **as s. as** en cuanto; **as s. as possible** cuanto antes; **I would just as s. stay at home** prefiero quedarme en casa; **I would (just) as s. read as watch TV** tanto me da leer como ver la tele.

soot [sʊt] hollín *m*.

soothe [su:ð] *vt* (*calm*) tranquilizar; (*pain*) aliviar.

sore [sɔ:ʳ] **1** *a* (*aching*) dolorido,-a; (*painful*) doloroso,-a; *fam* (*angry*) enfadado,-a; **to have a s. throat** tener dolor de garganta. **2** *n* llaga *f*.

sorrow ['sɒrəʊ] pena *f*.

sorry ['sɒrɪ] **1** *a* **I feel very s. for her** me da mucha pena; **to be s. (about sth)** sentir (algo); **I'm s. I'm late** siento llegar tarde. **2** *interj* (*apology*) ¡perdón!; *Br* (*for repetition*) ¿cómo?

sort [sɔːt] **1** *n* (*kind*) clase *f*, tipo *m*; (*brand*) marca *f*; **it's a s. of teapot** es una especie de tetera. **2** *vt* (*classify*) clasificar.

● **sort out** *vt* (*classify*) clasificar; (*put in order*) ordenar; (*problem*) solucionar.

soul [səʊl] alma *f*.

sound[1] [saʊnd] **1** *n* sonido *m*; (*noise*) ruido *m*; **I don't like the s. of it** no me gusta nada la idea. **2** *vt* (*bell, trumpet*) tocar. **3** *vi* (*trumpet, bell, alarm*) sonar; (*give an impression*) parecer; **it sounds interesting** parece interesante.

sound[2] **1** *a* (*healthy*) sano,-a; (*in good condition*) en buen estado; (*safe, dependable*) seguro,-a. **2** *adv* **to be s. asleep** estar profundamente dormido,-a.

soundproof *a* insonorizado,-a.

soup [suːp] sopa *f*; (*thin, clear*) caldo *m*.

sour [saʊəʳ] *a* (*fruit, wine*) agrio,-a; (*milk*) cortado,-a.

source [sɔːs] fuente *f*.

south [saʊθ] **1** *n* sur *m*; **in the s. of England** en el sur de Inglaterra. **2** *a* del sur. **3** *adv* (*location*) al sur; (*direction*) hacia el sur.

southbound *a* (con) dirección sur.

south'east *n & a* sudeste (*m*).

southern ['sʌðən] *a* del sur.

southerner sureño,-a *mf*.

southward ['saʊθwəd] *a & adv* hacia el sur.

south'west *n & a* suroeste (*m*).

souvenir [suːvə'nɪəʳ] recuerdo *m*.

sow* [səʊ] *vt* sembrar.

space [speɪs] **1** *n* espacio *m*; (*room*) sitio *m*. **2** *vt* (*also* **s. out**) espaciar.

space age era *f* espacial.

spaceship nave *f* espacial.

space shuttle transbordador *m* espacial.

spacious *a* espacioso,-a.

spade[1] [speɪd] (*for digging*) pala *f*.

spade[2] (*in cards*) (*international pack*) pica *f*; (*Spanish pack*) espada *f*.

spaghetti [spə'getɪ] espaguetis *mpl*.

Spaniard ['spænjəd] español,-a *mf*.

Spanish ['spænɪʃ] **1** *a* español,-a. **2** *n* (*language*) español *m*, castellano *m*; **the S.** los españoles.

spank [spæŋk] *vt* zurrar.

spanking cachete *m*.

spanner ['spænəʳ] llave f (para tuercas).

spare [speəʳ] **1** vt (do without) prescindir de; **can you s. me 10?** ¿me puedes dejar 10?; **I can't s. the time** no tengo tiempo; **there's none to s.** no sobra nada; **s. me the details** ahórrate los detalles. **2** a (left over) sobrante; (surplus) de sobra; **a s. moment** un momento libre; **s. part** (pieza f de) recambio m; **s. room** cuarto m de los invitados; **s. wheel** rueda f de recambio. **3** n (for car etc) (pieza f de) recambio m.

spark [spɑːk] chispa f.

sparkle ['spɑːkəl] vi (diamond, glass) destellar; (eyes) brillar.

sparkling a **s. wine** vino m espumoso.

spark plug bujía f.

sparrow ['spærəʊ] gorrión m.

speak* [spiːk] **1** vt (utter) decir; (language) hablar. **2** vi hablar; **to s. to sb** hablar con algn; **speaking!** ¡al habla!; **who's speaking, please?** ¿de parte de quién?

● **speak up** vi hablar más fuerte.

speaker (in dialogue) interlocutor,-a mf; (lecturer) conferenciante mf; (of language) hablante mf; (loudspeaker) altavoz m; **(public) s.** orador,-a mf.

spear [spiəʳ] lanza f.

special ['speʃəl] a especial.

specialist especialista mf.

speci'ality especialidad f.

specialize vi especializarse (in en).

specially adv (specifically) especialmente; (on purpose) a propósito.

specialty US especialidad f.

species ['spiːʃiːz] inv especie f.

specific [spɪ'sɪfɪk] a específico,-a; (precise) preciso,-a; **to be s.** concretar.

specimen ['spesɪmɪn] (sample) muestra f; (example) ejemplar m.

spectacular [spek'tækjʊləʳ] a espectacular.

spectator [spek'teɪtəʳ] espectador,-a mf.

speech [spiːtʃ] (faculty) habla f; (address) discurso m; **to give a s.** pronunciar un discurso.

speed [spiːd] **1** n velocidad f; (rapidity) rapidez f. **2** vi* (exceed speed limit) conducir con exceso de velocidad.

● **speed up 1** vt acelerar. **2** vi (person) darse prisa.

speedboat ['spiːdbəʊt] lancha f rápida.

speed limit velocidad f máxima.

spee'dometer [spɪ'dɒmɪtəʳ] velocímetro m.

spell¹* [spel] vt (write) escribir; (letter by letter) deletrear; **how is that spelled?** ¿cómo se escribe eso?

spell² (magical) hechizo m.

spell³ (*period*) periodo *m*; (*short period*) rato *m*; **cold s.** ola *f* de frío.

spelling ortografía *f*.

spend* [spend] *vt* (*money*) gastar (**on** en); (*time*) pasar.

sphere [sfɪəʳ] esfera *f*.

spice [spaɪs] **1** *n* especia *f*. **2** *vt* (*food*) sazonar.

spicy *a* sazonado,-a; (*hot*) picante.

spider ['spaɪdəʳ] araña *f*; **s.'s web** telaraña *f*.

spike [spaɪk] (*sharp point*) punta *f*.

spill* [spɪl] **1** *vt* (*liquid*) derramar. **2** *vi* (*liquid*) derramarse.

● **spill over** *vi* desbordarse.

spin* [spɪn] *vt* (*wheel etc*) hacer girar; (*washing*) centrifugar.

spinach ['spɪnɪtʃ] espinacas *fpl*.

spine [spaɪn] (*of back*) columna *f* vertebral.

spiral ['spaɪərəl] espiral *f*.

spire ['spaɪəʳ] aguja *f*.

spirits ['spɪrɪts] (*alcoholic drinks*) licores *mpl*.

spit¹ [spɪt] *vti* escupir.

spit² (*for cooking*) asador *m*.

spite [spaɪt] **in s. of** a pesar de; **in s. of the fact that** a pesar de que.

spiteful *a* (*remark*) malévolo,-a.

splash [splæʃ] **1** *vt* (*spray*) salpicar. **2** *vi* **to s. (about)** (*in water*) chapotear.

splendid ['splendɪd] *a* espléndido,-a.

splinter ['splɪntəʳ] (*wood*) astilla *f*.

split [splɪt] **1** *n* (*crack*) grieta *f*; (*tear*) desgarrón *m*. **2** *vt** (*crack*) hender; (*cut*) partir; (*tear*) rajar; (*divide*) dividir.

● **split up 1** *vt* (*break up*) partir; (*divide up*) dividir; (*share out*) repartir. **2** *vi* (*couple*) separarse.

spoil* [spɔɪl] *vt* (*ruin*) estropear; (*child*) mimar.

spoke¹ [spəʊk] *pt of* **speak**.

spoke² (*of wheel*) radio *m*.

spokesman portavoz *mf*.

sponge [spʌndʒ] **1** *n* esponja *f*. **2** *vt* (*wash*) lavar con esponja.

● **sponge down** *vt* lavar con esponja.

sponge bag bolsa *f* de aseo.

sponge cake bizcocho *m*.

spontaneous [spɒn'teɪnɪəs] *a* espontáneo,-a.

spool [spuːl] bobina *f*.

spoon [spuːn] cuchara *f*; (*small*) cucharita *f*.

spoonful cucharada *f*.

sport [spɔːt] deporte *m*.

sportsman deportista *m*.

sportswoman deportista f.

spot [spɒt] **1** n (dot) punto m; (on fabric) lunar m; (stain) mancha f; (pimple) grano m; (place) sitio m; **to decide sth on the s.** decidir algo en el acto. **2** vt (notice) notar; (see) ver.

spotless a (very clean) impecable.

spotlight foco m.

spotted a (speckled) moteado,-a.

spout [spaʊt] (of jug) pico m; (of teapot) pitorro m.

sprain [spreɪn] **1** n esguince m. **2** vt **to s. one's ankle** torcerse el tobillo.

spray [spreɪ] **1** n (aerosol) spray m. **2** vt (insecticide, perfume) pulverizar.

spray can aerosol m.

spread [spred] **1** n (for bread) pasta f; **cheese s.** queso para untar. **2** vt* (unfold) desplegar; (lay out) extender; (butter etc) untar; (news) difundir; (rumour) hacer correr; (panic) sembrar. **3** vi* (stretch out) extenderse; (news) difundirse; (rumour) correr; (disease, fire) propagarse.

spreadsheet hoja f de cálculo.

spring¹ [sprɪŋ] (season) primavera f.

spring² **1** n (of water) fuente f; (of watch etc) resorte m. **2** vi* (jump) saltar.

springboard trampolín m.

spring onion cebolleta f.

springtime primavera f.

sprinkle ['sprɪŋkəl] vt (with water) rociar (**with** de); (with sugar) espolvorear (**with** de).

sprinkler (for water) aspersor m.

sprout [spraʊt] (Brussels) sprouts coles fpl de Bruselas.

spur [spɜː'] espuela f.

spurt [spɜːt] vi (liquid) chorrear.

spy [spaɪ] **1** n espía mf. **2** vi espiar (**on** a).

spying espionaje m.

square [skweə'] **1** n cuadrado m; (in town) plaza f. **2** a cuadrado,-a; **a s. meal** una buena comida.

squash¹ [skwɒʃ] **1** n Br (drink) concentrado m. **2** vt (crush) aplastar.

squash² (sport) squash m.

squat [skwɒt] vi (crouch) agacharse.

squeak [skwiːk] vi (hinge, wheel) chirriar; (shoes) crujir.

squeal [skwiːl] **1** n chillido m. **2** vi (animal, person) chillar.

squeeze [skwiːz] **1** vt apretar; (lemon etc) exprimir; **to s. paste out of a tube** sacar pasta de un tubo apretando. **2** vi **to s. in** apretujarse.

● **squeeze up** vi (on bench etc) correrse.

squint [skwɪnt] **1** n bizquera f; **to have a s.** ser bizco,-a. **2** vi ser bizco,-a; **to s. at sth** (with eyes half-closed) mirar algo con los ojos entrecerrados.

squirrel ['skwɪrəl] ardilla f.

squirt [skwɜ:t] 1 vt lanzar a chorro. 2 vi **to s. out** salir a chorros.

stab [stæb] vt apuñalar.

stable[1] ['steɪbəl] a estable.

stable[2] (for horses) cuadra f.

stack [stæk] 1 n (pile) montón m; fam **stacks of** ... un montón de ... 2 vt (pile up) amontonar.

stadium ['steɪdɪəm] estadio m.

staff [stɑ:f] (personnel) personal m; (of army) estado m mayor.

staffroom sala f de profesores.

stag [stæg] venado m.

stage [steɪdʒ] 1 n (platform) plataforma f; (in theatre) escenario m; (of development, journey, rocket) etapa f; **in stages** por etapas. 2 vt (play) poner en escena.

stagger ['stægəʳ] 1 vi tambalearse. 2 vt (hours, work) escalonar.

stain [steɪn] 1 n mancha f. 2 vt manchar.

stained glass window vidriera f de colores.

stainless a (steel) inoxidable.

stair [steəʳ] peldaño m; **stairs** escalera f sing.

staircase escalera f.

stake [steɪk] (stick) estaca f.

stale [steɪl] a (food) pasado,-a; (bread) duro,-a.

stalk [stɔ:k] (of plant) tallo m; (of fruit) rabo m.

stall [stɔ:l] 1 n (in market) puesto m; (in theatre) **stalls** platea f sing. 2 vi (of engine) calarse.

stammer ['stæməʳ] 1 n tartamudeo m. 2 vi tartamudear.

stamp [stæmp] 1 n (postage stamp) sello m, Am estampilla f; (with foot) patada f. 2 vt (with postage stamp) poner el sello a; **stamped addressed envelope** sobre m franqueado; **to s. one's feet** patear.

• **stamp out** vt (racism etc) acabar con.

stamp collecting filatelia f.

stand [stænd] 1 n (of lamp, sculpture) pie m; (market stall) puesto m; (at exhibition) stand m; (in stadium) tribuna f; **newspaper s.** quiosco m de prensa. 2 vt* (place) poner, colocar; (tolerate) aguantar. 3 vi (be upright) estar de pie; (get up) levantarse; (be situated) encontrarse; (remain unchanged) permanecer.

• **stand about** or **around** vi estar sin hacer nada, (wait) esperar.

• **stand aside** vi apartarse.

• **stand back** vi (allow sb to pass) abrir paso.

• **stand by** 1 vi (do nothing) quedarse sin hacer nada; (be ready) estar listo,-a. 2 vt (person) apoyar.

• **stand down** vi fig retirarse.

● **stand for** vt (mean) significar; (tolerate) aguantar.

● **stand in** vi sustituir (for -).

● **stand out** vi (mountain etc, fig person) destacar(se).

● **stand up** vi (get up) ponerse de pie; fig **to s. up for sb** defender a algn; fig **to s. up to sb** hacer frente a algn.

standard ['stændəd] 1 n (level) nivel m; (criterion) criterio m; (norm) estándar m inv; **s. of living** nivel de vida. 2 a normal.

standby a **s. ticket** billete m sin reserva.

standing a (not sitting) de pie.

standpoint punto m de vista.

standstill **at a s.** (car, traffic) parado,-a; (industry) paralizado,-a; **to come to a s.** (car, traffic) pararse; (industry) paralizarse.

stank [stæŋk] pt of **stink.**

staple ['steipəl] 1 n (fastener) grapa f. 2 vt grapar.

stapler grapadora f.

star [stɑː^r] 1 n estrella f. 2 vt (film) tener como protagonista. 3 vi (in film) protagonizar.

stare [steə^r] 1 n mirada f fija. 2 vi mirar fijamente; **to s. at sb** mirar fijamente a algn.

start [stɑːt] 1 n (beginning) principio m; (of race) salida f; (advantage) ventaja f. 2 vt (begin) empezar, comenzar; **to s. doing sth** empezar a hacer algo. 3 vi (begin) empezar, comenzar; (engine) arrancar; (take fright) asustarse; **starting from Monday** a partir del lunes.

● **start off** vi (leave) salir.

● **start on** vt empezar.

● **start up** 1 vt (engine) arrancar. 2 vi (car) arrancar.

starter (in car) motor m de arranque; (food) entrada f.

startle ['stɑːtəl] vt asustar.

star'vation hambre m.

starve [stɑːv] vi pasar hambre; **to s. to death** morirse de hambre.

starving a **I'm s.!** estoy muerto,-a de hambre.

state [steit] 1 n estado m; **The States** (los) Estados Unidos. 2 vt declarar.

statement declaración f; (financial) estado m de cuenta; **monthly s.** balance m mensual.

statesman estadista m.

station ['steiʃən] estación f.

stationary ['steiʃənəri] a (not moving) inmóvil.

stationery ['steiʃənəri] (paper) papel m de escribir; (pens, ink etc) artículos mpl de escritorio.

stationmaster jefe m de estación.

station wagon camioneta f.

statistic [stə'tistik] estadística f.

statue ['stætjuː] estatua *f.*

stay [steɪ] **1** *n* estancia *f.* **2** *vi* (*remain*) quedarse; (*reside temporarily*) alojarse; **she's staying with us for a few days** ha venido a pasar unos días con nosotros.

● **stay away** *vi* (*not attend*) no asistir; **s. away from her** no te acerques a ella.

● **stay in** *vi* quedarse en casa.

● **stay out** *vi* **to s. out all night** no volver a casa en toda la noche.

● **stay out of** *vt* (*not interfere in*) no meterse en.

● **stay up** *vi* (*not go to bed*) no acostarse; (*fence etc*) mantenerse en pie.

steadily *adv* (*improve*) constantemente; (*walk*) con paso seguro; (*gaze*) fijamente; (*rain, work*) sin parar.

steady ['stedɪ] *a* firme; (*prices*) estable; (*demand, speed*) constante.

steak [steɪk] bistec *m.*

steal* [stiːl] *vti* robar.

steam [stiːm] **1** *n* vapor *m.* **2** *vt* (*food*) cocer al vapor.

● **steam up** *vi* (*window etc*) empañarse.

steamroller apisonadora *f.*

steel [stiːl] acero *m*; **s. industry** industria *f* siderúrgica.

steep [stiːp] *a* (*hill etc*) empinado,-a; (*price, increase*) excesivo,-a.

steeple ['stiːpəl] aguja *f.*

steer [stɪə^r] *vt* dirigir; (*car*) conducir; (*ship*) gobernar.

steering wheel volante *m.*

stem [stem] (*of plant*) tallo *m*; (*of glass*) pie *m.*

stenographer [stə'nɒgrəfə^r] *US* taquígrafo *m.*

step [step] **1** *n* paso *m*; (*measure*) medida *f*; (*stair*) peldaño *m*; **s. by s.** poco a poco; **steps** (*outdoor*) escalinata *f*; (*indoor*) escalera *f.* **2** *vi* dar un paso.

● **step aside** *vi* apartarse.

● **step back** *vi* retroceder.

● **step down** *vi fig* renunciar; (*resign*) dimitir.

● **step forward** *vi* (*volunteer*) ofrecerse.

● **step in** *vi fig* intervenir.

● **step into/out of** *vt* (*car etc*) entrar en/salir de.

stepbrother hermanastro *m.*

stepdaughter hijastra *f.*

stepfather padrastro *m.*

stepladder escalera *f* de tijera.

stepmother madrastra *f.*

stepsister hermanastra *f.*

stepson hijastro *m.*

stereo ['sterɪəʊ] **1** *n* estéreo *m.* **2** *a* estereo(fónico,-a).

sterilize ['sterɪlaɪz] *vt* esterilizar.

stew [stju:] estofado *m*, cocido *m*.

steward ['stjʊəd] (*on plane*) auxiliar *m* de vuelo.

stewardess (*on plane*) azafata *f*.

stick¹ [stɪk] palo *m*; (*walking stick*) bastón *m*.

stick²* **1** *vt* meter; (*with glue etc*) pegar; **he stuck his head out of the window** asomó la cabeza por la ventana. **2** *vi* (*become attached*) pegarse; (*window, drawer*) atrancarse.

● **stick down** *vt* (*stamp*) pegar.

● **stick on** *vt* (*stamp*) pegar.

● **stick out** **1** *vi* (*project*) sobresalir; (*be noticeable*) resaltar. **2** *vt* (*tongue*) sacar.

● **stick to** *vt* (*principles*) atenerse a.

● **stick up** *vt* (*poster*) fijar.

● **stick up for** *vt* defender.

sticker (*label*) etiqueta *f* adhesiva; (*with slogan*) pegatina *f*.

sticking plaster tirita *f*, curita *f*.

sticky *a* pegajoso,-a; (*label*) engomado,-a.

stiff [stɪf] *a* rígido,-a; (*joint*) entumecido,-a; **to have a s. neck** tener tortícolis.

stifle ['staɪfəl] **1** *vt* sofocar. **2** *vi* sofocarse.

stifling *a* sofocante.

still [stɪl] **1** *adv* (*up to this time*) todavía, aún; (*nonetheless*) no obstante; (*however*) sin embargo; (*with comparative*) (*even*) aún; **s. colder** aún más frío. **2** *a* (*calm*) tranquilo,-a; (*motionless*) inmóvil.

sting* [stɪŋ] **1** *n* picadura *f*. **2** *vt** picar.

stink* [stɪŋk] *vi* apestar (*of* a).

● **stink out** *vt* (*room*) apestar.

stir [stɜ:ʳ] *vt* (*liquid*) remover.

● **stir up** *vt* (*memories, curiosity*) despertar.

stirrup ['stɪrəp] estribo *m*.

stitch [stɪtʃ] puntada *f*; (*in knitting*) punto *m*; (*for surgery etc*) punto *m* (de sutura).

stock [stɒk] **1** *n* (*goods*) existencias *fpl*; (*selection*) surtido *m*; (*broth*) caldo *m*; **out of s.** agotado,-a; **to have sth in s.** tener existencias de algo; **stocks and shares** acciones *fpl*. **2** *vt* (*have in stock*) tener existencias de.

● **stock up** *vi* abastecerse (**on, with** de).

Stock Exchange Bolsa *f* (de valores).

stocking ['stɒkɪŋ] media *f*; **a pair of stockings** unas medias.

Stock Market Bolsa *f*.

stomach ['stʌmək] estómago *m*; **s. upset** trastorno *m* gástrico.

stone [stəʊn] piedra *f*; (*of fruit*) hueso *m*; (*weight*) *aprox* 6.348 kg.

stool [stu:l] taburete *m*.

stop [stɒp] **1** *n* parada *f*; (*break*) pausa *f*; **to come to a s.** pararse; **to put a s. to sth** poner fin a algo. **2** *vt* parar; (*gas, water supply*) cortar; (*prevent*) evitar; **to s. sb from doing sth** impedir a algn hacer algo; **to s. doing sth** dejar de hacer algo. **3** *vi* (*person, moving vehicle*) pararse; (*cease*) terminar; (*stay*) pararse.

● **stop by** *vi* pasarse; **I'll s. by at the office** me pasaré por la oficina.

● **stop off** *vi* pararse un rato.

● **stop over** *vi* (*spend the night*) pasar la noche.

● **stop up** *vt* (*hole*) tapar.

stopoff parada *f*; (*flying*) escala *f*.

stopover parada *f*.

stopwatch cronómetro *m*.

store [stɔːʳ] **1** *n* (*stock*) provisión *f*; (*warehouse*) almacén *m*; US (*shop*) tienda *f*; **department s.** gran almacén *m*. **2** *vt* (*furniture, computer data*) almacenar; (*keep*) guardar; **to s. (up)** acumular.

storeroom despensa *f*.

storey ['stɔːrɪ] piso *m*.

stork [stɔːk] cigüeña *f*.

storm [stɔːm] tormenta *f*; (*with wind*) vendaval *m*.

stormy *a* (*weather*) tormentoso,-a.

story[1] ['stɔːrɪ] (*tale*) historia *f*; (*account*) relato *m*; (*article*) artículo *m*; (*plot*) trama *f*; **tall s.** cuento *m* chino.

story[2] US piso *m*.

stove [stəʊv] (*for heating*) estufa *f*; (*cooker*) cocina *f*; (*oven*) horno *m*.

straight [streɪt] **1** *a* (*not bent*) recto,-a; (*hair*) liso,-a; (*honest*) honrado, -a; (*answer*) sincero,-a; (*drink*) solo,-a. **2** *adv* (*in a straight line*) en línea recta; (*directly*) directamente; (*frankly*) francamente; **keep s. ahead** sigue todo recto; **s. away** en seguida.

straighten *vt* (*tie, picture*) poner bien; (*hair*) alisar.

straight'forward *a* (*easy*) fácil.

strain [streɪn] **1** *vt* (*eyes, voice*) forzar; (*heart*) cansar; (*liquid*) filtrar; (*vegetables, tea*) colar. **2** *n* tensión *f*; (*effort*) esfuerzo *m*; (*exhaustion*) agotamiento *m*.

strainer colador *m*.

strange [streɪndʒ] *a* (*unknown*) desconocido,-a; (*unfamiliar*) nuevo,-a; (*odd*) extraño,-a.

stranger (*unknown person*) desconocido,-a *mf*; (*outsider*) forastero,-a *mf*.

strangle ['stræŋgəl] *vt* estrangular.

strap [stræp] (*leather*) correa *f*; (*on bag*) bandolera *f*; (*on dress*) tirante *m*.

straw [strɔː] paja *f*; (*for drinking*) pajita *f*.

strawberry ['strɔ:bərɪ] fresa *f*; (*large*) fresón *m*.

streak [stri:k] (*line*) raya *f*; (*in hair*) reflejo *m*; **s. of lightning** rayo *m*.

stream [stri:m] (*brook*) arroyo *m*; (*current*) corriente *f*; (*flow*) flujo *m*.

street [stri:t] calle *f*; **the man in the s.** el hombre de la calle.

streetcar *US* tranvía *m*.

streetlamp farol *m*.

street map *or* **plan** (plano *m*) callejero *m*.

strength [streŋθ] fuerza *f*; (*of rope etc*) resistencia *f*; (*of emotion, colour*) intensidad *f*.

strengthen *vt* reforzar; (*intensify*) intensificar.

stress [stres] **1** *n* estrés *m*; (*emphasis*) hincapié *m*; (*on word*) acento *m*. **2** *vt* (*emphasize*) subrayar; (*word*) acentuar.

stressful *a* estresante.

stretch [stretʃ] **1** *vt* (*elastic*) estirar; (*arm, hand*) alargar. **2** *vi* estirarse. **3** *n* (*of land*) extensión *f*; (*of time*) intervalo *m*.

● **stretch out 1** *vt* (*arm, hand*) alargar; (*legs*) estirar. **2** *vi* (*countryside, years etc*) extenderse.

stretcher camilla *f*.

strict [strɪkt] *a* estricto,-a.

strictly *adv* (*categorically*) terminantemente; (*precisely*) estrictamente; **s. speaking** en sentido estricto.

strictness severidad *f*.

stride [straɪd] **1** *n* zancada *f*. **2** *vi** **to s. (along)** andar a zancadas.

strike* [straɪk] **1** *vt* (*hit*) golpear; (*collide with*) chocar contra; (*match*) encender; (*impress*) impresionar; **the clock struck three** el reloj dio las tres; **it strikes me . . .** me parece . . . **2** *vi** (*workers*) declararse en huelga. **3** *n* (*by workers*) huelga *f*; **on s.** en huelga; **to go (out) on s.** declararse en huelga; **to call a s.** convocar una huelga.

● **strike up** *vt* (*friendship*) trabar; (*conversation*) entablar; (*tune*) empezar a tocar.

striker (*worker*) huelguista *mf*.

striking *a* (*eye-catching*) llamativo,-a; (*impressive*) impresionante.

string [strɪŋ] (*cord, of guitar*) cuerda *f*.

strip¹ [strɪp] (*undress*) desnudarse.

strip² tira *f*; (*of metal*) fleje *m*.

● **strip off** *vi* (*undress*) desnudarse.

stripe [straɪp] raya *f*.

striped [straɪpt] *a* a rayas.

stroke [strəʊk] **1** *n* (*blow*) golpe *m*; (*in swimming*) brazada *f*; (*illness*) apoplejía *f*; **a s. of luck** un golpe de suerte. **2** *vt* acariciar.

stroll [strəʊl] **1** *vi* dar un paseo; **he strolled across the square** cruzó la plaza a paso lento. **2** *n* paseo *m*.

stroller US (*for baby*) cochecito *m*.
strong [strɒŋ] *a* fuerte; (*durable*) sólido,-a.
structure ['strʌktʃəʳ] estructura *f*; (*building*) edificio *m*.
struggle ['strʌgəl] **1** *vi* luchar. **2** *n* lucha *f*; (*physical fight*) pelea *f*.
stub [stʌb] (*of cigarette*) colilla *f*; (*of cheque*) matriz *f*.
stubborn ['stʌbən] *a* testarudo,-a.
stubbornness testarudez *f*.
stuck [stʌk] **1** *pt & pp of* stick². **2** *a* (*caught, jammed*) atrancado; **I'm s.** (*unable to carry on*) no puedo seguir.
stud [stʌd] (*on clothing*) tachón *m*; (*on football boots*) taco *m*.
student ['stju:dənt] estudiante *mf*.
studio ['stju:dɪəʊ] (*TV etc*) estudio *m*; (*artist's*) taller *m*; **s. apartment, s. flat** estudio.
study ['stʌdɪ] **1** *vti* estudiar; **to s. to be a doctor** estudiar para médico. **2** *n* estudio *m*.
stuff [stʌf] **1** *vt* (*container*) llenar (**with** de); (*in cooking*) rellenar (**with** con *or* de); (*cram*) atiborrar (**with** de). **2** *n* (*material*) material *m*; (*things*) cosas *fpl*, trastos *mpl*.
stuffed up [stʌft] *a* (*nose*) tapado,-a.
stuffing relleno *m*.
stuffy *a* (*room*) mal ventilado,-a; (*atmosphere*) cargado,-a.
stumble ['stʌmbəl] *vi* tropezar; *fig* **to s. across** *or* **on** tropezar *or* dar con.
stump [stʌmp] (*of tree*) tocón *m*.
stun [stʌn] *vt* aturdir; (*news etc*) sorprender.
stunned *a* (*amazed*) estupefacto,-a.
stupid ['stju:pɪd] *a* estúpido,-a.
stu'pidity estupidez *f*.
sturdy ['stɜ:dɪ] *a* robusto,-a.
stutter ['stʌtəʳ] **1** *vi* tartamudear. **2** *n* tartamudeo *m*.
sty [staɪ] (*pen*) pocilga *f*.
style [staɪl] estilo *m*; (*of dress*) modelo *m*; (*fashion*) moda *f*.
stylish *a* con estilo.
subject ['sʌbdʒɪkt] **1** *n* (*citizen*) súbdito *m*; (*topic*) tema *m*; (*at school*) asignatura *f*; (*of sentence*) sujeto *m*. **2** [səb'dʒekt] *vt* someter.
subjunctive [səb'dʒʌŋktɪv] subjuntivo *m*.
submarine ['sʌbməri:n] submarino *m*.
subscribe [səb'skraɪb] *vi* suscribirse (**to** a).
subscriber abonado,-a *mf*.
subscription (*to magazine*) abono *m*.
subside [səb'saɪd] *vi* (*land*) hundirse; (*floodwater*) bajar.
substance ['sʌbstəns] sustancia *f*.
substantial [səb'stænʃəl] *a* (*sum, loss*) importante; (*meal*) abundante.

substitute ['sʌbstɪtjuːt] **1** vt sustituir. **2** n (person) suplente mf; (thing) sucedáneo m.

subtitle ['sʌbtaɪtəl] subtítulo m.

subtle ['sʌtəl] a sutil.

subtract [səb'trækt] vt restar.

subtraction resta f.

suburb ['sʌbɜːb] barrio m periférico; **the suburbs** las afueras.

su'burban a suburbano,-a.

subway ['sʌbweɪ] Br (underpass) paso m subterráneo; US (underground railway) metro m.

succeed [sək'siːd] vi (person) tener éxito; **to s. in doing sth** conseguir hacer algo.

success [sək'ses] éxito m.

successful a de éxito; (business) próspero,-a; **to be s. in doing sth** lograr hacer algo.

successfully adv con éxito.

such [sʌtʃ] **1** a (of that sort) tal, semejante; **artists s. as Monet** artistas como Monet. ‖ (so much, so great) tanto,-a; **he's always in s. a hurry** siempre anda con tanta prisa; **s. a lot of books** tantos libros. **2** adv (so very) tan; **it's s. a long time** hace tanto tiempo; **she's s. a clever woman** es una mujer tan inteligente.

suck [sʌk] **1** vt (liquid) sorber, chupar; (at breast) mamar. **2** vi (baby) mamar.

● **suck up** vt (with straw) aspirar.

sudden ['sʌdən] a (hurried) repentino,-a; (unexpected) imprevisto,-a; **all of a s.** de repente.

suddenly adv de repente.

suds [sʌdz] npl espuma f de jabón.

suede [sweɪd] ante m; (for gloves) cabritilla f.

suffer ['sʌfəʳ] vti sufrir; **to s. from** sufrir de.

suffering (affliction) sufrimiento m; (pain, torment) dolor m.

sufficient [sə'fɪʃənt] a suficiente, bastante.

sufficiently adv suficientemente, bastante.

suffix ['sʌfɪks] sufijo m.

suffocate ['sʌfəkeɪt] **1** vt asfixiar. **2** vi asfixiarse.

sugar ['ʃʊgəʳ] **1** n azúcar m & f. **2** vt azucarar.

sugar bowl azucarero m.

suggest [sə'dʒest] vt (propose) sugerir; (advise) aconsejar; (indicate, imply) indicar.

suggestion (proposal) sugerencia f.

suicide ['sjuːɪsaɪd] suicidio m.

suit [suːt] **1** n traje m de chaqueta; (in cards) palo m. **2** vt (be convenient *for*) convenir a; (*be right, appropiate for*) ir bien a; **red really suits you** el rojo te favorece mucho; **s. yourself!** ¡como quieras!

suitable *a* (*convenient*) conveniente; (*appropriate*) adecuado,-a; **the most s. woman for the job** la mujer más indicada para el puesto.

suitcase maleta *f*.

suite [swiːt] (*of furniture*) tresillo *m*; (*of hotel rooms, music*) suite *f*.

sulk [sʌlk] *vi* enfurruñarse.

sultana [sʌlˈtɑːnə] (*raisin*) pasa *f* (de Esmirna).

sum [sʌm] (*arithmetic problem, amount*) suma *f*; (*total amount*) total *m*; (*of money*) importe *m*.

● **sum up** *vt* resumir.

summarize [ˈsʌməraɪz] *vt* resumir.

summary resumen *m*.

summer [ˈsʌməʳ] **1** *n* verano *m*. **2** *a* (*holiday etc*) de verano; (*resort*) de veraneo.

summertime verano *m*.

sun [sʌn] sol *m*.

sunbathe *vi* tomar el sol.

sunburn quemadura *f* de sol.

sunburnt *a* (*burnt*) quemado,-a por el sol; (*tanned*) bronceado,-a.

sundae [ˈsʌndeɪ] helado *m* de fruta y nueces.

Sunday domingo *m*.

sunglasses *npl* gafas *fpl* de sol.

sunlamp lámpara *f* solar.

sunlight (luz *f* del) sol *m*.

sunny *a* (*day*) de sol; **it is s.** hace sol.

sunrise salida *f* del sol.

sunroof (*on car*) techo *m* corredizo.

sunset puesta *f* del sol.

sunshade sombrilla *f*.

sunshine (luz *f* del) sol *m*.

sunstroke insolación *f*.

suntan bronceado *m*; **s. oil** (aceite *m*) bronceador *m*; **s. lotion** leche *f* bronceadora.

suntanned *a* bronceado,-a.

super [ˈsuːpəʳ] *a fam* fenomenal.

superb [sʊˈpɜːb] *a* espléndido,-a.

superficial [suːpəˈfɪʃəl] *a* superficial.

superior [suːˈpɪərɪəʳ] *a* superior.

superi'ority superioridad *f*.

supermarket supermercado *m*.

superstition [suːpəˈstɪʃən] superstición *f*.

superstitious [suːpəˈstɪʃəs] *a* supersticioso,-a.

supervise [ˈsuːpəvaɪz] *vt* supervisar; (*watch over*) vigilar.

supervisor supervisor,-a *mf*.

supper [ˈsʌpə] cena *f*; **to have s.** cenar.

supple [ˈsʌpəl] *a* flexible.

supply [səˈplaɪ] **1** *n* (*provision*) suministro *m*; (*delivery*) provisión *f*; **supplies** (*food*) víveres *mpl*. **2** *vt* (*provide*) suministrar; (*with provisions*) aprovisionar; (*information*) facilitar.

support [səˈpɔːt] **1** *n* soporte *m*; (*moral*) apoyo *m*. **2** *vt* (*weight etc*) sostener; (*back*) apoyar; (*team*) ser (hincha) de; (*family*) mantener.

supporter (*political*) partidario,-a *mf*; (*in sport*) hincha *mf*.

suppose [səˈpəʊz] *vt* suponer; (*presume*) creer; **I s. not/so** supongo que no/sí; **you're not supposed to smoke in here** no está permitido fumar aquí dentro; **you're supposed to be in bed** deberías estar acostado,-a ya.

sure [ʃʊəʳ] *a* seguro,-a; **I'm s. (that) ...** estoy seguro,-a de que ...; **make s. that it's ready** asegúrate de que esté listo.

surely *adv* (*without a doubt*) seguramente; **s. not!** ¡no puede ser!

surface [ˈsɜːfɪs] superficie *f*; **s. area** área *f* de la superficie; **by s. mail** por vía terrestre *or* marítima.

surfboard [ˈsɜːfbɔːd] tabla *f* de surf.

surfing [ˈsɜːfɪŋ] surf *m*, surfing *m*.

surgeon [ˈsɜːdʒən] cirujano,-a *mf*.

surgery [ˈsɜːdʒərɪ] (*operation*) cirujía *f*; *Br* (*consulting room*) consultorio *m*; **s. hours** horas *fpl* de consulta.

surname [ˈsɜːneɪm] apellido *m*.

surprise [səˈpraɪz] **1** *n* sorpresa *f*; **to take sb by s.** coger desprevenido,-a a algn. **2** *a* (*visit*) inesperado,-a; **s. attack** ataque *m* sorpresa. **3** *vt* sorprender.

surprised *a* sorprendido,-a; **I should not be s. if it rained** no me extrañaría que lloviera.

surprising *a* sorprendente.

surprisingly *adv* de modo sorprendente.

surrender [səˈrendəʳ] *vi* (*give in*) rendirse.

surround [səˈraʊnd] *vt* rodear.

surrounding *a* circundante.

surroundings *npl* alrededores *mpl*.

survey [ˈsɜːveɪ] (*of trends etc*) encuesta *f*.

sur'veyor agrimensor,-a *mf*.

survive [səˈvaɪv] **1** *vi* sobrevivir. **2** *vt* sobrevivir a.

survivor superviviente *mf*.

suspect [ˈsʌspekt] **1** *n* sospechoso,-a *mf*. **2** [səˈspekt] *vt* (*person*) sospechar (**of** de); (*think likely*) imaginar.

suspend [sə'spend] *vt* suspender; (*pupil*) expulsar por un tiempo.

suspenders *npl US* tirantes *mpl*.

suspense [sə'spens] suspense *m*.

suspension suspensión *f*.

suspicion [sə'spɪʃən] sospecha *f*; (*mistrust*) recelo *m*; (*doubt*) duda *f*; (*trace*) pizca *f*.

suspicious *a* (*arousing suspicion*) sospechoso,-a; (*distrustful*) receloso, -a; **to be s. of sb** desconfiar de algn.

swallow[1] ['swɒləʊ] *vt* (*drink, food*) tragar.

swallow[2] (*bird*) golondrina *f*.

• **swallow down** *vt* tragarse.

swamp [swɒmp] ciénaga *f*.

swan [swɒn] cisne *m*.

swap [swɒp] **1** *n* intercambio *m*. **2** *vt* cambiar.

swarm [swɔ:m] enjambre *m*.

sway [sweɪ] *vi* (*swing*) balancearse; (*totter*) tambalearse.

swear[*] [sweə[r]] **1** *vt* (*vow*) jurar. **2** *vi* (*curse*) decir palabrotas.

swearword palabrota *f*.

sweat [swet] **1** *n* sudor *m*. **2** *vi* sudar.

sweater suéter *m*.

sweatshirt sudadera *f*.

Swede [swi:d] (*person*) sueco,-a *mf*.

Swedish ['swi:dɪʃ] **1** *a* sueco,-a. **2** *n* (*language*) sueco *m*.

sweep[*] [swi:p] *vti* barrer.

• **sweep away** *vt* (*dust*) barrer; (*storm*) arrastrar.

• **sweep out** *vt* (*room*) barrer.

• **sweep up** *vi* barrer.

sweet [swi:t] **1** *a* dulce; (*sugary*) azucarado,-a; (*pleasant*) agradable; (*person, animal*) encantador,-a. **2** *n* (*candy*) caramelo *m*; (*chocolate*) bombón *m*; (*dessert*) postre *m*.

sweetcorn maíz *m* dulce.

sweeten *vt* (*tea etc*) azucarar.

sweetly *adv* dulcemente.

sweet shop confitería *f*.

swell[*] (**up**) [swel] *vi* (*part of body*) hincharse.

swelling hinchazón *f*.

swerve [swɜ:v] *vi* (*car*) dar un viraje brusco.

swim[*] [swɪm] **1** *vi* nadar; **to go swimming** ir a nadar. **2** *vt* (*the Channel*) pasar a nado. **3** *n* baño *m*; **to go for a s.** ir a darse un baño.

swimmer nadador,-a *mf*.

swimming natación *f*.

swimming costume bañador *m*.

swimming pool piscina *f*.

swimming trunks bañador *m*.

swimsuit bañador *m*.

swing [swɪŋ] **1** *n* (*for playing*) columpio *m*. **2** *vi**** (*move to and fro*) balancearse; (*arms, legs*) menearse; (*on swing*) columpiarse. **3** *vt* (*arms, legs*) menear.

Swiss [swɪs] **1** *a* suizo,-a. **2** *n inv* (*person*) suizo,-a *mf*; **the S.** *pl* los suizos.

switch [swɪtʃ] **1** *n* (*for light etc*) interruptor *m*. **2** *vt* (*jobs, direction*) cambiar de.

● **switch off** *vt* apagar.

● **switch on** *vt* encender.

● **switch over** *vi* cambiar(**to** a).

swollen ['swəʊlən] *a* (*ankle, face*) hinchado,-a.

swop [swɒp] *vt* = **swap.**

sword [sɔːd] espada *f*.

syllable ['sɪləbəl] sílaba *f*.

syllabus ['sɪləbəs] programa *m* de estudios.

symbol ['sɪmbəl] símbolo *m*.

sym'bolic *a* simbólico,-a.

symmetry ['sɪmɪtrɪ] simetría *f*.

sympathetic *a* (*showing pity*) compasivo,-a; (*understanding*) comprensivo,-a; (*kind*) amable.

sympathize *vi* (*show pity*) compadecerse (**with** de); (*understand*) comprender.

sympathy ['sɪmpəθɪ] (*pity*) compasión *f*; (*condolences*) pésame *m*; (*understanding*) comprensión *f*; **to express one's s.** dar el pésame.

symphony ['sɪmfənɪ] sinfonía *f*.

symptom ['sɪmptəm] síntoma *m*.

synagogue ['sɪnəgɒg] sinagoga *f*.

synonym ['sɪnənɪm] sinónimo *m*.

syringe [sɪ'rɪndʒ] jeringuilla *f*.

syrup ['sɪrəp] jarabe *m*, almíbar *m*.

system ['sɪstəm] sistema *m*.

T

ta [tɑ:] *interj fam* gracias.
tab [tæb] (*flap*) lengüeta *f*.
table ['teɪbəl] mesa *f*; **to lay** *or* **set the t.** poner la mesa.
tablecloth mantel *m*.
tablemat salvamanteles *m inv*.
tablespoon cuchara *m* de servir.
tablespoonful cucharada *f* grande.
tablet ['tæblɪt] (*pill*) pastilla *f*.
tack [tæk] (*small nail*) tachuela *f*.
tackle ['tækəl] *vt* (*task*) emprender; (*problem*) abordar; (*grapple with*) agarrar; (*in sport*) placar; (*in football*) entrar a.
tacky ['tækɪ] *a fam* (*shoddy*) cutre.
tact [tækt] tacto *m*.
tactful *a* diplomático,-a.
tactic ['tæktɪk] táctica *f*; **tactics** táctica *f sing*.
taffy ['tæfɪ] *US* caramelo *m* duro.
tag [tæg] (*label*) etiqueta *f*.
tail [teɪl] cola *f*.
tailor ['teɪləʳ] sastre *m*.
take* [teɪk] *vt* tomar; (*bus etc*) coger; (*accept*) aceptar; (*win*) ganar; (*prize*) llevarse; (*eat, drink*) tomar; (*accompany*) llevar; (*endure*) aguantar; (*consider*) considerar; (*require*) requerir; **she's taking (a degree in) law** estudia derecho; **to t. an exam (in …)** examinarse (de …); **it takes an hour to get there** se tarda una hora en ir hasta allí; **it takes courage** se necesita valor.
● **take after** *vt* parecerse a.
● **take along** llevar (consigo).
● **take apart** *vt* (*machine*) desmontar.
● **take away** *vt* (*carry off*) llevarse; (*in maths*) restar (**from** de); **to t. sth away from sb** quitarle algo a algn.
● **take back** *vt* (*give back*) devolver; (*receive back*) recuperar; (*withdraw*) retirar.
● **take down** *vt* (*lower*) bajar; (*write*) apuntar.
● **take in** *vt* (*include*) abarcar; (*understand*) entender; (*deceive*) engañar.
● **take off 1** *vt* quitar; (*lead or carry away*) descontar; (*deduct*) descontar; **he took off his jacket** se quitó la chaqueta. **2** *vi* (*plane*) despegar.
● **take on** *vt* (*undertake*) encargarse de; (*acquire*) tomar; (*employ*) contratar.
● **take out** *vt* sacar; **he's taking me out to dinner** me ha invitado a cenar fuera; (*insurance*) sacarse; (*stain, tooth*) quitar.

● **take over 1** *vt* (*office, post*) tomar posesión de. **2** *vi* **to t. over from sb** relevar a algn.

● **take up** *vt* (*occupy*) ocupar; **I've taken up the guitar** he empezado a tocar la guitarra.

takeaway *Br* **1** *n* (*food*) comida *f* para llevar; (*restaurant*) restaurante *m* de comida para llevar. **2** *a* (*food*) para llevar.

takeoff (*of plane*) despegue *m*.

takings *npl* (*of shop, business*) recaudación *f sing*.

tale [teɪl] cuento *m*; **to tell tales** contar chismes.

talent ['tælənt] talento *m*.

talented *a* dotado,-a.

talk [tɔːk] **1** *vi* hablar; (*chat*) charlar; (*gossip*) chismorrear. **2** *vt* hablar; **to t. nonsense** decir tonterías. **3** *n* (*conversation*) conversación *f*; (*words*) palabras *fpl*; (*gossip*) chismes *mpl*; (*lecture*) charla *f*; **there's t. of ...** se habla de ...

● **talk into** *vt* **to t. sb into sth** convencer a algn para que haga algo.

● **talk out of** *vt* **to t. sb out of sth** disuadir a algn de que haga algo.

● **talk over** *vt* discutir.

talkative *a* hablador,-a.

tall [tɔːl] *a* alto,-a; **a tree ten metres t.** un árbol de diez metros (de alto); **how t. are you?** ¿cuánto mides?

tambourine [tæmbə'riːn] pandereta *f*.

tame [teɪm] **1** *a* (*animal*) domado,-a; (*by nature*) manso,-a. **2** *vt* domar.

tampon ['tæmpɒn] tampón *m*.

tan [tæn] **1** *n* (*of skin*) bronceado *m*. **2** *vt* (*skin*) broncear. **3** *vi* ponerse moreno,-a.

tangerine [tændʒə'riːn] clementina *f*.

tangled ['tæŋgəld] *a* enredado,-a.

tank [tæŋk] (*container*) depósito *m*; (*with gun*) tanque *m*.

tanker (*ship*) tanque *m*; (*for oil*) petrolero *m*.

tap¹ [tæp] **1** *vt* (*knock*) golpear suavemente; (*with hand*) dar una palmadita a. **2** *vi* **to t. at the door** llamar suavemente a la puerta. **3** *n* golpecito *m*.

tap² (*for water*) grifo *m*.

tape [teɪp] **1** *n* cinta *f*; **sticky t.** cinta *f* adhesiva. **2** *vt* pegar (con cinta adhesiva); (*record*) grabar (en cinta).

tape measure cinta *f* métrica.

tape recorder magnetófono *m*, cassette *m*.

tar [tɑːʳ] alquitrán *m*.

target ['tɑːgɪt] (*object aimed at*) blanco *m*; (*purpose*) meta *f*.

tarpaulin [tɑː'pɔːlɪn] lona *f*.

tart [tɑːt] (*to eat*) tarta *f*.

tartan ['tɑ:tən] tartán *m*.

task [tɑ:sk] tarea *f*.

taste [teɪst] **1** *n* (*sense*) gusto *m*; (*flavour*) sabor *m*; (*liking*) afición *f*; **it has a burnt t.** sabe a quemado; **in bad t.** de mal gusto; **to have (good) t.** tener (buen) gusto. **2** *vt* (*sample*) probar. **3** *vi* **to t. of sth** saber a algo.

tasty *a* sabroso,-a.

tattered ['tætəd] *a* hecho,-a jirones.

tattoo [tæ'tu:] **1** *vt* tatuar. **2** *n* (*mark*) tatuaje *m*.

tax [tæks] **1** *n* impuesto *m*. **2** *vt* gravar.

taxable *a* imponible.

taxi ['tæksɪ] taxi *m*.

taxi driver taxista *mf*.

taxi rank parada *f* de taxis.

taxpayer contribuyente *mf*.

tea [ti:] té *m*; (*meal*) merienda *f*.

tea bag bolsita *f* de té.

tea break descanso *m*.

teach* [ti:tʃ] **1** *vt* enseñar; (*subject*) dar clases de; **to t. sb (how) to do sth** enseñar a algn a hacer algo. **2** *vi* ser profesor,-a.

teacher profesor,-a *mf*.

teaching enseñanza *f*.

teacup taza *f* de té.

team [ti:m] equipo *m*.

• **team up to t. up with s.o.** juntarse con algn.

teapot tetera *f*.

tear¹ [tɪəʳ] lágrima *f*; **to be in tears** estar llorando.

tear² [teəʳ] **1** *vt** rasgar; **to t. sth out of sb's hands** arrancarle algo de las manos a algn. **2** *vi* (*cloth*) rasgarse. **3** *n* desgarrón *m*.

• **tear off** *vt* arrancar.

• **tear out** *vt* arrancar.

• **tear up** *vt* hacer pedazos.

tease [ti:z] *vt* tomar el pelo a.

tea service *or* **set** juego *m* de té.

teaspoon cucharilla *f*.

teaspoonful cucharadita *f*.

teat [ti:t] (*of bottle*) tetina *f*.

teatime hora *f* del té.

tea towel paño *m* (de cocina).

technical ['teknɪkəl] *a* técnico,-a.

tech'nician técnico,-a *mf*.

technique [tek'ni:k] técnica *f*.

technology [tek'nɒlədʒɪ] tecnología *f*.

teddy bear ['tedɪbeə'] oso *m* de felpa.

teenager ['tiːneɪdʒə'] quinceañero,-a *mf*.

tee-shirt ['tiːʃɜːt] camiseta *f*.

teeth [tiːθ] *npl see* tooth.

telegram ['telɪgræm] telegrama *m*.

telegraph pole ['telɪgrɑːf] poste *m* telegráfico.

telephone ['telɪfəʊn] **1** *n* teléfono *m*; **to speak to sb on the t.** hablar por teléfono con algn. **2** *vt* telefonear a, llamar por teléfono a.

telephone booth *or* **box** cabina *f* (telefónica).

telephone call llamada *f* telefónica.

telephone directory guía *f* telefónica.

telephone number número *m* de teléfono.

telescope ['telɪskəʊp] telescopio *m*.

televise ['telɪvaɪz] *vt* televisar.

television ['telɪvɪʒən] televisión *f*; **t. (set)** televisor *m*; **on t.** en la televisión.

tell* [tel] **1** *vt* decir; (*relate*) contar; (*inform*) comunicar; (*order*) mandar; (*distinguish*) distinguir; **to t. sb about sth** contarle algo a algn; **to t. sb to do sth** decir a algn que haga algo. **2** *vi* **who can t.?** (*know*) ¿quién sabe?
● **tell off** *vt* reñir.

teller (*cashier*) cajero,-a *mf*.

telltale chivato,-a *mf*.

telly ['telɪ] *Br fam* **the t.** la tele.

temper ['tempə'] (*mood*) humor *m*; **to keep one's t.** no perder la calma; **to lose one's t.** perder los estribos.

temperature ['temprɪtʃə'] temperatura *f*; **to have a t.** tener fiebre.

temple ['tempəl] (*building*) templo *m*.

temporary ['tempərərɪ] *a* provisional; (*setback, improvement*) momentáneo,-a; (*teacher*) sustituto,-a.

tempt [tempt] *vt* tentar; **to t. sb to do sth** incitar a algn a hacer algo.

temp'tation tentación *f*.

tempting *a* tentador,-a.

ten [ten] *a & n* diez (*m*) inv.

tenant ['tenənt] (*of house*) inquilino,-a *mf*.

tend [tend] *vi* (*be inclined*) tender, tener tendencia (**to** a).

tendency tendencia *f*.

tender ['tendə'] *a* (*affectionate*) cariñoso,-a; (*meat*) tierno,-a.

tennis ['tenɪs] tenis *m*.

tennis court pista *f* de tenis.

tenpin bowling bolos *mpl*.

tense¹ [tens] *a* tenso,-a.

tense² (*of verb*) tiempo *m*.

tension ['tenʃən] tensión f.
tent [tent] tienda f de campaña.
tenth [tenθ] a & n décimo,-a (mf).
term [tɜːm] (period) período m; (of study) trimestre m; (word) término m; **terms** (conditions) condiciones fpl; **to be on good/bad terms with sb** tener buenas/malas relaciones con algn.
terminal ['tɜːmɪnəl] terminal f; (for computer) terminal m.
terrace ['terəs] (of houses) hilera f de casas; (patio) terraza f.
terraced houses casas fpl (de estilo uniforme) en hilera.
terrible ['terəbəl] a terrible; **I feel t.** me encuentro fatal.
terribly adv terriblemente.
terrific [təˈrɪfɪk] a fenomenal.
terrify ['terɪfaɪ] vt aterrorizar.
terrifying a aterrador,-a.
territory ['terɪtərɪ] territorio m.
terror ['terəʳ] terror m.
terrorist a & n terrorista (mf).
terrorize vt aterrorizar.
test [test] **1** vt probar; (analyze) analizar. **2** n (of product) prueba f; (in school) examen m; (of blood) análisis m.
test tube probeta f.
text [tekst] texto m.
textbook libro m de texto.
textile ['tekstaɪl] **1** n tejido m. **2** a textil.
Thai [taɪ] a & n tailandés,-esa (mf).
than [ðæn, unstressed ðən] conj que; (with numbers) de; **he's older t. me** es mayor que yo; **more interesting t. we thought** más interesante de lo que creíamos; **more t. once** más de una vez; **more t. ten people** más de diez personas.
thank [θæŋk] vt agradecer; **t. you** gracias.
thankful a agradecido,-a.
thanks npl gracias fpl; **no t.** no gracias; **t. to** gracias a.
thanksgiving US T. Day Día m de Acción de Gracias.
that [ðæt, unstressed ðət] **1** dem a (pl those) (masculine) ese; (feminine) esa; (further away) (masculine) aquel; (feminine) aquella; **at t. time** en aquella época; **t. book** ese or aquel libro; **t. one** ése, aquél. **2** dem pron (pl those) ése m, ésa f; (further away) aquél m, aquélla f; (indefinite) eso; (remote) aquello; **after t.** después de eso; **like t.** así; **don't talk like t.** no hables así; **t.'s right** eso es; **t.'s where I live** allí vivo yo; **what's t.?** ¿qué es eso?; **who's t.?** ¿quién es?; **all those I saw** todos los que vi; **there are those who say that ...** hay quien dice que ... **3** rel pron que; **all t. you said** todo lo que dijiste; **the letter t. I sent you** la carta que te envié; **the car t. they**

came in el coche en el que vinieron; **the moment t. you arrived** el momento en que llegaste. **4** *conj* que; **come here so t. I can see you** ven aquí para que te vea; **he said (t.) he would come** dijo que vendría. **5** *adv* así de, tan; **that much** tanto,-a; **cut off t. much** córteme un trozo así de grande; **t. old** tan viejo; **we haven't got t. much money** no tenemos tanto dinero.

thaw [θɔː] **1** *vt* (*snow*) derretir; (*food, freezer*) descongelar. **2** *vi* descongelarse; (*snow*) derretirse. **3** *n* deshielo *m.*

the [ðə, *before vowel* ðɪ, *emphatic* ðiː] *def art* el, la; *pl* los, las; **at** *or* **to t.** al, a la; *pl* a los, a las; **of** *or* **from t.** del, de la; *pl* de los, de las; **the voice of the people** la voz del pueblo; **George t. Sixth** Jorge Sexto.

theatre, *US* **theater** [ˈθɪətəʳ] teatro *m.*

theft [θeft] robo *m.*

their [ðeəʳ] *poss a* su; (*pl*) sus.

theirs [ðeəz] *poss pron* (el) suyo, (la) suya; *pl* (los) suyos, (las) suyas.

them [ðem] *pers pron pl* (*direct object*) los, las; (*indirect object*) les; **I know t.** los *or* las conozco; **I shall tell t. so** se lo diré (a ellos *or* ellas); **it's t.!** ¡son ellos!; **speak to t.** hábleles. ‖ (*with preposition*) ellos, ellas; **walk in front of t.** camine delante de ellos; **with t.** con ellos.

them'selves [ðəmˈselvz] *pers pron pl* (*as subject*) ellos mismos, ellas mismas; (*as direct or indirect object*) se; (*after a preposition*) sí mismos, sí mismas; **they did it by t.** lo hicieron ellos solos.

then [ðen] **1** *adv* (*at that time, in that case*) entonces; (*next, afterwards*) luego; **since t.** desde entonces; **till t.** hasta entonces; **go t.** pues vete. **2** *conj* entonces.

theory [ˈθɪərɪ] teoría *f.*

there [ðeəʳ] *adv* (*indicating place*) allí, allá; (*nearer speaker*) ahí; **is Peter t.?** ¿está Peter?; **that man t.** aquel hombre; **t. is, t. are** hay; **t. were six of us** éramos seis.

therefore *adv* por lo tanto.

thermometer [θəˈmɒmɪtəʳ] termómetro *m.*

Thermos[(R)] [ˈθɜːməs] **T. (flask)** termo *m.*

thermostat [ˈθɜːməstæt] termostato *m.*

these [ðiːz] **1** *dem a pl* estos,-as. **2** *dem pron pl* éstos,-as; *see* **this.**

they [ðeɪ] *pron* ellos, ellas; **t. are dancing** están bailando; **t. alone** ellos solos. ‖ (*indefinite*) **t. say that . . .** se dice que . . .

thick [θɪk] *a* (*book, slice, material*) grueso,-a; (*wood, vegetation*) espeso, -a; **a wall two metres t.** un muro de dos metros de espesor.

thicken 1 *vt* espesar. **2** *vi* espesarse.

thickness (*of wall etc*) espesor *m*; (*of wire, lips*) grueso *m*; (*of liquid, forest*) espesura *f.*

thief [θiːf] (*pl* **thieves** [θiːvz]) ladrón,-ona *mf.*

thigh [θaɪ] muslo *m.*

thimble ['θɪmbəl] dedal *m*.

thin [θɪn] **1** *a* delgado,-a; (*hair, vegetation*) ralo,-a; (*liquid*) claro,-a; **a t. slice** una loncha fina. **2** *vt* **to t. (down)** (*paint*) diluir.

thing [θɪŋ] cosa *f*; **my things** (*clothing*) mi ropa *f sing*; (*possessions*) mis cosas.

think* [θɪŋk] **1** *vt* pensar, creer; **I t. so/not** creo que sí/no; **I thought as much** ya me lo imaginaba. **2** *vi* pensar (*of, about* en); **what do you t.?** ¿a ti qué te parece?

● **think over** *vt* reflexionar; **we'll have to t. it over** lo tendremos que pensar.

● **think up** *vt* idear.

thinly *adv* ligeramente.

third [θɜːd] **1** *a* tercero,-a; (*before masculine singular noun*) tercer; **(on) the t. of March** el tres de marzo. **2** *n* (*in series*) tercero,-a *mf*; (*fraction*) tercera parte.

thirdly *adv* en tercer lugar.

thirst [θɜːst] sed *f*.

thirsty *a* **to be t.** tener sed.

thirteen [θɜːˈtiːn] *a & n* trece (*m*).

'thirty *a & n* treinta (*m*).

this [ðɪs] **1** *dem a* (*pl* these) (*masculine*) este; (*feminine*) esta; **t. book/these books** este libro/estos libros; **t. one** éste, ésta. **2** (*pl* these) *dem pron* (*indefinite*) esto; **t. is different** esto es distinto; **it was like t.** fue así; **t. is where we met** fue aquí donde nos conocimos; **it should have come before t.** debería haber llegado ya; (*introduction*) **t. is Mr Álvarez** le presento al Sr. Álvarez; (*on the phone*) **t. is Julia (speaking)** soy Julia. ‖ (*specific person or thing*) éste *m*, ésta *f*; **I prefer these to those** me gustan más éstos que aquéllos. **3** *adv* **he got t. far** llegó hasta aquí; **t. small/big** así de pequeño/grande.

thorn [θɔːn] espina *f*.

thorough ['θʌrə] *a* (*careful*) minucioso,-a; (*work*) concienzudo,-a; (*knowledge*) profundo,-a; **to carry out a t. enquiry into a matter** investigar a fondo un asunto.

thoroughly *adv* (*carefully*) a fondo; (*wholly*) completamente.

those [ðəʊz] **1** *dem a* esos,-as; (*remote*) aquellos,-as. **2** *dem pron* ésos,-as; (*remote*) aquéllos,-as; (*with rel*) los, las; *see* **that 1 & 2**.

though [ðəʊ] **1** *conj* aunque; **as t.** como si; **it looks as t. he's gone** parece que se ha ido. **2** *adv* sin embargo.

thought [θɔːt] (*act of thinking*) pensamiento *m*; (*reflection*) reflexión *f*.

thoughtful *a* (*considerate*) atento,-a.

thoughtless *a* (*person*) desconsiderado,-a; (*action*) irreflexivo,-a.

thousand ['θaʊzənd] *a & n* mil (*m*) *inv*; **thousands of people** miles de personas.

thread [θred] **1** *n* hilo *m*. **2** *vt* (*needle*) enhebrar.

threat [θret] amenaza *f*.

threaten *vt* amenazar; **to t. to do sth** amenazar con hacer algo.

threatening *a* amenazador,-a.

three [θriː] *a & n* tres (*m*).

threw [θruː] *pt of* **throw.**

thrill [θrɪl] (*excitement*) emoción *f*.

thrilled *a* emocionado,-a; **I'm t. about the trip** estoy muy ilusionado,-a con el viaje.

thriller (*book*) novela *f* de suspense; (*film*) película *f* de suspense.

thrilling *a* emocionante.

thriving ['θraɪvɪŋ] *a* próspero,-a.

throat [θrəʊt] garganta *f*.

throne [θrəʊn] trono *m*.

through [θruː] **1** *prep* (*place*) a través de, por; **to look t. the window** mirar por la ventana. ▌ (*time*) a lo largo de; **all t. his life** durante toda su vida. ▌ (*by means of*) por, mediante. ▌ (*because of*) a *or* por causa de; **t. ignorance** por ignorancia. **2** *a* **a t. train** un tren directo. **3** *adv* (*from one side to the other*) de un lado a otro; **to let sb t.** dejar pasar a algn; **to get t. to sb** comunicar con algn; **I'm t. with him** he terminado con él.

through'out 1 *prep* por todo,-a; **t. the year** durante todo el año. **2** *adv* (*place*) en todas partes; (*time*) todo el tiempo.

throw[*] [θrəʊ] *vt* tirar; (*to the ground*) derribar; (*party*) dar.

● **throw away** *vt* (*rubbish, money*) tirar; (*money*) malgastar; (*opportunity*) perder.

● **throw out** *vt* (*rubbish*) tirar; (*person*) echar.

● **throw up** *vti* devolver.

thud [θʌd] ruido *m* sordo.

thug [θʌg] (*lout*) gamberro *m*; (*criminal*) criminal *m*.

thumb [θʌm] pulgar *m*.

thumbtack *US* chincheta *f*.

thunder ['θʌndəʳ] **1** *n* trueno *m*. **2** *vi* tronar.

thunderstorm tormenta *f*.

Thursday ['θɜːzdɪ] jueves *m*.

tick [tɪk] (*mark*) marca *f* de visto bueno.

● **tick off** *vt* (*mark*) marcar.

ticket ['tɪkɪt] (*for bus etc*) billete *m*; (*for theatre*) entrada *f*; (*for lottery*) décimo *m*; (*receipt*) recibo *m*.

ticket collector revisor,-a *mf*.

ticket office taquilla *f*.

tickle ['tɪkəl] *vt* hacer cosquillas a.

ticklish *a* **to be t.** (*person*) tener cosquillas.

tide [taɪd] marea *f*.

tidily *adv* (*to put away*) ordenadamente.

tidy ['taɪdɪ] **1** *a* (*room, habits*) ordenado,-a; (*appearance*) arreglado,-a. **2** *vt* arreglar. **3** *vi* **to t. (up)** ordenar las cosas.

● **tidy away** *vt* poner en su sitio.

tie [taɪ] **1** *vt* (*shoelaces etc*) atar; **to t. a knot** hacer un nudo. **2** *n* (*around neck*) corbata *f*; (*match*) partido *m*; (*draw*) empate *m*.

● **tie up** *vt* (*parcel, dog*) atar.

tiger ['taɪgə'] tigre *m*.

tight [taɪt] **1** *a* apretado,-a; (*clothing*) ajustado,-a; (*seal*) hermético,-a; **my shoes are too t.** me aprietan los zapatos. **2** *adv* estrechamente; (*seal*) herméticamente; **hold t.** agárrate fuerte; **shut t.** bien cerrado,-a.

tighten *vt* (*screw*) apretar; (*rope*) tensar.

tights *npl* (*thin*) panties *mpl*; (*thick*) leotardos *mpl*.

tile [taɪl] **1** *n* (*of roof*) teja *f*; (*glazed*) azulejo *m*; (*for floor*) baldosa *f*. **2** *vt* (*roof*) tejar; (*wall*) alicatar; (*floor*) embaldosar.

till[1] [tɪl] (*for cash*) caja *f*.

till[2] **1** *prep* hasta; **from morning t. night** de la mañana a la noche; **t. then** hasta entonces. **2** *conj* hasta que.

tilt [tɪlt] **1** *vi* **to t. over** volcarse; **to t. (up)** inclinarse. **2** *vt* inclinar.

timber ['tɪmbə'] madera *f* (de construcción).

time [taɪm] **1** *n* tiempo *m*; (*era*) época *f*; (*point in time*) momento *m*; (*time of day*) hora *f*; (*occasion*) vez *f*; **all the t.** todo el tiempo; **for some t. (past)** desde hace algún tiempo; **I haven't seen him for a long t.** hace mucho (tiempo) que no lo veo; **in a short t.** en poco tiempo; **in t.** a tiempo; **in three weeks' t.** dentro de tres semanas. **(at) any t. (you like)** cuando quiera; **at no t.** en ningún momento; **at that t.** (en aquel) entonces; **at the same t.** al mismo tiempo; **at times** a veces; **from t. to t.** de vez en cuando; **he may turn up at any t.** puede llegar en cualquier momento; **on t.** puntualmente; **what's the t.?** ¿qué hora es?; **t. of the year** época *f* del año; **to have a good/bad t.** pasarlo bien/mal; **four at a t.** cuatro a la vez; **next t.** la próxima vez; **three times four** tres (multiplicado) por cuatro; **four times as big** cuatro veces más grande. **2** *vt* (*speech*) calcular la duración de; (*race*) cronometrar; (*choose the time of*) escoger el momento oportuno para.

timer (*device*) temporizador *m*.

timetable horario *m*.

timid ['tɪmɪd] *a* tímido,-a.

timing ['taɪmɪŋ] (*timeliness*) oportunidad *f*; (*coordination*) coordinación *f*; (*in race*) cronometraje *m*.

tin [tɪn] (*metal*) estaño *m*; (*container*) lata *f*.

tinfoil papel *m* de estaño.

tinned *a* enlatado,-a; **t. food** conservas *fpl*.

tinned food conservas *fpl*.

tin-opener abrelatas *m inv*.

tiny ['taɪnɪ] *a* diminuto,-a.

tip² [tɪp] (*end*) punta *f*; (*of cigarette*) colilla *f*.

tip² 1 *n* (*gratuity*) propina *f*; (*advice*) consejo *m*. 2 *vt* dar una propina a.

tip³ 1 *n* (*rubbish*) **t.** vertedero *m*. 2 *vt* inclinar; (*rubbish*) verter. 3 *vi* to **t.** (*up*) ladearse; (*cart*) bascular.

● **tip over** 1 *vt* volcar. 2 *vi* volcarse.

tipped cigarette [tɪpt] cigarrillo *m* con filtro.

tiptoe on t. de puntillas.

tire¹ [taɪəʳ] *US* (*of vehicle*) neumático *m*.

tire² 1 *vt* cansar. 2 *vi* cansarse.

● **tire out** *vt* agotar.

tired *a* cansado,-a; **t. out** rendido,-a; **to be t. of sth** estar harto,-a de algo.

tiredness cansancio *m*.

tiring *a* agotador,-a.

tissue ['tɪʃuː] (*handkerchief*) kleenex⁽ᴿ⁾ *m*.

title ['taɪtəl] título *m*.

to [tə, *stressed* tuː] 1 *prep* (*with place*) a; (*towards*) hacia; **he went to France/Japan** fue a Francia/al Japón; **I'm going to Mary's** voy a casa de Mary; **it is thirty miles to London** Londres está a treinta millas; **the train to Madrid** el tren de Madrid; **to the east** hacia el este; **to the right** a la derecha. ‖ (*time*) **ten (minutes) to six** las seis menos diez. ‖ (*with indirect object*) a; **he gave it to his cousin** se lo dio a su primo. ‖ (*towards*) **he was very kind to me** se portó muy bien conmigo. ‖ (*with infinitive*) **to buy/to come** comprar/venir; (*in order to*) para; (*with verbs of motion*) a; **he did it to help me** lo hizo para ayudarme; **he stopped to talk** se detuvo a hablar; **difficult to do** difícil de hacer; **ready to listen** dispuesto,-a a escuchar; **the first to complain** el primero en quejarse; **this is the time to do it** éste es el momento de hacerlo; **to have a great deal to do** tener mucho que hacer.

toad [təʊd] sapo *m*.

toadstool hongo *m* (venenoso).

toast [təʊst] 1 *n* slice of **t.** tostada *f*. 2 *vt* tostar.

toaster tostador *m* (de pan).

tobacco [tə'bækəʊ] tabaco *m*.

tobacconist t.'s (shop) estanco *m*.

toboggan [tə'bɒgən] tobogán *m*.

today [tə'deɪ] *adv* hoy.

toddler ['tɒdləʳ] niño,-a *mf* pequeño,- a.

toe [təʊ] dedo *m* del pie.

toenail uña *f* del dedo del pie.

toffee ['tɒfɪ] caramelo *m*.

together [tə'geðəʳ] *adv* junto,-a, juntos,-as; **all t.** todos juntos; **t. with** junto con.

toilet ['tɔɪlɪt] wáter *m*; (*public*) servicios *mpl*.

toilet paper *or* **tissue** papel *m* higiénico.

toiletries *npl* artículos *mpl* de aseo.

toilet roll rollo *m* de papel higiénico.

toilet water (*perfume*) agua *f* de colonia.

token ['təʊkən] (*for telephone*) ficha *f*; **book t.** vale *m* para comprar libros.

told [təʊld] *pt & pp of* **tell.**

tolerant ['tɒlərənt] *a* tolerante.

tolerate *vt* tolerar.

toll [təʊl] (*for road*) peaje *m*.

tollfree number = US teléfono *m* gratuito.

tomato [tə'mɑːtəʊ, US tə'meɪtəʊ] (*pl* **tomatoes**) tomate *m*.

tomb [tuːm] tumba *f*.

tomorrow [tə'mɒrəʊ] *adv* mañana; **the day after t.** pasado mañana; **t. night** mañana por la noche.

ton [tʌn] tonelada *f*; *fam* **tons of** montones de.

tone [təʊn] tono *m*.

tongs [tɒŋz] *npl* (*for sugar, hair*) tenacillas *fpl*; (**fire**) **t.** tenazas *fpl*.

tongue [tʌŋ] lengua *f*.

tonic ['tɒnɪk] (*drink*) tónica *f*.

tonight [tə'naɪt] *adv* esta noche.

tonsil ['tɒnsəl] amígdala *f*.

tonsillitis [tɒnsɪ'laɪtɪs] amigdalitis *f*.

too [tuː] *adv* (*also*) también; (*excessively*) demasiado; **t. much/many** demasiado,-a, demasiados,-as; **ten pounds t. much** diez libras de más; **t. much money** demasiado dinero; **t. old** demasiado viejo.

took [tʊk] *pt of* **take.**

tool [tuːl] (*utensil*) herramienta *f*.

tooth [tuːθ] (*pl* **teeth** [tiːθ]) diente *m*.

toothache dolor *m* de muelas.

toothbrush cepillo *m* de dientes.

toothpaste pasta *f* dentífrica.

toothpick mondadientes *m inv*.

top[1] [tɒp] **1** *n* (*upper part*) parte *f* de arriba; (*of hill*) cumbre *f*; (*of tree*) copa *f*; (*surface*) superficie *f*; (*of list etc*) cabeza *f*; (*of bottle etc*) tapón *m*; (*best*) lo mejor; **on t. of** encima de. **2** *a* (*part*) superior, de arriba; (*best*) mejor; **the t. floor** el último piso.

- **top up** *vt* llenar hasta el tope.
top[2] (*toy*) peonza *f*.
topic ['tɒpɪk] tema *m*.
torch [tɔːtʃ] (*burning*) antorcha *f*; (*electric*) linterna *f*.
torment [tɔː'ment] *vt* atormentar.
tornado [tɔː'neɪdəʊ] tornado *m*.
tortoise ['tɔːtəs] tortuga *f* de tierra.
tortoiseshell *a* de carey.
torture ['tɔːtʃəʳ] **1** *vt* torturar; (*cause anguish*) atormentar. **2** *n* tortura *f*; (*anguish*) tormento *m*.
toss [tɒs] **1** *vt* (*ball*) tirar; (*throw about*) sacudir; **to t. a coin** echar a cara o cruz. **2** *vi* **to t. about** agitarse; (*in sport*) **to t. (up)** sortear.
total ['təʊtəl] total *m*; (*in bill*) importe *m*.
totally *adv* totalmente.
touch [tʌtʃ] **1** *vt* tocar; (*lightly*) rozar; (*emotionally*) conmover. **2** *vi* tocarse; (*lightly*) rozarse. **3** *n* toque *m*; (*light contact*) roce *m*; (*sense of touch*) tacto *m*; **in t. with sb** en contacto con algn.
- **touch down** *vi* (*plane*) aterrizar.
touchy *a* (*person*) susceptible.
tough [tʌf] *a* (*material, competitor etc*) fuerte; (*test, criminal, meat*) duro,-a; (*punishment*) severo,-a; (*problem*) difícil.
tour [tʊəʳ] **1** *n* (*journey*) viaje *m*; (*of palace etc*) visita *f*; (*of city*) recorrido *m* turístico; (*of theatrical company, team*) gira *f*; **on t.** de gira. **2** *vt* (*country*) viajar por; (*building*) visitar. **3** *vi* estar de viaje.
tourism turismo *m*.
tourist turista *mf*; **t. class** clase *f* turista.
tourist office oficina *f* de información turística.
tournament ['tʊənəmənt] torneo *m*.
tow [təʊ] *vt* remolcar.
towards [tə'wɔːdz] *prep* hacia; **our duty t. others** nuestro deber para con los demás.
towel ['taʊəl] toalla *f*.
towelling felpa *f*.
tower ['taʊəʳ] torre *f*.
tower block torre *f*.
town [taʊn] ciudad *f*; (*small*) pueblo *m*; **to go into t.** ir al centro.
town council ayuntamiento *m*.
town hall ayuntamiento *m*.
tow truck *US* grúa *f*.
toy [tɔɪ] juguete *m*.
toyshop juguetería *f*.
trace [treɪs] **1** *n* (*sign*) indicio *m*, vestigio *m*. **2** *vt* (*drawing*) calcar; (*locate*)

seguir la pista de.

tracing paper papel *m* de calco.

track [træk] (*mark*) huellas *fpl*; (*pathway*) camino *m*; (*for running*) pista *f*; (*of railway*) vía *f*; (*on record*) canción *f*; **to be on the right t.** ir por buen camino; **to be on the wrong t.** haberse equivocado.

tracksuit chandal *m*.

tractor ['træktə'] tractor *m*.

trade [treɪd] **1** *n* (*job*) oficio *m*; (*sector*) industria *f*; (*commerce*) comercio *m*. **2** *vi* comerciar (**in** en). **3** *vt* **to t. sth for sth** trocar algo por algo.

trademark marca *f* (de fábrica); **registered t.** marca registrada.

trade union sindicato *m*.

trading comercio *m*.

tradition [trə'dɪʃən] tradición *f*.

traditional *a* tradicional.

traffic ['træfɪk] *n* tráfico *m*.

traffic island refugio *m*.

traffic jam atasco *m*.

traffic lights *npl* semáforo *m sing*.

traffic sign señal *f* de tráfico.

tragedy ['trædʒɪdɪ] tragedia *f*.

tragic ['trædʒɪk] *a* trágico,-a.

trail [treɪl] **1** *vt* **to t. sth (along)** (*drag*) arrastrar algo. **2** *vi* (*drag*) arrastrarse; **to t. (along)** (*linger*) rezagarse. **3** *n* senda *f*; (*bigger*) pista *f* (*of smoke*) estela *f*.

trailer (*behind vehicle*) remolque *m*; US (*caravan*) caravana *f*.

train[1] [treɪn] *n* tren *m*; **to go by t.** ir en tren.

train[2] **1** *vt* (*in sport*) entrenar; (*animal*) amaestrar; (*teach*) formar. **2** *vi* entrenarse; (*be taught*) prepararse.

trained *a* (*skilled*) cualificado,-a.

trainers *npl* (*shoes*) zapatillas *fpl* de deporte.

training entrenamiento *m*; (*instruction*) formación *f*.

traitor ['treɪtə'] traidor,-a *mf*.

tram [træm] tranvía *m*.

tramp [træmp] (*person*) vagabundo,-a *mf*.

tranquillizer ['træŋkwɪlaɪzə'] tranquilizante *m*.

transfer [træns'fɜː'] **1** *vt* trasladar; (*funds*) trasferir; **a transferred charge call** una conferencia a cobro revertido. **2** ['trænsfɜː'] *n* traslado *m*; (*of funds*) trasferencia *f*; (*picture, design*) calcomanía *f*.

transfusion [træns'fjuːʒən] transfusión *f* (de sangre).

transistor [træn'zɪstə'] transistor *m*.

transitive ['trænzɪtɪv] *a* transitivo,-a.

translate [træns'leɪt] *vt* traducir.

translation traducción f.

translator traductor,-a mf.

transparent [træns'pærənt] a transparente.

transplant ['trænsplɑːnt] trasplante m.

transport [træns'pɔːt] **1** vt transportar. **2** ['trænspɔːt] n transporte m.

trap [træp] **1** n trampa f. **2** vt (animal, fugitive) atrapar; **to t. sb into doing sth** lograr con ardides que algn haga algo.

trap door trampilla f.

trash [træʃ] (inferior goods) bazofia f; US (rubbish) basura f.

trash can US cubo m de la basura.

travel ['trævəl] **1** vi viajar; (vehicle, electric current) ir; **to t. through** recorrer. **2** vt recorrer. **3** n viajar m.

travel agency agencia f de viajes.

travelsickness mareo m.

traveller, US **traveler** viajero,-a mf.

traveller's cheque, US **traveler's check** cheque m de viaje.

travelling, US **traveling 1** a (salesman) ambulante. **2** n los viajes mpl; **I'm fond of t.** me gusta viajar.

tray [treɪ] (for food) bandeja f.

treacherous ['tretʃərəs] a (dangerous) peligroso,-a.

tread* [tred] vi pisar.

• **tread on** vt pisar.

treasure ['treʒə'] tesoro m.

treat [triːt] **1** n (present) regalo m. **2** vt tratar; (regard) considerar; **he treated them to dinner** les invitó a cenar.

treatment (of person) trato m; (of subject, patient) tratamiento m.

treble ['trebəl] **1** vt triplicar. **2** vi triplicarse.

tree [triː] árbol m.

tremble ['trembəl] vi temblar.

trench [trentʃ] (ditch) zanja f; (for troops) trinchera f.

trial ['traɪəl] (in court) juicio m.

triangle ['traɪæŋgəl] triángulo m.

tri'angular a triangular.

tribe [traɪb] tribu f.

trick [trɪk] **1** n (ruse) ardid m; (dishonest) engaño m; (practical joke) broma f; (of magic, knack) truco m; **to play a t. on sb** gastarle una broma a algn. **2** vt engañar.

trickle ['trɪkəl] **1** vi (water) gotear. **2** n hilo m.

tricky ['trɪkɪ] a (situation) delicado,-a; (problem) difícil.

tricycle ['traɪsɪkəl] triciclo m.

trigger ['trɪgə'] (of gun) gatillo m.

trim [trɪm] vt (cut) recortar; (expenses) disminuir.

trip [trɪp] **1** n (*journey*) viaje m; (*excursion*) excursión f. **2** vi **to t. (up)** (*stumble*) tropezar (**over** con).

triple ['trɪpəl] **1** vt triplicar. **2** vi triplicarse.

triumph ['traɪəmf] **1** n triunfo m. **2** vi triunfar.

trivial ['trɪvɪəl] a trivial.

trolley ['trɒlɪ] Br carro m.

trombone [trɒm'bəʊn] trombón m.

troops [tru:ps] tropas fpl.

trophy ['trəʊfɪ] trofeo m.

tropical ['trɒpɪkəl] a tropical.

trot [trɒt] **1** vi trotar. **2** n trote m.

trouble ['trʌbəl] **1** n (*misfortune*) desgracia f; (*problems*) problemas mpl; (*effort*) esfuerzo m; **to be in t.** estar en un lío; **it's not worth the t.** no merece la pena; **to take the t. to do sth** molestarse en hacer algo; **to have liver t.** tener problemas de hígado. **2** vt (*distress*) afligir; (*worry*) preocupar; (*bother*) molestar.

trousers ['traʊzəz] npl pantalón m sing, pantalones mpl.

trout [traʊt] trucha f.

truant ['tru:ənt] **to play t.** hacer novillos.

truck [trʌk] camión m; Br (*on railway*) vagón m.

true [tru:] a verdadero,-a; (*faithful*) fiel; **to come t.** cumplirse; **it's not t.** no es verdad; **it's t. that ...** es verdad que ...

trump [trʌmp] (*in cards*) triunfo m.

trumpet ['trʌmpɪt] trompeta f.

trunk [trʌŋk] (*of tree, body*) tronco m; (*of elephant*) trompa f; (*case*) baúl m.

trunks [trʌŋks] npl (**swimming**) **t.** bañador m sing.

trust [trʌst] **1** n confianza f. **2** vt (*rely upon*) fiarse de; **to t. sb with sth** confiar algo a algn.

truth [tru:θ] verdad f.

try [traɪ] **1** vt (*attempt*) intentar; (*test*) probar. **2** vi intentar; **to t. to do sth** tratar de or intentar hacer algo. **3** n (*attempt*) tentativa f; (*in rugby*) ensayo m.

● **try on** vt (*dress*) probarse.

● **try out** vt probar.

T-shirt ['ti:ʃɜ:t] camiseta f.

tub [tʌb] (*container*) tina f; (*bath*) bañera f.

tube [tju:b] tubo m; (*in body*) conducto m; **the t.** (*underground*) el metro.

tuck [tʌk] vt **to t. in the bedclothes** remeter la ropa de la cama; **to t. one's shirt into one's trousers** meterse la camisa por dentro (de los pantalones).

Tuesday ['tju:zdɪ] martes m.

tuft [tʌft] (*of hair*) mechón m; (*of wool etc*) copo m.

tug [tʌg] **1** *vt* (*pull at*) tirar de; (*haul along*) arrastrar; (*boat*) remolcar. **2** *n* (*boat*) remolcador *m*.

tugboat remolcador *m*.

tuition [tjuːˈɪʃən] instrucción *f*; **private t.** clases *fpl* particulares; **t. fees** tasas *fpl*.

tulip [ˈtjuːlɪp] tulipán *m*.

tumble [ˈtʌmbəl] **1** *vi* (*person*) caerse. **2** *n* caída *f*.

tumble dryer secadora *f*.

tumbler (*glass*) vaso *m*.

tummy [ˈtʌmɪ] *fam* estómago *m*; (*belly*) barriga *f*.

tuna [ˈtjuːnə] atún *m*.

tune [tjuːn] **1** *n* (*melody*) melodía *f*; **in/out of t.** afinado/desafinado; **to sing out of t.** desafinar. **2** *vt* (*instrument*) afinar; (*engine*) poner a punto.

● **tune in to** *vt* (*on radio etc*) sintonizar.

tuning (*of instrument*) afinación *f*.

Tunisian [tjuːˈnɪzɪən] *a & n* tunecino,-a (*mf*).

tunnel [ˈtʌnəl] túnel *m*.

turban [ˈtɜːbən] turbante *m*.

turkey [ˈtɜːkɪ] pavo *m*.

Turkish [ˈtɜːkɪʃ] **1** *a* turco,-a. **2** *n* (*language*) turco *m*.

turn [tɜːn] **1** *vt* (*revolve*) girar; (*page, head, gaze*) volver; (*change*) transformar (**into** en); **he's turned forty** ha cumplido los cuarenta. **2** *vi* (*revolve*) girar; (*change direction*) torcer; (*turn round*) volverse; (*become*) volverse; **to t. to sb** (*for help*) acudir a algn. **3** *n* (*of wheel*) vuelta *f*; (*in road*) curva *f*; (*in game, queue*) turno *m*; **it's your t.** te toca a ti; **to take it in turns to do sth** turnarse para hacer algo.

● **turn around** *vi* (*of person*) volverse.

● **turn away 1** *vt* (*person*) rechazar. **2** *vi* volver la cabeza; (*move away*) alejarse.

● **turn back 1** *vt* (*person*) hacer retroceder. **2** *vi* volverse.

● **turn down** *vt* (*gas, radio etc*) bajar; (*reject*) rechazar.

● **turn into 1** *vt* convertir en. **2** *vi* convertirse en.

● **turn off** *vt* (*light, TV, radio, engine*) apagar; (*water, gas*) cortar; (*tap*) cerrar.

● **turn on** *vt* (*light, TV, radio, engine*) encender; (*water, gas*) abrir la llave de; (*tap*) abrir.

● **turn out 1** *vt* (*extinguish*) apagar. **2** *vi* **it turns out that . . .** resulta que . . .; **things have turned out well** las cosas han salido bien.

● **turn over 1** *vt* (*turn upside down*) poner al revés; (*page*) dar la vuelta a. **2** *vi* volverse.

● **turn round 1** *vt* volver. **2** *vi* (*rotate*) girar.

● **turn up 1** *vt* (*collar*) levantar; (*TV, volume*) subir; (*light*) aumentar la

intensidad de. **2** *vi* (*arrive*) presentarse.
turning (*in road*) salida *f.*
turnip ['tɜːnɪp] nabo *m.*
turnup (*of trousers*) vuelta *f.*
turtle ['tɜːtəl] tortuga *f.*
turtleneck a t. **sweater** un jersey de cuello alto.
tusk [tʌsk] colmillo *m.*
tutor ['tjuːtəʳ] (*at university*) tutor,-a *mf;* **private t.** profesor,-a *mf* particular.
TV [tiːˈviː] TV.
tweezers ['twiːzəz] *npl* pinzas *fpl.*
twelfth [twelfθ] *a & n* duodécimo,-a (*mf*).
twelve [twelv] *a & n* doce (*m*); **t. o'clock** las doce.
twentieth ['twentɪɪθ] *a & n* vigésimo,-a (*mf*).
twenty ['twentɪ] *a & n* veinte (*m*) *inv.*
twice [twaɪs] *adv* dos veces; **he's t. as old as I am** tiene el doble de años que yo; **t. as big** el doble de grande.
twig [twɪg] ramita *f.*
twilight ['twaɪlaɪt] crepúsculo *m.*
twin [twɪn] *n* mellizo,-a *mf;* **identical twins** gemelos *mpl* (idénticos); **t. beds** camas *fpl* gemelas.
twine [twaɪn] bramante *m.*
twist [twɪst] **1** *vt* torcer; **to t. one's ankle** torcerse el tobillo. **2** *n* (*movement*) torsión *f;* (*in road*) vuelta *f.*
● **twist off** (*lid*) desenroscar.
two [tuː] *a & n* dos (*m*) *inv.*
two-way *a* (*street*) de dos direcciones.
type [taɪp] **1** *n* (*kind*) tipo *m;* (*print*) caracteres *mpl.* **2** *vti* escribir a máquina.
typewriter máquina *f* de escribir.
typewritten *a* escrito,-a a máquina.
typical ['tɪpɪkəl] *a* típico,-a.
typing mecanografía *f.*
typist mecanógrafo,-a *mf.*
tyre [taɪəʳ] neumático *m.*

U

UFO [ˈjuːefˈəʊ] *abbr of* **unidentified flying object** OVNI *m.*

ugliness fealdad *f.*

ugly [ˈʌglɪ] *a* feo,-a; (*situation*) desagradable.

ulcer [ˈʌlsə] (*sore*) llaga *f*; (*internal*) úlcera *f.*

umbrella [ʌmˈbrelə] paraguas *m inv.*

umpire [ˈʌmpaɪə] árbitro *m.*

unable to be u. to do sth no poder hacer algo.

unacceptable *a* inaceptable.

unaccustomed *a* he's u. to this climate no está acostumbrado a este clima.

unanimous [juːˈnænɪməs] *a* unánime.

unanimously *adv* unánimemente.

unattractive *a* (*idea, appearance*) poco atractivo,-a.

unavailable *a* no disponible; **Mr Smith is u. today** Mr Smith no le puede atender hoy.

unavoidable *a* inevitable; (*accident*) imprevisible.

unavoidably *adv* inevitablemente.

unaware *a* to be u. of sth ignorar algo.

unawares *adv* (*without knowing*) inconscientemente; **it caught me u.** me cogió desprevenido.

unbearable *a* insoportable.

unbelievable *a* increíble.

unbreakable *a* irrompible.

unbutton *vt* desabrochar.

uncertain *a* (*not certain*) incierto,-a; (*doubtful*) dudoso,-a; (*hesitant*) indeciso,-a.

uncertainty incertidumbre *f.*

unchanged *a* igual.

uncle [ˈʌŋkəl] tío *m.*

unclear *a* poco claro,-a.

uncomfortable *a* incómodo,-a.

uncommon *a* (*rare*) poco común.

unconnected *a* no relacionado,-a.

unconscious *a* inconsciente (*of* de).

unconvincing *a* poco convincente.

uncooperative *a* poco cooperativo,-a.

uncork *vt* (*bottle*) descorchar.

uncover *vt* destapar; (*discover*) descubrir.

undamaged *a* (*article etc*) sin desperfectos.

undecided *a* (*person*) indeciso,-a.

undeniable *a* innegable.

under ['ʌndər] **1** *prep* debajo de; (*less than*) menos de; **u. the circumstances** dadas las circunstancias; **u. there** allí debajo. **2** *adv* debajo.

under- *prefix* (*below*) sub-, infra-; (*insufficiently*) insuficientemente.

under'charge *vt* cobrar menos de lo debido.

underclothes *npl* ropa *f sing* interior.

underdone *a* poco hecho,-a.

under'estimate *vt* subestimar.

under'go* *vt* experimentar; (*change*) sufrir; (*test etc*) pasar por.

under'graduate estudiante *mf* universitario,-a.

underground 1 *a* subterráneo,-a. **2** *n* **the u.** (*subway*) el metro.

under'line *vt* subrayar.

underneath [ʌndə'ni:θ] **1** *prep* debajo de. **2** *adv* debajo. **3** *n* parte *f* inferior.

underpants *npl* calzoncillos *mpl*.

underpass paso *n* subterráneo.

undershirt *US* camiseta *f*.

under'stand* *vti* entender.

under'standable *a* comprensible.

under'standing 1 *n* (*intellectual grasp*) comprensión *f*; (*agreement*) acuerdo *m*. **2** *a* comprensivo,-a.

under'stood *a* (*agreed on*) convenido,-a.

under'take* *vt* (*responsibility*) asumir; (*task, job*) encargarse de; (*promise*) comprometerse a.

undertaker empresario,-a *mf* de pompas fúnebres.

undertaker's funeraria *f*.

under'taking (*task*) empresa *f*.

under'water 1 *a* submarino,-a. **2** *adv* bajo el agua.

underwear *inv* ropa *f* interior.

undo* [ʌn'du:] *vt* deshacer; (*button*) desabrochar.

undone *a* (*knot etc*) deshecho,-a; **to come u.** (*shoelace*) desatarse; (*button, blouse*) desabrocharse; (*necklace etc*) soltarse.

undoubtedly *adv* indudablemente.

undress 1 *vt* desnudar. **2** *vi* desnudarse.

uneasy *a* (*worried*) preocupado,-a; (*disturbing*) inquietante; (*uncomfortable*) incómodo,-a.

unemployed 1 *a* **to be u.** estar en paro. **2** *npl* **the u.** los parados.

unemployment paro *m*.

uneven *a* (*not level*) desigual; (*bumpy*) accidentado,-a; (*variable*) irregular.

uneventful *a* sin acontecimientos.

unexpected *a* (*unhoped for*) inesperado,-a; (*event*) imprevisto,-a.

unexpectedly *adv* in esperadamente.
unfair *a* injusto,-a.
unfairly *adv* injustamente.
unfairness injusticia *f.*
unfaithful *a* (*friend*) desleal; (*husband, wife*) infiel.
unfamiliar *a* (*unknown*) desconocido,-a; **to be u. with sth** no conocer bien algo.
unfashionable *a* pasado,-a de moda; (*ideas etc*) poco popular.
unfasten *vt* (*knot*) desatar; (*clothing, belt*) desabrochar.
unfavourable, *US* **unfavorable** *a* desfavorable.
unfinished *a* inacabado,-a.
unfit *a* (*food, building*) inadecuado,-a; (*person*) no apto,-a (**for** para); (*incompetent*) incompetente; (*physically*) incapacitado,-a; **to be u.** no estar en forma.
unfold *vt* (*sheet*) desdoblar; (*newspaper*) abrir.
unforgettable *a* inolvidable.
unforgivable *a* imperdonable.
unfortunate *a* (*person, event*) desgraciado,-a; **how u.!** ¡qué mala suerte!
unfortunately *adv* desgraciadamente.
unfriendly *a* antipático,-a.
unfurnished *a* sin amueblar.
ungrateful *a* (*unthankful*) desagradecido,-a.
unhappiness tristeza *f.*
unhappy *a* triste.
unharmed *a* ileso,-a, indemne.
unhealthy *a* (*ill*) enfermizo,-a; (*unwholesome*) malsano,-a.
unhelpful *a* (*advice*) inútil; (*person*) poco servicial.
unhook *vt* (*from hook*) descolgar; (*clothing*) desabrochar.
unhurt *a* ileso,-a.
unhygienic *a* antihigiénico,-a.
uniform ['juːnifɔːm] *a & n* uniforme (*m*).
unimportant *a* poco importante.
uninhabited *a* despoblado,-a.
uninjured *a* ileso,-a.
unintentional *a* involuntario,-a.
uninteresting *a* poco interesante.
union ['juːnjən] **1** *n* unión *f*; (*organization*) sindicato *m*. **2** *a* sindical.
Union Jack bandera *f* del Reino Unido.
unique [juːˈniːk] *a* único,-a.
unit ['juːnɪt] unidad *f*; (*piece of furniture*) módulo *m*; (*team*) equipo *m*; **kitchen u.** mueble *m* de cocina.
unite [juːˈnaɪt] **1** *vt* unir. **2** *vi* unirse.

universal *a* universal.

universe ['juːnɪvɜːs] universo *m*.

university [juːnɪ'vɜːsɪtɪ] **1** *n* universidad *f*. **2** *a* universitario,-a.

unjust *a* injusto,-a.

unkind *a* (*not nice*) poco amable; (*cruel*) despiadado,-a.

unknown *a* desconocido,-a.

unleaded [ʌn'ledɪd] *a* (*petrol, US gasoline*) sin plomo.

unless [ʌn'les] *conj* a menos que + *subj*, a no ser que + *subj*.

unlike *prep* a diferencia de.

unlikely *a* (*improbable*) poco probable.

unlimited *a* ilimitado,-a.

unload *vti* descargar.

unlock *vt* abrir (con llave).

unlucky *a* (*unfortunate*) desgraciado,-a; **to be u.** (*person*) tener mala suerte; (*thing*) traer mala suerte.

unmade *a* (*bed*) deshecho,-a.

unmarried *a* soltero,-a.

unnecessary *a* innecesario,-a.

unnoticed *a* desapercibido,-a; **to let sth pass u.** pasar algo por alto.

unoccupied *a* (*house*) desocupado,-a; (*seat*) libre.

unpack 1 *vt* (*boxes*) desembalar; (*suitcase*) deshacer. **2** *vi* deshacer la(s) maleta(s).

unpaid *a* (*bill, debt*) impagado,-a; (*work*) no retribuido,-a.

unpleasant *a* (*not nice*) desagradable; (*unfriendly*) antipático,-a (**to** con).

unplug *vt* desenchufar.

unpopular *a* impopular; **to make oneself u.** ganarse la antipatía de algn.

unpredictable *a* imprevisible.

unprepared *a* (*speech etc*) improvisado,-a; (*person*) desprevenido,-a.

unreasonable *a* poco razonable; (*demands*) desmedido,-a.

unrecognizable *a* irreconocible.

unrelated *a* (*not connected*) no relacionado,-a.

unreliable *a* (*person*) de poca confianza; (*information*) que no es de fiar; (*machine*) poco fiable.

unrest (*social etc*) malestar *m*.

unroll *vt* desenrollar.

unsafe *a* (*activity, journey*) peligroso,-a; (*building, car, machine*) inseguro,-a; **to feel u.** sentirse expuesto,- a.

unsatisfactory *a* insatisfactorio,-a.

unscrew *vt* destornillar.

unskilled *a* (*worker*) no cualificado,-a.

unstable *a* inestable.

unsteadily *adv* (*to walk*) con paso inseguro.

unsteady *a* (*not firm*) inestable; (*table, chair*) cojo,-a; (*hand, voice*) tembloroso,-a.

unsuccessful *a* (*person, negociation*) fracasado,-a; (*attempt, effort*) vano,-a; (*candidate*) derrotado,-a; **to be u. at sth** no tener éxito con algo.

unsuccessfully *adv* sin éxito.

unsuitable *a* (*person*) no apto,-a; (*thing*) inadecuado,-a.

unsuited *a* (*person*) no apto,-a; (*thing*) impropio,-a (**to** para).

unsure *a* poco seguro,-a; **to be u. of sth** no estar seguro,-a de algo.

untangle *vt* desenmarañar.

untidy *a* (*room, person*) desordenado,-a; (*hair*) despeinado,-a; (*appearance*) desaseado,-a.

untie *vt* desatar.

until [ʌn'tɪl] **1** *conj* hasta que; **u. she gets back** hasta que vuelva. **2** *prep* hasta; **u. now** hasta ahora; **not u. Monday** hasta el lunes no.

untrue *a* (*false*) falso,-a.

unused *a* (*car*) sin usar; (*flat etc*) sin estrenar; (*stamp*) sin matar.

unusual *a* (*rare*) poco común; (*exceptional*) excepcional.

unusually *adv* excepcionalmente.

unwell *a* **to be u.** estar malo,-a.

unwilling *a* **to be u. to do sth** no estar dispuesto a hacer algo.

unwillingly *adv* de mala gana.

unworthy *a* indigno,-a.

unwrap *vt* (*gift*) desenvolver; (*package*) deshacer.

unzip *vt* bajar la cremallera de.

up [ʌp] **1** *prep* (*movement*) **to climb up the mountain** escalar la montaña; **to walk up the street** ir calle arriba. ‖ (*position*) en lo alto de; **further up the street** más adelante (en la misma calle). **2** *adv* (*upwards*) arriba; **further up** hacia arriba; **from ten pounds up** de diez libras para arriba; **right up (to the top)** hasta arriba (del todo); **to go** *or* **come up** subir; **to walk up and down** ir de un lado a otro. ‖ (*towards*) hacia; **to come** *or* **go up to sb** acercarse a algn. ‖ (*increased*) **bread is up** el pan ha subido. ‖ (*wrong*) **what's up (with you)?** ¿qué pasa (contigo)?; **something must be up** debe pasar algo. ‖ **up to** (*as far as, until*) hasta; **I can spend up to £5** puedo gastar un máximo de cinco libras; **up to here** hasta aquí; **up to now** hasta ahora. ‖ **to be up to** (*depend on*) depender de; (*be capable of*) estar a la altura de; **he's up to something** está tramando algo. **3** *a* (*out of bed*) levantado,-a; (*finished*) terminado,-a; **time's up** (ya) es la hora. **4** *vt* (*increase*) aumentar. **5** *n* **ups and downs** altibajos *mpl*.

uphill *adv* cuesta arriba.

upon [ə'pɒn] *prep* sobre.

upper ['ʌpəʳ] *a* superior.

upright 1 *a* (*vertical*) vertical; (*honest*) honrado,-a. **2** *adv* derecho.

uproar tumulto *m*.

upset [ʌp'set] **1** *vt** (*shock*) trastornar; (*worry*) preocupar; (*displease*) disgustar; (*spoil*) desbaratar; (*make ill*) sentar mal a. **2** *a* (*shocked*) alterado,-a; (*displeased*) disgustado,-a; **to have an u. stomach** sentirse mal del estómago.

upside down al revés.

up'stairs 1 *adv* arriba. **2** *n* piso *m* de arriba.

up to 'date *a* (*current*) al día; (*modern*) moderno,-a. **to be u. with sth** estar al tanto de algo.

upward(s) *adv* hacia arriba; **from ten (years) u.** a partir de los diez años.

urge [ɜːdʒ] *vt* (*incite*) incitar; (*press*) instar; (*plead*) exhortar; (*advocate*) preconizar; **to u. that sth should be done** insistir en que se haga algo.

urgency ['ɜːdʒənsɪ] urgencia *f*.

urgent *a* urgente; (*need, tone*) apremiante.

urgently *adv* urgentemente.

Uruguayan [jʊərə'gwaɪən] *a & n* uruguayo,-a (*mf*).

us [ʌs] *pers pron* (*as object*) nos; (*after prep, 'to be'*) nosotros,-as; **she wouldn't believe it was us** no creía que fuéramos nosotros; **let's forget it** olvidémoslo.

use [juːz] **1** *vt* utilizar; (*consume*) consumir; **what is it used for?** ¿para qué sirve? **2** [juːs] *n* uso *m*; **'not in u.'** 'no funciona'; **to be of u.** servir; **to make (good) u. of sth** aprovechar algo; **it's no u.** es inútil; **it's no u. crying** no sirve de nada llorar.

● **use up** *vt* acabar; (*food*) consumir; (*petrol*) agotar; (*money*) gastar.

used[1] [juːzd] *a* (*second-hand*) usado,-a.

used[2] [juːst] **1** *v aux* **where did you use to live?** ¿dónde vivías (antes)?; **I u. to play the piano** solía tocar el piano; **I u. not to like it** antes no me gustaba. **2 to be u. to sth** estar acostumbrado,-a a algo.

useful *a* útil; (*practical*) práctico,-a; **to come in u.** venir bien.

usefulness utilidad *f*.

useless *a* inútil.

user ['juːzəʳ] usuario,-a *mf*.

usual ['juːʒʊəl] *a* corriente; **as u.** como siempre.

usually *adv* normalmente.

utensil [juː'tensəl] utensilio *m*; **kitchen utensils** batería *f sing* de cocina.

utility utilidad *f*.

utter[1] ['ʌtəʳ] *vt* (*words*) pronunciar; (*cry, threat*) lanzar.

utter[2] *a* total.

utterly *adv* completamente.

U-turn ['juːtɜːn] cambio *m* de sentido.

V

vacancy ['veɪkənsɪ] (*job*) vacante *f*; (*room*) habitación *f* libre.

vacant *a* (*empty*) vacío,-a; (*room, seat*) libre.

vacation [və'keɪʃən] vacaciones *fpl*; **on v.** de vacaciones.

vacationer *US* **summer v.** veraneante *mf*.

vaccinate ['væksɪneɪt] *vt* vacunar.

vaccination vacuna *f*.

vaccine ['væksiːn] vacuna *f*.

vacuum ['vækjʊəm] *vt* limpiar con aspiradora.

vacuum cleaner aspiradora *f*.

vacuum flask termo *m*.

vague [veɪg] *a* (*imprecise*) vago,-a; (*indistinct*) borroso,-a.

vaguely *adv* vagamente.

vain [veɪn] *a* **in v.** en vano.

valid ['vælɪd] *a* válido,-a.

valley ['vælɪ] valle *m*.

valuable 1 *a* valioso,-a. 2 *npl* **valuables** objetos *mpl* de valor.

value ['væljuː] valor *m*; **to get good v. for money** sacarle jugo al dinero.

van [væn] furgoneta *f*.

vandal ['vændəl] gamberro,-a *mf*.

vandalize *vt* destrozar.

vanilla [və'nɪlə] vainilla *f*.

vanish ['vænɪʃ] *vi* desaparecer.

varied ['veərɪd] *a* variado,-a.

variety [və'raɪɪtɪ] (*diversity*) variedad *f*; (*assortment*) surtido *m*; **for a v. of reasons** por razones diversas.

variety show espectáculo *m* de variedades.

various ['veərɪəs] *a* diversos,-as.

varnish ['vɑːnɪʃ] 1 *n* barniz *m*. 2 *vt* barnizar.

vary ['veərɪ] *vti* variar.

vase [vɑːz] florero *m*.

Vaseline[R] ['væsɪliːn] vaselina *f*.

vast [vɑːst] *a* vasto,-a.

VAT [viːeɪ'tiː, væt] *abbr of* **value added tax** IVA *m*.

VCR [viːsiː'ɑːʳ] *abbr of* **video cassette recorder** (grabador *m* de) vídeo *m*.

VDU [viːdiː'juː] *abbr of* **visual display unit** pantalla *f*.

veal [viːl] ternera *f*.

vegetable ['vedʒtəbəl] verdura *f*.

vege'tarian *a & n* vegetariano,-a (*mf*).

vege'tation vegetación *f*.

vehicle ['viːɪkəl] vehículo *m*.

veil [veɪl] velo *m.*

vein [veɪn] vena *f.*

velvet ['velvɪt] terciopelo *m.*

vending machine ['vendɪŋ] máquina *f* expendedora.

venetian blind [vəˈniːʃən] persiana *f* graduable.

Venezuelan [venɪˈzweɪlən] *a & n* venezolano,-a (*mf*).

ventilation [ventɪˈleɪʃən] ventilación *f.*

verb [vɜːb] verbo *m.*

verdict ['vɜːdɪkt] veredicto *m*; (*opinion*) opinión *f.*

verge [vɜːdʒ] (*of road*) arcén *m.*

verse [vɜːs] (*stanza*) estrofa *f*; (*poetry*) versos *mpl*; (*of song*) copla *f.*

version ['vɜːʃən] versión *f.*

vertical ['vɜːtɪkəl] *a* vertical.

very ['verɪ] *adv* muy; **v. much** muchísimo; **at the v. latest** como máximo; **the v. first/last** el primero/último de todos; **at this v. moment** en este mismo momento.

vest [vest] (*undershirt*) camiseta *f*; *US* (*waistcoat*) chaleco *m.*

vet [vet] veterinario,-a *mf.*

via ['vaɪə] *prep* por.

vibrate [vaɪˈbreɪt] *vi* vibrar (**with** de).

vibration vibración *f.*

vicar ['vɪkəʳ] párroco *m.*

vice[1] [vaɪs] vicio *m.*

vice[2] (*tool*) torno *m* de banco.

vicious ['vɪʃəs] *a* (*violent*) violento,-a; (*malicious*) malintencionado,-a; (*cruel*) cruel.

victim ['vɪktɪm] víctima *f.*

victory ['vɪktərɪ] victoria *f.*

video ['vɪdɪəʊ] vídeo *m*; **v. (cassette)** videocasete *m*; **v. (cassette recorder)** vídeo *m.*

video camera videocámara *f.*

video game videojuego *m.*

video tape cinta *f* de vídeo.

view [vjuː] (*sight*) vista *f*; (*opinion*) opinión *f*; **to come into v.** aparecer; **in v. of the fact that ...** dado que ...

viewer (*of TV*) televidente *mf.*

viewpoint punto *m* de vista.

villa ['vɪlə] (*country house*) casa *f* de campo.

village ['vɪlɪdʒ] (*small*) aldea *f*; (*larger*) pueblo *m.*

villager aldeano,-a *mf.*

vinegar ['vɪnɪgəʳ] vinagre *m.*

vineyard ['vɪnjəd] viñedo *m.*

violence ['vaɪələns] violencia f.

violent a violento,-a.

violently adv violentamente.

violin [vaɪə'lɪn] violín m.

virus ['vaɪrəs] virus m inv.

visa ['viːzə] visado m, Am visa f.

visible ['vɪzɪbəl] a visible.

visit ['vɪzɪt] **1** vt visitar. **2** n visita f; **to pay sb a v.** hacerle una visita a algn.

visiting hours npl horas fpl de visita.

visitor (guest) invitado,-a mf; (tourist) turista mf.

vital ['vaɪtəl] a (essential) fundamental.

vitally adv **it's v. important** es de vital importancia.

vitamin ['vɪtəmɪn, US 'vaɪtəmɪn] vitamina f.

vivid ['vɪvɪd] a (colour) vivo,-a; (description) gráfico,-a.

vocabulary [və'kæbjʊlərɪ] vocabulario m.

vodka ['vɒdkə] vodka m & f.

voice [vɔɪs] voz f; **at the top of one's v.** a voz en grito.

volcano [vɒl'keɪnəʊ] (pl volcanoes) volcán m.

volume ['vɒljuːm] volumen m.

voluntary ['vɒləntərɪ] a voluntario,-a.

volunteer [vɒlən'tɪər] **1** n voluntario,-a mf. **2** vi ofrecerse (**for** para).

vomit ['vɒmɪt] vti vomitar.

vote [vəʊt] **1** n voto m; (voting) votación f. **2** vti votar.

voter votante mf.

voucher ['vaʊtʃər] Br vale m.

vowel ['vaʊəl] vocal f.

voyage ['vɔɪɪdʒ] viaje m; (crossing) travesía f.

vulgar ['vʌlgər] a (coarse) ordinario,-a; (in poor taste) de mal gusto.

W

wad [wɒd] (*of paper*) taco *m*; (*of cotton wool*) bolita *f*; (*of banknotes*) fajo *m*.

waddle ['wɒdəl] *vi* andar como los patos.

wade [weɪd] *vi* caminar por el agua.

wafer ['weɪfə^r] barquillo *m*.

wag [wæg] **1** *vt* menear. **2** *vi* (*tail*) menearse.

wage earner asalariado,-a *mf*.

wages [weɪdʒəz] *npl* salario *m sing*.

wa(g)gon ['wægən] (*lorry*) camión *m*; (*of train*) vagón *m*.

waist [weɪst] cintura *f*.

waistcoat *Br* chaleco *m*.

wait [weɪt] **1** *n* espera *f*; (*delay*) demora *f*. **2** *vi* esperar; **to keep sb waiting** hacer esperar a algn.

● **wait behind** *vi* quedarse.

● **wait up** *vi* **to w. up for s.o.** esperar a algn levantado,-a.

waiter camarero *m*.

waiting '**no w.**' prohibido aparcar'.

waiting room sala *f* de espera.

waitress camarera *f*.

wake° [weɪk] **1** *vt* **to w. sb (up)** despertar a algn. **2** *vi* **to w. (up)** despertar(se).

walk [wɔːk] **1** *n* (*long*) caminata *m*; (*short*) paseo *m*; **it's an hour's w.** está a una hora de camino; **to go for a w.** dar un paseo. **2** *vt* (*dog*) pasear. **3** *vi* andar; (*to a specific place*) ir andando.

● **walk away** *vi* alejarse.

● **walk in** *vi* entrar.

● **walk out** *vi* salir.

walker paseante *mf*; (*in sport*) marchador,-a *mf*.

walking (*hiking*) excursionismo *m*.

walking stick bastón *m*.

Walkman^(R) (*pl* **Walkmans**) walkman^(R) *m*.

wall [wɔːl] (*exterior*) muro *m*; (*interior*) pared *f*.

wallet ['wɒlɪt] cartera *f*.

wallpaper 1 *n* papel *m* pintado. **2** *vt* empapelar.

walnut ['wɔːlnʌt] nuez *f*.

walrus ['wɔːlrəs] morsa *f*.

wander ['wɒndə^r] *vi* (*aimlessly*) vagar.

● **wander about** *vi* deambular.

want [wɒnt] *vt* querer; (*desire*) desear; (*need*) necesitar; **to w. to do sth** querer hacer algo; **you're wanted on the phone** te llaman al teléfono.

war [wɔːʳ] guerra *f*; **to be at w.** estar en guerra (**with** con).

ward [wɔːd] (*of hospital*) sala *f*.

warden ['wɔːdən] (*of residence*) guardián,-ana *mf*; **game w.** guarda *m* de coto.

wardrobe ['wɔːdrəʊb] armario *m* (ropero).

warehouse ['weəhaʊs] almacén *m*.

warm [wɔːm] **1** *a* caliente; (*water*) tibio,-a; **a w. day** un día de calor; **I am w.** tengo calor; **it is (very) w. today** hoy hace (mucho) calor. **2** *vt* calentar.
● **warm up 1** *vt* calentar; (*soup*) (re)calentar. **2** *vi* calentarse; (*food*) (re)calentarse; (*person*) entrar en calor.

warmth calor *m*.

warn [wɔːn] *vt* advertir (**about** sobre; **against** contra); **he warned me not to go** me advirtió que no fuera; **to w. sb that …** advertir a algn que …

warning (*of danger*) advertencia *f*; (*notice*) aviso *m*.

warning light piloto *m*.

warship buque *m* de guerra.

wart [wɔːt] verruga *f*.

was [wɒz] *pt of* **be**.

wash [wɒʃ] **1** *n* **to have a w.** lavarse. **2** *vt* lavar; (*dishes*) fregar; **to w. one's hair** lavarse el pelo. **3** *vi* (*have a wash*) lavarse.
● **wash away** *vt* (*of sea*) llevarse; (*traces*) borrar.
● **wash off** *vi* quitarse lavando.
● **wash out 1** *vt* (*stain*) quitar lavando. **2** *vi* quitarse lavando.
● **wash up 1** *vt Br* (*dishes*) fregar. **2** *vi Br* fregar los platos; *US* lavarse rápidamente.

washable *a* lavable.

washbasin lavabo *m*.

washcloth *US* manopla *f*.

washing (*action*) lavado *m*; (*of clothes*) colada *f*; (**dirty**) **w.** ropa *f* sucia; **to do the w.** hacer la colada.

washing machine lavadora *f*.

washing powder detergente *m*.

washing-up *Br* (*action*) fregado *m*; (*dishes*) platos *mpl* (para fregar); **to do the w.** fregar los platos.

washing-up liquid (detergente *m*) lavavajillas *m*.

washroom *US* servicios *mpl*.

wasp [wɒsp] avispa *f*.

waste [weɪst] **1** *n* (*unnecessary use*) desperdicio *m*; (*of resources, effort, money*) derroche *m*; (*of time*) pérdida *f*; (*rubbish*) basura *f*; **radio-active w.** desechos radioactivos. **2** *vt* (*squander*) desperdiciar; (*resources*) derrochar; (*time, chance*) perder.

wastebin cubo *m* de la basura.

waste ground (*in town*) descampado *m*.

wastepaper papeles *mpl* usados.

wastepaper basket papelera *f*.

watch [wɒtʃ] **1** *n* reloj *m*. **2** *vt* (*observe*) observar; (*keep an eye on*) vigilar; (*be careful of*) tener cuidado con. **3** *vi* (*look*) mirar.

● **watch out** *vi* w. out! ¡cuidado!

● **watch out for** *vt* tener cuidado con; (*wait for*) esperar.

watchstrap correa *f* (de reloj).

water ['wɔːtə'] **1** *n* agua *f*. **2** *vt* (*plants*) regar.

● **water down** *vt* (*drink*) aguar.

watercolour, *US* **watercolor** acuarela *f*.

watercress berro *m*.

waterfall cascada *f*; (*very big*) catarata *f*.

watering can regadera *f*.

watermelon sandía *f*.

waterproof *a* (*material*) impermeable; (*watch*) sumergible.

water-skiing esquí *m* acuático.

watertight *a* hermético,-a.

wave [weɪv] **1** *n* (*at sea*) ola *f*; (*in hair, radio*) onda *f*. **2** *vt* agitar; (*brandish*) blandir. **3** *vi* agitar el brazo; **she waved (to me)** (*greeting*) me saludó con la mano; (*goodbye*) se despidió (de mí) con la mano.

wavelength longitud *f* de onda.

wavy ['weɪvɪ] *a* ondulado,-a.

wax [wæks] **1** *n* cera *f*. **2** *vt* encerar.

way [weɪ] *n* (*route, road*) camino *m*; (*distance*) distancia *f*; (*means, manner*) manera *f*; **on the w.** en el camino; **on the w. here** de camino para aquí; **which is the w. to the station?** ¿por dónde se va a la estación?; **w. in** entrada *f*; **w. out** salida *f*; **on the w. back** en el viaje de regreso; **on the w. up/down** en la subida/bajada; **(get) out of the w.!** ¡quítate de en medio!; **you're in the w.** estás estorbando; **come this w.** venga por aquí; **which w. did he go?** ¿por dónde se fue?; **that w.** por allá; **a long w. off** lejos; **do it this w.** hazlo así; **which w. did you do it?** ¿cómo lo hiciste?; **no w.!** ¡ni hablar!

WC [dʌblju:'si:] wáter *m*.

we [wiː] *pers pron* nosotros,-as.

weak [wiːk] *a* débil; (*team, piece of work, tea*) flojo,-a.

weaken 1 *vt* debilitar; (*argument*) quitar fuerza a. **2** *vi* debilitarse; (*concede ground*) ceder.

weakness debilidad *f*; (*character flaw*) punto *m* flaco.

wealth [welθ] riqueza *f*.

wealthy *a* rico,-a.

weapon ['wepən] arma *f*.

wear [weə'] **1** *vt** (*clothes*) llevar (puesto,-a); (*shoes*) calzar; **he wears**

glasses lleva gafas. **he was wearing a jacket** llevaba chaqueta. **2** *n* (*deterioration*) desgaste *m*; **normal w. and tear** desgaste *m* natural.

● **wear off** *vi* (*effect, pain*) pasar.

● **wear out 1** *vt* gastar; *fig* (*exhaust*) agotar. **2** *vi* gastarse.

weary ['wɪərɪ] *a* (*tired*) cansado,-a.

weasel ['wi:zəl] comadreja *f*.

weather ['weðə'] tiempo *m*; **the w. is fine** hace buen tiempo; **to feel under the w.** no encontrarse bien.

weather forecast parte *m* meteorológico.

weave* [wi:v] *vt* tejer; (*intertwine*) entretejer.

web [web] (*of spider*) telaraña *f*.

wedding ['wedɪŋ] boda *f*.

wedding ring alianza *f*.

wedge [wedʒ] **1** *n* cuña *f*; (*for table leg*) calce *m*. **2** *vt* calzar.

Wednesday ['wenzdɪ] miércoles *m*.

weed [wi:d] mala hierba *f*.

week [wi:k] semana *f*; **a w. (ago) today/yesterday** hoy hace/ayer hizo una semana; **a w. today** de aquí a ocho días.

weekday día *m* laborable.

weekend fin *m* de semana; **at** *or* **on the w.** el fin de semana.

weekly 1 *a* semanal. **2** *adv* semanalmente. **3** *n* (*magazine*) semanario *m*.

weep* [wi:p] *vi* llorar.

weigh [weɪ] *vti* pesar.

weight peso *m*; **to lose w.** adelgazar; **to put on w.** engordar.

weird [wɪəd] *a* raro,-a.

welcome ['welkəm] **1** *a* (*person*) bienvenido,-a; (*news*) grato,-a; (*change*) oportuno,-a; **to make sb w.** acoger a algn calurosamente; **you're w.!** ¡no hay de qué! **2** *n* (*greeting*) bienvenida *f*. **3** *vt* acoger; (*more formally*) darle la bienvenida a; (*news*) acoger con agrado; (*decision*) aplaudir.

weld [weld] *vt* soldar.

welfare ['welfeə'] *US* (*social security*) seguridad *f* social.

well¹ [wel] (*for water*) pozo *m*.

well² 1 *a* (*healthy*) bien; **he's w.** está bien (de salud); **to get w.** reponerse; **all is w.** todo va bien. **2** *adv* (*properly*) bien; **w. done!** ¡muy bien!; **as w.** también; **as w. as** así como; **children as w. as adults** tanto niños como adultos. **3** *interj* (*surprise*) ¡vaya!; **w., as I was saying** pues (bien), como iba diciendo.

well-behaved *a* (*child*) formal; (*dog*) manso.

wellingtons ['welɪŋtənz] *npl* botas *fpl* de goma.

well-informed *a* bien informado,-a.

well-known *a* (bien) conocido,-a.

well-mannered *a* educado,-a.
well-off *a* acomodado,-a.
Welsh [welʃ] **1** *a* galés,-esa. **2** *n* (*language*) galés *m*; **the W.** *pl* los galeses.
Welshman galés *m*.
Welshwoman galesa *f*.
went [went] *pt of* **go**.
were [wɜːʳ, *unstressed* wəʳ] *pt of* **be**.
west [west] **1** *n* oeste *m*; **in** *or* **to the w.** al oeste. **2** *a* occidental. **3** *adv* al oeste.
westbound *a* (con) dirección oeste.
western 1 *a* del oeste, occidental. **2** *n* (*film*) western *m*.
westward ['westwəd] *a* hacia el oeste.
westwards ['westwədz] *adv* hacia el oeste.
wet [wet] **1** *a* mojado,-a; (*slightly*) húmedo,-a; (*rainy*) lluvioso,-a; **'w. paint'** 'recién pintado'. **2** *vt** mojar.
whale [weɪl] ballena *f*.
wharf [wɔːf] (*pl* **wharves** [wɔːvz]) muelle *m*.
what [wɒt] **1** *a* qué; **ask her w. colour she likes** pregúntale qué color le gusta. **2** *pron* (*in questions*) qué; **w. are you talking about?** ¿de qué estás hablando?; **he asked me w.** I thought me preguntó lo que pensaba; **I didn't know w. to say** no sabía qué decir; **w. about your father?** ¿y tu padre (qué)?; **w. about going tomorrow?** ¿qué te parece si vamos mañana?; **w. did you do that for?** ¿por qué hiciste eso?; **w. (did you say)?** ¿cómo?; **w. is it?** (*definition*) ¿qué es?; **what's the matter?** ¿qué pasa?; **w.'s it called?** ¿cómo se llama?; **w.'s this for?** ¿para qué sirve esto? **3** *interj* **w. a goal!** ¡qué golazo!
whatever 1 *a* **w. day you want** cualquier día que quieras; **of w. colour** no importa de qué color; **nothing w.** nada en absoluto; **with no interest w.** sin interés alguno. **2** *pron* (*anything, all that*) (todo) lo que; **do w. you like** haz lo que quieras; **don't tell him w. you do** no se te ocurra decírselo; **w. (else) you find** cualquier (otra) cosa que encuentres.
wheat [wiːt] trigo *m*.
wheel [wiːl] **1** *n* rueda *f*. **2** *vt* (*bicycle*) empujar.
wheelbarrow carretilla *f*.
wheelchair silla *f* de ruedas.
when [wen] **1** *adv* cuando; (*in questions*) cuándo; **w. did he arrive?** ¿cuándo llegó?; **tell me w. to go** dime cuándo he de irme; **the days w. I work** los días en que trabajo. **2** *conj* cuando; **I'll tell you w. she comes** te lo diré cuando llegue.
whenever *conj* (*when*) cuando; (*every time*) siempre que.
where [weəʳ] *adv* (*in questions*) dónde; (*direction*) adónde; (*at, in which*) donde; (*direction*) adonde; **w. are you going?** ¿adónde vas?; **w. do you**

come from? ¿de dónde es usted?; **tell me w. you went** dime adónde fuiste.

whereabouts 1 adv **w. do you live?** ¿por dónde vives? **2** n paradero m.

whereas conj (but, while) mientras que.

wherever conj dondequiera; **I'll find him w. he is** le encontraré dondequiera que esté; **sit w. you like** siéntate donde quieras.

whether ['weðə] conj (if) si; **I don't know w. it is true** no sé si es verdad; **I doubt w. he'll win** dudo que gane.

which [wɪtʃ] **1** a ¿qué? **w. colour do you prefer?** ¿qué color prefieres?; **w. one?** ¿cuál?; **w. way?** ¿por dónde?; **tell me w. dress you like** dime qué vestido te gusta. **2** pron (in questions) cuál, cuáles; **w. of you did it?** ¿quién de vosotros lo hizo? ‖ (relative) que; (after preposition) que, el/la que, los/las que; **here are the books (w.) I have read** aquí están los libros que he leído; **the accident (w.) I told you about** el accidente de que te hablé; **the car in w. he was travelling** el coche en (el) que viajaba; **this is the one (w.) I like** éste es el que me gusta; **I played three sets, all of w. I lost** jugué tres sets, todos los cuales perdí. ‖ (referring to a clause) lo cual; **he won, w. made me very happy** ganó, lo cual me alegró mucho.

whichever 1 a el/la que, cualquiera que; **I'll take w. books you don't want** tomaré los libros que no quieras; **w. system you choose** cualquiera que sea el sistema que elijas. **2** pron el que, la que.

while [waɪl] **1** conj (time) mientras; (although) aunque; (whereas) mientras que; **he fell asleep w. driving** se durmió mientras conducía. **2** n (length of time) rato m; **in a little w.** dentro de poco.

whim [wɪm] capricho m.

whine [waɪn] vi (child) lloriquear; (complain) quejarse.

whip [wɪp] **1** n (for punishment) látigo m. **2** vt (as punishment) azotar; (cream etc) batir.

whirl [wɜːl] vi **to w. (round)** girar con rapidez; (leaves etc) arremolinarse.

whisk [wɪsk] **1** n (for cream) batidor m; (electric) batidora f. **2** vt (cream etc) batir.

whiskers ['wɪskəs] (of cat) bigotes mpl.

whisky, US whiskey ['wɪskɪ] whisky m.

whisper ['wɪspə] **1** n susurro m. **2** vt decir en voz baja. **3** vi susurrar.

whistle ['wɪsəl] **1** n (instrument) pito m; (sound) silbido m. **2** vt (tune) silbar. **3** vi (person, kettle, wind) silbar; (train) pitar.

white [waɪt] **1** a blanco,-a, **to go w.** (face) palidecer; (hair) encanecer; **w. coffee** café m con leche. **2** n (colour, person, of eye) blanco m; (of egg) clara f.

whitewash vt (wall) blanquear.

Whitsun ['wɪtsən] pentecostés m.

whiz(z) [wɪz] vi (sound) silbar; **to w. past** pasar volando.

who [huː] pron (in questions) sing quién; pl quiénes; **w. are they?** ¿quiénes son?; **w. is it?** ¿quién es?; **I don't know w. did it** no sé quién lo hizo. ‖ *rel* (*defining*) que; (*nondefining*) quien, quienes, el/la cual, los/las cuales; **those w. don't know** los que no saben; **Elena's mother, w. is very rich ...** la madre de Elena, la cual es muy rica ...

whoever *pron* quienquiera que; **give it to w. you like** dáselo a quien quieras; **w. you are** quienquiera que seas.

whole [həʊl] **1** *a* (*entire*) entero,-a; (*in one piece*) intacto,-a; **a w. week** una semana entera; **he took the w. lot** se los llevó todos. **2** *n* **the w. of London** todo Londres; **on the w.** en general.

wholemeal *a* integral.

wholesale *adv* al por mayor.

wholesaler mayorista *mf*.

whom [hu:m] *pron* (*question*) a quién. ‖ (*after preposition*) of *or* from w.? ¿de quién? ‖ *rel* a quien, a quienes; **those w. I have seen** aquéllos a quienes he visto. ‖ *rel* (*after preposition*) quien, quienes, el/la cual, los/las cuales; **my brothers, both of w. are miners** mis hermanos, que son mineros los dos.

whooping cough ['hu:pɪŋkɒf] tos *f* ferina.

whose [hu:z] **1** *pron* de quién, de quiénes; **w. are these gloves?** ¿de quién son estos guantes? ‖ *rel* cuyo(s), cuya(s); **the man w. children we saw** el hombre a cuyos hijos vimos. **2** *a* **w. car/house is this?** ¿de quién es este coche/esta casa?

why [waɪ] *adv* por qué; (*for what purpose*) para qué; **w. did you do that?** ¿por qué hiciste eso?; **w. not go to bed?** ¿por qué no te acuestas?; **I don't know w. he did it** no sé por qué lo hizo; **there's no reason w. you shouldn't** go no hay motivo para que no vayas.

wick [wɪk] mecha *f*.

wicked ['wɪkɪd] *a* malvado,-a; (*awful*) malísimo,-a.

wicker ['wɪkəʳ] **1** *n* mimbre *f*. **2** *a* de mimbre.

wide [waɪd] **1** *a* (*road, trousers*) ancho,-a; (*area, knowledge, support, range*) amplio,-a; **it is ten metres w.** tiene diez metros de ancho. **2** *adv* **w. awake** completamente despierto,-a; **w. open** abierto,-a de par en par.

widely *adv* (*to travel etc*) extensamente.

widen 1 *vt* ensanchar; (*interests*) ampliar. **2** *vi* ensancharse.

widespread *a* (*unrest, belief*) general; (*damage*) extenso,-a.

widow ['wɪdəʊ] viuda *f*.

widower viudo *m*.

width [wɪdθ] anchura *f*.

wife [waɪf] (*pl* wives) esposa *f*.

wig [wɪg] peluca *f*.

wild [waɪld] *a* (*animal, tribe*) salvaje; (*plant*) silvestre; (*temperament, behaviour*) alocado,-a; (*appearance*) desordenado,-a; (*passions etc*) desenfrenado,-a.

wilderness ['wɪldənɪs] desierto *m*.

will¹ [wɪl] **1** *n* voluntad *f*; (*testament*) testamento *m*; **good/ill w.** buena/mala voluntad; **of my own free w.** por mi propia voluntad; **to make one's w.** hacer testamento. **2** *vt* **fate willed that ...** el destino quiso que ...

will² *v aux* **they w. come** vendrán; **w. he be there? – yes, he w.** ¿estará allí? – sí, (estará); **you w. *or* you'll tell him, won't you?** se lo dirás, ¿verdad?; **you w. be here at eleven!** ¡debes estar aquí a las once!; **be quiet, w. you! – no, I won't!** ¿quiere callarse? – no quiero; **will you have a drink? – yes, I w.** ¿quiere tomar algo? – sí, por favor.

willing *a* (*obliging*) complaciente; **to be w. to do sth** estar dispuesto,-a a hacer algo.

willingly *adv* de buena gana.

willingness buena voluntad *f*.

willow ['wɪləʊ] **w. (tree)** sauce *m*.

win [wɪn] **1** *n* victoria *f*. **2** *vt** ganar; (*prize*) llevarse; (*victory*) conseguir. **3** *vi** ganar.

wind¹ [wɪnd] viento *m*; (*in stomach*) gases *mpl*.

wind² [waɪnd] **1** *vt* (*onto a reel*) enrollar; (*clock*) dar cuerda a. **2** *vi* (*road, river*) serpentear.

● **wind back** *vt* (*film, tape*) rebobinar.

● **wind on** *vt* (*film, tape*) avanzar.

windmill ['wɪndmɪl] molino *m* (de viento).

window ['wɪndəʊ] ventana *f*; (*of vehicle, of ticket office etc*) ventanilla *f*; (**shop**) **w.** escaparate *m*.

window box jardinera *f*.

window cleaner limpiacristales *mf inv*.

windowpane cristal *m*.

windowsill alféizar *m*.

windscreen ['wɪndskriːn], *US* **windshield** parabrisas *m inv*; **w. wiper** limpiaparabrisas *m inv*.

windsurfing ['wɪndsɜːfɪŋ] windsurfing *m*.

windy ['wɪndɪ] *a* **it is very w. today** hoy hace mucho viento.

wine [waɪn] vino *m*; **w. list** lista *f* de vinos.

wineglass copa *f* (para vino).

wing [wɪŋ] ala *f*.

wink [wɪŋk] **1** guiño *m*. **2** *vi* (*person*) guiñar el ojo.

winner ['wɪnəʳ] ganador,-a *mf*.

winning *a* (*person, team*) ganador,-a; (*number*) premiado,-a.

winnings *npl* ganancias *fpl*.

winter ['wɪntəʳ] **1** *n* invierno *m*. **2** *a* de invierno.

wipe [waɪp] *vt* limpiar; **to w. one's feet/nose** limpiarse los pies/la nariz.

● **wipe away** vt (tear) enjugar.

● **wipe off** vt quitar frotando.

● **wipe out** vt (erase) borrar.

● **wipe up** vi secar los platos.

wiper (in vehicle) limpiaparabrisas m.

wire [waɪəʳ] alambre m; (electric) cable m.

wire mesh/netting tela f metálica.

wiring (of house) instalación f eléctrica.

wise [waɪz] a sabio,-a; **a w. man** un sabio; **it would be w. to keep quiet** sería prudente callarse.

wish [wɪʃ] 1 n (desire) deseo m (for de); **give your mother my best wishes** salude a su madre de mi parte; **with best wishes, Peter** (at end of letter) saludos de Peter. 2 vt (want) desear; **I w. I could stay longer** me gustaría poder quedarme más tiempo; **I w. you had told me!** ¡ojalá me lo hubieras dicho!; **to w. for sth** desear algo.

witch [wɪtʃ] bruja f.

with [wɪð] prep con; **the man w. the glasses** el hombre de las gafas; **w. no hat** sin sombrero; **he went w. me/you** fue conmigo/contigo; **he's w. Lloyds** trabaja para Lloyds; **to fill a vase w. water** llenar un jarrón de agua; **it is made w. butter** está hecho con mantequilla.

withdraw* 1 vt retirar; (statement) retractarse de; **to w. money from the bank** sacar dinero del banco. 2 vi retirarse; (drop out) renunciar.

wither ['wɪðəʳ] vi marchitarse.

within [wɪð'ɪn] prep (inside) dentro de; **w. five kilometres of the town** a menos de cinco kilómetros de la ciudad; **w. the hour** dentro de una hora; **w. the next five years** durante los cinco próximos años.

without [wɪð'aʊt] prep sin; **w. a coat** sin abrigo; **he did it w. my knowing** lo hizo sin que lo supiera yo.

witness ['wɪtnɪs] 1 n (person) testigo mf. 2 vt (see) presenciar.

wobbly a poco firme; (table, chair) cojo,-a.

wolf [wʊlf] (pl wolves) lobo m.

woman ['wʊmən] (pl women ['wɪmɪn]) mujer f; **old w.** vieja f.

wonder ['wʌndəʳ] 1 n **no w. he hasn't come** con razón no ha venido. 2 vt (ask oneself) preguntarse; **I w. why** ¿por qué será? 3 vi **it makes you w.** te da qué pensar.

wonderful a maravilloso,-a.

won't [wəʊnt] = **will not.**

wood [wʊd] (forest) bosque m; (material) madera f; (for fire) leña f.

wooden a de madera.

woodwork (craft) carpintería f.

wool [wʊl] lana f.

woollen, US woolen 1 a de lana. **2** npl **woollens** géneros mpl de lana.

word [wɜ:d] palabra *f*; **in other words . . .** es decir . . .; **I'd like a w. with you** quiero hablar contigo un momento; **words** (*of song*) letra *f*.

wording expresión *f*; **I changed the w. slightly** cambié algunas palabras.

word processing procesamiento *m* de textos.

word processor procesador *m* de textos.

wore [wɔ:ʳ] *pt of* wear.

work [wɜ:k] **1** *n* trabajo *m*; **his w. in the field of physics** su labor en el campo de la física; **out of w.** parado,-a; **a piece of w.** un trabajo; **a w. of art** una obra de arte; **works** (*factory*) fábrica *f*. **2** *vt* (*drive*) hacer trabajar; (*machine*) manejar; (*mechanism*) accionar. **3** *vi* trabajar (**on, at** en); (*machine*) funcionar; (*drug*) surtir efecto; (*system*) funcionar.

● **work out 1** *vt* (*plan*) idear; (*problem*) solucionar; (*solution*) encontrar; (*amount*) calcular. **2** *vi* (*train*) hacer ejercicio; **it works out at 5 each** sale a 5 cada uno.

worked up *a* **to get worked up** excitarse.

worker trabajador,-a *mf*; (*manual*) obrero,-a *mf*.

working *a* (*population, capital*) activo,-a; **w. class** clase obrera; **it is in w. order** funciona.

workman (*manual*) obrero *m*.

workout entrenamiento *m*.

workshop taller *m*.

work station estación *f* trabajo.

world [wɜ:ld] **1** *n* mundo *m*; **all over the w.** en todo el mundo. **2** *a* (*record, war*) mundial; **w. champion** campeón,-ona *mf* mundial; **The W. Cup** el Mundial *m*.

worm [wɜ:m] lombriz *f*.

worn [wɔ:n] *a* gastado,-a.

worn-out *a* (*thing*) gastado,-a; (*person*) agotado,-a.

worry ['wʌrɪ] **1** *vt* preocupar. **2** *vi* preocuparse (**about** por); **don't w.** no te preocupes. **3** *n* inquietud *f*; **my main w.** mi principal preocupación.

worrying *a* preocupante.

worse [wɜ:s] *a & adv* peor; **to get w.** empeorar; **w. than ever** peor que nunca.

worsen *vti* empeorar.

worship ['wɜ:ʃɪp] *vt* adorar.

worst [wɜ:st] **1** *a & adv* peor; **the w. part about it is that . . .** lo peor es que . . . **2** *n* (*person*) el/la peor, los/las peores.

worth [wɜ:θ] **1** *a* **a house w. £50,000** una casa que vale 50.000 libras; **a book w. reading** un libro que merece la pena leer; **how much is it w.?** ¿cuánto vale?; **it's w. your while, it's w. it** vale la pena. **2** *n* valor *m*; **five pounds' w. of petrol** gasolina por valor de 5 libras.

worthy ['wɜ:ðɪ] *a* (*deserving*) digno,-a (**of** de).

would [wʊd, *unstressed* wəd] *v aux* (*conditional*) **I w. go if I had time** iría si tuviera tiempo; **he w. have won but for that** habría ganado si no hubiera sido por eso. ▌ (*willingness*) **w. you do me a favour?** ¿quiere hacerme un favor? **w. you like a cigarette?** ¿quiere un cigarrillo?; **the car wouldn't start** el coche no arrancaba. ▌ (*custom*) **we w. go for walks** solíamos dar paseos.

wound [wuːnd] **1** *n* herida *f.* **2** *vt* herir.

wrap [ræp] *vt* envolver.

● **wrap up 1** *vt* envolver. **2** *vi* **w. up well!** ¡abrígate!

wrapper (*of sweet*) envoltorio *m.*

wrapping paper papel *m* de envolver.

wreath [riːθ] (*pl* **wreaths** [riːðz, riːθs]) (*of flowers*) corona *f.*

wreck [rek] **1** *n* (*sinking*) naufragio *m;* (*ship*) barco *m* naufragado; (*of car, plane*) restos *mpl.* **2** *vt* (*car, machine*) destrozar; (*holiday*) estropear.

wrench [rentʃ] (*tool*) *Br* llave *f* inglesa; *US* llave *f.*

wrestle ['resəl] *vi* luchar.

wrestler luchador,-a *mf.*

wrestling lucha *f.*

wring* [rɪŋ] *vt* (*clothes*) escurrir.

wrinkle ['rɪŋkəl] arruga *f.*

wrist [rɪst] muñeca *f.*

wristwatch reloj *m* de pulsera.

write* [raɪt] *vti* escribir (**about** sobre).

● **write back** *vi* contestar.

● **write down** *vt* poner por escrito; (*note*) apuntar.

● **write off for** *vt* pedir por escrito.

● **write out** *vt* (*cheque*) extender; (*recipe*) escribir.

write-protected *a* protegido,-a contra escritura.

writer (*by profession*) escritor,-a *mf;* (*of book, letter*) autor,-a *mf.*

writing (*script*) escritura *f;* (*handwriting*) letra *f;* **in w.** por escrito.

writing paper papel *m* de escribir.

wrong [rɒŋ] **1** *a* (*erroneous*) incorrecto,-a; (*unsuitable*) inadecuado,-a; (*time*) inoportuno,-a; (*not right*) (*person*) equivocado,-a; (*immoral etc*) malo,-a; **my watch is w.** mi reloj anda mal; **to go the w. way** equivocarse de camino; **I was w. about that boy** me equivoqué con ese chico; **to be w.** no tener razón; **what's w. with smoking?** ¿qué tiene de malo fumar? **what's w. with you?** ¿qué te pasa? **2** *adv* mal; **to get it w.** equivocarse; **to go w.** (*plan*) salir mal. **3** *n* (*evil, bad action*) mal *m;* **you did w. to hit him** hiciste mal en pegarle; **to be in the w.** tener la culpa.

wrongly *adv* (*incorrectly*) incorrectamente.

X

Xmas ['krɪsməs] *abbr of* **Christmas** Navidad *f*.
X-ray [eks'reɪ] **1** *n* (*picture*) radiografía *f*; **to have an X.** hacerse una radiografía. **2** *vt* radiografiar.

Y

yacht [jɒt] yate *m*.
yard[1] [jɑːd] (*measure*) yarda *f* (*aprox* 0.914 metros).
yard[2] patio *m*; *US* jardín *m*; (*of school*) patio *m* (de recreo).
yarn [jɑːn] hilo *m*.
yawn [jɔːn] **1** *vi* bostezar. **2** *n* bostezo *m*.
year [jɪəʳ] año *m*; (*at school*) curso *m*; **I'm ten years old** tengo diez años.
yearly *a* anual.
yeast [jiːst] levadura *f*.
yell [jel] **1** *vi* gritar (**at** a). **2** *n* grito *m*.
yellow ['jeləʊ] *a & n* amarillo,-a (*m*).
yes [jes] *adv* sí.
yesterday ['jestədeɪ] *adv* ayer; **the day before y.** anteayer; **y. morning** ayer por la mañana.
yet [jet] **1** *adv* **not y.** todavía no; **as y.** hasta ahora; **I haven't eaten y.** no he comido todavía. ‖ (*in questions*) ya; **has he arrived y.?** ¿ha venido ya? **2** *conj* (*nevertheless*) sin embargo.
yog(h)urt ['jɒgət] yogur *m*.
yolk [jəʊk] yema *f*.
you [juː] *pers pron* (*subject*) (*familiar use*) (*sing*) tú; (*pl*) vosotros,-as; (*polite use*) (*sing*) usted; (*pl*) ustedes; **how are y.?** ¿cómo estás?, ¿cómo estáis? ‖ (*object*) (*familiar use*) (*sing*) (*before verb*) te; (*after preposition*) ti; (*pl*) (*before verb*) os; (*after preposition*) vosotros,-as; **I saw y.** te vi, os vi; **with you** contigo, con vosotros,-as ‖ (*object*) (*polite use*) (*sing*) (*before verb*) le; (*after preposition*) usted; (*pl*) (*before verb*) les; (*after preposition*) ustedes; **I saw y.** le vi, les vi; **with you** con usted, con ustedes. ‖ (*subject*) (*impers use*) **y. never know** nunca se sabe.
young [jʌŋ] **1** *a* joven; (*brother etc*) pequeño,-a. **2** *n* **the y.** los jóvenes *mpl*; (*animals*) las crías *fpl*.
youngster muchacho,-a *mf*.

your [jɔ:, *unstressed* jə] *poss adj* (*familiar use*) (*referring to one person*) tu, tus; (*referring to more than one person*) vuestro,-a, vuestros,-as. ‖ (*polite use*) su, sus. ‖ (*impers use*) **the house is on y. right** la casa queda a la derecha; **they clean y. shoes for you** tc limpian los zapatos.

yours *poss pron* (*familiar use*) (*referring to one person*) el tuyo, la tuya, los tuyos, las tuyas; (*referring to more than one person*) el vuestro, la vuestra, los vuestros, las vuestras; **the house is y.** la casa es tuya. ‖ (*polite use*) el suyo, la suya; (*pl*) los suyos, las suyas; **the house is y.** la casa es suya.

yourself (*pl* **yourselves**) **1** *pers pron* (*familiar use*) *sing* tú mismo,-a; *pl* vosotros,-as mismos,-as; **by y.** (tú) solo; **by yourselves** vosotros,-as solos,-as. ‖ (*polite use*) *sing* usted mismo,-a; *pl* ustedes mismos,-as; **by y.** (usted) solo,-a; **by yourselves** (ustedes) solos,-as. **2** *reflexive pron* **did you wash y.?** (*familiar use*) *sing* ¿te lavaste?; *pl* ¿os lavasteis?; (*polite use*) *sing* ¿se lavó?, *pl* ¿se lavaron?

youth [ju:θ] juventud *f*; (*young man*) joven *m*.

youth club club *m* juvenil.

Yugoslav ['ju:gəʊslɑ:v] *a & n* yugoslavo,-a (*mf*).

Z

zebra ['zi:brə] cebra *f*.

zero ['zɪərəʊ] cero *m*.

zigzag ['zɪgzæg] **1** *n* zigzag *m*. **2** *vi* zigzaguear.

zip [zɪp] *n* **z. (fastener)** cremallera *f*.

● **zip up** *vt* subir la cremallera de.

zip code *US* código *m* postal.

zipper *US* cremallera *f*.

zit [zɪt] *fam* (pimple) espinilla *f*.

zone [zəʊn] zona *f*.

zoo [zu:] zoo *m*.

zucchini [zu:'ki:nɪ] *US* calabacín *m*.

SPANISH VERBS

Models for regular conjugation

TOMAR to take

INDICATIVE

PRESENT	FUTURE	CONDITIONAL
1. tomo	tomaré	tomaría
2. tomas	tomarás	tomarías
3. toma	tomará	tomaría
1. tomamos	tomaremos	tomaríamos
2. tomáis	tomaréis	tomaríais
3. toman	tomarán	tomarían

IMPERFECT	PRETERITE	PERFECT
1. tomaba	tomé	he tomado
2. tomabas	tomaste	has tomado
3. tomaba	tomó	ha tomado
1. tomábamos	tomamos	hemos tomado
2. tomabais	tomasteis	habéis tomado
3. tomaban	tomaron	han tomado

FUTURE PERFECT	CONDITIONAL PERFECT	PLUPERFECT
1. habré tomado	habría tomado	había tomado
2. habrás tomado	habrías tomado	habías tomado
3. habrá tomado	habría tomado	había tomado
1. habremos tomado	habríamos tomado	habíamos tomado
2. habréis tomado	habríais tomado	habíais tomado
3. habrán tomado	habrían tomado	habían tomado

SUBJUNCTIVE

PRESENT	IMPERFECT	PERFECT/PLUPERFECT
1. tome	tom-ara/ase	haya/hubiera* tomado
2. tomes	tom-aras/ases	hayas/hubieras tomado
3. tome	tom-ara/ase	haya/hubiera tomado
1. tomemos	tom-áramos/ásemos	hayamos/hubiéramos tomado
2. toméis	tom-arais/aseis	hayáis/hubierais tomado
3. tomen	tom-aran/asen	hayan/hubieran tomado

IMPERATIVE	*INFINITIVE*	*PARTICIPLE*
(tú) toma	**PRESENT**	**PRESENT**
(Vd) tome	tomar	tomando
(nosotros) tomemos		
(vosotros) tomad	**PERFECT**	**PAST**
(Vds) tomen	haber tomado	tomado

* the alternative form 'hubiese' etc is also possible

COMER to eat

INDICATIVE

PRESENT	FUTURE	CONDITIONAL
1. como	comere	comería
2. comes	comerás	comerías
3. come	comera	comería
1. comemos	comeremos	comeríamos
2. coméis	comeréis	comeríais
3. comen	comerán	comerían

IMPERFECT	PRETERITE	PERFECT
1. comía	comí	he comido
2. comías	comiste	has comido
3. comía	comio	ha comido
1. comíamos	comimos	hemos comido
2. comíais	comisteis	habéis comido
3. comían	comieron	han comido

FUTURE PERFECT	CONDITIONAL PERFECT	PLUPERFECT
1. habré comido	habría comido	había comido
2. habrás comido	habrías comido	habías comido
3. habrá comido	habría comido	había comido
1. habremos comido	habríamos comido	habíamos comido
2. habréis comido	habríais comido	habíais comido
3. habrán comido	habrían comido	habían comido

SUBJUNCTIVE

PRESENT	IMPERFECT	PERFECT/PLUPERFECT
1. coma	com-iera/iese	haya/hubiera* comido
2. comas	com-ieras/ieses	hayas/hubieras comido
3. coma	com-iera/iese	haya/hubiera comido
1. comamos	com-iéramos/iésemos	hayamos/hubiéramos comido
2. comáis	com-ierais/ieseis	hayáis/hubierais comido
3. coman	com-ieran/iesen	hayan/hubieran comido

IMPERATIVE	*INFINITIVE*	*PARTICIPLE*
(tú) come	PRESENT	PRESENT
(Vd) coma	comer	comiendo
(nosotros) comamos		
(vosotros) comed	PERFECT	PAST
(Vds) coman	haber comido	comido

* the alternative form 'hubiese' etc is also possible

PARTIR to leave

INDICATIVE

PRESENT	FUTURE	CONDITIONAL
1. parto	partiré	partiría
2. partes	partirás	partirías
3. parte	partirá	partiría
1. partimos	partiremos	partiríamos
2. partís	partiréis	partiríais
3. parten	partirán	partirían

IMPERFECT	PRETERITE	PERFECT
1. partía	partí	he partido
2. partías	partiste	has partido
3. partía	partió	ha partido
1. partíamos	partimos	hemos partido
2. partíais	partisteis	habéis partido
3. partían	partieron	han partido

FUTURE PERFECT	CONDITIONAL PERFECT	PLUPERFECT
1. habré partido	habría partido	había partido
2. habrás partido	habrías partido	habías partido
3. habrá partido	habría partido	había partido
1. habremos partido	habríamos partido	habíamos partido
2. habréis partido	habríais partido	habíais partido
3. habrán partido	habrían partido	habían partido

SUBJUNCTIVE

PRESENT	IMPERFECT	PERFECT/PLUPERFECT
parta	parti-era/ese	haya/hubiera* partido
partas	parti-eras/eses	hayas/hubieras partido
parta	parti-era/ese	haya/hubiera partido
partamos	parti- éramos/ésemos	hayamos/hubiéramos partido
partáis	parti-erais/eseis	hayáis/hubierais partido
partan	parti-eran/esen	hayan/hubieran partido

IMPERATIVE	INFINITIVE	PARTICIPLE
(tú) parte	PRESENT	PRESENT
(Vd) parta	partir	partiendo
(nosotros) partamos		
(vosotros) partid	PERFECT	PAST
(Vds) partan	haber partido	partido

* the alternative form 'hubiese' etc is also possible

ESTAR to be

INDICATIVE

PRESENT	FUTURE	CONDITIONAL
1. estoy	estaré	estaría
2. estás	estarás	estarías
3. está	estará	estaría
1. estamos	estaremos	estaríamos
2. estáis	estaréis	estaríais
3. están	estarán	estarían

IMPERFECT	PRETERITE	PERFECT
1. estaba	estuve	he estado
2. estabas	estuviste	has estado
3. estaba	estuvo	ha estado
1. estábamos	estuvimos	hemos estado
2. estabais	estuvisteis	habéis estado
3. estaban	estuvieron	han estado

FUTURE PERFECT	CONDITIONAL PERFECT	PLUPERFECT
1. habré	estado habría	estado había estado
2. habrás	estado habrías	estado habías estado
3. habrá	estado habría	estado había estado
1. habremos	estado habríamos	estadohabíamos estado
2. habréis	estado habríais	estado habíais estado
3. habrán	estado habrían	estado habían estado

SUBJUNCTIVE

PRESENT	IMPERFECT	PERFECT/PLUPERFECT
1. este	estuv-iera/iese	haya/hubiera* estado
2. estés	estuv-ieras/ieses	hayas/hubieras estado
3. este	estuv-iera/iese	haya/hubiera estado
1. estemos	estuv-iéramos/iésemos	hayamos/hubiéramos estado
2. estéis	estuv-ierais/ieseis	hayáis/hubierais estado
3. estén	estuv-ieran/iesen	hayan/hubieran estado

IMPERATIVE	*INFINITIVE*	*PARTICIPLE*
(tú) esta	PRESENT	PRESENT
(Vd) esté	estar	estando
(nosotros) estemos		
(vosotros) estad	PERFECT	PAST
(Vds) esten	haber estado	estado

* the alternative form 'hubiese' etc is also possible

HABER to have (auxiliary)

INDICATIVE

PRESENT	FUTURE	CONDITIONAL
1. he	habré	habría
2. has	habrás	habrías
3. ha/hay*	habrá	habría
1. hemos	habremos	habríamos
2. habéis	habréis	habríais
3. han	habrán	habrían

IMPERFECT	PRETERITE	PERFECT
1. había	hube	
2. habías	hubiste	
3. había	hubo	ha habido*
1. habíamos	hubimos	
2. habíais	hubisteis	
3. habían	hubieron	

FUTURE PERFECT	CONDITIONAL PERFECT	PLUPERFECT
1.		
2.		
3. habrá habido*	habría habido*	había habido*
1.		
2.		
3.		

SUBJUNCTIVE

PRESENT	IMPERFECT	PERFECT/PLUPERFECT
1. haya	hub-iera/iese	
2. hayas	hub-ieras/ieses	
3. haya	hub-iera/iese	haya/hubiera** habido*
1. hayamos	hub-iéramos/iésemos	
2. hayáis	hub-ierais/ieseis	
3. hayan	hub-ieran/iesen	

INFINITIVE PARTICIPLE

PRESENT	PRESENT
haber	habiendo
PERFECT	**PAST**
haber habido*	habido

* 'haber' is an auxiliary verb used with the participle of another verb to form compound tenses (eg he bebido - I have drunk). 'hay' means 'there is/are' and all third person singular forms in their respective tenses have this meaning. The forms highlighted with an asterisk are used only for this latter construction.

** the alternative form 'hubiese' is also possible

Models for irregular conjugation

[1] **pensar** *PRES* pienso, piensas, piensa, pensamos, pensáis, piensan; *PRES SUBJ* piense, pienses, piense, pensemos, penséis, piensen; *IMPERAT* piensa, piense, pensemos, pensad, piensen

[2] **contar** *PRES* cuento, cuentas, cuenta, contamos, contáis, cuentan; *PRES SUBJ* cuente, cuentes, cuente, contemos, contéis, cuenten; *IMPERAT* cuenta, cuente, contemos, contad, cuenten

[3] **perder** *PRES* pierdo, pierdes, pierde, perdemos, perdéis, pierden; *PRES SUBJ* pierda, pierdas, pierda, perdamos, perdáis, pierdan; *IMPERAT* pierde, pierda, perdamos, perded, pierdan

[4] **morder** *PRES* muerdo, muerdes, muerde, mordemos, mordéis, muerden; *PRES SUBJ* muerda, muerdas, muerda, mordamos, mordáis, muerdan; *IMPERAT* muerde, muerda, mordamos, morded, muerdan

[5] **sentir** *PRES* siento, sientes, siente, sentimos, sentís, sienten; *PRES SUBJ* sienta, sientas, sienta, sintamos, sintáis, sientan; *PRES P* sintiendo; *IMPERAT* siente, sienta, sintamos, sentid, sientan

[6] **vestir** *PRES* visto, vistes, viste, vestimos, vestís, visten; *PRES SUBJ* vista, vistas, vista, vistamos, vistáis, vistan; *PRES P* vistiendo; *IMPERAT* viste, vista, vistamos, vestid, vistan

[7] **dormir** *PRES* duermo, duermes, duerme, dormimos, dormís, duermen; *PRES SUBJ* duerma, duermas, duerma, durmamos, durmáis, duerman; *PRES P* durmiendo; *IMPERAT* duerme, duerma, durmamos, dormid, duerman

---

caer *PRES* caigo, caes, cae, caemos, caéis, caen; *PRES SUBJ* caiga, caigas, caiga, caigamos, caigáis, caigan; *PRES P* cayendo; *PP* caído; *IMPERAT* cae, caiga, caigamos, caed, caigan

conocer *PRES* conozco, conoces, conoce, conocemos, conocéis, conocen; *PRES SUBJ* conozca, conozcas, conozca, conozcamos, conozcáis, conozcan; *IMPERAT* conoce, conozca, conozcamós, conoced, conozcan

dar *PRES* doy, das, da, damos, dais, dan; *PRES SUBJ* dé, des, dé, demos, deis, den; *PRET* di, diste, dio, dimos, disteis, dieron; *IMPERF SUBJ* diera/diese; *IMPERAT* da, dé, demos, dad, den

decir *PRES* digo, dices, dice, decimos, decís, dicen; *PRES SUBJ* diga, digas, diga, digamos, digáis, digan; *FUT* diré; *COND* diría; *PRET* dije, dijiste, dijo, dijimos, dijisteis, dijeron; *IMPERF SUBJ* dijera/dijese; *PRES P* diciendo; *PP* dicho; *IMPERAT* di, diga, digamos, decid, digan

hacer *PRES* hago, haces, hace, hacemos, hacéis, hacen; *PRES SUBJ* haga, hagas, haga, hagamos, hagáis, hagan; *FUT* haré; *COND* haría; *PRET* hice, hiciste, hizo, hicimos, hicisteis, hicieron; *IMPERF SUBJ* hiciera/hiciese; *PP* hecho; *IMPERAT* haz, haga, hagamos, haced, hagan

ir *PRES* voy, vas, va, vamos, vais, van; *PRES SUBJ* vaya, vayas, vaya, vayamos, vayáis, vayan; *IMPERF* iba, ibas, iba, íbamos, ibais, iban; *PRET* fui, fuiste, fue, fuimos, fuisteis, fueron; *IMPERF SUBJ* fuera/fuese; *PRES P* yendo; *IMPERAT* ve, vaya, vamos, id, vayan

leer *PRET* leí, leíste, leyó, leímos, leísteis, leyeron; *IMPERF SUBJ* leyera/leyese; *PRES P* leyendo; *PP* leído; *IMPERAT* lee, lea, leamos, leed, lean

poder *PRES* puedo, puedes, puede, podemos, podéis, pueden; *PRES SUBJ* pueda, puedas, pueda, podamos, podáis, puedan; *FUT* podré; *COND* podría; *PRET* pude, pudiste, pudo, pudimos, pudisteis, pudieron; *IMPERF SUBJ* pudiera/pudiese; *PRES P* pudiendo; *IMPERAT* puede, pueda, podamos, poded, puedan

poner *PRES* pongo, pones, pone, ponemos, ponéis, ponen; *PRES SUBJ* ponga, pongas, ponga, pongamos, pongáis, pongan; *FUT* pondré; *COND* pondría; *PRET* puse, pusiste, puso, pusimos, pusisteis, pusieron; *IMPERF SUBJ* pusiera/pusiese; *PP* puesto; *IMPERAT* pon, ponga, pongamos, poned, pongan

querer *PRES* quiero, quieres, quiere, queremos, queréis, quieren; *PRES SUBJ* quiera, quieras, quiera, queramos, queráis, quieran; *FUT* querré; *COND* querría; *PRET* quise, quisiste, quiso, quisimos, quisisteis, quisieron; *IMPERF SUBJ* quisiera/quisiese; *IMPERAT* quiere, quiera, queramos, quered, quieran

saber *PRES* sé, sabes, sabe, sabemos, sabéis, saben; *PRES SUBJ* sepa, sepas, sepa, sepamos, sepáis, sepan; *FUT* sabré; *COND* sabría; *PRET* supe, supiste, supo, supimos, supisteis, supieron; *IMPERF SUBJ* supiera/supiese; *IMPERAT* sabe, sepa, sepamos, sabed, sepan

ser *PRES* soy, eres, es, somos, sois, son; *PRES SUBJ* sea, seas, sea, seamos, seáis, sean; *IMPERF* era, eras, era, éramos, erais, eran; *PRET* fui, fuiste, fue, fuimos, fuisteis, fueron; *IMPERF SUBJ* fuera/fuese; *IMPERAT* sé, sea, seamos, sed, sean

tener *PRES* tengo, tienes, tiene, tenemos, tenéis, tienen; *PRES SUBJ* tenga, tengas, tenga, tengamos, tengáis, tengan; *FUT* tendré; *COND* tendría; *PRET* tuve, tuviste, tuvo, tuvimos, tuvisteis, tuvieron; *IMPERF SUBJ* tuviera/tuviese; *IMPERAT* ten, tenga, tengamos, tened, tengan

venir *PRES* vengo, vienes, viene, venimos, venís, vienen; *PRES SUBJ* venga, vengas, venga, vengamos, vengáis, vengan; *FUT* vendré; *COND* vendría; *PRET* vine, viniste, vino, vinimos, vinisteis, vinieron; *IMPERF SUBJ* viniera/viniese; *PRES P* viniendo; *IMPERAT* ven, venga, vengamos, venid, vengan

VERBOS IRREGULARES INGLESES

infinitive	*past simple*	*past participle*
arise	arose	arisen
awake	awoke	awoken
be	was, were	been
bear	bore	borne
beat	beat	beaten
become	became	become
begin	began	begun
bend	bent	bent
bet	bet, betted	bet, betted
bid (offer)	bid	bid
bind	bound	bound
bite	bit	bitten
bleed	bled	bled
blow	blew	blown
break	broke	broken
breed	bred	bred
bring	brought [brɔːt]	brought
broadcast	broadcast	broadcast
build	built	built
burn	burnt, burned	burnt, burned
burst	burst	burst
buy	bought [bɔːt]	bought
cast	cast	cast
catch	caught [kɔːt]	caught
choose	chose	chosen
cling	clung	clung
come	came	come
cost	cost	cost
creep	crept	crept
cut	cut	cut
deal	dealt [delt]	dealt
dig	dug	dug
dive	dived, US dove [dəʊv]	dived
do	did	done
draw	drew	drawn
dream	dreamt, dreamed [dremt]	dreamt, dreamed
drink	drank	drunk
drive	drove	driven
eat	ate	eaten
fall	fell	fallen
feed	fed	fed
feel	felt	felt
fight	fought [fɔːt]	fought
find	found	found
flee	fled	fled
fling	flung	flung
fly	flew	flown
forbid	forbad(e)	forbidden

forecast	forecast	forecast
foresee	foresaw	foreseen
forget	forgot	forgotten
forgive	forgave	forgiven
freeze	froze	frozen
get	got	got, *US* gotten
give	gave	given
go	went	gone
grind	ground	ground
grow	grew	grown
hang	hung, hanged	hung, hanged
have	had	had
hear	heard [hɜːd]	heard
hide	hid	hidden
hit	hit	hit
hold	held	held
hurt	hurt	hurt
keep	kept	kept
kneel	knelt, kneeled	knelt, kneeled
know	knew	known
lay	laid	laid
lead	led	led
lean	leant [lent], leaned	leant, leaned
leap	leapt [lept], leaped	leapt, leaped
learn	learnt, learned	learnt, learned
leave	left	left
lend	lent	lent
let	let	let
lie	lay	lain
light	lit, lighted	lit, lighted
lose	lost	lost
make	made	made
mean	meant [ment]	meant
meet	met	met
mislay	mislaid	mislaid
mislead	misled	misled
mistake	mistook	mistaken
misunderstand	misunderstood	misunderstood
mow	mowed	mown, mowed
outdo	outdid	outdone
overcome	overcame	overcome
overdo	overdid	overdone
overtake	overtook	overtaken
pay	paid	paid
put	put	put
quit	quit	quit
read	read [red]	read
redo	redid	redone
rend	rent	rent
rewind	rewound	rewound

ride	rode	ridden
ring	rang	rung
rise	rose	risen
run	ran	run
saw	sawed	sawn, sawed
say	said [sed]	said
see	saw	seen
seek	sought [sɔːt]	sought
sell	sold	sold
send	sent	sent
set	set	set
sew	sewed	sewn, sewed
shake	shook	shaken
shear	sheared	shorn, sheared
shed	shed	shed
shine	shone	shone
shoot	shot	shot
show	showed	shown, showed
shrink	shrank, shrunk	shrunk
shut	shut	shut
sing	sang	sung
sink	sank	sunk
sit	sat	sat
sleep	slept	slept
slide	slid	slid
sling	slung	slung
slink	slunk	slunk
slit	slit	slit
smell	smelt, smelled	smelt, smelled
sneak	sneaked, *US* snuck	sneaked, *US* snuck
sow	sowed	sown, sowed
speak	spoke	spoken
speed	sped, speeded	sped, speeded
spell	spelt, spelled	spelt, spelled
spend	spent	spent
spill	spilt	spilt
spin	spun	spun
spit	spat	spat
split	split	split
spoil	spoilt, spoiled	spoilt, spoiled
spread	spread	spread
spring	sprang	sprung
stand	stood	stood
steal	stole	stolen
stick	stuck	stuck
sting	stung	stung
stink	stank	stunk
stride	strode	stridden
strike	struck	struck, stricken

string	strung	strung
strive	strove	striven
swear	swore	sworn
sweep	swep	swept
swell	swelled	swollen, swelled
swim	swam	swum
swing	swung	swung
take	took	taken
teach	taught [tɔːt]	taught
tear	tore	torn
tell	told	told
think	thought [θɔːt]	thought
throw	threw	thrown
thrust	thrust	thrust
tread	trod	trodden
undergo	underwent	undergone
understand	understood	understood
undertake	undertook	undertaken
undo	undid	undone
upset	upset	upset
wake	woke	woken
wear	wore	worn
weave	wove	woven
weep	wept	wept
wet	wet, wetted	wet, wetted
win	won [wʌn]	won
wind	wound [waʊnd]	wound
withdraw	withdrew	withdrawn
wring	wrung	wrung
write	wrote	written

PAÍSES Y REGIONES	COUNTRIES AND REGIONS
Africa *f* (*africano,-a*)	Africa (*African*)
Albania *f* (*albanés,-esa*)	Albania (*Albanian*)
Alemania *f* (*alemán, ana*)	Germany (*German*)
América *f* (*americano,-a*)	America (*American*)
A. Central/del Norte/del Sur *f*	Central/North/South America (*Central/North/South American*)
Antártida, *f* el Antártico *m* (*antártico,-a*)	Antarctica, the Antarctic (*Antarctic*)
Antillas *f* (*antillano,-a*)	the West Indies (*West Indian*)
Arabia *f* (*árabe*)	Arabia (*Arab, Arabic*)
Arabia Saudita *f* (*saudita, saudí Saudí*)	Saudi Arabia (*Saudi Arabian, Saudi*)
Argelia *f* (*argelino,-a*)	Algeria (*Algerian*)
Argentina *f* (*argentino,-a*)	Argentina (*Argentinian, Argentine*)
el Artico *m* (*ártico,-a*)	the Arctic (*Arctic*)
Asia *f* (*asiático,-a*)	Asia (*Asian*)
Australia *f* (*australiano,-a*)	Australia (*Australian*)
Austria *f* (*austríaco,-a*)	Austria (*Austrian*)
Baleares *fpl* (*balear*)	the Balearic Islands (*Balearic*)
Bélgica *f* (*belga*)	Belgium (*Belgian*)
Birmania *f* (*birmano,-a*)	Burma (*Burmese*)
Bolivia *f* (*boliviano,-a*)	Bolivia (*Bolivian*)
Brasil *m* (*brasileño,-a, brasilero,-a*)	Brazil (*Brazilian*)
Bulgaria *f* (*búlgaro,-a*)	Bulgaria (*Bulgarian*)
Canadá *m* (*canadiense*)	Canada (*Canadian*)
Canarias *fpl* (*canario,-a*)	Canaries
Centroamérica *f* (*centroamericano,-a*)	Central America (*Central American*)
Chile *m* (*chileno,-a*)	Chile (*Chilean*)
China *f* (*chino,-a*)	China (*Chinese*)
Chipre *m* (*chipriota*)	Cyprus (*Cypriot*)
Colombia *f* (*colombiano,-a*)	Colombia (*Colombian*)
Comunidad de Estados Independientes *f*	Commonwealth of Independent States
Córcega *f* (*corso,-a*)	Corsica (*Corsican*)
Corea *f* (*coreano,-a*)	Korea (*Korean*)
Costa Rica *f* (*costarricense, costarriqueño,-a*)	Costa Rica (*Costa Rican*)
Creta *f* (*cretense*)	Crete (*Cretan*)
Cuba *f* (*cubano,-a*)	Cuba (*Cuban*)
Dinamarca *f* (*danés,-esa*)	Denmark (*Danish*)
Ecuador *m* (*ecuatoriano,-a*)	Ecuador (*Ecuadorian*)
EE.UU. *abr de* Estados Unidos *mpl* (*estadounidense*)	United States of America, USA (*United States, American*)

Egipto m (egipcio,-a)	Egypt (Egyptian)
Eire m (irlandés,-esa)	Eire, Republic of Ireland (Irish)
El Salvador m (salvadoreño,-a)	El Salvador (Salvadoran, Salvadorian)
Escandinavia f (escandinavo,-a)	Scandinavia (Scandinavian)
Escocia f (escocés,-a)	Scotland (Scottish, Scots)
Eslovaquia f (eslovaco,-a)	Slovakia (Slovak)
España f (español,-a)	Spain (Spanish)
Estados Unidos mpl (estadounidense)	the United States (United States, American)
Etiopía f (etiope, etíope)	Ethiopia (Ethiopian)
Europa f (europeo,-a)	Europe (European)
Filipinas fpl (filipino,-a)	(the) Philippines (Philippine, Filipino)
Finlandia f (finlandés,-a)	Finland (Finnish)
Francia f (francés,-a)	France (French)
Gales f (el país de m) (galés,-esa)	Wales (Welsh)
Gibraltar m (gibraltareño,-a)	Gibraltar (Gibraltarian)
Gran Bretaña f (británico,-a)	Great Britain (British)
Grecia f.(griego,-a)	Greece (Greek)
Hispanoamérica f (hispanoamericano,-a)	Latin America (Latin American)
Holanda f (holandés,-esa)	Holland (Dutch)
Honduras f (hondureño,-a)	Honduras (Honduran)
Hungría f (húngaro,-a)	Hungary (Hungarian)
Iberoamérica f (iberoamericano,-a)	Latin America (Latin American)
India f (indio,-a)	India (Indian)
Indonesia f (indonesio,-a)	Indonesia (Indonesian)
Inglaterra f (inglés,-esa)	England (English)
Irak, Iraq m (iraquí)	Iraq (Iraqi)
Irán m (iraní)	Iran (Iranian)
Irlanda f (irlandés,-esa)	Ireland (Irish)
Irlanda del Norte f	Northern Ireland (Northern Irish)
Islandia f (islandés,-esa)	Iceland (Icelandic)
Israel m (israelí)	Israel (Israeli)
Italia f (italiano,-a)	Italy (Italian)
Jamaica f (jamaicano,-a)	Jamaica (Jamaican)
Japón m (japonés,-esa)	Japan (Japanese)
Kenia f (keniano,-a)	Kenya (Kenyan)
Latinoamérica f (latinomericano,-a)	Latin America (Latin American)
Letonia f (letón,-ona)	Latvia (Latvian)
Líbano m (libanés,-esa)	the Lebanon (Lebanese)
Libia f (libio,-a)	Libya (Libyan)
Lituania f (lituano,-a)	Lithuania (Lithuanian)

Luxemburgo *m* (*luxemburgués,-a*)	Luxembourg
Malasia *f* (*malayo,-a*)	Malaysia (*Malay*)
Mallorca *f* (*mallorquín,-ina*)	Majorca (*Majorcan*)
Marruecos *m* (*marroquí*)	Morocco (*Moroccan*)
Méjico, México *m* (*mejicano,-a, mexicano,-a*)	Mexico (*Mexican*)
Mongolia *f* (*mongol*)	Mongolia (*Mongolian*)
Nicaragua *f* (*nicaragüense, nicaragüeño,-a*)	Nicaragua (*Nicaraguan*)
Norteáfrica *f* (*norteafricano,-a*)	North Africa (*North African*)
Norteamérica *f* (*norteamericano,-a*)	North America (*(North) American*)
Noruega *f* (*noruego,-a*)	Norway (*Norwegian*)
Países Bajos *mpl* (*neerlandés,-esa*)	the Netherlands, the Low Countries (*Dutch*)
Pakistán, Paquistán *m* (*pakistaní, paquistaní*)	Pakistan (*Pakistani*)
Palestina *f* (*palestino,-a*)	Palestine (*Palestinian*)
Panamá *m* (*panameño,-a*)	Panama (*Panamanian*)
Paraguay *m* (*paraguayo,-a*)	Paraguay (*Paraguayan*)
Perú (el) *m* (*peruano,-a*)	Peru (*Peruvian*)
Polonia *f* (*polaco,-a*)	Poland (*Polish*)
Portugal *m* (*portugués,-a*)	Portugal (*Portuguese*)
Puerto Rico *m* (*portorriqueño,-a, puertorriqueño,-a*)	Puerto Rico (*Puerto Rican*)
República Checa *f* (*checo,-a*)	Czech Republic (*Czech*)
República Dominicana *f* (*dominicano,-a*)	Dominican Republic (*Dominican*)
Rumanía *f* (*rumano,-a*)	Rumania, Roumania (*Rumanian*)
Rusia *f* (*ruso,-a*)	Russia (*Russian*)
Sicilia *f* (*siciliano,-a*)	Sicily (*Sicilian*)
Siria *f* (*sirio,-a*)	Syria (*Syrian*)
Sudáfrica *f* (*sudafricano,-a*)	South Africa (*South African*)
Sudamérica *f* (*sudamericano,-a*)	South America (*South American*)
Suecia *f* (*sueco,-a*)	Sweden (*Swedish*)
Suiza *f* (*suizo,-a*)	Switzerland (*Swiss*)
Suramérica *f* (*suramericano,-a*)	South America (*South American*)
Tailandia *f* (*tailandés,-esa*)	Thailand (*Thai*)
Túnez *m* (*tunecino,-a*)	Tunisia (*Tunisian*)
Turquía *f* (*turco,-a*)	Turkey (*Turkish*)
Ucrania *f* (*ucraniano,-a*)	Ukraine (*Ukrainian*)
Uruguay *m* (*uruguayo,-a*)	Uruguay (*Uruguayan*)
Venezuela *f* (*venezolano,-a*)	Venezuela (*Venezuelan*)
Vietnam *m* (*vietnamita*)	Vietnam (*Vietnamese*)

A

a *prep* (*dirección*) to; **llegar a Valencia** to arrive in Valencia; **subir al tren** to get on the train. ‖ (*lugar*) at, on; **a la derecha** on the right; **a lo lejos** in the distance; **a mi lado** next to me; **al sol** in the sun. ‖ (*tiempo*) at; **a las doce** at twelve o'clock; **a los tres meses/la media hora** three months/half an hour later; **al final** in the end; **al principio** at first. ‖ (*distancia*) **a cien kilómetros de aquí** a hundred kilometres from here. ‖ (*manera*) **a mano** by hand. ‖ (*proporción*) **a 90 kilómetros por hora** at 90 kilometres an hour; **a 300 pesetas el kilo** three hundred pesetas a kilo; **tres veces a la semana** three times a week. ‖ **ganar cuatro a dos** to win four (to) two. ‖ (*complemento*) to; (*procedencia*) from; **díselo a Javier** tell Javier; **te lo di a ti** I gave it to you; **comprarle algo a algn** to buy sth from sb; (*para algn*) to buy sth for sb; **saludé a tu tía** I said hello to your aunt. ‖ *fam* **ir a por algn/algo** to go and fetch sb/sth. ‖ (*verbo* + *a* + *infinitivo*) to; **aprender a nadar** to learn (how) to swim. ‖ **a decir verdad** to tell (you) the truth; **a no ser que** unless; **a ver** let's see; **¡a comer!** food's ready!; **¡a dormir!** bedtime!; **¿a que no lo haces?** (*desafío*) I bet you don't do it!

abajo 1 *adv* (*en una casa*) downstairs; (*dirección*) down; **el piso de a.** the flat downstairs; **ahí/aquí a.** down there/here; **la parte de a.** the bottom (part); **más a.** further down; **hacia a.** down; **venirse a.** (*edificio*) to fall down. **2** *interj* **¡a. la censura!** down with censorship!

abalanzarse [4] *vr* **a. sobre/contra** to rush towards.

abalear *vt Am* to shoot at.

abandonar *vt* (*lugar*) to leave; (*persona, cosa*) to abandon; (*proyecto, plan*) to give up.

abanico *m* fan; (*gama*) range.

abarcar [1] *vt* to embrace; *Am* (*acaparar*) to monopolize.

abarrotado,-a *a* crammed (**de** with).

abarrotes *mpl Am* groceries.

abastecer 1 *vt* to supply. **2 abastecerse** *vr* to stock up (**de** *o* **con** with).

abatible *a* folding; **asiento a.** folding seat.

abatir 1 *vt* (*derribar*) to knock down; (*desanimar*) to depress. **2 abatirse** *vr* (*desanimarse*) to become depressed.

abdicar [1] *vti* to abdicate.

abdominales *mpl* sit-ups.

abecedario *m* alphabet.

abedul *m* birch.

abeja *f* bee; **a. reina** queen bee.

abejorro *m* bumblebee.

abertura *f* (*hueco*) opening; (*grieta*) crack.

abeto *m* fir (tree).

abierto,-a *a* open; (*grifo*) (turned) on; (*persona*) open-minded.

abismo *m* abyss.

ablandar 1 *vt* to soften. **2 ablandarse** *vr* to go soft; *fig* (*persona*) to mellow.

abnegado,-a *a* selfless.

abogado,-a *mf* lawyer; (*en tribunal supremo*) barrister; **a. defensor** counsel for the defence.

abolir *vt defectivo* to abolish.

abollar *vt* to dent.

abonado,-a *mf* subscriber.

abono *m* (*producto*) fertilizer; (*estiércol*) manure; (*pago*) payment; (*billete*) season ticket.

aborrecer *vt* to detest.

aborto *m* miscarriage; (*provocado*) abortion.

abrasar 1 *vti* to scorch. **2 abrasarse** *vr* to burn.

abrazadera *f* clamp.

abrazar 1 [4] *vt* to embrace. **2 abrazarse** *vr* **abrazarse a algn** to embrace sb; **se abrazaron** they embraced each other.

abrazo *m* hug.

abrelatas *m inv* can opener.

abreviar 1 *vt* to shorten; (*texto*) to abridge; (*palabra*) to abbreviate. **2** *vi* to be quick *o* brief; **para a.** to cut a long story short.

abreviatura *f* abbreviation.

abridor *m* (*de latas, botellas*) opener.

abrigado,-a *a* wrapped up.

abrigar [7] **1** *vt* to keep warm; (*esperanza*) to cherish; (*duda*) to harbour. **2** *vi* **esta chaqueta abriga mucho** this cardigan is very warm.

abrigo *m* (*prenda*) coat; **ropa de a.** warm clothes *pl*.

abril *m* April.

abrir[1] *m* **en un a. y cerrar de ojos** in the twinkling of an eye.

abrir[2] (*pp* **abierto**) **1** *vi* to open. **2** *vt* to open; (*cremallera*) to undo; (*gas, grifo*) to turn on. **3 abrirse** *vr* to open; **abrirse paso** to make one's way.

abrochar *vt*, **abrocharse** *vr* (*botones*) to do up; (*camisa*) to button (up); (*cinturón*) to fasten; (*zapatos*) to tie up; (*cremallera*) to do up.

abrumar *vt* to overwhelm.

abrupto,-a *a* (*terreno*) steep.

absceso *m* abscess.

absolutamente *adv* absolutely.

absoluto,-a *a* absolute; **en a.** not at all.

absolver [4] (*pp* **absuelto**) *vt* to acquit.

absorbente *a* (*papel*) absorbent; (*fascinante*) engrossing.

absorber *vt* to absorb.

absorto,-a *a* engrossed (**en** in).

abstenerse *vr* to abstain (**de** from); (*privarse*) refrain (**de** from).

abstracto,-a *a* abstract.

abstraído,-a *a* (*ensimismado*) engrossed (**en** in).

absuelto,-a *a pp de* **absolver.**

absurdo,-a *a* absurd.

abuchear *vt* to boo.

abuela *f* grandmother; *fam* grandma, granny.

abuelo *m* grandfather; *fam* grandad, grandpa; **abuelos** grandparents.

abultado,-a *a* bulky.

abundancia *f* abundance; ... **en a.** plenty of ...

abundante *a* abundant.

aburrido,-a *a* **ser a.** to be boring; **estar a.** to be bored; (*harto*) to be tired (**de** of).

aburrimiento *m* boredom; **¡qué a.!** what a bore!.

aburrir 1 *vt* to bore. 2 **aburrirse** *vr* to get bored.

abusar *vi* (*propasarse*) to go too far; **a. de** (*situación, persona*) to take (unfair) advantage of; (*poder, amabilidad*) to abuse; **a. de la bebida/del tabaco** to drink/smoke too much *o* to excess.

abuso *m* abuse.

a. C. *abr de* **antes de Cristo** before Christ, BC.

acá *adv* (*lugar*) over here; **más a.** nearer; **¡ven a.!** come here!

acabar 1 *vt* to finish (off); (*completar*) to complete. 2 *vi* to finish; **a. de ...** to have just ...; **acaba de entrar** he has just come in; **acabaron casándose** *o* **por casarse** they ended up getting married. 3 **acabarse** *vr* to finish; **se nos acabó la gasolina** we ran out of petrol.

acacia *f* acacia.

academia *f* academy.

académico,-a *a & mf* academic.

acalorado,-a *a* hot; (*debate etc*) heated.

acampar *vi* to camp.

acantilado *m* cliff.

acaparar *vt* (*productos*) to hoard; (*mercado*) to corner.

acariciar *vt* to caress; (*pelo, animal*) to stroke.

acarrear *vt* (*transportar*) to transport; (*conllevar*) to entail.

acaso *adv* perhaps, maybe; **por si a.** just in case; **si a. viene ...** if he should come ...

acatar *vt* to comply with.

acatarrado,-a *a* **estar a.** to have a cold.

acceder *vi* **a. a** (*consentir*) to consent to.

accesible *a* accessible; (*persona*) approachable.

acceso *m* (*entrada*) access; (*en carretera*) approach.

accesorio,-a *a & m* accessory.

accidentado,-a 1 *a* (*terreno*) uneven; (*viaje, vida*) eventful. **2** *mf* casualty.

accidental *a* accidental; **un encuentro a.** a chance meeting.

accidente *m* accident; **a. laboral** industrial accident.

acción *f* action; (*acto*) act; (*en la bolsa*) share; **poner en a.** to put into action; **película de a.** adventure film.

accionar *vt* to drive.

accionista *mf* shareholder.

acechar *vt* to lie in wait for.

aceite *m* oil; **a. de girasol/maíz/oliva** sunflower/corn/olive oil.

aceituna *f* olive; **a. rellena** stuffed olive.

acelerador *m* accelerator.

acelerar *vti* to accelerate.

acento *m* accent; (*énfasis*) stress.

acentuar 1 *vt* to stress. **2 acentuarse** *vr* to become more pronounced.

aceptar *vt* to accept.

acequia *f* irrigation ditch *o* channel.

acera *f* pavement, *US* sidewalk.

acerca *adv* **a. de** about.

acercar [1] **1** *vt* to bring (over). **2 acercarse** *vr* to approach (**a -**); (*ir*) to go; (*venir*) to come.

acero *m* steel; **a. inoxidable** stainless steel.

acérrimo,-a *a* (*partidario*) staunch; (*enemigo*) bitter.

acertado,-a *a* (*solución*) correct; (*decisión*) wise.

acertar [1] **1** *vt* (*pregunta*) to get right; (*adivinar*) to guess correctly. **2** *vi* to be right.

acertijo *m* riddle.

achacar [1] *vt* (*atribuir*) to attribute.

achaque *m* ailment.

achicharrar *vt* to burn to a crisp.

acholado,-a *a Am* half-caste.

achuchar *vt* (*empujar*) to shove.

aciago,-a *a* ill-fated.

acicalarse *vr* to dress up.

acidez *f* (*de sabor*) sharpness; **a. de estómago** heartburn.

ácido,-a 1 *a* (*sabor*) sharp. **2** *m* acid.

acierto *m* (*buena decisión*) good choice.

aclamar *vt* to acclaim.

aclarado *m* rinse.

aclarar 1 *vt* (*explicar*) to clarify; (*color*) to make lighter; (*enjuagar*) to rinse. **2** *v impers* (*tiempo*) to clear (up). **3 aclararse** *vr* **aclararse la voz** to clear one's throat.

aclimatarse *vr* **a. a algo** to get used to sth.

acné *f* acne.

acogedor,-a *a* (*habitación*) cosy.

acoger [5] **1** *vt* (*recibir*) to receive; (*persona desvalida*) to take in. **2 acogerse** *vr* **acogerse a** to take refuge in; **acogerse a la ley** to have recourse to the law.

acometer *vt* (*emprender*) to undertake; (*atacar*) to attack.

acomodado,-a *a* well-off.

acomodador,-a *mf* (*hombre*) usher; (*mujer*) usherette.

acomodar 1 *vt* (*alojar*) to accommodate; (*en cine etc*) to find a place for. **2 acomodarse** *vr* (*instalarse*) to make oneself comfortable; (*adaptarse*) to adapt.

acompañante 1 *mf* companion. **2** *a* accompanying.

acompañar *vt* to accompany; **¿te acompaño a casa?** can I walk you home?; (*en funeral*) **le acompaño en el sentimiento** my condolences.

acomplejar 1 *vt* to give a complex. **2 acomplejarse** *vr* **acomplejarse por** to develop a complex about.

acondicionado,-a *a* **aire a.** air conditioning.

acondicionador *m* conditioner.

aconsejar *vt* to advise.

acontecimiento *m* event.

acopio *m* **hacer a. de** to store.

acordar [2] **1** *vt* to agree; (*decidir*) to decide. **2 acordarse** *vr* to remember.

acordeón *m* accordion.

acordonar *vt* (*zona*) to cordon off.

acorralar *vt* to corner.

acortar *vt* to shorten.

acoso *m* harassment; **a. sexual** sexual harassment.

acostar [2] **1** *vt* to put to bed. **2 acostarse** *vr* to go to bed.

acostumbrado,-a *a* usual; **es lo a.** it is the custom; **a. al frío/calor** used to the cold/heat.

acostumbrar 1 *vi* **a. a** (*soler*) to be in the habit of. **2** *vt* **a. a algn a algo** (*habituar*) to get sb used to sth. **3 acostumbrarse** *vr* (*habituarse*) to get used (**a** to).

acotejar *vt Am* to arrange.

acre *m* (*medida*) acre.

acreditar *vt* to be a credit to; (*probar*) to prove.

acreedor,-a *mf* creditor.

acrílico,-a *a* acrylic.

acriollarse *vr Am* to adopt local customs.

acrobacia *f* acrobatics *sing*.

acta *f* (*de reunión*) minutes *pl*; (*certificado*) certificate.

actitud *f* attitude.

actividad *f* activity.

activo,-a *a* active.

acto *m* act; (*ceremonia*) ceremony; (*de teatro*) act; **en el a.** at once; **a. seguido** immediately afterwards.

actor *m* actor.

actriz *f* actress.

actuación *f* performance; (*intervención*) intervention.

actual *a* current, present.

actualidad *f* present time; (*hechos*) current affairs *pl*; **en la a.** at present.

actualmente *adv* (*hoy en día*) nowadays.

actuar *vi* to act.

acuarela *f* watercolour.

acuario *m* aquarium.

acuciante *a* urgent.

acudir *vi* (*ir*) to go; (*venir*) to come.

acuerdo *m* agreement; **¡de a.!** all right!, OK!; **de a. con** in accordance with; **ponerse de a.** to agree.

acumular *vt*, **acumularse** *vr* to accumulate.

acuñar *vt* (*moneda*) to mint; (*frase*) to coin.

acurrucarse [1] *vr* to curl up.

acusación *f* accusation; (*en juicio*) charge.

acusado,-a 1 *mf* accused. 2 *a* (*marcado*) marked.

acusar 1 *vt* to accuse (*de* of); (*en juicio*) to charge (*de* with). 2 **acusarse** *vr* (*acentuarse*) to become more pronounced.

acústica *f* acoustics *sing*.

acústico,-a *a* acoustic.

adaptador *m* adapter.

adaptar 1 *vt* to adapt; (*ajustar*) to adjust. 2 **adaptarse** *vr* to adapt (oneself) (**a** to).

adecuado,-a *a* appropriate.

a. de J.C. *abr de* **antes de Jesucristo** before Christ, BC.

adelantado,-a *a* advanced; (*desarrollado*) developed; (*reloj*) fast; **pagar por a.** to pay in advance.

adelantamiento *m* overtaking.

adelantar 1 *vt* to bring forward; (*reloj*) to put forward; (*en carretera*) to overtake; (*fecha*) to bring forward. 2 *vi* to advance; (*progresar*) to make progress; (*reloj*) to be fast. 3 **adelantarse** *vr* (*ir delante*) to go ahead; (*reloj*) to be fast.

adelante 1 *adv* forward; **más a.** (*lugar*) further on; (*tiempo*) later. 2

interj **¡a!** *(pase)* come in!

adelanto *m* advance; *(progreso)* progress; **el reloj lleva diez minutos de a.** the watch is ten minutes fast.

adelgazar [4] *vi* to slim.

ademán *m* gesture.

además *adv* moreover, furthermore; **a. de él** besides him.

adherir [5] **1** *vt* to stick on. **2 adherirse** *vr* **adherirse a** to adhere to.

adhesión *f* adhesion.

adicción *f* addiction.

adicto,-a 1 *mf* addict. **2** *a* addicted (**a** to).

adiestrar *vt* to train.

adinerado,-a *a* wealthy.

adiós *(pl* **adioses)** *interj* goodbye; *fam* bye-bye; *(al cruzarse)* hello.

aditivo,-a *a* & *m* additive.

adivinanza *f* riddle.

adivinar *vt* to guess.

adjetivo,-a *m* adjective.

adjudicar 1 *vt* *(premio, contrato)* to award; *(en subasta)* to sell. **2 adjudicarse** *vr* to appropriate.

adjuntar *vt* to enclose.

adjunto,-a 1 *a* enclosed, attached. **2** *mf* *(profesor)* assistant teacher.

administración *f* *(gobierno)* authorities *pl*; *(de empresa)* management; *(oficina)* (branch) office; **a. central** *(gobierno)* central government; **a. pública** civil service.

administrador,-a 1 *mf* administrator. **2** *a* administrating.

administrar *vt* to administer; *(dirigir)* to run.

administrativo,-a 1 *a* administrative. **2** *mf* *(funcionario)* official.

admiración *f* admiration; *(ortográfica)* exclamation mark.

admirar 1 *vt* to admire; *(sorprender)* to amaze. **2 admirarse** *vr* to be amazed.

admisión *f* admission.

admitir *vt* to let in; *(aceptar)* to accept; *(permitir)* to allow; *(reconocer)* to acknowledge.

ADN *m abr de* **ácido desoxirribonucleico** desoxyribonucleic acid, DNA.

adobe *m* adobe.

adobo *m* marinade.

adolescencia *f* adolescence.

adolescente *a* & *mf* adolescent.

adónde *adv* where (to)?

adonde *adv* where.

adondequiera *adv* wherever.

adopción *f* adoption.

adoptar *vt* to adopt.

adoptivo,-a *a* (*hijo*) adopted; (*padres*) adoptive.

adorar *vt* to worship.

adormecer 1 *vt* to make sleepy. **2 adormecerse** *vr* (*dormirse*) to doze off; (*brazo etc*) to go numb.

adornar *vt* to adorn.

adorno *m* decoration; **de a.** decorative.

adosado,-a *a* adjacent; (*casa*) semidetached.

adquirir *vt* to acquire; (*comprar*) to purchase.

adquisición *f* acquisition; (*compra*) purchase.

adrede *adv* deliberately, on purpose.

aduana *f* customs *pl*.

aduanero,-a *mf* customs officer.

aducir *vt* to adduce.

adueñarse *vr* **a. de** to take over.

aduje *pt indef de* **aducir.**

adular *vt* to adulate.

adulterar *vt* to adulterate.

adulterio *m* adultery.

adulto,-a *a & mf* adult.

aduzco *indic pres de* **aducir.**

adverbio *m* adverb.

adversario,-a 1 *mf* opponent. **2** *a* opposing.

adversidad *f* adversity; (*revés*) setback.

adverso,-a *a* adverse.

advertencia *f* warning.

advertir [5] *vt* to warn; (*informar*) to advise; (*notar*) to notice.

adviento *m* Advent.

adyacente *a* adjacent.

aéreo,-a *a* aerial; (*correo, transporte*) air; **por vía aerea** by air.

aerodinámico,-a *a* aerodynamic; **de línea aerodinámica** streamlined.

aeromoza *f Am* air hostess.

aeronáutico,-a *a* **la industria aeronáutica** the aeronautics industry.

aeroplano *m* light aeroplane.

aeropuerto *m* airport.

aerosol *m* aerosol.

afable *a* affable.

afán *m* (*pl* **afanes**) (*esfuerzo*) effort; (*celo*) zeal.

afanarse *vr* **a. por conseguir algo** to do one's best to achieve sth.

afección *f* disease.

afectar *vi* **a. a** to affect; **le afectó mucho** she was deeply affected.

afecto,-a *m* affection; **tomarle a. a algn** to become fond of sb.

afectuoso,-a *a* affectionate.

afeitar *vt*, **afeitarse** *vr* to shave.

afeminado,-a *a* effeminate.

aferrarse *vr* to cling (**a** to).

afianzar [4] *vt* to strengthen.

afición *f* liking; **tiene a. por la música** he is fond of music; (*de deporte*) **la a.** the fans *pl*.

aficionado,-a 1 *mf* enthusiast; (*no profesional*) amateur. **2** *a* keen; (*no profesional*) amateur; **ser a. a algo** to be fond of sth.

aficionarse *vr* to take a liking (**a** to).

afilado,-a *a* sharp.

afiliarse *vr* **a. a** to become a member of.

afinar *vt* (*puntería*) to sharpen; (*instrumento*) to tune.

afinidad *f* affinity.

afirmación *f* statement.

afirmar *vt* (*aseverar*) to state; (*afianzar*) to strengthen.

afligir [6] **1** *vt* to afflict. **2 afligirse** *vr* to be distressed.

aflojar 1 *vt* to loosen. **2 aflojarse** *vr* (*rueda*) to work loose.

afluencia *f* influx; **gran a. de público** great numbers of people.

afluente *m* tributary.

afónico,-a *a* **estar a.** to have lost one's voice.

afortunado,-a *a* fortunate.

afrontar *vt* to confront; **a. las consecuencias** to face the consequences.

afuera 1 *adv* outside; **la parte de a.** the outside; **más a.** further out. **2 afueras** *fpl* outskirts.

agachar 1 *vt* to lower. **2 agacharse** *vr* to duck.

agarrar 1 *vt* to grasp; *Am* to take; **agárralo fuerte** hold it tight. **2 agarrarse** *vr* to hold on.

agasajar *vt* to smother with attentions.

agazaparse *vr* to crouch (down).

agencia *f* agency; (*sucursal*) branch; **a. de viajes** travel agency; **a. de seguros** insurance agency; **a. inmobiliaria** estate agency.

agenda *f* diary.

agente *mf* agent; **a. de policía** (*hombre*) policeman; (*mujer*) policewoman; **a. de seguros** insurance broker.

ágil *a* agile.

agilidad *f* agility.

agilizar [4] *vt* (*trámites*) to speed up.

agitación *f* agitation; (*inquietud*) restlessness.

agitado,-a *a* agitated; (*persona*) anxious; (*mar*) rough.

agitar 1 *vt* (*botella*) to shake. **2 agitarse** *vr* (*persona*) to become agitated.

aglomeración *f* (*de gente*) crowd.

agobiante *a* (*trabajo*) overwhelming; (*lugar*) claustrophobic; (*calor*) oppressive; (*persona*) tiresome.

agobiar 1 *vt* to overwhelm. **2 agobiarse** *vr* (*angustiarse*) to worry too much.

agobio *m* (*angustia*) anxiety; (*sofoco*) suffocation.

agolparse *vr* to crowd.

agonía *f* last days.

agonizar [4] *vi* to be dying.

agosto *m* August.

agotado,-a *a* (*cansado*) exhausted; (*existencias*) sold out; (*provisiones*) exhausted; (*libro*) out of print.

agotador,-a *a* exhausting.

agotamiento *m* exhaustion.

agotar 1 *vt* (*cansar*) to exhaust; (*acabar*) to use up (completely). **2 agotarse** *vr* (*acabarse*) to run out; (*producto*) to be sold out; (*persona*) to become exhausted *o* tired out.

agradable *a* pleasant.

agradar *vi* to please; **no me agrada** I don't like it.

agradecer *vt* (*dar las gracias*) to thank for; (*estar agradecido*) to be grateful to; **te lo agradezco mucho** thank you very much.

agradecimiento *m* gratitude.

agrandar 1 *vt* to enlarge. **2 agrandarse** *vr* to become larger.

agrario,-a *a* agrarian.

agravar 1 *vt* to aggravate. **2 agravarse** *vr* to get worse.

agredir *vt defectivo* to assault.

agregado,-a *a* **profesor a.** (*de escuela*) secondary school teacher; (*de universidad*) assistant teacher.

agregar [7] *vt* (*añadir*) to add.

agresión *f* aggression.

agresivo,-a *a* aggressive.

agrícola *a* agricultural.

agricultor,-a *mf* farmer.

agricultura *f* agriculture.

agrietar 1 *vt* to crack; (*piel, labios*) to chap. **2 agrietarse** *vr* to crack; (*piel*) to get chapped.

agringarse [7] *vr Am* to behave like a gringo.

agrio,-a *a* sour.

agropecuario,-a *a* agricultural.

agrupación *f* association.

agua** *f* water; **a. potable** drinking water; **a. corriente/del grifo** running/tap water; **a. dulce/salada** fresh/salt water; **a. mineral sin/con gas** still/fizzy mineral water.

aguacate *m* (*fruto*) avocado (pear).

aguacero *m* downpour.

aguanieve *f* sleet.

aguantar 1 *vt* (*soportar*) to tolerate; (*sostener*) to support; **no lo aguanto más** I can't stand it any longer; **aguanta la respiración** hold your breath. **2 aguantarse** *vr* (*contenerse*) to keep back; (*resignarse*) to resign oneself; **no pude aguantarme la risa** I couldn't help laughing.

aguardar 1 *vt* to await. **2** *vi* to wait.

aguardiente *m* brandy.

aguarrás *m* turpentine.

aguatero,-a *mf Am* water carrier *o* seller.

agudizar [4] *vt*, **agudizarse** *vr* to intensify.

agudo,-a *a* (*dolor*) acute; (*voz*) high-pitched; (*sonido*) high.

aguijón *m* sting.

águila** *f* eagle.

aguja *f* needle; (*de reloj*) hand; (*de tocadiscos*) stylus.

agujerear *vt* to make holes in.

agujero *m* hole; **a. negro** black hole.

agujetas *fpl* **tener a.** to be stiff.

aguzar [4] *vt* **a. el oído** to prick up one's ears; **a. la vista** to look attentively.

ahí *adv* there; **a. está** there he/she/it is; **por a.** (*en esa dirección*) that way; (*aproximadamente*) over there.

ahínco *m* **con a.** eagerly.

ahogado,-a 1 *a* (*en líquido*) drowned; (*asfixiado*) suffocated; **morir a.** to drown. **2** *mf* drowned person.

ahogar [7] *vt*, **ahogarse** *vr* (*en líquido*) to drown; (*asfixiar*) to suffocate; (*motor*) to flood.

ahora 1 *adv* now; **a. mismo** right now; **de a. en adelante** from now on; **por a.** for the time being; **a. voy** I'm coming; **hasta a.** (*hasta el momento*) until now, so far; (*hasta luego*) see you later. **2** *conj* **a. bien** (*sin embargo*) however.

ahorcar [1] **1** *vt* to hang. **2 ahorcarse** *vr* to hang oneself.

ahorita *adv Am* right now.

ahorrar *vt* to save.

ahorros *mpl* savings; **caja de a.** savings bank.

ahuevado *a Am* stupid.

ahumado,-a *a* (*smoked*; (*bacon*) smoky.

ahuyentar *vt* to scare away.

aindiado,-a *a Am* Indian-like.

airado,-a *a* angry.

aire *m* air; (*de automóvil*) choke; (*viento*) wind; (*aspecto*) appearance; **a.**

acondicionado air conditioning; **al a.** (*al descubierto*) uncovered; **al a. libre** in the open air; **en el a.** (*pendiente*) in the air; **tomar el a.** to get some fresh air; **cambiar de aires** to change one's surroundings; **darse aires** to put on airs.

aislado,-a *a* isolated; *(cable)* insulated.

aislante 1 *a* **cinta a.** insulating tape. **2** *m* insulator.

aislar *vt* to isolate; *(cable)* to insulate.

ajedrez *m* (*juego*) chess; (*piezas y tablero*) chess set.

ajeno,-a *a* belonging to other people; **por causas ajenas a nuestra voluntad** for reasons beyond our control.

ajetreado,-a *a* hectic.

ajo *m* garlic; **cabeza/diente de a.** head/clove of garlic.

ajustado,-a *a* tight.

ajustar *vt* to adjust; *(apretar)* to tighten.

ajuste *m* adjustment; *(de precio)* fixing; *(de cuenta)* settlement; **a. de cuentas** settling of scores.

ajusticiar *vt* to execute.

al (*contracción de* **a** & **el**) *ver* **a**; (**al** + *infinitivo*) **al salir** on leaving.

ala *f* wing; (*de sombrero*) brim.

alabar *vt* to praise.

alabastro *m* alabaster.

alambrada *f*, **alambrado** *m* wire fence.

alambre *m* wire; **a. de púas** barbed wire.

álamo *m* poplar.

alarde *m* (*ostentación*) bragging; **hacer a. de** to show off.

alardear *vi* to brag.

alargadera *f* (*cable*) extension.

alargado,-a *a* elongated.

alargar [7] **1** *vt* to lengthen; (*estirar*) to stretch; (*prolongar*) to prolong; (*dar*) to pass. **2 alargarse** *vr* to get longer; (*prolongarse*) to go on.

alarido *m* shriek; **dar un a.** to howl.

alarma *f* alarm; **falsa a.** false alarm; **señal de a.** alarm (signal).

alarmar 1 *vt* to alarm. **2 alarmarse** *vr* to be alarmed.

alba** *f* dawn.

albañil *m* bricklayer; (*obrero*) building worker.

albaricoque *m* (*fruta*) apricot; (*árbol*) apricot tree.

alberca *f* (*poza*) (small) reservoir.

albergar [7] **1** *vt* (*alojar*) to house. **2 albergarse** *vr* to stay.

albergue *m* (*lugar*) hostel; (*refugio*) refuge; **a. juvenil** youth hostel.

albino,-a *a* & *mf* albino.

albóndiga *f* meatball.

albornoz *m* bathrobe.

alborotar 1 *vt* (*desordenar*) to turn upside down. **2** *vi* to kick up a racket. **3 alborotarse** *vr* to get excited; (*mar*) to get rough.

albufera *f* lagoon.

álbum *m* album.

alcachofa *f* artichoke.

alcalde *m* mayor.

alcaldesa *f* mayoress.

alcance *m* reach; **dar a. a** to catch up with; **fuera del a. de los niños** out of the reach of children.

alcantarilla *f* sewer; (*boca*) drain.

alcanzar [4] **1** *vt* to reach; (*persona*) to catch up with; (*conseguir*) to achieve. **2** *vi* (*ser suficiente*) to be sufficient.

alcaparra *f* (*fruto*) caper.

alcayata *f* hook.

alcazaba *f* citadel.

alcázar *m* (*fortaleza*) fortress; (*castillo*) castle.

alcoba *f* bedroom.

alcohol *m* alcohol.

alcoholemia *f* **prueba de a.** breath test.

alcohólico,-a *a & mf* alcoholic.

alcoholímetro *m* Breathalyzer(R).

alcornoque *m* cork oak.

alcurnia *f* ancestry.

aldea *f* village.

aleccionador,-a *a* (*ejemplar*) exemplary.

alegar [7] *vt* (*aducir*) to claim.

alegrar 1 *vt* (*complacer*) to make glad; **me alegra que se lo hayas dicho** I am glad you told her. **2 alegrarse** *vr* to be glad; **me alegro de verte** I am pleased to see you.

alegre *a* (*contento*) glad; (*color*) bright; (*música*) lively.

alegría *f* happiness.

alejado,-a *a* remote.

alejar 1 *vt* to move further away. **2 alejarse** *vr* to go away.

alemán,-ana 1 *a & mf* German. **2** *m* (*idioma*) German.

alentar [1] *vt* to encourage.

alergia *f* allergy.

alérgico,-a *a* allergic.

alerta *f & a* alert.

aleta *f* (*de pez*) fin; (*de foca, de nadador*) flipper.

aletargar [7] **1** *vt* to make lethargic. **2 aletargarse** *vr* to become lethargic.

aletear *vi* to flutter *o* flap its wings.

alfabetización *f* **campaña de a.** literacy campaign.

alfabeto *m* alphabet.

alfalfa *f* alfalfa grass.

alfarería *f* pottery.

alféizar *m* windowsill.

alférez *m* second lieutenant.

alfil *m* (*ajedrez*) bishop.

alfiler *m* pin.

alfombra *f* rug; (*moqueta*) carpet.

alga *f* (*marina*) seaweed.

álgebra** *f* algebra.

álgido,-a *a* **el punto a.** the climax.

algo 1 *pron indef* (*afirmativo*) something; (*interrogativo*) anything; (*cantidad indeterminada*) some; **a. así** something like that; **¿a. más?** anything else?; **¿queda a. de pastel?** is there any cake left? **2** *adv* (*un poco*) somewhat; **está a. mejor** she's feeling a bit better.

algodón *m* cotton; **a. (hidrófilo)** cotton wool, *US* absorbent cotton.

alguacil *m* bailiff.

alguien *pron indef* (*afirmativo*) somebody, someone; (*interrogativo*) anybody, anyone.

algún *a* (*delante de nombres masculinos en singular*) *ver* **alguno,-a.**

alguno,-a 1 *a* (*delante de nombre*) (*afirmativo*) some; (*interrogativo*) any; **alguna que otra vez** now and then; **¿le has visto alguna vez?** have you ever seen him?; **no vino persona alguna** nobody came. **2** *pron indef* someone, somebody; **algunos,-as** some (people).

alhaja *f* jewel.

alhelí *m* (*pl* **alhelíes**) wallflower.

aliado,-a *a* allied.

alianza *f* (*pacto*) alliance; (*anillo*) wedding ring.

aliarse *vr* to become allies.

alicates *mpl* pliers *pl.*

aliciente *m* (*atractivo*) charm; (*incentivo*) incentive.

aliento *m* breath; **sin a.** breathless.

aligerar 1 *vt* (*carga*) to lighten; (*acelerar*) to speed up; **a. el paso** to quicken one's pace. **2** *vi fam* **¡aligera!** hurry up!

alijo *m* haul; **un a. de drogas** a consignment of drugs.

alimaña *f* vermin.

alimentación *f* (*comida*) food; (*acción*) feeding.

alimentar 1 *vt* (*dar alimento*) to feed; (*ser nutritivo para*) to be nutritious for. **2 alimentarse** *vr* **alimentarse con** *o* **de** to live on.

alimenticio,-a *a* nutritious; **valor a.** nutritional value.

alimento *m* food.

alinear 1 *vt* to align. **2 alinearse** *vr* to line up.

aliñar *vt* to season; (*ensalada*) to dress.

alistar *vt*, **alistarse** *vr* (*en el ejército*) to enlist.

aliviar 1 *vt* (*dolor*) to relieve; (*carga*) to lighten. **2 aliviarse** *vr* (*dolor*) to diminish.

allá *adv* (*lugar alejado*) over there; **a. abajo/arriba** down/up there; **más a.** further on; **más a. de** beyond; **a. tú** that's your problem.

allí *adv* there; **a. abajo/arriba** down/up there; **por a.** (*movimiento*) that way; (*posición*) over there.

alma** *f* soul.

almacén *m* (*local*) warehouse; **grandes almacenes** department store.

almacenar *vt* to store.

almanaque *m* calendar.

almeja *f* clam.

almendra *f* almond.

almendro *m* almond tree.

almíbar *m* syrup.

almirante *m* admiral.

almizcle *m* musk.

almohada *f* pillow.

almohadón *m* large pillow.

almorrana *f fam* pile.

almorzar [2] **1** *vi* to have lunch. **2** *vt* to have for lunch.

almuerzo *m* lunch.

aló *interj Am* hello.

alojar 1 *vt* to accommodate. **2 alojarse** *vr* to stay.

alojamiento *m* accommodation, *US* accommodations; **dar a.** to accommodate.

alondra *f* lark.

alpargata *f* canvas sandal.

alpinismo *m* mountaineering.

alpinista *mf* mountaineer.

alquilar *vt* to hire; (*pisos, casas*) to rent; **'se alquila'** 'to let', 'for rent'.

alquiler *m* (*acción*) hiring; (*de pisos, casas*) letting; (*precio*) rental; (*de pisos, casas*) rent; **a. de coches** car hire; **de a.** (*pisos, casas*) to let; (*coche*) for hire; **en una casa de a.** in a rented house.

alquitrán *m* tar.

alrededor 1 *adv* (*lugar*) round. **2** *prep* **a. de** round; **a. de quince** about fifteen. **3 alrededores** *mpl* surrounding area *sing*.

alta *f* **dar de** *o* **el a.** (*a un enfermo*) to discharge from hospital.

altamente *adv* extremely.

altanero,-a *a* arrogant.

altar *m* altar.

altavoz *m* loudspeaker.

alteración *f* (*cambio*) alteration; (*alboroto*) quarrel; (*excitación*) agitation.

alterar 1 *vt* to alter. **2 alterarse** *vr* (*inquietarse*) to be upset.

altercado *m* argument.

alternar 1 *vt* to alternate. **2** *vi* (*relacionarse*) to socialize. **3 alternarse** *vr* to alternate.

alternativa *f* alternative.

alterno,-a *a* alternate.

altibajos *mpl* ups and downs.

altitud *f* altitude.

altivez *f* arrogance.

alto¹ *m* (*interrupción*) stop; **dar el a. a algn** to tell sb to stop; **un a. el fuego** a cease-fire.

alto,-a² *a* (*persona, árbol, edificio*) tall; (*montaña, techo, presión*) high; (*sonido*) loud; (*precio, tecnología*) high; (*agudo*) high; **en lo a.** at the top; **clase alta** upper class; **en voz alta** aloud; **a altas horas de la noche** late at night. **2** *adv* high; (*fuerte*) loud; **¡habla más a.!** speak up. **3** *m* (*altura*) height; **¿cuánto tiene de a.?** how tall/high is it?

altoparlante *m Am* loudspeaker.

altura *f* height; (*nivel*) level; **de diez metros de a.** ten metres high; **estar a la a. de las circunstancias** to meet the challenge; *fig* **a estas a.** by now.

alubia *f* bean.

alud *m* avalanche.

aludir *vi* to allude.

alumbrar 1 *vt* (*iluminar*) to illuminate. **2** *vi* (*parir*) to give birth.

aluminio *m* aluminium, *US* aluminum.

alumno,-a *mf* (*de colegio*) pupil; (*de Universidad*) student.

alusión *f* allusion.

alverjana *f Am* pea.

alza** *f* rise; **en a.** rising.

alzamiento *m* (*rebelión*) uprising.

alzar [4] **1** *vt* to raise; **a. los ojos/la vista** to look up. **2 alzarse** *vr* (*levantarse*) to rise; (*rebelarse*) to rebel.

ama *f* (*dueña*) owner; **a. de casa** housewife.

amabilidad *f* kindness; **tenga la a. de esperar** would you be so kind as to wait.

amable *a* kind, nice.

amaestrar *vt* (*animal*) to train; (*domar*) to tame.

amainar *vi* (*viento etc*) to die down.

amamantar *vt* to breast-feed; (*entre animales*) to suckle.

amanecer 1 *v impers* **¿a qué hora amanece?** when does it get light?; **amaneció lluvioso** it was rainy at daybreak. **2** *vi* **amanecimos en Finlandia** we were in Finland at daybreak; **amaneció muy enfermo** he woke up feeling very ill. **3** *m* dawn; **al a.** at dawn.

amanerado,-a *a* affected.

amante *mf* lover.

amapola *f* poppy.

amar 1 *vt* to love. **2 amarse** *vr* to love each other.

amargar [7] **1** *vt* to make bitter; (*relación*) to embitter. **2 amargarse** *vr* to become embittered.

amargo,-a *a* bitter.

amargor *m*, **amargura** *f* bitterness.

amarillo,-a *a & m* yellow.

amarilloso,-a *Am* yellowish.

amarrar *vt* (*atar*) to tie (up).

amasar *vt* to knead.

amateur *a & mf* amateur.

ámbar *m* amber.

ambición *f* ambition.

ambicioso,-a 1 *a* ambitious. **2** *mf* ambitious person.

ambiental *a* environmental.

ambiente 1 *m* environment. **2** *a* environmental; **temperatura a.** room temperature.

ambiguo,-a *a* ambiguous.

ámbito *m* field.

ambos,-as *a pl* both.

ambulancia *f* ambulance.

ambulatorio *m* surgery.

amedrentar *vt* to frighten.

amenaza *f* threat.

amenazador,-a, amenazante *a* threatening.

amenazar [4] *vt* to threaten.

ameno,-a *a* entertaining.

americana *f* (*prenda*) jacket.

americano,-a *a* American.

ametralladora *f* machine gun.

amígdala *f* tonsil.

amigdalitis *f* tonsillitis.

amigo,-a *mf* friend; **hacerse amigos** to become friends; **son muy amigos** they are very good friends.

aminorar *vt* to reduce; **a. el paso** to slow down.

amistad *f* friendship; **amistades** friends.

amnistía *f* amnesty.

amo *m* (*dueño*) owner.

amodorrarse *vr* to become sleepy.

amoldar *vt*, **amoldarse** *vr* to adapt.

amonestación *f* reprimand.

amontonar 1 *vt* to pile up. **2 amontonarse** *vr* to pile up; (*gente*) to crowd together.

amor *m* love; **hacer el a.** to make love; **a. propio** self-esteem.

amoratado,-a *a* (*de frío*) blue with cold; (*de un golpe*) black and blue.

amordazar [4] *vt* (*a una persona*) to gag.

amoroso,-a *a* loving.

amortiguador *m* (*de vehículo*) shock absorber.

amortiguar *vt* (*golpe*) to cushion; (*ruido*) to muffle.

amortizar [4] *vt* to pay off.

amotinar 1 *vt* to incite to riot. **2 amotinarse** *vr* to rise up.

amparar 1 *vt* to protect. **2 ampararse** *vr* to seek refuge.

ampliación *f* enlargement; (*de plazo, casa*) extension.

ampliar *vt* to enlarge; (*casa, plazo*) to extend.

amplificador *m* amplifier.

amplio,-a *a* large; (*ancho*) broad.

ampolla *f* blister; (*de medicina*) ampoule.

amputar *vt* (*vejiga*) to amputate.

amueblar *vt* to furnish.

amuleto *m* amulet.

anaconda *f* anaconda.

anacronismo *m* anachronism.

anales *mpl* annals.

analfabeto,-a *mf* illiterate.

analgésico,-a *a* & *m* analgesic.

análisis *m inv* analysis; **a. de sangre** blood test.

analizar [4] *vt* to analyze.

analogía *f* analogy.

análogo,-a *a* analogous.

ananá *m* (*pl* **ananaes**), **ananás** *m* (*pl* **ananases**) pineapple.

anarquista *a* & *mf* anarchist.

andaluz,-a *a* & *mf* Andalusian.

antártico,-a 1 *a* Antarctic. **2 m el A.** the Antarctic.

anatomía *f* anatomy.

ancho,-a 1 *a* wide, broad; **a lo a.** breadthwise; **te está muy a.** it's too big for you. **2** *m* (*anchura*) width, breadth; **dos metros de a.** two metres wide; **¿qué a. tiene?** how wide is it?

anchoa *f* anchovy.

anchura *f* width, breadth.

anciano,-a *a* **1** very old. **2** *mf* old person.

ancla** *f* anchor.

andamiaje *m* scaffolding.

andamio *m* scaffold.

andar *m*, **andares** *mpl* gait *sing*.

andar 1 *vi* to walk; (*coche etc*) to move; (*funcionar*) to work; *fam* **anda por los cuarenta** he's about forty; **¿cómo andamos de tiempo?** how are we off for time?; **tu bolso debe a. por ahí** your bag must be over there somewhere. **2** *vt* (*recorrer*) to walk.

andariego,-a *a* fond of walking.

andén *m* platform.

andinismo *m* *Am* mountaineering.

andino,-a *a* & *mf* Andean.

andrajo *m* rag.

anécdota *f* anecdote.

anegar *vt*, **anegarse** *vr* [7] to flood.

anejo,-a *a* attached (**a** to).

anemia *f* anaemia.

anestesia *f* anaesthesia.

anexión *f* annexation.

anexionar *vt* to annex.

anexo,-a **1** *a* attached (**a** to). **2** *m* appendix.

anfitrión,-ona **1** *m* host. **2** *f* hostess.

ángel *m* angel; *Am* (*micrófono*) hand microphone.

angina *f* **tener anginas** to have tonsillitis; **a. de pecho** angina pectoris.

anglosajón,-ona *a* & *mf* Anglo-Saxon.

angosto,-a *a* narrow.

anguila *f* eel.

angula *f* elver.

ángulo *m* angle.

angustia *f* anguish.

anhídrido *m* **a. carbónico** carbon dioxide.

anilla *f* ring.

anillo *m* ring.

animado,-a *a* (*fiesta etc*) lively.

animadversión *f* animosity.

animal 1 *m* animal; *fig* (*basto*) brute. **2** *a* animal.

animar 1 *vt* (*alentar*) to encourage; (*alegrar*) (*persona*) to cheer up; (*fiesta, bar*) to liven up. **2 animarse** *vr* (*persona*) to cheer up; (*fiesta, reunión*) to brighten up.

ánimo *m* (*valor, coraje*) courage; **estado de á.** state of mind; **con á. de**

with the intention of; **¡a.!** cheer up!

aniquilar *vt* to annihilate.

anís *m* (*bebida*) anisette.

aniversario *m* anniversary.

anoche *adv* last night; (*por la tarde*) yesterday evening; **antes de a.** the night before last.

anochecer 1 *v impers* to get dark. **2** *m* nightfall.

anodino,-a *a* (*insustancial*) insubstantial; (*soso*) insipid.

anómalo,-a *a* anomalous.

anónimo,-a 1 *a* (*desconocido*) anonymous; **sociedad anónima** public liability company, *US* corporation. **2** *m* (*carta*) anonymous letter.

anorak *m* (*pl* **anoraks**) anorak.

anormal *a* abnormal; (*inhabitual*) unusual.

anotar *vt* (*apuntar*) to note down.

anquilosarse *vr* to stagnate.

ansiar *vt* to long for.

ansiedad *f* anxiety; **con a.** anxiously.

antagonismo *m* antagonism.

antaño *adv* in the past.

ante¹ *m* (*piel*) suede.

ante² *prep* (*delante de*) in the presence of; (*en vista de*) faced with; **a. todo** most of all.

anteanoche *adv* the night before last.

anteayer *adv* the day before yesterday.

antecedente 1 *a* previous. **2 antecedentes** *mpl* (*historial*) record *sing*; **a. penales** criminal record *sing*.

antecesor,-a *mf* (*en un cargo*) predecessor.

antelación *f* **con un mes de a.** a month beforehand.

antemano *adv* **de a.** beforehand, in advance.

antena *f* (*de radio, television*) aerial; (*de animal*) antenna; **a. parabólica** dish aerial; **en a.** on the air.

anteojo *m* telescope; **anteojos** (*binoculares*) binoculars; *Am* (*gafas*) glasses, spectacles.

antepecho *m* (*de ventana*) sill.

antepenúltimo,-a *a* **el capítulo a.** the last chapter but two.

anteproyecto *m* draft; **a. de ley** draft bill.

antepuesto,-a *pp* de **anteponer.**

antepuse *pt indef* de **anteponer.**

anterior *a* previous; (*delantero*) front.

anteriormente *adv* previously.

antes 1 *adv* before; (*antaño*) in the past; **mucho a.** long before; **cuanto a.** as soon as possible; **a. prefiero hacerlo yo** I'd rather do it myself; **a. (bien)**

on the contrary. **2** *prep* **a. de** before.

antiadherente *a* nonstick.

antibiótico,-a *a & m* antibiotic.

anticaspa *a* anti-dandruff.

anticipar 1 *vt* (*acontecimiento*) to bring forward; (*dinero*) to pay in advance. **2 anticiparse** *vr* (*llegar pronto*) to arrive early; **él se me anticipó** he beat me to it.

anticonceptivo,-a *a & m* contraceptive.

anticongelante *a & m* (*de radiador*) antifreeze; (*de parabrisas*) de-icer.

anticonstitucional *a* unconstitutional.

anticuado,-a *a* antiquated.

anticuario,-a *mf* antique dealer.

anticuerpo *m* antibody.

antídoto *m* antidote.

antifaz *m* mask.

antigüedad *f* (*período histórico*) antiquity; (*en cargo*) seniority; **tienda de antigüedades** antique shop.

antiguo,-a *a* old; (*pasado de moda*) old-fashioned; (*anterior*) former.

antihistamínico *m* antihistamine.

antiniebla *a inv* **luces a.** foglamps.

antipático,-a *a* unpleasant.

antirrobo 1 *a inv* **alarma a.** burglar alarm; (*para coche*) car alarm. **2** *m* burglar alarm; (*para coche*) car alarm.

antiséptico,-a *a & m* antiseptic.

antojarse *vr* **cuando se me antoja** when I feel like it; **se le antojó un helado** he fancied an ice-cream.

antojo *m* (*capricho*) whim; (*de embarazada*) craving.

antorcha *f* torch.

antropología *f* anthropology.

anual *a* annual.

anudar *vt* (*atar*) to knot.

anular *vt* (*matrimonio*) to annul; (*ley*) to repeal.

anunciar *vt* (*producto etc*) to advertise; (*avisar*) to announce.

anuncio *m* (*comercial*) advertisment; (*aviso*) announcement; (*cartel*) notice.

anzuelo *m* (fish) hook.

añadir *vt* to add (**a** to).

añejo,-a *a* (*vino, queso*) mature.

año *m* year; **el a. pasado** last year; **el a. que viene** next year; **hace años** a long time ago; **los años noventa** the nineties; **todo el a.** all the year (round); **¿cuántos a. tienes?** how old are you?; **tiene seis a.** he's six years old.

añorar *vt* to long for.

apacible *a* mild.

apagar [7] *vt* (*fuego*) to put out; (*luz, tele etc*) to switch off.

apagón *m* power cut.

apaisado,-a *a* (*papel*) landscape.

aparador *m* (*mueble*) sideboard.

aparato *m* (piece of) apparatus; (*dispositivo*) device; (*instrumento*) instrument; **a. de radio/televisión** radio/television set; **a. digestivo** digestive system.

aparcamiento *m* (*en la calle*) parking place; (*parking*) car park, US parking lot.

aparcar [1] *vti* to park.

aparecer 1 *vi* to appear; **no aparece en mi lista** he is not on my list; (*en un sitio*) to turn up; **¿apareció el dinero?** did the money turn up?; **no apareció nadie** nobody turned up. 2 **aparecerse** *vr* to appear.

aparejador,-a *mf* quantity surveyor.

aparejo *m* (*equipo*) equipment.

aparentar 1 *vt* (*simular*) to affect; (*tener aspecto*) **no aparenta esa edad** she doesn't look that age. 2 *vi* to show off.

apariencia *f* appearance; **en a.** apparently; **guardar las apariencias** to keep up appearances.

apartamento *m* (small) flat, apartment.

apartar 1 *vt* (*alejar*) to remove; (*guardar*) to put aside. 2 *vi* **aparta** move out of the way. 3 **apartarse** *vr* (*alejarse*) to move away.

aparte 1 *adv* aside; **modestia/bromas a.** modesty/joking apart; **eso hay que pagarlo a.** (*separadamente*) you have to pay for that separately; **punto y a.** full stop, new paragraph. 2 *prep* **a. de eso** (*además*) besides that; (*excepto*) apart from that.

apasionado,-a *a* passionate.

apasionante *a* exciting.

apasionar *vt* to excite.

apático,-a 1 *a* apathetic. 2 *mf* apathetic person.

apearse *vi* (*de un autobús, tren*) to get off; (*de un coche*) to get out.

apedrear *vt* to throw stones at.

apelar *vi* (*sentencia*) to appeal; (*recurrir*) to resort (**a** to).

apellido *m* surname; **a. de soltera** maiden name.

apenar 1 *vt* to grieve. 2 **apenarse** *vr* to be grieved; *Am* (*avergonzarse*) to be ashamed.

apenas *adv* (*casi no*) hardly, scarcely; **a. (si) hay nieve** there is hardly any snow; **a. llegó, sonó el teléfono** scarcely had he arrived when the phone rang.

apéndice *m* appendix.

apendicitis *f* appendicitis.

aperitivo *m* (*bebida*) apéritif; (*comida*) appetizer.

apertura *f* (*comienzo*) opening.

apestar *vi* to stink (**a** of).

apetecer *vi* ¿**qué te apetece para cenar?** what would you like for supper?; ¿**te apetece ir al cine?** do you fancy going to the cinema?

apetito *m* appetite; **tengo mucho apetito** I'm really hungry.

apiadarse *vr* to take pity (**de** on).

apilar *vt*, **apilarse** *vr* to pile up.

apiñarse *vr* to crowd together.

apio *m* celery.

apisonadora *f* steamroller, *US* roadroller.

aplacar [1] *vt*, **aplacarse** *vr* to calm down.

aplanar *vt* to level.

aplastar *vt* to squash.

aplaudir *vt* to applaud.

aplauso *m* applause.

aplazamiento *m* postponement.

aplazar [4] *vt* to postpone.

aplicar [1] **1** *vt* to apply. **2 aplicarse** *vr* (*esforzarse*) to apply oneself; (*usar*) to apply.

aplique *m* wall lamp.

aplomo *m* aplomb.

apoderado,-a *mf* representative.

apoderarse *vr* to take possession (**de** of).

apodo *m* nickname.

apogeo *m* **estar en pleno a.** (*fama etc*) to be at its height.

apoplejía *f* apoplexy.

aporrear *vt* to beat; (*puerta*) to bang.

aportar *vt* to contribute.

aposento *m* (*cuarto*) room.

aposta *adv* on purpose.

apostar [2] *vti*, **apostarse** *vr* to bet (**por** on).

apoyar **1** *vt* to lean; (*causa*) to support. **2 apoyarse** *vr* **apoyarse en** to lean on; (*basarse*) to be based on.

apoyo *m* support.

apreciar **1** *vt* to appreciate; (*percibir*) to see. **2 apreciarse** *vr* (*notarse*) to be noticeable.

aprecio *m* regard; **tener a. a algn** to be fond of sb.

aprender *vt* to learn.

aprendiz,-a *mf* apprentice.

aprensivo,-a *a* & *mf* apprehensive.

apresar *vt* to capture.

apresurar 1 *vt* (*paso etc*) to speed up. **2 apresurarse** *vr* to hurry up.

apretado,-a *a* (*ropa, cordón*) tight; **íbamos todos apretados en el coche** we were all squashed together in the car.

apretar [1] **1** *vt* (*botón*) to press; (*nudo, tornillo*) to tighten; **me aprietan las botas** these boots are too tight for me. **2 apretarse** *vr* to squeeze together.

aprieto *m* tight spot; **poner a algn en un a.** to put sb in an awkward position.

aprisa *adv* quickly.

aprisionar *vt* to trap.

aprobado *m* (*nota*) pass.

aprobar [2] *vt* (*autorizar*) to approve; (*estar de acuerdo con*) to approve of; (*examen*) to pass; (*ley*) to pass.

apropiado,-a *a* suitable.

aprovechamiento *m* use.

aprovechar 1 *vt* to make good use of; (*recursos etc*) to take advantage of. **2** *vi* **¡que aproveche!** enjoy your meal! **3 aprovecharse** *vr* **aprovecharse de algo/algn** to take advantage of sth/sb.

aproximadamente *adv* approximately.

aproximado,-a *a* approximate.

aproximar 1 *vt* to bring nearer. **2 aproximarse** *vr* to approach (**a** -).

apto,-a *a* (*apropiado*) suitable; (*capacitado*) capable; (*examen*) passed.

apuesta *f* bet.

apuntador,-a *mf* (*en el teatro*) prompter.

apuntalar *vt* to prop up.

apuntar 1 *vt* (*con arma*) to aim; (*anotar*) to note down; (*indicar*) to suggest. **2 apuntarse** *vr* (*en una lista*) to put one's name down; *fam* to take part (**a** in).

apuntes *mpl* notes; **tomar apuntes** to take notes.

apuñalar *vt* to stab.

apurar 1 *vt* (*terminar*) to finish off; (*preocupar*) to worry. **2 apurarse** *vr* (*preocuparse*) to worry; (*darse prisa*) to hurry.

apuro *m* (*situación difícil*) tight spot; (*escasez de dinero*) hardship; (*vergüenza*) embarrassment; **pasar apuros** to be hard up; **¡qué a.!** how embarrassing!

aquel,-ella *a dem* that; **a. niño** that boy; **aquellos,-as** those; **aquellas niñas** those girls.

aquél,-élla *pron dem mf* that one; (*el anterior*) the former; **todo a. que** anyone who; **aquéllos,-as** those; (*los anteriores*) the former.

aquella *a dem f ver* **aquel.**

aquélla *pron dem f ver* **aquél.**

aquello *pron dem neutro* that, it.

aquellos,-as *a dem pl ver* **aquel,-ella.**

aquéllos,-as *pron dem mfpl ver* **aquél,-ella.**

aquí *adv* (*lugar*) here; **a. arriba/fuera** up/out here; **a. mismo** right here; **de a. para allá** up and down, to and fro; **hasta a.** this far; **por a., por favor** this way please; **está por a.** it's around here somewhere; (*tiempo*) **de a. en adelante** from now on.

árabe 1 *a* & *mf* Arab. **2** *m* (*idioma*) Arabic.

arado *m* plough, *US* plow.

aragonés,-esa *a* & *mf* Aragonese.

arancel *m* customs duty.

arandela *f* (*anilla*) ring.

araña *f* spider.

arañazo *m* scratch.

arar *vti* to plough, *US* plow.

arbitrario,-a *a* arbitrary.

árbitro,-a *mf* referee; (*de tenis*) umpire; (*mediador*) arbitrator.

árbol *m* tree; **á. genealógico** family tree.

arbusto *m* bush.

arcada *f* (*de puente*) arch; (*náusea*) retching.

arcén *m* verge; (*de autopista*) hard shoulder.

archipiélago *m* archipelago.

archivador *m* filing cabinet.

archivar *vt* (*documento etc*) to file (away); (*caso, asunto*) to shelve; (*en ordenador*) to save.

archivo *m* file; (*archivador*) filing cabinet; **archivos** archives.

arcilla *f* clay.

arco *m* (*de edificio etc*) arch; (*de violín, para flechas*) bow; **a. iris** rainbow.

arder *vi* to burn.

ardilla *f* squirrel.

ardor *m* fervour; **a. de estómago** heartburn.

área *f* area; (*medida*) are (100 square metres).

arena *f* sand; (*en plaza de toros*) bullring; **playa de a.** sandy beach.

arenisca *f* sandstone.

arenque *m* herring.

arete *m* earring.

argelino,-a *a* & *mf* Algerian.

argentino,-a *a* & *mf* Argentinian, Argentine.

argolla *f* (*large*) ring; *Am* (*alianza*) wedding ring.

argot *m* (*popular*) slang; (*técnico*) jargon.

argumento *m* (*trama*) plot; (*razonamiento*) argument.

árido,-a *a* arid.

arisco,-a *a* (*persona*) unfriendly; (*áspero*) gruff; (*animal*) unfriendly.

aristócrata *mf* aristocrat.

aritmética *f* arithmetic.

arma *f* weapon; **a. de fuego** firearm; **a. nuclear** nuclear weapon.

armada *f* navy.

armador,-a *mf* shipowner.

armadura *f* (*armazón*) frame.

armamento *m* (*armas*) armaments; **a. nuclear** nuclear weapons.

armar 1 *vt* (*tropa, soldado*) to arm; (*montar*) to assemble. **2 armarse** *vr* to arm oneself; **armarse de paciencia** to summon up one's patience; **armarse de valor** to pluck up courage.

armario *m* (*para ropa*) wardrobe; (*de cocina*) cupboard; **a. empotrado** built-in wardrobe/cupboard.

armazón *m* frame; (*de madera*) timberwork.

armisticio *m* armistice.

armonioso,-a *a* harmonious.

aro *m* hoop; (*servilletero*) serviette ring.

aroma *m* aroma; (*de vino*) bouquet.

arpa** *f* harp.

arpón *m* harpoon.

arqueología *f* archaeology.

arquitecto,-a *mf* architect.

arquitectura *f* architecture.

arrabales *mpl* slums.

arraigado,-a *a* deeply rooted.

arrancar [1] **1** *vt* (*planta*) to uproot; (*diente, pelo*) to pull out; (*coche, motor*) to start; **a. de raíz** to uproot. **2** *vi* (*coche, motor*) to start; (*empezar*) to begin.

arrasar *vt* to devastate; (*terreno*) to level.

arrastrar 1 *vt* to drag (along); **lo arrastró la corriente** he was swept away by the current. **2 arrastrarse** *vr* to drag oneself.

arrebatar 1 *vt* (*coger*) to seize. **2 arrebatarse** *vr* (*enfurecerse*) to become furious; (*exaltarse*) to get carried away.

arrebato *m* outburst.

arreciar *vi* (*viento, tormenta*) to get worse.

arrecife *m* reef.

arreglado,-a *a* (*reparado*) repaired; (*solucionado*) settled; (*habitación*) tidy; (*persona*) smart.

arreglar 1 *vt* to arrange; (*problema*) to sort out; (*habitación*) to tidy; (*papeles*) to put in order; (*reparar*) to repair. **2 arreglarse** *vr* (*vestirse*) to get ready; *fam* **arreglárselas** to manage.

arreglo *m* arrangement; (*acuerdo*) compromise; (*reparación*) repair; **no**

tiene a. it is beyond repair; **con a.** a in accordance with.
arremangarse [7] *vr* to roll one's sleeves/trousers up.
arrendar [1] *vt* (*piso*) to rent; (*dar en arriendo*) to let on lease; (*tomar en arriendo*) to take on lease.
arrepentirse [5] *vr* **a. de** to regret; (*en confesión*) to repent.
arrestar *vt* to arrest; (*encarcelar*) to put in prison.
arriba 1 *adv* up; (*encima*) on the top; (*en casa*) upstairs; **ahí a.** up there; **de a. abajo** from top to bottom; **mirar a algn de a. abajo** to look sb up and down; **desde a.** from above; **hacia a.** upwards; **más a.** further up; **la parte de a.** the top (part); **vive a.** he lives upstairs; **véase más a.** see above. **2** *interj* up you get!; **¡a. la República!** long live the Republic!; **¡a. las manos!** hands up! **3** *prep Am* **a. de** on top of.
arribeño,-a *Am* **1** *a* highland. **2** *mf* highlander.
arriendo *m* lease.
arriesgado,-a *a* (*peligroso*) risky; (*persona*) daring.
arriesgar [7] *vt*, **arriesgarse** *vr* to risk.
arrimar 1 *vt* to move closer; *fam* **a. el hombro** to lend a hand. **2 arrimarse** *vr* to move nearer.
arrinconar *vt* (*poner en un rincón*) to put in a corner; (*acorralar*) to corner.
arrodillarse *vr* to kneel down.
arrogante *a* arrogant.
arrojar 1 *vt* (*tirar*) to throw. **2 arrojarse** *vr* to throw oneself.
arrollador,-a *a* overwhelming; (*éxito*) resounding; (*personalidad*) captivating.
arropar 1 *vt* to wrap up; (*en cama*) to tuck in. **2 arroparse** *vr* to wrap oneself up.
arroyo *m* stream.
arroz *m* rice; **a. con leche** rice pudding.
arruga *f* (*en piel*) wrinkle; (*en ropa*) crease.
arrugar [7] **1** *vt* (*piel*) to wrinkle; (*ropa*) to crease; (*papel*) to crumple (up). **2 arrugarse** *vr* (*piel*) to wrinkle; (*ropa*) to crease.
arruinar 1 *vt* to ruin. **2 arruinarse** *vr* to be ruined.
arsenal *m* arsenal.
arte *m & f* art; (*habilidad*) skill; **bellas artes** fine arts.
artefacto *m* device.
arteria *f* artery.
artesanía *f* craftsmanship; (*objetos*) crafts *pl*.
ártico,-a 1 *a* arctic; **el océano a.** the Arctic Ocean. **2** *m* **el A.** the Arctic.
articulación *f* (*de huesos*) joint.
artículo *m* article.
artificial *a* artificial; (*sintético*) man-made, synthetic.

artillería *f* artillery.
artista *mf* artist; **a. de cine** film star.
artritis *f* arthritis.
arveja *f Am* pea.
as *m* ace.
asa** *f* handle.
asado,-a 1 *a* roast; **pollo a.** roast chicken. **2** *m* roast.
asaltar *vt* to attack; (*banco*) to rob.
asamblea *f* meeting; **a. general** general meeting.
asar 1 *vt* to roast. **2 asarse** *vr fig* to be roasting.
ascender [3] **1** *vt* (*en un cargo*) to promote. **2** *vi* move upward; (*temperatura etc*) to rise; **a. de categoría** to be promoted; **la factura asciende a ...** the bill adds up to ...
ascenso *m* promotion; (*subida*) rise.
ascensor *m* lift, *US* elevator.
asco *m* disgust; **me da a.** it makes me (feel) sick; **¡qué a.!** how disgusting!
ascua** *f* live coal.
asear 1 *vt* to tidy up. **2 asearse** *vr* to wash.
asedio *m* siege.
asegurar 1 *vt* to insure; (*garantizar*) to assure; (*cuerda*) to fasten. **2 asegurarse** *vr* to insure onself; **asegurarse de que ...** to make sure that ...
asemejarse *vr* **a. a** to look like.
asentamiento *m* settlement.
asentir [5] *vi* to agree; **a. con la cabeza** to nod.
aseo *m* (*limpieza*) tidiness; (*cuarto de baño*) toilet.
asequible *a* affordable; (*alcanzable*) attainable.
aserrín *m* sawdust.
asesinar *vt* to murder; (*rey, ministro*) to assassinate.
asesinato *m* murder; (*de rey, ministro*) assassination.
asesino,-a 1 *a* murderous. **2** *mf* (*hombre*) murderer; (*mujer*) murderess; (*de político*) assassin.
asesorar *vt* to advise.
asesoría *f* consultancy.
asfalto *m* asphalt.
asfixiar *vt*, **asfixiarse** *vr* to asphyxiate.
así 1 *adv* (*de esta manera*) like this *o* that, this way; **ponlo a.** put this way; **a. de grande/alto** this big/tall; **algo a.** something like this *o* that; **¿no es a.?** isn't that so *o* right?; **a. las seis o a.** around six o'clock; **a. como** as well as; **aun a.** and despite that. **2** *conj* **a. pues ...** so...; **a. que ...** so ...
asiático,-a *a & mf* Asian.
asiduo,-a 1 *a* assiduous. **2** *mf* regular customer.
asiento *m* seat; **a. trasero/delantero** front/back seat; **tome a.** take a seat.

asignar *vt* to allocate; (*nombrar*) to appoint.

asignatura *f* subject.

asilo *m* asylum; **a. de ancianos** old people's home.

asimismo *adv* also, as well.

asistencia *f* (*presencia*) attendance; (*público*) audience; **falta de a.** absence; **a. médica/técnica** medical/technical assistance.

asistenta *f* cleaning lady.

asistente 1 *a* **el público a.** the audience; (*en estadio*) spectators *pl.* **2** *mf* (*ayudante*) assistant; **a. social** social worker; **los asistentes** the audience; (*en estadio*) the spectators.

asistir 1 *vt* to assist. **2** *vi* to attend (**a -**).

asma *f* asthma.

asno *m* donkey.

asociación *f* association.

asociar 1 *vt* to associate. **2 asociarse** *vr* to be associated.

asomar 1 *vt* to stick out; **asomó la cabeza por la ventana** he put his head out the window. **2** *vi* to appear. **3 asomarse** *vr* to lean out; **asomarse a la ventana** to lean out of the window.

asombrar 1 *vt* to astonish. **2 asombrarse** *vr* to be astonished; **asombrarse de algo** to be amazed at sth.

asombro *m* astonishment.

asorocharse *vr* *Am* to suffer from altitude sickness.

aspa *f* (*de molino*) arm; (*de ventilador*) blade; (*cruz*) cross.

aspecto *m* look; (*de un asunto*) aspect.

áspero;-a *a* rough; (*carácter*) surly.

aspersor *m* sprinkler.

aspiradora *f* vacuum cleaner.

aspirante *mf* candidate.

aspirar *vt* (*respirar*) to inhale.

aspirina *f* aspirin.

asqueroso,-a 1 *a* (*sucio*) filthy; (*desagradable*) disgusting. **2** *mf* filthy *o* revolting person.

asterisco *m* asterisk.

astilla *f* splinter.

astillero *m* shipyard.

astringente *a & m* astringent.

astro *m* star.

astrología *f* astrology.

astronauta *mf* astronaut.

astronave *f* spaceship.

astronomía *f* astronomy.

asturiano,-a *a & mf* Asturian.

astuto,-a *a* astute.

asunto *m* subject; **no es a. tuyo** it's none of your business.

asustar 1 *vt* to frighten. **2 asustarse** *vr* to be frightened.

atacar [1] *vt* to attack.

atajo *m* shortcut.

atañer *v impers* to concern.

ataque *m* attack; (*de nervios, tos*) fit; **a. cardíaco** *o* **al corazón** heart attack.

atar 1 *vt* (*ligar*) to tie; **a. cabos** to put two and two together; *fam* **loco de a.** as mad as a hatter. **2 atarse** *vr fig* to get tied up; **átate los zapatos** do your shoes up.

atardecer 1 *v impers* to get dark. **2** *m* evening.

atareado,-a *a* busy.

atascar [1] **1** *vt* (*bloquear*) to block. **2 atascarse** *vr* (*bloquearse*) to become blocked.

atasco *m* traffic jam.

ataúd *m* coffin.

atemorizar [4] *vt* to frighten.

atención 1 *f* attention; **llamar la a.** to attract attention; **prestar/poner a.** to pay attention (**a** to). **2** *interj* attention!; (*cuidado*) watch out!

atender [3] **1** *vt* to attend to. **2** *vi* (*alumno*) to pay attention (**a** to).

atentado *m* attack.

atentamente *adv* (*con atención*) attentively; **le saluda a.** (*en carta*) yours sincerely.

atento,-a *a* attentive; (*amable*) thoughtful; **estar a. a** to aware of.

aterrador,-a *a* terrifying.

aterrar 1 *vt* to terrify. **2 aterrarse** *vr* to be terrified.

aterrizaje *m* landing.

aterrizar [4] *vi* to land.

aterrorizar [4] **1** *vt* to terrify. **2 aterrorizarse** *vr* to be terrified.

ático *m* attic; (*vivienda*) attic flat.

atingencia *f Am* connection.

atizar [4] *vt* (*fuego*) to poke.

atlas *m inv* atlas.

atleta *mf* athlete.

atletismo *m* athletics *sing*.

atmósfera *f* atmosphere.

atolondrado,-a *a* (*tonto*) silly; (*aturdido*) bewildered.

atómico,-a *a* atomic.

átomo *m* atom.

atónito,-a *a* astonished.

atontado,-a *a* stunned; (*atontado*) stupid.

atorarse *vr* to get stuck.

atormentar 1 *vt* to torment. 2 **atormentarse** *vr* to torment oneself.

atornillar *vt* to screw on.

atracar [1] 1 *vt* to hold up; (*persona*) to rob. 2 *vi* (*barco*) to come alongside. 3 **atracarse** *vr* (*de comida*) to stuff oneself (**de** with).

atracción *f* attraction; **parque de atracciones** funfair.

atraco *m* hold-up; **a. a mano armada** armed robbery.

atracón *m fam* binge.

atractivo,-a 1 *a* attractive. 2 *m* attraction.

atraer *vt* to attract.

atragantarse *vr* to choke (**con** on).

atraigo *indic pres de* **atraer.**

atraje *pt indef de* **atraer.**

atrancar [1] 1 *vt* (*puerta*) to bolt. 2 **atrancarse** *vr* to get stuck.

atrapar *vt* to catch.

atrás *adv* (*lugar*) at the back, behind; **hacia/para a.** backwards; **puerta de a.** back *o* rear door; **echarse a.** to back out; **venir de muy a.** to go back a long time.

atrasado,-a *a* late; (*pago*) overdue; (*reloj*) slow; (*país*) backward.

atrasar 1 *vt* to put back. 2 *vi* (*reloj*) to be slow. 3 **atrasarse** *vr* to lag behind; (*tren*) to be late.

atravesar [1] 1 *vt* (*cruzar*) to cross; (*traspasar*) to go through; (*poner a través*) to put across. 2 **atravesarse** *vr* to get in the way.

atreverse *vr* to dare; **a. a hacer algo** to dare to do sth.

atrevido,-a *a* (*osado*) daring; (*insolente*) insolent; (*ropa etc*) daring.

atropellar *vt* to knock down.

atroz *a* (*bárbaro*) atrocious; *fam* (*hambre, frío*) tremendous.

ATS *mf abr de* **ayudante técnico sanitario** nurse.

atuendo *m* attire.

atún *m* tuna.

aturdido,-a *a* stunned.

aturdir *vt* (*con un golpe*) to stun; (*confundir*) to bewilder.

audaz *a* audacious.

audición *f* hearing; (*en el teatro*) audition.

audiencia *f* (*público*) audience; (*entrevista*) audience; (*tribunal*) high court.

audiovisual *a* audio-visual.

auditor *m* auditor.

auge *m* peak; (*económico*) boom; **estar en a.** to be booming.

aula** *f* (*en colegio*) classroom; (*en universidad*) lecture room.

aulaga *f* gorse.

aullido *m* howl.

aumentar 1 *vt* to increase; (*precios*) to put up; (*producción*) to step up; (*imagen*) to magnify. **2** *vi* (*precios*) to go up; (*valor*) to appreciate.

aumento *m* increase; (*de imagen*) magnification; **ir en a.** to be on the increase.

aun *adv* even; **a. así** even so; **a. más** even more.

aún *adv* still; (*en negativas*) yet; **a. está aquí** he's still here; **ella no ha venido a.** she hasn't come yet.

aunque *conj* although, though; (*enfático*) even if, even though.

aureola *f* halo.

auricular *m* (*del teléfono*) receiver; **auriculares** headphones.

aurora *f* dawn.

auscultar *vt* to sound (with a stethoscope).

ausencia *f* absence.

ausentarse *vr* (*irse*) to go missing.

ausente 1 *a* absent. **2** *mf* absentee.

austero,-a *a* austere.

australiano,-a *a & mf* Australian.

austríaco,-a *a & mf* Austrian.

auténtico,-a *a* authentic.

autista 1 *a* autistic. **2** *mf* autistic person.

auto[1] *m* car.

auto[2] *m* (*sentencia*) writ; **autos** (*pleito*) documents.

autobiografía *f* autobiography.

autobiográfico,-a *a* autobiographical.

autobús *m* bus.

autocar *m* coach.

autóctono,-a *a* indigenous.

autodefensa *f* self-defence.

autoescuela *f* driving school.

autógrafo *m* autograph.

automático,-a *a* automatic.

automotor,-a *m* diesel train.

automóvil *m* car.

automovilista *mf* motorist.

automovilístico,-a *a* car.

autonomía *f* autonomy; (*región*) autonomous region.

autonómico,-a *a* autonomous.

autopista *f* motorway.

autopsia *f* autopsy.

autor,-a *mf* author; (*de crimen*) perpetrator.

autoridad *f* authority.

autoritario,-a *a* authoritarian.

autorizar [4] *vt* to authorize.
autoservicio *m* self-service; (*tienda*) supermarket.
autostop *m* hitch-hiking; **hacer a.** to hitch-hike.
autostopista *mf* hitch-hiker.
autosuficiencia *f* self-sufficiency.
auxiliar 1 *a* & *mf* auxiliary. **2** *vt* to assist.
auxilio *m* assistance; **primeros auxilios** first aid *sing*.
avalancha *f* avalanche.
avance *m* advance.
avanzado,-a *a* advanced; **de avanzada edad** advanced in years.
avanzar [4] *vt* to advance.
avaricia *f* avarice.
avaro,-a 1 *a* miserly. **2** *mf* miser.
ave** *f* bird.
avellana *f* hazelnut.
avellano *m* hazelnut tree.
avena *f* oats *pl*.
avenida *f* avenue.
avenido,-a *a* **bien/mal avenidos** on good/bad terms.
aventajar *vt* (*ir por delante de*) to be ahead, be in front (**a** of); (*superar*) to outdo.
aventura *f* adventure; (*amorosa*) (love) affair.
aventurarse *vr* to venture.
aventurero,-a 1 *a* adventurous. **2** *mf* adventurous person.
avergonzar [2] **1** *vt* to shame. **2 avergonzarse** *vr* to be ashamed (**de** of).
avería *f* breakdown.
averiar 1 *vt* to break. **2 averiarse** *vr* (*estropearse*) to malfunction; (*coche*) to break down.
averiguar *vt* to find out.
aversión *f* aversion.
avestruz *m* ostrich.
aviación *f* aviation; (*militar*) air force; **accidente de a.** plane crash.
aviador,-a *mf* aviator; (*piloto militar*) air force pilot.
ávido,-a *a* avid; **a. de** eager for.
avión *m* aeroplane, *US* airplane; **por a.** (*en carta*) airmail.
avioneta *f* light aircraft.
avisar *vt* (*informar*) to inform; (*advertir*) to warn; (*llamar*) to call for.
aviso *m* notice; (*advertencia*) warning; (*nota*) note; **sin previo a.** without notice.
avispa *f* wasp.
avivar *vt* (*fuego*) to stoke (up); (*paso*) to quicken.
axila *f* armpit.

ay *interj* (*dolor*) ouch!

ayer *adv* yesterday; **a. por la mañana/por la tarde** yesterday morning/ afternoon; **a. por la noche** last night; **antes de a.** the day before yesterday.

ayuda *f* help.

ayudante *mf* assistant.

ayudar 1 *vt* to help. 2 **ayudarse** *vr* (*unos a otros*) to help; **ayudarse de** to make use of.

ayunas en a. without having eaten breakfast.

ayuntamiento *m* (*institución*) town council; (*edificio*) town hall.

azafata *f* (*de avión*) air hostess; (*de congresos*) stewardess; (*de concurso*) hostess.

azafrán *m* saffron.

azahar *m* (*del naranjo*) orange blossom.

azar *m* chance; **al a.** at random.

azorado,-a *a* embarrassed.

azorar 1 *vt* to embarrass. 2 **azorarse** *vr* to be embarrassed.

azotar *vt* to beat; (*lluvia*) to beat down on; (*con látigo*) to whip.

azotea *f* flat roof.

azteca *a* & *mf* Aztec.

azúcar *m* & *f* sugar; **a. blanco** refined sugar; **a. moreno** brown sugar.

azucarero,-a 1 *m* & *f* sugar bowl. 2 *a* sugar.

azucena *f* lily.

azul *a* & *m* blue; **a. celeste** sky blue; **a. marino** navy blue.

azulejo *m* (glazed) tile.

B

baba *f* dribble.

babero *m* bib.

babor *m* port.

babosa *f* slug.

baboso,-a *a fam* slimy; *Am* stupid.

baca *f* roof rack.

bacalao *m* cod.

bache *m* (*en carretera*) pot hole; (*mal momento*) bad patch.

bachillerato *m* ≈ General Certificate of Secondary Education, *US* high school degree.

bacon *m* bacon.

bacteriológico,-a *a* bacteriological; **guerra b.** germ warfare.

badén *m* (*en carretera*) bump.

bádminton *m* badminton.

bafle *m* loudspeaker.

bahía *f* bay.

bailar *vti* to dance.

bailarín,-ina *mf* dancer.

baile *m* (*danza*) dance; (*formal*) ball; **b. de disfraces** fancy dress ball.

baja *f* (*disminución*) drop; (*en batalla*) loss; **dar de b. a algn** (*despedir*) to lay sb off; **darse de b.** (*por enfermedad*) to take sick leave.

bajada *f* (*descenso*) descent; (*señal*) way down; (*cuesta*) slope.

bajar 1 *vt* to come/go down; (*descender*) to get down; (*volumen*) to turn down; (*voz, telón*) to lower; (*precios etc*) to cut; (*cabeza*) to lower; **b. la escalera** to come/go downstairs. **2** *vi* to go/come down; (*apearse*) to get off; (*de un coche*) to get out (**de** of); (*disminuir*) to fall. **3 bajarse** *vr* to come/go down; (*apearse*) to get off; (*de un coche*) to get out (**de** of).

bajío *m Am* lowland.

bajo,-a 1 *a* low; (*persona*) short; (*sonido*) faint; **en voz baja** in a low voice; **planta baja** ground floor; **de baja calidad** of poor quality. **2** *adv* low; **hablar b.** to speak quietly. **3** *prep* (*lugar*) under, underneath; **b. tierra** underground; **b. cero** below zero; **b. juramento** under oath; **b. fianza** on bail.

bajón *m* (*bajada*) sharp fall.

bala *f* bullet; **como una b.** like a shot.

balance *m* balance; (*declaración*) balance sheet.

balanza *f* scales *pl*; **b. comercial** balance of trade; **b. de pagos** balance of payments.

balbucear *vi* (*adulto*) to stutter, stammer; (*niño*) to babble.

balbucir *vi defectivo ver* **balbucear.**

balcón *m* balcony.
balde de b. free; **en b.** in vain.
baldosa *f* (ceramic) floor tile; (*para pavimentar*) paving stone.
baliza *f* (*boya*) buoy; (*en avación*) beacon.
ballena *f* whale.
ballet *m* ballet.
balneario *m* health resort.
balón *m* ball.
baloncesto *m* basketball.
balonmano *m* handball.
balonvolea *m* volleyball.
balsa *f* raft.
bálsamo *m* balm.
bambú *m* (*pl* **bambúes**) bamboo.
banana *f* banana.
banca *f* (*asiento*) bench; **la b.** (the) banks.
bancarrota *f* bankruptcy.
banco *m* bank; (*asiento*) bench.
banda *f* (*de música*) band; (*cinta*) sash; **b. sonora** sound track; **(línea de) b.** touchline; **saque de b.** throw-in.
bandada *f* flock.
bandeja *f* tray.
bandera *f* flag.
bandido *m* bandit.
bando *m* side.
bandolero *m* bandit.
banquero,-a *mf* banker.
banqueta *f* stool.
banquete *m* banquet; **b. de bodas** wedding reception.
bañador *m* (*de mujer*) swimming costume; (*de hombre*) swimming trunks *pl*.
bañar 1 *vt* to bath. **2 bañarse** *vr* (*en baño*) to have a bath; (*en mar, piscina*) to go for a swim.
bañera *f* bath.
bañista *mf* swimmer.
baño *m* bath; (*de chocolate etc*) coating; (*cuarto de baño*) bathroom; (*lavabo*) toilet; **tomar un b.** to have a bath.
bar *m* bar, pub.
baraja *f* pack, deck.
baranda, barandilla *f* (*de escalera*) banister; (*de balcón*) handrail.
baratija *f* knick-knack.
barato,-a 1 *a* cheap. **2** *adv* cheaply.

barba *f* (*pelo*) beard; (*mentón*) chin.

barbacoa *f* barbecue.

barbaridad *f* atrocity; (*disparate*) piece of nonsense; **una b.** a lot.

barbería *f* barber's (shop).

barbilla *f* chin.

barbo *m* barbel.

barbudo,-a *a* with a heavy beard.

barca *f* small boat.

barcaza *f* lighter.

barco *m* ship; **b. de vapor** steamer.

barlovento *m* windward.

barman *m* barman.

barniz *m* (*en madera*) varnish; (*en cerámica*) glaze.

barómetro *m* barometer.

barquillo *m* wafer.

barra *f* bar; **b. de pan** French loaf; **b. de labios** lipstick.

barraca *f* (*caseta*) hut; (*en Valencia y Murcia*) thatched farmhouse.

barranco *m* (*despeñadero*) cliff; (*torrentera*) ravine.

barrendero,-a *mf* (street) sweeper.

barreno *m* (*taladro*) large drill; (*explosivo*) charge.

barreño *m* tub.

barrer *vt* to sweep.

barrera *f* barrier.

barricada *f* barricade.

barriga *f* belly, *fam* tummy.

barril *m* barrel; **cerveza de b.** draught beer.

barrio *m* district; **del b.** local; **b. chino** red-light district; **barrios bajos** slums.

barro *m* (*lodo*) mud; (*arcilla*) clay; **objetos de b.** earthenware *sing*.

bártulos *mpl fam* bits and pieces.

barullo *m* (*alboroto*) row; (*confusión*) confusion.

basar 1 *vt* to base (**en** on). **2 basarse** *vr* (*teoría, película*) to be based (**en** on).

báscula *f* scales *pl* .

base *f* base; (*de argumento, teoría*) basis; (*de partido*) grass roots; **sueldo b.** minimum wage; **b. de datos** database; **a b. de estudiar** by studying; **a b. de productos naturales** using natural products.

básico,-a *a* basic.

básquet *m* basketball.

bastante 1 *a* (*suficiente*) enough; **b. tiempo/comida** enough time/food; (*abundante*) quite a lot of; **hace b. calor/frío** it's quite hot/cold; **bastantes amigos** quite a lot of friends. **2** *adv* (*suficiente*) enough; (*considerable-*

mente) fairly, quite; **con esto hay b.** that is enough; **no soy lo b. rico (como) para ...** I am not rich enough to ...; **me gusta b.** I quite like it; **vamos b. al cine** we go to the cinema quite often.

bastar *vi* to be sufficient *o* enough; **basta con tres** three will be enough; **¡basta (ya)!** that's enough!

basto,-a *a* (*cosa*) rough; (*persona*) coarse.

bastos *m* (*in Spanish pack of cards*) ≈ clubs.

bastón *m* stick.

basura *f* rubbish, *US* trash.

basurero *m* (*persona*) dustman, *US* garbage collector; (*lugar*) rubbish dump, *US* garbage dump.

bata *f* (*para casa*) dressing gown; (*de médico etc*) white coat.

batalla *f* battle.

bate *m* (*de béisbol*) bat.

batería 1 *f* battery; (*percusión*) drums *pl* ; **b. de cocina** set of pans. **2** *mf* drummer.

batida *f* (*de la policía*) raid.

batido,-a 1 *a* (*huevo, crema*) whipped. **2** *m* milk shake.

batidora *f* whisk.

batir *vt* to beat; (*huevo*) to beat; (*nata*) to whip; (*récord*) to break.

baudio *m* baud.

baúl *m* trunk; *Am* (*de coche*) boot, *US* trunk.

bautizar *vt* to baptize, christen.

bautizo *m* baptism.

baya *f* berry.

bayeta *f* floorcloth.

bazar *m* bazaar.

bazo *m* spleen.

bazofia *f* *fam* rubbish.

beato,-a *a* *peyorativo* sanctimonious.

bebé *m* baby.

beber *vti* to drink.

bebida *f* drink.

beca *f* grant.

becario,-a *mf* grant holder.

becerro *m* calf.

bechamel *f* bechamel; **salsa b.** white sauce.

bedel *m* janitor.

beige *a & m inv* beige.

béisbol *m* baseball.

belga *a & mf* Belgian.

bélico,-a *a* warlike; (*preparativos etc*) war.

belleza *f* beauty.

bello,-a *a* beautiful.

bellota *f* acorn.

bencina *f Am* petrol.

bendición *f* blessing.

bendito,-a *a* blessed.

beneficencia *f* charity.

beneficiar 1 *vt* to benefit. **2 beneficiarse** *vr* **beneficiarse de** *o* **con algo** to profit from sth.

beneficio *m* profit; (*bien*) benefit; **en b. propio** in one's own interest; **un concierto a b. de ...** a concert in aid of ...

beneficioso,-a *a* beneficial.

benevolencia *f* benevolence.

bengala *f* flare.

benigno,-a *a* (*persona*) gentle.

benjamín,-ina *mf* youngest child.

berberecho *m* (common) cockle.

berbiquí *m* drill.

berenjena *f* aubergine, *US* eggplant.

Bermudas 1 *fpl* **las (Islas) B.** Bermuda *sing.* **2** *mpl* **bermudas** (*prenda*) Bermuda shorts.

berrear *vi* to bellow.

berrinche *m fam* tantrum.

berro *m* watercress.

berza *f* cabbage.

besar *vt,* **besarse** *vr* to kiss.

beso *m* kiss.

best-seller *m* best-seller.

bestia 1 *f* beast. **2** *mf fam* brute. **3** *a fig* brutish.

besugo *m* (*pez*) sea bream.

betún *m* (*para el calzado*) shoe polish.

biberón *m* baby's bottle.

Biblia *f* Bible.

bibliografía *f* bibliography.

biblioteca *f* (*edificio*) library; (*estantería*) bookcase.

bicarbonato *m* bicarbonate; **b. sódico** bicarbonate of soda.

bíceps *m inv* biceps.

bicho *m* bug.

bici *f fam* bike.

bicicleta *f* bicycle; **montar en b.** to ride a bicycle.

bidón *m* drum.

bien¹ **1** *adv* (*correctamente*) well; **responder b.** to answer correctly; **hiciste**

b. en decírmelo you were right to tell me; **las cosas le van b.** things are going well for him; **¡b.!** good!, great!; **¡muy b.!** excellent!; **¡qué b.!** great!; **vivir b.** to be comfortably off; **¡está b.!** (*¡de acuerdo!*) fine!, all right!; **¡ya está b.!** that's (quite) enough!; **esta falda te está b.** this skirt suits you; **ese libro está muy b.** that book is very good. ‖ (*intensificador*) very; **b. temprano** nice and early; **b. caliente** pretty hot; **más b.** rather. **2** *conj* **o b.** or else; **b. ... o b. ...** either ... or ...; **no b. llegó ...** no sooner had she arrived than ...; **si b.** although.

bien² *m* (*bondad*) good; **el b. y el mal** good and evil; **por el b. de** for the good of; **lo hace por tu b.** he does it for your sake; **bienes** goods; **bienes inmuebles** real estate; **bienes de consumo** consumer goods.

bienestar *m* well-being.

bienvenida *f* welcome; **dar la b. a algn** to welcome sb.

bienvenido,-a *a* welcome.

bifurcación *f* (*de la carretera*) fork.

bigote *m* (*de persona*) moustache, US mustache; **bigotes** (*de animal*) whiskers *pl*.

bilateral *a* bilateral.

bilingüe *a* bilingual.

bilis *f* bile.

billar *m* (*juego*) billiards *sing*; (*mesa*) billiard table; **b. americano** pool; **b. ruso** snooker.

billete *m* ticket; (*de banco*) note, US bill; **b. de ida y vuelta** return (ticket), US round-trip ticket; **b. sencillo** *o* **de ida** single (ticket); **un b. de mil pesetas** a thousand peseta note.

billetera *f*, **billetero** *m* wallet.

billón *m* thousand billion.

bingo *m* (*juego*) bingo; (*sala*) bingo hall.

biografía *f* biography.

biología *f* biology.

biombo *m* (folding) screen.

biopsia *f* biopsy.

bioquímica *f* biochemistry.

bióxido *m* **b. de carbono** carbon dioxide.

biquini *m* bikini.

birria *f fam* rubbish.

bisabuela *f* great-grandmother.

bisabuelo *m* great-grandfather; **bisabuelos** great-grandparents.

bisagra *f* hinge.

bisiesto *a* **año b.** leap year.

bisonte *m* bison.

bisté, bistec *m* steak.

bisturí *m* scalpel.

bisutería *f* imitation jewellery *o US* jewelry.

bizco,-a 1 *a* cross-eyed. **2** *mf* cross-eyed person.

bizcocho *m* sponge cake.

blanco,-a[1] **1** *a* white; (*tez*) fair. **2** *mf* (*hombre*) white man; (*mujer*) white woman; **los blancos** whites.

blanco[2] *m* (*color*) white; (*hueco*) blank; (*diana*) target; **pasar la noche en b.** to have a sleepless night; **me quedé en b.** my mind went blank; **ser el b. de todas las miradas** to be the centre of attention.

blancura *f* whiteness.

blando,-a *a* soft.

blanquear *vt* (*encalar*) to whitewash.

blasfemar *vi* to blaspheme (**contra** against).

blindado,-a *a* (*carro*) armoured; (*antibalas*) bullet-proof; **coche b.** bullet-proof car; **puerta blindada** reinforced door.

bloc *m* pad; **b. de notas** notepad.

bloque *m* block; **b. de pisos** block (of apartments).

bloquear *vt* to block; (*sitiar*) to blockade.

blusa *f* blouse.

blusón *m* loose blouse.

bobada *f* nonsense; **decir bobadas** to talk nonsense.

bobina *f* reel.

bobo,-a 1 *a* (*tonto*) stupid, silly; (*ingenuo*) naïve. **2** *mf* fool.

boca *f* mouth; **b. abajo** face downward; **b. arriba** face upward; *fam* **¡cierra la b!** shut up!; **con la b. abierta** open-mouthed; **se le hizo la b. agua** his mouth watered; **la b. del metro** the entrance to the underground station.

bocacalle *f* entrance to a street.

bocadillo *m* sandwich; **un b. de jamón/tortilla** a ham/omelette sandwich.

bocado *m* bite.

bocanada *f* (*de humo*) puff; **una b. de viento** a gust of wind.

bocata *m fam* sandwich.

bocazas *mf inv fam* bigmouth.

boceto *m* (*de cuadro etc*) sketch; (*esquema*) outline.

bochorno *m* (*tiempo*) sultry weather; (*calor sofocante*) stifling heat; (*vergüenza*) embarrassment.

bocina *f* horn; **tocar la b.** to sound one's horn.

boda *f* marriage; **bodas de plata** silver wedding *sing*.

bodega *f* (*en casa*) wine cellar; (*tienda*) wine shop; *Am* grocery store, grocer's.

body *m* bodystocking.

bofetada *f*, **bofetón** *m* slap on the face; **dar una b./un b. a algn** to slap sb's face.

bohío *m Am* hut.

boicotear *vt* to boycott.

boina *f* beret.

bola *f* ball; (*canica*) marble; *Am* (*rumor*) rumour; **b. de nieve** snowball; **no dar pie con b.** to be unable to do anything right.

bolera *f* bowling alley.

boletería *f Am* (*de estadio, estación*) ticket office; (*de teatro*) box office.

boletín *m* bulletin.

boleto *m* ticket.

boli *m* biro[(R)].

bólido *m* (*coche*) racing car.

bolígrafo *m* ballpoint (pen).

boliviano,-a *a & mf* Bolivian.

bollar *vt* to dent.

bollo *m* (*de pan*) roll; (*abolladura*) dent.

bolo *m* skittle; **bolos** (*juego*) skittles.

bolsa[1] *f* bag; **b. de deportes** sports bag; **b. de la compra** shopping bag; **b. de viaje** travel bag.

bolsa[2] *f* (*de valores*) Stock Exchange.

bolsillo *m* (*prenda*) pocket; **de b.** pocket; **libro de b.** paperback.

bolso *m* handbag, bag, *US* purse.

bomba[1] *f* pump; **b. de incendios** fire engine.

bomba[2] *f* (*explosivo*) bomb; **b. atómica/de hidrógeno/de neutrones** atom/hydrogen/neutron bomb; **b. de relojería** time bomb; *fam* **pasarlo b.** to have a great time.

bombardear *vt* to bomb.

bombero,-a *mf* (*hombre*) fireman; (*mujer*) firewoman; (*ambos sexos*) firefighter; **cuerpo de bomberos** fire brigade; **parque de bomberos** fire station.

bombilla *f* (light) bulb.

bombín *m* bowler hat.

bombo *m* (*de percusión*) bass drum; (*de sorteo*) lottery drum; (*de lavadora*) drum.

bombón *m* chocolate.

bombona *f* cylinder; **b. de butano** butane gas cylinder.

bonachón,-ona *a* good-natured.

bonanza *f* (*tiempo*) fair weather; (*prosperidad*) prosperity.

bondadoso,-a *a* good-natured.

boniato *m* sweet potato.

bonificación *f* bonus.

bonito,-a[1] *a* pretty, nice.

bonito[2] *m* tuna.

bono *m* (*vale*) voucher; (*título*) bond.

bono-bus *m* bus pass.

boquerón *m* anchovy.

boquete *m* hole.

boquiabierto,-a *a* open-mouthed; **se quedó b.** he was flabbergasted.

boquilla *f* (*de cigarro*) tip; (*de pipa*) mouthpiece.

borda *f* gunwale; **arrojar** *o* **echar por la b.** to throw overboard; **fuera b.** (*motor*) outboard motor.

bordado,-a 1 *a* embroidered. **2** *m* embroidery.

bordar *vt* to embroider.

borde *m* (*de mesa, camino*) edge; (*de prenda*) hem; (*de vasija*) rim; **al b. del mar** at the seaside.

bordear *vt* to skirt.

bordillo *m* kerb, *US* curb.

bordo *m* **a b.** on board; **subir a b.** to go on board.

borrachera *f* (*embriaguez*) drunkenness; (*curda*) binge; **coger** *o* **pillar una b.** to get drunk.

borracho,-a 1 *a* (*bebido*) drunk; (*bizcocho*) with rum; **estar b.** to be drunk. **2** *mf* drunk.

borrador *m* (*escrito*) rough copy; (*de pizarra*) duster.

borrar *vt* (*con goma*) to rub out; (*pizarra*) to clean; (*en pantalla*) to delete.

borrasca *f* area of low pressure.

borrego,-a *mf* yearling lamb; (*persona*) sheep.

borroso,-a *a* blurred; **veo b.** I can't see clearly.

bosque *m* wood.

bosquejo *m* (*de dibujo*) sketch; (*de plan*) draft.

bostezar [4] *vi* to yawn.

bota *f* boot; (*de vino*) wineskin.

botana *f* *Am* snack.

botánico,-a *a* botanic; **jardín b.** botanic gardens *pl*.

botar 1 *vi* (*saltar*) to jump; (*pelota*) to bounce. **2** *vt* (*barco*) to launch; (*pelota*) to bounce; *Am* (*arrojar*) to throw out.

bote[1] *m* jump; (*de pelota*) bounce.

bote[2] *m* (*lata*) can, tin; (*para propinas*) jar *o* box for tips.

bote[3] *m* (*lancha*) boat; **b. salvavidas** lifeboat.

botella *f* bottle.

botellín *m* small bottle.

botijo *m* earthenware pitcher (with spout and handle).

botín *m* (*de un robo*) loot.

botiquín *m* medicine cabinet; (*portátil*) first aid kit; (*enfermería*) first aid post.

botón *m* button.

botones *m inv* (*en hotel*) bellboy, *US* bellhop; (*recadero*) errand boy.

boutique *f* boutique.

boxeador *m* boxer.

boxeo *m* boxing.

boya *f* (*baliza*) buoy; (*corcho*) float.

boy-scout *m* boy scout.

bozal *m* muzzle.

bracear *vi* (*nadar*) to swim.

bragas *fpl* panties *pl*, knickers *pl*.

bragueta *f* (*de pantalón etc*) fly, flies *pl*.

braille *m* braille.

bramido *m* bellowing.

brandy *m* brandy.

brasa *f* ember; **chuletas a la b.** barbecued chops.

brasero *m* brazier.

bravo,-a 1 *a* (*valiente*) brave; **un toro b.** a fighting bull. **2** *interj* ¡**b.!** well done!

braza *f* breast stroke; **nadar a b.** to do the breast stroke.

brazada *f* stroke.

brazalete *m* (*pulsera*) bracelet; (*insignia*) armband.

brasileño,-a, brasilero,-a *a & mf* Brazilian.

brazo *m* arm; **en brazos** in one's arms; **ir del b.** to walk arm in arm; **con los brazos abiertos** with open arms.

brecha *f* (*en muro*) gap; (*herida*) wound.

brécol *m* broccoli.

breva *f* (*higo*) early fig; *fam* ¡**no caerá esa b.!** no such luck!

breve *a* brief; **en b., en breves momentos** shortly, soon.

brezo *m* heather.

bribón,-ona 1 *a* roguish. **2** *mf* rogue.

bricolaje *m* do-it-yourself, DIY.

bridge *m* bridge.

brigada *f* brigade; (*de policías*) squad.

brillante 1 *a* brilliant. **2** *m* diamond.

brillantina *f* brilliantine.

brillar *vi* (*resplandecer*) to shine; (*ojos, joyas*) to sparkle; (*lentejuelas etc*) to glitter.

brillo *m* (*resplandor*) shine; (*del sol, de la luna*) brightness; (*de lentejuelas etc*) glittering; (*del cabello, tela*) sheen; (*de zapatos*) shine; **sacar b. a** to polish.

brincar [1] *vi* to skip.

brindar 1 *vi* to drink a toast; **b. por algn/algo** drink to sb/sth. **2 brindarse** *vr* to volunteer (**a** to).

brindis *m* toast.

brío *m* energy.

brisa *f* breeze; **b. marina** sea breeze.

británico,-a 1 *a* British; **las Islas Británicas** the British Isles. **2** *mf* Briton; **los británicos** the British.

brocha *f* (*para pintar*) paintbrush; (*de afeitar*) shaving brush.

broche *m* (*joya*) brooch; (*de vestido*) fastener.

bróculi *m* broccoli.

broma *f* (*chiste*) joke; **en b.** as a joke; **¡ni en b.!** not on your life!; **b. pesada** practical joke; **gastar una b.** to play a joke.

bronca *f* (*riña*) row; **echar una b. a algn** to bawl sb out.

bronce *m* bronze.

bronceado,-a 1 *a* (sun)tanned. **2** *m* (sun)tan.

bronceador,-a 1 *a* **leche bronceadora** suntan lotion. **2** *m* suntan lotion.

bronquitis *f inv* bronchitis.

brotar *vi* (*planta*) to sprout; (*agua*) to gush; (*epidemia*) to break out.

bruces de b. face downwards; **se cayó de b.** he fell flat on his face.

bruja *f* witch.

brújula *f* compass.

bruma *f* mist.

brusco,-a *a* (*persona*) brusque; (*repentino*) sudden.

bruto,-a 1 *a* (*necio*) stupid; (*grosero*) coarse; (*no neto*) gross; **un diamante en b.** an uncut diamond. **2** *mf* blockhead.

bucear *vi* to swim under water.

bucle *m* curl.

budín *m* pudding.

budista *a* Buddhist.

buen *a* (*delante de un nombre masculino singular*) good; **¡b. viaje!** have a good trip!; *ver* **bueno,-a**.

buenamente *adv* **haz lo que b. puedas** just do what you can; **si b. puedes** if you possibly can.

bueno,-a 1 *a* good; (*amable*) (*con ser*) good, kind; (*sano*) (*con estar*) well, in good health; **un alumno muy b.** a very good pupil; **lo b.** the good thing; **hoy hace buen tiempo** it's fine today; **un buen número de** a good number of; **una buena cantidad** a considerable amount; **un buen trozo de pastel** a nice *o* good big piece of cake; **¡en buen lío te has metido!** that's a fine mess you've got yourself into!; **¡buenas!** (*saludos*) hello!; **buenas tardes** (*desde mediodía hasta las cinco*) good afternoon; (*desde las cinco*) good evening; **buenas noches** (*al llegar*) good evening; (*al irse*) good night; **buenos días** good morning; **de buenas a primeras** all at once; **por las buenas** willingly; **por las buenas o por las malas** willy-nilly; **¡buena la has hecho!** that's done it!; **¡estaría b.!** I should jolly well hope not!; **librarse dc una buena** to get off scot free. **2** *interj* **¡b.!** (*vale*) all right, OK.

buey *m* ox.

búfalo,-a *mf* buffalo.

bufanda *f* scarf.

bufete *m* (*despacho de abogado*) lawyer's office.

buhardilla *f* attic.

búho *m* owl.

buitre *m* vulture.

bujía *f* (*de coche*) spark plug.

bulbo *m* bulb.

bulla *f* (*ruido*) din; **armar b.** to kick up a din.

bullicio *m* din.

bulto *m* (*cosa indistinta*) shape; (*maleta, caja*) piece of luggage; (*hinchazón*) lump; **hacer mucho b.** to be very bulky.

búnker *m* bunker.

buñuelo *m* doughnut.

buque *m* ship; **b. de guerra** warship; **b. de pasajeros** passenger ship.

burbuja *f* bubble.

burdel *m* brothel.

burguesía *f* bourgeoisie.

burladero *m* refuge in bullring.

burlarse *vr* to make fun (**de** of).

burlón,-ona *a* mocking.

burocracia *f* bureaucracy.

burocrático,-a *a* bureaucratic.

burro,-a *mf* donkey; *fam* (*estúpido*) blockhead. **2** *a fam* (*necio*) stupid; (*obstinado*) stubborn.

bursátil *a* stock market.

busca *f* search; **ir en b. de** to go in search of.

buscar [1] **1** *vt* to look *o* search for; **ir a b. algo** to go and get sth; **fue a buscarme a la estación** she picked me up at the station. **2 buscarse** *vr fam* **buscarse la vida** to try and earn one's living; **se busca** wanted.

búsqueda *f* search.

busto *m* bust.

butaca *f* (*sillón*) armchair; (*de teatro, cine*) seat; **b. de platea** *o* **patio** seat in the stalls.

butano *m* (*gas*) **b.** butane gas.

buzo *m* diver.

buzón *m* letter box, *US* mailbox; **echar una carta al b.** to post a letter.

C

cabalgar [7] *vti* to ride.

caballa *f* mackerel.

caballería *f* (*cuerpo*) cavalry; (*cabalgadura*) mount, steed.

caballero *m* gentleman; **ropa de c.** menswear; **caballeros** (*en letrero*) gents.

caballo *m* horse; (*de ajedrez*) knight; (*de naipes*) queen; **a c.** on horseback; **montar a c.** to ride; *fig* **a c. entre ...** halfway between ...

cabaña *f* (*choza*) cabin.

cabaret *m* (*pl* **cabarets**) cabaret.

cabecera *f* top, head.

cabecilla *mf* leader.

cabello *m* hair.

caber *vi* to fit; **cabe en el maletero** it fits in the boot; **en este coche/jarro caben ...** this car/jug holds ...; **no cabe duda** there is no doubt; **cabe la posibilidad de que ...** there is a possibility that ...; **no está mal dentro de lo que cabe** it isn't bad, under the circumstances.

cabestrillo *m* sling.

cabeza *f* head; **en c.** in the lead; **por c.** a head, per person; **a la c. de** at the head of; **estar mal de la c.** to be a mental case; *mf* **el** *o* **la c. de familia** the head of the family.

cabida *f* capacity.

cabina *f* cabin; **c. telefónica** telephone box, *US* telephone booth.

cable *m* cable.

cabo *m* (*extremo*) end; (*rango*) corporal; (*policía*) sergeant; (*de barco*) rope, cable; (*geográfica*) cape; **al c. de** after; **atar cabos** to put two and two together.

cabra *f* goat; *fam* **estar como una c.** to be off one's head.

cabré *indic fut de* **caber.**

cabriola *f* skip.

cacahuete *m* peanut.

cacao *m* cacao; (*polvo, bebida*) cocoa.

cacatúa *f* cockatoo.

cacería *f* (*actividad*) hunting; (*partida*) hunt.

cacerola *f* saucepan.

cacharro *m* earthenware pot *o* jar; *fam* (*cosa*) thing, piece of junk; **cacharros** (*de cocina*) pots and pans.

cachear *vt* to frisk, search.

cachetada *f Am* slap.

cachete *m* (*bofetada*) slap; *Am* (*mejilla*) cheek.

cachimba *m* pipe.

cachivache *m fam* thing, knick-knack.

cacho[1] *m fam* (*pedazo*) bit, piece.

cacho[2] *m Am* (*cuerno*) horn.

cachondeo *m fam* laugh; **tomar algo a c.** to take sth as a joke.

cachorro,-a *mf* (*de perro*) pup, puppy; (*de gato*) kitten; (*de otros animales*) cub, baby.

cacique *m* (*jefe*) local boss.

caco *m fam* thief.

cacto *m*, **cactus** *m inv* cactus.

cada *a* (*de dos*) each; (*de varios*) each, every; **c. día** every day; **c. dos días** every second day; **c. vez más** more and more; **¿c. cuánto?** how often?; **cuatro de c. diez** four out of (every) ten.

cadáver *m* (*de persona*) corpse, body; (*de animal*) body, carcass.

cadena *f* chain; (*correa de perro*) lead, leash; (*canal*) channel; (*de montañas*) range; **trabajo en c.** assembly line work; **c. perpetua** life imprisonment; (*para ruedas*) **cadenas** tyre chains.

cadera *f* hip.

caducar [1] *vi* to expire.

caducidad *f* expiry; **fecha de c.** (*en alimentos*) ≈ sell-by date; (*en medicinas*) to be used before.

caer 1 *vi* to fall; (*entender*) to understand, see; (*hallarse*) to be; **dejar c.** to drop; **ya caigo** I get it; **cae por Granada** it is somewhere near Granada; **me cae bien/mal** I like/don't like her. **2 caerse** *vr* to fall (down); **me caí de la moto** I fell off the motorbike; **se le cayó el pañuelo** she dropped her handkerchief.

café *m* coffee; (*cafetería*) café; **c. solo/con leche** black/white coffee.

cafeína *f* caffeine.

cafetera *f* (*para hacerlo*) coffee-maker; (*para servirlo*) coffeepot.

cafetería *f* snack bar, coffee bar; (*en tren*) buffet car.

caída *f* fall; (*de pelo, diente*) loss; (*de gobierno*) downfall, collapse.

caigo *indic pres de* **caer.**

caimán *m* caiman.

caja *f* box; (*de embalaje*) crate, case; (*en tienda*) cash desk; (*en banco*) cashier's desk; (*féretro*) coffin, *US* casket; **c. fuerte** safe; **c. de cerveza** crate of beer; **c. de cambios** gearbox; **c. de ahorros** *o* **de pensiones** savings bank.

cajero,-a *mf* cashier; **c. automático** cash point.

cajón *m* (*en un mueble*) drawer; (*caja grande*) crate, chest.

cal *f* lime; **a c. y canto** hermetically.

calabacín *m* (*pequeño*) courgette, *US* zucchini; (*grande*) marrow, *US* squash.

calabaza *f* pumpkin, gourd.

calabozo m (*prisión*) jail, prison; (*celda*) cell.

calado,-a a (*mojado*) soaked.

calamar m squid *inv*; **calamares a la romana** squid fried in batter.

calambre m (*descarga*) electric shock; (*en músculo*) cramp; **ese cable da c.** that wire is live.

calamidad f calamity.

calar 1 vt (*mojar*) to soak, drench. **2** vi (*prenda*) to let in water. **3 calarse** vr (*prenda, techo*) to let in water; (*mojarse*) to get soaked; (*coche*) to stall; **calarse el sombrero** to pull one's hat down.

calavera f skull.

calcar [1] vt (*dibujo*) to trace; (*imitar*) to copy, imitate.

calcetín m sock.

calcio m calcium.

calco m tracing; **papel de c.** carbon paper.

calculadora f calculator.

calcular vt to calculate; (*evaluar*) to (make an) estimate; (*suponer*) to guess.

cálculo m calculation; (*matemático*) calculus.

caldera f boiler.

caldo m stock, broth; **c. de cultivo** breeding ground.

calefacción f heating; **c. central** central heating.

calendario m calendar.

calentador m heater.

calentar [1] **1** vt (*agua, horno*) to heat; (*comida, habitación*) to warm up. **2 calentarse** vr to get hot, heat up.

calentura f fever, temperature.

calidad f quality; **de primera c.** first-class; **un vino de c.** good-quality wine.

cálido,-a a warm.

caliente a hot; (*debate*) heated.

calificar [1] vt to describe (**de,** as); (*examen*) to mark, grade.

caligrafía f calligraphy; (*modo de escribir*) handwriting.

caliza f limestone.

callar 1 vi (*dejar de hablar*) to stop talking; (*no hablar*) to keep quiet, say nothing; **¡calla!** be quiet!, shut up! **2** vt (*noticia*) not to mention, keep to oneself. **3 callarse** vr to be quiet, shut up; **¡cállate!** shut up!

calle f street, road; (*de piscina, pista*) lane; **c. de dirección única** one-way street.

callejón m back alley, back street; **c. sin salida** cul-de-sac, dead end.

callista mf chiropodist.

callo m callus, corn; **callos** tripe *sing*.

calma f calm; **¡c.!** calm down!; **en c.** calm; **tómatelo con c.** take it easy.

calmante *m* painkiller; (*relajante*) tranquillizer.

calmar 1 *vt* (*persona*) to calm (down); (*dolor*) to soothe, relieve. **2 calmarse** *vr* (*persona*) to calm down; (*dolor, viento*) to ease off.

calor *m* heat, (*entusiamo*) warm; **hace c.** it's hot; **tengo c.** I'm hot; **entrar en c.** to warm up.

caloría *f* calorie.

calumnia *f* slander.

caluroso,-a *a* hot; (*acogida etc*) warm.

calvicie *f* baldness.

calvo,-a 1 *a* bald. **2** *m* bald man.

calzada *f* road.

calzado *m* shoes *pl.*

calzador *m* shoehorn.

calzar [4] **1** *vt* (*poner calzado*) to put shoes on; (*mueble*) to wedge; **¿qué número calzas?** what size shoe do you take? **2 calzarse** *vr* **calzarse los zapatos** to put on one's shoes.

calzones *nmpl* trousers.

calzoncillos *nmpl* underpants, pants.

cama *f* bed; **estar en** *o* **guardar c.** to be confined to bed; **hacer la c.** to make the bed; **irse a la c.** to go to bed; **c. doble/sencilla** double/single bed.

cámara 1 *f* (*aparato*) camera; (*de diputados etc*) Chamber, House; (*de rueda*) inner tube; **a c. lenta** in slow motion; **c. frigorífica** cold-storage room. **2** *mf* (*hombre*) cameraman; (*mujer*) camerawoman.

camarada *mf* comrade.

camarera *f* (*de hotel*) (chamber)maid.

camarero,-a *mf* (*de restaurante*) (*hombre*) waiter; (*mujer*) waitress; (*tras la barra*) (*hombre*) barman; (*mujer*) barmaid.

camarón *m* prawn.

camarote *m* cabin.

cambiar 1 *vt* to change; (*intercambiar*) to swap, exchange; **c. algo de sitio** to move sth. **2** *vi* to change; **c. de casa** to move (house); **c. de idea** to change one's mind. **3 cambiarse** *vr* (*de ropa*) to change (clothes); (*de casa*) to move (house).

cambio *m* change; (*de impresiones*) exchange; (*de divisas*) exchange; **c. de marcha** gear change; **a c. de** in exchange for; **en c.** on the other hand; **¿tienes c. de mil pesetas?** have you got change for a thousand pesetas?

camello,-a *mf* camel.

camilla *f* stretcher.

caminar 1 *vi* to walk. **2** *vt* walk; **caminaron diez kilómetros** they walked for ten kilometres.

camino *m* (*ruta*) route, way; (*vía*) path, track; **ponerse en c.** to set off; **abrirse c.** to break through; **a medio c.** half-way; **estar en c.** to be on the way; **nos coge** *o* **pilla de c.** it is on the way.

camión *m* lorry, *US* truck; **c. cisterna** tanker; **c. de la basura** refuse lorry, *US* garbage truck; **c. frigorífico** refrigerator lorry.

camionero,-a *mf* lorry driver, *US* truck driver.

camioneta *f* van.

camisa *f* shirt; **en mangas de c.** in one's shirtsleeves; **c. de fuerza** straightjacket.

camiseta *f* (*de uso interior*) vest, *US* undershirt; (*de uso exterior*) T-shirt; (*de deporte*) shirt.

camisón *m* nightdress, nightie.

camote *m Am* sweet potato.

campamento *m* camp.

campana *f* bell.

campanada *f* peal of a bell.

campanilla *f* small bell.

campaña *f* campaign; **c. electoral** election campaign; **c. publicitaria** advertising campaign.

campeón,-ona *mf* champion; **c. mundial** world champion.

campeonato *m* championship.

campesino,-a *mf* (*hombre*) countryman; (*mujer*) countrywoman.

camping *m* campsite; **hacer** *o* **ir de c.** to go camping.

campista *mf* camper.

campo *m* country, countryside; (*de fútbol*) pitch; (*de tenis*) court; (*de golf*) course; (*parcela, ámbito*) field; **a c. traviesa** *o* **través** cross-country; **c. de batalla** battlefield; **c. de concentración** concentration camp; **c. de trabajo** work camp.

camposanto *m* cemetery.

cana *f* (*gris*) grey hair; (*blanco*) white hair; **tener canas** to have grey hair.

canal *m* (*artificial*) canal; (*natural, de televisión*) channel; **C. de la Mancha** English Channel.

canalla *mf* swine, rotter.

canalón *m* gutter.

canalones *mpl* (*pasta*) cannelloni.

canapé *m* canapé; (*sofá*) couch, sofa.

canario,-a 1 *a & mf* Canarian; **Islas Canarias** Canary Islands, Canaries. **2** *m* (*pájaro*) canary.

canasta *f* basket.

cancela *f* wrought-iron gate.

cancelar *vt* to cancel; (*deuda*) to pay off.

cáncer *m* cancer; **c. de pulmón/mama** lung/breast cancer.

cancerígeno,-a *a* carcinogenic.

canceroso,-a *a* cancerous.

cancha f ground; (de tenis, baloncesto) court.
canciller mf chancellor.
canción f song.
candado m padlock.
candelabro m candelabra.
candidato,-a mf candidate; (a un puesto) applicant.
candidatura f (lista) list of candidates.
cándido,-a a candid.
candoroso,-a a innocent, pure.
canela f cinnamon.
cangrejo m (de mar) crab; (de río) freshwater crayfish.
canguro 1 m kangaroo. 2 mf fam baby-sitter.
caníbal a & mf cannibal.
canica f marble.
canícula f dog days, midsummer heat.
caniche m poodle.
canillera f Am (cobardía) cowardice; (miedo) fear.
canillita m Am newspaper boy.
canino,-a 1 a canine. 2 m (colmillo) canine.
canoa f canoe.
canoso,-a a (de pelo blanco) white-haired; (de pelo gris) grey-haired;
(pelo) white; grey.
cansado,-a a (agotado) tired, weary.
cansancio m tiredness, weariness.
cansar 1 vt to tire. 2 vi to be tiring. 3 **cansarse** vr to get tired; **se cansó de
esperar** he got tired of waiting, he got fed up (with) waiting.
cantante 1 mf singer. 2 a singing.
cantaor,-a mf flamenco singer.
cantar vti to sing.
cántaro m pitcher; **llover a cántaros** to rain cats and dogs.
cante m (canto) singing; **c. hondo, c. jondo** flamenco.
cantera f (de piedra) quarry; (de equipo) young players pl.
cantidad f quantity; (de dinero) sum; fam **c. de gente** thousands of
people.
cantina f canteen.
canto[1] m (arte) singing; (canción) song.
canto[2] m (borde) edge; **de c.** on its side.
canturrear vi to hum, croon.
caña f (de cerveza) glass of draught o US draft beer; (tallo) cane, stem;
(de pescar) rod; **c. de azúcar** sugar cane.
cañada f (barranco) gully, ravine.
cañería f (piece of) piping; **cañerías** plumbing sing.

caño m (tubería) pipe; (tubo) tube; (chorro) spout.

cañón m cannon; (de fusil) barrel; (garganta) canyon.

cañonazo m gunshot.

caoba f mahogany.

caos m chaos.

caótico,-a a chaotic.

capa f (prenda) cloak, cape; (de pintura) layer, coat.

capacidad f capacity.

caparazón m shell.

capataz mf (hombre) foreman; (mujer) forewoman.

capaz a capable, able; **ser c. de hacer algo** (tener la habilidad de) to be able to do sth; (atreverse a) to dare to do sth; Am **es c. que** it is likely that.

capicúa a **número c.** reversible number; **palabra c.** palindrome.

capilla f chapel.

capital 1 f capital. **2** m (dinero) capital. **3** a capital, main; **pena c.** capital punishment.

capitalismo m capitalism.

capitalista a & mf capitalist.

capitán,-ana mf captain.

capitulación f agreement; (pacto) capitulation.

capítulo m (de libro) chapter; (tema) subject.

capó m (de coche) bonnet, US hood.

capota f (de coche) soft top.

capote m (de torero) cape.

capricho m (antojo) whim, caprice.

caprichoso,-a a whimsical.

cápsula f capsule.

captar vt (ondas) to receive, pick up; (comprender) to understand, grasp; (interés etc) to attract.

captura f capture.

capturar vt (criminal) to capture; (cazar, pescar) to catch.

capucha f hood.

capullo m (de insecto) cocoon; (de flor) bud.

caqui 1 a (color) khaki. **2** m (fruto) persimmon.

cara 1 f face; (lado) side; (de moneda) right side; fam (desfachatez) cheek, nerve; **c. a c.** face to face; **tener buena/mala c.** to look good/bad; **(de) c. a** with a view to; **echarle a algn algo en c.** to reproach sb for sth; **¿c. o cruz?** heads or tails?; **echar algo a c.** o **cruz** to toss (a coin) for sth; **¡qué c. (más dura) tienes!** you've got a cheek! **2** m fam (desvergonzado) cheeky person.

caracol m (de tierra) snail; Am shell.

caracola f conch.

carácter m (pl caracteres) character; (índole) nature; **tener buen/mal c.**

to be good-natured/bad-tempered.

característica f characteristic.

característico,-a a characteristic.

caramba interj (sorpresa) good grief!; (enfado) damn it!

carámbano m icicle.

caramelo m (dulce) sweet, US candy; (azúcar quemado) caramel.

caravana f caravan; (cola) tailback.

carbón m coal; **c. vegetal** charcoal; **c. mineral** coal.

carbonizar [4] vt, **carbonizarse** vr to char.

carbono m carbon.

carburador m carburettor, US carburetor.

carburante m fuel.

carcajada f guffaw.

cárcel f prison, jail.

carcelero,-a mf jailer, warder, US warden.

cardenal m cardinal; (en la piel) bruise.

cardiaco,-a, cardíaco,-a a cardiac, heart; **ataque c.** heart attack.

cardinal a cardinal; **punto/número c.** cardinal point/number.

cardiólogo,-a mf cardiologist.

cardo m (con espinas) thistle.

carecer vi c. de to lack.

carencia f lack (de, of).

careta f mask; **c. antigás** gas mask.

carezco indic pres de **carecer**.

carga f (acción) loading; (cosa cargada) load; (de avión, barco) cargo, freight; (explosiva, eléctrica) charge; (obligación) burden.

cargado,-a a loaded; (bebida) strong; **un café c.** a strong coffee; **atmósfera cargada** stuffy atmosphere; **c. de deudas** up to one's eyes in debt.

cargamento m (carga) load; (mercancías) cargo, freight.

cargar [7] **1** vt to load; (mechero, pluma) to fill; (batería) to charge; **cárguelo a mi cuenta** charge it to my account. **2** vi c. con (llevar) to carry; **c. con las consecuencias** to suffer the consequences. **3 cargarse** vr to load oneself with; fam (estropear) to smash, ruin; fam (matar) to kill, bump off.

cargo m (puesto) post, position; (persona) top person; (débito) charge, debit; (acusación) charge, accusation; **alto c.** (puesto) top job; **estar al c. de** to be in charge of; **correr a c. de** (gastos) to be met by; **hacerse c. de** to take charge of; **hazte c. de mi situación** please try to understand my situation; **con c. a mi cuenta** charged to my account.

caricatura f caricature.

caricia f caress, stroke.

caridad *f* charity.

caries *f inv* decay, caries.

cariño *m* (*amor*) affection; (*querido*) darling; **coger/tener c. a algo/algn** to grow/to be fond of sth/sb; **con c.** (*en carta*) love.

cariñoso,-a *a* loving, affectionate.

cariz *m* look.

carmín *m* (*de color*) **c.** carmine; **c. (de labios)** lipstick.

carnaval *m* carnival.

carne *f* flesh; (*alimento*) meat; **ser de c. y hueso** to be only flesh and blood; **c. de gallina** goose pimples; **c. de cerdo/cordero/ternera/vaca** pork/lamb/veal/beef.

carné, carnet *m* card; **c. de conducir** driving licence, *US* driver's license; **c. de identidad** identity card.

carnero *m* ram; (*carne*) mutton.

carnicería *f* butcher's (shop).

caro,-a 1 *a* expensive, dear. **2** *adv* **salir c.** to cost a lot; **te costará c.** (*amenaza*) you'll pay dearly for this.

carpa *f* (*pez*) carp; (*de circo*) big top, marquee; *Am* (*de camping*) tent.

carpeta *f* folder.

carpintería *f* (*oficio*) carpentry; (*taller*) carpenter's (shop).

carpintero,-a *mf* carpenter.

carraspear *vi* to clear one's throat.

carrera *f* run; (*de media*) run, ladder; (*competición*) race; (*estudios*) degree; (*profesión*) career, profession; **c. de coches** rally, meeting; **echar una c. a algn** to race sb.

carrerilla *f* **tomar c.** to take a run; **de c.** parrot fashion.

carrete *m* (*de hilo*) reel; (*de película*) spool.

carretera *f* road; (*en autopista*) slip road; **c. comarcal/nacional** A/B road; **c. de circunvalación** ring road; **c. de acceso** access road.

carretilla *f* wheelbarrow.

carril *m* (*de trenes*) rail; (*de carretera*) lane.

carrillo *m* cheek.

carro *m* (*carreta*) cart; (*de máquina de escribir*) carriage; *Am* car; **c. de combate** tank.

carrocería *f* bodywork.

carta *f* letter; (*menú*) menu; (*de baraja*) card; **c. certificada/urgente** registered/express letter; **a la c.** à la carte; **c. de vinos** wine list; **tomar cartas en un asunto** to take part in an affair.

cartel *m* poster.

cartera *f* (*de bolsillo*) wallet; (*de mano*) handbag; (*para documentos etc*) briefcase; (*de colegial*) satchel, schoolbag; *Am* (*bolso*) handbag, *US* purse.

cartero,-a *mf* (*hombre*) postman; (*mujer*) postwoman.

cartilla *f* (*libreta*) book; (*para leer*) first reader; **c. de ahorros** savings book.

cartón *m* (*material*) card, cardboard; (*de cigarrillos*) carton.

cartucho *m* cartridge; (*de papel*) cone.

cartulina *f* card.

casa *f* (*edificio*) house; (*hogar*) home; (*empresa*) company, firm; **c. de huéspedes** boarding house; **c. de socorro** first aid post.

casado,-a 1 *a* married. **2** *mf* married person; **los recién casados** the newlyweds.

casar 1 *vt* to marry. **2 casarse** *vr* to marry, get married.

cascabel *m* bell.

cascada *f* waterfall, cascade.

cascar [1] *vt*, **cascarse** *vr* to crack.

cáscara *f* shell; (*de fruta*) skin, peel; (*de grano*) husk.

casco *m* helmet; (*de caballo*) hoof; (*envase*) empty bottle; (*de barco*) hull; **c. urbano** city centre; **cascos** (*auriculares*) headphones.

casero,-a 1 *a* (*hecho en casa*) home-made; (*persona*) home-loving. **2** *mf* (*dueño*) (*hombre*) landlord; (*mujer*) landlady.

caseta *f* hut, booth; (*de feria, exposición*) stand, stall.

casete 1 *m* (*magnetófono*) cassette player *o* recorder. **2** *f* (*cinta*) cassette (tape).

casi *adv* almost, nearly; **c. nunca** hardly ever; **c. nadie** hardly anyone; **c. me caigo** I almost fell.

casino *m* casino.

caso *m* case; **el c. es que ...** the thing is that ...; **el c. Mattei** the Mattei affair; **(en) c. contrario** otherwise; **en c. de necesidad** if need be; **en cualquier c.** in any case; **en el mejor/peor de los casos** at best/worst; **en ese c.** in such a case; **en todo c.** in any case; **hacer c. a** *o* **de algn** to pay attention to sb; **no venir al c.** to be beside the point; **pongamos por c.** let's say.

caspa *f* dandruff.

cassette *m* & *f* = **casete.**

castaña *f* chestnut.

castaño,-a 1 *a* chestnut-brown; (*pelo, ojos*) brown, dark. **2** *m* (*árbol*) chestnut.

castigar [7] *vt* to punish; (*penalizar*) to penalize.

castigo *m* punishment; (*pena*) penalty.

castillo *m* castle.

casual *a* accidental, chance.

casualidad *f* chance, coincidence; **de** *o* **por c.** by chance; **dió la c. que ...** it so happened that ...; **¿tienes un lápiz, por c.?** do you happen to have a pencil?; **¡que c.!** what a coincidence!

casualmente *adv* by chance.

cataclismo *m* cataclysm.

catalejo *m* telescope.

catalogar [7] *vt* to catalogue, *US* catalog; (*clasificar*) to classify.

catálogo *m* catalogue, *US* catalog.

catapulta *f* catapult.

catarata *f* waterfall; (*enfermedad*) cataract.

catarro *m* (common) cold.

catástrofe *f* catastrophe.

cátedra *f* (*professorial*) chair.

catedral *f* cathedral.

catedrático,-a *mf* (*de universidad*) professor; (*de instituto*) head of department.

categoría *f* category; **de c.** (*persona*) important.

cateto,-a *mf* (*paleto*) yokel, bumpkin.

católico,-a *mf* Catholic.

catorce *a & m inv* fourteen.

cauce *m* (*de un río*) bed; *fig* channel.

caucho *m* rubber; *Am* (*cubierta*) tyre, *US* tire.

caudal *m* (*de un río*) flow; (*riqueza*) wealth.

caudillo *m* leader, head.

causa *f* cause; **a** *o* **por c. de** because of.

causante 1 *a* causal. **2** *mf* **el c. del incendio** the person who caused the fire.

causar *vt* to cause; **c. buena/mala impresión** to made a good/bad impression.

cautela *f* caution.

cautivar *vt* to capture, take prisoner.

cautiverio *m*, **cautividad** *f* captivity.

cautivo,-a *a & mf* captive.

cava 1 *f* (*bodega*) wine cellar. **2** *m* (*vino espumoso*) champagne.

cavar *vt* to dig.

caverna *f* cave.

caviar *f* caviar.

cavidad *f* cavity.

cavilar *vt* to ponder.

cayado *m* (*de pastor*) crook.

caza *f* hunting; (*animales*) game; (*persecución*) hunt; **ir de c.** to go hunting; **c. furtiva** poaching; **c. mayor/menor** big/small game.

cazador,-a *mf* hunter.

cazadora *f* (waist-length) jacket.

cazar [4] *vt* to hunt.

cazo *m* (*cacerola*) saucepan; (*cucharón*) ladle.

cazuela *f* saucepan; (*guiso*) casserole, stew; **a la c.** stewed.

cebada *f* barley.

cebo *m* bait.

cebolla *f* onion.

cebolleta *f* spring onion.

cebra *f* zebra; **paso c.** zebra crossing, *US* crosswalk.

ceder 1 *vt* to give, hand over; **c. el paso** to give way. **2** *vi* (*cuerda, cable*) to give way; (*consentir*) to give in.

cédula *f* document, certificate; *Am* **c. de identidad** identity card.

C(E)E *f abr de* **Comunidad (Económica) Europea** European (Economic) Community, E(E)C.

cegar [1] *vt* to blind; (*puerta, ventana*) to wall up.

ceguera *f* blindness.

ceja *f* eyebrow.

celador,-a *mf* attendant; (*de cárcel*) warder.

celda *f* cell.

celebración *f* (*festejo*) celebration; (*de juicio etc*) holding.

celebrar 1 *vt* to celebrate; (*reunión, juicio, elecciones*) to hold. **2 celebrarse** *vr* to take place, be held.

célebre *a* famous, well-known.

celeste 1 *a* (*de cielo*) celestial; (*color*) sky-blue. **2** *m* sky blue.

celibato *m* celibacy.

celo *m* zeal; **en c.** (*macho*) in rut; (*hembra*) in heat; **celos** jealousy *sing*; **tener celos (de algn)** to be jealous (of sb).

celo[R] *m* sellotape[R], *US* Scotch tape[R].

celofán *m* cellophane.

celoso,-a *a* jealous.

célula *f* cell.

celulitis *f inv* cellulite.

cementerio *m* cemetery.

cemento *m* cement.

cena *f* dinner.

cenar 1 *vi* to have dinner. **2** *vt* to have for dinner.

cenicero *m* ashtray.

cenit *m* zenith.

censo *m* census; **c. electoral** electoral roll.

censura *f* censorship; **moción de c.** vote of no confidence.

censurar *vt* (*libro, película*) to censor.

centavo,-a *Am* cent, centavo.

centellear *vi* to flash, sparkle.

centena *f*, **centenar** *m* hundred.
centenario *m* centenary.
centeno *m* rye.
centésimo,-a *a & mf* hundredth.
centígrado,-a *a* centigrade.
centilitro *m* centilitre.
centímetro *m* centimetre.
céntimo *m* cent.
centinela *m* sentry.
centollo *m* spider crab.
central 1 *a* central. 2 *f* (*oficina principal*) head office; **c. nuclear/térmica** nuclear/coal-fired power station.
centralismo *m* centralism.
centralita *f* switchboard.
centralizar [4] *vt* to centralize.
céntrico,-a *a* centrally situated.
centrifugar [7] *vt* (*ropa*) to spin-dry.
centro *m* centre; **c. de la ciudad** city centre; **c. comercial** shopping centre.
ceñido,-a *a* tight-fitting, clinging.
cepillar *vt*, **cepillarse** *vr* to brush.
cepillo *m* brush; (*en carpintería*) plane; **c. de dientes** toothbrush; **c. del pelo** hairbrush.
cera *f* wax; (*de abeja*) beeswax.
cerámica *f* ceramics *sing*.
cerca¹ 1 *adv* near, close; **de c.** closely. 2 *prep* **c. de** (*al lado de*) near, close to; (*casi*) nearly, around; **el colegio está c. de mi casa** the school is near my house; **c. de cien personas** about one hundred people.
cerca² *f* enclosure.
cercano,-a *a* nearby; **el C. Oriente** the Near East.
cercar [1] *vt* (*tapiar*) to fence, enclose; (*rodear*) to surround.
cerdo *m* pig; (*carne*) pork.
cereal *m* cereal.
cerebro *m* brain; (*inteligencia*) brains *pl*.
ceremonia *f* ceremony.
cereza *f* cherry.
cerezo *m* cherry tree.
cerilla *f* match.
cero *m* zero; (*en resultado*) nil; **ser un c. a la izquierda** to be useless.
cerrado,-a *a* closed, shut; (*intransigente*) uncompromising; (*acento*) broad; (*curva*) sharp.
cerradura *f* lock.
cerrar [1] 1 *vt* to shut, close; (*grifo, gas*) to turn off; (*cremallera*) to do

up; (*negocio*) to close down; (*cuenta*) to close; (*sobre*) to seal; **c. con llave** to lock; **c. el paso a algn** to block sb's way. **2** *vi* to close, shut. **3 cerrarse** *vr* to close, shut.

cerril *a* (*obstinado*) pig-headed, headstrong.

cerro *m* hill.

cerrojo *m* bolt; **echar el c. (de una puerta)** to bolt (a door).

certamen *m* competition, contest.

certeza, certidumbre *f* certainty; **tener la c. de que ...** to be certain that ...

certificado,-a 1 *a* certified; (*correo*) registered. **2** *m* certificate; **c. médico** medical certificate.

cervecería *f* (*bar*) pub, bar; (*fábrica*) brewery.

cerveza *f* beer; **c. de barril** draught beer; **c. negra** stout.

cesar 1 *vi* to stop, cease (**de** -); **sin c.** incessantly. **2** *vt* (*empleado*) to dismiss.

césped *m* lawn, grass.

cesta *f* basket.

cesto *m* basket.

chabola *f* shack.

chacinería *f* pork butcher's shop.

chacra *f* *Am* small farm.

chafar *vt fam* (*plan etc*) to ruin; (*aplastar*) to squash.

chal *m* shawl.

chalado,-a *a fam* crazy, nuts (**por** about).

chalé *m* (*pl* **chalés**) villa.

chaleco *m* waistcoat, *US* vest; (*de punto*) sleeveless pullover; **c. salvavidas** life jacket.

chalet *m* villa.

champán, champaña *m* champagne.

champiñón *m* mushroom.

champú *m* shampoo.

chamuscar [1] *vt* to singe, scorch.

chancaca *f* *Am* syrup cake.

chance *m* *Am* opportunity.

chancear *vi* to joke, horse around.

chanchada *f* *Am fam* dirty trick.

chancho,-a *mf* *Am* pig.

chancla *f* flipflop.

chándal *m* track suit, jogging suit.

chantaje *m* blackmail; **hacer c. a algn** to blackmail sb.

chantajear *vt* to blackmail.

chapa *f* (*tapón*) bottle top, cap; (*de adorno*) badge; *Am* lock.

chapado,-a *a* (*metal*) plated; **c. en oro** gold-plated.

chaparrón *m* downpour, heavy shower.

chapotear *vi* to splash about, paddle.

chapurrear *vt* (*idioma*) to speak badly.

chapuza *f* (*trabajo mal hecho*) shoddy piece of work; (*trabajo ocasional*) odd job.

chapuzón *m* (*baño corto*) dip; **darse un c.** to have a dip.

chaqueta *f* jacket.

charca *f* pond, pool.

charco *m* puddle.

charcutería *f* delicatessen.

charla *f* (*conversación*) talk, chat; (*conferencia*) informal lecture.

charlar *vi* to talk, chat.

charlatán,-ana 1 *a* (*parlanchín*) talkative. **2** *mf* (*parlanchín*) chatterbox; (*embaucador*) charlatan.

charol *m* patent leather.

chárter *a inv* (**vuelo**) **c.** charter (flight).

chasca *f Am* (*cabellera revuelta*) mop of hair, tangled hair.

chasco *m fam* (*decepción*) disappointment; **llevarse un c.** to be disappointed.

chasis *m inv* chassis.

chasqui *m Am* messenger, courier.

chasquido *m* (*de la lengua*) click; (*de los dedos*) snap; (*de látigo, madera*) crack.

chatarra *f* scrap (metal), scrap iron; (*cosa inservible*) junk.

chato,-a *a* (*nariz*) snub; (*persona*) snub-nosed.

chauvinista *a & mf* chauvinist.

chaval,-a *mf* (*chico*) boy, lad; (*chica*) girl, lass.

chepa *f* hump.

cheque *m* cheque, *US* check; **c. de viaje** *o* **(de) viajero** traveller's cheque, *US* traveler's check.

chequeo *m* checkup.

chicano,-a *a & mf* chicano.

chicha *f Am* maize liquor.

chícharo *m Am* (*guisante*) pea.

chicharra *f* cicada.

chichón *m* bump, lump.

chicle *m* chewing gum.

chico,-a 1 *mf* (*muchacho*) boy, lad; (*muchacha*) girl, lass. **2** *a* (*pequeño*) small, little.

chicote *m Am* whip.

chiflado,-a *a fam* mad, crazy (**por** about).

chillar vi (*persona*) to scream, shriek.

chillido m (*de persona*) scream, shriek.

chillón,-ona a (*voz*) shrill, high-pitched; (*sonido*) harsh; (*color*) loud.

chimenea f fireplace, hearth; (*conducto*) chimney.

chincheta f drawing pin, US thumbtack.

chingana f Am bar.

chip m (pl **chips**) chip.

chipirón m baby squid.

chiquillo,-a mf kid, youngster.

chiringuito m (*en playa etc*) refreshment stall; (*en carretera*) roadside snack bar.

chirriar vi (*puerta*) to creak; (*frenos*) to screech.

chirrido m (*de puerta*) creak, creaking; (*de frenos*) screech.

chisme m (*habladuría*) piece of gossip; *fam* (*trasto*) knick-knack; (*cosa*) thing.

chismear vi to gossip.

chismoso,-a 1 a (*murmurador*) gossipy. 2 mf gossip.

chispa f spark.

chispear vi to spark; (*lloviznar*) to spit.

chiste m joke; **contar un c.** to tell a joke.

chivatazo m *fam* (*soplo*) tip-off; **dar el c.** to squeal.

chivato,-a mf *fam* (*acusica*) telltale; (*delator*) grass.

chocante a (*sorprendente*) surprising; (*raro*) strange.

chocar [1] 1 vi (*topar*) to crash, collide; (*pelota*) to hit, strike; **c. con** o **contra** to run into, collide with. 2 vt to knock; (*sorprender*) to surprise.

chochear vi (*viejo*) to be senile.

chocolate m chocolate.

chocolatina f bar of chocolate, chocolate bar.

chófer m (pl **chóferes**), **chofer** m Am (pl **choferes**) driver; (*particular*) chauffeur.

chomba f Am jumper, pullover.

chonta f Am palm tree.

chopo m poplar.

choque m impact; (*de coches etc*) crash, collision.

chorizo m highly-seasoned pork sausage.

chorrear vi to gush, spurt; (*gotear*) to drip, trickle; *fam* **estoy chorreando** I am soaking wet.

chorro m (*de agua etc*) spurt; (*muy fino*) trickle; **salir a chorros** to gush forth.

chovinista 1 a chauvinistic. 2 mf chauvinist.

choza f hut, shack.

chubasco m heavy shower, downpour.

chubasquero *m* cagoule.

chuleta *f* chop, cutlet; **c. de cerdo** pork chop.

chulo,-a *fam* **1** *mf* show-off. **2** *a* (*bonito*) smashing.

chupachup⁽ᴿ⁾ *m* lollipop.

chupar 1 *vt* to suck; (*lamer*) to lick; (*absorber*) to soak up, absorb. **2** *vi* to suck. **3 chuparse** *vr* **está para chuparse los dedos** it's really mouth-watering.

chupete *m* dummy, *US* pacifier.

churrete *m* dirty mark, grease spot.

churro *m* fritter, *US* cruller.

chutar *vi* (*a gol*) to shoot.

cicatriz *f* scar.

cicatrizar [4] *vti* to heal.

ciclismo *m* cycling.

ciclista 1 *a* cycling. **2** *mf* cyclist.

ciclo *m* cycle; (*de conferencias etc*) series.

ciclomotor *m* moped.

ciclón *m* cyclone.

ciego,-a 1 *a* blind; **a ciegas** blindly. **2** *mf* blind person; **los ciegos** the blind *pl*.

cielo *m* sky; (*gloria*) heaven; (*de la boca*) roof.

ciempiés *m inv* centipede.

cien *a & m inv* hundred; **c. libras** a *o* one hundred pounds; **c. por c.** one hundred per cent.

ciencia *f* science; **saber algo a c. cierta** to know something for certain; **c. ficción** science fiction.

cieno *m* mud.

científico,-a 1 *a* scientific. **2** *mf* scientist.

ciento *a* hundred; **c. tres** one hundred and three; **por c.** per cent.

cierre *m* (*acción*) closing, shutting; (*de fábrica*) shutdown; (*de emisión*) close-down; (*de bolso*) clasp; (*de puerta*) catch.

cierto,-a 1 *a* certain; (*verdadero*) true; **lo c. es que ...** the fact is that ...; **por c.** by the way. **2** *adv* certainly.

ciervo,-a *mf* deer; (*macho*) stag; (*hembra*) doe, hind.

cifra *f* (*número*) figure, number; (*suma*) amount.

cigala *f* Norway lobster.

cigarra *f* cicada.

cigarrillo *m* cigarette.

cigarro *m* (*cigarrillo*) cigarette; (*puro*) cigar.

cigüeña *f* stork.

cilindro *m* cylinder.

cima *f* summit.

cimientos *nmpl* foundations.

cinco *a & m inv* five.

cincuenta *a & m inv* fifty.

cine *m* cinema, *US* movie theater; (*arte*) cinema.

cinematográfico,-a *a* cinematographic; **la industria cinematográfica** the film *o US* movie industry.

cínico,-a 1 *a* cynical. **2** *mf* cynic.

cinta *f* (*tira*) band, strip; (*para adornar*) ribbon; (*película*) film; **c. adhesiva/aislante** adhesive/insulating tape; **c. de vídeo** video tape; **c. transportadora** conveyor belt.

cintura *f* waist.

cinturón *m* belt; **c. de seguridad** safety belt.

ciprés *m* cypress.

circo *m* circus.

circuito *m* circuit.

circulación *f* circulation; (*tráfico*) traffic.

circular 1 *a & f* circular. **2** *vi* (*moverse*) to circulate; (*líquido*) to flow; (*tren, autobús*) to run; (*rumor*) to go round.

círculo *m* circle.

circuncisión *f* circumcision.

circundante *a* surrounding.

circunferencia *f* circumference.

circunscripción *f* district.

circunstancia *f* circumstance.

cirio *m* wax candle.

ciruela *f* plum; **c. claudia** greengage; **c. pasa** prune.

ciruelo *m* plum tree.

cirugía *f* surgery; **c. estética** *o* **plástica** plastic surgery.

cirujano,-a *mf* surgeon.

cisne *m* swan.

cisterna *f* cistern, tank.

cita *f* appointment; (*amorosa*) date; (*mención*) quotation.

citar *vt* (*mencionar*) to quote; **me ha citado el dentista** I have an appointment with the dentist.

cítrico,-a 1 *a* citric, citrus. **2** *nmpl* **cítricos** citrus fruits.

ciudad *f* town; (*grande*) city.

ciudadano,-a 1 *mf* citizen. **2** *a* civic.

cívico,-a *a* civic.

civil *a* civil; (*no militar*) civilian; **matrimonio c.** civil marriage.

civilización *f* civilization.

civilizado,-a *a* civilized.

civismo *m* civility.

clamoroso,-a *a* resounding.

clan *m* clan.

clandestino,-a *a* clandestine.

clara *f* (*de huevo*) white.

claraboya *f* skylight.

clarear *vi* (*amanecer*) to dawn; (*despejar*) to clear up.

clarete *a* & *m* claret.

claridad *f* (*luz*) brightness; (*inteligibilidad*) clarity; **con c.** clearly.

clarificar [1] *vt* to clarify.

clarinete *m* clarinet.

claro,-a 1 *a* clear; (*líquido, salsa*) thin; (*color*) light. **2** *interj* of course!; **¡c. que no!** of course not!; **¡c. que sí!** certainly! **3** *m* (*en un bosque*) clearing; (*tiempo despejado*) bright spell. **4** *adv* clearly.

clase *f* class; (*tipo*) kind, sort; (*curso*) class; (*aula*) classroom; **c. alta/media** upper/middle class; **primera/segunda c.** first/second class; **toda c. de ...** all kinds of ...

clásico,-a 1 *a* classical; (*típico, en el vestir*) classic. **2** *m* classic.

clasificación *f* classification; (*para campeonato, concurso*) qualification.

clasificar [1] **1** *vt* to classify, class. **2 clasificarse** *vr* to qualify.

claustrofobia *f* claustrophobia.

cláusula *f* clause.

clausura *f* (*cierre*) closure.

clavar **1** *vt* to nail; (*clavo*) to hammer in; (*estaca*) to drive in. **2 clavarse** *vr* **clavarse una astilla** to get a splinter.

clave *f* key; **la palabra c.** the key word.

clavel *m* carnation.

clavícula *f* collarbone.

clavo *m* nail; *fig* **dar en el c.** to hit the nail on the head; (*especia*) clove.

claxon *m* (*pl* **cláxones**) horn; **tocar el c.** to sound the horn.

clemencia *f* mercy, clemency.

clementina *f* clementine.

clérigo *m* priest.

clero *m* clergy.

cliché *m* (*tópico*) cliché; (*negativo*) negative.

cliente *mf* customer, client.

clima *m* climate.

climatizado,-a *a* air-conditioned.

clínica *f* clinic.

clip *m* (*para papel*) clip.

cloaca *f* sewer, drain.

cloro *m* chlorine.

cloroformo *m* chloroform.

club *m* (*pl* **clubs** *o* **clubes**) club; **c. náutico** yacht club.

coacción *f* coercion.

coalición *f* coalition.

coartada *f* alibi.

cobarde 1 *a* cowardly. **2** *mf* coward.

cobaya *f* guinea pig.

cobertizo *m* shed, shack.

cobertor *m* bedspread.

cobija *f Am* blanket.

cobijar *vt*, **cobijarse** *vr* to shelter.

cobra *f* cobra.

cobrador,-a *mf* (*de autobús*) (*hombre*) conductor; (*mujer*) conductress; (*de luz, agua etc*) collector.

cobrar *vt* (*dinero*) to charge; (*cheque*) to cash; (*salario*) to earn; **c. importancia** to become important.

cobre *m* copper; *Am* (*moneda*) copper cent.

cobro *m* (*pago*) collecting; (*de cheque*) cashing; **llamada a c. revertido** reverse-charge call, *US* collect call.

coca *f* coca.

cocaína *f* cocaine.

cocción *f* cooking; (*en agua*) boiling; (*en horno*) baking.

cocer [4] *vt*, **cocerse** *vr* (*comida*) to cook; (*hervir*) to boil; (*en horno*) to bake.

coche *m* car; **en c.** by car; **c. de bomberos** fire engine; (*vagón*) carriage, coach; **c. cama** sleeper.

cochecito *m* (*de niño*) pram, *US* baby carriage.

cochera *f* garage; (*de autobuses*) depot.

cochino,-a 1 *mf* (*macho*) pig; (*hembra*) sow; *fam* (*persona*) pig. **2** *a* (*sucio*) filthy.

cocido *m* stew.

cocina *f* kitchen; (*aparato*) cooker; (*arte*) cooking; **c. eléctrica/de gas** electric/gas cooker; **c. casera** home cooking.

cocinar *vti* to cook.

cocinero,-a *mf* cook.

coco *m* coconut.

cocodrilo *m* crocodile.

cocotero *m* coconut palm.

cóctel *m* cocktail.

codazo *m* (*señal*) nudge with one's elbow; (*golpe*) blow with one's elbow.

codicia *f* greed.

codicioso,-a 1 *a* covetous. **2** *mf* greedy person.

código *m* code; **c. de circulación** highway code.

codo *m* elbow; *fam* **hablar por los codos** to talk nonstop.

coeficiente *m* **c. intelectual** IQ.

coetáneo,-a *a* & *mf* contemporary.

coexistir *vi* to coexist.

cofre *m* trunk, chest.

coger [5] **1** *vt* to take; (*del suelo*) to pick (up); (*fruta, flores*) to pick; (*asir*) to seize, take hold of; (*coche, bus*) to take, catch; (*pelota, ladrón, resfriado*) to catch; (*atropellar*) to run over. **2 cogerse** *vr* (*agarrarse*) to hold on.

cogote *m* back of the neck.

cohabitar *vi* to live together, cohabit.

coherente *a* coherent.

cohete *m* rocket.

cohibir 1 *vt* to inhibit. **2 cohibirse** *vr* to feel inhibited.

coincidencia *f* coincidence.

coincidir *vi* to coincide; (*concordar*) to agree; (*encontrarse*) to meet by chance.

cojear *vi* (*persona*) to limp; (*mesa etc*) to wobble.

cojín *m* cushion.

cojinete *m* bearing.

cojo,-a 1 *a* (*persona*) lame; (*mueble*) rickety. **2** *mf* lame person.

col *f* cabbage; **c. de Bruselas** Brussels sprout.

cola[1] *f* tail; (*de vestido*) train; (*de pelo*) ponytail; (*fila*) queue, *US* line; **a la c.** at the back; **hacer c.** to queue (up), *US* stand in line.

cola[2] *f* glue.

colaboración *f* collaboration.

colaborador,-a 1 *mf* collaborator. **2** *a* collaborating.

colaborar *vi* to collaborate.

colada *f* wash, laundry; **hacer la c.** to do the washing.

colador *m* colander, sieve; (*de té, café*) strainer.

colapso *m* collapse; **c. circulatorio** traffic jam.

colar [2] **1** *vt* (*líquido*) to strain. **2 colarse** *vr* to slip in; (*a fiesta*) to gatecrash; (*en una cola*) to jump the queue.

colcha *f* bedspread.

colchón *m* mattress.

colchoneta *f* air bed.

colección *f* collection.

coleccionar *vt* to collect.

colecta *f* collection.

colectivo,-a 1 *a* collective. **2** *m* (*asociación*) association; *Am* long-distance taxi.

colega *mf* colleague.

colegial, -a 1 *a* (*escolar*) school. **2** *mf* (*alumno*) schoolboy; (*alumna*) schoolgirl; **los colegiales** the schoolchildren.

colegio *m* (*escuela*) school; **c. privado** *Br* public *o* independent school; **c. mayor** *o* **universitario** (*residencia*) hall of residence.

cólera¹ *f* anger, rage.

cólera² *m* (*enfermedad*) cholera.

colesterol *m* cholesterol.

colgante 1 *m* (*joya*) pendant. **2** *a* hanging.

colgar [2] **1** *vt* to hang (up); (*colada*) to hang (out); (*ahorcar*) to hang. **2** *vi* to hang (**de** from); (*teléfono*) to hang up. **3 colgarse** *vr* (*ahorcarse*) to hang oneself.

cólico *m* colic.

coliflor *f* cauliflower.

colilla *f* cigarette end.

colina *f* hill.

colirio *m* eyedrops.

colisión *f* collision, crash.

collar *m* (*adorno*) necklace; (*de perro*) collar.

colmado, -a *a* full, filled; (*cucharada*) heaped.

colmena *f* beehive.

colmillo *m* eye tooth; (*de carnívoro*) fang; (*de jabalí, elefante*) tusk.

colmo *m* ¡eso es el c.! that's the last straw!; **para c.** to top it all.

colocación *f* (*acto*) positioning; (*situación*) situation; (*empleo*) job.

colocar [1] **1** *vt* to place, put; (*emplear*) to give work to. **2 colocarse** *vr* (*situarse*) to put oneself; (*emplearse*) to take a job (**de** as).

Colón *n* Columbus.

colonia¹ *f* colony; (*campamento*) summer camp.

colonia² *f* (*agua de colonia*) cologne.

colonial *a* colonial.

colonizar [4] *vt* to colonize.

coloquio *m* discussion.

color *m* colour; **de colores** multicoloured; **persona de c.** coloured person.

colorado, -a 1 *a* red; **ponerse c.** to blush. **2** *m* red.

colorante *m* colouring.

colorear *vt* to colour.

colorete *m* rouge.

colorido *m* colour.

columna *f* column; **c. vertebral** spinal column.

columpio *m* swing.

coma¹ *f* (*ortográfica*) comma.

coma² *m* (*estado*) coma.
comadrona *f* midwife.
comandante *m* commander, commanding officer; (*de avión*) captain.
comarca *f* region.
combate *m* combat; (*de boxeo*) fight; (*batalla*) battle; **fuera de c.** out for the count.
combatir *vti* to fight.
combinación *f* combination; (*prenda*) slip.
combinar *vt*, **combinarse** *vr* to combine.
combustible 1 *m* fuel. **2** *a* combustible.
comedia *f* comedy.
comedor *m* dining room.
comentar *vt* (*escribir*) to comment on; (*discutir*) to discuss.
comentario *m* comment; **sin c.** no comment.
comenzar [1] *vti* to begin, start; **comenzó a llover** it started raining *o* to rain; **comenzó diciendo que . . .** he started by saying that . . .
comer 1 *vti* to eat; **dar de c. a algn** to feed sb. **2 comerse** *vr* to eat.
comercial *a* commercial.
comercializar [4] *vt* to market.
comerciante *mf* merchant.
comercio *m* commerce, trade; (*tienda*) shop.
comestible 1 *a* edible. **2** *nmpl* **comestibles** food *sing.*
cometa 1 *m* comet. **2** *f* (*juguete*) kite.
cometer *vt* (*error, falta*) to make; (*delito, crimen*) to commit.
comezón *m* itch.
comicios *nmpl* elections.
cómico,-a 1 *a* (*divertido*) comical, funny; **actor c.** comedian. **2** *mf* comic; (*hombre*) comedian; (*mujer*) comedienne.
comida *f* (*alimento*) food; (*almuerzo, cena*) meal.
comienzo *m* beginning, start; **dar c. (a algo)** to start (sth).
comillas *nfpl* inverted commas; **entre c.** in inverted commas.
comisaría *f* police station.
comisión *f* (*retribución*) commission; (*comité*) committee.
comité *m* committee.
como 1 *adv* (*manera*) how; **me gusta c. cantas** I like the way you sing. ▌ (*comparación*) as; **blanco c. la nieve** as white as snow; **habla c. su padre** he talks like his father. ▌ (*según*) as; **c. decíamos ayer** as we were saying yesterday. ▌ (*en calidad de*) as; **lo compré c. recuerdo** I bought it as a souvenir. ▌ (*aproximadamente*) about; **c. unos diez** about ten. **2** *conj* **c. + subj** (*si*) if; **c. no estudies vas a suspender** if you don't study hard, you'll fail. ▌ (*porque*) as, since; **c. no venías me marché** as you didn't come I left. ▌ **c. si** as if; **c. si nada** *o* **tal cosa** as if nothing had happened.

cómo *adv* ¿c.? (*¿perdón?*) what? ‖ (*interrogativo*) how; **¿c. estás?** how are you?; **¿a c. están los tomates?** (*a cuánto*) how much are the tomatoes?; (*por qué*) **¿c. fue que no viniste a la fiesta?** how come you didn't come to the party? ‖ (*exclamativo*) how; **¿c. es eso?** how come?; **¡c. has crecido!** you've really grown a lot!; **¡c. no!** but of course!

cómoda *f* chest of drawers.

comodidad *f* comfort; (*convenciencia*) convenience.

comodín *m* joker.

cómodo,-a *a* comfortable; (*útil*) handy, convenient.

compacto,-a *a* compact; **disco c.** compact disc.

compadecer 1 *vt* to feel sorry for, pity. 2 **compadecerse** *vr* to take pity (**de** on).

compañero,-a *mf* companion; **c. de piso** flatmate, *US* room-mate.

compañía *f* company; **hacer c. a algn** to keep sb company.

comparación *f* comparison; **en c.** comparatively; **en c. con** compared to; **sin c.** beyond compare.

comparar *vt* to compare (**con** with).

compartimento, compartimiento *m* compartment.

compartir *vt* to share.

compás *m* (pair of) compasses; (*brújula*) compass; (*ritmo*) rhythm; **al c. de** in time to.

compasión *f* compassion, pity; **tener c. de algn** to feel sorry for sb.

compatible *a* compatible.

compatriota *mf* compatriot; (*hombre*) fellow countryman; (*mujer*) fellow countrywoman.

compensar 1 *vt* (*pérdida, error*) to make up for; (*indemnizar*) to compensate (for). 2 *vi* to be worthwhile.

competencia *f* (*rivalidad, empresas rivales*) competition; (*capacidad*) competence; (*incumbencia*) field.

competición *f* competition.

competir [6] *vi* to compete.

competitivo,-a *a* competitive.

compinche *mf* (*cómplice*) accomplice.

complacer *vt* to please.

complejo,-a *a* & *m* complex.

complemento *m* complement; (*objeto*) object.

completar *vt* to complete.

completo,-a *a* (*terminado*) complete; (*lleno*) full; **por c.** completely.

completamente *adv* completely.

complicado,-a *a* (*complejo*) complicated; (*implicado*) involved.

complicar [1] 1 *vt* to complicate; (*involucrar*) to involve (**en** in). 2 **complicarse** *vr* to get complicated.

cómplice *mf* accomplice.

complot *m* (*pl* **complots**) conspiracy, plot.

componer (*pp* **compuesto**) **1** *vt* to compose; (*reparar*) to mend, repair. **2** **componerse** *vr* (*consistir*) to be made up (**de** of), consist (**de** of).

comportamiento *m* behaviour.

composición *f* composition.

compra *f* (*acción*) buying; (*cosa comprada*) purchase, buy; **ir de c.** to go shopping.

comprar *vt* to buy.

comprobar [2] *vt* to check.

comprender *vt* (*entender*) to understand; (*contener*) to comprise, include.

comprensión *f* understanding.

comprensivo,-a *a* understanding.

compresa *f* (*para mujer*) sanitary towel.

comprimido,-a **1** *m* tablet. **2** *a* compressed.

comprobar [2] *vt* to check.

comprometer **1** *vt* (*arriesgar*) to compromise; (*obligar*) to compel. **2** **comprometerse** *vr* (*involucrarse*) to involve oneself; (*novios*) to become engaged; **comprometerse a hacer algo** to undertake to do sth.

compromiso *m* (*obligación*) obligation, commitment; (*acuerdo*) agreement; **por c.** out of a sense of duty; **poner a algn en un c.** to put sb in a difficult situation.

compuesto,-a **1** *a* compound; **c. de** composed of. **2** *m* compound.

compuse *pt indef de* **componer.**

computadora *f* computer.

común **1** *a* common; (*compartido*) shared; **poco c.** unusual; **por lo c.** generally. **2** *m Br* **los Comunes** the Commons.

comunicación *f* communication; (*oficial*) communiqué; (*telefónica*) connection; (*unión*) link, connection.

comunicar [1] **1** *vt* to communicate; **comuníquenoslo lo antes posible** let us know as soon as possible. **2** *vi* to communicate; (*teléfono*) to be engaged. **3** **comunicarse** *vr* to communicate.

comunidad *f* community; **C. Europea** European Community.

comunión *f* communion.

con *prep* with; **c. ese frío/niebla** in that cold/fog; **estar c. (la) gripe** to have the flu; **una bolsa c. dinero** a bag (full) of money; **habló c. todos** he spoke to everybody. ▌ (*con infinitivo*) **c. llamar será suficiente** it will be enough just to phone. ▌ (*con subj* + **que**) **bastará c. que lo esboces** a general idea will do; **c. tal (de) que ...** provided that ...

concebir [6] **1** *vt* (*plan, hijo*) to conceive; (*entender*) to understand. **2** *vi* (*mujer*) to conceive.

conceder *vt* to grant; (*premio*) to award; (*admitir*) to concede.

concejal,-a *mf* town councillor.
concentración *f* concentration; (*de manifestantes*) gathering.
concentrar *vt,* **concentrarse** *vr* to concentrate (**en** on).
concepción *f* conception.
concepto *m* concept; **bajo/por ningún c.** under no circumstances.
concernir [5] *v impers* (*afectar*) to concern; (*corresponder*) to be up to;
en lo que a mí concierne as far as I am concerned; **en lo que concierne a**
with regard/respect to.
concesión *f* concession; (*de premio, contrato*) awarding.
concha *f* (*caparazón*) shell; (*carey*) tortoiseshell.
conciencia *f* conscience; (*conocimiento*) consciousness, awareness; **a c.**
conscientiously.
concienzudo,-a *a* conscientious.
concierto *m* concert; (*composición*) concerto; (*acuerdo*) agreement.
concluir *vt* to conclude.
conclusión *f* conclusion; **sacar una c.** to draw a conclusion.
concreto,-a 1 *a* (*preciso, real*) concrete; (*particular*) specific; **en c.**
specifically. **2** *m Am* concrete.
concretamente *adv* specifically.
concurrido,-a *a* crowded, busy.
concursante *mf* contestant, competitor.
concurso *m* (*competición*) competition; (*de belleza etc*) contest;
(*televisivo*) quiz show.
condena *f* sentence; (*desaprobación*) condemnation, disapproval.
condenado,-a 1 *a* convicted; **c. a muerte** condemned to death. **2** *mf*
convicted person; (*a muerte*) condemned person.
condenar *vt* to convict, find guilty; (*desaprobar*) to condemn.
condensado,-a *a* condensed; **leche condensada** condensed milk.
condensar *vt,* **condensarse** *vr* to condense.
condición *f* condition; **en buenas/malas condiciones** in good/bad
condition; **con la c. de que ...** on condition that ...
condimento *m* seasoning, flavouring.
condón *f* condom.
conducir 1 *vt* (*coche*) to drive; (*electricidad*) to conduct. **2** *vi* to drive;
(*llevar*) to lead; **permiso de c.** driving licence, *US* driver's license.
conducta *f* behaviour, conduct.
conducto *m* (*tubería*) pipe.
conductor,-a *mf* driver.
conectar *vt* to connect up; (*enchufar*) to plug in, switch on.
conejillo *m* **c. de Indias** guinea pig.
conejo *m* rabbit.
conexión *f* connection.

confección *f* dressmaking; (*de ropa masculina*) tailoring; (*de plan*) making.

conferencia *f* lecture; (*de telefónica*) long-distance call.

confesar [1] **1** *vti* to confess. **2 confesarse** *vr* to confess; (*de pecados*) to go to confession; **confesarse culpable** to admit one's guilt.

confianza *f* (*seguridad*) confidence; **tener c. en uno mismo** to be self-confident; **de c.** reliable; **tener c. con algn** to be on intimate terms with sb.

confiar 1 *vt* (*entregar*) to entrust; (*información, secreto*) to confide. **2** *vi* **c. en** to trust; **no confíes en su ayuda** don't count on his help. **3 confiarse** *vr* to confide (**en, a** in).

confidencial *a* confidential.

confirmar *vt* to confirm.

confiscar [1] *vt* to confiscate.

confitería *f* confectioner's (shop), *US* candy store; *Am* café.

confitura *f* preserve, jam.

conflicto *m* conflict.

conformarse *vr* **tendrás que conformate (con esto)** you will have to be content with that.

conforme 1 *a* (*satisfecho*) satisfied; **no estoy c.** I don't agree. **2** *conj* as. **3** *prep* **c. a** in accordance with.

confort *m* (*pl* **conforts**) comfort.

confortable *a* comfortable.

confrontación *f* confrontation.

confundir 1 *vt* to confuse (**con** with); (*engañar*) to mislead; **c. a una persona con otra** to mistake somebody for somebody else. **2 confundirse** *vr* (*equivocarse*) to be mistaken; (*mezclarse*) to mingle; (*colores, formas*) to blend.

confusión *f* confusion.

confuso,-a *a* confused; (*formas, recuerdo*) vague.

congelado,-a 1 *a* frozen. **2** *nmpl* **congelados** frozen food *sing*.

congelador *m* freezer.

congelar 1 *vt* to freeze. **2 congelarse** *vr* to freeze.

congoja *f* sorrow, grief.

congreso *m* congress, conference; **c. de los Diputados** ≈ Parliament, *US* Congress.

congrio *m* conger eel.

conjugación *f* conjugation.

conjunción *f* conjunction.

conjunto,-a 1 *m* (*grupo*) collection, group; (*todo*) whole; (*pop*) group, band; (*prenda*) outfit; **de c.** overall; **en c.** on the whole. **2** *a* joint.

conmemoración *f* commemoration.

conmigo *pron pers* with me; **él habló c.** he talked to me.

conmoción *f* commotion, shock; **c. cerebral** concussion.

conmovedor,-a *a* touching.

conmover [4] *vt* to touch, move.

conmutador *m* switch; *Am* switchboard.

cono *m* cone.

conocedor,-a *a* & *mf* expert; (*de vino, arte etc*) connoisseur.

conocer 1 *vt* to know; (*por primera vez*) to meet; (*reconocer*) to recognize; **dar (algo/algn) a c.** to make (sth/sb) known. **2 conocerse** *vr* (*dos personas*) to know each other; (*por primera vez*) to meet.

conocido,-a 1 *a* known; (*famoso*) well-known. **2** *mf* acquaintance.

conocimiento *m* knowledge; (*conciencia*) consciousness; **perder/recobrar el c.** to lose/regain consciousness; **conocimientos** knowledge.

conquistador,-a *mf* conqueror.

conquistar *vt* (*país, ciudad*) to conquer; **c. a una persona** to win over.

consabido,-a *a* (*bien conocido*) well-known; (*usual*) familiar, usual.

consagrar 1 *vt* (*artista*) to establish; (*vida, tiempo*) to devote. **2 consagrarse** *vr* (*dedicarse*) to devote oneself (**a** to); (*lograr fama*) to establish oneself.

consciente *a* conscious.

consecuencia *f* consequence; (*coherencia*) consistency; **a** *o* **como c. de** as a consequence of; **en c.** therefore.

consecuente *a* consistent.

consecutivo,-a *a* consecutive; **tres días consecutivos** three days in a row.

conseguir [6] *vt* to get, obtain; (*objetivo*) to achieve; (*lograr*) to manage.

consejero,-a *mf* (*asesor*) adviser; (*ministro*) regional minister.

consejo *m* (*recomendación*) advice; (*junta*) council; (*reunión*) cabinet meeting; **un c.** a piece of advice; **c. de ministros** cabinet; **c. de administración** board of directors.

consentido,-a *a* spoiled.

consentimiento *m* consent.

consentir [5] **1** *vt* (*tolerar*) to allow, permit; (*mimar*) to spoil; **no consientas que haga eso** don't allow him to do that. **2** *vi* to consent; **c. en** to agree to.

conserje *m* (*bedel*) janitor.

conserva *f* tinned *o* canned food.

conservador,-a *a* & *mf* conservative; (*derechista*) Conservative.

conservante *m* preservative.

conservar 1 *vt* to conserve, preserve; (*mantener*) to keep up; (*alimentos*) to preserve. **2 conservarse** *vr* (*tradición etc*) to survive.

conservatorio *m* conservatory.

considerado,-a *a* (*atento*) considerate, thoughtful.

considerar *vt* to consider; **lo considero imposible** I think it's impossible.

consigna *f (para maletas)* left-luggage office, *US* checkroom.

consigo[1] *pron pers (tercera persona) (hombre)* with him; *(mujer)* with her; *(cosa, animal)* with it; *(plural)* with them; *(usted)* with you; **hablar c. mismo** to speak to oneself.

consigo[2] *indic pres de* **conseguir.**

consiguiente *a* consequent; **por c.** therefore, consequently.

consistente *a (firme)* firm, solid.

consistir *vi* to consist (**en** of).

consola *f* console.

consolar [2] **1** *vt* to console, comfort. **2 consolarse** *vr* to console oneself.

consomé *m* clear soup, consommé.

consonante *a & f* consonant.

consorte *mf (cónyuge)* partner, spouse.

conspiración *f* conspiracy, plot.

conspirar *vi* to conspire, plot.

constancia *f* perseverance; *(testimonio)* proof, evidence.

constante 1 *a* constant; *(persona)* steadfast. **2** *f* constant feature.

constantemente *adv* constantly.

constar *vi (figurar)* to figure in, be included (in); **me consta que ...** I am absolutely certain that ...; **c. de** *(consistir)* to consist of.

constatar *vt* to state; *(comprobar)* to check.

constipado,-a 1 *a* **estar c.** to have a cold. **2** *m* cold.

constiparse *vr* to catch a cold.

constitución *f* constitution.

constituir 1 *vt (formar)* to constitute; *(suponer)* to represent; *(fundar)* to constitute, set up; **estar constituido por** to consist of. **2 constituirse** *vr* to set oneself up (**en** as).

construcción *f* construction; *(sector)* building industry.

constructor,-a 1 *mf* builder. **2** *a* **empresa constructora** builders *pl*, construction company.

construir *vt* to construct, build.

consuelo *m* consolation.

cónsul *mf* consul.

consulado *m* consulate.

consulta *f* consultation; *(médica)* surgery; *(despacho)* consulting room; **horas de c.** surgery hours.

consultar *vt* to consult.

consultivo,-a *a* consultative, advisory.

consultorio *m (médico)* medical centre.

consumidor,-a 1 *mf* consumer. **2** *a* consuming.

consumir 1 *vt* to consume. **2 consumirse** *vr (agua, jugo)* to boil away.

consumo *m* consumption; **bienes de c.** consumer goods; **sociedad de c.** consumer society.

contabilidad *f* (*profesión*) accountancy; (*de empresa, sociedad*) accounting.

contable *mf* accountant.

contactar *vi* **c. con** to contact.

contacto *m* contact; (*en coche*) ignition; **ponerse en c.** to get in touch.

contado,-a *a* (*pocos*) few and far between; **contadas veces** very seldom. **2 m pagar al c.** to pay cash.

contador *m* meter.

contagiar 1 *vt* (*enfermedad*) to pass on. **2 contagiarse** *vr* (*enfermar*) to get infected; (*transmitirse*) to be contagious.

contagioso,-a *a* contagious; (*risa*) infectious.

contaminación *f* contamination; (*del aire*) pollution.

contar [2] **1** *vt* (*sumar*) to count; (*narrar*) to tell. **2** *vi* to count; **c. con** (*confiar en*) to count on; (*tener*) to have.

contemplar *vt* to contemplate; (*considerar*) to consider.

contemporáneo,-a *a & mf* contemporary.

contenedor *m* container.

contener 1 *vt* to contain; (*reprimir*) to restrain, hold back. **2 contenerse** *vr* to control oneself, hold (oneself) back.

contenido *m* content, contents *pl*.

contentar 1 *vt* (*satisfacer*) to please; (*alegrar*) to cheer up. **2 contentarse** *vr* (*conformarse*) to make do (**con**, with), be satisfied (**con** with).

contento,-a *a* happy, pleased (**con** with).

contestador *m* **c. automático** answering machine.

contestación *f* answer.

contestar *vt* to answer.

contienda *f* struggle.

contigo *pron pers* with you.

contiguo,-a *a* adjoining.

continente *m* continent.

continuación *f* continuation; **a c.** next.

continuar *vti* to continue.

continuo,-a *a* continuous; (*reiterado*) continual, constant.

continuamente *adv* continuously.

contra 1 *prep* against; **en c. de** against. **2** *nmpl* **los pros y los contras** the pros and cons.

contrabajo *m* double bass.

contrabando *m* smuggling; **pasar algo de c.** to smuggle sth in.

contracción *f* contraction.

contracepción *f* contraception.

contradecir (*pp* **contradicho**) *vt* to contradict.

contradicción *f* contradiction.

contraer 1 *vt* to contract; **c. matrimonio** to get married. **2 contraerse** *vr* to contract.

contraigo *indic pres de* **contraer.**

contraje *pt indef de* **contraer.**

contrapeso *m* counterweight.

contraproducente *a* counterproductive.

contrariedad *f* (*contratiempo*) obstacle, setback; (*decepción*) annoyance.

contrario,-a 1 *a* opposite; **en el lado/sentido c.** on the other side/in the other direction; **al c., por el c.** on the contrary; **de lo c.** otherwise; **todo lo c.** quite the opposite. **2** *mf* opponent, rival. **3** *f* **llevar la contraria** to be contrary.

contrariamente *adv* **c. a ...** contrary to ...

contrarrestar *vt* to offset, counteract.

contrastar *vt* to contrast (**con** with).

contraste *m* contrast.

contratar *vt* (*empleado*) to hire, engage.

contratiempo *m* setback, hitch.

contratista *mf* contractor.

contrato *m* contract.

contribución *f* contribution; (*impuesto*) tax.

contribuir *vti* to contribute (**a** to).

contribuyente *mf* taxpayer.

contrincante *mf* rival, opponent.

control *m* control; (*inspección*) check; (*de policía etc*) checkpoint; **c. a distancia** remote control.

controlador,-a *mf* **c. (aéreo)** air traffic controller.

controlar 1 *vt* to control. **2 controlarse** *vr* to control oneself.

controversia *f* controversy.

convalecencia *f* convalescence.

convalidar *vt* to validate; (*documento*) to ratify.

convencer [2] *vt* to convince; **c. a algn de algo** to convince sb about sth.

convencional *a* conventional.

convenio *m* agreement.

convenir *vti* (*acordar*) to agree; (*ser oportuno*) to suit, be good for; **c. en** to agree on; **conviene recordar que ...** it's as well to remember that ...

convento *m* (*de monjas*) convent.

conversación *f* conversation.

conversión *f* conversion.

convertir [5] **1** *vt* to change, convert. **2 convertirse** *vr* **convertirse en** to turn into, become.

convicción *f* conviction.

convidado,-a *a & mf* guest.

convidar *vt* to invite.

convivencia *m* life together.

convivir *vi* to live together.

convocar [1] *vt* to summon; (*reunión, elecciones*) to call.

convocatoria *f* (*a huelga etc*) call.

convulsión *f* convulsion.

conyugal *a* conjugal; **vida c.** married life.

cónyuge *mf* spouse; **cónyuges** married couple *sing,* husband and wife.

coñac *m* brandy, cognac.

cooperación *f* co-operation.

cooperar *vi* to co-operate (**a, en** in; **con** with).

cooperativa *f* co-operative.

coordenada *f* co-ordinate.

coordinar *vt* to co-ordinate.

copa *f* glass; (*de árbol*) top; (*premio*) cup; **tomar una c.** to have a drink.

copia *f* copy.

copiar *vt* to copy.

copla *f* verse, couplet.

copo *m* flake; **c. de nieve** snowflake; **copos de maíz** cornflakes.

coquetear *vi* to flirt.

coqueto,-a *a* coquettish.

coraje *m* (*valor*) courage; (*ira*) anger, annoyance.

coral[1] *m* coral.

coral[2] *f* (*composición*) choral, chorale.

Corán *m* Koran.

coraza *f* armour.

corazón *m* heart; (*de fruta*) core; **tener buen c.** to be kind-hearted.

corbata *f* tie, *US* necktie.

corcho *m* cork; (*de pesca*) float.

cordel *m* rope, cord.

cordero,-a *mf* lamb.

cordial *a* cordial, warm.

cordillera *f* mountain range.

cordón *m* string; (*de zapatos*) shoelace.

cornada *f* (*de toro*) goring.

córner *m* corner (kick).

corneta *f* bugle.

cornisa *f* cornice.

coro *m* (*musical*) choir; (*en tragedia*) chorus; **a c.** all together.

corona *f* crown; (*de flores etc*) wreath, garland.

coronación *f* coronation.

coronel *m* colonel.

coronilla *f* crown of the head; *fam* **estar hasta la c.** to be fed up (**de** with).

corporación *f* corporation.

corporal *a* corporal; **olor c.** body odour, BO.

corpulento,-a *a* corpulent, stout.

corral *m* farmyard, *US* corral.

correa *f* (*tira*) strap; (*de pantalón*) belt; (*de perro*) lead, leash; (*de motor*) belt.

corrección *f* (*rectificación*) correction; (*educación*) courtesy, politeness.

correcto,-a *a* (*sin errores*) correct; (*educado*) polite, courteous (**con** to); (*conducta*) proper.

corredizo,-a *a* (*puerta etc*) sliding; **nudo c.** slipknot.

corredor,-a *mf* (*deportista*) runner; (*balconada*) gallery.

corregir [6] **1** *vt* to correct. **2 corregirse** *vr* (*persona*) to mend one's ways.

correo *m* post, mail; **echar al c.** to post; **por c.** by post; **c. aéreo** airmail; **c. certificado** registered post; **correos** (*edificio*) post office *sing*.

correr 1 *vi* to run; (*coche*) to go fast; (*conductor*) to drive fast; (*viento*) to blow; **c. prisa** to be urgent. **2** *vt* (*cortina*) to draw; (*cerrojo*) to close; (*mover*) to pull up, draw up; **c. el riesgo** to run the risk. **3 correrse** *vr* (*moverse*) to move over.

correspondencia *f* correspondence.

corresponder 1 *vi* to correspond (**a** to; **con** with); (*ajustarse*) to go (**con** with); (*incumbir*) to concern; (*pertenecer*) to be one's due; **me dieron lo que me correspondía** they gave me my share. **2 corresponderse** *vr* (*ajustarse*) to correspond; (*dos cosas*) to tally; **no se corresponde con la descripción** it does not match the description.

correspondiente *a* corresponding (**a** to).

corresponsal *mf* correspondent.

corrida *f* **c. (de toros)** bullfight.

corriente 1 *a* (*común*) common; (*agua*) running; (*mes, año*) current, present; (*cuenta*) current; **estar al c.** to be up to date. **2** *f* current, stream; (*de aire*) draught, *US* draft; (*tendencia*) trend, current; *fam* **seguirle o llevarle la c. a algn** to humour sb; **c. (eléctrica)** (electric) current.

corrijo *indic pres de* **corregir.**

corro *m* circle, ring; (*juego*) ring-a-ring-a-roses.

corromper *vt*, **corromperse** *vr* to go bad, rot.

corrupción *f* corruption.

corrupto,-a *a* corrupt.

cortacésped *m & f* lawnmower.

cortar 1 *vt* to cut; (*carne*) to carve; (*árbol*) to cut down; (*piel*) to chap, crack; (*luz, teléfono*) to cut off; (*paso, carretera*) to block. **2 cortarse** *vr* (*herirse*) to cut oneself; (*leche etc*) to curdle; **cortarse el pelo** to have one's hair cut; **se cortó la comunicación** we were cut off.

corte *m* cut; (*sección*) section; **c. de pelo** haircut.

cortés *a* courteous, polite.

corteza *f* (*de árbol*) bark; (*de queso*) rind; (*de pan*) crust.

cortijo *m* Andalusian farmhouse.

cortina *f* curtain.

corto,-a *a* (*distancia, tiempo*) short; **c. de vista** short-sighted; **luz corta** dipped headlights *pl*; **quedarse c.** (*calcular mal*) to underestimate.

cortocircuito *m* short circuit.

cosa *f* thing; (*asunto*) matter, business; **eso es c. tuya** that's your business; **eso es otra c.** that's different; **hace c. de una hora** about an hour ago.

coscorrón *m* knock on the head.

cosecha *f* harvest, crop; (*año del vino*) vintage.

coser *vt* to sew.

cosmético,-a *a & m* cosmetic.

cosmonauta *mf* cosmonaut.

coso *m* (*taurino*) bullring.

cosquillas *fpl* **hacer c. a algn** to tickle sb; **tener c.** to be ticklish.

costa *f* coast; (*litoral*) coastline; (*playa*) beach, seaside.

costado *m* (*lado*) side; **de c.** sideways.

costar [2] *vi* to cost; **¿cuánto cuesta?** how much is it?; **c. barato/caro** to be cheap/expensive; **c. trabajo** *o* **mucho** to be hard; **me cuesta hablar francés** I find it hard to speak French.

coste *m* cost; **c. de la vida** cost of living.

costear 1 *vt* to afford, pay for. **2 costearse** *vr* to pay for.

costilla *f* (*hueso*) rib; (*chuleta*) cutlet.

costo *m* cost.

costra *f* crust; (*de herida*) scab.

costumbre *f* (*hábito*) habit; (*tradición*) custom; **como de c.** as usual; **tengo la c. de levantarme temprano** I usually get up early; **tenía la c. de ...** he used to ...

costura *f* sewing; (*confección*) dressmaking; (*línea de puntadas*) seam; **alta c.** haute couture.

costurero *m* sewing basket.

cotidiano,-a *a* daily.

cotilla *mf fam* busybody, gossip.

cotilleo *m fam* gossip.

cotización *f* (market) price, quotation.

coto *m* enclosure; **c. de caza** game reserve.

cotorra *f* parrot; (*persona*) chatterbox.

COU *m abr de* **Curso de Orientacion Universitaria** ≈ GCE A-level studies, sixth-form studies.

coz *f* kick.

cráneo *m* cranium, skull.

cráter *m* crater.

creación *f* creation.

crear *vt* to create.

creativo,-a *a* creative.

crecer *vi* to grow.

crecimiento *m* growth.

credencial *a* credential; **(cartas) credenciales** credentials.

crédito *m* credit; **dar c. a** to believe.

creer 1 *vt* to believe; (*pensar*) to think; **creo que no** I don't think so; **creo que sí** I think so; **ya lo creo** I should think so. **2** *vi* to believe. **3 creerse** *vr* **se cree guapo** he thinks he's good-looking.

crema *f* cream.

cremallera *f* zip, *US* zipper.

crematorio *m* crematorium.

cremoso,-a creamy.

crepe *f* pancake.

crepúsculo *m* twilight.

cresta *f* crest; (*de gallo*) comb.

crezco *indic pres de* **crecer.**

cría *f* (*cachorro*) young; (*crianza*) breeding.

criada *f* maid.

criado,-a 1 *a* **mal c.** spoilt. **2** *mf* servant.

criar *vt* (*animales*) to breed; (*niños*) to bring up.

criatura *f* (living) creature; (*crío*) baby, child.

criba *f* sieve.

crimen *m* (*pl* **crímenes**) murder.

criminal *mf & a* criminal.

crin *f*, **crines** *fpl* mane *sing.*

crío,-a *m* kid.

criollo,-a *a & mf* Creole.

crisis *f inv* crisis; **c. nerviosa** nervous breakdown.

crispar *vt* to make tense; **me crispa los nervios** it sets my nerves on edge.

cristal *m* crystal; (*vidrio*) glass; (*de gafas*) lens; (*de ventana*) (window) pane.

cristiano,-a *a & mf* Christian.
Cristo *m* Christ.
criterio *m* (*pauta*) criterion; (*opinión*) opinion.
crítica *f* criticism; (*reseña*) review.
criticar [1] **1** *vt* to criticize. **2** *vi* (*murmurar*) to gossip.
crítico,-a 1 *a* critical. **2** *mf* critic.
croissant *m* croissant.
crol *m* (*en natación*) crawl.
cromo *m* (*metal*) chromium, chrome; (*estampa*) picture card.
cromosoma *m* chromosome.
crónica *f* feature.
crónico,-a *a* chronic.
cronológico,-a *a* chronological.
cronometrar *vt* to time.
cronómetro *m* stopwatch.
croqueta *f* croquette.
croquis *m inv* sketch.
cruce *m* crossing; (*de carreteras*) crossroads.
crucero *m* (*viaje*) cruise; (*barco*) cruiser.
crucifijo *m* crucifix.
crucigrama *m* crossword (puzzle).
crudo,-a 1 *a* (*natural*) raw; (*comida*) underdone; (*color*) cream. **2** *m* (*petróleo*) crude.
cruel *a* cruel.
crueldad *f* cruelty.
crujiente *a* crunchy.
crujir *vi* (*madera*) to creak; (*comida*) to crunch; (*hueso*) to crack.
cruz *f* cross; **C. Roja** Red Cross; **¿cara o c.?** ≈ heads or tails?
cruzado,-a *a* crossed; (*atravesado*) lying across; **con los brazos cruzados** arms folded.
cruzar [4] **1** *vt* to cross; (*palabra, mirada*) to exchange. **2** *vi* (*atravesar*) to cross. **3 cruzarse** *vr* to cross; **cruzarse con algn** to pass sb.
cuaderno *m* notebook.
cuadra *f* (*establo*) stable; *Am* block (of houses).
cuadrado,-a *a & m* square; **elevar (un número) al c.** to square (a number).
cuadriculado,-a *a* **papel c.** squared paper.
cuadro *m* square; (*gráfico*) chart, graph; (*pintura*) painting, picture; **tela a cuadros** checked cloth; **c. de mandos** control panel.
cual *pron rel* **el/la c.** (*persona*) who; (*cosa*) which; **con el/la c.** with whom/which; **lo c.** which.
cuál 1 *pron interr* which (one)?; **¿c. quieres?** which one do you want? **2** *a*

interr which.

cualidad *f* quality.

cualquier *a indef* any; **c. cosa** anything; **en c. momento** at any moment.

cualquiera (*pl* **cualesquiera**) **1** *a indef* (*indefinido*) any; (*corriente*) ordinary. **2** *pron indef* (*persona*) anybody, anyone; (*cosa, animal*) any one; **c. que sea** whatever it is.

cuando *adv & conj* when; **de c. en c., de vez en c.** from time to time; **c. quieras** whenever you want; **c. vengas** when you come; **(aun) c.** even if.

cuándo *adv interr* when?; **¿desde c.?** since when?; **¿para c. lo quieres?** when do you want it for?

cuanto,-a 1 a toma cuantos caramelos quieras take all the sweets you want; **unas cuantas niñas** a few girls. **2** *pron rel* as much as; **coma (todo) c. quiera** eat as much as you want. **3** *pron indef pl* **unos cuantos** a few. **4** *adv* (*tiempo*) **c. antes** as soon as possible; **en c.** as soon as; **c. más ... más** the more ... the more; **en c. a** with respect to, regarding.

cuánto,-a 1 *a & pron interr* (*sing*) how much?; (*pl*) how many?; **¿cuántas veces?** how many times?; **¿c. es?** how much is it? **2** *adv* how, how much; **¡cuánta gente hay!** what a lot of people there are!

cuarenta *a & m inv* forty.

cuartel *m* (*militar*) barracks *pl*; **c. general** headquarters.

cuartilla *f* sheet of paper.

cuarto,-a 1 *m* (*habitación*) room; (*cuarta parte*) quarter; **c. de baño** bathroom; **c. de estar** living room; **c. de hora** quarter of an hour. **2** *a & mf* fourth.

cuatro *m inv* four.

cuatrocientos,-as *a & mf* four hundred.

cubano,-a *a & mf* Cuban.

cubata *m fam* cubalibre.

cubierta *f* cover; (*de rueda*) tyre, *US* tire; (*de barco*) deck.

cubierto,-a 1 *a* covered; (*piscina etc*) indoor; (*cielo*) overcast. **2** *mpl* **cubiertos** cutlery *sing*.

cubo *m* bucket; (*en matemática*) cube; **c. de la basura** rubbish bin.

cubrir (*pp* **cubierto**) **1** *vt* to cover. **2** **cubrirse** *vr* (*cielo*) to become overcast.

cucaracha *f* cockroach.

cuchara *f* spoon.

cucharada *f* spoonful.

cucharilla *f* teaspoon; **c. de café** coffee spoon.

cucharón *m* ladle.

cuchichear *vi* to whisper.

cuchilla *f* blade; **c. de afeitar** razor blade.

cuchillo *m* knife.

cuco m cuckoo.
cucurucho m (de helado) cornet; (envoltorio) paper cone.
cuello m neck; (de camisa etc) collar.
cuenco m bowl.
cuenta f (factura) bill; (de banco) account; (cálculo) count; (de collar) bead; **c. corriente** current account; **caer en la c., darse c.** to realize; **tener en c.** to take into account; **traer c.** to be worthwhile; **en resumidas cuentas** in short; **trabajar por c. propia** to be self-employed.
cuentakilómetros m inv (distancia) milometer; (velocidad) speedometer.
cuento m story; **contar un c.** to tell a story; **c. de hadas** fairy story.
cuerda f (cordel) rope; (de instrumento) string; (del reloj) spring; **dar c. al reloj** to wind up a watch.
cuerdo,-a a sane.
cuerno m horn; (de ciervo) antler; fam **¡vete al c.!** get lost!
cuero m leather; **chaqueta de c.** leather jacket; **c. cabelludo** scalp.
cuerpo m body; (cadáver) corpse; **c. de bomberos** fire brigade; **c. diplomático** diplomatic corps; **c. de policía** police force.
cuesta 1 f slope; **c. abajo** downhill; **c. arriba** uphill. 2 adv **a cuestas** on one's back.
cuestión f (asunto) matter, question; (pregunta) question; **en c. de unas horas** in just a few hours.
cuestionario m questionnaire.
cueva f cave.
cuezo indic pres de **cocer**.
cuidado,-a 1 m care; **con c.** carefully; **tener c.** to be careful; **estar al c. de** to be in charge of; (persona) to look after; **me trae sin c.** I couldn't care less; **cuidados intensivos** intensive care sing. 2 interj **¡c.!** look out!
cuidadoso,-a a careful.
cuidar 1 vt to care for, look after. 2 **cuidarse** vr **cuídate** look after yourself.
culebra f snake.
culebrón m soap opera.
culo m fam (trasero) backside; (de recipiente) bottom.
culpa f blame; (culpabilidad) guilt; **echar la c. a algn** to put the blame on sb; **fue c. mía** it was my fault; **por tu c.** because of you.
culpable 1 mf offender, culprit. 2 a guilty; **declararse c.** to plead guilty.
cultivar vt to cultivate.
culto,-a 1 a educated; (palabra) learned. 2 m cult; (devoción) worship.
cultura f culture.
culturismo m body building.
cumbre f (de montaña) summit, top; (conferencia) **c.** summit conference.

cumpleaños *m inv* birthday; **¡feliz c.!** happy birthday!

cumplir 1 *vt* to carry out; (*deseo*) to fulfil; (*promesa*) to keep; **ayer cumplí veinte años** I was twenty (years old) yesterday. **2** *vi* (*plazo*) to expire, end; **c. con el deber** to do one's duty. **3 cumplirse** *vr* (*deseo*) to come true; (*plazo*) to expire.

cuna *f* cot.

cuneta *f* (*de la carretera*) gutter.

cuñado,-a *mf* (*hombre*) brother-in-law; (*mujer*) sister-in-law.

cuota *f* (*de club etc*) membership fees *pl*; (*porción*) quota, share; *Am* **carretera de c.** toll road.

cupe *pt indef de* **caber.**

cupiera *subj imperfecto de* **caber.**

cupón *m* coupon, voucher.

cura 1 *m* (*religioso*) priest. **2** *f* (*de enfermedad*) cure.

curación *f* cure, treatment.

curar 1 *vt* to cure; (*herida*) to dress; (*enfermedad*) to treat. **2** *vi & vr* **curar(se)** (*sanar*) to recover, get well; (*herida*) to heal up.

curiosidad *f* curiosity.

curioso,-a 1 *a* (*extraño*) strange, odd; (*indiscreto*) curious, inquisitive. **2** *mf* (*mirón*) onlooker.

currículum *m* (*pl* **curricula**) **c. vitae** curriculum vitae.

cursi *a* posh.

cursillo *m* short course; **c. de reciclaje** refresher course.

curso *m* (*año académico*) year; (*clase*) class; (*de acontecimientos, río*) course; **en el c. de** in the course of; **moneda de c. legal** legal tender.

cursor *m* cursor.

curtir *vt* (*cuero*) to tan; (*endurecer*) to harden.

curva *f* curve; (*en carretera*) bend; **c. cerrada** sharp bend.

cutis *m* complexion.

cuyo,-a *pron rel & pos* (*persona*) whose; (*de cosa*) of which; **en c. caso** in which case.

D

D. *abr de* **don** Mister, Mr.

D.ª *abr de* **doña** Mrs; Miss.

dado *m* dice.

dálmata *m* Dalmatian.

dama *f* (*señora*) lady; **damas** (*juego*) draughts, *US* checkers.

danés,-esa 1 *a* Danish. **2** *mf* (*persona*) Dane. **3** *m* (*idioma*) Danish; **gran d.** (*perro*) Great Dane.

danza *f* dancing; (*baile*) dance.

daño *m* (*a cosa*) damage; (*a persona*) (*físico*) hurt; (*perjuicio*) harm.

dar 1 *vt* to give; (*noticia*) to tell; (*mano de pintura, cera*) to apply; (*fruto, flores*) to bear; (*beneficio, interés*) to yield; (*hora*) to strike; **dale a la luz** switch the light on; **d. la mano a algn** to shake hands with sb; **d. los buenos días/las buenas noches a algn** to say good morning/good evening to sb; **me da lo mismo** *or* **me da igual** it's all the same to me; **¿qué más da?** what difference does it make?; **d. de comer a** to feed; **d. a conocer** (*noticia*) to release; **d. a entender que...** to imply that...; **d. por** (*considerar*) to consider; **d. por descontado/sabido** to take for granted. **2** *ví* **me dio un ataque de tos/risa** I had a coughing fit/an attack of the giggles; **d. a** (*ventana, habitación*) to overlook; (*puerta*) to open onto; **d. con la solución** to hit upon the solution; **d. de sí** (*ropa*) to stretch; **el presupuesto no da para más** the budget will not stretch any further; **d. que hablar** to set people talking. **3 darse** *vr* **se dio la circunstancia de que** it happened that; **se dio a la bebida** he took to drink; **darse con** *o* **contra** to bump into; **darse por satisfecho** to feel satisfied; **darse por vencido** to give in; **se le da bien/mal el francés** she's good/bad at French.

dardo *m* dart.

dársena *f* dock.

dátil *m* date.

dato *m* piece of information; **datos** (*de ordenador*) data.

d.C. *abr de* **después de Cristo** Anno Domini, AD.

dcha. *abr de* **derecha** right.

de *prep* (*pertenencia*) of; **el título de la novela** the title of the novel; **el coche/hermano de Sofía** Sofía's car/brother. ‖ (*procedencia*) from; **vino de Madrid** he came from Madrid. ‖ (*descripción*) **el niño de ojos azules** the boy with blue eyes; **una avenida de quince kilómetros** an avenue fifteen kilometres long; **una botella de litro** a litre bottle; **el señor de la chaqueta** the man in the jacket; **un reloj de oro** a gold watch; (*contenido*) of; **un saco de patatas** a sack of potatoes. ‖ (*oficio*) by, as; **trabaja de secretaria** she's working as a secretary. ‖ (*acerca de*) about; **curso de informática** computer course. ‖ (*tiempo*) **a las tres de la tarde** at three in the afternoon; **de día** by day; **de noche** at night; **de lunes a jueves** from Monday to Thursday; **de pequeño** as a child. ▌ (*con superlativo*) in; **el más largo de España** the longest in Spain. ▌ (*causa*) with, because of; **llorar de alegría** to cry with joy; **morir de hambre** to die of hunger. ▌ **de cuatro en cuatro** four at a time; **de semana en semana** every week.

debajo 1 *adv* underneath, below. **2** *prep* **d. de** under(neath); **por d. de lo normal** below normal

debate *m* debate.

debatir 1 *vt* to debate. **2 debatirse** *vr* to struggle.

deber¹ *m* duty; (*en el colegio*) **deberes** homework *sing*.

deber² **1** *vt* (*dinero, explicación*) to owe. **2** *vi* **debe (de) irse ahora** she has to leave now; **la factura debe pagarse mañana** the bill must be paid tomorrow; **deberías visitar a tus padres** you ought to visit your parents; **debería haber ido ayer** I should have gone yesterday; **no debiste hacerlo** you shouldn't have done it; **deben de estar fuera** they must be out. **3 deberse** *vr* **deberse a** to be due to.

debidamente *adv* duly.

debido,-a *a* **d. a** due to.

débil *a* weak; (*luz*) dim; **punto d.** weak spot.

debutar *vi* to make one's debut.

década *f* **en la d. de los noventa** during the nineties.

decadencia *f* decadence.

decano,-a *mf* dean.

decena *f* (about) ten; **una d. de veces** (about) ten times; **por decenas** in tens.

decenio *m* decade.

decente *a* decent; (*decoroso*) modest.

decepción *f* disappointment.

decidido,-a *a* determined.

decidir 1 *vti* to decide. **2 decidirse** *vr* **decidirse (a hacer algo)** to make up one's mind (to do sth); **decidirse por algo** to decide on sth.

décima *f* tenth.

decimal *a & m* decimal.

décimo,-a 1 *a & mf* tenth. **2** *m* (*parte*) tenth.

decir (*pp* **dicho**) **1** *vt* to say; **d. una mentira/la verdad** to tell a lie/the truth; (*al teléfono*) **dígame** hello; **esta película no me dice nada** this film doesn't appeal to me; **querer d.** to mean; (*locuciones*) **es d.** that is (to say); **por así decirlo** so to speak; **digamos** let's say; **digo yo** in my opinion; **ni que d. tiene** needless to say; **¡no me digas!** really! **2 decirse** *vr* **¿cómo se dice 'mesa' en inglés?** how do you say 'mesa' in English?; **se dice que ...** they say that ...

decisión *f* decision; (*resolución*) determination; **tomar una d.** to make a

decision; **con d.** decisively.
declaración *f* declaration; **d. de (la) renta** tax return; (*afirmación*) statement; **hacer declaraciones** to comment.
declarar 1 *vt* to declare; (*afirmar*) to state; **d. la guerra a** to declare war on. **2** *vi* (*en juicio*) to testify. **3 declararse** *vr* (*guerra, incendio*) to break out; **declararse a favor/en contra de** to declare oneself in favour of/ against; **declararse en huelga** to go on strike; **declararse a algn** to declare one's love for sb.
decoración *f* decoration.
decorar *vt* to decorate.
decreto *m* decree.
decorativo,-a *a* decorative.
decreto-ley *m* decree.
dedal *m* thimble.
dedicar [1] **1** *vt* to dedicate; (*tiempo, esfuerzos*) to devote (**a** to). **2 dedicarse** *vr* **¿a qué se dedica Vd.?** what do you do for a living?; **los fines de semana ella se dedica a pescar** at weekends she spends her time fishing.
dedo *m* (*de la mano*) finger; (*del pie*) toe; **d. anular/corazón/índice/ meñique** ring/middle/index/little finger; **d. pulgar, d. gordo** thumb.
deducir 1 *vt* to deduce. **2 deducirse** *vr* **de aquí se deduce que ...** from this it follows that ...
defecar [1] *vi* to defecate.
defecto *m* defect.
defectuoso,-a *a* defective.
defender [3] **1** *vt* to defend (**contra** against; **de** from). **2 defenderse** *vr* to defend oneself.
defensa 1 *f* defence; **en d. propia, en legítima d.** in self-defence. **2** *m* (*en equipo*) defender.
deficiente 1 *a* deficient. **2** *m* (*nota*) fail.
definición *f* definition.
definir *vt* to define.
deformar 1 *vt* to deform; (*cara*) to disfigure; (*la verdad, una imagen*) to distort. **2 deformarse** *vr* to become distorted.
defraudar *vt* to disappoint; **d. a Hacienda** to evade taxes.
defunción *f* demise.
degenerado,-a *a & mf* degenerate.
degollar [2] *vt* to behead.
degradante *a* degrading.
degustación *f* tasting.
dejar 1 *vt* to leave; (*prestar*) to lend; (*abandonar*) to give up; (*permitir*) to let, allow; **déjame en paz** leave me alone; **dejé el tabaco y la bebida** I gave up smoking and drinking; **d. caer** to drop; **d. entrar/salir** to let in/out; **d.**

triste to make sad; **d. preocupado/sorprendido** to worry/surprise. **2** *v aux* **d. de** + *inf* to stop; (*renunciar*) give up; **no deja de llamarme** she's always phoning me up. **3 dejarse** *vr* **me he dejado las llaves dentro** I've left the keys inside; **dejarse barba** to grow a beard; **dejarse llevar por** to be influenced by.

del (*contracción de* **de** + **el**) *ver* **de.**

delantal *m* apron.

delante 1 *adv* in front; **la entrada de d.** the front entrance; **por d.** in front; **se lo lleva todo por d.** he destroys everything in his path; **tiene toda la vida por d.** he has his whole life ahead of him. **2** *prep* **d. de** in front of; (*en serie*) ahead of.

delatar *vt* to inform against.

delegación *f* (*acto, delegados*) delegation; (*oficina*) local office.

delegado,-a *mf* delegate.

deletrear *vt* to spell (out).

delfín *m* dolphin.

delgado,-a *a* slim; (*capa*) fine.

deliberado,-a *a* deliberate.

delicadeza *f* (*finura*) daintiness; (*tacto*) tactfulness; **falta de d.** tactlessness.

delicado,-a *a* delicate.

delicioso,-a *a* (*comida*) delicious; (*agradable*) delightful.

delincuente *a & mf* delinquent.

delineante *mf* (*hombre*) draughtsman; (*mujer*) draughtswoman.

delirar *vi* to be delirious.

delirio *m* delirium.

delito *m* crime.

delta *m* delta.

demanda *f* (*judicial*) lawsuit.

demandar *vt* to sue.

demás 1 *a* **los/las d.** the rest of. **2** *pron* **lo/los/las d.** the rest; **por lo d.** otherwise, apart from that.

demasiado,-a 1 *a* (*singular*) too much; (*plural*) too many. **2** *adv* too (much); **es d. grande/caro** it is too big/dear; **fumas/trabajas d.** you smoke/work too much.

demencia *f* insanity.

democracia *f* democracy.

democrático,-a *a* democratic.

demográfico,-a *a* demographic; **crecimiento d.** population growth.

demonio *m* devil.

demora *f* delay.

demorar 1 *vt* to delay, hold up. **2 demorarse** *vr* (*retrasarse*) to be delayed, be held up.

demostrar [2] *vt* (*mostrar*) to show; (*evidenciar*) to prove.

denegar [1] *vt* to refuse.

denigrante *a* humiliating.

denominación *f* denomination.

denominar *vt* to name.

denotar *vt* to denote.

densidad *f* density.

denso,-a *a* dense.

dentadura *f* teeth; **d. postiza** false teeth *pl*, dentures *pl*.

dental *a* dental.

dentera *f* **me da d.** it sets my teeth on edge.

dentífrico,-a 1 *a* **pasta/crema dentífrica** toothpaste. **2** *m* toothpaste.

dentista *mf* dentist.

dentro 1 *adv* (*en el interior*) inside; **aquí d.** in here; **por d.** (on the) inside. **2** *prep* **d. de** (*lugar*) inside; **d. de poco** shortly, soon; **d. de un mes** in a month's time.

denunciar *vt* (*delito*) to report (**a** to).

departamento *m* department; (*territorial*) province; *Am* (*piso*) flat.

depender *vi* to depend (**de** on); (*económicamente*) to be dependent (**de on**).

dependienta *f* shop assistant.

dependiente 1 *a* dependent (**de** on). **2** *m* shop assistant.

depilación *f* depilation.

depilar *vt* to remove the hair from; (*cejas*) to pluck.

depilatorio,-a *a & m* depilatory; **crema depilatoria** hair-remover.

deportar *vt* to deport.

deporte *m* sport; **hacer d.** to go in for sports.

deportista 1 *mf* (*hombre*) sportsman; (*mujer*) sportswoman. **2** *a* sporty.

deportivo,-a 1 *a* sports; **club/chaqueta d.** sports club/jacket. **2** *m* (*coche*) sports car.

depositar 1 *vt* (*colocar*) to put. **2 depositarse** *vr* to settle.

depósito *m* (*dinero*) deposit; (*de agua, gasolina*) tank.

depresión *f* depression.

deprimente *a* depressing.

deprimir 1 *vt* to depress. **2 deprimirse** *vr* to get depressed.

deprisa *adv* quickly.

derecha *f* (*mano*) right hand; (*lugar*) right, right-hand side; **a la d.** on the right, on the right-hand side; (*en politica*) **la d.** the right.

derecho,-a 1 *a* (*de la derecha*) right; (*recto*) straight. **2** *m* (*privilegio*) right; (*carrera*) law; **derechos civiles/humanos** civil/human rights; **tener d. a** to be entitled to; **no hay d.** it's not fair. **3** *adv* **siga todo d.** go straight ahead.

derivar 1 *vi* to drift; **d. de** to derive from. **2 derivarse** *vr* to stem (**de** from).

dermatólogo,-a *mf* dermatologist.

derramar 1 *vt* to spill; (*lágrimas*) to shed. **2 derramarse** *vr* to spill.

derrapar *vi* to skid.

derretir [6] *vt*, **derretirse** *vr* to melt; (*hielo, nieve*) to thaw.

derribar *vt* (*demoler*) to knock down; (*gobierno*) to bring down.

derrochar *vt* to waste.

derroche *m* waste.

derrota *f* defeat.

derrotar *vt* to defeat.

derruir *vt* to demolish.

derrumbar 1 *vt* (*edificio*) to knock down. **2 derrumbarse** *vr* to collapse; (*techo*) to fall in.

desabrido,-a *a* (*tono*) harsh; (*persona*) irritable.

desabrochar 1 *vt* to undo. **2 desabrocharse** *vr* (*prenda*) to come undone; **desabróchate la camisa** undo your shirt.

desacato *m* lack of respect (**a** for).

desacertado,-a *a* unwise.

desacreditar *vt* (*desprestigiar*) to discredit; (*criticar*) to disparage.

desactivar *vt* (*bomba*) to defuse.

desacuerdo *m* disagreement.

desafiante *a* defiant.

desafiar *vt* to challenge.

desafinar 1 *vi* to sing out of tune; (*instrumento*) to play out of tune. **2 desafinarse** *vr* to go out of tune.

desafío *m* challenge.

desafortunado,-a *a* unfortunate.

desagradable *a* unpleasant.

desagradar *vi* to displease.

desagradecido,-a 1 *a* ungrateful. **2** *mf* ungrateful person.

desagrado *m* displeasure.

desagüe *m* (*cañería*) drainpipe; (*vaciado*) drain.

desaguisado *m* mess.

desahogado,-a *a* (*acomodado*) well-off; (*espacioso*) spacious.

desahogarse [7] *vr* to let off steam.

desahuciar *vt* (*desalojar*) to evict; (*enfermo*) to deprive of all hope.

desairar *vt* to slight.

desajuste *m* upset.

desalentar [1] **1** *vt* to dishearten. **2 desalentarse** *vr* to get discouraged.

desaliento *m* discouragement.

desaliñado,-a *a* untidy.

desalmado,-a *a* heartless.

desalojar *vt* (*inquilino*) to evict; (*público*) to move on; (*lugar*) to evacuate; (*abandonar*) to abandon.

desamparado,-a *a* (*persona*) helpless.

desangrarse *vr* to lose (a lot of) blood.

desanimado,-a *a* (*persona*) downhearted; (*fiesta etc*) dull.

desanimar 1 *vt* to dishearten. **2 desanimarse** *vr* to lose heart.

desánimo *m* dejection.

desapacible *a* unpleasant.

desaparecer *vi* to disappear.

desaparición *f* disappearance.

desapercibido,-a *a* **pasar d.** to go unnoticed.

desaprovechar *vt* (*dinero, tiempo*) to waste.

desarmar *vt* (*desmontar*) to dismantle; (*ejército*) to disarm.

desarme *m* disarmament; **d. nuclear** nuclear disarmament.

desarraigado,-a *a* rootless.

desarreglar *vt* to mess up.

desarrollado,-a *a* developed.

desarrollar 1 *vt* to develop. **2 desarrollarse** *vr* (*persona, enfermedad*) to develop; (*tener lugar*) to take place.

desarrollo *m* development; **países en vías de d.** developing countries.

desarticular *vt* to dismantle.

desasir 1 *vt* to release. **2 desasirse** *vr* to get loose; **desasirse de** to free oneself of.

desasosiego *m* uneasiness.

desastrado,-a 1 *a* scruffy. **2** *mf* scruff.

desastre *m* disaster.

desastroso,-a *a* disastrous.

desatar 1 *vt* to untie, undo. **2 desatarse** *vr* (*zapato, cordón*) to come undone.

desatascar [1] *vt* to clear.

desatornillar *vt* to unscrew.

desatrancar [1] *vt* to unblock; (*puerta*) to unbolt.

desautorizar [4] *vt* to disallow; (*huelga etc*) to ban.

desavenencia *f* disagreement.

desayunar 1 *vi* to have breakfast. **2** *vt* to have for breakfast.

desayuno *m* breakfast.

desbarajuste *m* confusion.

desbaratar *vt* to ruin.

desbordar 1 *vt* to overflow. **2** *vi* to overflow (**de** with). **3 desbordarse** *vr* to overflow.

descabellado,-a *a* crazy.

descafeinado,-a *a* decaffeinated.

descalabro *m* misfortune.

descalificar [1] *vt* to disqualify.

descalzarse [4] *vr* to take one's shoes off.

descalzo,-a *a* barefoot.

descampado *m* waste ground.

descansado,-a *a* (*persona*) rested; (*vida, trabajo*) restful.

descansar *vi* to rest, have a rest; (*corto tiempo*) to take a break.

descansillo *m* landing.

descanso *m* rest; (*en teatro, cine*) interval; (*en deporte*) half-time; **un día de d.** a day off.

descapotable *a & m* convertible.

descarado,-a **1** *a* (*insolente*) cheeky; (*desvergonzado*) shameless. **2** *mf* cheeky person.

descarga *f* unloading; (*eléctrica, explosiva*) discharge.

descargar [7] **1** *vt* to unload; (*golpe*) to deal. **2** *vi* (*tormenta*) to burst. **3** **descargarse** *vr* to go flat.

descaro *m* cheek.

descarrilar *vi* to be derailed.

descartar *vt* to rule out.

descender [3] **1** *vi* (*temperatura, nivel*) to fall; **d. de** to descend from. **2** *vt* to lower.

descendiente *mf* descendant.

descenso *m* descent; (*de temperatura*) fall.

descifrar *vt* to decipher; (*mensaje*) decode; (*misterio*) to solve.

descolgar [2] *vt* (*el teléfono*) to pick up; (*cuadro, cortinas*) to take down.

descolorido,-a *a* faded.

descomponer (*pp* **descompuesto**) **1** *vt* to break down; (*corromper*) to decompose. **2** **descomponerse** *vi* (*corromperse*) to decompose; (*ponerse nervioso*) to lose one's cool.

descomposición *f* (*de carne*) decomposition.

descompuse *pt indef de* **descomponer.**

descomunal *a* massive.

desconcertar [1] **1** *vt* to disconcert. **2** **desconcertarse** *vr* to be bewildered.

desconectar *vt* to disconnect.

desconfiado,-a *a* distrustful.

desconfiar *vi* to distrust (**de** -).

descongelar *vt* to defrost.

desconocer *vt* not to know.

desconocido,-a **1** *a* unknown; (*irreconocible*) unrecognizable. **2** *m* **lo**

d. the unknown. **3** *mf* stranger.

desconsolado,-a *a* disconsolate.

descontar [2] *vt* to deduct.

descontento,-a 1 *a* unhappy. **2** *m* dissatisfaction.

descorchar *vt* to uncork.

descorrer *vt* to draw back.

descoser *vt* to unpick.

descoyuntar *vt* to dislocate.

descrédito *m* disrepute.

descremado,-a *a* skimmed.

describir (*pp* **descrito**) *vt* to describe.

descripción *f* description.

descuartizar [4] *vt* to cut into pieces.

descubierto,-a 1 *a* open. **2** *m* **al d.** in the open; **poner al d.** to bring out into the open.

descubrimiento *m* discovery.

descubrir (*pp* **descubierto**) *vt* to discover; (*conspiración*) to uncover; (*placa*) to unveil.

descuento *m* discount.

descuidado,-a *a* (*negligente*) careless; (*desaseado*) untidy; (*desprevenido*) off one's guard.

descuido *m* oversight; (*negligencia*) carelessness; **por d.** inadvertently.

desde *adv* (*tiempo*) since; (*lugar*) from; **no lo he visto d. hace un año** I haven't seen him for a year; **d. siempre** always; **d. luego** of course; **d. que** ever since.

desdén *m* disdain.

desdeñar *vt* to disdain.

desdichado,-a 1 *a* unfortunate. **2** *mf* poor devil.

desdoblar *vt* to unfold.

desear *vt* to desire; (*querer*) to want; **¿qué desea?** can I help you?; **estoy deseando que vengas** I'm looking forward to your coming; **te deseo buena suerte/feliz Navidad** I wish you good luck/a merry Christmas.

desechable *a* disposable.

desechar *vt* (*tirar*) to discard; (*idea, proyecto*) to drop.

desembarcar [1] **1** *vt* (*mercancías*) to unload; (*personas*) to disembark. **2** *vi* to disembark.

desembarco, desembarque *m* (*de mercancías*) unloading; (*de personas*) disembarkation.

desembocar [1] *vi* (*río*) to flow (**en** into); (*calle, situación*) to lead (**en,** to).

desembolsar *vt* to pay out.

desempaquetar *vt* to unpack.

desempate *m* play-off.

desempeñar *vt* (*cargo*) to hold; (*función*) to fulfil; (*papel*) to play.

desempleado,-a 1 *a* unemployed, out of work. **2** *mf* unemployed person; **los desempleados** the unemployed.

desempleo *m* unemployment; **cobrar el d.** to be on the dole.

desencadenar 1 *vt* (*provocar*) to unleash. **2 desencadenarse** *vr* (*viento, pasión*) to rage; (*conflicto*) to break out.

desencanto *m* disillusion.

desenchufar *vt* to unplug.

desenfadado,-a *a* free and easy.

desenfocado,-a *a* out of focus.

desenganchar *vt* to unhook; (*vagón*) to uncouple.

desengaño *m* disappointment.

desengrasar *vt* to remove the grease from.

desenlace *m* outcome; (*de historia*) ending.

desenmascarar *vt* to unmask.

desenredar *vt* to disentangle.

desenrollar *vt* to unroll; (*cable*) to unwind.

desenroscar [1] *vt* to unscrew.

desentenderse [3] *vr* **se desentendió de mi problema** he didn't want to have anything to do with my problem.

desentonar *vi* to be out of tune; (*colores etc*) not to match; (*persona, comentario*) to be out of place.

desentrañar *vt* to unravel.

desentrenado,-a *a* out of training.

desenvolver [4] (*pp* desenvuelto) **1** *vt* to unwrap. **2 desenvolverse** *vr* (*persona*) to manage.

desenvuelto,-a *a* relaxed.

deseo *m* wish; (*sexual*) desire.

desequilibrado,-a 1 *a* unbalanced. **2** *mf* unbalanced person.

desértico,-a *a* desert.

desertor,-a *mf* deserter.

desesperado,-a *a* (*sin esperanza*) desperate; (*exasperado*) exasperated.

desesperante *a* exasperating.

desesperar **1** *vt* to drive to despair; (*exasperar*) to exasperate. **2 desesperarse** *vr* to despair.

desfachatez *f* cheek.

desfallecer *vi* (*debilitarse*) to feel faint; (*desmayarse*) to faint.

desfavorable *a* unfavourable.

desfigurar *vt* (*cara*) to disfigure.

desfiladero *m* narrow pass.

desfilar *vi* to march in single file; (*soldados*) to march past.

desfile *m* (*militar*) parade; **d. de modas** fashion show.

desganado,-a *a* (*apático*) apathetic; **estar d.** (*inapetente*) to have no appetite.

desgarrador,-a *a* bloodcurdling.

desgarrar *vt* to tear.

desgastar *vt*, **desgastarse** *vr* to wear out.

desgaste *m* wear.

desgracia *f* misfortune; **por d.** unfortunately.

desgraciadamente *adv* unfortunately.

desgraciado,-a 1 *a* unfortunate; (*infeliz*) unhappy. **2** *mf* unfortunate person.

desgravación *f* deduction; **d. fiscal** tax deduction.

desgravar *vt* to deduct.

deshabitado,-a *a* uninhabited.

deshacer (*pp* **deshecho**) **1** *vt* (*paquete*) to undo; (*maleta*) to unpack; (*destruir*) to destroy; (*disolver*) to dissolve; (*derretir*) to melt. **2 deshacerse** *vr* to come undone; **deshacerse de algn/algo** to get rid of sb/sth; (*disolverse*) to dissolve; (*derretirse*) to melt.

deshielo *m* thaw.

deshonesto,-a *a* dishonest; (*indecente*) indecent.

deshonrar *vt* to dishonour; (*a la familia etc*) to bring disgrace on.

deshora (a) *adv* at an inconvenient time.

deshuesar *vt* (*carne*) to bone; (*fruta*) to stone.

desierto,-a 1 *m* desert. **2** *a* (*deshabitado*) uninhabited; (*vacío*) deserted.

designar *vt* to designate; (*fecha, lugar*) to fix.

desigual *a* uneven.

desigualdad *f* inequality; (*del terreno*) unevenness.

desilusión *f* disappointment.

desilusionar *vt* to disappoint.

desinfectante *a & m* disinfectant.

desinflar 1 *vt* to deflate; (*rueda*) to let down. **2 desinflarse** *vr* to go flat.

desintegrar *vt*, **desintegrarse** *vr* to disintegrate.

desinteresado,-a *a* selfless.

desistir *vi* to desist.

deslenguado,-a *a* (*insolente*) insolent.

desliz *m* slip.

deslizar [4] **1** *vi* to slide. **2 deslizarse** *vr* (*patinar*) to slide; (*bajar*) to slide down.

deslumbrador,-a, deslumbrante *a* dazzling; *fig* stunning.

deslumbrar *vt* to dazzle.

desmandarse *vr* to get out of hand.

desmantelar *vt* to dismantle.

desmaquillador,-a 1 *m* make-up remover. **2** *a* **leche desmaquilladora** cleansing cream.

desmaquillarse *vr* to remove one's make-up.

desmayarse *vr* to faint.

desmayo *m* fainting fit; **tener un d.** to faint.

desmedido,-a *a* out of all proportion.

desmejorar(se) *vi & vr* to deteriorate.

desmemoriado,-a *a* forgetful.

desmentir [5] *vt* to deny.

desmenuzar [4] *vt* to crumble.

desmesurado,-a *a* excessive.

desmontar *vt* to dismantle.

desmoralizar [4] *vt* to demoralize.

desmoronarse *vr* to crumble.

desnatado,-a *a* (*leche*) skimmed.

desnivel *m* drop.

desnudar *vt*, **desnudarse** *vr* to undress.

desnudista *a & mf* nudist.

desnudo,-a *a* naked.

desnutrido,-a *a* undernourished.

desobedecer *vt* to disobey.

desobediente 1 *a* disobedient. **2** *mf* disobedient person.

desocupado,-a *a* (*vacío*) empty; (*ocioso*) free.

desodorante *a & m* deodorant.

desolar [2] *vt* to devastate.

desollar [2] **1** *vt* to skin. **2 desollarse** *vr* to scrape; **me desollé el brazo** I scraped my arm.

desorbitado,-a *a* (*precio*) exhorbitant.

desorden *m* mess; **d. público** civil disorder.

desordenado,-a *a* untidy.

desordenar *vt* to make untidy, mess up.

desorientar 1 *vt* to disorientate. **2 desorientarse** *vr* to lose one's bearings.

despabilado,-a *a* (*sin sueño*) wide awake; (*listo*) quick.

despachar *vt* (*asunto*) to get through; (*en tienda*) to serve.

despacho *m* (*oficina*) office; (*en casa*) study.

despacio *adv* **1** (*lentamente*) slowly. **2** (*en voz baja*) quietly.

desparramar *vt*, **desparramarse** *vr* to scatter; (*líquido*) to spill.

despavorido,-a *a* terrified.

despectivo,-a *a* derogatory.

despedida *f* goodbye.

despedir [6] **1** vt (empleado) to sack; (decir adiós) to say goodbye to; (olor, humo etc) to give off. **2 despedirse** vr (decir adiós) to say goodbye (**de** to).

despegar [7] **1** vt to detach. **2** vi (avión) to take off. **3 despegarse** vr to come unstuck.

despegue m takeoff.

despeinado,-a a dishevelled.

despejar 1 vt to clear. **2 despejarse** vr (cielo) to clear; (persona) to clear one's head.

despeje m (de balón) clearance.

despensa f pantry.

despeñarse vr to go over a cliff.

desperdiciar vt to waste; (oportunidad) to throw away.

desperdicio m waste; **desperdicios** (basura) rubbish sing; (desechos) leftovers.

desperdigar [7] vt, **desperdigarse** vr to scatter.

desperezarse [4] vr to stretch (oneself).

desperfecto m (defecto) flaw; (daño) damage.

despertador m alarm clock.

despertar [1] vt, **despertarse** vr to wake (up).

despiadado,-a a merciless.

despido m dismissal.

despierto,-a a (desvelado) awake; (listo) quick.

despilfarrar vt to squander.

despistado,-a 1 a (olvidadizo) scatterbrained. **2** mf scatterbrain.

despistar 1 vt (hacer perder la pista a) to lose. **2 despistarse** vr (perderse) to get lost; (distraerse) to switch off.

desplazamiento m (viaje) journey.

desplazar [4] **1** vt to displace. **2 desplazarse** vr to travel.

despojar vt to strip (de of); fig to deprive (de of).

desposar vt to marry.

déspota mf despot.

despreciar vt (desdeñar) to scorn; (rechazar) to reject.

desprender 1 vt (separar) to remove; (olor, humo etc) to give off. **2 desprenderse** vr (soltarse) to come off; **desprenderse de** to rid oneself (**de** of).

despreocupado,-a a (tranquilo) unconcerned; (descuidado) careless; (estilo) casual.

desprestigiar vt to discredit.

desprevenido,-a a unprepared; **coger** o **pillar a algn d.** to catch sb unawares.

desproporcionado,-a a disproportionate.

desprovisto,-a a lacking (**de -**).

después 1 adv afterwards, later; (*entonces*) then; (*seguidamente, lugar*) next; **poco d.** soon after. **2** prep **d. de** after. **3** conj **d. de que** after.

destacar [1] **1** vt to stress. **2 destacar(se)** vi & vr to stand out.

destapar 1 vt to take the lid off; (*botella*) to open. **2 destaparse** vr to get uncovered.

destartalado,-a a rambling; (*desvencijado*) ramshackle.

destello m sparkle.

desteñir [6] **1** vti to discolour. **2 desteñirse** vr to fade.

desternillarse vi **d. (de risa)** to split one's sides laughing.

desterrar [1] vt to exile.

destierro m exile.

destilería f distillery.

destinar vt (*dinero etc*) to assign; (*empleado*) to appoint.

destino m (*rumbo*) destination; (*sino*) fate; (*de empleo*) post; **el avión con d. a Bilbao** the plane to Bilbao.

destituir vt to remove from office.

destornillador m screwdriver.

destreza f skill.

destrozar [4] vt (*destruir*) to destroy; (*abatir*) to shatter.

destrucción f destruction.

destruir vt to destroy.

desuso m disuse; **caer en d.** to fall into disuse.

desvalijar vt (*robar*) to rob; (*casa, tienda*) to burgle.

desván m loft.

desvanecerse vr (*disiparse*) to vanish; (*desmayarse*) to faint.

desvariar vi to talk nonsense.

desvelar 1 vt to keep awake. **2 desvelarse** vr to stay awake.

desvencijarse vr to fall apart.

desventaja f disadvantage; (*inconveniente*) drawback; **estar en d.** to be at a disadvantage.

desvergonzado,-a 1 a (*indecente*) shameless; (*descarado*) insolent. **2** mf (*sinvergüenza*) shameless person; (*fresco*) insolent person.

desvestir [6] vt, **desvestirse** vr to undress.

desviar 1 vt (*río, carretera*) to divert; (*golpe, conversación*) to deflect. **2 desviarse** vr to go off course; (*coche*) to turn off.

desvío m diversion.

detallado,-a a detailed.

detalle m detail; (*delicadeza*) nice thought.

detallista a perfectionist.

detectar vt to detect.

detective mf detective; **d. privado** private detective.

detener 1 *vt* to stop; (*arrestar*) to arrest. **2 detenerse** *vr* to stop.

detenidamente *adv* carefully.

detenido,-a 1 *a* (*parado*) stopped; (*arrestado*) detained; (*minucioso*) thorough. **2** *mf* detainee.

detergente *a & m* detergent.

deteriorar 1 *vt* to spoil. **2 deteriorarse** *vr* (*estropearse*) to get damaged.

determinado,-a *a* (*preciso*) definite; (*resuelto*) resolute.

determinar 1 *vt* (*fecha etc*) to set; (*decidir*) to decide on. **2 determinarse** *vr* **determinarse a** to make up one's mind to.

detestar *vt* to hate.

detrás 1 *adv* behind. **2** *prep* **d. de** behind.

detuve *pt indef de* **detener.**

deuda *f* debt; **d. pública** national debt.

deudor,-a *mf* debtor.

devaluar *vt* to devalue.

devastador,-a *a* devastating.

devoción *f* devoutness; (*al trabajo etc*) devotion.

devolución *f* return; (*de dinero*) refund.

devolver [4] (*pp* **devuelto**) **1** *vt* to give back; (*dinero*) to refund. **2** *vi* (*vomitar*) to vomit. **3 devolverse** *vr Am* to go/come back.

devorar *vt* to devour.

devoto,-a 1 *a* devout. **2** *mf* pious person; (*seguidor*) devotee.

devuelto,-a *pp de* **devolver.**

DF *m abr de* **Distrito Federal** Federal District.

di *pt indef de* **dar;** *imperativo de* **decir.**

día *m* day; **¿qué d. es hoy?** what's the date today?; **d. a d.** day by day; **de d.** by day; **durante el d.** during the daytime; **un d. sí y otro no** every other day; **pan del d.** fresh bread; **hoy (en) d.** nowadays; **el d. de mañana** in the future; **d. festivo** holiday; **d. laborable** working day; **d. libre** day off; **es de d.** it is daylight; **hace buen/mal d.** it's a nice/rotten day.

diabético,-a *a & mf* diabetic.

diablo *m* devil.

diadema *f* tiara.

diagnóstico *m* diagnosis.

diagonal *a & f* diagonal; **en d.** diagonally.

dial *m* dial.

diálogo *m* dialogue.

diamante *m* diamond.

diámetro *m* diameter.

diana *f* (*blanco*) bull's eye.

diapositiva *f* slide.

diariamente *adv* daily.

diario,-a 1 *a* daily; **a d.** daily. **2** *m* (*daily*) newspaper; (*memorias*) diary.

diarrea *f* diarrhoea.

dibujante *mf* drawer; (*de cómic*) cartoonist; (*delineante*) (*hombre*) draughtsman; (*mujer*) draughtswoman.

dibujar *vt* to draw.

dibujo *m* drawing; **dibujos animados** cartoons.

diccionario *m* dictionary.

dicho,-a *a* said; **mejor d.** or rather; **d. y hecho** no sooner said than done; **dicha persona** the above-mentioned person.

dichoso,-a *a* (*feliz*) happy; *fam* (*maldito*) damned.

diciembre *m* December.

dictado *m* dictation.

dictadura *f* dictatorship.

dictáfono[R] *m* Dictaphone[R].

dictar *vt* to dictate; (*ley*) to enact.

didáctico,-a *a* didactic.

diecinueve *a* & *m inv* nineteen.

dieciocho *a* & *m inv* eighteen.

dieciséis *a* & *m inv* sixteen.

diecisiete *a* & *m inv* seventeen.

diente *m* tooth; **d. de ajo** clove of garlic; **d. de leche** milk tooth; **dientes postizos** false teeth.

diera *subj imperfecto de* **dar**.

diesel *a* & *m* diesel.

diestro,-a 1 *a* (*hábil*) skilful. **2** *m* bullfighter.

dieta *f* (*paga*) diet; **estar a d.** to be on a diet; **dietas** expenses.

diez *a* & *m inv* ten.

diferencia *f* difference; **a d. de** unlike.

diferenciar 1 *vt* to differentiate (**entre** between). **2 diferenciarse** *vr* to differ (**de** from).

diferente 1 *a* different (**de** from, *US* than). **2** *adv* differently.

diferido,-a *a* en **d.** recorded.

difícil *a* difficult; **d. de creer/hacer** difficult to believe/do; **es d. que venga** it is unlikely that she'll come.

dificultad *f* difficulty; (*aprieto*) problem.

difundir *vt*, **difundirse** *vr* to spread.

difunto,-a *mf* deceased.

digestión *f* digestion.

digestivo,-a *a* easy to digest.

digital *a* digital; **huellas digitales** fingerprints; **tocadiscos d.** CD player.

dígito *m* digit.

digno,-a *a* (*merecedor*) worthy; (*decoroso*) decent.

digo *indic pres de* **decir.**

dije *pt indef de* **decir.**

dilatar *vt,* **dilatarse** *vr* to expand.

dilema *m* dilemma.

diluir *vt,* **diluirse** *vr* to dilute.

diluviar *v impers* to pour with rain.

diluyo *indic pres de* **diluir.**

dimensión *f* dimension; **de gran d.** very large.

dimisión *m* resignation; **presentar la d.** to hand in one's resignation.

dimitir *vi* to resign (**de** from).

dinamita *f* dynamite.

dinamo *f,* **dínamo** *f* dynamo.

dinero *m* money; **d. efectivo** *o* **en metálico** cash.

dinosaurio *m* dinosaur.

dios *m* god; **¡D. mío!** my God!; **¡por D.!** for goodness sake!

diploma *m* diploma.

diplomacia *f* diplomacy.

diplomarse *vr* to graduate.

diplomático,-a 1 *a* diplomatic. **2** *mf* diplomat.

diptongo *m* diphthong.

diputación *f* **d. provincial** ≈ county council.

diputado,-a *mf* ≈ Member of Parliament, MP; *US (hombre)* Congressman; *(mujer)* Congresswoman; **Congreso de Diputados** ≈ House of Commons, *US* Congress.

dique *m* dike.

diré *fut de* **decir.**

dirección *f* direction; *(señas)* address; *(destino)* destination; *(de vehículo)* steering; *(dirigentes)* management; *(cargo)* directorship; *(de un partido)* leadership; **d. prohibida** no entry; **calle de d. única** one-way street.

directa *f (marcha)* top gear.

directiva *f* board of directors.

directamente *adv* directly.

directo,-a *a* direct; **en d.** live.

director,-a *mf* director; *(de colegio) (hombre)* headmaster; *(mujer)* headmistress; *(de periódico)* editor; **d. de cine** (film) director; **d. de orquesta** conductor; **d. gerente** managing director.

dirigir [6] **1** *vt* to direct; *(empresa)* to manage; *(negocio, colegio)* to run; *(orquesta)* to conduct; *(partido)* to lead; *(periódico)* to edit; **d. la palabra a algn** to speak to sb. **2 dirigirse** *vr* **dirigirse a** *o* **hacia** *(ir)* to make one's way towards; *(hablar)* to speak to.

disciplina *f* discipline.

discípulo,-a *mf* disciple.

disco *m* disk; (*de música*) record; **d. compacto** compact disc; **d. duro** hard disk; **d. óptico** optical disk.

discoteca *f* discotheque.

díscrepar *vi* (*disentir*) to disagree (**de** with; **en** on).

discreto,-a *a* discreet.

discriminación *f* discrimination.

disculpa *f* excuse; **dar disculpas** to make excuses; **pedir disculpas a algn** to apologize to sb.

disculpar 1 *vt* to excuse. 2 **disculparse** *vr* to apologize (**por** for).

discurrir *vi* to think.

discurso *m* speech; **dar** *o* **pronunciar un d.** to make a speech.

discusión *f* argument.

discutir 1 *vi* to argue (**de** about). 2 *vt* to discuss.

diseñar *vt* to design.

diseño *m* design.

disfrazar [4] 1 *vt* to disguise. 2 **disfrazarse** *vr* to disguise oneself.

disfrutar 1 *vi* (*gozar*) to enjoy oneself; (*poseer*) to enjoy (**de** -). 2 *vt* to enjoy.

disgustar 1 *vt* to upset. 2 **disgustarse** *vr* (*molestarse*) to get upset; (*dos amigos*) to quarrel.

disgusto *m* (*preocupación*) upset; (*desgracia*) trouble; **llevarse un d.** to get upset; **dar un d. a algn** to upset sb; **a d.** unwillingly.

disimular *vt* to conceal.

disipar 1 *vt* (*niebla*) to drive away; (*temor, duda*) to dispel. 2 **disiparse** *vr* (*niebla, temor etc*) to disappear.

dislocar [1] *vt* to dislocate.

disminuir 1 *vt* to reduce. 2 *vi* to diminish.

disolvente *a* & *m* solvent.

disolver [4] (*pp* **disuelto**) *vt* to dissolve.

disparar 1 *vt* (*pistola etc*) to fire; (*flecha, balón*) to shoot. 2 **dispararse** *vr* (*arma*) to go off; (*precios*) to rocket.

disparate *m* (*dicho*) nonsense; **decir disparates** to talk nonsense; (*acto*) foolish act.

dispersar *vt*, **dispersarse** *vr* to disperse.

disponer (*pp* **dispuesto**) 1 *vt* (*arreglar*) to arrange; (*ordenar*) to order. 2 *vi* **d. de** to have at one's disposal. 3 **disponerse** *vr* to get ready.

disposición *f* (*colocación*) layout; (*orden*) law; **a su d.** at your service.

dispositivo *m* device.

disputa *f* (*discusión*) argument; (*contienda*) contest.

disquete *m* diskette, floppy disk.

disquetera *f* disk drive.

distancia *f* distance.
distante *a* distant.
distinguir 1 *vt* (*diferenciar*) to distinguish; (*reconocer*) to recognize. **2** *vi* (*diferenciar*) to discriminate. **3 distinguirse** *vr* to distinguish oneself.
distintivo,-a 1 *a* distinctive. **2** *m* distinctive mark.
distinto,-a *a* different.
distracción *f* entertainment; (*pasatiempo*) pastime; (*descuido*) absent-mindedness.
distraer 1 *vt* (*atención*) to distract; (*divertir*) to entertain. **2 distraerse** *vr* (*divertirse*) to amuse oneself; (*abstraerse*) to let one's mind wander.
distraído,-a *a* entertaining; (*abstraído*) absent-minded.
distribuidor,-a 1 *a* distributing. **2** *mf* distributor.
distribuir *vt* to distribute; (*trabajo*) to share out.
distrito *m* district; **d. postal** postal district.
disturbio *m* riot.
disuadir *vt* to dissuade.
disuelto,-a *pp de* **disolver.**
diván *m* couch.
diversión *f* fun.
diverso,-a *a* different; **diversos** various.
divertido,-a *a* funny.
divertir [5] **1** *vt* to amuse. **2 divertirse** *vr* to enjoy oneself.
dividir *vt,* **dividirse** *vr* to divide (**en** into).
divisa *f* **divisas** foreign currency *sing*.
división *f* division.
divorciado,-a 1 *a* divorced. **2** *mf* (*hombre*) divorcé; (*mujer*) divorcée.
divorciarse *vr* to get divorced.
divorcio *m* divorce.
divulgación *f* disclosure.
DNI *m abr de* **Documento Nacional de Identidad** Identity Card, ID card.
doberman *m* Doberman (pinscher).
dobladillo *m* hem.
doblar 1 *vt* to double; (*plegar*) to fold up; (*torcer*) to bend; (*la esquina*) to go round. **2** *vi* (*girar*) to turn. **3 doblarse** *vr* (*plegarse*) to fold; (*torcerse*) to bend.
doble 1 *a* double. **2** *m* double; **gana el d. que tú** she earns twice as much as you do.
doce *a & m inv* twelve.
docena *f* dozen.
docente *a* teaching; **centro d.** educational centre.
dócil *a* docile.
doctor,-a *mf* doctor.

doctorado *m* doctorate, PhD.

documentación *f* documentation; (*DNI, de conducir etc*) papers *pl.*

documental *a & m* documentary.

documento *m* document; **d. nacional de identidad** identity card.

dogo *m* bulldog.

dólar *m* dollar.

doler [4] *vi* to ache; **me duele la cabeza** I've got a headache.

dolor *m* pain; (*pena*) grief; **d. de cabeza** headache; **d. de muelas** toothache.

domar *vt* to tame; (*caballo*) to break in.

doméstico,-a *a* domestic; **animal d.** pet.

domicilio *m* residence; (*señas*) address.

dominante *a* dominant; (*déspota*) domineering.

dominar 1 *vt* to dominate; (*situación*) to control; (*idioma*) to speak very well. **2** *vi* to dominate; (*resaltar*) to stand out. **3 dominarse** *vr* to control oneself.

domingo *m inv* Sunday; **D. de Resurrección** *o* **Pascua** Easter Sunday.

dominical 1 *a* Sunday. **2** *m* (*suplemento*) Sunday supplement.

dominicano,-a *a & mf* Dominican; **República Dominicana,** Dominican Republic.

dominio *m* (*poder*) control; (*de un idioma*) command; (*territorio*) dominion.

dominó, dómino *m* dominoes *pl.*

don[1] *m* (*habilidad*) gift; **tener el d. de** to have a knack for.

don[2] *m* Señor **D. José García** Mr José Garcia; **D. Fulano de Tal** Mr So-and-So.

donar *vt* (*sangre etc*) to give.

donativo *m* donation.

dónde *adv* where (*in questions*); **¿por d. se va a la playa?** which way is it to the beach?

donde *adv rel* where; **a** *o* **en d.** where; **de** *o* **desde d.** from where.

doña *f* Señora **D. Leonor Benítez** Mrs Leonor Benítez.

dorada *f* (*pez*) gilthead bream.

dorado,-a *a* golden.

dormido,-a *a* asleep; **quedarse d.** to fall asleep; (*no despertarse*) to oversleep.

dormilón,-ona *fam* **1** *a* sleepyheaded. **2** *mf* sleepyhead.

dormir [7] **1** *vi* to sleep. **2** *vt* **d. la siesta** to have an afternoon nap. **3 dormirse** *vr* to fall asleep; **se me ha dormido el brazo** my arm has gone to sleep.

dormitorio *m* (*de una casa*) bedroom; (*de colegio, residencia*) dormitory.

dorsal 1 *a* **espina d.** spine. **2** *m* (*de camiseta*) number.

dorso *m* back; **instrucciones al d.** instructions over; **véase al d.** see overleaf.

dos 1 *a* two. **2** *m inv* two; **los d.** both; **nosotros/vosotros d.** both of us/you.

doscientos,-as *a & mf* two hundred.

dosis *f inv* dose.

doy *indic pres de* **dar.**

Dr. *abr de* **doctor** doctor, Dr.

Dra. *abr de* **doctora** doctor, Dr.

dragón *m* dragon.

drama *m* drama.

dramático,-a *a* dramatic.

drástico,-a *a* drastic.

droga *f* drug; **d. blanda/dura** soft/hard drug.

drogadicto,-a *mf* drug addict.

drogar [7] **1** *vt* to drug. **2 drogarse** *vr* to take drugs.

droguería *f* hardware and household goods shop.

ducha *f* shower; **darse/tomar una d.** to take/have a shower.

ducharse *vr* to take a shower.

duda *f* doubt; **sin d.** without a doubt; **no cabe d.** (there is) no doubt.

dudar 1 *vi* to doubt; (*vacilar*) to hesitate (**en** to). **2** *vt* to doubt.

dueña *f* owner; (*de pensión*) landlady.

dueño *m* owner; (*de casa etc*) landlord.

dulce 1 *a* (*sabor*) sweet; (*carácter, voz*) gentle; (*agua*) fresh. **2** *m* (*pastel*) cake; (*caramelo*) sweet, *US* candy.

duna *f* dune.

duodécimo,-a *a & mf* twelfth.

duplicar [1] **1** *vt* to duplicate; (*cifras*) to double. **2 duplicarse** *vr* to double.

duración *f* duration.

durante *prep* during.

durar *vi* to last.

durazno *m* (*fruto*) peach; (*árbol*) peach tree.

dureza *f* hardness; (*severidad*) severity; (*callosidad*) corn.

duro,-a 1 *a* hard; (*resistente*) tough. **2** *m* (*moneda*) five-peseta coin. **3** *adv* hard.

E

e *conj* (*before words beginning with* **i** *or* **hi**) and.

ébano *m* ebony.

ebullición *f* boiling; **punto de e.** boiling point.

echar 1 *vt* to throw; (*carta*) to post; (*vino, agua*) to pour; (*expulsar*) to throw out; (*despedir*) to sack; (*humo, olor etc*) to give off; **e. una mano** to give a hand; **e. una mirada/una ojeada** to have a look/a quick look; **e. gasolina al coche** to put petrol in the car; **e. de menos** *o* **en falta** to miss. **2** *vi* (**+ a +** *infinitivo*) (*empezar*) to begin to; **echó a correr** he ran off. **3** **echarse** *vr* (*tumbarse*) to lie down; (*lanzarse*) to throw oneself; (**+ a +** *infinitivo*) (*empezar*) to begin to; *fig* **echarse atrás** to get cold feet; **echarse a llorar** to burst into tears; **echarse a perder** (*comida*) to go bad.

eclesiástico,-a 1 *a* ecclesiastical. **2** *m* clergyman.

eclipse *m* eclipse.

eco *m* echo.

ecológico,-a *a* ecological.

ecologista 1 *a* ecological. **2** *mf* ecologist.

economía *f* economy; (*ciencia*) economics *sing*.

económico,-a *a* economic; (*barato*) economical.

economizar [4] *vti* to economize.

ecuación *f* equation.

ecuador *m* equator.

ecuatoriano,-a *a* & *mf* Ecuadorian.

ecuánime *a* (*temperamento*) even-tempered; (*juicio*) impartial.

ecuestre *a* equestrian.

edad *f* age; **¿qué e. tienes?** how old are you?; **E. Media** Middle Ages *pl*.

edición *f* (*publicación*) publication; (*conjunto de ejemplares*) edition.

edicto *m* edict.

edificio *m* building.

edil,-a *mf* town councillor.

editar *vt* (*libro, periódico*) to publish; (*disco*) to release; (*en odenador*) to edit.

editor,-a 1 *a* publishing. **2** *mf* publisher. **3** *m* **e. de textos** text editor.

editorial 1 *a* publishing. **2** *f* publishing house. **3** *m* editorial.

edredón *m* continental quilt.

educación *f* education; (*formación*) upbringing; **buena/mala e.** (*modales*) good/bad manners; **falta de e.** bad manners.

educado,-a *a* polite.

educar [1] *vt* (*hijos*) to raise.

educativo,-a *a* educational.

efectivamente *adv* yes indeed!

efectivo,-a *a* effective; **hacer e. un cheque** to cash a cheque. **2** *m* **en e.** in cash.

efecto *m* (*resultado*) effect; (*impresión*) impression; **efectos personales** personal belongings; **en e.** yes indeed!

efectuar *vt* to carry out; (*viaje*) to make; (*pedido*) to place.

eficacia *f* (*de persona*) efficiency; (*de remedio etc*) effectiveness.

eficaz *a* (*persona*) efficient; (*remedio, medida etc*) effective.

eficiente *a* efficient.

efusivo,-a *a* effusive.

EGB *f abr de* **Enseñanza General Básica** ≈ Primary School Education.

egipcio,-a *a & mf* Egyptian.

egoísmo *m* egoism.

egoísta **1** *a* selfish. **2** *mf* ego(t)ist.

egresar *vi Am* to leave school, *US* graduate.

ej. *abr de* **ejemplo** example.

eje *m* (*de rueda*) axle; (*de máquina*) shaft.

ejecutar *vt* (*ajusticiar*) to execute; (*sinfonía*) to perform.

ejecutiva *f* (*gobierno*) executive.

ejecutivo,-a **1** *a* executive; **el poder e.** the government. **2** *m* executive.

ejemplar **1** *m* (*de libro*) copy; (*de revista, periódico*) issue; (*especimen*) specimen. **2** *a* exemplary.

ejemplo *m* example; **por e.** for example; **dar e.** to set an example.

ejercer [2] *vt* (*profesión etc*) to practise; (*influencia*) to exert.

ejercicio *m* exercise; (*de profesión*) practice; **hacer e.** to take exercise.

ejercitar *vt* to practise.

ejército *m* army.

el **1** *art def m* the; **el Sr. García** Mr. García. ‖ (*no se traduce*) **el hambre/ destino** hunger/fate. ‖ (*con partes del cuerpo, prendas de vestir*) **me he cortado el dedo** I've cut my finger; **métetelo en el bolsillo** put it in your pocket. ‖ (*con días de la semana*) **el lunes** on Monday. **2** *pron* the one; **el de las once** the eleven o'clock one; **el que tienes en la mano** the one you've got in your hand; **el que quieras** whichever one you want; **el de tu amigo** your friend's.

él *pron pers* (*sujeto*) (*persona*) he; (*animal, cosa*) it; (*complemento*) (*persona*) him; (*animal, cosa*) it.

elaboración *f* (*de un producto*) production.

elaborar *vt* (*producto*) to produce.

elasticidad *f* elasticity; *fig* flexibility.

elástico,-a *a & m* elastic.

elección *f* choice; (*votación*) election.

electorado *m* electorate *pl*.

electoral *a* electoral; **campaña e.** election campaign; **colegio e.** polling

empujón *m* push, shove.
emulsión *f* emulsion.
en *prep* (*posición*) in; at; (*sobre*) on; **en Madrid/Bolivia** in Madrid/Bolivia; **en casa/el trabajo** at home/work; **en la mesa** on the table. ‖ (*movimiento*) into; **entrar en la casa** to go into the house. ‖ (*tiempo*) in; on; at; **en 1940** in 1940; *Am* **en la mañana** in the morning; **cae en martes** it falls on a Tuesday; **en ese momento** at that moment. ‖ (*transporte*) by; **en coche/tren** by car/train. ‖ (*modo*) **en español** in Spanish; **en broma** jokingly; **en serio** seriously. ‖ (*reducción, aumento*) by; **los precios aumentaron en un diez por ciento** the prices went up by ten percent. ‖ (*tema, materia*) at, in; **bueno en deportes** good at sports; **experto en política** expert in politics. ‖ (*división, separación*) in; **lo dividió en tres partes** he divided it in three. ‖ (*con infinitivo*) **fue rápido en responder** he was quick to answer.
enaguas *fpl* petticoat *sing*.
enamorado,-a 1 *a* in love. **2** *mf* person in love.
enamorar 1 *vt* to win the heart of. **2 enamorarse** *vr* to fall in love (**de** with).
enano,-a *a* & *mf* dwarf.
encabezamiento *m* (*de carta*) heading; (*de periódico*) headline.
encabezar [4] *vt* (*carta, lista*) to head; (*periódico*) to lead; (*rebelión, carrera, movimiento*) to lead.
encajar 1 *vt* (*ajustar*) to insert; **e. un golpe a algn** to land sb a blow. **2** *vi* (*ajustarse*) to fit; **e. con** to fit (in) with.
encaje *m* lace.
encallar *vi* to run aground.
encantado,-a *a* (*contento*) delighted; (*embrujado*) enchanted; **e. de conocerle** pleased to meet you;
encantador,-a 1 *a* charming. **2** *mf* magician.
encantar *vt* (*hechizar*) to cast a spell on; **me encanta nadar** I love swimming.
encanto *m* charm; **ser un e.** to be charming.
encapricharse *vr* to set one's mind (**con** on).
encaramarse *vr* to climb up.
encarar 1 *vt* to face. **2 encararse** *vr* **encararse con** to face up to.
encarcelar *vt* to imprison.
encarecer 1 *vt* to put up the price of. **2 encarecerse** *vr* to go up (in price).
encargado,-a 1 *mf* (*hombre*) manager; (*mujer*) manageress; (*responsable*) person in charge. **2** *a* in charge.
encargar [7] **1** *vt* to entrust with; (*mercancías*) to order. **2 encargarse** *vr* **encargarse de** to see to.
ncargo *m* order; (*recado*) errand; (*tarea*) job.

station.
electricidad *f* electricity.
electricista *mf* electrician.
eléctrico,-a *a* electric.
electrocutar *vt* to electrocute.
electrodoméstico *m* (domestic) electrical appliance.
electrónico,-a *a* electronic.
elefante *m* elephant.
elegancia *f* elegance.
elegante *a* elegant.
elegir [6] *vt* to choose; (*en votación*) to elect.
elemental *a* (*fundamental*) basic; (*simple*) elementary.
elemento *m* element; (*componente*) component.
elepé *m* LP (record).
elevación *f* elevation; (*de precios*) rise.
elevado,-a *a* high; (*edificio*) tall.
elevalunas *m inv* **e. eléctrico** electric windows *pl*.
elevar 1 *vt* to raise. **2 elevarse** *vr* (*subir*) to rise; **elevarse a** (*cantidad*) to come to.
elijo *indic pres de* **elegir.**
eliminar *vt* to eliminate.
eliminatorio,-a *a* qualifying.
ella *pron pers f* (*sujeto*) she; (*animal, cosa*) it, she; (*complemento*) her; (*animal, cosa*) it, her.
ellas *pron pers fpl* (*sujeto*) they; (*complemento*) them.
ello *pron pers neutro* it; **por e.** for that reason.
ellos *pron pers mpl* (*sujeto*) they; (*complemento*) them.
elocuente *a* eloquent.
elogiar *vt* to praise.
elote *m Am* tender corncob.
eludir *vt* to avoid.
embajada *f* embassy.
embajador,-a *mf* ambassador.
embalaje *m* packing.
embalse *m* reservoir; (*presa*) dam.
embarazada 1 *a* pregnant. **2** *f* pregnant woman.
embarazo *m* (*preñez*) pregnancy; (*turbación*) embarrassment.
embarazoso,-a *a* embarrassing.
embarcación *f* (*nave*) boat; (*embarco*) embarkation.
embarcadero *m* quay.
embarcar [1] **1** *vt* to ship. **2** *vi* to go on board. **3 embarcarse** *vr* to go on board (**en** -); (*en avión*) to board (**en** -).

embarque *m* (*de persona*) boarding; (*de mercancías*) loading; **tarjeta de e.** boarding card.

embestida *f* onslaught; (*de toro*) charge.

embestir [6] *vt* (*a torero*) to charge; (*atacar*) to attack.

emblema *m* emblem.

embobado,-a *a* fascinated.

émbolo *m* piston.

embolsar *vt*, **embolsarse** *vr* to pocket.

emborrachar *vt*, **emborracharse** *vr* to get drunk.

emboscada *f* ambush.

embotellamiento *m* traffic jam.

embotellar *vt* to bottle; (*tráfico*) to block.

embrague *m* clutch.

embriagar [7] **1** *vt* to intoxicate. **2 embriagarse** *vr* to get drunk.

embriaguez *f* intoxication.

embrollar 1 *vt* to confuse. **2 embrollarse** *vr* to get confused.

embrujado,-a *a* (*sitio*) haunted.

embudo *m* funnel.

embuste *m* lie.

embustero,-a *mf* cheat.

embutido *m* sausage.

emergencia *f* emergency; **salida de e.** emergency exit; **en caso de e.** in an emergency.

emigración *f* emigration.

emigrante *a* & *mf* emigrant.

emigrar *vi* to emigrate.

emisión *f* emission; (*de radio, TV*) broadcasting.

emisora *f* (*de radio*) radio station; (*de televisión*) television station.

emitir *vt* to emit; (*luz, calor*) to give off; (*opinión, juicio*) to express; (*programa*) to transmit.

emoción *f* emotion; (*excitación*) excitement; **¡qué e.!** how exciting!

emocionante *a* (*conmovedor*) moving; (*excitante*) exciting.

emocionar 1 *vt* (*conmover*) to move; (*excitar*) to thrill. **2 emocionarse** *vr* (*conmoverse*) to be moved; (*excitarse*) to get excited.

empacar [1] *vt* (*mercancías*) to pack; *Am* to annoy.

empacho *m* (*de comida*) indigestion.

empalagoso,-a *a* (*dulce*) sickly sweet.

empalizada *f* fence.

empalmar 1 *vt* (*unir*) to join; (*cuerdas, cables*) to splice. **2** *vi* to converge; (*trenes*) to connect.

empanada *f* pie.

empanadilla *f* pasty.

empañar *vt*, **empañarse** *vr* (*cristales*) to steam up.

empapado,-a *a* soaked.

empapar 1 *vt* (*mojar*) to soak; (*absorber*) to soak up. **2 empaparse** *vr* (*persona*) to get soaked.

empapelar *vt* to wallpaper.

empaquetar *vt* to pack.

emparedado *m* sandwich.

empaste *m* (*de diente*) filling.

empatar *vi* to draw; *Am* (*unir*) to join.

empate *m* draw.

empedrado,-a 1 *a* cobbled. **2** *m* (*adoquines*) cobblestones *pl*.

empeine *m* (*de pie, de zapato*) instep.

empellón *m* shove.

empeñar 1 *vt* to pawn. **2 empeñarse** *vr* (*insistir*) to insist (**en** on); (*endeudarse*) to get into debt.

empeño *m* (*insistencia*) insistence; (*deuda*) pledge.

empeorar 1 *vi* to deteriorate. **2** *vt* to make worse. **3 empeorarse** *vr* to deteriorate.

emperador *m* emperor.

empezar [1] *vti* to begin, start (**a hacer algo** to do sth).

empinado,-a *a* (*cuesta*) steep.

empinar 1 *vt* to raise. **2 empinarse** *vr* (*persona*) to stand on tiptoe.

emplazamiento *m* (*colocación*) location.

empleado,-a *mf* employee; (*de oficina, banco*) clerk.

emplear *vt* (*usar*) to use; (*contratar*) to employ; (*dinero, tiempo*) to spend.

empleo *m* employment; (*oficio*) job; (*uso*) use; **modo de e.** instructions for use.

emplomar *vt* *Am* (*diente*) to fill.

empobrecer 1 *vi* to impoverish. **2 empobrecerse** *vr* to become impoverished.

empobrecimiento *m* impoverishment.

empollón,-ona *mf fam* swot.

emporio *m* *Am* department store.

empotrado,-a *a* fitted.

emprendedor,-a *a* enterprising.

empresa *f* firm; (*tarea*) undertaking.

empresarial *a* (*de empresa*) business; (*espíritu*) entrepreneurial; (**ciencias) empresariales** business studies.

empresario,-a *mf* (*hombre*) businessman; (*mujer*) businesswoman; (*patrón*) employer.

empujar *vt* to push, shove.

encariñarse *vr* to become fond (**con** of).
encarnado,-a *a* (*rojo*) red.
encarnizado,-a *a* fierce.
encauzar [4] *vt* to channel.
encendedor *m* lighter.
encender [3] **1** *vt* (*luz, radio, tele*) to switch on, put on; (*cigarro, vela, fuego*) to light; (*cerilla*) to strike. **2 encenderse** *vr* (*fuego*) to catch; (*lámpara etc*) to go *o* come on.
encendido *m* ignition.
encerado *m* (*pizarra*) blackboard.
encerrar [1] **1** *vt* to shut in; (*con llave*) to lock in. **2 encerrarse** *vr* to shut oneself in; (*con llave*) to lock oneself in.
encharcar [1] *vt*, **encharcarse** *vr* to flood.
enchufado,-a 1 *a fig fam* **estar e.** to have good connections. **2** *mf* (*favorito*) pet.
enchufar *vt* to plug in; (*unir*) to join.
enchufe *m* (*hembra*) socket; (*macho*) plug; *fam* contact.
encía *f* gum.
enciclopedia *f* encyclopedia.
encima 1 *adv* on top; (*arriba*) above; (*en el aire*) overhead; (*además*) besides. **2** *prep* **e. de** (*sobre*) on; (*además*) besides; **ahí e.** up there; **por e.** above; **leer un libro por e.** to skip through a book.
encina *f* holm oak.
encinta *a* pregnant.
enclenque *a* (*débil*) puny; (*enfermizo*) sickly.
encoger [5] **1** *vti* to contract; (*prenda*) to shrink. **2 encogerse** *vr* (*contraerse*) to contract; (*prenda*) to shrink; **encogerse de hombros** to shrug (one's shoulders).
encolar *vt* (*papel*) to paste; (*madera*) to glue.
encolerizar [4] **1** *vt* to infuriate. **2 encolerizarse** *vr* to become furious.
encono *m* spitefulness.
encontrar [2] **1** *vt* (*hallar*) to find; (*a persona*) to meet; (*problema*) to come up against. **2 encontrarse** *vr* (*sentirse*) to feel, be; (*estar*) to be; **encontrarse a gusto** to feel comfortable; **encontrarse con algn** to meet sb.
encontronazo *m* (*choque*) clash.
encorvarse *vr* to bend (over).
encrucijada *f* crossroads.
encuadernar *vt* to bind.
encubrir *vt* to conceal.
encuentro *m* meeting; (*deportivo*) match.
encuesta *f* (*sondeo*) (opinion) poll; (*investigación*) investigation.
encuestar *vt* to poll.

endeble *a* weak.

endémico,-a *a* endemic.

enderezar [4] **1** *vt* (*poner derecho*) to straighten out; (*poner vertical*) to set upright. **2 enderezarse** *vr* to straighten up.

endeudarse *vr* to get into debt.

endiablado,-a *a* mischievous.

endibia *f* endive.

endulzar [4] *vt* to sweeten.

endurecer *vt*, **endurecerse** *vr* to harden.

enemigo,-a *a & mf* enemy.

enemistar 1 *vt* to set at odds. **2 enemistarse** *vr* to become enemies; **enemistarse con algn** to fall out with sb.

energía *f* energy; **e. nuclear** nuclear power; **e. vital** vitality.

enérgico,-a *a* energetic; (*tono*) emphatic.

enero *m* January.

enfadado,-a *a* angry.

enfadar 1 *vt* to make angry. **2 enfadarse** *vr* to get angry (**con** with); (*dos personas*) to fall out.

enfado *m* anger.

énfasis *m inv* emphasis.

enfermar *vi*, **enfermarse** *vr Am* to fall ill.

enfermedad *f* illness; (*contagiosa*) disease.

enfermería *f* infirmary.

enfermero,-a *mf* (*mujer*) nurse; (*hombre*) male nurse.

enfermizo,-a *a* unhealthy.

enfermo,-a 1 *a* ill. **2** *mf* ill person; (*paciente*) patient.

enfocar [1] *vt* (*imagen*) to focus; (*tema*) to approach; (*con linterna*) to shine a light on.

enfrentamiento *m* clash.

enfrentar 1 *vt* (*situación, peligro*) to confront; (*enemistar*) to set at odds. **2 enfrentarse** *vr* **enfrentarse con** *o* **a** (*encararse*) to confront.

enfrente 1 *adv* opposite; **la casa de e.** the house opposite. **2** *prep* **e. de** opposite.

enfriamiento *m* (*proceso*) cooling; (*catarro*) chill.

enfriar 1 *vt* to cool (down). **2 enfriarse** *vr* to get cold; (*resfriarse*) to catch a cold.

enfurecer 1 *vt* to enrage. **2 enfurecerse** *vr* to get furious.

enganchar 1 *vt* to hook. **2 engancharse** *vr* (*ropa*) to get caught; (*persona*) to get hooked.

engañar 1 *vt* to deceive; (*estafar*) to cheat; (*mentir a*) to lie to; (*al marido, mujer*) to be unfaithful to. **2 engañarse** *vr* to deceive oneself.

engaño *m* deceit; (*estafa*) fraud; (*mentira*) lie.

engañoso,-a *a* (*palabras*) deceitful; (*apariencias*) deceptive.

engarzar [4] *vt* (*unir*) to link; (*engastar*) to mount.

engastar *vt* to mount.

engendrar *vt fig* to engender.

englobar *vt* to include.

engordar 1 *vt* to make fat. **2** *vi* to put on weight; (*comida, bebida*) to be fattening.

engorro *m* nuisance.

engranaje *m* gearing.

engrasar *vt* (*lubricar*) to lubricate; (*manchar*) to make greasy.

engreído,-a *a* conceited.

engrudo *m* paste.

engullir *vt* to gobble up.

enhebrar *vt* to thread.

enhorabuena *f* congratulations *pl*; **dar la e. a algn** to congratulate sb.

enigma *m* enigma.

enjabonar *vt* to soap.

enjambre *m* swarm.

enjaular *vt* (*animal*) to cage.

enjuagar [7] *vt* to rinse.

enjugar [7] *vt*, **enjugarse** *vr* (*secar*) to mop up; (*lágrimas*) to wipe away.

enjuiciar *vt* (*criminal*) to prosecute.

enlace *m* connection; (*casamiento*) marriage.

enlatado,-a *a* canned, tinned.

enlazar [4] *vti* to connect (**con** with).

enloquecer 1 *vi* to go mad. **2** *vt* to drive mad. **3 enloquecerse** *vr* to go mad.

enmarañar 1 *vt* (*pelo*) to tangle; (*complicar*) to complicate. **2 enmarañarse** *vr* (*pelo*) to get tangled.

enmascarar *vt* (*problema, la verdad*) to disguise.

enmendar [1] **1** *vt* (*corregir*) to put right. **2 enmendarse** *vr* (*persona*) to mend one's ways.

enmienda *f* correction; (*de ley*) amendment.

enmohecerse *vr* (*metal*) to rust; (*comida*) to go mouldy.

enmudecer *vi* to fall silent; (*por sorpresa etc*) to be dumbstruck.

ennegrecer *vt*, **ennegrecerse** *vr* to turn black.

enojado,-a *a* angry.

enojar 1 *vt* to anger. **2 enojarse** *vr* to get angry.

enorgullecer 1 *vt* to fill with pride. **2 enorgullecerse** *vt* to be proud (**de** of).

enorme *a* enormous.

enraizar *vi*, **enraizarse** *vr* (*planta, costumbre*) to take root.

enrarecerse *vr* (*aire*) to become rarefied.

enredadera *f* climbing plant.

enredar 1 *vt* (*enmarañar*) to entangle; *fig* (*implicar*) to involve (**en** in). **2 enredarse** *vr* (*enmarañarse*) to get tangled up; *fig* (*involucrarse*) to get involved, to get entangled (**con** with).

enriquecer 1 *vt* to make rich; *fig* to enrich. **2 enriquecerse** *vr* to become rich; *fig* to become enriched.

enrojecer(se) *vi & vr* (*ruborizarse*) to blush.

enrollado,-a *a* rolled up.

enrollar 1 *vt* to roll up; (*cable*) to coil; (*hilo*) to wind up. **2 enrollarse** *vr fam* (*hablar*) to go on and on.

enroscar [1] **1** *vt* to coil (round); (*tornillo*) to screw in; (*tapón*) to screw on. **2 enroscarse** *vr* to coil.

ensaimada *f* kind of spiral pastry from Majorca.

ensalada *f* salad.

ensaladilla rusa *f* Russian salad.

ensanchar 1 *vt* to widen; (*ropa*) to let out. **2 ensancharse** *vr* to widen.

ensangrentado,-a *a* bloodstained.

ensayar *vt* to try out; (*obra, canción*) to rehearse.

ensayo *m* trial; (*de obra*) rehearsal; **e. general** dress rehearsal.

enseguida, en seguida *adv* (*inmediatamente*) at once, straight away; (*poco después*) in a minute, soon.

ensenada *f* inlet.

enseñanza *f* (*educación*) education; (*de idioma etc*) teaching.

enseñar *vt* to teach; (*mostrar*) to show; (*señalar*) to point out; **e. a algn a hacer algo** to teach sb how to do sth.

ensimismado,-a *a* (*absorbido*) engrossed; (*abstraído*) lost in thought.

ensimismarse *vr* (*absorberse*) to become engrossed; (*abstraerse*) to be lost in thought.

ensombrecer 1 *vt* to cast a shadow over. **2 ensombrecerse** *vr* to darken.

ensopar *vt Am* to soak.

ensordecedor,-a *a* deafening.

ensuciar *vt*, **ensuciarse** *vr* to get dirty.

ensueño *m* dream.

entablar *vt* (*conversación*) to begin; (*amistad*) to strike up.

entallado,-a *a* (*vestido*) close-fitting; (*camisa*) fitted.

entender [3] **1** *vt* (*comprender*) to understand; **dar a algn a e. que ...** to give sb to understand that ... **2** *vi* (*comprender*) to understand; **e. de** (*saber*) to know about. **3 entenderse** *vr* (*comprenderse*) to be understood.

entendimiento *m* understanding.

enteramente *adv* entirely.

enterarse *vr* to find out; **me he enterado de que ...** I understand ...; **ni me enteré** I didn't even realize it.

entereza *f* strength of character.

enternecer 1 *vt* to move. **2 enternecerse** *vr* to be moved.

entero,-a *a* (*completo*) entire, whole.

enterrar [1] *vt* to bury.

entidad *f* organization.

entierro *m* burial; (*ceremonia*) funeral.

entonar *vt* (*canción*) to sing.

entonces *adv* then; **por aquel e.** at that time.

entornar *vt* (*ojos etc*) to half-close; (*puerta*) to leave ajar.

entorpecer *vt* (*obstaculizar*) to hinder.

entrada *f* entrance; (*billete*) ticket; (*recaudación*) takings *pl*; (*plato*) entrée; **entradas** (*en la frente*) receding hairline.

entrar 1 *vi* to enter; (*venir dentro*) to come in; (*ir dentro*) go in; (*encajar*) to fit; **me entró dolor de cabeza** I got a headache; **me entraron ganas de reír** I felt like laughing. **2** *vt* (*datos*) to enter.

entre *prep* (*dos*) between; (*más de dos*) among(st).

entreabierto,-a *a* (*ojos etc*) half-open; (*puerta*) ajar.

entreacto *m* interval.

entrecejo *m* space between the eyebrows.

entrecortado,-a *a* (*voz*) faltering.

entrega *f* (*de productos*) delivery; (*de premios*) presentation; (*devoción*) selflessness.

entregar [7] **1** *vt* (*dar*) to hand over; (*deberes etc*) to hand in; (*mercancía*) to deliver. **2 entregarse** *vr* (*rendirse*) to give in; **entregarse a** to devote oneself to.

entrelazar [4] *vt*, **entrelazarse** *vr* to entwine.

entremedias *adv* in between.

entremés *m* hors d'oeuvres.

entremeterse *vr* = **entrometerse.**

entrenador,-a *mf* trainer.

entrenamiento *m* training.

entrenar *vi*, **entrenarse** *vr* to train.

entresuelo *m* mezzanine.

entretanto *adv* meanwhile.

entretención *f Am* entertainment.

entretener 1 *vt* (*divertir*) to entertain; (*retrasar*) to delay; (*detener*) to detain. **2 entretenerse** *vr* (*distraerse*) to amuse oneself; (*retrasarse*) to be held up.

entretenido,-a *a* entertaining.

entretenimiento *m* entertainment.

entretiempo *a* **ropa de e.** lightweight clothing.

entrevista *f* interview.

entrevistar 1 *vt* to interview. **2 entrevistarse** *vr* **entrevistarse con algn** to have an interview with sb.

entristecer 1 *vt* to sadden. **2 entristecerse** *vr* to be sad (**por** about).

entrometerse *vr* to meddle (**en** in, with).

entumecerse *vr* to go numb.

enturbiar 1 *vt* to make cloudy. **2 enturbiarse** *vr* to become cloudy.

entusiasmar 1 *vt* to fill with enthusiasm. **2 entusiasmarse** *vr* to get enthusiastic (**con** about).

entusiasmo *m* enthusiasm; **con e.** enthusiastically.

enumerar *vt* to enumerate.

envasar *vt* (*embotellar*) to bottle; (*empaquetar*) to pack; (*enlatar*) to can, tin.

envase *m* (*recipiente*) container; (*botella vacía*) empty.

envejecer [4] *vti* to age.

envenenar *vt* to poison.

envergadura *f* **de gran e.** large-scale.

enviar *vt* to send.

envidia *f* envy; **tener e. de algn** to envy sb.

envidiable *a* enviable.

envidiar *vt* to envy.

envidioso,-a *a* envious.

envío *m* sending; (*remesa*) consignment; (*paquete*) parcel; **gastos de e.** postage and packing.

envoltorio *m*, **envoltura** *f* wrapping.

envolver [4] (*pp* **envuelto**) **1** *vt* (*con papel*) to wrap; (*en complot etc*) to involve (**en** in). **2 envolverse** *vr* to wrap oneself up (**en** in).

enyesar *vt* to put in plaster.

epidemia *f* epidemic.

episodio *m* episode.

época *f* time; (*periodo*) period.

equilibrio *m* balance.

equilibrista *mf* tightrope walker; *Am* opportunist.

equipaje *m* luggage; **hacer el e.** to pack.

equipar *vt* to equip (**con, de** with).

equiparar *vt* to compare (**con** with).

equipo *m* (*de expertos, jugadores*) team; (*aparatos*) equipment; (*ropas*) outfit; **e. de alta fidelidad** hi-fi stereo system.

equitación *f* horseriding.

equitativo,-a *a* equitable.

equivalente *a* equivalent.

equivaler *vi* to be equivalent (**to** a).

equivocación *f* error.

equivocado,-a *a* mistaken.

equivocar [1] **1** *vt* to mix up. **2 equivocarse** *vr* to make a mistake.

equívoco,-a *a* misleading.

era *pt imperfecto de* **ser.**

eras *pt imperfecto de* **ser.**

eres *indic pres de* **ser.**

erguir [5] *vt* to erect.

erizarse [4] *vr* to stand on end.

erizo *m* hedgehog; **e. de mar, e. marino** sea urchin.

ermita *f* shrine.

erosión *f* erosion.

erótico,-a *a* erotic.

erradicar [1] *vt* to eradicate.

errante *a* wandering.

errata *f* misprint.

erróneo,-a *a* erroneous.

error *m* mistake.

eructar *vi* to belch.

eructo *m* belch, burp.

erudito,-a **1** *a* erudite. **2** *mf* scholar.

erupción *f* (*de volcán*) eruption; (*en la piel*) rash.

es *indic pres de* **ser.**

esa *a dem* that.

ésa *pron dem ver* **ése.**

esbelto,-a *a* slender.

escabeche *m* brine.

escabullirse *vr* to scurry off.

escala *f* scale; (*parada*) (*de barco*) port of call; (*de avión*) stopover; (*escalera*) ladder; **en gran e.** on a large scale; **hacer e. en** to stop over in.

escalada *f* climb.

escalador,-a *mf* climber.

escalar *vt* to climb.

escaldar *vt* to scald.

escalera *f* stair; (*escala*) ladder; **e. de incendios** fire escape; **e. mecánica** escalator.

escalerilla *f* steps *pl.*

escalfar *vt* to poach.

escalofrío *m* shiver.

escalón *m* step; **e. lateral** (*en letrero*) ramp.
escalonar *vt* to space out.
escama *f* (*de animal*) scale; (*de jabón*) flake.
escamotear *vt* to do out of.
escampar *vi* to clear up.
escandalizar [4] **1** *vt* to scandalize. **2 escandalizarse** *vr* to be shocked (**de** at, by).
escándalo *m* (*alboroto*) racket; (*desvergüenza*) scandal; **armar un e.** to kick up a fuss.
escanear *vt* to scan.
escáner *m* scanner.
escaño *m* (*parlamentario*) seat.
escapada *f* (*de prisión*) escape.
escapar 1 *vi* to escape. **2 escaparse** *vr* to escape; (*gas etc*) to leak.
escaparate *m* shop window.
escape *m* (*huida*) escape; (*de gas etc*) leak; **tubo de e.** exhaust (pipe).
escarabajo *m* beetle.
escarbar *vt* (*suelo*) to scratch.
escarcha *f* frost.
escarlata *a* scarlet.
escarlatina *f* scarlet fever.
escarmentar [1] *vi* to learn one's lesson.
escarmiento *m* lesson.
escarola *f* curly endive, *US* escarole.
escarpado,-a *a* (*paisaje*) craggy.
escasear *vi* to be scarce.
escasez *f* scarcity.
escaso,-a *a* scarce; (*dinero*) tight; (*conocimientos*) scant.
escayola *f* plaster of Paris; (*para brazo etc*) plaster.
escayolar *vt* (*brazo etc*) to put in plaster.
escena *f* scene; (*escenario*) stage.
escenario *m* (*en teatro*) stage; (*de película*) setting.
escéptico,-a *a* & *mf* sceptic.
esclarecer *vt* to shed light on.
esclavo,-a *a* & *mf* slave.
esclusa *f* lock.
escoba *f* brush.
escocer [4] *vi* to sting.
escocés,-a 1 *a* Scottish, Scots; **falda escocesa,** kilt. **2** *mf* Scot.
escoger [5] *vt* to choose.
escolar 1 *a* (*curso, año*) school. **2** *mf* (*niño*) schoolboy; (*niña*) schoolgirl.
escollo *m* reef; (*obstáculo*) pitfall.

escolta *f* escort.
escoltar *vt* to escort.
escombros *mpl* debris *sing.*
esconder *vt*, **esconderse** *vr* to hide (**de** from).
escondidas *adv* **a e.** secretly.
escondite *m* (*lugar*) hiding place; (*juego*) hide-and-seek.
escondrijo *m* hiding place.
escopeta *f* shotgun; **e. de aire comprimido** air gun.
escorpión *m* scorpion.
escotado,-a *a* low-cut.
escote *m* low neckline.
escotilla *f* hatch.
escozor *m* stinging.
escribir (*pp* **escrito**) **1** *vt* to write; **e. a máquina** to type. **2 escribirse** *vr* (*dos personas*) to write to each other.
escrito,-a 1 *a* written; **por e.** in writing. **2** *m* (*documento*) document.
escritor,-a *mf* writer.
escritorio *m* (*mueble*) writing desk.
escritura *f* (*documento*) document.
escrúpulo *m* (*recelo*) scruple; **una persona sin escrúpulos** an unscrupulous person.
escrupuloso,-a *a* squeamish; (*honesto*) scrupulous; (*meticuloso*) painstaking.
escrutinio *m* (*de votos*) count.
escuadra *f* (*intrumento*) square; (*militar*) squad; (*de barcos*) squadron.
escuálido,-a *a* emaciated.
escuchar 1 *vt* to listen to; (*oir*) to hear. **2** *vi* to listen.
escudo *m* (*arma defensiva*) shield; (*blasón*) coat of arms.
escuela *f* school; **e. de idiomas** language school.
escueto,-a *a* plain.
escuezo *indic pres de* **escocer.**
esculcar [1] *vt Am* (*registrar*) to search.
escultor,-a *mf* (*hombre*) sculptor; (*mujer*) sculptress; (*de madera*) woodcarver.
escultura *f* sculpture.
escupidera *f* (*recipiente*) spittoon, *US* cuspidor; (*orinal*) chamberpot.
escupir 1 *vi* to spit. **2** *vt* to spit out.
escurreplatos *m inv* dish rack.
escurridizo,-a *a* slippery.
escurridor *m* colander; (*escurreplatos*) dish rack.
escurrir 1 *vt* (*plato, vaso*) to drain; (*ropa*) to wring out; **e. el bulto** to wriggle out. **2 escurrirse** *vr* (*resbalarse*) to slip.

ese,-a *a dem* that; **esos,-as** those.

ése,-a *pron dem mf* that one; **ésos,-as** those (ones); *fam* **¡ni por ésas!** no way!

esencia *f* essence.

esencial *a* essential; **lo e.** the main thing.

esencialmente *adv* essentially.

esfera *f* sphere; (*de reloj de pulsera*) dial; (*de reloj de pared*) face.

esforzarse [2] *vr* to endeavour (**por** to).

esfuerzo *m* effort.

esfumarse *vr fam* to beat it.

esgrima *f* fencing.

esguince *m* sprain.

eslabón *m* link.

eslogan *m* (*pl* **eslóganes**) slogan.

esmalte *m* enamel; (*de uñas*) nail polish.

esmeralda *f* emerald.

esmerarse *vr* to be careful; (*esforzarse*) to go to great lengths.

esmoquin *m* (*pl* **esmóquines**) dinner jacket, *US* tuxedo.

esnob (*pl* **esnobs**) **1** *a* (*persona*) snobbish; (*restaurante etc*) posh. **2** *mf* snob.

eso *pron dem neutro* that; **¡e. es!** that's it!; **por e.** that's why; **a e. de las diez** around ten.

esos,-as *a dem pl* **those.**

ésos,-as *pron dem mfpl* **those.**

espabilado,-a *a* (*despierto*) wide awake; (*listo*) clever.

espabilar *vt*, **espabilarse** *vr* to wake up.

espacial *a* spatial; **nave e.** spaceship.

espacio *m* space; (*de tiempo*) length; (*programa*) programme.

espacioso,-a *a* spacious.

espada *f* sword; **pez e.** swordfish.

espaguetis *mpl* spaghetti *sing.*

espalda *f* back; (*en natación*) backstroke; **espaldas** back *sing*; **a espaldas de algn** behind sb's back; **por la e.** from behind; **volver la e. a algn** to turn one's back on sb.

espantajo *m* (*muñeco*) scarecrow.

espantapájaros *m inv* scarecrow.

espantar 1 *vt* (*asustar*) to frighten; (*ahuyentar*) to frighten away. **2** **espantarse** *vr* to become frightened (**de** of).

espantoso,-a *a* dreadful.

español,-a 1 *a* Spanish. **2** *mf* Spaniard; **los españoles** the Spanish. **3** *m* (*idioma*) Spanish.

esparadrapo *m* sticking plaster.

esparcir [3] **1** *vt* (*papeles, semillas*) to scatter; (*rumor*) to spread. **2**
  esparcirse *vr* to be scattered.
espárrago *m* asparagus.
espátula *f* spatula.
especia *f* spice.
especial *a* special; **en e.** especially.
especialidad *f* speciality, *US* specialty.
especialista *mf* specialist.
especializarse [4] *vr* to specialize (**en** in).
especialmente *adv* (*exclusivamente*) specially; (*muy*) especially.
especie *f* species *inv*; (*clase*) kind.
específicamente *adv* specifically.
especificar [1] *vt* to specify.
específico,-a *a* specific.
espectacular *a* spectacular.
espectáculo *m* show.
espectador,-a *mf* spectator; (*en teatro, cine*) member of the audience;
  los espectadores the audience *sing*; (*de televisión*) viewers.
especulación *f* speculation.
espejismo *m* mirage.
espejo *m* mirror; **e. retrovisor** rear-view mirror.
espeluznante *a* horrifying.
espera *f* wait; **en e. de** waiting for; **a la e. de** expecting; **sala de e.** waiting
  room.
esperanza *f* hope; **e. de vida** life expectancy.
esperar **1** *vi* (*aguardar*) to wait; (*tener esperanza*) to hope. **2** *vt*
  (*aguardar*) to wait for; (*tener esperanza*) to hope for; (*estar a la espera
  de, bebé*) to expect; **espero que sí** I hope so; **espero que vengas** I hope
  you'll come.
esperma *m* sperm; *Am* (*vela*) candle.
espesar *vt*, **espesarse** *vr* to thicken.
espeso,-a *a* (*bosque, niebla*) dense; (*líquido*) thick; (*masa*) stiff.
espesor *m* thickness; **tres metros de e.** three metres thick.
espía *mf* spy.
espiar **1** *vi* to spy. **2** *vt* to spy on.
espiga *f* (*de trigo*) ear.
espigado,-a *a* slender.
espina *f* (*de planta*) thorn; (*de pescado*) bone; **e. dorsal** spine.
espinaca *f* spinach.
espinazo *m* spine.
espinilla *f* shin; (*en la piel*) spot.
espionaje *m* spying.

espiral *a & f* spiral.

espirar *vi* to breathe out.

espíritu *m* spirit; (*alma*) soul.

espiritual *a* spiritual.

espléndido,-a *a* (*magnífico*) splendid; (*generoso*) lavish.

esplendor *m* splendour.

espliego *m* lavender.

esponja *f* sponge.

espontáneo,-a *a* spontaneous.

esposado,-a *a* (*con esposas*) handcuffed.

esposas *fpl* handcuffs.

esposo,-a *mf* spouse; (*hombre*) husband; (*mujer*) wife.

esprint *m* sprint.

espuela *f* spur.

espuma *f* foam; (*de cerveza*) head; (*de jabón*) lather; **e. de afeitar** shaving foam.

espumoso,-a *a* frothy; (*vino*) sparkling.

esqueleto *m* skeleton.

esquema *m* diagram.

esquemático,-a *a* (*escueto*) schematic; (*con diagramas*) diagrammatic.

esquí *m* (*objeto*) ski; (*deporte*) skiing; **e. acuático** water-skiing.

esquiador,-a *mf* skier.

esquiar *vi* to ski.

esquimal *a & mf* Eskimo.

esquina *f* corner.

esquivar *vt* (*a una persona*) to avoid; (*un golpe*) to dodge.

esta *a dem* this.

está *indic pres de* **estar.**

ésta *pron dem f* this (one).

estabilidad *f* stability.

estable *a* stable.

establecer 1 *vt* to establish; (*récord*) to set. **2 establecerse** *vr* (*instalarse*) to settle.

establecimiento *m* establishment.

establo *m* cow shed.

estaca *f* stake; (*de tienda de campaña*) peg.

estación *f* station; (*del año*) season; **e. de servicio** service station; **e. de esquí** ski resort; **e. de trabajo** work station.

estacionamiento *m* (*acción*) parking.

estacionar *vt*, **estacionarse** *vr* to park.

estacionario,-a *a* stationary.

estada *f*, **estadía** *f Am* stay.

estadio *m* (*de portivo*) stadium; (*fase*) stage.

estadística *f* statistics *sing*; **una e.** a statistic.

estado *m* state; **e. civil** marital status; **e. de cuentas** statement of account.

estadounidense 1 *a* United States, American. **2** *mf* United States citizen.

estafa *f* swindle.

estafar *vt* to swindle.

estafeta *f* **e. de Correos** sub post office.

estallar *vi* to burst; (*bomba*) to explode; (*guerra*) to break out.

estallido *m* explosion; (*de guerra*) outbreak.

estampa *f* illustration.

estampado,-a 1 *a* (*tela*) printed. **2** *m* (*de tela*) print.

estampilla *f Am* (*postage*) stamp.

estancar [1] **1** *vt* (*agua*) hold back; (*paralizar*) to block; (*negociaciones*) to bring to a standstill. **2 estancarse** *vr* to stagnate.

estancia *f* (*permanencia*) stay; (*habitación*) room; *Am* (*hacienda*) ranch.

estanco,-a *m* tobacconist's.

estándar (*pl* **estándares**) *a & m* standard.

estanque *m* pond.

estante *m* shelf; (*para libros*) bookcase.

estantería *f* shelves.

estaño *m* tin.

estar 1 *vi* to be; **¿está tu madre?** is your mother in?; **¿cómo estás?** how are you?; **está escribiendo** she is writing; **estamos a 2 de Noviembre** it is the 2nd of November; **están a 100 pesetas el kilo** they're 100 pesetas a kilo. **¿estamos?** OK?; **e. de más** not to be needed. ‖ (+ **para**) **estará para las seis** it will be finished by six; **hoy no estoy para bromas** I'm in no mood for jokes today; **el tren está para salir** the train is just about to leave. ‖ (+ **por**) **está por hacer** it has still to be done; **eso está por ver** it remains to be seen. ‖ (+ **con**) to have; **e. con la gripe** to have the flu. ‖ (+ **sin**) to have no. **2 estarse** *vr* **¡estáte quieto!** keep still!

estatal *a* state.

estatua *f* statue.

estatura *f* height.

estatuto *m* statute; (*de empresa etc*) rules *pl*.

este 1 *a* eastern; (*dirección*) easterly. **2** *m* east; **al e. de** to the east of.

esté *subj pres de* **estar**.

este,-a *a dem* this; **estos,-as** these.

éste,-a *pron dem mf* this one; **aquél ... é.** the former ... the latter; **éstos,-as** these (ones); **aquéllos ... éstos** the former ... the latter.

estela *f* (*de barco*) wake; (*de avión*) vapour trail.

estepa _f_ steppe.
estera _f_ rush mat.
estéreo _m_ & _a_ stereo.
estereofónico,-a _a_ stereophonic.
estereotipo _m_ stereotype.
estéril _a_ sterile.
esterlina _a_ **libra e.** pound (sterling).
esternón _m_ breastbone.
estero _m_ _Am_ marsh.
esteticienne, esteticista _f_ beautician.
estético,-a _a_ aesthetic; **cirugía estética** plastic surgery.
estiércol _m_ manure.
estilarse _vr_ to be in vogue.
estilo _m_ style; (_modo_) manner; (_en natación_) stroke.
estilográfica _f_ **(pluma) e.** fountain pen.
estima _f_ esteem.
estimación _f_ (_estima_) esteem; (_valoración_) evaluation; (_cálculo aproximado_) estimate.
estimado,-a _a_ respected; **E. Señor** (_en carta_) Dear Sir.
estimar _vt_ (_apreciar_) to esteem; (_considerar_) to think; (_valuar_) to value.
estimulante 1 _a_ stimulating. **2** _m_ stimulant.
estimular _vt_ to stimulate.
estímulo _m_ stimulus.
estirar _vt_, **estirarse** _vr_ to stretch.
estival _a_ summer.
esto _pron dem_ (_esta cosa_) this, this thing; (_este asunto_) this matter.
estocada _f_ stab.
estofado _m_ stew.
estómago _m_ stomach; **dolor de e.** stomach ache.
estoque _m_ sword.
estorbar 1 _vt_ (_dificultar_) to hinder. **2** _vi_ to be in the way.
estorbo _m_ (_obstáculo_) obstacle.
estornudar _vi_ to sneeze.
estornudo _m_ sneeze.
estos,-as _a dem pl_ these.
éstos,-as _pron dem mfpl_ these.
estoy _indic pres de_ **estar**.
estrangular _vt_ to strangle.
estraperlo _m_ black market.
estratagema _f_ ruse.
estratégico,-a _a_ strategic.
estrechamente _adv_ (_íntimamente_) closely.

estrechamiento *m* narrowing; **'e. de calzada'** (*en letrero*) 'road narrows'.

estrechar 1 *vt* to make narrow; **e. la mano a algn** to shake sb's hand; (*lazos de amistad*) to tighten. **2 estrecharse** *vr* to narrow.

estrechez *f* narrowness; **pasar estrecheces** to be hard up.

estrecho,-a 1 *a* narrow; (*ropa, zapato*) tight; (*amistad, relación*) close. **2** *m* strait.

estrella *f* star; **e. de cine** film star; **e. de mar** starfish; **e. fugaz** shooting star.

estrellar 1 *vt fam* to smash. **2 estrellarse** *vr* (*chocar*) to crash (**contra** into).

estremecer *vt*, **estremecerse** *vr* to shake.

estrenar *vt* to use for the first time; (*ropa*) to wear for the first time; (*obra, película*) to premiere.

estreno *m* (*teatral*) first performance; (*de película*) premiere.

estreñimiento *m* constipation.

estrépito *m* din.

estrés *m* stress.

estribillo *m* (*en canción*) chorus; (*en poema*) refrain.

estribo *m* stirrup; *fig* **perder los estribos** to fly off the handle.

estribor *m* starboard.

estricto,-a *a* strict.

estropajo *m* scourer.

estropear 1 *vt* (*máquina, cosecha*) to damage; (*fiesta, plan*) to spoil; (*pelo, manos*) to ruin. **2 estropearse** *vr* to be ruined; (*máquina*) to break down.

estructura *f* structure; (*armazón*) framework.

estrujar *vt* (*limón etc*) to squeeze; (*ropa*) to wring; (*apretar*) to crush.

estuche *m* case.

estudiante *mf* student.

estudiar *vti* to study.

estudio *m* study; (*encuesta*) survey; (*sala*) studio; (*apartamento*) studio (flat).

estudioso,-a 1 *a* studious. **2** *mf* specialist.

estufa *f* heater.

estupefaciente *m* drug.

estupefacto,-a *a* astounded.

estupendamente *adv* marvellously.

estupendo,-a *a* marvellous; **¡e.!** great!

estupidez *f* stupidity.

estúpido,-a 1 *a* stupid. **2** *mf* idiot.

estuve *pt indef de* **estar**.

ETA *f abr de* **Euzkadi Ta Askatasuna** (*Patria Vasca y Libertad*) ETA.

etapa *f* stage.

etcétera *adv* etcetera.

eterno,-a *a* eternal.

ético,-a *a* ethical.

etílico,-a *a* **alcohol e.** ethyl alcohol.

etiqueta *f* (*de producto*) label; (*ceremonia*) etiquette; **de e.** formal.

étnico,-a *a* ethnic.

eucalipto *m* eucalyptus.

eufórico,-a *a* euphoric.

europeo,-a *a & mf* European.

euskera *a & m* Basque.

eutanasia *f* euthanasia.

evacuación *f* evacuation.

evacuar *vt* to evacuate.

evadir 1 *vt* (*respuesta, peligro, impuestos*) to avoid; (*responsabilidad*) to shirk. **2 evadirse** *vr* to escape.

evaluación *f* evaluation; (*en colegio*) assessment.

evaluar *vt* to assess.

evangelio *m* gospel.

evaporación *f* evaporation.

evaporar *vt,* **evaporarse** *vr* to evaporate.

evasión *f* (*fuga*) escape; (*escapismo*) escapism; **e. de capitales** flight of capital.

evasiva *f* evasive answer.

evento *m* (*acontecimiento*) event; (*incidente*) unforeseen event.

eventual *a* (*posible*) possible; (*trabajo, obrero*) casual.

evidencia *f* obviousness; **poner a algn en e.** to show sb up.

evidente *a* obvious.

evidentemente *adv* obviously.

evitar *vt* to avoid; (*problema futuro*) to prevent; (*desastre*) to avert.

evocar [1] *vt* (*traer a la memoria*) to evoke.

evolución *f* evolution; (*desarrollo*) development.

evolucionar *vi* to develop; (*especies*) to evolve.

ex *prefijo* former, ex-; **ex alumno** former pupil; **ex marido** ex-husband; *fam* **mi ex** my ex.

exacerbar 1 *vt* (*agravar*) to exacerbate. **2 exacerbarse** *vr* (*irritarse*) to feel exasperated.

exactamente *adv* exactly.

exactitud *f* accuracy; **con e.** precisely.

exacto,-a *a* exact; **¡e.!** precisely!

exageración *f* exaggeration.

exagerado,-a *a* exaggerated; (*excesivo*) excessive.

exagerar *vti* to exaggerate.

exaltarse *vr* (*acalorarse*) to get carried away.

examen *m* examination, exam; **e. de conducir** driving test.

examinar 1 *vt* to examine. **2 examinarse** *vr* to sit an examination.

exasperante *a* exasperating.

exasperar 1 *vt* to exasperate. **2 exasperarse** *vr* to become exasperated.

excavación *f* excavation; (*en arqueología*) dig.

excavadora *f* digger.

excedencia *f* leave (of absence).

excedente *a* & *m* surplus.

exceder 1 *vt* to exceed. **2 excederse** *vr* to go too far.

excelencia *f* excellence.

excelente *a* excellent.

excéntrico,-a *a* eccentric.

excepción *f* exception; **a e. de** except for.

excepcional *a* exceptional.

excepto *adv* except (for).

exceptuar *vt* to except.

excesivo,-a *a* excessive.

exceso *m* excess; **e. de velocidad** speeding.

excitación *f* (*sentimiento*) excitement; (*acción*) excitation.

excitante *a* exciting.

excitar 1 *vt* to excite. **2 excitarse** *vr* to get excited.

exclamación *f* exclamation.

exclamar *vti* to exclaim.

excluir *vt* to exclude.

exclusive *adv* (*en fechas*) exclusive.

exclusivo,-a *a* exclusive.

excremento *m* excrement.

excursión *f* excursion.

excursionista *mf* tripper; (*a pie*) hiker.

excusa *f* (*pretexto*) excuse; (*disculpa*) apology.

excusar 1 *vt* (*justificar*) to excuse; (*eximir*) to exempt (**de** from). **2 excusarse** *vr* (*disculparse*) to apologize.

exención *f* exemption.

exento,-a *a* exempt (**de** from).

exhalar *vt* to breathe out.

exhaustivo,-a *a* exhaustive.

exhausto,-a *a* exhausted.

exhibición *f* exhibition.

exhibir 1 *vt* (*mostrar*) to exhibit; (*lucir*) to show off. **2 exhibirse** *vr* to show off.

exigente *a* demanding.

exigir [6] *vt* to demand.

exilado,-a 1 *a* exiled. **2** *mf* exile.

exilar 1 *vt* to exile. **2 exilarse** *vr* to go into exile.

exiliado,-a = **exilado,-a.**

exiliar *vt* = **exilar.**

exilio *m* exile.

existencia *f* (*vida*) existence; **existencias** stocks.

existente *a* existing.

existir *vi* to exist.

éxito *m* success; **con é.** successfully; **tener é.** to be successful.

éxodo *m* exodus.

exorbitante *a* exorbitant.

exótico,-a *a* exotic.

expandir *vt*, **expandirse** *vr* to expand.

expansión *f* expansion; (*de noticia*) spreading; (*diversión*) relaxation.

expectación *f* (*interés*) excitement.

expectativa *f* expectancy.

expedición *f* expedition.

expediente *m* (*informe*) record; (*ficha*) file; **e. académico** student's record.

expedir [6] *vt* (*pasaporte etc*) to issue.

expendeduría *f* tobacconist's.

expensas *fpl* **a e. de** at the expense of.

experiencia *f* experience; (*experimento*) experiment.

experimentado,-a *a* experienced.

experimental *a* experimental.

experimentar 1 *vi* to experiment. **2** *vt* to undergo; (*aumento*) to show; (*pérdida*) to suffer; (*sensación*) to experience.

experimento *m* experiment.

experto,-a *mf* expert.

expirar *vi* to expire.

explanada *f* esplanade.

explicación *f* explanation.

explicar [1] **1** *vt* to explain. **2 explicarse** *vr* (*persona*) to explain (oneself); **no me lo explico** I can't understand it.

exploración *f* exploration.

explorador,-a *mf* (*persona*) explorer.

explorar *vt* to explore.

explosión *f* explosion; **hacer e.** to explode.

explosivo,-a *a & m* explosive.

explotación *f* exploitation.

explotar 1 *vi* (*bomba*) to explode, go off. **2** *vt* to exploit.

exponer (*pp* **expuesto**) **1** *vt* (*mostrar*) to exhibit; (*presentar*) to put forward; (*arriesgar*) to expose. **2 exponerse** *vr* to expose oneself (**a** to).

exportación *f* export.

exportar *vt* to export.

exposición *f* exhibition.

exprés *a* express; **olla e.** pressure cooker; **café e.** espresso (coffee).

expresamente *adv* expressly.

expresar 1 *vt* to express; (*manifestar*) to state. **2 expresarse** *vr* to express oneself.

expresión *f* expression.

expreso,-a 1 *a* express. **2** *m* express (train). **3** *adv* on purpose.

exprimidor *m* squeezer, *US* juicer.

exprimir *vt* (*limón*) to squeeze; (*zumo*) to squeeze out.

expulsar *vt* to expel; (*jugador*) to send off.

expuse *pt indef de* **exponer.**

exquisito,-a *a* exquisite; (*comida*) delicious; (*gusto*) refined.

extender [3] **1** *vt* to extend; (*agrandar*) to enlarge; (*mantel, mapa*) to spread (out); (*mano, brazo*) to stretch (out); (*crema, mantequilla*) to spread. **2 extenderse** *vr* (*en el tiempo*) to last; (*en el espacio*) to stretch; (*rumor, noticia*) to spread.

extendido,-a *a* extended; (*mapa, plano*) open; (*mano, brazo*) outstretched; (*costumbre, rumor*) widespread.

extensión *f* (*de libro etc*) length; (*de terreno*) expanse.

extenso,-a *a* (*terreno*) extensive; (*libro, película*) long.

extenuar 1 *vt* to exhaust. **2 extenuarse** *vr* to exhaust oneself.

exterior 1 *a* (*de fuera*) outer; (*puerta*) outside; (*política, deuda*) foreign; **Ministerio de Asuntos Exteriores** Ministry of Foreign Affairs, *Br* Foreign Office, *US* State Department. **2** *m* (*parte de fuera*) outside; (*extranjero*) abroad.

exteriormente *adv* outwardly.

exterminar *vt* to exterminate.

externo,-a *a* external.

extinguir 1 *vt* (*fuego*) to exinguish; (*raza*) to wipe out. **2 extinguirse** *vr* (*fuego*) to go out; (*especie*) to become extinct.

extintor *m* fire extinguisher.

extorsionar *vt* to extort.

extra 1 *a* extra; (*superior*) top quality; **horas e.** overtime; **paga e.** bonus. **2** *mf* extra.

extracto *m* extract; **e. de cuenta** statement of account.

extraer *vt* to extract.

extranjero,-a 1 *a* foreign. **2** *mf* foreigner. **3** *m* abroad; **en el e.** abroad.

extrañar 1 *vt* (*sorprender*) to surprise; *Am* (*echar de menos*) to miss. **2 extrañarse** *vr* **extrañarse de** (*sorprenderse*) to be surprised at.

extrañeza *f* (*sorpresa*) surprise; (*singularidad*) strangeness.

extraño,-a 1 *a* strange. **2** *mf* stranger.

extraoficial *a* unofficial.

extraordinario,-a *a* extraordinary.

extrarradio *m* suburbs *pl*.

extraterrestre *mf* alien.

extravagante *a* outlandish.

extravertido,-a *a* = **extrovertido,-a.**

extraviar 1 *vt* to mislay. **2 extraviarse** *vr* to be missing.

extremeño,-a *a* & *mf* Estremaduran.

extremidad *f* (*extremo*) tip; (*miembro*) limb.

extremo,-a 1 *m* (*de calle, cable*) end; (*máximo*) extreme; **en último e.** as a last resort; *f* **e. derecha/izquierda** outside-right/-left. **2** *a* extreme; **E. Oriente** Far East.

extrovertido,-a *a* & *mf* extrovert.

exuberante *a* exuberant; (*vegetación*) lush.

F

fabada *f* stew of beans, pork sausage and bacon.
fábrica *f* factory.
fabricación *f* manufacture.
fabricante *mf* manufacturer.
fabricar [1] *vt* to manufacture.
fabuloso,-a *a* fabulous.
facción *f* faction; **facciones** (*rasgos*) features.
facha *f fam* look.
fachada *f* facade.
facial *a* facial.
fácil *a* easy; **es f. que ...** it's (quite) likely that ...
facilidad *f* (*sencillez*) easiness; (*soltura*) ease; **facilidades de pago** easy terms.
facilitar *vt* (*simplificar*) to make easy *o* easier; **f. algo a algn** to provide sb with sth.
fácilmente *adv* easily.
facsímil, facsímile *m* facsimile.
factoría *f* factory.
factura *f* invoice.
facturación *f* (*en aeropuerto*) check-in; (*en estación*) registration.
facturar *vt* (*en aeropuerto*) to check in; (*en estación*) to register.
facultad *f* faculty.
faena *f* (*tarea*) task; (*en corrida*) performance.
faisán *m* pheasant.
faja *f* (*corsé*) corset.
fajo *m* (*de billetes*) wad.
falda *f* (*prenda*) skirt; (*de montaña*) slope; **f. pantalón** culottes *pl*.
falla *f Am* (*defecto*) fault.
fallar 1 *vi* to fail; **le falló la puntería** he missed his aim. **2** *vt* to miss.
fallecer *vi* to pass away, die.
fallo *m* (*error*) mistake; (*del corazón, de los frenos*) failure.
falsear *vt* (*hechos, la verdad*) to distort.
falsificar [1] *vt* to falsify; (*cuadro, firma, moneda*) to forge.
falso,-a *a* false; (*persona*) insincere.
falta *f* (*carencia*) lack; (*escasez*) shortage; (*ausencia*) absence; (*error*) mistake; (*defecto*) fault, defect; (*fútbol*) foul; (*tenis*) fault; **sin f.** without fail; **echar algo/a algn en f.** to miss sth/sb; **f. de ortografía** spelling mistake; **hacer f.** to be necessary; **(nos) hace f. una escalera** we need a ladder; **harán f. dos personas para mover el piano** it'll take two people to move the piano; **no hace f. que ...** there is no need for ...

faltar vi (no estar) to be missing; (escasear) to be lacking o needed; (quedar) to be left; **¿quién falta?** who is missing?; **le falta confianza en sí mismo** he lacks confidence in himself; **¡lo que me faltaba!** that's all I needed!; **¡no faltaría o faltaba más!** (por supuesto) (but) of course!; **¿cuántos kilómetros faltan para Managua?** how many kilometres is it to Managua?; **ya falta poco para las vacaciones** it won't be long now till the holidays; **f. a la verdad** not to tell the truth.

fama f fame; (reputación) reputation.

familia f family.

familiar 1 a (de la familia) family; (conocido) familiar. **2** mf relation, relative.

famoso,-a a famous.

fan mf fan.

fanático,-a 1 a fanatical. **2** mf fanatic.

fanfarrón,-ona 1 a boastful. **2** mf show-off.

fango m (barro) mud.

fantasía f fantasy.

fantasma m ghost.

fantástico,-a a fantastic.

fardo m bundle.

farmacéutico,-a 1 a pharmaceutical. **2** mf pharmacist.

farmacia f (tienda) chemist's (shop), US pharmacy.

faro m (torre) lighthouse; (de coche) headlight.

farol m (luz) lantern; (en la calle) streetlight, streetlamp.

farola f streetlight, streetlamp.

fascículo m instalment, US installment.

fascinar vt to fascinate.

fascista a & mf fascist.

fase f phase, stage.

fastidiar 1 vt (molestar) to annoy, bother. **2 fastidiarse** vr (aguantarse) to put up with it; **que se fastidie** that's his tough luck; **fastidiarse el brazo** to hurt one's arm.

fastuoso,-a a (acto) splendid, lavish.

fatal 1 a (muy malo) awful; (mortal) fatal. **2** adv awfully; **lo pasó f.** he had a rotten time.

fatiga f (cansancio) fatigue.

fatigar, [7] vt, **fatigarse** vr to tire.

fauna f fauna.

favor m favour; **¿puedes hacerme un f.?** can you do me a favour?; **estar a f. de** to be in favour of; **por f.** please; **haga el f. de sentarse** please sit down.

favorable a favourable.

favorecer *vt* to favour; (*sentar bien*) to flatter.
favorito,-a *a & mf* favourite.
fe *f* faith; **fe de bautismo/matrimonio** baptism/marriage certificate.
fealdad *f* ugliness.
febrero *m* February.
fecha *f* date; **f. de caducidad** sell-by date; **hasta la f.** so far.
fechar *vt* to date.
fecundación *f* fertilization.
federación *f* federation.
felicidad *f* happiness; **(muchas) felicidades** (*en cumpleaños*) many happy returns.
felicitar *vt* to congratulate (**por** on); **¡te felicito!** congratulations!
feliz *a* (*contento*) happy; **¡felices Navidades!** Happy *o* Merry Christmas!
felpa *f* (*tela*) plush; (*para el pelo*) hairband; **oso** *o* **osito de f.** teddy bear.
felpudo *m* mat.
femenino,-a *a* a feminine; (*equipo, ropa*) women's; **sexo f.** female sex.
feminista *a & mf* feminist.
fémur *m* femur.
fenomenal **1** *a* phenomenal; *fam* (*fantástico*) great. **2** *adv fam* wonderfully.
fenómeno,-a *m* phenomenon; (*prodigio*) genius; (*monstruo*) freak.
feo,-a *a* ugly.
féretro *m* coffin.
feria *f* fair; **f. de muestras/del libro** trade/book fair.
fermentar *vi* to ferment.
feroz *a* fierce, ferocious.
ferretería *f* ironmonger's (shop), hardware store.
ferrocarril *m* railway, *US* railroad.
ferroviario,-a *a* railway, rail.
ferry *m* ferry.
fértil *a* fertile.
fertilizante *m* fertilizer.
fertilizar [4] *vt* to fertilize.
festejar *vt* to celebrate.
festín *m* feast.
festival *m* festival.
festividad *f* festivity.
festivo,-a **1** *a* (*ambiente etc*) festive; **día f.** holiday. **2** *m* holiday.
feto *m* fetus.
fiable *a* reliable, trustworthy.
fiador,-a *mf* guarantor.
fiambre *m* cold meat.

fiambrera *f* lunch box.

fianza *f* (*depósito*) deposit; (*jurídica*) bail.

fiarse *vr* to trust (**de -**).

fibra *f* fibre.

ficción *f* fiction.

ficha *f* (*de archivo*) filing card; (*en juegos*) counter; (*de ajedrez*) piece.

fichaje *m* signing.

fichero *m* card index; (*de ordenador*) file.

ficticio,-a *a* fictitious.

fidelidad *f* faithfulness; **alta f.** high fidelity, hi-fi.

fideo *m* noodle.

fiebre *f* fever; **tener f.** to have a temperature.

fiel 1 *a* (*leal*) faithful, loyal. **2** *mpl* **los fieles** the congregation.

fieltro *m* felt.

fiera *f* wild animal.

fierro *m Am* (*hierro*) iron; (*navaja*) knife.

fiesta *f* (*entre amigos*) party; (*vacaciones*) holiday; (*festividad*) celebration.

figura *f* figure.

figurar 1 *vi* (*aparecer*) to figure. **2 figurarse** *vr* to imagine; **ya me lo figuraba** I thought as much; **¡figúrate!, ¡figúrese!** just imagine!

fijador *m* (*gomina*) gel.

fijamente *adv* **mirar f.** to stare.

fijar 1 *vt* to fix. **2 fijarse** *vr* (*darse cuenta*) to notice; (*poner atención*) to pay attention, watch.

fijo,-a *a* fixed; (*trabajo*) steady.

fila *f* file; (*de cine, teatro*) row; **en f. india** in single file.

filántropo,-a *mf* philanthropist.

filarmónico,-a *a* philharmonic.

filatelia *f* philately, stamp collecting.

filete *m* fillet.

filial 1 *a* (*de hijos*) filial. **2** *f* (*empresa*) subsidiary.

filmar *vt* to film.

film(e) *m* film.

filo *m* edge.

filosofía *f* philosophy.

filosófico,-a *a* philosophical.

filósofo,-a *mf* philosopher.

filtración *f* filtration; (*de noticia*) leak(ing).

filtrar 1 *vt* to filter; (*noticia*) to leak. **2 filtrarse** *vr* (*líquido*) to seep; (*noticia*) to leak out.

filtro *m* filter.

fin *m* (*final*) end; (*objetivo*) purpose, aim; **dar** *o* **poner f. a** to put an end to; **en f.** anyway; **¡por** *o* **al f.!** at last!; **f. de semana** weekend; **al f. y al cabo** when all's said and done; **a f. de** in order to, so as to.

final 1 *a* final. **2** *m* end; **al f.** in the end; **a finales de octubre** at the end of October. **3** *f* (*de campeonato*) final.

finalizar [4] *vti* to end, finish.

finalmente *adv* finally.

financiación *f* financing.

financiar *vt* to finance.

financiero,-a *a* financial.

financista *mf Am* financier.

finanzas *fpl* finances.

finca *f* (*de campo*) country house.

fingir [6] **1** *vt* to feign. **2** *vi* to pretend.

fino,-a 1 *a* (*hilo, capa*) fine; (*flaco*) thin; (*educado*) refined, polite; (*oído*) sharp, acute. **2** *m* (*vino*) type of dry sherry.

firma *f* signature; (*empresa*) firm.

firmar *vt* to sign.

firme 1 *a* firm; **tierra f.** terra firma. **2** *adv* hard.

firmemente *adv* firmly.

fiscal 1 *a* fiscal, tax. **2** *mf* (*en juicio*) public prosecutor, *US* district attorney.

fisco *m* treasury, exchequer.

física *f* physics *sing*.

físico,-a *a* physical.

fisioterapia *f* physiotherapy.

flaco,-a *a* (*delgado*) skinny.

flamenco,-a 1 *a* (*música*) flamenco; (*de Flandes*) Flemish. **2** *m* (*música*) flamenco.

flan *m* caramel custard.

flanco *m* flank, side.

flaquear *vi* (*fuerzas, piernas*) to weaken, give way.

flash *m* flash.

flauta *f* flute.

flecha *f* arrow.

flechazo *m* (*enamoramiento*) love at first sight.

fleco *m* fringe.

flema *f* phlegm.

flemático,-a *a* phlegmatic.

flemón *m* gumboil.

flequillo *m* fringe, *US* bangs *pl*.

fletar *vt* to charter.

flexible *a* flexible.

flexión *f* flexion.

flexionar *vt* to bend; (*músculo*) to flex.

flexo *m* reading lamp.

flirtear *vi* to flirt.

flojera *f fam* weakness, faintness.

flojo,-a *a* (*tornillo, cuerda etc*) loose, slack; (*perezoso*) lazy, idle.

flor *f* flower.

flora *f* flora.

floreado,-a *a* flowery.

florecer *vi* (*plantas*) to flower; (*negocio*) to flourish, thrive.

floreciente *a* flourishing, prosperous.

florero *m* vase.

floristería *f* florist's (shop).

flota *f* fleet.

flotador *m* (*para nadar*) rubber ring.

flotar *vi* to float.

flote *m* **a f.** afloat.

flotilla *f* flotilla.

fluctuar *vi* to fluctuate.

fluido,-a 1 *a* fluid; (*estilo etc*) fluent. **2** *m* liquid.

fluir *vi* to flow.

flujo *m* flow; (*de la marea*) rising tide.

flúor *m* fluorine.

fluorescente *a* fluorescent.

fluvial *a* river.

FMI *m abr de* **Fondo Monetario Internacional** International Monetary Fund, IMF.

fobia *f* phobia (**a** of).

foca *f* seal.

foco *m* spotlight, floodlight; *Am* (*bombilla*) (electric light) bulb; (*de coche*) (car) headlight; (*farola*) street light.

fogata *f* bonfire.

fogón *m* (*de cocina*) ring.

folio *m* sheet of paper.

folklórico,-a *a* **música f.** folk music.

follaje *m* foliage.

folletín *m* (*relato*) newspaper serial.

folleto *m* leaflet; (*turístico*) brochure.

follón *m fam* (*alboroto*) rumpus; (*enredo, confusión*) mess.

fomentar *vt* to promote.

fomento *m* promotion.

fonda *f* inn.

fondear *vi* to anchor.

fondista *mf* (*corredor*) long-distance runner.

fondo[1] *m* (*parte más baja*) bottom; (*de habitación*) back; (*de pasillo*) end; (*segundo término*) background; **a f.** thoroughly; **al f. de la calle** at the bottom of the street; **en el f. es bueno** deep down he's kind; **música de f.** background music.

fondo[2] (*dinero*) fund; **cheque sin fondos** bad cheque.

fonético,-a *a* phonetic.

fontanero,-a *mf* plumber.

footing *m* jogging; **hacer f.** to go jogging.

forastero,-a *mf* outsider.

forcejear *vi* to wrestle.

forense 1 *a* forensic. **2** *mf* (**médico**) **f.** forensic surgeon.

forestal *a* forest; **repoblación f.** reafforestation.

forjar *vt* to forge.

forma *f* form, shape; (*manera*) way; **¿qué f. tiene?** what shape is it?; **de esta f.** in this way; **de f. que** so that; **de todas formas** anyway, in any case; **estar en f.** to be on form; **estar en baja f.** to be off form.

formación *f* formation; (*enseñanza*) training; **f. profesional** vocational training.

formal *a* formal; (*serio*) serious; (*fiable*) reliable.

formalizar [4] *vt* (*hacer formal*) to formalize; (*contrato*) to legalize.

formar 1 *vt* to form; **f. parte de algo** to be a part of sth; (*enseñar*) to educate, train. **2 formarse** *vr* to be formed, form.

formidable *a* (*estupendo*) terrific.

fórmula *f* formula.

formular *vt* (*quejas, peticiones*) to make; (*deseo*) to express; (*pregunta*) to ask; (*una teoría*) to formulate.

formulario *m* form.

forrar *vt* (*por dentro*) to line; (*por fuera*) to cover.

forro *m* (*por dentro*) lining; (*por fuera*) cover.

fortalecer *vt* to fortify, strengthen.

fortificar [1] *vt* to fortify.

fortísimo,-a *a* very strong.

fortuito,-a *a* fortuitous.

fortuna *f* (*suerte*) luck; (*capital*) fortune; **por f.** fortunately.

forzado,-a *a* forced; **trabajos forzados** hard labour.

forzar [2] *vt* to force.

forzosamente *adv* necessarily.

forzoso,-a *a* obligatory, compulsory.

fosa *f* (*sepultura*) grave; (*hoyo*) pit.

fósforo *m* (*cerilla*) match.

fósil *a & m* fossil.

foso *m* (*hoyo*) pit.

foto *f* photo.

fotocopia *f* photocopy.

fotocopiadora *f* photocopier.

fotocopiar *vt* to photocopy.

fotografía *f* photograph; **hacer fotografías** to take photographs.

fotografiar *vt* to photograph, take a photograph of.

fotógrafo,-a *mf* photographer.

FP *f Educ abr de* **Formación Profesional** vocational training.

frac *m* (*pl* **fracs** *o* **fraques**) dress coat, tails *pl*.

fracasar *vi* to fail.

fraccionar *vt,* **fraccionarse** *vr* to break up.

fractura *f* fracture.

fragancia *f* fragrance.

frágil *a* (*quebradizo*) fragile; (*débil*) frail.

fragmento *m* fragment; (*de novela etc*) passage.

fraile *m* friar, monk.

frambuesa *f* raspberry.

francamente *adv* frankly.

franco,-a[1] *a* (*persona*) frank; **puerto f.** free port.

franco[2] *m* (*moneda*) franc.

franela *f* flannel.

franja *f* (*de terreno*) strip; (*de bandera*) stripe.

franqueo *m* postage.

frasco *m* small bottle, flask.

frase *f* (*oración*) sentence; (*expresión*) phrase.

fraterno,-a *a* fraternal, brotherly.

fraude *m* fraud.

frecuencia *f* frequency; **con f.** frequently.

frecuentar *vt* to frequent.

frecuente *a* frequent.

frecuentemente *adv* frequently, often.

fregadero *m* (kitchen) sink.

fregar [1] *vt* (*lavar*) to wash; (*suelo*) to mop; *Am* to annoy.

fregona *f* mop.

freidora *f* (deep) fryer.

freír [5] (*pp* **frito**) *vt* to fry.

frenar *vti* to brake.

frenazo *m* sudden braking.

frenético,-a *a* frantic.

freno *m* brake; **pisar/soltar el f.** to press/release the brake; **f. de mano** handbrake.

frente 1 *m* front; **chocar de f.** to crash head on; **hacer f. a algo** to face up to sth. **2** *f* (*de la cara*) forehead; **f. a f.** face to face. **3** *adv* **f. a** opposite.

fresa *f* strawberry.

fresco,-a 1 *a* (*frío*) cool; (*comida, fruta*) fresh; (*descarado*) cheeky. **2** *m* (*frescor*) fresh air; (*caradura*) cheek; **hace f.** it's chilly.

frescura *f* freshness; (*desvergüenza*) cheek, nerve.

fresón *m* (large) strawberry.

fríamente *adv* coolly.

fricción *f* friction.

frígido,-a *a* frigid.

frigorífico,-a *m* refrigerator, fridge.

frijol, fríjol *m* kidney bean.

frío,-a 1 *a* cold; (*indiferente*) cold, cool. **2** *m* cold; **hace f.** it's cold.

friolero,-a *a* sensitive to the cold, chilly.

frívolo,-a *a* frivolous.

frontera *f* frontier.

frontón *m* pelota.

frotar 1 *vt* to rub. **2 frotarse** *vr* **f. las manos** to rub one's hands together.

fruncir [3] *vt* **f. el ceño** to frown.

frustrar 1 *vt* to frustrate. **2 frustrarse** *vr* (*esperanza*) to fail; (*persona*) to be frustrated *o* disappointed.

fruta *f* fruit; **f. del tiempo** fresh fruit.

frutería *f* fruit shop.

frutero *m* fruit dish *o* bowl.

fruto *m* fruit; **frutos secos** nuts.

fucsia *f* fuchsia.

fuego *m* fire; (*lumbre*) light; **fuegos artificiales** fireworks; **¿me da f., por favor?** have you got a light, please?

fuel, fuel-oil *m* diesel.

fuente *f* (*artificial*) fountain; (*recipiente*) dish; (*origen*) source; (*de caracteres*) font.

fuera¹ 1 *adv* outside; **desde f.** from (the) outside; **por f.** on the outside; **la puerta de f.** the outer door. **2** *prep* **f. de** out of; **f. de serie** extraordinary.

fuera² 1 *subj imperfecto de* **ir. 2** *subj imperfecto de* **ser.**

fuerte 1 *a* strong; (*dolor*) severe; (*sonido*) loud; (*comida*) heavy. **2** *m* (*fortaleza*) fort. **3** *adv* **¡abrázame f.!** hold me tight!; **¡habla más f.!** speak up!; **¡pégale f.!** hit him hard!

fuerza *f* (*fortaleza*) strength; (*cuerpo*) force; **a f. de** by dint of; **a la f.** (*por obligación*) of necessity; (*con violencia*) by force; **por f.** of necessity; **Fuerzas Aéreas** ≈ *Br* Royal Air Force; **Fuerzas Armadas** Armed Forces.

fuese 1 *subj imperfecto de* **ir**. **2** *subj imperfecto de* **ser**.

fuete *m Am* whip.

fuga *f* (*huida*) escape; (*de gas etc*) leak.

fugarse [7] *vr* to escape.

fui 1 *pt indef de* **ir**. **2** *pt indef de* **ser**.

fulminante *a* (*muerte, enfermedad*) sudden; (*mirada*) withering.

fumador,-a *mf* smoker; **los no fumadores** non-smokers.

fumar 1 *vti* to smoke; **no f.** (*en letrero*) no smoking. **2 fumarse** *vr* **f. un cigarro** to smoke a cigarette.

función *f* function; (*cargo*) duties *pl*; (*de teatro, cine*) performance.

funcionamiento *m* operation; **poner/entrar en f.** to put/come into operation.

funcionar *vi* to work; **no funciona** (*en letrero*) out of order.

funcionario,-a *mf* civil servant.

funda *f* cover; (*de gafas etc*) case; **f. de almohada** pillowcase.

fundación *f* foundation.

fundamental *a* fundamental.

fundar 1 *vt* (*crear*) to found. **2 fundarse** *vr* (*empresa*) to be founded; (*teoría, afirmación*) to be based.

fundir *vt*, **fundirse** *vr* (*derretirse*) to melt; (*bombilla, plomos*) to blow; (*unirse*) to merge.

fúnebre *a* (*mortuorio*) funeral; **coche f.** hearse.

funeral *m* funeral.

funeraria *f* undertaker's, *US* funeral parlor.

fungir *vi Am* to act (**de** as).

furgoneta *f* van.

furia *f* fury.

furioso,-a *a* furious.

furor *m* fury.

furtivo,-a *a* furtive; **cazador/pescador f.** poacher.

furúnculo *m* boil.

fusible *m* fuse.

fusil *m* gun, rifle.

fusilar *vt* to shoot, execute.

fusión *f* (*de metales*) fusion; (*del hielo*) thawing, melting; (*de empresas*) merger.

fusionar *vt*, **fusionarse** *vr* (*metales*) to fuse; (*empresas*) to merge.

fútbol *m* football, soccer.

futbolín *m* table football.

futbolista *mf* footballer, football *o* soccer player.

futuro,-a 1 *a* future. **2** *m* future.

G

gabardina *f* (*prenda*) raincoat.

gabinete *m* (*despacho*) study; (*de gobierno*) cabinet.

gacho,-a *a* **con la cabeza gacha** hanging one's head.

gafas *fpl* glasses, spectacles; **g. de sol** sunglasses.

gafe *m* **ser (un) g.** to be a jinx.

gaita *f* bagpipes *pl*.

gajo *m* (*de naranja, pomelo etc*) segment.

gala *f* (*espectáculo*) gala; **de g.** dressed up; (*ciudad*) decked out.

galán *m* handsome young man; (*personaje*) leading man.

galante *a* gallant.

galápago *m* turtle.

galardón *m* prize.

galardonar *vt* to award a prize to.

galería *f* (*corredor*) covered balcony; (*museo*) art gallery.

Gales *m* **(el país de) G.** Wales.

galés,-esa 1 *a* Welsh. **2** *mf* (*hombre*) Welshman; (*mujer*) Welshwoman; **los galeses** the Welsh. **3** *m* (*idioma*) Welsh.

galgo *m* greyhound.

Galicia *f* Galicia.

galimatías *m inv* gibberish.

gallego,-a 1 *a* Galician; *Am fam* Spanish. **2** *mf* Galician; *Am fam* Spaniard. **3** *m* (*idioma*) Galician.

galleta *f* biscuit.

gallina *f* hen.

gallinero *m* hen run.

gallo *m* cock.

galopante *a* (*inflación etc*) galloping.

galopar *vi* to gallop.

gama *f* range.

gamba *f* prawn.

gamberro,-a 1 *mf* hooligan. **2** *a* uncouth.

gamo *m* fallow deer.

gamuza *f* (*trapo*) chamois *o* shammy leather.

gana *f* (*deseo*) wish (**de** for); (*apetito*) appetite; **de buena g.** willingly; **de mala g.** reluctantly; **tener ganas de (hacer) algo** to feel like (doing) sth.

ganado *m* livestock.

ganador,-a 1 *a* winning. **2** *mf* winner.

ganancia *f* profit.

ganar 1 *vt* (*sueldo*) to earn; (*premio*) to win; (*aventajar*) to beat. **2 ganarse** *vr* to earn.

ganchillo *m* crochet work.

gancho *m* hook; *Am* (*horquilla*) hairpin.

ganga *f* bargain.

ganso,-a *mf* goose; (*macho*) gander; *fam* dolt.

garabato *m* scrawl.

garaje *m* garage.

garantía *f* guarantee.

garantizar [4] *vt* (*cosa*) to guarantee; (*a persona*) to assure.

garbanzo *m* chickpea.

garfio *m* hook.

garganta *f* throat; (*desfiladero*) narrow pass.

garra *f* claw; (*de ave*) talon; **tener g.** to be compelling.

garrafa *f* carafe.

garrapata *f* tick.

garrote *m* (*porra*) club.

gas *m* gas; (*en bebida*) fizz; **g. ciudad** town gas; **gases (nocivos)** fumes; **g. de escape** exhaust fumes; **agua con g.** fizzy water.

gasa *f* gauze.

gaseosa *f* lemonade.

gasoducto *m* gas pipeline.

gasoil, gasóleo *m* diesel oil.

gasolina *f* petrol, *US* gasoline.

gasolinera *f* petrol *o US* gas station.

gastar 1 *vt* (*consumir*) (*dinero, tiempo*) to spend; (*gasolina, electricidad*) to consume; (*malgastar*) to waste; (*ropa*) to wear; **g. una broma a algn** to play a practical joke on sb. **2 gastarse** *vr* (*zapatos etc*) to wear out.

gasto *m* expenditure; **gastos** expenses.

gatas a gatas on all fours.

gatear *vi* to crawl.

gatillo *m* (*de armas*) trigger.

gato *m* cat; (*de coche*) jack.

gaviota *f* seagull.

gay *a inv & m* (*pl* **gays**) gay.

gazpacho *m* gazpacho.

gel *m* gel; **g. (de ducha)** shower gel.

gelatina *f* (*ingrediente*) gelatin; (*para postre*) jelly.

gema *f* gem.

gemelo,-a 1 *a & mf* (*identical*) twin. **2** *mpl* **gemelos** (*de camisa*) cufflinks; (*anteojos*) binoculars.

gemido *m* groan.

gemir [6] *vi* to groan.

generación *f* generation.

general a general; **por lo** o **en g.** in general.
generalizar [4] **1** vt to generalize. **2 generalizarse** vr to become widespread o common.
generalmente adv generally.
generar vt to generate.
género m (clase) kind, sort; (mercancía) article; (gramatical) gender.
generoso,-a a generous (**con, para** to).
genético,-a a genetic.
genial a brilliant.
genio mf inv genius; (mal carácter) temper; **estar de mal g.** to be in a bad mood.
genocidio m genocide.
gente f people pl; Am respectable people.
gentuza f riffraff.
genuino,-a a (puro) genuine; (verdadero) authentic.
geografía f geography.
geología f geology.
geometría f geometry.
geranio m geranium.
gerente mf manager.
gérmen m germ.
gerundio m gerund.
gestación f gestation.
gesticular vi to gesticulate.
gestión f (administración) management; **gestiones** (negociaciones) negotiations; (trámites) formalities.
gesto m (mueca) face; (con las manos) gesture.
gigante,-a a & mf giant.
gigantesco,-a a gigantic.
gimnasia f gymnastics pl.
gimnasio m gymnasium.
ginecólogo,-a mf gynaecologist.
gira f (musical, teatral) tour.
girar vi (dar vueltas) to spin; **g. a la derecha/izquierda** to turnright/left.
girasol m sunflower.
giratorio,-a a revolving.
giro m (vuelta) turn; (frase) turn of phrase; (libranza) draft; **g. telegráfico** giro o money order; **g. postal** postal o money order.
gitano,-a a & mf gypsy, gipsy.
glaciar m glacier.
glándula f gland.
global a comprehensive.

globo *m* balloon; (*esfera*) globe.

gloria *f* (*fama*) glory; (*cielo*) heaven.

glorieta *f* (*plazoleta*) small square; (*encrucijada de calles*) roundabout, US traffic circle.

glosario *m* glossary.

glotón,-ona 1 *a* greedy. **2** *mf* glutton.

glucosa *f* glucose.

gobernación *f* government; **Ministerio de la Gobernación,** ≈ *Br* Home Office, *US* Department of the Interior.

gobernador,-a *mf* governor.

gobernante 1 *a* ruling. **2** *mpl* **los gobernantes** the rulers.

gobernar [1] *vt* to govern; (*un país*) to rule.

gobierno *m* government; (*mando*) running.

gofio *m* (*en América y Canarias*) roasted maize meal.

gol *m* goal.

golf *m* golf; **palo de g.** golf club.

golfo,-a¹ *mf* good for nothing.

golfo² *m* gulf.

golondrina *f* swallow.

golosina *f* sweet, *US* candy.

goloso,-a *a* sweet-toothed.

golpe *m* blow; (*llamada*) knock; (*puñetazo*) punch; (*choque*) bump; (*desgracia*) blow; **de g.** all of a sudden; **g. de estado** coup d'état.

golpear *vt* to hit; (*con el puño*) to punch; (*puerta, cabeza*) to bang.

goma *f* rubber; (*elástica*) rubber band; **g. de borrar** rubber, *US* eraser.

gomal *m Am* rubber plantation.

gomero *m Am* gum tree; (*recolector*) rubber collector.

gordo,-a 1 *a* (*carnoso*) fat; (*grueso*) thick. **2** *mf* fat person, *fam* fatty. **3** *m* **el g.** (*de lotería*) first prize.

gorila *m* gorilla.

gorra *f* cap.

gorrión *m* sparrow.

gorro *m* cap.

gota *f* drop; **g. a g.** drop by drop; **ni g.** not a bit.

gotear *v impers* to drip; **el techo gotea** there's a leak in the ceiling.

gotera *f* leak.

gozar [4] **1** *vt* to enjoy. **2** *vi* (*disfrutar*) to enjoy (**de -**).

gozne *m* hinge.

grabación *f* recording.

grabado,-a *m* (*arte*) engraving; (*dibujo*) drawing.

grabadora *f* tape recorder.

grabar *vt* (*sonidos, imágenes*) to record; (*en ordenador*) to save.

gracia *f* (*chiste*) joke; (*indulto*) pardon; **hacer** *o* **tener g.** to be funny.

gracias *fpl* thanks; **muchas** *o* **muchísimas g.** thank you very much.

gracioso,-a 1 *a* (*divertido*) funny. **2** *mf* (*personaje*) comic character.

grada *f* (*peldaño*) step; **gradas** flight *sing* of steps, *US* forecourt *sing* (*estadio*) terracing.

grado *m* degree; **de buen g.** willingly.

gradual *a* gradual.

gradualmente *adv* gradually.

graduar [30] **1** *vt* (*regular*) to regulate. **2 graduarse** *vr* (*soldado, alumno*) to graduate; **g. la vista** to have one's eyes tested.

gráfico,-a 1 *a* graphic. **2** *mf* graph; **gráficos** (*de ordenador*) graphics.

gragea *f* pill.

gral. *abr de* **General** Gen.

gramática *f* grammar.

gramo *m* gram, gramme.

gran *a ver* **grande.**

granada *f* (*fruto*) pomegranate; (*explosivo*) grenade.

granate 1 *a inv* maroon. **2** *m* maroon.

grande *a* (*before singular noun* **gran** *is used*) (*tamaño*) big, large; *fig* (*persona*) great; (*cantidad*) large; **pasarlo en g.** to have a great time.

granel a granel (*sin medir exactamente*) loose.

granito *m* granite.

granizada *f*, **granizado** *m* iced drink.

granizo *m* hail.

granja *f* farm.

granjear(se) *vt & vr* to gain.

granjero,-a *mf* farmer.

grano *m* grain; (*de café*) bean; (*espinilla*) spot.

granuja *m* **1** (*pilluelo*) ragamuffin. **2** (*estafador*) con-man.

grapa *f* staple.

grapadora *f* stapler.

grasa *f* grease.

grasiento *a* greasy.

graso,-a *a* (*pelo*) greasy; (*materia*) fatty.

gratis *adv* free.

gratitud *f* gratitude.

gratuito,-a *a* (*de balde*) free (of charge); (*arbitrario*) gratuitous.

grava *f* (*guijas*) gravel; (*en carretera*) chippings *pl*.

gravar *vt* (*impuestos*) to tax.

grave *a* (*importante*) serious; (*muy enfermo*) seriously ill; (*voz, nota*) low.

gravedad *f* seriousness; (*fuerza*) gravity.

gravilla *f* (*en carretera*) chippings *pl*.

grieta *f* crack; (*en la piel*) chap.

grifo *m* tap, *US* faucet.

grillo *m* cricket.

gringo,-a *a* & *mf Am* gringo, yankee.

gripe *f* flu.

gris *a m* grey, *US* gray.

grisáceo,-a *a* greyish.

gritar *vti* to shout.

grito *m* shout.

grosella *f* (*fruto*) redcurrant; **g. negra** blackcurrant; **g. silvestre** gooseberry.

grosería *f* (*ordinariez*) rude word *o* expression.

grosor *m* thickness.

grotesco,-a *a* grotesque.

grúa *f* (*en construcción*) crane; (*para coches*) breakdown van, *US* tow truck.

grueso,-a 1 *a* thick; (*persona*) stout. **2** *m* (*parte principal*) bulk.

grumo *m* lump.

gruñido *m* grunt.

gruñón,-ona *a* grumpy.

grupo *m* group.

gruta *f* cave.

guacamol, guacamole *m Am* avocado sauce.

guachafita *f Am* uproar.

guacho,-a *a* & *mf Am* orphan.

guagua[1] *f* (*en Canarias y Cuba*) bus.

guagua[2] *f Am* baby.

guante *m* glove.

guantera *f* (*en coche*) glove compartment.

guapo,-a *a* good-looking; (*mujer*) beautiful, pretty; (*hombre*) handsome.

guaraca *f Am* sling.

guarango,-a *a Am* rude.

guarda *mf* guard; **g. jurado** security guard.

guardacoches *mf inv* parking attendant.

guardacostas *m inv* (*persona*) coastguard; (*embarcación*) coastguard vessel.

guardaespaldas *mf inv* bodyguard.

guardameta *mf* goalkeeper.

guardar *vt* (*conservar, reservar*) to keep; (*un secreto*) to keep; (*poner en un sitio*) to put away; (*en ordenador*) to save.

guardería infantil *f* nursery (school).

guardia 1 *f* (*vigilancia*) watch; (*turno de servicio*) duty; **la g. civil** the civil guard; **farmacia de g.** duty chemist. **2** *mf* (*hombre*) policeman; (*mujer*) policewoman.

guardián,-ana *mf* watchman.

guarecerse *vr* to take shelter *o* refuge (**de** from).

guaso,-a *a Am* peasant.

guasón,-ona 1 *a* humorous. **2** *mf* joker.

guata *f* (*relleno*) padding; *Am* (*barriga*) paunch.

guayabo,-a *mf* (*chica bonita*) pretty young girl; (*chico guapo*) good-looking boy.

guerra *f* war; **g. civil/fría/mundial/nuclear** civil/cold/world/nuclear war.

guerrilla *f* (*partida armada*) guerrilla force *o* band; (*lucha*) guerrilla warfare.

guía 1 *mf* (*persona*) guide. **2** *f* (*libro*) guide; **la g. de teléfonos** the telephone directory.

guiar [29] **1** *vt* (*indicar el camino*) to guide; (*automóvil*) to drive. **2 guiarse** *vr* to be guided (**por** by).

guijarro *m* pebble.

guindilla *f* chilli.

guiñapo *m* (*andrajo*) rag.

guiñar *vt* to wink.

guión *m* (*de cine, televisión*) script; (*ortográfico*) hyphen; (*esquema*) sketch.

guirnalda *f* garland.

guisante *m* pea.

guisar *vt* to cook.

guita *f* rope.

guitarra 1 *f* guitar. **2** *mf* guitarist.

gula *f* gluttony.

gusano *m* worm; (*oruga*) caterpillar.

gustar 1 *vt* **me gusta el vino** I like wine; **me gustaban los caramelos** I used to like sweets; **me gusta nadar** I like swimming; **me gustaría ir** I would like to go. **2** *vi* **g. de** to enjoy.

gusto *m*.taste; **con (mucho) g.** with (great) pleasure; **tanto g.** pleased to meet you; **estar a g.** to feel comfortable *o* at ease; **ser de buen/mal g.** to be in good/bad taste; **tener buen/mal g.** to have good/bad taste.

H

ha *indic pres de* **haber.**

haba *f* broad bean.

habano *m* Havana (cigar).

haber 1 *v aux (en tiempos compuestos)* to have; **lo he visto** I have seen it; **ya lo había hecho** he had already done it. ‖ **h. de** + *infin (obligación)* to have to; **has de ser bueno** you must be good. **2** *v impers (special form of present tense:* **hay**) *(existir, estar) (singular used also with plural nouns)* **hay** there is *o* are; **había** there was *o* were; **habrá una fiesta** there will be a party; **había una vez** ... once upon a time...; **no hay de qué** you're welcome; **¿qué hay?** how are things? ‖ **h. que** + *infinitivo* it is necessary to.

habichuela *f* kidney bean.

hábil *a (diestro)* skilful; **días hábiles** working days.

habitación *f (cuarto)* room; *(dormitorio)* bedroom; **h. individual/doble** single/double room.

habitante *mf* inhabitant.

hábito *m (costumbre)* habit; *(de monje)* habit.

habitual *a* usual, habitual.

habituar 1 *vt* to accustom (**a** to). **2 habituarse** *vr* to get used (**a** to), become accustomed (**a** to).

hablador,-a *a (parlanchín)* talkative.

hablar 1 *vi* to speak, talk; **h. con algn** to speak to sb; **¡ni h.!** no way!; *fam* **¡quién fue a h.!** look who's talking! **2** *vt (idioma)* to speak. **3 hablarse** *vr* to speak *o* talk to one another; **'se habla español'** 'Spanish spoken'.

habré *indic fut de* **haber.**

hacer 1 *vt* to do; *(crear, fabricar)* to make; **hazme un favor** do me a favour; **¿qué haces?** *(en este momento)* what are you doing?; *(para vivir)* what do you do (for a living)?; **tengo mucho que h.** I have a lot to do; **lo hizo con sus proprias manos** he made it with his own hands; **h. la cama** to make the bed; **h. la cena** to make dinner; **el negro le hace más delgado** black makes him look slimmer; **ya no puedo leer como solía hacerlo** I can't read as well as I used to; **¡bien hecho!** well done! **2** *vi (actuar)* to play; **hizo de Desdémona** she played Desdemona; **h. por** *o* **para** + *infinitivo* to try to; **haz por venir** try and come. **3** *v impers* **hace calor/ frío** it's hot/cold; **hace mucho (tiempo)** a long time ago; **hace dos días que no le veo** I haven't seen him for two days; **hace dos años que vivo en Glasgow** I've been living in Glasgow for two years. **4 hacerse** *vr (volverse)* to become, grow; *(simular)* to pretend; **hacerse el dormido** to pretend to be sleeping; **hacerse con** *(apropiarse)* to get hold of; **hacerse a** *(habituarse)* to get used to.

hacha *f* (*herramienta*) axe, *US* ax.

hachís *m* hashish.

hacia *prep* (*dirección*) towards, to; (*aproximadamente*) at about, at around; **h. abajo** down, downwards; **h. adelante** forwards; **h. arriba** up, upwards; **h. atrás** back, backwards.

hacienda *f* ranch; **Ministerio de H.** = Exchequer, Treasury.

hada *f* fairy; **cuento de hadas** fairy tale.

hago *indic pres de* **hacer.**

halagar [7] *vt* to flatter.

halago *m* flattery.

halcón *m* falcon.

hallar 1 *vt* (*encontrar*) to find; (*descubrir*) to discover. **2 hallarse** *vr* (*estar*) to be, find oneself; (*estar situado*) to be situated.

hallazgo *m* (*descubrimiento*) discovery; (*cosa encontrada*) find.

hamaca *f* hammock.

hambre *f* (*apetito*) hunger; (*inanición*) starvation; (*catástrofe*) famine; **tener h.** to be hungry.

hamburguesa *f* hamburger.

han *indic pres de* **haber.**

haré *indic fut de* **hacer.**

harina *f* flour.

hartar 1 *vt* (*cansar, fastidiar*) to annoy; (*atiborrar*) to satiate. **2 hartarse** *vr* (*saciar el apetito*) to eat one's fill; (*cansarse*) to get fed up (**de** with).

harto,-a *a* (*lleno*) full; (*cansado*) fed up; **estoy h. de trabajar** I'm fed up (with) working.

has *indic pres de* **haber.**

hasta 1 *prep* (*lugar*) up to, as far as; (*tiempo*) until, up to; (*con cantidad*) up to, as many as; (*incluso*) even; **h. la fecha** up to now; **h. luego** see you later. **2** *conj* **h. que** until.

hay *indic pres de* **haber.**

haya *subj pres de* **haber.**

haz *imperativo de* **hacer.**

he *indic pres de* **haber.**

hebilla *f* buckle.

hebra *f* thread.

hebreo,-a 1 *a* Hebrew. **2** *mf* Hebrew.

hechizo *m* (*embrujo*) spell.

hecho,-a 1 *a* made, done; (*carne*) done; (*ropa*) ready-made. **2** *m* (*realidad*) fact; (*acto*) act, deed; (*suceso*) event, incident; **de h.** in fact.

hectárea *f* hectare.

hedor *m* stink, stench.

helada *f* frost.

heladería *f* ice-cream parlour.

helado,-a 1 *m* ice cream. **2** *a* (*muy frío*) freezing cold; *fig* **quedarse h.** (*atónito*) to be flabbergasted.

helar [1] **1** *vt* (*congelar*) to freeze. **2** *v impers* to freeze; **anoche heló** there was a frost last night. **3 helarse** *vr* (*congelarse*) to freeze.

helecho *m* fern.

hélice *f* (*de avión, barco*) propeller.

helicóptero *m* helicopter.

hembra *f* *Bot Zool* female; (*mujer*) woman.

hemorragia *f* haemorrhage.

hemos *indic pres de* **haber.**

hendidura *f* crack.

heno *m* hay.

herbolario *m* (*tienda*) herbalist's (shop).

heredar *vt* to inherit.

heredero,-a *mf* (*hombre*) heir; (*mujer*) heiress.

herencia *f* inheritance, legacy; (*biológica*) heredity.

herida *f* (*lesión*) injury; (*corte*) wound.

herido,-a *mf* injured person.

herir [5] **1** *vt* (*físicamente*) (*lesionar*) to injure; (*cortar*) to wound. **2 herirse** *vr* to injure *o* hurt oneself.

hermana *f* sister.

hermano *m* brother; **primo h.** first cousin; **hermanos** brothers and sisters.

herméticamente *adv* **h. cerrado** hermetically sealed.

hermético,-a *a* (*cierre*) hermetic, airtight; *fig* (*grupo*) secretive.

hermoso,-a *a* beautiful, lovely; (*grandioso*) fine.

héroe *m* hero.

heroína *f* (*mujer*) heroine; (*droga*) heroin.

herradura *f* horseshoe.

herramienta *f* tool.

hervir [5] **1** *vt* (*hacer bullir*) to boil. **2** *vi* (*bullir*) to boil.

heterogéneo,-a *a* heterogeneous.

hice *pt indef de* **hacer.**

hiciste *pt indef de* **hacer.**

hidratante *a* moisturizing; **crema/leche h.** moisturizing cream/lotion.

hidráulico,-a *a* hydraulic.

hidroavión *m* seaplane, *US* hydroplane.

hiedra *f* ivy.

hielo *m* ice.

hiena *f* hyena.

hierba *f* grass; **mala h.** weed.

meante a (chimenea) smoky, smoking.
umedad f (atmosférica) humidity; (de lugar) dampness.
umedecer 1 vt to moisten, dampen. **2 humedecerse** vr to become damp o moist.
húmedo,-a a (casa, ropa) damp; (clima) humid, damp.
humildad f (de persona) humility; (de cosa) humbleness.
humilde a humble; (familia) poor.
humillar 1 vt (rebajar) to humiliate. **2 humillarse** vr humiullarse ante algn to humble oneself before sb.
humo m smoke; (gas) fumes pl; (vapor) vapour, steam.
humor m (genio) mood; (gracia) humour; **estar de buen** o **mal h.** to be in a good o bad mood; **sentido del h.** sense of humour.
hundimiento m (de edificio) collapse; (de barco) sinking; (de tierra) subsidence; (ruina) downfall.
hundir 1 vt (barco) to sink; (derrumbar) to bring o knock down. **2 hundirse** vr (barco) to sink; (edificio, empresa) to collapse.
huracán m hurricane.
huraño,-a a unsociable.
hurgar [7] **1** vi (fisgar) to poke one's nose (**en** in). **2** vt (fuego etc) to poke.
hurto m petty theft.
huyo indic pres de **huir.**

hierbabuena f mint.
hierro m iron.
hígado m liver.
higiénico,-a a hygienic; **papel h.** toilet paper.
hija f daughter.
hijo m son; **hijos** children.
hilera f line, row.
hilo m thread; (grueso) yarn; (fibra) linen; **perder el h.** to lose the thread; **h. musical** background music.
himno m hymn; **h. nacional** national anthem.
hincapié m hacer **h. en** (insistir) to insist on; (subrayar) to emphasize.
hincar [1] **1** vt (clavar) to drive (in). **2 hincarse** vr **h. de rodillas** to kneel (down).
hincha 1 mf (de equipo) fan, supporter. **2** f (antipatía) grudge, dislike.
hinchado,-a a swollen.
hinchar 1 vt (inflar) to inflate, blow up. **2 hincharse** vr to swell (up); fam (hartarse) to stuff oneself.
hindú a & mf Hindu.
hipermercado m hypermarket.
hípico,-a a horse.
hipnotizar [4] vt to hypnotize.
hipo m tener **h.** to have the hiccups.
hipócrita 1 a hypocritical. **2** mf hypocrite.
hipopótamo m hippopotamus.
hipoteca f mortgage.
hipótesis f inv hypothesis.
hispánico,-a a Hispanic.
hispano,-a 1 a Hispanic. **2** mf Spanish American, Hispanic.
hispanohablante 1 a Spanish-speaking. **2** mf Spanish speaker.
histérico,-a a hysterical.
historia f (estudio del pasado) history; (narración) story.
historial m record; (antecedentes) background.
histórico,-a a historical; (de gran importancia) historic, memorable.
historieta f (tira cómica) comic strip.
hizo indic indef de **hacer.**
hocico m (de animal) snout.
hogar m (casa) home; (de la chimenea) hearth.
hoguera f bonfire.
hoja f leaf; (de papel) sheet; (de cuchillo, espada) blade; (impreso) handout.
hojalata f tin.
hojaldre m puff pastry.

hojear vt (libro) to leaf through.

hola interj hello!

holgado,-a a (ropa) loose, baggy; (económicamente) comfortable; (espacio) roomy.

holgazán,-ana 1 a lazy. **2** mf lazybones inv.

hollín m soot.

hombre 1 m man; **h. de negocios** businessman. **2** interj (saludo) hey!; **¡sí h.!, ¡h. claro!** (enfático) sure! you bet!

hombrera f shoulder pad.

hombro m shoulder; **a hombros** on one's shoulders; **encogerse de hombros** to shrug one's shoulders; **mirar a algn por encima del h.** to look down one's nose at sb.

homenaje m homage, tribute.

homicida 1 mf (hombre) murderer; (mujer) murderess. **2** a homicidal.

homicidio m homicide.

homogéneo,-a a homogeneous, uniform.

homosexual a & mf homosexual.

hondo,-a a (vacío) deep; **plato h.** soup dish.

honesto,-a a (honrado) honest; (recatado) modest.

hongo m fungus; (sombrero) bowler (hat); **h. venenoso** toadstool.

honor m honour; **palabra de h.** word of honour.

honorario,-a 1 a honorary. **2** mpl **honorarios** fees.

honra f (dignidad) dignity; (honor) honour; **¡a mucha h.!** and proud of it!

honradez f honesty.

honrado,-a a (de fiar) honest.

hora f hour; (cita) appointment; **media h.** half an hour; **h. punta** rush hour; **horas extra** overtime (hours); **¿qué h. es?** what time is it?; **a última h.** at the last moment; **pedir h.** (al médico etc) to ask for an appointment.

horario-a m timetable, US schedule.

horca f gallows pl.

horchata f sweet milky drink made from chufa nuts or almonds.

horizonte m horizon.

hormiga f ant.

hormigón m concrete.

hormiguero m anthill.

hormona f hormone.

horno m (de cocina) oven; (para metales) furnace; (para cerámica etc) kiln; **pescado al h.** baked fish.

horóscopo m horoscope.

horquilla f (del pelo) hair-grip.

horrible a horrible.

horror m horror; **¡qué h.!** how awful!; fam **tengo h. a las motos** I hate

motorbikes.

horrorizar [4] vt to horrify; (dar miedo) to terrify.

horroroso,-a a horrifying; (que da miedo) terrifying; fam hideous; fam (malísimo) awful.

hortaliza f vegetable.

hortera a fam (persona) flashy; (cosa) tacky.

hospedar 1 vt to put up. **2 hospedarse** vr to stay (**en** at).

hospicio m (para huérfanos) orphanage.

hospital m hospital.

hospitalizar [4] vt to send into hospital, hospitalize.

hostal m guest house.

hostelería f (negocio) catering business; (estudios) hotel management.

hostería f Am inn, lodging house.

hostil a hostile.

hotel m hotel.

hoy adv (día) today; **h. (en) día** nowadays.

hoyo m hole.

hube pt indef de **haber.**

hubiera subj imperfecto de **haber.**

hucha f piggy bankecto.

hueco,-a 1 a (vacío) empty, hollow; (sonido) resonant. **2** m (cavidad) hollow, hole; (sitio no ocupado) empty space.

huele indic pres de **oler.**

huelga f strike; **estar en** o **de h.** to be on strike; **hacer h.** to go on strike.

huella f (del pie) footprint; (coche) track; **h. dactilar** fingerprint; fig (vestigio) trace.

huérfano,-a mf orphan.

huerta f (parcela) market o US truck garden; (región) irrigated area used for cultivation.

huerto m (de verduras) vegetable garden; (de frutales) orchard.

hueso m (del cuerpo) bone; (de fruto) stone, US pit; Am (enchufe) contact.

huésped,-a mf guest; **casa de huéspedes** guesthouse.

huevo m egg; **h. duro** hard-boiled egg; **h. frito** fried egg; **h. pasado por agua,** Am **h. tibio** soft-boiled egg; **huevos revueltos** scrambled eggs.

huida f flight, escape.

huir vi (escaparse) to run away (**de** from), flee; (evadirse) to escape (**de** from).

hule m (tela impermeable) oilcloth; (de mesa) tablecloth; Am rubber.

humanitario,-a a humanitarian.

humano,-a 1 a (relativo al hombre) human; (compasivo) humane; **ser h.** human being. **2** m human (being).

I

ibérico,-a *a* Iberian.

iberoamericano,-a *a & mf* Latin American.

iceberg *m* (*pl* **icebergs**) iceberg.

ICONA *m abr de* **Instituto para la Conservación de la Naturaleza** Institute for the Protection of Nature.

icono *m* icon.

ida *f* **billete de i. y vuelta** return ticket, *US* round trip ticket.

idea *f* idea; **hacerse a la i. de** to get used to the idea of; **ni i.** no idea; **cambiar de i.** to change one's mind.

ideal *a & m* ideal.

idear *vt* (*inventar*) to devise; (*concebir*) to think up.

idéntico,-a *a* identical.

identidad *f* identity; **carnet de i.** identity card.

identificación *f* identification.

identificar [1] **1** *vt* to identify. **2 identificarse** *vr* to identify oneself; (*simpatizar*) to identify (**con** with).

idilio *m* (*romance*) romance.

idioma *m* language.

idiota 1 *a* idiotic. **2** *mf* idiot.

ídolo *m* idol.

idóneo,-a *a* suitable.

iglesia *f* (*edificio*) church; **la I.** the Church.

ignorante 1 *a* (*sin instrucción*) ignorant; (*no informado*) unaware (**de** of). **2** *mf* ignoramus.

ignorar 1 *vt* (*algo*) not to know; (*algn*) to ignore. **2 ignorarse** *vr* to be unknown.

igual 1 *a* (*lo mismo*) the same; (*equivalente*) equal; **es i.** it doesn't matter; **i. que** the same as; **a partes iguales** fifty-fifty; **al i. que** just like; **por i.** equally; **6 más 7 i. a 13** 6 plus 7 equals 13. **2** *m* equal. **3** *adv* **lo haces i. que yo** you do it the same way I do.

igualmente *adv* equally; (*también*) also, likewise; **¡gracias! – ¡i.!** thank you! – the same to you!

igualar *vt* to make equal; (*nivelar*) to level.

igualdad *f* equality; (*identidad*) sameness; **en i. de condiciones** on equal terms.

ilegal *a* illegal.

ilegalmente *adv* illegally.

ilegítimo,-a *a* illegitimate.

ileso,-a *a* unharmed.

ilícito,-a *a* unlawful.

ilimitado 488

ilimitado,-a *a* unlimited.
iluminación *f* (*alumbrado*) illumination.
iluminar *vt* to illuminate.
ilusión *f* (*esperanza*) hope; (*esperanza vana*) illusion; (*emoción*) excitement; **hacerse ilusiones** to build up one's hopes; **me hace i. verla** I'm looking forward to seeing her; **¡qué i.!** how exciting!
ilusionar 1 *vt* (*esperanzar*) **i. a algn** to build up sb's hopes; (*entusiasmar*) to excite. **2 ilusionarse** *vr* (*esperanzarse*) to build up one's hopes; (*entusiasmarse*) to be excited (**con** about).
ilustración *f* (*grabado*) illustration; (*erudición*) learning.
ilustrar *vt* to illustrate.
ilustre *a* distinguished.
imagen *f* image; (*de televisión*) picture.
imaginación *f* imagination.
imaginar 1 *vt* to imagine. **2 imaginarse** *vr* to imagine; **me imagino que sí** I suppose so.
imán *m* magnet.
imbécil 1 *a* stupid. **2** *mf* imbecile.
imitar *vt* to imitate; (*gestos*) to mimic.
impacientar 1 *vt* **i. a algn** to exasperate sb. **2 impacientarse** *vr* to get impatient (**por** at).
impaciente *a* (*deseoso*) impatient; (*intranquilo*) anxious.
impacto *m* impact.
impar *a* odd.
imparcial *a* impartial.
impasible *a* impassive.
impecable *a* impeccable.
impedimento *m* impediment; (*obstáculo*) hindrance.
impedir [6] *vt* (*obstaculizar*) to impede; (*imposibilitar*) to prevent, stop.
impenetrable *a* impenetrable.
imperante *a* (*gobernante*) ruling; (*predominante*) prevailing.
imperativo,-a 1 *a* imperative. **2** *m* imperative.
imperdible *m* safety pin.
imperfecto,-a *a* imperfect; (*defectuoso*) defective; (*tiempo verbal*) imperfect.
imperio *m* empire.
impermeable 1 *a* impervious; (*ropa*) waterproof. **2** *m* raincoat, mac.
impertinente *a* (*insolente*) impertintent; (*inoportuno*) irrelevant.
impetuoso,-a *a* (*violento*) violent; (*fogoso*) impetuous.
implacable *a* implacable.
implicar [1] *vt* (*involucrar*) to involve (**en** in); (*conllevar*) to imply.
implícito,-a *a* implicit.

implorar *vt* to implore.

imponente *a* (*impresionante*) imposing; (*sobrecogedor*) stunning.

imponer (*pp* **impuesto**) **1** *vt* to impose; (*impresionar*) to be impressive; **i. respeto** to inspire respect. **2 imponerse** *vr* (*prevalecer*) to prevail; (*ser necesario*) to be necessary.

importación *f* (*mercancía*) import; (*acción*) importing; **artículos de i.** imported goods.

importancia *f* importance; (*tamaño*) size.

importante *a* important; (*grande*) significant.

importar[1] **1** *vi* (*tener importancia*) to be important; **no importa** it doesn't matter; **eso no te importa a tí** that doesn't concern you; **¿te importa si fumo?** do you mind if I smoke? **2** *vt* (*valer*) to amount to.

importar[2] *vt* to import.

importe *m* amount.

imposibilitar *vt* (*impedir*) to make impossible; (*incapacitar*) to disable.

imposible *a* impossible; **me es i. hacerlo** I can't (possibly) do it.

impostor,-a *mf* impostor.

impotencia *f* powerlessness.

imprenta *f* (*taller*) printer's; (*aparato*) printing press.

imprescindible *a* essential.

impresión *f* (*efecto, opinión*) impression; (*acto, de revista etc*) printing; (*edición*) edition.

impresionante *a* impressive.

impresionar *vt* (*causar admiración*) to impress; (*sorprender*) to stun.

impresionismo *m* impressionism.

impreso,-a **1** *a* printed. **2** *m* (*papel, folleto*) printed matter; (*formulario*) form; **i. de solicitud** application form.

impresora *f* printer; **i. de inyección** inkjet (printer); **i. láser** laser (printer); **i. matricial** dot matrix (printer).

imprevisible *a* unforeseeable.

imprevisto,-a **1** *a* unforeseen. **2** *m* unforeseen event.

imprimir (*pp* **impreso**) *vt* to print.

impropio,-a *a* (*inadecuado*) inappropriate.

improvisado,-a *a* (*espontáneo*) improvised; (*provisional*) makeshift.

improvisar *vt* to improvise.

imprudencia *f* rashness; (*indiscreción*) indiscretion.

impuesto *m* tax; **i. sobre la renta** income tax; **libre de impuestos** tax-free.

impulsar *vt* to drive.

impulso *m* impulse.

impunemente *adv* with impunity.

impureza *f* impurity.

impuse *pt indef de* **imponer.**

inacabable *a* endless.

inaccesible *a* inaccessible.

inaceptable *a* unacceptable.

inadaptado,-a 1 *a* maladjusted. **2** *mf* misfit.

inadecuado,-a *a* unsuitable.

inadmisible *a* inadmissible.

inagotable *a* (*recursos etc*) inexhaustible; (*persona*) tireless.

inaguantable *a* unbearable.

inapreciable *a* (*valioso*) invaluable; (*insignificante*) insignificant.

inasequible *a* (*producto*) unaffordable; (*meta*) unattainable; (*persona*) unapproachable.

inaudito,-a *a* unprecedented.

inauguración *f* inauguration.

inaugurar *vt* to inaugurate.

inca *a & mf* Inca.

incalculable *a* incalculable.

incandescente *a* white hot.

incansable *a* tireless.

incapacidad *f* inability; (*incompetencia*) incompetence.

incapacitar *vt* to incapacitate; (*inhabilitar*) to disqualify.

incapaz *a* incapable (**de** of).

incendiar 1 *vt* to set alight. **2 incendiarse** *vr* to catch fire.

incendio *m* fire; **i. forestal** forest fire.

incentivo *m* incentive.

incertidumbre *f* uncertainty.

incierto,-a *a* uncertain.

incinerar *vt* (*basura*) to incinerate; (*cadáveres*) to cremate.

incipiente *a* incipient.

incitar *vt* to incite.

inclinación *f* (*de terreno*) slope; (*del cuerpo*) stoop; (*reverencia*) bow.

inclinar 1 *vt* to incline; (*cabeza*) to nod. **2 inclinarse** *vr* to lean; (*al saludar*) to bow; (*optar*) **inclinarse a** to be inclined to.

incluir *vt* to include; (*contener*) to contain; (*adjuntar*) to enclose.

inclusive *adv* (*incluido*) inclusive; (*incluso*) even; **hasta la lección ocho i.** up to and including lesson eight.

incluso *adv* even.

incógnita *f* (*misterio*) mystery.

incoherente *a* incoherent.

incoloro,-a *a* colourless.

incombustible *a* incombustible.

incomodidad *f* discomfort; (*molestia*) inconvenience.

incómodo,-a *a* uncomfortable.

incompatible *a* incompatible.

incompetencia *f* incompetence.

incompetente *a & mf* incompetent.

incompleto,-a *a* incomplete; (*inacabado*) unfinished.

incomprensible *a* incomprehensible.

incomunicado,-a *a* (*aislado*) isolated; (*en la cárcel*) in solitary confinement; **el pueblo se quedó i.** the town was cut off.

inconcebible *a* inconceivable.

incondicional *a* unconditional; (*apoyo*) wholehearted; (*amigo*) faithful; (*partidario*) staunch.

inconfundible *a* unmistakable.

incongruente *a* incongruous.

inconsciencia *f* unconsciousness; (*irresponsabilidad*) irresponsibility.

inconsciente 1 *a* (*con estar*) (*desmayado*) unconscious; (*con ser*) (*despreocupado*) unaware (**de** of); (*irreflexivo*) thoughtless.

inconsistente *a* (*argumento*) weak.

inconstante *a* fickle.

incontrolable *a* uncontrollable.

inconveniente 1 *a* inconvenient; (*inapropiado*) unsuitable. **2** *m* (*objeción*) objection; (*desventaja*) disadvantage; (*problema*) difficulty.

incorporación *f* incorporation.

incorporar 1 *vt* to incorporate (**en** into); (*levantar*) to help to sit up. **2 incorporarse** *vr* (*en la cama*) to sit up; **incorporarse a** (*sociedad*) to join; (*trabajo*) to start.

incorrecto,-a *a* (*equivocado*) incorrect.

incorregible *a* incorrigible.

incrédulo,-a 1 *a* incredulous. **2** *mf* disbeliever.

increíble *a* incredible.

incrementar 1 *vt* to increase. **2 incrementarse** *vr* to increase.

inculto,-a 1 *a* uneducated. **2** *mf* ignoramus.

incumplimiento *m* (*de un deber*) non-fulfilment; (*de una orden*) failure to execute.

incurrir *vi* to fall (**en** into).

indagar [7] *vt* to investigate.

indebido,-a *a* (*desconsiderado*) undue; (*ilegal*) unlawful.

indecente *a* indecent.

indeciso,-a 1 *a* hesitant. **2** *m* (*en elecciones*) don't know.

indefenso,-a *a* defenceless.

indefinidamente *adv* indefinitely.

indefinido,-a *a* (*indeterminado*) indefinite; (*impreciso*) vague; (*tiempo verbal*) indefinite.

indemnización f (*acto*) indemnification; (*compensación*) compensation.

indemnizar [4] *vt* to compensate (**de, por** for).

independencia f independence.

independiente a (*libre*) independent; (*individualista*) self-reliant.

independientemente *adv* independently (**de** of); (*aparte de*) irrespective (**de** of).

indescriptible a indescribable.

indeseable a & *mf* undesirable.

indeterminado,-a a indefinite; (*impreciso*) vague; (*artículo*) indefinite.

indicación f (*señal*) indication; (*instrucción*) instruction.

indicador,-a *m* indicator.

indicar [1] *vt* to indicate.

indicativo,-a a indicative (**de** of); (**modo**) **i.** indicative (mode).

índice *m* (*de libro*) index; (*relación*) rate; **i. de natalidad/mortalidad** birth/death rate; (**dedo**) **i.** index finger.

indicio *m* indication (**de** of).

índico,-a *adj* Indian; **Océano I.** Indian Ocean.

indiferente a indifferent; **me es i.** it makes no difference to me.

indígena 1 a indigenous (**de** to). 2 *mf* native (**de** of).

indigestión f indigestion.

indignación f indignation.

indignar 1 *vt* to infuriate. 2 **indignarse** *vr* to be indignant (**por** at, about).

indio,-a a & *mf* Indian.

indirecta f *fam* insinuation.

indirecto,-a *adj* indirect.

indiscreto,-a a indiscreet.

indiscutible a indisputable.

indispensable a indispensable.

indisponer (*pp* **indispuesto**) 1 *vt* to make unwell. 2 **indisponerse** *vr* to become unwell.

indispuse *pt indef de* **indisponer.**

indistintamente *adv* **pueden escribir en inglés o en español i.** you can write in English or Spanish, it doesn't matter which.

individual a individual; **habitación i.** single room.

individuo *m* individual; (*tío*) bloke, guy.

índole f (*carácter*) character; (*clase, tipo*) kind.

inducir *vt* to lead.

indudable a indubitable; **es i. que** there is no doubt that.

induje *pt indef de* **inducir.**

indultar *vt* to pardon.

indumentaria *f* clothing.
industria *f* industry.
industrial *a* industrial.
industrialización *f* industrialization.
induzco *indic pres de* **inducir.**
ineficacia *f* (*ineptitud*) inefficiency; (*inutilidad*) ineffectiveness.
ineficaz *adj* (*inepto*) inefficient; (*inefectivo*) ineffective.
ineptitud *nf* ineptitude, incompetence.
inepto,-a 1 *a* inept. 2 *mf* incompetent person.
inerte *a* (*inanimado*) inert; (*inmóvil*) motionless.
inesperado,-a *a* (*fortuito*) unexpected; (*imprevisto*) sudden.
inestabilidad *f* instability.
inevitable *a* inevitable.
inexistente *a* non-existent.
inexperiencia *f* lack of experience.
inexplicable *a* inexplicable.
infalible *a* infallible.
infancia *f* childhood.
infantería *f* infantry.
infantil *a* **literatura i.** (*para niños*) children's literature. **2** (*aniñado*) childlike; (*peyorativo*) childish.
infarto *m* **i. (de miocardio)** heart attack.
infección *f* infection.
infeliz 1 *a* unhappy; (*desdichado*) unfortunate. **2** *mf fam* simpleton.
inferior 1 *a* (*más bajo*) lower; (*calidad*) inferior; (*cantidad*) lower. **2** *mf* (*persona*) subordinate.
infestado,-a *a* **i. de** infested with; **infestado de turistas** swarming with tourists.
infidelidad *f* unfaithfulness.
infierno *m* hell; (*horno*) inferno; *fam* **¡vete al i.!** go to hell!
infinidad *f* infinity; (*sinfín*) great number; **en i. de ocasiones** on countless occasions.
infinitivo,-a *a & m* infinitive.
infinito,-a 1 *a* infinite. **2** *m* infinity.
inflable *a* inflatable.
inflación *f* inflation.
inflamable *a* flammable.
inflamación *f* inflammation.
inflamar 1 *vt* to inflame; (*encender*) to set on fire. **2 inflamarse** *vr* to become inflamed; (*incendiarse*) to catch fire.
inflar 1 *vt* to inflate. **2 inflarse** *vr* to inflate.
inflexible *a* inflexible.

influencia *f* influence; **ejercer** *o* **tener i. sobre algn** to have an influence on sb.

influir 1 *vt* to influence. **2** *vi* to have influence; **i. en** *o* **sobre** to influence.

información *f* information; (*servicio telefónico*) directory enquiries *pl.*

informal *a* (*reunión, cena*) informal; (*comportamiento*) casual; (*persona*) unreliable.

informar 1 *vt* (*enterar*) to inform (**de** of); (*dar informes*) to report. **2 informarse** *vr* (*procurarse noticias*) to find out (**de** about); (*enterarse*) to enquire (**de** about).

informática *f* information technology, IT.

informe *m* report; **informes** references.

infracción *f* infringement.

infraestructura *f* infrastructure.

infringir [6] *vt* **i. una ley** to break a law.

infundir *vt* to infuse; (*idea etc*) to instil.

infusión *f* infusion.

ingeniero,-a *mf* engineer; **i. de caminos** civil engineer; **i. técnico** technician.

ingenio *m* (*talento*) talent; (*inventiva*) inventiveness; (*agudeza*) wit.

ingenioso,-a *a* ingenious; (*vivaz*) witty.

ingenuo,-a 1 *a* naïve. **2** *mf* naïve person.

ingle *f* groin.

inglés,-esa 1 *a* English. **2** *mf* (*hombre*) Englishman; (*mujer*) Englishwoman; **los ingleses** the English. **3** *m* (*idioma*) English.

ingratitud *f* ingratitude.

ingrediente *m* ingredient.

ingresar 1 *vt* (*dinero*) to pay in; (*enfermo*) to admit; **la ingresaron en el hospital** she was admitted to hospital. **2** *vi* to enter.

ingreso *m* (*dinero*) deposit; (*entrada*) entry (**en** into); (*admisión*) admission (**en** to); **ingresos** (*sueldo, renta*) income *sing;* (*beneficios*) revenue *sing.*

inhalador *m* inhaler.

inhalar *vt* to inhale.

inhumano,-a *a* inhumane; (*cruel*) inhuman.

inicial *a & f* initial.

iniciar 1 *vt* (*empezar*) to begin, start; (*discusión*) to initiate; (*una cosa nueva*) to pioneer. **2 iniciarse** *vr* to begin, start.

iniciativa *f* initiative; **por i. propia** on one's own initiative.

inicio *m* beginning, start.

ininterrumpido,-a *a* uninterrupted.

injerirse *vr* to interfere (**en** in).

injuria *f* insult.

injusticia *f* injustice.

injustificado,-a *a* unjustified.

injusto,-a *a* unjust.

inmaduro,-a *a* immature.

inmediatamente *adv* immediately, at once.

inmediato,-a *a* (*en el tiempo*) immediate; (*en el espacio*) next (**a** to); **de i.** at once.

inmejorable *a* (*trabajo*) excellent; (*precio*) unbeatable.

inmenso,-a *a* immense.

inmigración *f* immigration.

inmigrante *mf* immigrant.

inminente *a* imminent.

inmiscuirse *vr* to interfere (**en** in).

inmobiliaria *f* estate agency, *US* real estate company.

inmoral *a* immoral.

inmortal *a & mf* immortal.

inmóvil *a* motionless.

inmovilizar [4] *vt* to immobilize.

inmueble *m* building.

inmune *a* immune (**a** to).

inmunidad *f* immunity (**contra** to).

inmunizar [4] *vt* to immunize (**contra** against).

innato,-a *a* innate.

innecesario,-a *a* unnecessary.

innegable *a* undeniable.

innovación *f* innovation.

innumerable *a* countless.

inocencia *f* innocence; (*ingenuidad*) naïvety.

inocentada *f* ≈ April Fools' joke.

inocente **1** *a* innocent. **2** *mf* innocent; **día de los Inocentes** Holy Innocents' Day, 28th December, ≈ April Fools' Day.

inocuo,-a *a* innocuous.

inofensivo,-a *a* harmless.

inolvidable *a* unforgettable.

inoportuno,-a *a* inappropriate.

inoxidable *a* **acero i.** stainless steel.

inquietante *a* worrying.

inquietar **1** *vt* to worry. **2 inquietarse** *vr* to worry (**por** about).

inquieto,-a *a* (*preocupado*) worried (**por** about); (*intranquilo*) restless.

inquietud *f* (*preocupación*) worry; (*agitación*) restlessness.

inquilino,-a *mf* tenant.

insaciable *a* insatiable.

insatisfecho,-a *a* dissatisfied.

inscribir (*pp* **inscrito**) **1** *vt* (*registrar*) to register; (*matricular*) to enrol; (*grabar*) to inscribe. **2 inscribirse** *vr* (*registrarse*) to register; (*hacerse miembro*) to join; (*matricularse*) to enrol; **inscribirse en un club** to join a club.

inscripción *f* (*matriculación*) enrolment; (*escrito etc*) inscription.

insecticida *m* insecticide.

insecto *m* insect.

inseguridad *f* (*falta de confianza*) insecurity; (*duda*) uncertainty; (*peligro*) lack of safety.

insensato,-a 1 *a* foolish. **2** *mf* fool.

insensible *a* (*indiferente*) unfeeling; (*imperceptible*) imperceptible; (*miembro*) numb.

inseparable *a* inseparable.

insertar *vt* to insert.

inservible *a* useless.

insignia *f* badge.

insignificante *a* insignificant.

insinuar *vt* to insinuate.

insistir *vi* to insist (**en** on).

insolación *f* sunstroke.

insolente *a* insolent.

insólito,-a *a* (*poco usual*) unusual; (*extraño*) strange, odd.

insomnio *m* insomnia.

insoportable *a* unbearable.

insospechado,-a *a* unsuspected.

inspección *f* inspection.

inspeccionar *vt* to inspect.

inspector,-a *mf* inspector; **i. de Hacienda** tax inspector.

inspiración *f* inspiration; (*inhalación*) inhalation.

inspirar 1 *vt* to inspire; (*inhalar*) to inhale. **2 inspirarse** *vr* **inspirarse en** to be inspired by.

instalación *f* installation; **instalaciones deportivas** sports facilities.

instalar 1 *vt* to install; (*erigir*) to set up. **2 instalarse** *vr* to settle (down).

instancia *f* (*solicitud*) request; **a instancia(s) de** at the request of; **en última i.** as a last resort.

instantáneamente *adv* instantly.

instantáneo,-a *a* instantaneous; **café i.** instant coffee.

instante *m* instant; **a cada i.** constantly; **al i.** immediately.

instaurar *vt* to found.

instigar [7] *vt* to instigate.

instintivo,-a *a* instinctive.
instinto *m* instinct; **por i.** instinctively.
institución *f* institution.
instituto *m* institute; (*colegio*) state secondary school, *US* high school.
institutriz *f* governess.
instrucción *f* (*educación*) education; **instrucciones para el** *o* **de uso**
   instructions *o* directions for use.
instructivo,-a *a* instructive.
instruir *vt* to instruct; (*enseñar*) to educate.
instrumento *m* instrument.
insubordinarse *vr* to rebel (**contra** against).
insuficiente 1 *a* insufficient. **2** *m* (*nota*) fail.
insultar *vt* to insult.
insulto *m* insult.
insurrección *f* insurrection.
intacto,-a *a* intact.
integral *a* integral; **pan i.** wholemeal bread.
integrar 1 *vt* to integrate; (*formar*) to compose. **2 integrarse** *vr* to
   integrate (**en** with).
integridad *f* integrity.
íntegro,-a *a* (*entero*) whole; (*honrado*) upright; **versión íntegra** un-
   abridged version.
intelectual *a* & *mf* intellectual.
inteligencia *f* intelligence.
inteligente *a* intelligent.
inteligible *a* intelligible.
intemperie *f* **a la i.** in the open (air).
intención *f* intention; **con i.** deliberately; **tener la i. de hacer algo** to
   intend to do sth.
intencionadamente *adv* on purpose.
intencionado,-a *a* deliberate.
intensidad *f* intensity; (*del viento*) force.
intensificar [1] *vt*, **intensificarse** *vr* to intensify; (*relación*) to
   strengthen.
intenso,-a *a* intense.
intentar *vt* to try.
intento *m* attempt; **i. de suicidio** attempted suicide.
intercambiar *vt* to exchange.
interceder *vi* to intercede.
interceptar *vt* (*detener*) to intercept; (*carretera*) to block; (*tráfico*) to
   hold up.
interés *m* interest; (*provecho personal*) self-interest; **tener i. en** *o* **por** to be

interested in; **tipos de i.** interest rates.
interesante *a* interesting.
interesar 1 *vt* (*tener interés*) to interest; (*concernir*) to concern. **2** *vi* (*ser importante*) to be of interest. **3 interesarse** *vr* **interesarse por** *o* **en** to be interested in.
interferencia *f* interference; (*en radio, televisión*) jamming.
interfono *m* intercom.
interior 1 *a* inner; **ropa i.** underwear; (*política, vuelo*) domestic; (*región*) inland. **2** *m* inside; (*de un país*) interior; **Ministerio del I.** Home Office, *US* Department of the Interior.
interjección *f* interjection.
interlocutor,-a *mf* speaker.
intermediario *m* middleman.
intermedio,-a 1 *a* intermediate. **2** *m* (*en televisión*) break.
interminable *a* endless.
intermitente 1 *a* intermittent. **2** *m* (*de automóvil*) indicator.
internacional *a* international.
internado *m* (*colegio*) boarding school.
interno,-a 1 *a* internal; (*política*) domestic. **2** *mf* (*alumno*) boarder.
interpretación *f* interpretation.
interpretar *vt* to interpret; (*papel*) to play; (*obra*) to perform; (*concierto*) to perform; (*canción*) to sing.
intérprete *mf* (*traductor*) interpreter; (*actor, músico*) performer; (*cantante*) singer.
interrogación *f* interrogation; **(signo de) i.** question mark.
interrogar [7] *vt* to question; (*testigo etc*) to interrogate.
interrogatorio *m* interrogation.
interrumpir *vt* to interrupt; (*tráfico*) to block.
interruptor *m* switch.
interurbano,-a *a* intercity; **conferencia interurbana** long-distance call.
intervalo *m* interval.
intervenir 1 *vi* (*mediar*) to intervene (**en** in); (*participar*) take part (**en** in). **2** *vt* (*teléfono*) to tap.
interviú *m* (*pl* **interviús**) interview.
intestino *m* intestine.
intimidar *vt* to intimidate.
íntimo,-a *a* intimate; (*vida*) private; (*amigo*) close.
intolerante 1 *a* intolerant. **2** *mf* intolerant person.
intoxicación *f* poisoning; **i. alimenticia** food poisoning.
intranquilizarse *vr* to get worried.
intransitivo,-a *a* intransitive.
intriga *f* intrigue; (*trama*) plot.

intrigar [7] **1** *vt* (*interesar*) to intrigue. **2** *vi* (*maquinar*) to plot.

intrínseco,-a *a* intrinsic.

introducir *vt* to introduce; (*meter*) to insert.

introvertido,-a 1 *a* introverted. **2** *mf* introvert.

intruso,-a *mf* intruder.

intuición *f* intuition.

intuir *vt* to know by intuition.

inundación *f* flood.

inusitado,-a *a* unusual.

inútil 1 *a* useless; (*esfuerzo*, *intento*) pointless. **2** *mf fam* good-for-
nothing.

inutilizar [4] *vt* to make useless.

invadir *vt* to invade; **los estudiantes invadieron la calle** students poured
out onto the street.

inválido,-a 1 *a* (*nulo*) invalid; (*minusválido*) disabled. **2** *mf* disabled
person.

invariable *a* invariable.

invasión *f* invasion.

invencible *a* (*enemigo*) invincible; (*obstáculo*) insurmountable.

invención *f* (*invento*) invention; (*mentira*) fabrication.

inventar *vt* (*crear*) to invent; (*excusa*, *mentira*) to concoct.

inventario *m* inventory.

invento *m* invention.

invernadero *m* greenhouse.

invernal *a* winter.

inversión *f* inversion; (*de dinero*) investment.

inverso,-a *a* **en sentido i.** in the opposite direction; **en orden i.** in reverse
order.

invertir [5] *vt* (*orden*) to invert; (*dinero*) to invest (**en** in); (*tiempo*) to
spend (**en** on).

investigación *f* (*policial etc*) investigation; (*científica*) research.

investigar [7] *vt* (*indagar*) to investigate; (*científicamente*) to research.

invierno *m* winter.

invisible *a* invisible.

invitado,-a 1 *a* invited. **2** *mf* guest.

invitar *vt* to invite; **me invitó a una copa** he treated me to a drink.

involuntario,-a *a* involuntary; (*impremeditado*) unintentional.

inyección *f* injection; **poner una i.** to give an injection.

ir 1 *vi* to go; **¡vamos!** let's go!; **¡ya voy!** (I'm) coming!; **¿cómo le va el nuevo
trabajo?** how is he getting on in his new job?; **el negro no te va** black
doesn't suit you; **ir con falda** to wear a skirt; **ir de blanco/de uniforme** to
be dressed in white/in uniform; **va para abogado** he's studying to be a

lawyer; **ir por la derecha** to keep (to the) right; **ve (a) por agua** go and fetch some water; **voy por la página noventa** I've got as far as page ninety; **en lo que va de año** so far this year; **ir a parar** to end up; **¡qué va!** of course not!; **va a lo suyo** he looks after his own interests; **¡vamos a ver!** let's see!; **¡vaya!** fancy that; **¡vaya moto!** what a bike! **2** *v aux* **ir andando** to go on foot; **va mejorando** she's improving; **ya van rotos tres** three (of them) have already been broken; **iba a decir que . . .** I was going to say that . . .; **va a llover** it's going to rain. **3 irse** *vr* (*marcharse*) to go away; **me voy** I'm off; **¡vete!** go away!; **¡vámonos!** let's go!; **¡vete a casa!** go home!; **¿por dónde se va a . . .?** which is the way to . . .?

ira *f* rage.

iraní *a & mf* (*pl* **iraníes**) Iranian.

iraquí *a & mf* (*pl* **iraquíes**) Iraqi.

irascible *a* irascible.

iris *m inv* **arco i.** rainbow.

irlandés,-esa 1 *adj* Irish. **2** *mf* (*hombre*) Irishman; (*mujer*) Irish-woman; **los irlandeses** the Irish. **3** *m* (*idioma*) Irish.

ironía *f* irony.

irónico,-a *a* ironic.

irracional *a* irrational.

irreal *a* unreal.

irregular *a* irregular.

irremediable *a* incurable.

irresistible *a* (*impulso, persona*) irresistible; (*insoportable*) unbearable.

irresponsable *a* irresponsible.

irritar 1 *vt* to irritate. **2 irritarse** *vr* to become irritated.

irrompible *a* unbreakable.

irrumpir *vi* to burst (**en** into).

isla *f* island.

islámico,-a *a* Islamic.

israelí *a & mf* (*pl* **israelíes**) Israeli.

italiano,-a 1 *a* Italian. **2** *mf* (*persona*) Italian. **3** *m* (*idioma*) Italian.

itinerario *m* itinerary.

IVA *m abr de* **impuesto sobre el valor añadido** value-added tax, VAT.

izqda., izqd^a *abr de* **izquierda** left.

izqdo., izqd^o *abr de* **izquierdo** left.

izquierda *f* left; (*mano*) left hand; **a la i.** on the left; **girar a la i.** to turn left.

izquierdo,-a *a* left.

J

jabalí m (pl **jabalíes**) wild boar.

jabalina f javelin.

jabón m soap; **j. de afeitar/tocador** shaving/toilet soap.

jabonera f soap dish.

jaca f gelding.

jacaré m Am caiman.

jacinto m hyacinth.

jactarse vr to boast (**de** about).

jadear vi to pant.

jalea f jelly.

jaleo m (alboroto) din; (confusión) muddle.

jalón m Am lift.

jamás adv never; **j. he estado allí** I have never been there; **el mejor libro que j. se ha escrito** the best book ever written; **nunca j.** never again.

jamón m ham; **j. de York/serrano** boiled/cured ham.

japonés,-esa a & mf Japanese; **los japoneses** the Japanese.

jaque m check; **j. mate** checkmate; **j. al rey** check.

jaqueca f migraine.

jarabe m syrup; **j. para la tos** cough mixture.

jardín m garden; **j. botánico** botanical garden; **j. de infancia** nursery school.

jardinero,-a mf gardener.

jarra f pitcher.

jarro m (recipiente) jug; (contenido) jugful.

jarrón m vase.

jaula f cage.

jazmín m jasmine.

J.C. abr de **Jesucristo** Jesus Christ, J.C.

jeep m jeep.

jefa f manageress.

jefatura f (cargo, dirección) leadership; (sede) central office.

jefe m head; (de empresa) manager; (de partido) leader; **J. de Estado** Head of State.

jengibre m ginger.

jerez m sherry.

jerga f (técnica) jargon; (vulgar) slang.

jeringa f syringe.

jeringuilla f (hypodermic) syringe.

jeroglífico m hieroglyphic; (juego) rebus.

jersey m (pl **jerseis**) pullover.

Jesucristo *m* Jesus Christ.
Jesús 1 *m* Jesus. **2** *interj* (*al estornudar*) bless you!
jíbaro,-a *mf Am* peasant.
jícara *f Am* gourd.
jilguero *m* goldfinch.
jinete *m* horseman.
jirafa *f* giraffe.
jirón *m* (*trozo desgarrado*) strip; (*pedazo suelto*) scrap; **hecho jirones** in tatters.
JJOO *mpl abr de* **Juegos Olímpicos** Olympic Games.
jornada *f* **j. (laboral)** (*día de trabajo*) working day; **trabajo de media j./j. completa** part-time/full-time work.
jornal *m* day's wage.
jornalero,-a *mf* day labourer.
joroba *f* hump.
jorobado,-a 1 *a* hunchbacked. **2** *mf* hunchback.
joven 1 *a* young; **de aspecto j.** young-looking. **2** *mf* (*hombre*) young man; (*mujer*) young woman; **de j.** as a young man/woman; **los jóvenes** young people.
joya *f* jewel; **ser una j.** (*persona*) to be a gem.
joyería *f* (*tienda*) jewellery shop.
joyero,-a 1 *mf* jeweller. **2** *m* jewel case.
jubilado,-a 1 *a* retired. **2** *mf* retired person; **los jubilados** retired people.
judía *f* bean; **j. verde** green bean.
judío,-a 1 *a* Jewish. **2** *mf* Jew.
judo *m* judo.
juego *m* game; (*conjunto de piezas*) set; (*apuestas*) gambling; **j. de azar** game of chance; **j. de cartas** card game; **Juegos Olímpicos** Olympic Games; **terreno de j.** field; **fuera de j.** offside; **j. de café/té** coffee/tea service; **ir a j. con** to match.
juerga *f fam* rave-up; **ir de j.** to go on a binge.
jueves *m inv* Thursday; **J. Santo** Maundy Thursday.
juez,-a *mf* judge; **j. de línea** linesman.
jugada *f* move; *fam* dirty trick.
jugador,-a player; (*apostador*) gambler.
jugar 1 *vi* to play; **j. a(l) fútbol** to play football; **j. sucio** to play dirty. **2** *vt* to play; (*apostar*) to bet. **3 jugarse** *vr* (*arriesgar*) to risk; (*apostar*) to bet.
jugo *m* juice.
juguete *m* toy; **pistola de j.** toy gun.
juicio *m* (*facultad mental*) judgement; (*sensatez*) reason; (*opinión*) opinion; (*en tribunal*) trial; **a j. de** in the opinion of; **a mi j.** in my opinion; **perder el j.** to go mad.

julio *m* July.

junco *m* rush.

jungla *f* jungle.

junio *m* June.

júnior *a* junior.

junta *f* (*reunión*) meeting; (*dirección*) board; (*gobierno militar*) junta; (*parlamento regional*) regional parliament.

juntar 1 *vt* (*unir*) to join; (*piezas*) to assemble; (*dinero*) to raise. 2 **juntarse** *vr* (*unirse*) to join; (*ríos, caminos*) to meet; (*personas*) to gather.

junto,-a 1 *a* together. 2 **junto** *adv* **j. con** together with; **j. a** next to.

jurado *m* jury.

juramento *m* oath; **bajo j.** under oath.

jurar 1 *vi* to swear. 2 *vt* to swear; **j. el cargo** to take the oath of office.

jurídico,-a *a* legal.

justicia *f* justice; **tomarse la j. por su mano** to take the law into one's own hands.

justificado,-a *a* justified.

justificante *m* written proof.

justamente *adv* **¡j.!** precisely! **j. detrás de.** right behind.

justo,-a 1 *a* just; (*apretado*) (*ropa*) tight; (*exacto*) accurate; **un trato j.** a fair deal; **estamos justos de tiempo** we're pressed for time; **llegamos en el momento j. en que salían** we arrived just as they were leaving; **lo j.** just enough. 2 **justo** *adv* (*exactamente*) precisely; **j. al lado de** right beside.

juvenil *a* young; **ropa j.** (*de joven*) young people's clothes; **delincuencia j.** juvenile delinquency.

juventud *f* (*edad*) youth; (*jóvenes*) young people.

juzgado *m* court.

juzgar [7] *vt* to judge; **a j. por ...** judging by ...

K

kárate *m* karate.
kilo *m* (*medida*) kilo.
kilogramo *m* kilogram.
kilometraje *m* ≈ mileage.
kilómetro *m* kilometre.
kiosco *m* kiosk.
kiwi *m* (*fruto*) kiwi (fruit).
kleenex^(R) *m* tissue.

L

la¹ 1 *art def f* the. **2** *pron dem* the one; **la del vestido azul** the one in the blue dress.

la² ** *pron pers f* (*persona*) her; (*usted*) you; (*cosa*) it; **la invitaré I'll invite her along; **ya la avisaremos, señora** we'll let you know, madam; **no la dejes abierta** don't leave it open.

labio *m* lip.

labor *f* job; (*de costura*) needlework.

laborable *a* **día l.** working day.

laboral *a* industrial; **accidente l.** industrial accident; **jornada l.** working day.

laboratorio *m* laboratory.

laborista *a* **partido l.** Labour Party.

laca *f* hairspray; **l. de uñas** nail polish.

ladera *f* slope.

lado *m* side; **a un l.** aside; **al l.** close by, nearby; **al l. de** next to; **ponte de l.** stand sideways; **por todos lados** on all sides; **por otro l.** (*además*) moreover; **por un l. ..., por otro l. ...** on the one hand ..., on the other hand ...

ladrar *vi* to bark.

ladrillo *m* brick.

ladrón,-ona *mf* thief.

lagartija *f* small lizard.

lagarto *m* lizard.

lago *m* lake.

lágrima *f* tear.

laguna *f* small lake.

lamentar 1 *vt* to regret; **lo lamento** I'm sorry. **2 lamentarse** *vr* to complain.

lamer *vt* to lick.

lámina *f* sheet.

lámpara *f* lamp; (*bombilla*) bulb.

lana *f* wool.

lancha *f* motorboat; **l. motora** speedboat; **l. neumática** rubber dinghy; **l. salvavidas** lifeboat.

langosta *f* lobster; (*insecto*) locust.

langostino *m* king prawn.

lanza *f* spear.

lanzar [4] **1** *vt* (*arrojar*) to throw; (*grito*) to let out; (*ataque, producto*) to launch. **2 lanzarse** *vr* to throw oneself.

lápiz *m* pencil; **l. de labios** lipstick; **l. de ojos** eyeliner.

largo,-a 1 *a* long; **a lo l. de** (*espacio*) along; (*tiempo*) through; **a la larga** in the long run. **2** *m* (*longitud*) length; **¿cuánto tiene de l.?** how long is it? **3** **largo** *adv fam* **¡l. (de aquí)!** clear off!; **esto va para l.** this is going to last a long time.

largometraje *m* feature film.

las¹ **1** *art def fpl* the. **2** *pron dem* **l. que** (*personas*) those who; (*objetos*) those that; **toma l. que quieras** take whichever ones you want.

las² *pron pers fpl* (*ellas*) them; (*ustedes*) you; **no l. rompas** don't break them; **l. llamaré mañana (a ustedes)** I'll call you tomorrow.

lástima *f* pity; **¡qué l.!** what a pity!; **es una l. que ...** it's a pity (that) ...

lata¹ *f* (*envase*) tin, can; (*hojalata*) tin(plate); **en l.** tinned, canned.

lata² *f fam* drag; **dar la l.** to be a nuisance.

lateral *a* side; **escalón l.** (*en letrero*) ramp.

latido *m* beat.

látigo *m* whip.

latín *m* Latin.

latinomericano,-a *a & mf* Latin American.

latir *vi* to beat.

latón *m* brass.

laucha *f Am* mouse.

laurel *m* bay leaf.

lava *f* lava.

lavable *a* washable.

lavabo *m* (*pila*) washbasin; (*cuarto de aseo*) washroom; (*retrete*) toilet.

lavado *m* washing; **l. en seco** dry-cleaning.

lavadora *f* washing machine.

lavanda *f* lavender.

lavandería *f* (*autoservicio*) launderette, *US* laundromat; (*atendida por personal*) laundry.

lavaplatos *m inv* dishwasher.

lavar *vt* to wash.

lavavajillas *m inv* dishwasher.

laxante *a & m* laxative.

lazo *m* (*adorno*) bow; (*nudo*) knot; **lazos** (*vínculo*) links.

le 1 *pron pers mf* (*objeto indirecto*) (*a él*) (to/for) him; (*a ella*) (to/for) her; (*a cosa*) (to/for) it; (*a usted*) (to/for) you; **lávale la cara** wash his face; **le compraré uno** I'll buy one for her; **¿qué le pasa (a usted)?** what's the matter with you? **2** *pron pers m* (*objeto directo*) (*él*) him; (*usted*) you; **no le oigo** I can't hear him; **no quiero molestarle** I don't wish to disturb you.

leal *a* faithful.

lección *f* lesson.

leche *f* milk; **dientes de l.** milk teeth; **l. descremada** *o* **desnatada** skimmed milk.

lechuga *f* lettuce.

lechuza *f* owl.

lector,-a *mf (persona)* reader; *(de colegio)* (language) assistant.

lectura *f* reading.

leer *vt* to read.

legal *a* legal.

legalizar [4] *vt* to legalize; *(documento)* to authenticate.

legislación *f* legislation.

legítimo,-a *a* legitimate; *(auténtico)* real; **en legítima defensa** in self-defence; **oro l.** pure gold.

legumbres *fpl* pulses.

lejano,-a *a* far-off.

lejía *f* bleach.

lejos *adv* far (away); **a lo l.** in the distance; **de l.** from a distance; *fig* **sin ir más l.** to take an obvious example.

lema *m* motto.

lencería *f (prendas)* lingerie; *(ropa blanca)* linen (goods *pl*).

lengua *f* tongue; *(idioma)* language; **l. materna** mother tongue.

lenguado *m* sole.

lenguaje *m* language; **l. corporal** body language.

lente *mf* lens; **lentes de contacto** contact lenses.

lenteja *f* lentil.

lentilla *f* contact lens.

lento,-a *a* slow; **a fuego l.** on a low heat.

leña *f* firewood.

leño *m* log.

león *m* lion.

leopardo *m* leopard.

leotardos *mpl* thick tights.

les *pron pers mfpl (a ellos/ellas)* them; *(a ustedes)* you; **dales el dinero** give them the money; **les he comprado un regalo** I've bought you/them a present; **l. esperaré** I shall wait for you/them; **no quiero molestarles** I don't wish to disturb you/them.

lesión *f (física)* injury.

lesionar *vt* to injure.

letal *a* lethal.

letargo *m* lethargy.

letra *f* letter; *(escritura)* (hand)writing; *(de canción)* lyrics *pl*; **l. de imprenta** block capitals; **l. mayúscula** capital letter; **l. minúscula** small letter; **l. (de cambio)** bill of exchange; *(carrera)* **letras** arts.

letrero *m* (*aviso*) notice; (*cartel*) poster.

levadura *f* yeast; **l. en polvo** baking powder.

levantamiento *m* lifting; (*insurrección*) uprising; **l. de pesos** weight-lifting.

levantar 1 *vt* to lift; (*mano, voz*) to raise; (*edificio*) to erect; (*ánimos*) to raise. **2** *vr* **levantarse** to get up; (*ponerse de pie*) to stand up.

levante *m* (**el**) **L.** Levante, the regions of Valencia and Murcia.

leve *a* (*ligero*) light; (*de poca importancia*) slight.

levemente *adv* slightly.

ley *f* law; **aprobar una l.** to pass a bill; **oro de l.** pure gold; **plata de l.** sterling silver.

leyenda *f* (*relato*) legend; (*bajo ilustración*) caption.

liar 1 *vt* (*envolver*) to wrap up; (*cigarrillo*) to roll; (*enredar*) to muddle up; (*confundir*) to confuse. **2 liarse** *vr* (*embarullarse*) to get muddled up.

liberal 1 *a* liberal; (*generoso*) generous; (*carácter*) open-minded; **profesión l.** profession. **2** *mf* liberal.

liberar *vt* (*país*) to liberate; (*prisionero*) to release.

libertad *f* freedom; (**en**) **l. bajo palabra/fianza** (on) parole/bail; (**en**) **l. condicional** (on) parole.

libio,-a *a & mf* Libyan.

libra *f* pound; **l. esterlina** pound sterling.

librar 1 *vt* to free; (*preso*) to release. **2 librarse** *vr* to escape; **librarse de algn** to get rid of sb.

libre *a* free; (*sin restricción*) open to the public; **entrada l.** admission free; **l. de impuestos** tax-free.

librería *f* (*tienda*) bookshop, *US* bookstore; (*estante*) bookcase.

libreta *f* notebook.

libro *m* book; **l. de texto** textbook.

licencia *f* (*permiso*) permission; (*documentos*) licence; *Am* driving licence, *US* driver's license.

licenciado,-a *mf* graduate; *Am* lawyer; **l. en Ciencias** Bachelor of Science.

licenciatura *f* (*título*) (bachelor's) degree (course); (*carrera*) degree (course).

licor *m* spirits *pl*, *US* licor.

licuadora *f* liquidizer.

líder *mf* leader.

lidia *f* bullfighting.

lidiar *vt* to fight.

liebre *f* hare.

liga *f* league.

ligar [7] **1** *vt* to join. **2** *vi fam* **l. con una chica** to chat up a girl.

ligereza *f* lightness; (*frivolidad*) flippancy; (*acto*) indiscretion; (*rapidez*) speed.

ligeramente *adv* (*levemente*) lightly; (*un poco*) slightly.

ligero,-a 1 *a* (*peso*) light; (*veloz*) quick; (*leve*) slight; **l. de ropa** lightly clad; **brisa/comida ligera** light breeze/meal. **2** *adv* **ligero** (*rápido*) fast.

liguero *m* suspenders *pl*, *US* garter belt.

lija *f* sandpaper; **papel de l.** sandpaper.

lima *f* (*herramienta*) file; **l. de uñas** nailfile.

limar *vt* to file.

limitar 1 *vt* to restrict. **2** *vi* **l. con** to border on.

límite *m* limit; (*de país*) border; **fecha l.** deadline; **velocidad l.** maximum speed.

limón *m* lemon.

limonada *f* lemon squash.

limonero *m* lemon tree.

limpiaparabrisas *m inv* windscreen *o US* windshield wiper.

limpiar *vt* to clean; (*con un trapo*) to wipe; (*zapatos*) to polish.

limpieza *f* (*calidad*) cleanliness; (*acción*) cleaning.

limpio,-a 1 *a* (*aseado*) clean; (*neto*) net; **juego l.** fair play. **2** *adv* **limpio** fairly; **jugar l.** to play fair.

lindar *vi* **l. con** to border on.

lindo,-a 1 *a* (*bonito*) pretty; **de lo l.** a great deal. **2** *adv* *Am* (*bien*) nicely.

línea *f* line; **l. aérea** airline; **en líneas generales** roughly speaking; **guardar la l.** to watch one's figure.

lino *m* (*fibra*) linen.

linterna *f* torch.

lío *m* (*paquete*) bundle; (*embrollo*) mess; **hacerse un l.** to get mixed up; **meterse en líos** to get into trouble.

liquidación *f* (*saldo*) clearance sale; (*de deuda, cuenta*) settling.

liquidar 1 *vt* (*deuda, cuenta*) to settle; (*mercancías*) to sell off. **2** *vr* **liquidarse a algn** (*matar*) to bump sb off.

líquido,-a 1 *a* liquid; (*cantidad*) net. **2** *m* liquid.

lirio *m* iris.

lisiado,-a 1 *a* crippled. **2** *mf* cripple.

liso,-a *a* (*superficie*) smooth; (*pelo, falda*) straight; (*tela*) self-coloured; *Am* (*desvergonzado*) rude.

lista *f* (*relación*) list; (*franja*) stripe; **l. de espera** waiting list; (*en avión*) standby; **pasar l.** to call the register; **de/a listas** striped.

listín *m* **l. telefónico** telephone directory.

listo,-a *a* **ser l.** to be clever; **estar l.** to be ready.

litera *f* (*cama*) bunk bed; (*en tren*) couchette.

literatura *f* literature.

litigio *m* lawsuit.

litoral 1 *m* coast. **2** *a* coastal.

litro *m* litre.

llaga *f* sore; (*herida*) wound.

llama *f* flame; **en llamas** in flames.

llamada *f* call; **l. interurbana** long-distance call.

llamar 1 *vt* to call; **l. (por teléfono)** to call; **l. la atención** to attract attention. **2** *vi* (*a la puerta*) to knock. **3 llamarse** *vr* to be called; **¿cómo te llamas?** what's your name?

llano,-a 1 *a* (*superficie*) flat. **2** *m* plain.

llanta *f* (*de rueda*) wheel rim; *Am* tyre, *US* tire.

llanto *m* crying.

llanura *f* plain.

llave *f* key; (*interruptor*) switch; (*herramienta*) spanner; **cerrar con l.** to lock; (*de coche*) **l. de contacto** ignition key; **l. inglesa** adjustable spanner; **l. de paso** stopcock.

llavero *m* key ring.

llegada *f* arrival; (*meta*) finish.

llegar [7] *vi* to arrive; **l. a Madrid** to arrive in Madrid; **¿llegas al techo?** can you reach the ceiling?; **l. a** + *infinitivo* to go so far as to; **l. a ser** to become.

llenar 1 *vt* to fill; (*satisfacer*) to satisfy. **2** *vi* (*comida*) to be filling. **3 llenarse** *vr* to fill (up).

lleno,-a *a* full (up).

llevar 1 *vt* to take; (*hacia el oyente*) to bring; (*transportar*) to carry; (*prenda*) to wear; (*negocio*) to be in charge of; **llevo dos años aquí** I've been here for two years; **esto lleva mucho tiempo** this takes a long time. **2** *v aux* **l.** + *gerundio* to have been + *present participle*; **llevo dos años estudiando español** I've been studying Spanish for two years. ‖ **l.** + *participio pasado* to have + *past participle*; **llevaba escritas seis cartas** I had written six letters. **3 llevarse** *vr* to take away; (*premio*) to win; (*estar de moda*) to be fashionable; **l. bien con algn** to get on well with sb.

llorar *vi* to cry.

llover [4] *v impers* to rain.

llovizna *f* drizzle.

lluvia *f* rain.

lluvioso,-a *a* rainy.

lo¹ *art def neutro* the; **lo mismo** the same thing; **lo mío** mine; **lo tuyo** yours.

lo² *pron pers m & neutro* (*cosa*) it; **debes hacerlo** you must do it; (*no se traduce*) **no se lo dije** I didn't tell her; **lo que ...** what ...; **lo cual ...** which ...; **lo de ...** the business of ...; **cuéntame lo del juicio** tell me about the trial.

lobo *m* wolf; **como boca de l.** pitch-dark.

local 1 *a* local. **2** *m* (*recinto*) premises *pl*.

localidad *f* (*pueblo*) locality; (*asiento*) seat.

localizar [4] *vt* (*encontrar*) to find; (*fuego, dolor*) to localize.

loción *f* lotion.

loco,-a 1 *a* mad; **a lo l.** crazily; **l. por** crazy about; **volverse l.** to go mad. **2** *mf* madman; madwoman.

locomotora *f* locomotive.

locura *f* madness.

locutor,-a *mf* presenter.

locutorio *m* telephone booth.

lodo *m* mud.

lógico,-a *a* logical; **era l. que ocurriera** it was bound to happen.

lograr *vt* to get, obtain; (*premio*) to win; (*meta*) to achieve; **l. hacer algo** to manage to do something.

lombriz *f* earthworm.

lomo *m* back; (*para filete*) loin.

lona *f* canvas.

loncha *f* slice.

lonchería *f Am* snack bar.

longaniza *f* spicy (pork) sausage.

longitud *f* length; **dos metros de l.** two metres long; **salto de l.** long jump.

lonja *f* market.

loquería *f Am* mental hospital.

lord *m* (*pl* **lores**) lord; **Cámara de los Lores** House of Lords.

loro *m* parrot.

los¹ *art def mpl* the. **2** *pron* **l. que** (*personas*) those who; (*cosas*) the ones (that); **toma l. que quieras** take whichever ones you want. **esos son l. míos/tuyos** these are mine/yours.

los² *pron pers mpl* them; **¿l. has visto?** have you seen them?

losa *f* slab.

lote *m* set; (*de productos*) lot.

lotería *f* lottery; **tocarle la l. a algn** to win a prize in the lottery.

loza *f* (*material*) earthenware; (*vajilla*) crockery.

lubricante *m* lubricant.

lucir 1 *vi* (*brillar*) to shine. **2** *vt* (*ropas*) to sport. **3 lucirse** *vr* (*hacer buen papel*) to do very well; (*pavonearse*) to show off.

lucha *f* fight; (*deporte*) wrestling; **l. libre** free-style wrestling.

luchar *vi* to fight; (*como deporte*) to wrestle.

luego 1 *adv* (*después*) then, next; (*más tarde*) later (on); **¡hasta l.!** so long!; *Am* **l. de** after; **desde l.** of course. **2** *conj* therefore.

lugar *m* place; **en primer l.** in the first place; **en l. de** instead of; **sin l. a dudas** without a doubt; **tener l.** to take place; **dar l. a** to give rise to.

lujo *m* luxury.

lujuria *f* lust.

lumbre *f* fire.

luminoso,-a *a* luminous; *fig* bright.

luna *f* moon; (*espejo*) mirror; *fig* **estar en la l.** to have one's head in the clouds; **l. llena** full moon; **l. de miel** honeymoon.

lunar *m* (*en la ropa*) dot; (*en la piel*) mole.

lunes *m inv* Monday.

lupa *f* magnifying glass.

lustre *m* shine.

luto *m* mourning.

luz *f* light; **apagar la l.** to put out the light; **dar a l.** (*parir*) to give birth to; **luces de cruce** dipped headlights; **luces de posición** sidelights; **luces largas** headlights *pl*; **traje de luces** bullfighter's costume.

luzco *indic pres de* **lucir**.

M

macana *f Am* (*palo*) club; (*trasto*) rubbish.

macanear *vt Am* to make up.

macarrones *mpl* macaroni *sing*.

macedonia *f* fruit salad.

maceta *f* flowerpot.

machacar [1] *vt* to crush.

machista *a & m* male chauvinist.

macho 1 *a* male; *fam* (*viril*) manly. **2** *m* male; *fam* (*hombre viril*) macho.

machote *m Am* rough draft.

macizo,-a *a* solid.

macuto *m* haversack.

madeja *f* hank.

madera *f* wood; (*de construcción*) timber, *US* lumber; **de m.** wooden.

madrastra *f* stepmother.

madre 1 *f* mother; **m. de familia** housewife; **m. política** mother-in-law; **m. soltera** unmarried mother. **2** *interj* **¡m. mía!** good heavens!

madrina *f* (*de bautizo*) godmother; (*de boda*) ≈ bridesmaid.

madrugada *f* small hours *pl*; **de m.** in the (wee) small hours; **las tres de la m.** three o'clock in the morning.

madrugador,-a 1 *a* early rising. **2** *mf* early riser.

madrugar [7] *vi* to get up early.

madurar *vi* (*persona*) to mature; (*fruta*) to ripen.

maduro,-a *a* mature; (*fruta*) ripe; **de edad madura** middle-aged.

maestro,-a 1 *mf* teacher; (*especialista*) master; (*músico*) maestro. **2** *a* **obra maestra** masterpiece.

magdalena *f* bun.

magia *f* magic; **por arte de m.** as if by magic.

magnetofón, magnetófono *m* tape recorder.

magnífico,-a *a* magnificent.

mago,-a *mf* wizard; **los (tres) Reyes Magos** the Three Wise Men, the Three Kings.

magullar 1 *vt* to bruise. **2 magullarse** *vr* to get bruised.

mahonesa *f* mayonnaise.

maíz *m* maize, *US* corn.

majestad *f* majesty.

majo,-a *a* (*bonito*) pretty, nice; *fam* (*simpático*) nice.

mal 1 *m* evil; (*daño*) harm; (*enfermedad*) illness. **2** *a* bad; **un m. año** a bad year; **ver malo,-a. 3** *adv* badly; **menos m. que ...** it's a good job (that) ...; **no está (nada) m.** it is not bad (at all); **te oigo/veo (muy) m.** I can hardly hear/see you.

malabarista *mf* juggler.

malcriado,-a 1 *a* ill-mannered. **2** *mf* ill-mannered person.

maldad *f* badness; (*acción perversa*) evil thing.

maldecir *vti* to curse.

maldición 1 *f* curse. **2** *interj* damnation!

maldito,-a *a fam* (*molesto*) damned; **¡maldita sea!** damn it!

maleducado,-a 1 *a* bad-mannered. **2** *mf* bad-mannered person.

malentendido *m* misunderstanding.

malestar *m* (*molestia*) discomfort; (*inquietud*) uneasiness.

maleta *f* suitcase; **hacer la m.** to pack one's case.

maletero *m* (*de coche*) boot, *US* trunk.

maletín *m* briefcase.

maleza *f* (*arbustos*) undergrowth; (*malas hierbas*) weeds *pl*.

malgastar *vt* to waste.

malhablado,-a 1 *a* foul-mouthed. **2** *mf* foul-mouthed person.

malhechor,-a *mf* wrongdoer.

malhumor *m* bad mood; **de m.** in a bad mood.

malicia *f* (*mala intención*) malice; (*astucia*) cunning; (*maldad*) badness.

malintencionado,-a 1 *a* ill-intentioned. **2** *mf* ill-intentioned person.

malla *f*; (*red*) mesh; *Am* (*bañador*) swimsuit; (*mallas*) leotard;.

malo,-a *a* bad; (*persona*) (*malvado*) wicked; (*travieso*) naughty; (*cosa*) bad; (*perjudicial*) harmful; (*enfermo*) ill; **por las malas** by force; **lo m. es que ...** the problem is that ...

malpensado,-a 1 *a* nasty-minded. **2** *mf* nasty-minded person.

malta *f* malt.

maltratado,-a *a* battered.

maltratar *vt* to ill-treat.

mama *f* (*de mujer*) breast; (*de animal*) teat; (*mamá*) mum.

mamá *f fam* mum, mummy.

mamadera *f Am* feeding bottle.

mamar *vt* to suck.

mamífero,-a *mf* mammal.

mampara *f* screen.

manada *f* (*de vacas, elefantes*) herd; (*de ovejas*) flock; (*de lobos, perros*) pack; (*de leones*) pride.

manantial *m* spring.

mancha *f* stain.

manchar 1 *vt* to stain. **2 mancharse** *vr* to get dirty.

manco,-a 1 *a* (*de un brazo*) one-armed; (*de una mano*) one-handed. **2** *mf* (*de un brazo*) one-armed person; (*de una mano*) one-handed person.

mancornas *fpl Am* cufflinks.

mandado *m* (*recado*) errand; **hacer un m.** to run an errand.

mandar *vt* (*ordenar*) to order; (*dirigir*) to be in charge of; (*ejército*) to command; (*enviar*) to send; **m. (a) por** to send for; **m. algo por correo** to send sth by post.

mandarina *f* mandarin.

mandíbula *f* jaw.

mando *m* (*autoridad*) command; (*control*) controls *pl*; **cuadro** *o* **tablero de mandos** dashboard; **m. a distancia** remote control.

manecilla *f* (*de reloj*) hand.

manejar 1 *vt* (*máquina, situación*) to handle; (*dirigir*) to manage; *Am* (*coche*) to drive. **2 manejarse** *vr* to manage.

manera *f* way, manner; **de cualquier m.** (*mal*) carelessly; (*en cualquier caso*) in any case; **de esta m.** in this way; **de ninguna m.** certainly not; **de todas maneras** anyway; **de m. que** so; **de tal m. que** in such a way that; **maneras** manners; **con buenas maneras** politely.

manga *f* sleeve; (*de riego*) hose; (*vuelta*) leg; (*en tenis*) set; **de m. corta/ larga** short-/long-sleeved; **sin mangas** sleeveless; *fig* **sacarse algo de la m.** to pull sth out of one's hat.

mango *m* handle.

manguera *f* hose.

maní *m* (*pl* **manises**) peanut.

maniático,-a 1 *a* fussy. **2** *mf* fusspot.

manicomio *m* mental hospital.

manifestación *f* demonstration; (*expresión*) expression.

manifestar [1] **1** *vt* (*declarar*) to state; (*mostrar*) to show. **2 manifestarse** *vr* (*por la calle*) to demonstrate.

manilla *f* (*de reloj*) hand; *Am* (*palanca*) lever.

manillar *m* handlebar.

maniobra *f* manoeuvre.

manipular *vt* to manipulate; (*máquina*) to handle.

maniquí *m* dummy.

manivela *f* crank.

manjar *m* dish.

mano *f* hand; **a m.** (*sin máquina*) by hand; (*asequible*) at hand; **escrito a m.** hand-written; **hecho a m.** hand-made; **estrechar la m. a algn** to shake hands with sb; **de segunda m.** second-hand; **¡manos a la obra!** shoulders to the wheel!; **equipaje de m.** hand luggage; **a m. derecha/izquierda** on the right/left(-hand side); **m. de pintura** coat of paint; **m. de obra** labour (force).

manojo *m* bunch.

manopla *f* mitten.

manso,-a *a* (*animal*) tame.

manta *f* blanket.

manteca *f* fat; **m. de cacao/cacahuete** cocoa/peanut butter.

mantecado *m* shortcake.

mantel *m* tablecloth.

mantener 1 *vt* (*conservar*) to keep; (*entrevista, reunión*) to have; (*familia*) to support; (*sostener*) to hold up; **m. la línea** to keep in trim. **2 mantenerse** *vr* (*sostenerse*) to stand; (*sustentarse*) to live (**de** on); **mantenerse firme** (*perseverar*) to hold one's ground.

mantenimiento *m* (*de máquina*) maintenance; (*alimento*) sustenance.

mantequilla *f* butter.

manto *m* cloak.

mantón *m* shawl.

mantuve *pt indef de* **mantener.**

manual 1 *a* manual; **trabajos manuales** handicrafts. **2** *m* (*libro*) manual.

manufactura *f* manufacture.

manzana *f* apple; (*de edificios*) block.

manzanilla *f* (*infusión*) camomile tea; (*vino*) manzanilla.

maña *f* (*astucia*) cunning; (*habilidad*) skill.

mañana 1 *f* (*parte de día*) morning; **de m.** early in the morning; **por la m.** in the morning. **2** *m* el **m.** tomorrow. **3** *adv* tomorrow; **¡hasta m.!** see you tomorrow! **m. por la m.** tomorrow morning; **pasado m.** the day after tomorrow.

mañoso,-a *a* skilful.

mapa *m* map.

maquillaje *m* make-up.

maquillar 1 *vt* to make up. **2 maquillarse** *vr* (*ponerse maquillaje*) to put one's make-up on; (*usar maquillaje*) to wear make-up.

máquina *f* machine; **escrito a m.** typewritten; **hecho a m.** machine-made; **m. de afeitar (eléctrica)** (electric) shaver; **m. de coser** sewing machine; **m. de escribir** typewriter; **m. fotográfica** *o* **de fotos** camera.

maquinaria *f* machinery; (*mecanismo*) mechanism.

maquinilla *f* **m. de afeitar** safety razor.

mar *m & f* sea; **en alta m.** on the high seas; *fam* **está la m. de guapa** she's looking really beautiful; **llover a mares** to rain cats and dogs.

maratón *mf* marathon.

maravilla *f* marvel; **de m.** wonderfully; **¡qué m. de película!** what a wonderful film!

marca *f* mark; (*de producto*) brand; (*récord*) record; **m. registrada** registered trademark.

marcar [1] *vt* to mark; (*número*) to dial; (*indicar*) to indicate; (*gol, puntos*) to score; (*cabello*) to set.

marcha *f* march; (*de coche*) gear; **hacer algo sobre la m.** to do sth as one goes along; **estar en m.** (*vehículo*) to be in motion; (*máquina*) to be working; **poner en m.** to start; **m. atrás** reverse (gear).

marchar 1 *vi* (*ir*) to walk; (*aparato*) to be on; **m. bien** (*negocio*) to be going well. **2 marcharse** *vr* to leave, go away.

marco *m* (*de cuadro etc*) frame; (*moneda*) mark.

marea *f* tide; **m. alta/baja** high/low tide; **m. negra** oil slick.

marear 1 *vt* to make sick; (*en el mar*) to make seasick; (*en un avión*) to make airsick; (*en un coche*) to make carsick; (*aturdir*) to make dizzy; *fam* (*fastidiar*) to annoy. **2 marearse** *vr* to get sick/seasick/airsick/carsick; (*quedar aturdido*) to get dizzy.

marejada *f* swell.

mareo *m* (*náusea*) sickness; (*en el mar*) seasickness; (*en un avión*) airsickness; (*en un coche*) carsickness; (*aturdimiento*) dizziness.

marfil *m* ivory.

margarina *f* margarine.

margarita *f* daisy.

margen *m* edge; (*de folio*) margin; *fig* **mantenerse al m.** not to get involved.

marginado,-a 1 *a* excluded. **2** *mf* dropout.

marginar *vt* (*a una persona*) to exclude.

marido *m* husband.

mariguana, marihuana, marijuana *f* marijuana.

marinero,-a *m* sailor.

marioneta *f* marionette.

mariposa *f* butterfly.

mariquita *f* ladybird.

marisco *m* shellfish; **mariscos** seafood.

marítimo,-a *a* maritime; **paseo m.** promenade.

mármol *m* marble.

marqués *m* marquis.

marrano,-a 1 *a* (*sucio*) filthy. **2** *mf fam* slob; (*animal*) pig.

marrón *a & m* brown.

marroquí *a & mf* Moroccan.

Marte *m* Mars.

martes *m inv* Tuesday.

martillo *m* hammer.

mártir *mf* martyr.

marzo *m* March.

más 1 *adv* more; **m. gente de la que esperas** more people than you're expecting; **m. de** more than, over; **cada día** *o* **vez m.** more and more; **es m.** what's more, furthermore; **lo m. posible** as much as possible; **m. bien** rather; **m. o menos** more or less; **m. aún** even more; **¿qué m. da?** what's the difference? ▌ (*comparativo*) **es m. alta/inteligente que yo** she's taller/more intelligent than me. ▌ (*superlativo*) **el m. bonito/caro** the prettiest/most expensive. ▌ (*exclamación*) **¡qué casa m. bonita!** what a lovely house!; **¡está m. guapa!** she looks so beautiful!. ▌ (*después de pron interr e indef*) else; **¿algo m.?** anything else?; **no, nada m.** no, nothing else; **quién m.?** who else?; **nadie/alguien m.** nobody/somebody else. ▌ **por m.** + (*a/adv* +) *que* + *subjuntivo* however (much); **por m. fuerte que sea** however strong he may be. **2** *m inv* **los/las m.** most people. **3** *prep* (*en sumas*) plus.

masa *f* mass; (*de cosas*) bulk; (*de pan etc*) dough; **medios de comunicación de masas** mass media.

masaje *m* massage; **dar masaje(s) (a)** to massage.

mascar [1] *vti* to chew.

máscara *f* mask; **m. de gas** gas mask.

mascarilla *f* mask; **m. de oxígeno** oxygen mask; (*cosmética*) face pack.

masculino,-a *a* male; (*para hombre*) men's; (*género*) masculine.

máster *m* master's degree.

masticar [1] *vt* to chew.

mástil *m* mast.

mastín *m* mastiff.

mata *f* (*matorral*) shrub.

matador *m* matador, bullfighter.

matar *vt* to kill.

mate[1] *a* (*sin brillo*) matt.

mate[2] *m* mate; **jaque m.** checkmate.

matemática *f*, **matemáticas** *fpl* mathematics *sing*.

materia *f* matter; (*tema*) question; (*asignatura*) subject; **m. prima** raw material; **índice de materias** table of contents.

material 1 *a* material. **2** *m* material; **m. escolar/de construcción** teaching/building materials; **m. de oficina** office equipment.

materialmente *adv* physically.

maternal *a* maternal.

materno,-a *a* maternal; **abuelo m.** maternal grandfather; **lengua materna** mother tongue.

matiz *m* (*de color*) shade.

matorral *m* thicket.

matrero,-a *Am* (*bandolero*) bandit.

matrícula *f* registration; (*de coche*) (*número*) registration number; (*placa*) number *o US* license plate.

matrimonio *m* marriage; (*pareja casada*) married couple; **m. civil/religioso** registry office/church wedding; **contraer m.** to marry; **cama de m.** double bed.

matriz *f* womb.

matrona *f* (*comadrona*) midwife.

maullar *vi* to miaow.

maxilar *m* jaw.

máximo,-a 1 *a* maximum. **2** *m* maximum; **al m.** to the utmost; **como m.** (*como mucho*) at the most; (*lo más tarde*) at the latest.

mayo *m* May.

mayonesa *f* mayonnaise.

mayor *a* (*comparativo*) (*tamaño*) bigger (**que** than); (*edad*) older, elder; (*superlativo*) (*tamaño*) biggest; (*edad*) oldest, eldest; (*adulto*) grown-up; (*maduro*) mature; (*principal*) major; **la m. parte** the majority; **la m. parte de las veces** most often; **ser m. de edad** to be of age; **al por m.** wholesale.

mayoría *f* majority; **la m. de los niños** most children; **m. de edad** majority.

mayúscula *f* capital letter.

mazapán *m* marzipan.

me *pron pers* (*objeto directo*) me; **no me mires** don't look at me. ‖ (*objeto indirecto*), me, to me, for me; **¿me das un caramelo?** will you give me a sweet?; **me lo dio** he gave it to me. ‖ (*pron reflexivo*) myself; **me he cortado** I've cut myself; **me voy/muero** (*no se traduce*) I'm off/dying.

mecánico,-a 1 *a* mechanical. **2** *mf* mechanic.

mecanismo *m* mechanism.

mecanografía *f* typing.

mecanógrafo,-a *mf* typist.

mecedora *f* rocking chair.

mecer [2] **1** *vt* to rock. **2 mecerse** *vr* to rock.

mecha *f* (*de vela*) wick; (*de pelo*) streak.

mechero,-a *m* (cigarette) lighter.

mechón *m* (*de pelo*) lock; (*de lana*) tuft.

medalla *f* medal.

media *f* stocking; *Am* (*calcetín*) sock; (*promedio*) average; **a medias** (*incompleto*) unfinished; (*entre dos*) half and half.

mediano,-a *a* (*tamaño*) medium-sized.

medianoche *f* midnight.

mediante *prep* by means of.

medicación *f* medication.

medicamento *m* medicine.

medicina *f* medicine; **estudiante de m.** medical student.

médico,-a 1 *mf* doctor; **m. de cabecera** family doctor. **2** *a* medical.

medida *f* measure; (*dimensión*) measurement; **a (la) m.** (*ropa*) made-to-measure; **a m. que avanzaba** as he advanced; **adoptar** *o* **tomar medidas** to take steps.

medieval *a* medieval.

medio,-a 1 *a* half; (*intermedio*) middle; (*normal*) average; **una hora y**

media an hour and a half; **a media mañana/tarde** in the middle of the morning/afternoon; **clase media** middle class; **salario m.** average wage. **2** *adv* half; **está m. muerta** she is half dead. **3** *m* (*mitad*) half; (*centro*) middle; **en m. (de)** (*en el centro*) in the middle (of); (*entre dos*) in between; **medios de transporte** means of transport; **por m. de** by means of; **medios de comunicación** (mass) media; **m. ambiente** environment.

medioambiental *a* environmental.

mediocre *a* mediocre.

mediodía *m* (*hora exacta*) midday; (*período aproximado*) early afternoon; (*sur*) south.

medir [6] **1** *vt* to measure. **2** *vi* to measure; **mide 2 metros** he is 2 metres tall; **mide dos metros de alto/ancho/largo** it is two metres high/wide/long.

médula *f* marrow; **m. ósea** bone marrow.

megafonía *f* public-address system.

mejicano,-a *a & mf* Mexican.

mejilla *f* cheek.

mejillón *m* mussel.

mejor **1** *a* (*comparativo*) better (**que** than); (*superlativo*) best; **tu m. amiga** your best friend; **lo m.** the best thing. **2** *adv* (*comparativo*) better (**que** than); (*superlativo*) best; **cada vez m.** better and better; **m. dicho** or rather; **es el que m. canta** he is the one who sings the best; **a lo m.** (*quizás*) perhaps; (*ojalá*) hopefully.

mejora *f* improvement.

mejorar **1** *vti* to improve. **2 mejorarse** *vr* to get better; **¡que te mejores!** get well soon!

melancolía *f* melancholy.

melancólico,-a *a* melancholic.

melena *f* (head of) hair; (*de león*) mane.

mellizo,-a *a & mf* twin.

melocotón *m* peach.

melodía *f* tune.

melón *m* melon.

membrana *f* membrane.

membrillo *m* quince.

memoria *f* memory; (*informe*) report; **memorias** (*biografía*) memoirs; **aprender/saber algo de m.** to learn/know sth by heart.

mencionar *vt* to mention.

mendigo,-a *mf* beggar.

mendrugo *m* crust (of stale bread).

menear **1** *vt* to shake; (*cola*) to wag. **2 menearse** *vr* to shake.

menestra *f* vegetable stew.

menguar *vti* to diminish.

meñique *a & m* **(dedo)** m. little finger.

menor 1 *a* (*comparativo*) (*de tamaño*) smaller (**que** than); (*de edad*) younger (**que** than); (*superlativo*) (*de tamaño*) smallest; (*de intensidad*) least, slightest; (*de edad*) youngest; **ser m. de edad** to be a minor, to be under age; **al por m.** retail. **2** *mf* minor.

menos 1 *a* (*comparativo*) (*con singular*) less; (*con plural*) fewer; **m. dinero/leche/tiempo que** less money/milk/time than; **m. libros/pisos que** fewer books/flats than; **tiene m. años de lo que parece** he's younger than he looks; (*superlativo*) **fui el que perdí m. dinero** I lost the least money. **2** *adv* **m. de** (*con singular*) less than; (*con plural*) fewer than, less than. ‖ (*superlativo*) (*con singular*) least; **el m. inteligente de la clase** the least intelligent boy in the class. ‖ (*con plural*) the fewest; **ayer fue cuando vinieron m. personas** yesterday was when the fewest people came. ‖ (*locuciones*) **a m. que** + *subjuntivo* unless; **al** *o* **por lo m.** at least; **echar a algn de m.** to miss sb; **¡m. mal!** just as well! **ni mucho m.** far from it. **3** *prep* except; (*en restas*) minus.

menosprecio *m* contempt.

mensaje *m* message.

mensajero,-a *mf* messenger.

mensual *a* monthly.

menta *f* mint; (*licor*) crème de menthe.

mental *a* mental.

mente *f* mind.

mentir [5] *vi* to lie.

mentira *f* lie.

mentón *m* chin.

menú *m* menu.

menudo,-a 1 *a* minute; **¡m. lío/susto!** what a mess/fright! **2** *adv* **a m.** often.

mercado *m* market; **M. Común** Common Market.

mercadotecnia *f* marketing.

mercancías *fpl* goods.

mercantil *a* commercial.

mercería *f* haberdasher's (shop), *US* notions store.

merecer *vt* **1** to deserve; (*uso impers*) **no merece la pena hacerlo** it's not worth while doing it. **2 merecerse** *vr* to deserve.

merendar [1] **1** *vt* to have for tea. **2** *vi* to have tea.

merendero *m* (*en el campo*) picnic spot.

merezco *indic pres de* **merecer**.

meridional *a* southern.

merienda *f* afternoon snack.

mérito *m* merit.

merluza *f* hake.

mermelada *f* jam; (*de agrios*) marmalade; **m. de fresa** strawberry jam; **m. de naranja** orange marmalade.

mes *m* month; **el m. pasado/que viene** last/next month.

mesa *f* table; (*de despacho etc*) desk; **poner/recoger la m.** to set/clear the table.

meseta *f* plateau.

mesilla *f* **m. de noche** bedside table.

mesón *m* old-style tavern.

meta *f* (*objetivo, portería*) goal; (*de carrera*) finishing line.

metal *m* metal.

metálico,-a *a* metallic. **2** *m* **pagar en m.** to pay (in) cash.

meteorológico,-a *a* meteorological; **parte** *m* **m.** weather report.

meter 1 *vt* (*poner*) to put (**en**, in); (*comprometer*) to involve (**en** in). **2 meterse** *vr* (*entrar*) to go/come in; (*entrometerse*) to meddle; (*estar*) **¿dónde te habías metido?** where have you been (all this time)?; **m. con algn** (*en broma*) to get at sb.

método *m* method.

métrico,-a *a* metric; **sistema m.** metric system.

metro *m* metre; (*tren*) underground, tube, *US* subway.

mexicano,-a *a* & *mf* Mexican.

mezcla *f* (*producto*) mixture; (*acción*) mixing.

mezclar 1 *vt* to mix; (*involucrar*) to involve. **2 mezclarse** *vr* (*cosas*) to get mixed up; (*gente*) to mingle.

mezquino,-a *a* (*tacaño*) mean; (*escaso*) miserable.

mezquita *f* mosque.

mi *a* my; **mis cosas/libros** my things/books.

mí *pron pers* me; **a mí me dio tres** he gave me three; **compra otro para mí** buy one for me too; **por mí mismo** just by myself.

mía *a* & *pron pos f ver* **mío**.

microbús *m* minibus.

micrófono *m* microphone.

microonda *f* **un** (*horno*) **microondas** a microwave (oven).

microprocesador *m* microprocessor.

microscopio *m* microscope.

miedo *m* (*pavor*) fear; (*temor*) apprehension; **una película de m.** a horror film; **tener m. de algo/algn** to be afraid of sth/sb.

miedoso,-a *a* fearful.

miel *f* honey.

miembro *m* (*socio*) member; (*de cuerpo*) limb.

mientras 1 *conj* while; (*cuanto más*) **m. más/menos ...** the more/less ... **2** *adv* **m. (tanto)** meanwhile, in the meantime.

miércoles *m inv* Wednesday; **M. de Ceniza** Ash Wednesday.

miga *f (de pan etc)* crumb.

mil *a & m* thousand; **m. pesetas** a *o* one thousand pesetas.

milagro *m* miracle.

milésimo,-a *a & mf* thousandth.

mili *f* military service; **hacer la m.** to do one's military service.

milímetro *m* millimetre.

militar 1 *a* military. **2** *m* soldier.

milla *f* mile.

millar *m* thousand.

millón *m* million.

millonario,-a *a & mf* millionaire.

mimar *vt* to spoil.

mimbre *f* wicker.

mina *f* mine; *(de lápiz)* lead; **lápiz de m.** propelling pencil.

mineral 1 *a* mineral. **2** *m* ore.

minero,-a 1 *mf* miner. **2** *a* mining.

miniatura *f* miniature.

minifalda *f* miniskirt.

mínimo,-a 1 *a (muy pequeño)* minute; *(en matemáticas)* minimum. **2** *m* minimum; **como m.** at least.

ministerio *m* ministry, *US* department.

ministro,-a *mf* minister; **primer m.** Prime Minister.

minoría *f* minority; **m. de edad** minority.

minúsculo,-a *a* minute; **letra minúscula** small letter.

minusválido,-a 1 *a* disabled. **2** *mf* disabled person.

minuto *m* minute.

mío,-a 1 *a pos* of mine; **un amigo m.** a friend of mine; **no es asunto m.** it is none of my business. **2** *pron pos* mine.

miope *mf* short-sighted person.

mirada *f* look; **lanzar** *o* **echar una m.** to glance at.

mirar 1 *vt* to look at; *(observar)* to watch; *(cuidar)* **mira que no le pase nada** see that nothing happens to him. **2** *vi* **la casa mira al norte** the house faces north.

mirlo *m* blackbird.

misa *f* mass.

miserable *a (mezquino) (persona)* despicable; *(sueldo etc)* miserable; *(pobre)* wretched.

miseria *f (pobreza extrema)* extreme poverty; *(insignificancia)* pittance; *(tacañería)* meanness.

misión *f* mission.

mismo,-a 1 *a* same; *(uso enfático)* **yo m.** I myself; **por eso m.** that is why;

por uno *o* sí m. by oneself; **aquí m.** right here. **2** *pron* same; **es el m. de ayer**
it's the same one as yesterday; **lo m.** the same (thing); **dar** *o* **ser lo m.** to
make no difference. **3** *adv* **así m.** likewise.

misterio *m* mystery.

mitad *f* half; (*centro*) middle; **a m. de camino** half-way there; **a m. de
precio** half price; **en la m. del primer acto** half-way through the first act.

mitote *m Am* uproar.

mixto *a* mixed.

mobiliario *m* furniture.

moca *m* mocha.

mochila *f* rucksack.

moco *m* snot; **sonarse los mocos** to blow one's nose.

mocoso,-a *mf fam* brat.

moda *f* fashion; **a la m., de m.** in fashion; **pasado de m.** old-fashioned.

modales *mpl* manners.

modelo 1 *a inv* & *m* model. **2** *mf* (fashion) model; **desfile** *m* **de modelos**
fashion show.

módem *m* modem.

moderado,-a *a* moderate.

modernizar [4] *vt*, **modernizarse** *vr* to modernize.

moderno,-a *a* modern.

modesto,-a *a* modest.

modificar [1] *vt* to modify.

modisto,-a *mf* fashion designer.

modo *m* (*manera*) way, manner; (*en lingüística*) mood; **m. de empleo**
instructions for use; **modos** manners.

mofarse *vr* to laugh (**de** at).

moflete *m* chubby cheek.

mohoso,-a *a* (*oxidado*) rusty.

mojar 1 *vt* to wet; (*humedecer*) to dampen. **2 mojarse** *vr* to get wet.

molde *m* mould.

moldeador *m* (*del pelo*) wave.

mole *f* mass.

moler [4] *vt* to grind.

molestar 1 *vt* (*incomodar*) to disturb; (*causar malestar*) to hurt; **¿le
molestaría esperar fuera?** would you mind waiting outside? **2 molestarse**
vr (*tomarse la molestia*) to bother; (*ofenderse*) to take offence.

molestia *f* bother; (*dolor*) slight pain.

molesto,-a *a* (*irritante*) annoying; **estar m. con algn** (*enfadado*) to be
annoyed with sb.

molino *m* mill; **m. de viento** windmill.

momentáneo,-a *a* momentary.

momento *m* (*instante*) moment; (*periodo*) time; **al m.** at once; **de m.** for the time being; **en cualquier m.** at any time.

monasterio *m* monastery.

mondar 1 *vt* to peel. **2 mondarse** *vr fam* **m. (de risa)** to laugh one's head off.

moneda *f* (*pieza*) coin; (*dinero*) currency; **m. suelta** small change.

monedero *m* purse.

monetario,-a *a* monetary.

monigote *m* (*persona*) wimp; (*dibujo*) rough sketch (of a person).

monitor,-a *mf* monitor; (*profesor*) instructor.

monja *f* nun.

monje *m* monk.

mono,-a 1 *m* monkey; (*prenda*) (*de trabajo*) overalls *pl*; (*de vestir*) catsuit. **2** *a fam* (*bonito*) pretty.

monopolio *m* monopoly.

monótono,-a *a* monotonous.

monstruo *m* monster; (*genio*) genius.

montaje *m* (*instalación*) fitting; (*ensamblaje*) assembling.

montaña *f* mountain; **m. rusa** big dipper.

montañismo *m* mountaineering.

montañoso,-a *a* mountainous.

montar 1 *vi* (*en bici, a caballo*) to ride; (*en coche, tren*) to travel; (*subirse*) to get in. **2** *vt* (*colocar*) to put on; (*máquina etc*) to assemble; (*negocio*) to set up. **3 montarse** *vr* (*subirse*) to get on; (*en coche*) to get in.

monte *m* (*montaña*) mountain; (*con nombre propio*) mount.

montón *m* heap; **un m. de** a load of.

montura *f* (*cabalgadura*) mount; (*de gafas*) frame.

monumento *m* monument.

moño *m* bun.

moqueta *f* fitted carpet.

mora *f* (*zarzamora*) blackberry.

morado,-a *a & m* purple.

moral 1 *a* moral. **2** *f* (*ética*) morals *pl*; (*ánimo*) morale.

morboso,-a *a* (*malsano*) morbid.

morcilla *f* black pudding.

mordaz *a* biting.

morder [4] *vt* to bite.

mordida *f Am* (*soborno*) bribe.

mordisco *m* bite.

moreno,-a 1 *a* (*pelo*) dark-haired; (*piel*) dark-skinned; (*bronceado*) tanned; **ponerse m.** to get a suntan; **pan/azúcar m.** brown bread/sugar. **2** *mf* (*persona*) (*de pelo*) dark-haired person; (*mujer*) brunette; (*de piel*) dark-skinned person.

morgue *f Am* morgue.

morir [7] **1** *vi* to die; **m. de frío/hambre/cáncer** to die of cold/hunger/cancer. **2 morirse** *vr* to die; **morirse de hambre** to starve to death; *fig* to be starving; **morirse de aburrimiento** to be bored to death; **morirse de risa** to die laughing.

moro,-a *a & mf* Moor; *fam* (*musulmán*) Muslim; (*árabe*) Arab.

morocho,-a *a Am* (*moreno*) swarthy.

morro *m* (*hocico*) snout.

mortadela *f* mortadella.

mortal *a* mortal; (*mortífero*) fatal; **un accidente m.** a fatal accident.

mosca *f* fly; *fam* **estar m.** (*suspicaz*) to be suspicious; *fam* **por si las moscas** just in case.

moscardón *m* blowfly.

mosquito *m* mosquito.

mostaza *f* mustard.

mostrador *m* (*de tienda*) counter; (*de bar*) bar.

mostrar 1 *vt* to show. **2 mostrarse** *vr* to be; **se mostró muy comprensiva** she was very understanding.

mota *f* speck.

mote[1] *m* (*apodo*) nickname.

mote[2] *m Am* boiled salted maize *o US* corn.

motín *m* (*amotinamiento*) mutiny; (*disturbio*) riot.

motivo *m* (*causa*) reason; **motivos** grounds; **con m. de** on the occasion of; **sin m.** for no reason at all.

moto *f* motorbike.

motocicleta *f* motorbike.

motociclista *mf* motorcyclist.

motor,-a *m* (*grande*) engine; (*pequeño*) motor; **m. de reacción** jet engine.

motora *f* motorboat.

motorista *mf* motorcyclist.

mover [4] **1** *vt* to move; (*hacer funcionar*) to drive; **2 moverse** *vr* to move.

movimiento *m* movement; (*en física*) motion; (*actividad*) activity; (**poner algo**) **en m.** (to set sth) in motion.

moza *f* young girl.

mozo *m* boy; (*de estación*) porter; (*de hotel*) bellboy, *US* bellhop.

mucamo,-a *mf Am* servant.

muchacha *f* girl.

muchacho *m* boy.

muchedumbre *f* crowd.

mucho,-a 1 *a sing* lots of; (*en frases negativas e interrogativas*) much; **hay m. tonto suelto** there are lots of idiots around; **no tengo m. dinero** I

.don't have much money; **¿bebes m. café?** do you drink a lot of coffee?; **m. tiempo** a long time; **tengo m. sueño/mucha sed** I am very sleepy/thirsty. ▌ **muchos,-as** lots of; (*en frases negativas e interrogativas*) many; **no hay muchas chicas** there aren't many girls; **¿tienes muchos amigos?** do you have many friends?; **tiene muchos años** he is very old. **2** *pron* lots; **¿cuánta leche queda? – mucha** how much milk is there left? – a lot; **muchos,-as** lots; **¿cuántos libros tienes? – muchos** how many books have you got? – lots; **muchos creemos que ...** many of us believe that ... **3** *adv* a lot; **lo siento m.** I'm very sorry; **como m.** at the most; **con m.** by far; **m. antes/ después** long before/after; **¡ni m. menos!** no way!; **por m. (que)** + *subj* however much; **hace m. que no viene por aquí** he has not been to see us for a long time.

mudanza *f* move; **estar de m.** to be moving; **camión de m.** removal van.

mudar 1 *vt* (*ropa*) to change; (*plumas, pelo*) to moult; (*de piel*) to shed. **2 mudarse** *vr* **mudarse de casa/ropa** to move house/to change one's clothes.

mudo,-a *a* (*que no habla*) dumb. **2** *mf* mute.

mueble *m* piece of furniture; **muebles** furniture *sing;* **con/sin muebles** furnished/unfurnished.

muela *f* molar; **dolor de muelas** toothache; **m. del juicio** wisdom tooth.

muelle[1] *m* spring.

muelle[2] *m* (*en puerto*) dock.

muerte *f* death; **dar m. a algn** to kill sb; **odiar a algn a m.** to loathe sb; **un susto de m.** the fright of one's life.

muerto,-a 1 *a* dead; **m. de hambre** starving; **m. de frío** frozen to death; **m. de miedo** scared stiff; **m. de risa** laughing one's head off; **(en) punto m.** (in) neutral. **2** *mf* (*difunto*) dead person; **hacerse el m.** to pretend to be dead.

muestra *f* (*espécimen*) sample; (*modelo a copiar*) model; (*prueba, señal*) sign; **dar muestras de** to show signs of; **m. de cariño/respeto** token of affection/respect.

mugido *m* (*de vaca*) moo; (*de toro*) bellow.

mugre *f* filth.

mujer *f* woman; (*esposa*) wife; **m. de la limpieza** cleaning lady; **m. de su casa** houseproud woman.

muleta *f* (*prótesis*) crutch; (*de torero*) muleta.

mulo,-a *mf* mule.

multa *f* fine; (*de tráfico*) ticket.

multicopista *f* duplicator.

multinacional *a & f* multinational.

múltiple *a* multiple.

multiplicación *f* multiplication.

multiplicar [1] **1** *vti* to multiply (**por** by). **2 multiplicarse** *vr* to multiply.

multitud *f* (*de personas*) crowd; (*de cosas*) multitude.

mundial 1 *a* worldwide; **campeón m.** world champion; **de fama m.** world-famous. **2** *m* world championship.

mundialmente *adv* **m. famoso** world-famous.

mundo *m* world; **todo el m.** everyone.

muñeca *f* wrist; (*juguete, muchacha*) doll.

muñeco *m* (*juguete*) (little) boy doll; **m. de trapo** rag doll; **m. de nieve** snowman.

munición *f* ammunition.

municipal *a* municipal; (*policía*) local.

municipio *m* municipality; (*ayuntamiento*) town council.

murciélago *m* bat.

murmullo *m* murmur.

murmurar *vi* (*criticar*) to gossip; (*susurrar*) to whisper; (*producir murmullo*) to murmur.

muro *m* wall.

músculo *m* muscle.

museo *m* museum.

musgo *m* moss.

música *f* music; **m. clásica** classical music.

musical *a* musical.

músico,-a *mf* musician.

muslo *m* thigh.

musulmán,-ana *a & mf* Muslim.

mutilado,-a *mf* disabled person.

mutuo,-a *a* mutual.

muy *adv* very; **m. bueno/malo** very good/bad; **¡m. bien!** very good!; **M. señor mío** Dear Sir; **m. de mañana/noche** very early/late.

N

nabo *m* turnip.

nácar *m* mother-of-pearl.

nacer *vi* to be born; *(pelo)* to begin to grow; *(río)* to rise; **nací en Montoro** I was born in Montoro.

nacimiento *m* birth; *(de río)* source; *(belén)* Nativity scene; **lugar de n.** place of birth.

nación *f* nation; **las Naciones Unidas** the United Nations.

nacional 1 *a* national; *(producto, mercado, vuelo)* domestic. **2** *mf* national.

nacionalidad *f* nationality.

nada 1 *pron* nothing; *(con verbo)* not ... anything, nothing; **no sé n.** I don't know anything; **yo no digo n.** I'm saying nothing, I'm not saying anything; **más que n.** more than anything; **sin decir n.** without saying anything; **casi n.** hardly anything; **gracias – de n.** thanks – don't mention it; **para n.** not at all; **como si n.** just like that; **n. de eso** nothing of the kind; **n. de n.** nothing at all; **n. más verla** as soon as he saw her. **2** *adv* not at all; **no me gusta n.** I don't like it at all.

nadar *vi* to swim; **n. a braza** to do the breaststroke.

nadie *pron* no-one, nobody; *(con verbo)* not ... anyone, anybody; **no conozco a n.** I don't know anyone *o* anybody; **más que n.** more than anyone; **sin decírselo a n.** without telling anyone; **casi n.** hardly anyone.

nafta *f Am (gasolina)* petrol, *US* gasoline.

nailon *m* nylon; **medias de n.** nylons.

naipe *m* playing card.

nalga *f* buttock.

nana *f* lullaby.

naranja 1 *f* orange. **2** *a & m (color)* orange.

naranjada *f* orangeade.

naranjo *m* orange tree.

narcotráfico *m* drug trafficking.

nariz *f* nose; **narices** nose *sing*; *fam* **meter las narices en algo** to poke one's nose into sth.

nata *f* cream; *(de leche hervida)* skin; **n. batida/montada** whipped cream.

natación *f* swimming.

natillas *fpl* custard *sing*.

natural 1 *a* natural; *(fruta, flor)* fresh; *(bebida)* at room temperature; **de tamaño n.** life-size. **2** *mf* native.

naturaleza *f* nature; **en plena n.** in unspoilt countryside.

naturalidad *f (sencillez)* naturalness; *(espontaneidad)* ease; **con n.** straightforwardly.

naturalizar [4] **1** *vt* to naturalize. **2 naturalizarse** *vr* to become naturalized.

naturalmente *adv* naturally; ¡n.! of course!

naturismo *m* naturism.

naufragar [7] *vi* (*barco*) to be wrecked.

naufragio *m* shipwreck.

náusea *f* nausea; **me da n.** it makes me sick; **sentir náuseas** to feel sick.

navaja *f* (*cuchillo*) penknife; **n. de afeitar** razor.

nave *f* ship; (*de iglesia*) nave; **n. (espacial)** spaceship; **n. industrial** plant.

navegar [7] *vi* to sail.

Navidad(es) *f(pl)* Christmas; **árbol de Navidad** Christmas tree; **Feliz Navidad/Felices Navidades** Merry Christmas.

navideño,-a *a* Christmas.

navío *m* ship.

neblina *f* mist.

necesario,-a *a* necessary; **es n. hacerlo** it has to be done; **es n. que vayas** you must go; **no es n. que vayas** it's not necessary for you to go; **si fuera n.** if need be.

neceser *m* toilet bag.

necesidad *f* need; **por n.** of necessity; **tener n. de** to need.

necesitar *vt* to need.

necio,-a 1 *a* silly. **2** *mf* fool.

nectarina *f* nectarine.

neerlandés,-esa 1 *a* Dutch. **2** *mf* (*hombre*) Dutchman; (*mujer*) Dutchwoman; **los neerlandeses** the Dutch. **3** *m* (*idioma*) Dutch.

nefasto,-a *a* (*perjudicial*) harmful; (*funesto*) ill-fated.

negación *f* negation; (*negativa*) denial; (*gramatical*) negative.

negar [1] **1** *vt* to deny; (*rechazar*) to refuse; **negó haberlo robado** he denied stealing it; **le negaron la beca** they refused him the grant. **2 negarse** *vr* to refuse (**a** to).

negativo,-a *a & m* negative.

negligencia *f* negligence.

negociación *f* negotiation.

negociar **1** *vt* to negotiate. **2** *vi* (*comerciar*) to do business.

negocio *m* business; (*transacción*) deal; (*asunto*) affair; **hombre de negocios** businessman; **mujer de negocios** businesswoman.

negro,-a 1 *a* black; **verlo todo n.** to be very pessimistic. **2** *mf* (*hombre*) black; (*mujer*) black (woman); *fam* **trabajar como un n.** to work like a dog. **3** *m* (*color*) black.

nene,-a *mf* (*niño*) baby boy; (*niña*) baby girl.

neocelandés,-esa 1 *a* New Zealand. **2** *mf* New Zealander.

neoyorkino,-a 1 *a* New York. **2** *mf* New Yorker.

neozelandés,-esa *a & mf* = **neocelandés,-esa.**

nervio *m* nerve; (*de la carne*) sinew; **nervios** nerves; **ataque de n.** a fit of hysterics; **ser un manojo de n.** to be a bundle of nerves.

nervioso,-a *a* nervous; **poner n. a algn** to get on sb's nerves.

neto,-a *a* (*peso, cantidad*) net.

neumático,-a 1 *a* pneumatic. **2** *m* tyre, *US* tire; **n. de recambio** spare tyre.

neumonía *f* pneumonia.

neurótico,-a *a & mf* neurotic.

neutral *a* neutral.

neutro,-a *a* (*imparcial*) neutral; (*género*) neuter.

nevada *f* snowfall.

nevar [1] *v impers* to snow.

nevera *f* (*frigorífico*) fridge; (*portátil*) cool box.

ni *conj* no ... **ni, ni** ... **ni** neither ... nor, not ... or; **ni se te ocurra** don't even think about it

nicaragüense, nicaragüeño,-a *a & mf* Nicaraguan.

nido *m* nest.

niebla *f* fog; **hay mucha n.** it is very foggy.

nieto,-a *mf* (*niño*) grandson; (*niña*) granddaughter; **mis nietos** my grandchildren.

nieve *f* snow.

nigeriano,-a *a & mf* Nigerian.

ningún *a* (*delante de m sing*) *ver* **ninguno,-a.**

ninguno,-a 1 *a* (*con verbo*) not ... any; **en ninguna parte** nowhere; **de ningún modo** no way. **2** *pron* (*persona*) nobody, no one; **n. de los dos** neither of the two; **n. de ellos** none of them; (*cosa*) not ... any of them; (*enfático*) none of them; **n. me gusta** I don't like any of them; **no vi n.** I saw none of them.

niña *f* girl; (*pupila*) pupil.

niñera *f* nanny.

niño,-a *mf* child; (*bebé*) baby; (*muchacho*) (small) boy; (*muchacha*) (little) girl; **de n.** as a child; **niños** children.

nitrógeno *m* nitrogen.

nivel *m* (*altura*) level; (*categoría*) standard; **a n. del mar** at sea level; **n. de vida** standard of living.

n° *abr de* **número** number, n.

no *adv* not; (*como respuesta*) no; **n. vi a nadie** I did not see anyone, I didn't see anyone; **aún no** not yet; **ya no** no longer; **¿por qué no?** why not?; **no fumar/aparcar** (*en letrero*) no smoking/parking; **no sea que** + *subjuntivo* in case; **es rubia, ¿no?** she's blonde, isn't she?; **llegaron anoche, ¿no?** they arrived yesterday, didn't they?

noble 1 *a* noble. **2** *mf* (*hombre*) nobleman; (*mujer*) noblewoman; **los nobles** the nobility *sing*.

noche *f* evening; (*después de las diez*) night; **de n., por la n.** at night; **esta n.** tonight; **mañana por la n.** tomorrow night/evening; **buenas noches** (*saludo*) good evening; (*despedida*) good night.

nochebuena *f* Christmas Eve.

nochevieja *f* New Year's Eve.

nocturno,-a *a* night; **clases nocturnas** evening classes.

nombrar *vt* to name.

nombre *m* name; (*sustantivo*) noun; **n. de pila** Christian name; **n. y apellidos** full name; **n. propio** proper noun.

nordeste *m* northeast.

nórdico,-a 1 *a* (*del norte*) northern; (*escandinavo*) Nordic. **2** *mf* Nordic person.

noreste *m* northeast.

norma *f* norm.

normal *a* normal; **lo n.** the usual.

normalizar [4] **1** *vt* to normalize. **2 normalizarse** *vr* to return to normal.

noroeste *m* northwest.

norte *m* north; **al n. de** to the north of.

norteafricano,-a *a & mf* North African.

norteamericano,-a *a & mf* (North) American.

noruego,-a 1 *a* Norwegian. **2** *mf* Norwegian. **3** *m* (*idioma*) Norwegian.

nos *pron pers* us; (*con verbo reflexivo*) ourselves; (*con verbo recíproco*) each other; **n. hemos divertido mucho** we enjoyed ourselves a lot; **n. queremos mucho** we love each other very much.

nosotros,-as *pron pers* (*sujeto*) we; (*complemento*) us; **con n.** with us.

nostalgia *f* nostalgia; (*morriña*) homesickness.

nota *f* note; (*de examen*) mark; **sacar buenas notas** to get good marks.

notable 1 *a* (*apreciable*) noticeable; (*digno de notar*) outstanding. **2** *m* (*nota*) very good.

notar 1 *vt* (*percibir*) to notice. **2 notarse** *vr* (*percibirse*) to show; **no se nota** it doesn't show.

notario,-a *mf* notary (public).

noticia *f* news *sing*; **una n.** a piece of news; **una buena n.** (some) good news.

notificar [1] *vt* to notify.

novato,-a 1 *a* (*persona*) inexperienced. **2** *mf* (*principiante*) novice.

novecientos,-as *a inv & mf inv* nine hundred.

novedad *f* (*cosa nueva*) novelty; (*cambio*) change; (*cualidad*) newness.

novela *f* novel; (*corta*) story.

noveno,-a *a & m* ninth; **novena parte** ninth.

noventa *a & m inv* ninety.

novia *f* (*amiga*) girlfriend; (*prometida*) fiancée; (*en boda*) bride.

noviembre *m* November.

novillada *f* bullfight with young bulls.

novillo,-a *mf* (*toro*) young bull; (*vaca*) young cow; **hacer novillos** to play truant *o US* hooky.

novio *m* (*amigo*) boyfriend; (*prometido*) fiancé; (*en boda*) bridegroom; **los novios** the bride and groom.

nube *f* cloud.

nublarse *vr* to cloud over.

nuca *f* back of the neck.

nuclear *a* nuclear; **central n.** nuclear power station.

núcleo *m* nucleus; (*parte central*) core.

nudillo *m* knuckle.

nudista *a & mf* nudist.

nudo *m* knot; **hacer un n.** to tie a knot.

nuera *f* daughter-in-law.

nuestro,-a 1 *a pos* our; **un amigo n.** a friend of ours. **2** *pron pos* ours; **este libro es n.** this book is ours.

nuevamente *adv* again.

nueve *a & m inv* nine.

nuevo,-a *a* new.

nuez *f* walnut; **n. (de Adán)** Adam's apple.

numérico,-a *a* digital.

número *m* number; (*de zapatos*) size; **n. de matrícula** registration number, *US* license number.

numeroso,-a *a* numerous.

nunca *adv* never; (*enfático*) not … ever; **no he estado n. en España** I've never been to Spain; **yo no haría n. eso** I wouldn't ever do that; **casi n.** hardly ever; **más que n.** more than ever; **n. jamás** never ever; (*futuro*) never again.

nutrición *f* nutrition.

nutritivo,-a *a* nutritious; **valor n.** nutritional value.

ñame *m Am* yarn.

ñapa *f Am* bonus.

ñato,-a *a Am* snub-nosed.

ñoño,-a 1 *a* (*soso*) dull. **2** *mf* dullard.

o

o *conj* or; **o ... o** either ... or; **o sea** in other words.

oasis *m inv* oasis.

obedecer *vt* to obey.

obediente *a* obedient.

obeso,-a *a* obese.

obispo *m* bishop.

objetivo,-a 1 *m* (*fin, meta*) objective; (*de cámara*) lens. **2** *a* objective.

objeto *m* object; (*fin*) purpose; **con o. de ...** in order to ...

obligación *f* (*deber*) obligation; **por o.** out of a sense of duty.

obligar [7] *vt* to force.

obligatorio,-a *a* obligatory.

obra *f* (*trabajo*) work; **o. maestra** masterpiece; (*acto*) deed; (*construcción*) building site; **'carretera en o.'** 'roadworks'.

obrar *vi* (*proceder*) to act; **o. bien/mal** to do the right/wrong thing.

obrero,-a 1 *mf* worker. **2** *a* working; **clase obrera** working class.

obsceno,-a *a* obscene.

obscurecer 1 *vi impers* to get dark. **2** *vt* (*ensombrecer*) to darken. **3** **obscurecerse** *vr* (*nublarse*) to become cloudy.

obscuridad *f* darkness; *fig* obscurity.

obscuro,-a *a* dark; (*origen, idea*) obscure; (*nublado*) overcast.

obsequio *m* gift.

observador,-a 1 *mf* observer. **2** *a* observant.

observar *vt* (*mirar*) to watch; (*notar*) to notice; (*cumplir*) to observe.

obsesión *f* obsession.

obstáculo *m* obstacle.

obstante (**no**) **1** *adv* nevertheless. **2** *prep* notwithstanding.

obstinado,-a *a* obstinate.

obstinarse *vr* to persist (**en** in).

obstruir 1 *vt* (*salida, paso*) to block. **2 obstruirse** *vr* to get blocked up.

obtener *vt* (*alcanzar*) to obtain, get.

obvio,-a *a* obvious.

oca *f* goose.

ocasión *f* (*momento*) occasion; (*oportunidad*) opportunity; (*saldo*) bargain; **en cierta o.** once; **aprovechar la o.** to make the most of an opportunity.

ocasional *a* (*eventual*) occasional; **de forma o.** occasionally.

ocasionar *vt* to cause.

occidental *a* western.

océano *m* ocean.

ochenta *a & m inv* eighty.

ocho *a & m inv* eight.

ochocientos,-as *a & m inv* eight hundred.

ocio *m* leisure.

octavo,-a *a & mf* eighth.

octubre *m* October.

oculista *mf* ophthalmologist.

ocultar 1 *vt* to conceal; **o. algo a algn** to hide sth from sb. **2 ocultarse** *vr* to hide.

ocupación *f* (*tarea*) occupation.

ocupado,-a *a* (*persona*) busy; (*asiento*) taken; (*aseos, teléfono*) engaged; (*puesto de trabajo*) filled.

ocupante *mf* occupant; (*ilegal*) squatter.

ocupar 1 *vt* to occupy; (*espacio, tiempo*) to take up; (*cargo*) to hold. **2 ocuparse** *vr* **ocuparse de** (*cuidar*) to look after; (*encargarse*) to see to.

ocurrencia *f* (*agudeza*) witty remark; (*idea*) idea.

ocurrente *a* witty.

ocurrir 1 *v impers* to happen; **¿qué te ocurre?** what's the matter with you? **2 ocurrirse** *vr* **no se me ocurre nada** I can't think of anything.

odiar *vt* to hate.

odio *m* hatred.

odontólogo,-a *mf* dental surgeon.

oeste *m* west.

ofender 1 *vt* to offend. **2 ofenderse** *vr* to take offence (**con, por** at).

ofensa *f* offence.

oferta *f* offer; (*presupuesto*) bid.

oficial,-a 1 *a* official. **2** *m* (*rango*) officer; (*obrero*) skilled worker.

oficialismo *m Am* (*gobierno*) government.

oficina *f* office; **o. de turismo** tourist office; **o. de correos** post office.

oficinista *mf* office worker.

oficio *m* (*ocupación*) occupation; (*profesión*) trade.

ofrecer 1 *vt* to offer; (*aspecto*) to present. **2 ofrecerse** *vr* (*prestarse*) to offer; (*situación*) to present itself.

ofrezco *indic pres de* ofrecer.

oftalmólogo,-a *mf* ophthalmologist.

oído *m* (*sentido*) hearing; (*órgano*) ear.

oír *vt* to hear; **¡oye!** hey!; **¡oiga!** excuse me!

ojal *m* buttonhole.

ojalá 1 *interj* let's hope so! **2** *conj* + *subjuntivo* **¡o. sea cierto!** I hope it is true!

ojeada *f* **echar una o.** to have a quick look (**a** at).

ojeras *fpl* bags under the eyes.

ojo 1 *m* eye; (*de cerradura*) keyhole; **calcular a o.** to guess. **2** *interj* careful!

ojota *f Am* sandal.

ola *f* wave.

oleaje *m* swell.

oleoducto *m* pipeline.

oler [4] **1** *vt* to smell. **2** *vi* (*exhalar*) to smell; **o. a** to smell of; **o. bien/mal** to smell good/bad.

olfato *m* sense of smell.

olimpiada *f* Olympic Games *pl*; **las olimpiadas** the Olympic Games.

olímpico,-a *a* Olympic.

oliva *f* olive; **aceite de o.** olive oil.

olivo *m* olive (tree).

olmo *m* elm.

olor *m* smell.

olvidar **1** *vt* to forget; (*dejar*) to leave. **2 olvidarse** *vr* **olvidarse de algo** to forget sth.

olla *f* saucepan; **o. exprés** *o* **a presión** pressure cooker.

ombligo *m* navel.

omisión *f* omission.

omitir *vt* to omit.

omnipotente *a* almighty.

omóplato, omoplato *m* shoulder blade.

once *inv a & m* eleven.

onda *f* wave; (*en el agua*) ripple; **o. larga/media/corta** long/medium/short wave.

ondulado,-a *a* (*pelo*) wavy; (*paisaje*) rolling.

ONU *f abr de* **Organización de las Naciones Unidas** United Nations (Organization), UN(O).

opaco,-a *a* opaque.

opcional *a* optional.

ópera *f* opera.

operación *f* operation; (*financiera*) transaction.

operador,-a *mf* operator; (*de la cámara*) (*hombre*) cameraman; (*mujer*) camerawoman.

operar **1** *vt* to operate (**a** on). **2 operarse** *vr* to have an operation (**de** for); (*producirse*) to take place.

opinar *vi* (*pensar*) to think; (*declarar*) to give one's opinion.

opinión *f* opinion; **cambiar de o.** to change one's mind.

oponer (*pp* **opuesto**) **1** *vt* (*resistencia*) to offer. **2 oponerse** *vr* (*estar en contra*) to be against.

oporto *m* (*vino*) port.

oportunidad *f* opportunity.

oportuno,-a *a* timely; (*conveniente*) appropriate.

oposición *f* opposition; (*examen*) competitive examination.
opresión *f* oppression.
oprimir *vt* (*pulsar*) to press; (*subyugar*) to oppress.
optativo,-a *a* optional.
óptica *f* (*tienda*) optician's (shop).
óptico,-a 1 *a* optical. **2** *mf* optician.
optimista 1 *a* optimistic. **2** *mf* optimist.
óptimo,-a *a* excellent; (*condiciones*) optimum.
opuesto,-a *a* (*contrario*) contrary; (*de enfrente*) opposite; **en direcciones opuestas** in opposite directions.
opuse *pt indef de* **oponer.**
oración *f* (*plegaria*) prayer.
oral *a* oral; **por vía o.** to be taken orally.
orar *vi* to pray.
orden 1 *m* order; **o. público** law and order; **por o. alfabético** in alphabetical order; **del o. de** in the order of. **2** *f* order; (*judicial*) warrant; **¡a la o.!** sir!
ordenado,-a *a* tidy.
ordenador,-a *m* computer; **o. de sobremesa** desktop (computer); **o. doméstico** home computer.
ordenanza 1 *m* (*empleado*) office boy. **2** *f* regulations *pl*.
ordenar *vt* (*organizar*) to put in order; (*habitación*) to tidy up; (*mandar*) to order.
ordeñar *vt* to milk.
ordinario,-a *a* (*corriente*) ordinary; (*grosero*) common.
orégano *m* oregano.
oreja *f* ear.
orejero,-a *a Am* (*soplón*) grass.
orfanato, orfelinato *m* orphanage.
orgánico,-a *a* organic.
organismo *m* organism; (*institución*) body.
organización *f* organization.
organizar [4] **1** *vt* to organize. **2 organizarse** *vr* (*armarse*) to happen.
órgano *m* organ.
orgullo *m* (*propia estima*) pride; (*arrogancia*) arrogance.
orgulloso,-a *a* **estar o.** (*satisfecho*) to be proud; **ser o.** (*arrogante*) to be arrogant.
orientación *f* (*dirección*) orientation; (*guía*) guidance.
oriental 1 *a* eastern. **2** *mf* Oriental.
orientar 1 *vt* (*indicar camino*) to give directions to; **una casa orientada al sur** a house facing south. **2 orientarse** *vr* (*encontrar el camino*) to get one's bearings.

oriente *m* East; **el Extremo** *o* **Lejano/Medio/Próximo O.** the Far/Middle/Near East.

orificio *m* hole; (*del cuerpo*) orifice.

origen *m* origin; **dar o. a** to give rise to.

original *a & mf* original.

orilla *f* (*borde*) edge; (*del río*) bank; (*del mar*) shore.

orinal *m* chamberpot, *fam* potty.

orinar 1 *vi* to urinate. **2 orinarse** *vr* to wet oneself.

oro *m* gold; **de o.** golden; **o. de ley** fine gold.

orquesta *f* orchestra; (*de verbena*) dance band.

ortiga *f* (stinging) nettle.

ortodoxo,-a *a & mf* orthodox.

ortografía, *f* spelling.

ortográfico,-a *a* spelling.

ortopédico,-a *a* orthopaedic.

oruga *f* caterpillar.

orzuelo *m* sty(e).

os *pron pers* (*complemento directo*) you; (*complemento indirecto*) (to) you; (*con verbo reflexivo*) yourselves; (*con verbo recíproco*) each other; **os veo mañana** I'll see you tomorrow; **os daré el dinero** I'll give you the money; **os escribiré** I'll write to you.

osadía *f* (*audacia*) daring; (*desvergüenza*) impudence.

oscilar *vi* (*variar*) to fluctuate.

oscuras (a) *adv* in the dark.

oscurecer *vi impers & vt* = **obscurecer.**

oscuro,-a *a* = **obscuro,-a.**

osito *m* **o. (de peluche)** teddy bear.

oso *m* bear; **o. polar** polar bear.

ostentación *f* ostentation.

osteópata *mf* osteopath.

ostra *f* oyster; **aburrirse como una o.** to be bored stiff.

OTAN *f abr de* **Organización del Tratado del Atlántico Norte** North Atlantic Treaty Organization, NATO.

otoño *m* autumn, *US* fall.

otorgar [7] *vt* (*premio*) to award (**a** to).

otorrinolaringólogo,-a *mf* ear, nose and throat specialist.

otro,-a 1 *a indef* **otro/otra** ... another ...; **otros/otras** ... other ...; **el otro/la otra** ... the other ...; **otra cosa** something else; **otra vez** again. **2** *pron indef* another (one); **otros/otras** others; **el otro/la otra** the other (one); **los otros/las otras** the others.

oval, ovalado,-a *a* oval.

oveja *f* sheep; (*hembra*) ewe; **la o. negra** the black sheep.

overol *m Am* overalls *pl.*

ovillo *m* ball (of wool).

OVNI *m abr de* **objeto volador no identificado** UFO.

oxidar 1 *vt* (*metales*) to rust. **2 oxidarse** *vr* (*metales*) to rust.

oxígeno *m* oxygen.

oye *indic pres & imperativo de* **oír.**

ozono *m* ozone; **capa** *f* **de o.** ozone layer.

P

pabellón *m* (*en feria*) stand; (*bloque*) wing; **p. de deportes** sports centre.

paciencia *f* patience.

pacificar [1] *vt* to pacify.

pacotilla *f* **de p.** second-rate.

pactar *vt* to agree.

padecer *vti* to suffer; **padece del corazón** he suffers from heart trouble.

padrastro *m* stepfather; (*pellejo*) hangnail.

padre *m* father; **padres** parents.

padrenuestro *m* Lord's Prayer.

padrino *m* (*de bautizo*) godfather; (*de boda*) best man; **padrinos** godparents.

padrón *m* census.

paella *f* paella (rice dish made with vegetables, meat and/or seafood).

pág *abr de* **página** page, p.

paga *f* (*salario*) wage; **p. extra** bonus.

pagar [7] *vti* to pay; (*recompensar*) to repay; **p. en metálico** *o* **al contado** to pay cash.

página *f* page.

pago *m* payment; **p. adelantado** *o* **anticipado** advance payment.

paila *f* *Am* (frying) pan.

país *m* country; **P. Vasco** Basque Country; **P. Valenciano** Valencia.

paisaje *m* landscape.

paja *f* straw.

pajarita *f* bow tie; (*de papel*) paper bird.

pájaro *m* bird; **p. carpintero** woodpecker.

pakistaní *a & mf* Pakistani.

pala *f* shovel; (*de jardinero*) spade; (*de ping-pong, frontón*) bat; (*de remo*) blade.

palabra *f* word; **dirigir la p. a algn** to address sb; **juego de palabras** pun; **p. de honor** word of honour.

palabrota *f* swearword.

palacio *m* (*grande*) palace; (*más pequeño*) mansion.

paladar *m* palate.

paladear *vt* to savour.

palanca *f* lever; (*manecilla*) handle; **p. de cambio** gearstick, *US* gearshift.

palco *m* box.

palestino,-a *a & mf* Palestinian.

paleta *f* (*espátula*) slice; (*de pintor*) palette; (*de albañil*) trowel; (*de cricket, pingpong*) bat.

paletilla *f* shoulder blade.

paleto,-a 1 *a* boorish. **2** *mf* country bumpkin.
paliar *vt* to alleviate.
palidecer *vi* (*persona*) to turn pale.
palidez *f* paleness.
pálido,-a *a* pale.
palillero *m* toothpick case.
palillo *m* (*mondadientes*) toothpick; **palillos chinos** chopsticks; (*de tambor*) drumstick.
paliza *f* beating; **darle a algn una p.** to give sb a thrashing.
palma *f* palm; (*árbol*) palm tree; **hacer palmas** to applaud.
palmada *f* (*golpe*) slap.
palmera *f* palm tree.
palmo *m* **p. a p.** inch by inch.
palo *m* stick; (*vara*) rod; (*de escoba*) broomstick; (*golpe*) blow; (*madera*) wood; (*de portería*) woodwork; (*de golf*) club.
paloma *f* pigeon; (*como símbolo*) dove.
palomar *m* pigeon house.
palomitas (de maíz) *fpl* popcorn *sing*.
palpar *vt* to feel.
palpitar *vi* to palpitate.
palurdo,-a *a* boorish.
pamela *f* broad-brimmed hat.
pampa *f* pampa, pampas *pl*.
pan *m* bread; **p. de molde** loaf of sliced bread; **p. integral** wholemeal bread; **p. rallado** breadcrumbs *pl*.
pana *f* corduroy.
panadería *f* bakery.
panameño,-a *a & mf* Panamanian.
pancarta *f* placard; (*en manifestación*) banner.
panda¹ *m* panda.
panda² *f* (*de amigos*) gang.
pandilla *f* gang.
panfleto *m* political pamphlet.
pánico *m* panic; **sembrar el p.** to cause panic.
panorama *m* panorama.
pantaletas *fpl Am* panties.
pantalones *mpl* trousers *pl*; **p. vaqueros** jeans *pl*.
pantalla *f* (*monitor*) screen; (*de lámpara*) shade.
pantano *m* (*natural*) marsh; (*artificial*) reservoir.
pantera *f* panther.
pantorrilla *f* calf.
pantufla *f* slipper.

panty *m* (pair of) tights *pl*.

panza *f fam* belly.

pañal *m* nappy, *US* diaper.

paño *m* cloth.

pañuelo *m* handkerchief; (*pañoleta*) shawl.

papa *f* (*patata*) potato.

Papa *m* **el P.** the Pope.

papá *m fam* dad, daddy.

papada *f* double chin.

papagayo *m* parrot.

papel *m* paper; (*hoja*) piece of paper; (*rol*) role; **papeles** (*documentos*) identification papers; **p. higiénico** toilet paper; **p. de aluminio** aluminium foil; **p. pintado** wallpaper.

papelera *f* (*en despacho*) wastepaper basket; (*en calle*) litter bin.

papelería *f* (*tienda*) stationer's.

papeleta *f* (*de rifa*) ticket; (*de votación*) ballot paper.

paperas *fpl* mumps *sing*.

papilla *f* mush; (*de niños*) baby food.

paquete *m* packet; (*postal*) parcel.

par 1 *a* (*número*) even. **2** *m* (*pareja*) pair; (*dos*) couple; **a la p.** (*a la vez*) at the same time; **de p. en p.** wide open.

para *prep* for; (*finalidad*) to, in order to; (*tiempo*) by; (*a punto de*) **está p. salir** it's about to leave; **p. terminar antes** (in order) to finish earlier; **p. entonces** by then; **¿p. qué?** what for?; **ir p. viejo** to be getting old; **no es p. tanto** it's not as bad as all that; **p. mí** in my opinion.

parabólico,-a *a* **antena parabólica** satellite dish.

parabrisas *m inv* windscreen, *US* windshield.

paracaidista *mf* parachutist; (*soldado*) paratrooper.

parachoques *m inv* bumper, *US* fender.

parada *f* stop; **p. de autobús** bus stop; **p. de taxis** taxi rank.

paradero *m* (*lugar*) whereabouts *pl*; *Am* (*apeadero*) stop.

parado,-a 1 *a* stopped; (*quieto*) still; (*fábrica*) at a standstill; (*desempleado*) unemployed; *Am* (*de pie*) standing; *fig* **salir bien/mal p.** to come off well/badly. **2** *mf* unemployed person.

parador *m* roadside inn; **p. nacional** *o* **de turismo** luxury hotel.

paraguas *m inv* umbrella.

paraíso *m* paradise.

paralelo,-a *a & m* parallel.

paralítico,-a *a & mf* paralytic.

paralizar [1] **1** *vt* to paralyse; (*circulación*) to stop. **2 paralizarse** *vr* to come to a standstill.

parapeto *m* parapet; (*de defensa*) barricade.

parar 1 *vt* to stop; (*balón*) to save. **2** *vi* to stop; (*alojarse*) to stay; **sin p.** nonstop; **fue a p. a la cárcel** he ended up in jail. **3 pararse** *vi* to stop; *Am* (*ponerse en pie*) to stand up.

pararrayos *m inv* lightning conductor, *US* lightning rod.

parásito,-a *a & m* parasite.

parcela *f* plot.

parche *m* patch; (*emplasto*) plaster.

parchís *m* ludo.

parcial *a* (*partidario*) biased; (*no completo*) partial; **a tiempo p.** part-time.

parcialmente *adv* partly.

pardo,-a *a* (*marrón*) brown; (*gris*) dark grey.

parecer 1 *vi* to seem; **parece que no arranca** it looks as if it won't start; **como te parezca** whatever you like; **¿te parece?** is that okay with you?; **¿qué te parece?** what do you think of it? **2 parecerse** *vr* to be alike; **parecerse a** to look like.

parecido,-a 1 *a* similar; **bien p.** good-looking. **2** *m* resemblance.

pared *f* wall.

pareja *f* pair; (*hombre y mujer*) couple; (*de baile, juego*) partner; **por parejas** in pairs; **hacen buena p.** they make a nice couple.

parentesco *m* relationship.

paréntesis *m inv* bracket; **entre p.** in brackets.

parezco *indic pres de* **parecer.**

pariente *mf* relative, relation.

parir 1 *vt* to give birth to. **2** *vi* to give birth.

parlamento *m* parliament.

paro *m* (*huelga*) strike; (*desempleo*) unemployment; **estar en p.** to be unemployed; **cobrar el p.** to be on the dole.

parpadear *vi* (*ojos*) to blink; (*luz*) to flicker.

párpado *m* eyelid.

parque *m* park; (*de niños*) playpen; **p. de atracciones** funfair; **p. zoológico** zoo; **p. nacional/natural** national park/nature reserve.

parquear *vti Am* to park.

parquímetro *m* parking meter.

parra *f* grapevine.

párrafo *m* paragraph.

parrilla *f* grill; **pescado a la p.** grilled fish.

párroco *m* parish priest.

parroquia *f* parish; (*iglesia*) parish church.

parte 1 *f* (*sección*) part; (*en una repartición*) share; (*lugar*) place; (*en juicio*) party; **en o por todas partes** everywhere; **por mi p.** as far as I am concerned; **de p. de ...** on behalf of ...; **¿de p. de quién?** who's calling?; **en gran p.** to a large extent; **en p.** partly; **la mayor p.** the majority; **por otra p.** on the other hand. **2** *m* (*informe*) report.

participación *f* participation; (*acción*) share; (*notificación*) notification.

participar 1 *vi* to take part, participate (**en** in). **2** *vt* (*notificar*) to notify.

participio *m* participle.

particular 1 *a* (*concreto*) particular; (*privado*) private; (*raro*) peculiar. **2** *mf* (*individuo*) private individual.

partida *f* (*salida*) departure; (*remesa*) batch; (*juego*) game; (*certificado*) certificate; **p. de nacimiento** birth certificate.

partidario,-a 1 *a* **ser/no ser p. de algo** to be for/against sth. **2** *mf* supporter.

partido,-a *m* party; (*de fútbol*) match, game; **sacar p. de** to profit from.

partir 1 *vt* to break; (*dividir*) to split; (*cortar*) to cut. **2** *vi* (*marcharse*) to leave; **a p. de** from. **3 partirse** *vr* to split (up); **partirse de risa** to split one's sides laughing.

partitura *f* score.

parto *m* labour; childbirth.

pasa *f* raisin.

pasadizo *m* corridor.

pasado,-a 1 *a* (*último*) last; (*anticuado*) old-fashioned; (*alimento*) bad; (*cocido*) cooked; **p. (de moda)** out of date; **p. mañana** the day after tomorrow. **2** *m* past.

pasaje *m* passage; (*calle*) alley; (*pasajeros*) passengers *pl;* (*billete*) ticket.

pasajero,-a 1 *a* passing. **2** *mf* passenger.

pasamanos *m inv* (*barra*) handrail; (*de escalera*) ban(n)ister.

pasaporte *m* passport.

pasar 1 *vt* to pass; (*página*) to turn; (*trasladar*) to move; (*tiempo*) to spend, pass; (*padecer*) to suffer; (*cruzar*) to cross; (*límite*) to go beyond; **p. hambre** to go hungry. **2** *vi* to pass; (*entrar*) to come in; **p. a** (*continuar*) to go on to; **p. de largo** to go by (without stopping). **3** *v impers* (*suceder*) to happen; **¿qué pasa aquí?** what's going on here?; **¿qué te pasa?** what's the matter?; **pase lo que pase** come what may. **4 pasarse** *vr* (*comida*) to go off; (*excederse*) to go too far; **se me pasó la ocasión** I missed my chance; **se le pasó llamarme** he forgot to phone me; **pasarse el día haciendo algo** to spend the day doing sth; **pasárselo bien/mal** to have a good/bad time.

pasatiempo *m* pastime, hobby.

pascua *f* Easter; **pascuas** (*Navidad*) Christmas *sing;* **¡Felices Pascuas!** Merry Christmas!

pasear 1 *vi* to go for a walk. **2** *vt* (*perro*) to walk. **3 pasearse** *vr* to go for a walk.

paseo *m* walk; (*en bicicleta, caballo*) ride; (*en coche*) drive; (*avenida*) avenue; **dar un p.** to go for a walk/ride/drive.

pasillo *m* corridor.

pasión *f* passion.

pasivo,-a *a* passive; (*inactivo*) inactive.

paso *m* step; (*modo de andar*) gait; (*ruido al andar*) footstep; (*camino*) way; (*acción*) passage; (*de montaña*) mountain pass; **abrirse p.** to force one's way through; **'ceda el p.'** 'give way'; **'prohibido el p.'** 'no entry'; **p. a nivel** level *o* US grade crossing; **p. de peatones** pedestrian crossing, US crosswalk; **el p. del tiempo** the passage of time; **estar de p.** to be just passing through.

pasta *f* paste; (*italiana*) pasta; (*galleta*) biscuit; *fam* (*dinero*) dough; **p. de dientes** *o* **dentífrica** toothpaste.

pastel *m* cake; (*de carne, fruta*) pie.

pastelería *f* confectioner's (shop).

pastilla *f* tablet; (*de jabón*) bar; **pastillas para la tos** cough drops.

pastor,-a 1 *mf* shepherd; (*mujer*) shepherdess; **p. alemán** Alsatian. **2** *m* (*sacerdote*) pastor.

pata *f* leg; **patas arriba** upside down; **mala p.** bad luck; **meter la p.** to put one's foot in it.

patada *f* kick; (*en el suelo*) stamp.

patalear *vi* to stamp one's feet (with rage).

patán *m* bumpkin.

patata *f* potato; **patatas fritas** French fries, *Br* chips; (*de bolsa*) crisps, US potato chips.

paté *m* pâté.

patentar *vt* to patent.

paternal *a* paternal.

paterno,-a *a* paternal.

patilla *f* (*de gafas*) leg; **patillas** (*pelo*) sideboards, US sideburns.

patín *m* skate; (*hidropedal*) pedal boat; **p. de ruedas/de hielo** roller/ice skate.

patinaje *m* skating; **p. artístico** figure skating; **p. sobre hielo/ruedas** ice-/roller-skating.

patinar *vi* to skate; (*sobre ruedas*) to roller-skate; (*sobre hielo*) to ice-skate; (*deslizarse*) to slide; (*resbalar*) to slip; (*vehículo*) to skid.

patinete *m* scooter.

patio *m* (*de una casa*) patio; (*de recreo*) playground; **p. de butacas** stalls.

pato *m* duck.

patria *f* fatherland.

patrimonio *m* (*bienes*) wealth; (*heredado*) inheritance.

patriotismo *m* patriotism.

patrocinar *vt* to sponsor.

patrón,-ona 1 *mf* (*jefe*) boss; (*de pensión*) (*hombre*) landlord; (*mujer*) landlady. **2** *m* pattern.

patronal 1 *a* employers'. **2** *f* (*dirección*) management.

patronato, patronazgo *m* (*institución benéfica*) foundation; (*protección*) patronage.

patrono,-a *mf* boss; (*empresario*) employer.

patrulla *f* patrol.

paulatino,-a *a* gradual.

pausa *f* pause; (*musical*) rest.

pavimento *m* (*de calle*) paving.

pavo *m* turkey.

pavor *m* terror.

payaso *m* clown.

payo,-a *mf* non-Gipsy.

paz *f* peace; (*sosiego*) peacefulness; **¡déjame en p.!** leave me alone!

peaje *f* toll; **autopista de p.** toll motorway, *US* turnpike.

peatón *m* pedestrian.

peca *f* freckle.

pecado *m* sin.

pecera *f* fishtank.

pecho *m* chest; (*de mujer, animal*) breast; **dar el p. (a un bebé)** to breastfeed (a baby).

pechuga *f* (*de ave*) breast.

pectoral *a* chest.

peculiar *a* (*raro*) peculiar; (*característico*) characteristic.

pedagógico,-a *a* pedagogical.

pedal *m* pedal.

pedante 1 *a* pedantic. **2** *mf* pedant.

pedazo *m* piece, bit; **hacer pedazos** to smash to pieces; (*papel, tela*) to tear to pieces.

pediatra *mf* paediatrician.

pedido *m* (*remesa*) order.

pedir [6] *vt* to ask (for); (*en bar etc*) to order; (*mendigar*) to beg; **p. algo a algn** to ask sb for sth; **p. prestado** to borrow; **p. cuentas** to ask for an explanation.

pedrada *f* (*golpe*) blow from a stone; (*lanzamiento*) throw of a stone.

pega *f fam* (*objeción*) objection; **de p.** (*falso*) sham.

pegajoso,-a *a* (*pegadizo*) sticky.

pegamento *m* glue.

pegar [7] **1** *vt* (*adherir*) to stick; (*con pegamento*) to glue; (*golpear*) to hit; *fam* **no pegó ojo** he didn't sleep a wink; **p. un grito** to shout; **p. un salto** to jump. **2** *vi* (*adherirse*) to stick; (*armonizar*) to match; (*sol*) to beat down. **3 pegarse** *vr* (*adherirse*) to stick; (*pelearse*) to fight; (*comida*) to get burnt; (*arrimarse*) to get close; **pegarse un tiro** to shoot oneself; **se me ha pegado el sol** I've got a touch of the sun.

pegatina *f* sticker.

peinado,-a *m* hairstyle, *fam* hairdo.

peinar 1 *vt* (*pelo*) to comb. **2 peinarse** *vr* to comb one's hair.

peine *m* comb.

pelado,-a *a* (*fruta, patata*) peeled; (*cabeza*) shorn.

pelar 1 *vt* (*cortar el pelo a*) to cut the hair of; (*fruta, patata*) to peel. **2 pelarse** *vr* (*cortarse el pelo*) to get one's hair cut.

peldaño *m* step; (*de escalera de mano*) rung.

pelea *f* fight; (*riña*) row.

pelear 1 *vi* to fight; (*reñir*) to quarrel. **2 pelearse** *vr* to fight; (*reñir*) to quarrel; (*enemistarse*) to fall out.

peletería *f* (*tienda*) fur shop.

película *f* film, *US* movie; (*fotográfica*) film; **p. de miedo** *o* **terror** horror film; **p. del Oeste** Western.

peligro *m* danger; (*riesgo*) risk; **correr (el) p. de ...** to run the risk of ...; **poner en p.** to endanger.

peligroso,-a *a* dangerous.

pelirrojo,-a 1 *a* red-haired; (*anaranjado*) ginger-haired. **2** *mf* redhead.

pellejo *m* (*piel*) skin; **jugarse el p.** to risk one's neck.

pellizco *m* pinch.

pelma *mf*, **pelmazo,-a** *mf* (*persona*) bore.

pelo *m* hair; (*de animal*) coat; **cortarse el p.** (*uno mismo*) to cut one's hair; (*en la peluquería*) to have one's hair cut; **tomar el p. a algn** to pull sb's leg; **por los pelos** by the skin of one's teeth.

pelota *f* ball; **hacer la p. a algn** to suck up to sb.

pelotón *m* squad.

pelotudo,-a *a Am* slack.

peluca *f* wig.

peluche *m* **osito de p.** teddy bear.

peludo,-a *a* hairy.

peluquería *f* hairdresser's (shop).

pena *f* (*tristeza*) sorrow; **¡qué p.!** what a pity!; **no merece** *o* **vale la p. (ir)** it's not worthwhile (going); **a duras penas** with great difficulty; **p. de muerte** *o* **capital** death penalty.

penalti *m* (*pl* **penaltis**) penalty.

pendejo *m Am* jerk.

pendiente 1 *a* (*por resolver*) pending; (*colgante*) hanging (**de** from); **asignatura p.** (*en colegio*) subject not yet passed; **estar p. de** (*esperar*) to

...e waiting for; (*vigilar*) to be on the lookout for. **2** *m* (*joya*) earring. **3** *f* slope.

penetrante *a* penetrating; (*frío, voz, mirada*) piercing.

penetrar 1 *vt* to penetrate. **2** *vi* (*entrar*) to enter (**en** -).

penicilina *f* penicillin.

península *f* peninsula.

penique *m* penny, *pl* pence.

penitenciario,-a *a* prison.

pensamiento *m* thought; (*flor*) pansy.

pensar [1] **1** *vi* to think (**en** of, about; **sobre** about, over); **sin p.** (*con precipitación*) without thinking; (*involuntariamente*) involuntarily. **2** *vt* (*considerar*) to think about; (*proponerse*) to intend; (*concebir*) to make; *fam* **¡ni pensarlo!** not on your life!

pensativo,-a *a* thoughtful.

pensión *f* (*residencia*) boarding house; (*hotel*) guesthouse; (*paga*) allowance; **media p.** half board; **p. completa** full board.

pensionista *mf* pensioner.

penúltimo,-a *a & mf* penultimate.

penumbra *f* half-light.

peña *f* rock; (*de amigos*) club.

peñón *m* rock; **el P. de Gibraltar** the Rock of Gibraltar.

peón *m* unskilled labourer; (*en ajedrez*) pawn.

peor *a & adv* (*comparativo*) worse; (*superlativo*) worst; **en el p. de los casos** if the worst comes to the worst.

pepinillo *m* gherkin.

pepino *m* cucumber.

pequeño,-a 1 *a* small, little; (*bajo*) short. **2** *mf* child; **de p.** as a child.

pera *f* pear.

peral *m* pear tree.

percance *m* mishap.

percha *f* (*colgador*) (coat) hanger.

perchero *m* clothes rack.

percibir *vt* (*notar*) to perceive; (*cobrar*) to receive.

percusión *f* percussion.

perder [3] **1** *vt* to lose; (*tren, autobús, oportunidad*) to miss; (*tiempo*) to waste. **2** *vi* to lose; **echar (algo) a p.** to spoil (sth); **echarse a p.** to be spoilt; **salir perdiendo** to come off worst. **3 perderse** *vr* (*extraviarse*) (*persona*) to get lost; **se me ha perdido la llave** I've lost my key.

pérdida *f* loss; (*de tiempo, esfuerzos*) waste.

perdiz *f* partridge.

perdón *m* pardon; **¡perdón!** sorry!; **pedir p.** to apologize

perdonar *vt* to forgive; (*eximir*) to pardon; **¡perdone!** sorry!; **perdonarle**

la vida a algn to spare sb's life.
perecedero,-a *a* perishable; **artículos perecederos** perishables.
perecer *vi* to perish.
perejil *m* parsley.
perenne *a* perennial.
perezoso,-a *a* (*vago*) lazy.
perfección *f* perfection; **a la p.** to perfection.
perfeccionar *vt* to perfect; (*mejorar*) to improve.
perfeccionista *a & mf* perfectionist.
perfectamente *adv* perfectly; **¡p.!** (*de acuerdo*) agreed!, all right!
perfecto,-a *a* perfect.
perfil *m* profile; (*contorno*) outline; **de p.** in profile.
perforar *vt* to perforate.
perfumar 1 *vti* to perfume. **2 perfumarse** *vr* to put on perfume.
perfume *m* perfume.
pericia *f* expertise.
periferia *f* periphery; (*alrededores*) outskirts *pl*.
periférico *m* peripheral.
periódico,-a 1 *m* newspaper. **2** *a* periodic.
periodista *mf* journalist.
periodo, período *m* period.
periquito *m* budgerigar, *fam* budgie.
perjudicar [1] *vt* to harm; (*intereses*) to prejudice.
perjudicial *a* harmful.
perjuicio *m* damage.
perla *f* pearl.
permanecer *vi* to remain, stay.
permanente 1 *a* permanent. **2** *f* (*de pelo*) perm; **hacerse la p.** to have one's hair permed.
permiso *m* (*autorización*) permission; (*licencia*) licence, *US* license; **p. de conducir** driving licence, *US* driver's license.
permitir 1 *vt* to permit, allow. **2 permitirse** *vr* (*costearse*) to afford; **'no se permite fumar'** 'no smoking'.
pero *conj* but.
perpendicular *a & f* perpendicular.
perpetuo,-a *a* perpetual; **cadena perpetua** life imprisonment.
perplejo,-a *a* perplexed.
perra *f* bitch.
perrera *f* kennel; (*para muchos perros*) kennels *pl*.
perro *m* dog; *fam* **vida de perros** dog's life; **p. caliente** hot dog.
persecución *f* pursuit; (*represión*) persecution.
perseguir [6] *vt* to pursue; (*seguir*) to run after; (*reprimir*) to persecute.

perseverar *vi* to persevere; (*durar*) to last.

persiana *f* blinds *pl.*

persistente *a* persistent.

persistir *vi* to persist.

persona *f* person; *fam* **p. mayor** grown-up.

personaje *m* character; (*celebridad*) celebrity.

personal 1 *a* personal. **2** *m* (*plantilla*) personnel.

personalidad *f* personality.

perspectiva *f* perspective; (*futuro*) prospect.

perspicaz *a* perspicacious.

persuadir *vt* to persuade.

persuasión *f* persuasion.

pertenecer *vi* to belong (**a** to).

pertinaz *a* persistent; (*obstinado*) obstinate.

perturbación *f* disturbance.

peruano,-a *a & mf* Peruvian.

perverso,-a *a* perverse.

pervertir [5] *vt* to pervert.

pesa *f* weight; **levantamiento** *m* **de pesas** weightlifting.

pesadez *f* heaviness; (*de estómago*) fullness; (*fastidio*) drag.

pesadilla *f* nightmare.

pesado,-a *a* heavy; (*aburrido*) tedious.

pésame *m* **dar el p.** to offer one's condolences.

pesar 1 *vt* to weigh; (*entristecer*) to grieve. **2** *vi* to weigh; (*ser pesado*) to be heavy. **3** *m* (*pena*) sorrow; (*arrepentimiento*) regret; **a p. de** in spite of.

pesca *f* fishing.

pescadería *f* fish shop.

pescadilla *f* young hake.

pescado *m* fish.

pescador,-a 1 *a* fishing. **2** *mf* (*hombre*) fisherman; (*mujer*) fisher-woman.

pescar [1] *vti* to fish.

pescuezo *m fam* neck.

peseta *f* peseta.

pesimismo *m* pessimism.

pesimista 1 *a* pessimistic. **2** *mf* pessimist.

pésimo,-a *a* awful.

peso *m* weight; **p. bruto/neto** gross/net weight; **de p.** (*razón*) convincing.

pestaña *f* eyelash.

peste *f* (*hedor*) stench; (*epidemia*) plague.

esticida *m* pesticide.

stillo *m* bolt.

petaca f (*para cigarrillos*) cigarette case; (*para bebidas*) flask; *Am* (*maleta*) suitcase.

pétalo m petal.

petardo m firecracker.

petición f request.

petróleo m oil.

petrolero m oil tanker.

pez m fish.

pezón m nipple.

pezuña f hoof.

piadoso,-a a (*devoto*) pious; (*compasivo*) compassionate; **mentira piadosa** white lie.

pianista mf pianist.

piano m piano.

pibe,-a mf *Am* (*niño*) kid.

picadero m riding school.

picado,-a 1 a (*carne*) minced, *US* ground; (*fruta*) bad; (*diente*) decayed; (*mar*) choppy. **2** m **caer en p.** to plummet.

picador m picador.

picadora f mincer.

picadura f (*de insecto, serpiente*) bite; (*de avispa, abeja*) sting; (*en fruta*) spot.

picante a hot; (*chiste etc*) risqué.

picaporte m (*aldaba*) door knocker; (*pomo*) door handle.

picar [1] **1** vt (*insecto, serpiente*) to bite; (*avispas, abejas*) to sting; (*comer*) (*aves*) to peck (at); (*persona*) to pick at; (*anzuelo*) to bite; (*perforar*) to prick; (*carne*) to mince. **2** vi (*escocer*) to itch; (*herida*) to smart; (*el sol*) to burn; (*estar picante*) to be hot; (*pez*) to bite; *fig* (*dejarse engañar*) to swallow it. **3 picarse** vr (*fruta*) to spot; (*dientes*) to decay; (*enfadarse*) to get cross.

pícaro,-a 1 a (*travieso*) mischievous; (*astuto*) crafty. **2** mf rogue.

pico m (*de ave*) beak, bill; (*punta*) corner; (*de montaña*) peak; (*herramienta*) pick, *US* pickax; **cincuenta y p.** fifty odd; **las dos y p.** a little after two.

picor m tingling.

pie m foot; (*de instrumento*) stand; (*de copa*) stem; (*de una ilustración*) caption; **a p.** on foot; **de p.** standing up; **de pies a cabeza** from head to foot; **en p.** standing; **hacer p.** to touch the bottom; **perder p.** to get out of one's depth; **al p. de la letra** to the letter.

piedad f piety; (*compasión*) pity.

piedra f stone; (*de mechero*) flint.

piel f skin; (*de patata*) peel; (*cuero*) leather; (*con pelo*) fur; **p. de gallina**

goose pimples *pl.*

pienso *m* fodder.

pierna *f* leg.

pieza *f* piece, part; (*habitación*) room; (*teatral*) play; **p. de recambio** spare part.

pijama *m* pyjamas *pl.*

pila *f* battery; (*montón*) pile; (*de la cocina*) sink; **nombre de p.** Christian name.

píldora *f* pill.

pileta *f* (*pila*) sink; *Am* (*piscina*) swimming pool.

pillar 1 *vt* (*coger*) to catch; (*alcanzar*) to catch up with; **lo pilló un coche** he was run over by a car. **2 pillarse** *vr* to catch; **pillarse un dedo/una mano** to catch one's finger/hand.

pillo,-a 1 *a* (*travieso*) naughty; (*astuto*) cunning. **2** *mf* rogue.

piloto *m* (*de avión, barco*) pilot; (*de coche*) driver; (*de moto*) rider; (*luz*) pilot lamp; **piso p.** show flat.

pimentón *m* red pepper.

pimienta *f* pepper.

pimiento *m* (*fruto*) pepper; (*planta*) pimiento.

pinar *m* pine wood.

pincel *m* paintbrush.

pinchadiscos *mf inv* disc jockey, DJ.

pinchar 1 *vt* (*punzar*) to jag; (*balón, globo*) to burst; (*rueda*) to puncture. **2** *vi* (*coche*) to get a puncture.

pinchazo *m* (*punzadura*) prick; (*de rueda*) puncture; (*de dolor*) sharp pain.

pincho *m* (*púa*) barb; **p. moruno** shish kebab.

ping-pong *m* table tennis.

pingüino *m* penguin.

pino *m* pine; *fig* **hacer el p.** to do a handstand.

pinole *m Am* maize drink.

pinta *f* (*medida*) pint; *fam* (*aspecto*) look.

pintada *f* graffiti.

pintar 1 *vt* (*dar color*) to paint; (*dibujar*) to draw. **2 pintarse** *vr* (*maquillarse*) to put make-up on.

pintor,-a *mf* painter.

pintoresco,-a *a* (*lugar*) picturesque; (*persona*) eccentric.

pintura *f* painting; (*materia*) paint.

pinza *f* (*para depilar*) tweezers *pl*; (*para tender*) clothes peg; (*de animal*) pincer.

piña *f* (*de pino*) pine cone; (*ananás*) pineapple.

piñón *m* pine seed.

piojo *m* louse.

pipa *f* (*de fumar*) pipe; (*de fruta*) pip; (*de girasol*) sunflower seed.

piragua *f* canoe.

piragüismo *m* canoeing.

pirámide *f* pyramid.

piraña *f* piranha.

pirata *a* & *mf* pirate.

piropo *m* **echar un p.** to pay a compliment.

pisada *f* footstep; (*huella*) footprint.

pisapapeles *m inv* paperweight.

pisar *vt* to step on.

piscifactoría *f* fish farm.

piscina *f* swimming pool.

piso *m* flat, apartment; (*planta*) floor; (*de carretera*) surface.

pisotear *vt* (*aplastar*) to stamp on; (*pisar*) to trample on.

pisotón *m* **me dio un p.** he stood on my foot.

pista *m* track; (*rastro*) trail; (*indicio*) clue; **p. de baile** dance floor; **p. de esquí** ski slope; **p. de patinaje** ice rink; **p. de tenis** tennis court; **p. de aterrizaje** landing strip; **p. de despegue** runway.

pistacho *m* pistachio (nut).

pistola *f* pistol.

pitar 1 *vt* (*silbato*) to blow. **2** *vi* to whistle; (*coche*) to toot one's horn.

pitillo *m* cigarette, *fam* fag.

pito *m* whistle; (*de vehículo*) horn.

pizarra *f* (*encerado*) blackboard; (*piedra*) slate.

pizca *f* little bit; **ni p.** not a bit.

placa *f* plate; (*conmemorativa*) plaque.

placer *m* pleasure; **tengo el p. de ...** it gives me great pleasure to ...

plaga *f* plague.

plagiario,-a *mf Am* (*secuestrador*) kidnapper.

plagio *m* plagiarism.

plan *m* (*proyecto*) plan; (*programa*) programme; **p. de estudios** syllabus; **estar a p.** to be on a diet.

plana *f* page; **primera p.** front page.

plancha *f* iron; (*de metal*) plate; (*de cocina*) hotplate; **sardinas a la p.** grilled sardines.

planchar *vt* to iron.

planeta *m* planet.

planificación *f* planning.

planilla *f Am* application form.

plano,-a 1 *m* (*de ciudad*) map; (*proyecto*) plan. **2** *a* flat.

planta *f* plant; (*del pie*) sole; (*piso*) floor, storey; **p. baja** ground floor, *US* first floor.

plantar 1 vt (*árboles, campo*) to plant; (*poner*) to put, place; **2 plantarse** vr to stand; (*llegar*) to arrive.

plantear 1 vt (*problema*) to raise; (*proponer*) to put forward; (*exponer*) to present. **2 plantearse** vt & vr (*considerar*) to consider; (*problema*) to arise.

plantilla f (*personal*) staff; (*de zapato*) insole.

plantón m fam **dar un p. a algn** to stand sb up.

plástico,-a a & m plastic.

plastilina[R] f Plasticine[R].

plata f silver; (*objetos de plata*) silverware; *Am* money; **p. de ley** sterling silver.

plataforma m platform.

plátano m (*fruta*) banana; (*árbol*) plane tree.

platillo m saucer; **p. volante** flying saucer.

platina f (*de tocadiscos*) deck.

plato m plate, dish; (*parte de una comida*) course; (*guiso*) dish; (*de balanza*) tray; (*de tocadiscos*) turntable; **de primer p.** for starters; **p. combinado** one-course meal.

playa f beach; (*costa*) seaside; *Am* **p. de estacionamiento** car park, *US* parking lot.

playera f sandshoe, *US* sneaker; *Am* (*camiseta*) teeshirt.

plaza f square; (*mercado*) marketplace; (*de vehículo*) seat; (*laboral*) post; **p. de toros** bullring.

plazo m (*periodo*) period; (*término*) deadline; **a corto/largo p.** in the short term/in the long run; **comprar a plazos** to buy on hire purchase, *US* buy on an installment plan.

plegable a folding.

plegar vt to fold.

pleito m lawsuit; **poner un p. (a algn)** to sue (sb).

pleno,-a 1 a full. **2** m plenary meeting.

pliego m sheet of paper.

pliegue m fold; (*de vestido*) pleat.

plomero,-a m *Am* plumber.

plomo m (*metal*) lead; (*fusible*) fuse.

pluma f feather; (*de escribir*) fountain pen.

plumero m feather duster.

plumier m pencil box.

plural a & m plural.

pluriempleo m moonlighting.

población f (*ciudad*) town; (*pueblo*) village; (*habitantes*) population.

poblado,-a a populated.

pobre 1 *a* poor; **¡p.!** poor thing! **2** *mf* poor person; **los pobres** the poor.

pobreza *f* (*indigencia*) poverty; (*escasez*) scarcity.

pocillo *m Am* cup.

poco,-a 1 *m* **un p.** a little; **un p. de azúcar** a little sugar. **2** *a* not much, little; **p. sitio/tiempo** not much space/time, little space/time; **pocos,-as** not many, few; **pocas personas** not many people, few people; **unos,-as pocos,-as** a few. **3** *pron* not much; **pocos,-as** few, not many; **queda p.** there isn't much left. **4** *adv* (*con verbo*) not (very) much, little; (*con a*) not very; **p. generoso** not very generous; **un p. tarde/frío** a little late/cold; **dentro de p.** soon; **p. a p.** little by little; **p. antes/después** shortly before/afterwards; **por p.** almost.

pocho,-a *a* (*fruta*) overripe.

poder¹ *m* power.

poder² 1 *vt* to be able to; **no puede hablar** she can't speak; **no podré llamarte** I won't be able to phone. ‖ (*permiso*) may, can; **¿se puede (entrar)?** may *o* can I (come in)?; **aquí no se puede fumar** you can't smoke here. ‖ (*posibilidad*) may, might; **puede que no lo sepan** they may *o* might not know; **no puede ser** that's impossible; **puede (ser) (que sí)** maybe, perhaps. ‖ (*deber*) **podrías haberme advertido** you might have warned me. **2** *vi* to cope (**con** with).

poderoso,-a *a* powerful.

podré *indic fut de* **poder.**

podrido,-a *a* rotten.

podrir *vt defectivo de* **pudrir.**

poesía *f* (*género*) poetry; (*poema*) poem.

poeta *mf* poet.

póker *m* poker.

polaco,-a 1 *a* Polish. **2** *mf* Pole. **3** *m* (*idioma*) Polish.

polea *f* pulley.

polémica *f* controversy.

polémico,-a *a* controversial.

polen *m* pollen.

policía 1 *f* police (force). **2** *mf* (*hombre*) policeman; (*mujer*) policewoman.

polideportivo *m* sports centre.

poliéster *m* polyester.

polietileno *m* polythene.

polígono *m* polygon; **p. industrial** industrial estate.

polilla *f* moth.

politécnico,-a *a & m* polytechnic.

política *f* politics *sing*; (*estrategia*) policy.

político,-a 1 *a* political; (*pariente*) in-law; **su familia política** her in-laws. **2** *mf* politician.

póliza *f* (*sello*) stamp; **p. de seguros** insurance policy.

polo *m* pole; (*helado*) ice lolly, *US* Popsicle(R); (*deporte*) polo; **P. Norte/ Sur** North/South Pole.

polución *f* pollution.

polvera *f* powder compact.

polvo *m* dust; **limpiar** *o* **quitar el p.** to dust; **en p.** powdered; **polvo(s) de talco** talcum powder; *fam* **estar hecho p.** (*cansado*) to be knackered; (*deprimido*) to be depressed.

pólvora *f* gunpowder.

polvoriento,-a *a* dusty.

polvorón *m* sweet pastry.

pollo *m* chicken.

pomada *f* ointment.

pomelo *m* (*fruto*) grapefruit; (*árbol*) grapefruit tree.

pómez *a inv* **piedra p.** pumice (stone).

pomo *m* (*de puerta*) knob.

pómulo *m* cheekbone.

ponche *m* punch.

poncho *m* poncho.

pondré *indic fut de* **poner.**

poner (*pp* **puesto**) **1** *vt* to put; (*mesa, huevo*) to lay; (*gesto*) to make; (*multa*) to impose; (*telegrama*) to send; (*negocio*) to set up; (*encender*) to switch on; (*película*) to put on; (+ *adjetivo*) to make; **p. triste a algn** to make sb sad; **¿qué llevaba puesto?** what was he wearing?; (*decir*) **¿qué pone aquí?** what does it say here? **2 ponerse** *vr* to put oneself; (*vestirse*) to put on; (+ *adjetivo*) to become; (*sol*) to set; **p. al teléfono** to answer the phone; **p. a** to start to; **p. a trabajar** to get down to work.

poney *m* pony.

pongo *indic pres de* **poner.**

poniente *m* (*occidente*) West.

popa *f* stern.

popular *a* (*música, costumbre*) folk; (*famoso*) popular.

póquer *m* poker.

por *prep* (*agente*) by; **pintado p. Picasso** painted by Picasso; **p. qué** why ▌ (*causa*) because of; **p. necesidad/amor** out of need/love. ▌ (*tiempo*) **p. la mañana/noche** in the morning/at night; **p. ahora** for the time being. ▌ (*en favor de*) for; **lo hago p. mi hermano** I'm doing it for my brother('s sake). ▌ (*lugar*) **pasamos p. Córdoba** we went through Cordoba; **p. ahí** over there; **¿p. dónde vamos?** which way are we taking?; **mirar p. la ventana** to look out of the window; **entrar p. la ventana** to get in through the window. ▌ (*medio*) by; **p. avión/correo** by plane/post. ▌ (*a cambio de*) for; **cambiar algo p. algo** to exchange sth for sth. ‖ (*distributivo*) **p. cabeza** per person; **p. hora/mes** per hour/month. ‖ (*multiplicación*) **dos p. tres, seis** two times three is six; **un diez p. ciento** ten per cent. ‖ (*con infinitivo*) in order to. ‖ **p. más/muy . . . que sea** no matter how . . . he/she is; **p. mí** as far as I'm concerned.

porcelana *f* porcelain.

porcentaje *m* percentage.

porción *f* portion.

porche *m* porch.

pormenor *m* detail; **venta al p.** retail.

porno *a inv* porn.

pornográfico,-a *a* pornographic.

poro *m* pore.

porque *conj* because; **¡p. no!** just because!

porqué *m* reason.

porquería *f* (*suciedad*) dirt; (*birria*) rubbish.

porra *f* (*de policía*) truncheon; *fam* **¡vete a la p.!** get lost!

porrazo *m* thump.

porrón *m* glass bottle with a spout coming out of its base, used for drinking wine.

portada *f* (*de libro etc*) cover; (*de periódico*) front page; (*de disco*) sleeve; (*fachada*) facade.

portaequipajes *m inv* (*maletero*) boot, *US* trunk; (*baca*) roof rack.

portal *m* entrance hall; (*porche*) porch; (*puerta de la calle*) main door.

portarse *vr* to behave.

portátil *a* portable.

portazo *m* slam of a door; **dar un p.** to slam the door.

portento *m* (*cosa*) marvel; (*persona*) genius.

portería *f* porter's lodge; (*de fútbol etc*) goal.

portero,-a *mf* (*de vivienda*) caretaker; (*de edificio público*) doorman; (*guardameta*) goalkeeper. **p. automático** entryphone.

portorriqueño,-a *a & mf* Puerto Rican.

portugués,-a *a & mf* Portuguese.

porvenir *m* future.

posada *f* inn.

posar 1 *vi* (*para retrato etc*) to pose. **2** *vt* to put down. **3 posarse** *vr* to settle.

posdata *f* postscript.

poseer *vt* to possess.

posibilidad *f* possibility; (*oportunidad*) chance.

posible *a* possible; **de ser p.** if possible; **lo antes p.** as soon as possible; **es p. que venga** he might come.

posición *f* position.
positivo,-a *a* positive.
posponer *vt* (*aplazar*) to postpone; (*relegar*) to relegate.
postal 1 *a* postal. **2** *f* postcard.
poste *m* pole; (*de portería*) post.
póster *m* poster.
posterior *a* (*lugar*) rear; (*tiempo*) subsequent (**a** to).
posteriormente *adv* subsequently.
postgraduado,-a *a & mf* postgraduate.
postigo *m* (*de puerta*) wicket; (*de ventana*) shutter.
postizo,-a *a* false; **dentadura postiza** dentures *pl*.
postre *m* dessert.
póstumo,-a *a* posthumous.
postura *f* position.
potable *a* drinkable; **agua p./no p.** drinking water/not drinking water.
potaje *m* hotpot.
potencia *f* power; **en p.** potential.
potencial *a & m* potential.
potente *a* powerful.
potro *m* colt; (*de gimnasia*) horse.
pozo *m* well; (*minero*) shaft.
PP *m abr de* **Partido Popular.**
práctica *f* practice; **en la p.** in practice.
practicar [1] *vti* to practise, *US* practice; (*operación*) to carry out.
práctico,-a *a* practical; (*útil*) handy.
pradera *f*, **prado** *m* meadow.
pragmático,-a 1 *a* pragmatic. **2** *mf* pragmatist.
preámbulo *m* (*introducción*) preamble; (*rodeo*) circumlocution.
precario,-a *a* precarious.
precaución *f* (*cautela*) caution; (*medida*) precaution; **con p.** cautiously.
precavido,-a *a* cautious.
precedente 1 *a* preceding. **2** *mf* predecessor. **3** *m* precedent; **sin p.**
unprecedented.
precepto *m* precept.
precintar *vt* to seal off.
precinto *m* seal.
precio *m* price.
preciosidad *f* (*cosa*) lovely thing; (*persona*) darling.
precioso,-a *a* (*hermoso*) lovely, beautiful; (*valioso*) precious.
precipicio *m* precipice.
precipitación *f* (*prisa*) haste; (*lluvia*) rainfall.
precipitado,-a *a* (*apresurado*) hurried; (*irreflexivo*) rash.

precipitar 1 *vt* (*acelerar*) to hurry; (*arrojar*) to hurl down. **2 precipitarse** *vr* (*persona*) to hurl oneself; (*acontecimientos*) to gather speed; (*actuar irreflexivamente*) to rush.

precisamente *adv* (*con precisión*) precisely; (*exactamente*) exactly.

precisar *vt* (*especificar*) to specify; (*necesitar*) to require.

precisión *m* (*exactitud*) precision; (*aclaración*) clarification; **con p.** precisely.

preciso,-a *a* (*necesario*) necessary; (*exacto*) accurate; (*claro*) clear.

precoz *a* (*persona*) precocious.

predecesor,-a *mf* predecessor.

predecir (*pp* **predicho**) *vt* to predict.

predicado *m* predicate.

predicción *f* prediction.

predigo *indic pres de* **predecir.**

predije *pt indef de* **predecir.**

predilecto,-a *a* favourite.

predisponer (*pp* **predispuesto**) *vt* to predispose.

predominar *vi* to predominate.

preescolar *a* preschool.

preferencia *f* preference.

preferible *a* preferable; **es p. que no vengas** you'd better not come.

preferido,-a *mf* favourite.

preferir [5] *vt* to prefer.

prefijo *m* (*telefónico*) code, *US* area code; (*gramatical*) prefix.

pregunta *f* question; **hacer una p.** to ask a question.

preguntar 1 *vti* to ask; **p. algo a algn** to ask sb sth; **p. por algn** to ask about sb. **2 preguntarse** *vr* to wonder.

prehistórico,-a *a* prehistoric.

prejuicio *m* prejudice.

preliminar *a & m* preliminary.

prematuro,-a *a* premature.

premeditado,-a *a* premeditated.

premiar *vt* to award a prize (**a** to); (*recompensar*) to reward.

premio *m* prize; (*recompensa*) reward.

prenatal *a* prenatal.

prenda *f* garment.

prender 1 *vt* (*sujetar*) to fasten; (*con alfileres*) to pin; **p. fuego a** to set fire to. **2** *vi* (*fuego*) to catch; (*madera*) to catch fire. **3 prenderse** *vr* to catch fire.

prensa *f* press.

prensar *vt* to press.

preñado,-a *a* pregnant.

preocupación *f* worry.

preocupar 1 *vt* to worry. **2 preocuparse** *vr* to worry (**por** about); **no te preocupes** don't worry.

preparación *f* preparation; (*formación*) training.

preparar 1 *vt* to prepare. **2 prepararse** *vr* to get ready.

preparativo *m* preparation.

preposición *f* preposition.

presa *f* prey; (*embalse*) dam; *fig* **ser p. de** to be a victim of.

presagiar *vt* to predict.

presagio *m* (*señal*) omen; (*premonición*) premonition.

prescindir *vi* **p. de** to do without.

presencia *m* presence; **p. de ánimo** presence of mind.

presenciar *vt* to witness.

presentación *f* presentation; (*de personas*) introduction.

presentador,-a *mf* presenter.

presentar 1 *vt* to present; (*una persona a otra*) to introduce. **2 presentarse** *vr* (*comparecer*) to present oneself; (*inesperadamente*) to turn up; (*ocasión, oportunidad*) to arise; (*candidato*) to stand; (*darse a conocer*) to introduce oneself (**a** to).

presente 1 *a* present; **tener p.** (*tener en cuenta*) to bear in mind. **2** *m* present.

presentimiento *m* premonition.

preservar *vt* to preserve (**de** from; **contra** against).

preservativo,-a *m* condom.

presidente,-a *mf* president; (*de una reunión*) chairperson; **p. del gobierno** Prime Minister.

presidiario,-a *mf* prisoner.

presidio *m* prison.

presidir *vt* to head; (*reunión*) to chair.

presión *f* pressure; **a** *o* **bajo p.** under pressure.

presionar *vt* to press; *fig* to pressurize.

preso,-a 1 *a* imprisoned. **2** *mf* prisoner.

préstamo *m* loan.

prestar 1 *vt* to lend; (*atención*) to pay; (*ayuda*) to give; (*servicio*) to do. **2 prestarse** *vr* (*ofrecerse*) to offer oneself (**a** to).

prestidigitador,-a *mf* conjuror.

prestigio *m* prestige.

presumido,-a 1 *a* conceited. **2** *mf* vain person.

presumir 1 *vt* (*suponer*) to presume. **2** *vi* (*ser vanidoso*) to show off.

presuntuoso,-a *a* (*vanidoso*) conceited; (*pretencioso*) pretentious.

presupuesto,-a *m* budget; (*cálculo*) estimate.

pretender *vt* (*intentar*) to try; (*aspirar a*) to try for; (*cortejar*) to court.

pretendiente,-a *mf* (*al trono*) pretender; (*amante*) suitor.

pretérito,-a *m* preterite.

pretexto *m* pretext.

prevenir *vt* (*precaver*) to prevent; (*evitar*) to avoid; (*advertir*) to warn.

prever (*pp* **previsto**) *vt* to forecast.

previo,-a *a* prior; **sin p. aviso** without notice.

previsible *a* predictable.

previsto,-a *a* forecast.

primario,-a *a* primary.

primavera *f* spring.

primer *a* (*delante de m*) first.

primera *f* (*en tren*) first class; (*marcha*) first (gear).

primero,-a 1 *a* first; **de primera necesidad** basic. **2** *mf* first; **a primero(s) de mes** at the beginning of the month. **3** *adv* first.

primitivo,-a *a* primitive; (*tosco*) rough.

primo,-a 1 *mf* cousin; **p. hermano** first cousin. **2** *a* **materia prima** raw material.

primogénito,-a *a & mf* first-born.

primoroso,-a *a* exquisite.

princesa *f* princess.

principal *a* main, principal; **puerta p.** front door.

príncipe *m* prince.

principiante 1 *a* novice. **2** *mf* beginner.

principio *m* beginning, start; (*fundamento*) principle; **a principio(s) de** at the beginning of; **al p., en un p.** at first; **en p.** in principle; **principios** basics.

pringar [7] **1** *vt* (*ensuciar*) to make greasy. **2 pringarse** *vr* (*ensuciarse*) to get greasy.

pringoso,-a *a* (*grasiento*) greasy.

prisa *f* hurry; **date p.** hurry up; **tener p.** to be in a hurry; **de** *o* **a p.** in a hurry.

prisión *f* prison.

prisionero,-a *mf* prisoner.

prismáticos *mpl* binoculars.

privado,-a *a* private.

privar 1 *vt* (*despojar*) to deprive (**de** of). **2 privarse** *vr* (*abstenerse*) to go without.

privilegio *m* privilege.

pro 1 *m* advantage; **los pros y los contras** the pros and cons. **2** *prep* in favour of.

proa *f* prow.

probable *a* probable, likely; **es p. que llueva** it'll probably rain.

probador *m* fitting room.

probar [2] **1** *vt* to try; (*comprobar*) to check; (*demostrar*) to prove. **2** *vi* to try. **3 probarse** *vr* (*ropa*) to try on.

probeta *f* test tube.

problema *m* problem.

proceder 1 *vi* (*actuar*) to act; (*ser oportuno*) to be advisable; **p. de** (*provenir*) to come from; **p. a** (*continuar*) to go on to. **2** *m* (*comportamiento*) behaviour.

procedimiento *m* (*método*) procedure.

procesador *m* processor; **p. de textos** word processor.

procesar *vt* to prosecute; (*información*) to process.

procesión *f* procession.

proceso *m* process; (*juicios*) trial; **p. de datos** data processing.

proclamar *vt* to proclaim.

procurar *vt* (*intentar*) to attempt; (*proporcionar*) (to manage) to get; **procura que no te vean** make sure they don't see you.

prodigioso,-a *a* (*sobrenatural*) prodigious; (*maravilloso*) wonderful.

producción *f* (*acción*) production; (*producto*) product; **p. en cadena/ serie** assembly-line/mass production.

producir 1 *vt* to produce; (*fruto, cosecha, rendir*) to yield; (*originar*) to bring about. **2 producirse** *vr* to take place.

productivo,-a *a* productive; (*beneficioso*) profitable.

producto *m* product; (*producción*) produce.

productor,-a 1 *a* producing. **2** *mf* producer.

profesión *f* profession.

profesional *a & mf* professional.

profesor,-a *mf* teacher; (*de universidad*) lecturer.

profesorado *m* (*grupo de profesores*) staff.

profetizar [4] *vt* to prophesy.

prófugo,-a *a & mf* fugitive.

profundidad *f* depth; **un metro de p.** one metre deep.

profundo,-a *a* deep; (*idea, sentimiento*) profound.

progenitor,-a *mf* **progenitores** (*padres*) parents.

programa *m* programme, *US* program; (*informático*) program; (*de estudios*) syllabus.

programación *f* programming.

programar *vt* to programme, *US* program; (*para ordenador*) to program.

progresar *vi* to make progress.

progresivamente *adv* progressively.

progresivo,-a *a* progressive.

progreso *m* progress.

prohibido,-a *a* forbidden; **'prohibida la entrada'** 'no admittance'; **p. aparcar/fumar** no parking/smoking.

prohibir *vt* to forbid.

prójimo,-a *mf* one's fellow man.

proliferar *vi* to proliferate.

prólogo *m* prologue.

prolongar [7] **1** *vt* (*alargar*) to extend. **2 prolongarse** *vr* (*continuar*) to carry on.

promedio *m* average.

promesa *f* promise.

prometer 1 *vt* to promise. **2** *vi* to be promising. **3 prometerse** *vr* to get engaged.

prometido,-a 1 *a* promised. **2** *mf* (*hombre*) fiancé; (*mujer*) fiancée.

promocionar *vt* to promote.

pronombre *m* pronoun.

pronosticar [1] *vt* to forecast.

pronóstico *m* (*del tiempo*) forecast; (*médico*) prognosis.

pronto,-a 1 *a* quick, prompt. **2** *adv* (*deprisa*) quickly; (*temprano*) early; **de p.** suddenly; **por de** *o* **lo p.** (*para empezar*) to start with; **¡hasta p.!** see you soon!

pronunciación *f* pronunciation.

pronunciar *vt* to pronounce; (*discurso*) to deliver.

propaganda *f* (*política*) propaganda; (*comercial*) advertising.

propagar [7] **1** *vt* to spread. **2 propagarse** *vr* to spread.

propiamente *adv* **p. dicho** strictly speaking.

propiedad *f* (*posesión*) ownership; (*cosa poseída*) property; **con p.** properly.

propietario,-a *mf* owner.

propina *f* tip.

propio,-a *a* (*de uno*) own; (*correcto*) suitable; (*característico*) typical; (*mismo*) (*hombre*) himself; (*mujer*) herself; (*animal, cosa*) itself; **el p. autor** the author himself; **propios,-as** themselves.

proponer (*pp* **propuesto**) **1** *vt* to propose. **2 proponerse** *vr* to intend.

proporción *f* proportion; **proporciones** (*tamaño*) size *sing*.

proporcional *a* proportional.

proporcionar *vt* (*dar*) to give; (*suministrar*) to supply.

proposición *f* (*propuesta*) proposal.

propósito *m* (*intención*) intention; **a p.** (*por cierto*) by the way; (*adrede*) on purpose.

propuesta *f* suggestion.

propuse *pt indef de* **proponer**.

prórroga *f* (*prolongación*) extension; (*en partido*) extra time, *US* overtime; (*aplazamiento*) postponement.

prosa *f* prose.

proseguir [6] *vti* to carry on.

prospecto *m* leaflet.

prosperar *vi* (*negocio, país*) to prosper; (*propuesta*) to be accepted.

próspero,-a *a* prosperous.

prostitución *f* prostitution.

prostituta *f* prostitute.

protagonista *mf* main character.

protección *f* protection; **p. de escritura** write protection.

protector,-a 1 *a* protective. **2** *mf* protector.

proteger [5] *vt* to protect.

protesta *f* protest.

protestante *a & mf* Protestant.

protestar *vi* to protest; (*quejarse*) to complain.

protocolo *m* protocol.

protuberante *a* bulging.

provecho *m* benefit; **¡buen p.!** enjoy your meal!; **sacar p. de algo** to benefit from sth.

proveedor,-a *mf* supplier.

proveer (*pp* **provisto**) *vt* to supply.

provenir *vi* **p. de** to come from.

proverbio *m* proverb.

provincia *f* province.

provisional *a* provisional.

provisto,-a *a* **p. de** equipped with.

provocación *f* provocation.

provocador,-a 1 *mf* instigator. **2** *a* provocative.

provocar [1] *vt* (*causar*) to cause; (*instigar*) to provoke; *Am* **si no le provoca** if he doesn't feel like it.

provocativo,-a *a* provocative.

próximamente *adv* soon.

proximidad *f* closeness; **en las proximidades de** in the vicinity of.

próximo,-a *a* (*cercano*) near, close; (*siguiente*) next.

proyección *f* projection; (*de película*) showing.

proyectar *vt* (*luz*) to project; (*planear*) to plan; (*película*) to show.

proyectil *m* projectile.

proyecto *m* project.

proyector *m* projector.

prudencia *f* prudence; (*moderación*) care.

prudente *a* prudent; (*conductor*) careful.

prueba *f* (*argumento*) proof; (*examen etc*) test; **a p. de agua/balas**

waterproof/bullet-proof.

psicoanálisis *m inv* psychoanalysis.

psicología *f* psychology.

psicológico,-a *a* psychological.

psicólogo,-a *mf* psychologist.

psicópata *mf* psychopath.

psiquiatra *mf* psychiatrist.

psiquiátrico,-a *a* psychiatric.

psíquico,-a *a* psychic.

PSOE *m abr de* **Partido Socialista Obrero Español** Socialist Workers'
Party.

pta(s). *abr de* **peseta(s)** peseta(s).

pts *abr de* **pesetas.**

púa *f* (*de planta*) thorn; (*de animal*) spine; (*de peine*) tooth.

pub *m* (*pl* **pubs, pubes**) pub.

publicación *f* publication.

publicar [1] *vt* to publish; (*divulgar*) to publicize.

publicidad *f* advertising; (*conocimiento público*) publicity.

público,-a 1 *a* public. **2** *m* public; (*de teatro*) audience; (*de estadio*)
spectators *pl*.

puchero *m* (*olla*) cooking pot; (*cocido*) stew; **hacer pucheros** to pout.

pucho *m Am* dog-end.

pude *pt indef de* **poder.**

pudor *m* modesty.

pudrir *vt defective,* **pudrirse** *vr* to rot.

pueblo *m* village; (small) town; (*gente*) people.

puente *m* bridge; **p. aéreo** (*civil*) air shuttle service.

puerco,-a 1 *a* filthy. **2** *m* pig; *f* sow.

puericultura *f* p(a)ediatrics *sing*.

pueril *a* childish.

puerro *m* leek.

puerta *f* door; (*verja*) gate.

puerto *m* (*de mar, ordenador*) port; (*de montaña*) (mountain) pass; **p.**
deportivo marina.

puertorriqueño,-a *a & mf* Puerto Rican.

pues *conj* (*puesto que*) as, since; (*por lo tanto*) therefore; (*entonces*) so;
(*para reforzar*) **¡p. claro que sí!** but of course!; **p. como iba diciendo** well,
as I was saying; **¡p. no!** certainly not!

puestero,-a *mf Am* stallholder.

puesto,-a 1 *conj* **p. que** since, as. **2** *m* (*lugar*) place; (*empleo*) post;
(*tienda*) stall; **p. de trabajo** job. **3** *a* (*colocado*) put; **llevar p.** (*ropa*) to have
on.

pugna *f* fight.

pulcro,-a *a* (extremely) neat.

pulga *f* flea.

pulgada *f* inch.

pulgar *m* thumb.

pulir *vt* (*metal, madera*) to polish.

pulmón *m* lung.

pulpería *f* *Am* store.

pulpo *m* octopus.

pulsación *f* pulsation; (*en mecanografía*) keystroke.

pulsar *vt* (*timbre, botón*) to press; (*tecla*) to hit.

pulsera *f* (*aro*) bracelet; **reloj de p.** wristwatch.

pulso *m* pulse; (*mano firme*) steady hand; **echarse un p.** to arm-wrestle.

puma *m* puma.

puna *f* *Am* high moor; (*mal*) mountain sickness.

punta *f* (*extremo*) tip; (*extremo afilado*) point; (*de cabello*) end; **sacar p. a un lápiz** to sharpen a pencil; **tecnología p.** state-of-the-art technology; **hora p.** rush hour.

puntapié *m* kick.

puntería *f* aim; **tener buena/mala p.** to be a good/bad shot.

puntiagudo,-a *a* sharp.

puntilla *f* (*encaje*) lace; **dar la p.** to finish (the bull) off; **de puntillas** on tiptoe.

punto *m* point; (*marca*) dot; (*lugar*) point; (*de costura, sutura*) stitch; **a p. ready**; **a p. de** on the point of; **hasta cierto p.** to a certain extent; **p. muerto** neutral; **p. de vista** point of view; **p. y seguido** full stop; **p. y coma** semicolon; **dos puntos** colon; **p. y aparte** full stop, new paragraph; **las ocho en p.** eight o'clock sharp; **hacer p.** to knit.

puntuación *f* (*ortográfica*) punctuation; (*deportiva*) score; (*nota*) mark.

puntual 1 *a* punctual. **2** *adv* punctually.

puntualidad *f* punctuality.

puñado *m* handful.

puñal *m* dagger.

puñalada *f* stab.

puñetazo *m* punch.

puño *m* fist; (*de camisa etc*) cuff; (*de herramienta*) handle.

pupa *f* (*herida*) sore.

pupila *f* pupil.

pupitre *m* desk.

puré *m* purée; **p. de patata** mashed potatoes.

pureza *f* purity.

purificar [1] *vt* to purify.

puritano,-a 1 *a* puritanical. **2** *mf* puritan.

puro,-a 1 *a* (*sin mezclas*) pure; (*mero*) sheer; **aire p.** fresh air; **la pura verdad** the plain truth. **2** *m* (*cigarro*) cigar.

púrpura *a inv* purple.

puse *pt indef de* **poner.**

puzzle *m* jigsaw puzzle.

P.V.P. *m abr de* **precio de venta al público** recommended retail price.

Pza., Plza. *abr de* **plaza** square, Sq.

Q

que[1] *pron rel* (*sujeto, persona*) who, that; (*cosa*) that, which. ‖ (*complemento, persona*) *no se traduce o* that; (*cosa*) *no se traduce o* that, which; **la chica q. conocí** the girl (that) I met; **el coche q. compré** the car (that *o* which) I bought. ‖ **lo q.** what. ‖ (*con infinitivo*) **hay mucho q. hacer** there's a lot to do.

que[2] *conj no se traduce o* that; **dijo que llamaría** he said (that) he would call. ‖ (*consecutivo*) *no se traduce o* that; **habla tan bajo q. no se le oye** he speaks so quietly (that) he can't be heard. ‖ (*en comparativas*) than; **mejor que tú** better than you ‖ (*causal*) because; **date prisa q. no tenemos mucho tiempo** hurry up, because we haven't got much time. ‖ (*enfático*) **¡q. no!** no! ‖ (*deseo, mandato*) (+ *subjuntivo*) **¡q. te diviertas!** enjoy yourself! ‖ (*final*) so that; **ven q. te dé un beso** come and let me give you a kiss. ‖ (*disyuntivo*) whether; **me da igual que suba o no** I couldn't care whether he comes up or not. ‖ (*locuciones*) **q. yo sepa** as far as I know; **yo q. tú** if I were you.

qué 1 *pron interr* what; **¿q. quieres?** what do you want? ‖ (*exclamativo*) (+ *a*) how; (+ *n*) what a; **¡q. bonito!** how pretty!; **¡q. lástima!** what a pity! **2** *a interr* which; **¿q. libro quieres?** which book do you want?

quebrada *f Am* stream.

quebrar [1] **1** *vt* (*romper*) to break. **2** *vi* (*empresa*) to go bankrupt. **3 quebrarse** *vr* to break.

quedar 1 *vi* (*restar*) to be left; (*con amigo*) to arrange to meet; (*acordar*) to agree (**en** to); (*estar situado*) to be; **quedan dos** there are two left; **quedaría muy bien allí** it would look very nice there; **q. en ridículo** to make a fool of oneself; **q. bien/mal** to make a good/bad impression. **2 quedarse** *vr* (*permanecer*) to stay; **quedarse sin dinero/pan** to run out of money/bread; **quedarse con hambre** to be still hungry; **quedarse (con)** (*retener*) to keep; **quédese (con) el cambio** keep the change.

quehacer *m* chore.

queja *f* complaint; (*de dolor*) groan.

quejarse *vr* to complain (**de** about).

quemadura *f* burn.

quemar 1 *vt* to burn. **2** *vi* to be burning hot. **3 quemarse** *vr fig* to burn oneself out.

quemazón *f* smarting.

quepo *indic pres de* **caber**.

querella *f* lawsuit.

querer **1** *vt* to want; (*amar*) to love; **sin q.** without meaning to; **¡por lo que más quieras!** for heaven's sake!; **¿quiere pasarme el pan?** would you pass me the bread?; **q. decir** to mean; **no quiso darme permiso** he refused me permission. **2 quererse** *vr* to love each other.

querido,-a *a* dear.

querré *indic fut de* **querer.**

queso *m* cheese.

quicio *m* (*de puerta*) doorpost; **sacar de q. (a algn)** to infuriate (sb).

quien *pron rel* **el hombre con q. vino** the man she came with, (*formal*) the man with whom she came. ‖ (*indefinido*) **q. quiera venir ...** whoever wants to come ...; **hay q. dice lo contrario** there are some people who say the opposite.

quién *pron interr* who; **¿q. es?** who is it?; **¿para q. es?** who is it for?; **¿de q. es esa bici?** whose bike is that?

quienquiera *pron indef* (*pl* **quienesquiera**) whoever.

quieto,-a *a* still; **¡estáte q.!** keep still!

quilo *m* = **kilo.**

químico,-a *a* chemical.

quince *a & m inv* fifteen.

quiniela *f* football pools *pl*.

quinientos,-as *a & mf inv* five hundred.

quinqué *m* oil lamp.

quintal *m* (*medida*) 46 kg; **q. métrico** = 100 kg.

quinto,-a *a & mf* fifth.

quiosco *m* kiosk; **q. de periódicos** newspaper stand.

quirófano *m* operating theatre, *US* operating room.

quirúrgico,-a *a* surgical.

quise *indic fut de* **querer.**

quitaesmalte(s) *m inv* nail varnish remover.

quitamanchas *m inv* stain remover.

quitanieves *m* (*máquina*) **q.** snowplough, *US* snowplow.

quitar 1 *vt* to remove, take away; (*ropa*) to take off; (*dolor*) to relieve; (*sed*) to quench; (*hambre*) to take away; (*robar*) to steal; (*tiempo*) to take up; (*asiento*) to take; (*cantidad*) to take away. **2** *vi* **¡quita!** get out of the way! **3 quitarse** *vr* (*apartarse*) to move away; (*mancha*) to come out; (*dolor*) to go away; (*ropa, gafas*) to take off; **quitarse de fumar** to give up smoking; **quitarse a algn de encima** to get rid of sb.

quizá(s) *adv* perhaps, maybe.

R

rábano *m* radish.

rabia *f* (*ira*) rage; (*enfermedad*) rabies *sing*; **¡qué r.!** how annoying!; **me da r.** it gets up my nose.

rabiar *vi* (*enfadarse*) to rage; **hacer r. a algn** to make sb see red.

rabioso,-a *a* rabid; (*enfadado*) furious.

rabo *m* tail; (*de fruta etc*) stalk.

racha *f* (*de viento*) gust; (*período*) spell.

racial *a* racial.

racimo *m* bunch.

ración *f* portion.

racionar *vt* to ration.

racismo *m* racism.

racista *a & mf* racist.

radar *m* (*pl* **radares**) radar.

radiación *f* radiation.

radiactividad *f* radioactivity.

radiactivo,-a *a* radioactive.

radiador *m* radiator.

radiante *a* radiant (**de** with).

radical *a* radical.

radio 1 *f* radio. **2** *m* radius; (*de rueda*) spoke.

radioactividad *f* radioactivity.

radiocasete *m* (*pl* **radiocasetes**) radio cassette.

radiografía *f* (*imagen*) X-ray.

ráfaga *f* (*de viento*) gust; (*de disparos*) burst.

raído,-a *a* (*gastado*) worn.

raíz *f* (*pl* **raíces**) root; **r. cuadrada** square root; **a r. de** as a result of.

raja *f* (*corte*) cut; (*hendidura*) crack.

rajar 1 *vt* (*tela*) to tear; (*hender*) to crack. **2 rajarse** *vr* (*tela*) to tear; (*partirse*) to crack; *fam* (*echarse atrás*) to back out; *Am* (*acobardarse*) to chicken out.

rallado,-a *a* **queso r.** grated cheese; **pan r.** breadcrumbs *pl*.

rallador *m* grater.

rallar *vt* to grate.

ralo,-a *a* thin.

rama *f* branch.

ramillete *m* (*de flores*) posy.

ramo *m* (*de flores*) bunch; (*sector*) branch.

rampa *f* ramp.

rana *f* frog.

rancho *m* (*granja*) ranch.

rancio,-a *a* (*comida*) stale.

rango *m* rank; (*jerarquía elevada*) high social standing.

ranura *f* slot; **r. de expansión** expansion slot.

rapar *vt* to crop.

rapaz 1 *a* predatory; **ave r.** bird of prey. **2** *mf* youngster; (*muchacho*) lad;
  (*muchacha*) lass.

rape *m* (*pez*) angler fish; **cortado al r.** close-cropped.

rapidez *f* speed.

rápido,-a 1 *a* quick, fast. **2** *adv* quickly. **3** *m* fast train.

raptar *vt* to kidnap.

rapto *m* (*secuestro*) kidnapping.

raqueta *f* (*de tenis*) racket; (*de ping-pong*) bat, *US* paddle.

raquítico,-a *a* (*delgado*) emaciated; *fam* (*escaso*) meagre.

raro,-a *a* rare; (*extraño*) strange.

rascacielos *m inv* skyscraper.

rascar [1] *vt* (*con las uñas*) to scratch.

rasgar [7] *vt* to tear.

rasgo *m* feature.

rasguño *m* scratch.

raso,-a 1 *a* (*llano*) flat; (*cielo*) clear. **2** *m* satin.

raspa *f* (*de pescado*) bone.

raspar 1 *vt* (*limar*) to scrape (off). **2** *vi* (*ropa etc*) to chafe.

rastrear *vt* (*zona*) to comb.

rastrillo *m* rake; (*mercadillo*) flea market.

rastro *m* trace; (*en el suelo*) trail.

rasurar *vt*, **rasurarse** *vr* to shave.

rata *f* rat.

ratero,-a *mf* pickpocket.

ratificar [1] *vt* to ratify.

rato *m* (*momento*) while; **a ratos** at times; **al poco r.** shortly after; **pasar un
  buen/mal r.** to have a good/bad time; **ratos libres** free time *sing*.

ratón *m* (*también de ordenador*) mouse.

raya *f* (*línea*) line; (*del pantalón*) crease; (*del pelo*) parting, *US* part;
  camisa a rayas striped shirt.

rayar *vt* to scratch.

rayo *m* ray; (*relámpago*) (flash of) lightning.

raza *f* (*humana*) race; (*de animal*) breed.

razón *f* reason; (*justicia*) justice; (*proporción*) rate; **uso de r.** power of
  reasoning; **dar la r. a algn** to say that sb is right; **tener r.** to be right.

razonable *a* reasonable.

razonar 1 *vt* (*argumentar*) to reason out. **2** *vi* (*discurrir*) to reason.

reacción *f* reaction; **avión de r.** jet (plane).

reaccionar *vi* to react.

reactor *m* reactor; (*avión*) jet (plane).

reajuste *m* readjustment.

real[1] *a* (*efectivo, verdadero*) real.

real[2] *a* (*regio*) royal.

realidad *f* reality; **en r.** in fact.

realismo *m* realism.

realizador,-a *mf* producer.

realizar [4] **1** *vt* (*hacer*) to carry out; (*ambición*) to achieve; **2 realizarse** *vr* (*persona*) to fulfil oneself; (*sueño*) to come true.

realmente *adv* really.

realzar [4] *vt* (*recalcar*) to highlight; (*belleza, importancia*) to heighten.

reanimar *vt*, **reanimarse** *vr* to revive.

reanudar 1 *vt* to renew. **2 reanudarse** *vr* to resume.

rebaja *f* (*descuento*) reduction; **rebajas** sales.

rebajar 1 *vt* (*precio*) to cut; (*tanto por ciento*) to take off. **2 rebajarse** *vr* (*humillarse*) to humble oneself.

rebanada *f* slice.

rebaño *m* herd; (*de ovejas*) flock.

rebasar *vt* (*exceder*) to exceed.

rebeca *f* cardigan.

rebelarse *vr* to rebel.

rebelde 1 *mf* rebel. **2** *a* rebellious.

rebelión *f* rebellion.

rebobinar *vt* to rewind.

rebosar *vi* to overflow.

rebotar *vi* (*pelota*) to bounce; (*bala*) to ricochet.

rebuznar *vi* to bray.

recado *m* (*mandado*) errand; (*mensaje*) message; **dejar un r.** to leave a message.

recalcar [1] *vt fig* to stress.

recalentar [1] *vt* (*comida*) to reheat.

recambio *m* (*repuesto*) spare (part); (*de pluma etc*) refill; **rueda de r.** spare wheel.

recapacitar *vt* to think over.

recargado,-a *a* (*estilo*) overelaborate.

recargar [7] *vt* (*batería*) to recharge; (*adornar mucho*) to overelaborate.

recatado,-a *a* (*prudente*) cautious; (*modesto*) modest.

recaudador,-a *mf* tax collector.

recaudar *vt* to collect.

recelar *vt* **r. de** to distrust.

receloso,-a *a* suspicious.

recepción *f* reception.

recepcionista *mf* receptionist.

receptor,-a 1 *mf* (*persona*) recipient. **2** *m* (*aparato*) receiver.

receta *f* recipe; **r. (médica)** prescription.

recetar *vt* to prescribe.

rechazar [4] *vt* to reject.

rechinar *vi* (*metal*) to squeak; (*dientes*) to chatter.

rechoncho,-a *a* chubby.

recibidor *m* entrance hall.

recibimiento *m* reception.

recibir 1 *vt* to receive; (*acoger*) to welcome. **2 recibirse** *vr* *Am* **recibirse de** to qualify as.

recibo *m* (*factura*) bill; (*resguardo*) receipt.

reciclar *vt* to recycle.

recién *adv* recently; **r. casados** newlyweds; **r. nacido** newborn baby.

reciente *a* recent.

recientemente *adv* recently.

recinto *m* (*cercado*) enclosure; **r. comercial** shopping precinct.

recio,-a *a* (*robusto*) sturdy; (*grueso*) thick; (*voz*) loud.

recipiente *m* container.

recíproco,-a *a* reciprocal.

recitar *vt* to recite.

reclamación *f* (*demanda*) claim; (*queja*) complaint.

reclamar 1 *vt* to claim. **2** *vi* to protest (**contra** against).

reclinar 1 *vt* to lean (**sobre** on). **2 reclinarse** *vr* to lean back.

recluir *vt* to shut away.

recluso,-a *mf* inmate.

recobrar 1 *vt* to recover; (*conocimiento*) to regain; **r. el aliento** to get one's breath back. **2 recobrarse** *vr* to recover.

recodo *m* bend.

recoger [5] **1** *vt* to pick up; (*datos etc*) to collect; (*ordenar, limpiar*) to clean; (*cosecha*) to gather. **2 recogerse** *vr* (*pelo*) to lift up.

recogida *f* collection; (*cosecha*) harvest.

recomendación *f* recommendation; (*para persona*) reference.

recomendar [1] *vt* to recommend.

recompensa *f* reward.

reconciliar 1 *vt* to reconcile. **2 reconciliarse** *vr* to be reconciled.

reconfortante *a* comforting.

reconocer *vt* to recognize; (*admitir*) to admit; (*paciente*) to examine.

reconocimiento *m* recognition; (*médico*) examination.

reconstituyente *m* tonic.

reconstruir *vt* to reconstruct.

recopilación *f* compilation.

recopilar *vt* to compile.

récord *m* record.

recordar [2] *vti* to remember; **r. algo a algn** to remind sb of sth.

recorrer *vt* (*distancia*) to travel; (*país*) to tour; (*ciudad*) to walk round.

recorrido *m* (*trayecto*) journey; (*itinerario*) route.

recortar *vt* to cut out.

recorte *m* cutting; (*de pelo*) trim.

recostar [2] **1** *vt* to lean. **2 recostarse** *vr* (*tumbarse*) to lie down.

recreo *m* recreation; (*en colegio*) break, playtime.

recriminar *vt* to recriminate; (*reprochar*) to reproach.

recrudecer *vt*, **recrudecerse** *vr* to worsen.

recta *f* (*de carretera*) straight stretch.

rectangular *a* rectangular.

rectángulo *m* rectangle.

rectificar [1] *vt* to rectify; (*corregir*) to remedy.

recto,-a 1 *a* (*derecho*) straight; (*ángulo*) right. **2** *adv* straight (on).

rector,-a *mf* rector.

recuerdo *m* (*memoria*) memory; (*regalo etc*) souvenir; **recuerdos** regards.

recuperación *f* recovery.

recuperar 1 *vt* (*salud*) to recover; (*conocimiento*) to regain; (*tiempo, clases*) to make up. **2 recuperarse** *vr* to recover.

recurrir *vi* (*sentencia*) to appeal; **r. a** (*a algn*) to turn to; (*a algo*) to resort to.

recurso *m* resource; (*de sentencia*) appeal.

red *f* net; (*sistema*) network; **r. local** local area network, LAN.

redacción *f* (*escrito*) composition; (*acción*) writing.

redactar *vt* to draft.

redactor,-a *mf* editor.

redondel *m* (*círculo*) ring.

redondo,-a *a* round; (*rotundo*) categorical.

reducción *f* reduction.

reducir 1 *vt* (*disminuir*) to reduce. **2 reducirse** *vr* (*disminuirse*) to diminish; (*limitarse*) to confine oneself (**a** to).

reembolso *m* reimbursement; **contra r.** cash on delivery.

reemplazar [4] *vt* to replace (**con** with).

ref. *abr de* **referencia** reference, ref.

refaccionar *vt* *Am* to repair.

refectorio *m* refectory.

referencia *f* reference.

referéndum *m* (*pl* **referéndums**) referendum.
referente referente a concerning, regarding.
referir [5] **1** *vt* to tell. **2 referirse** *vr* (*aludir*) to refer (**a** to).
refilón de refilón (*de pasada*) briefly.
refinería *f* refinery.
reflector *m* spotlight.
reflejar 1 *vt* to reflect. **2 reflejarse** *vr* to be reflected (**en** in).
reflejo,-a 1 *m* (*imagen*) reflection; (*destello*) gleam; **reflejos** (*en el cabello*) highlights. **2** *a* (*movimiento*) reflex.
reflexión *f* reflection.
reflexionar *vi* to think (**sobre** about).
reflexivo,-a *a* (*persona*) thoughtful; (*verbo etc*) reflexive.
reforma *f* reform; (*reparación*) repair.
reformar *vt* to reform; (*edificio*) to renovate.
reformatorio *m* reform school.
reforzar [2] *vt* to strengthen.
refrán *m* saying.
refrescante *a* refreshing.
refrescar [1] **1** *vt* to refresh. **2** *vi* (*bebida*) to be refreshing. **3 refrescarse** *vr* to cool down.
refresco *m* soft drink.
refrigeración *f* refrigeration; (*aire acondicionado*) air conditioning.
refrigerado,-a *a* (*local*) air-conditioned.
refuerzo *m* strengthening.
refugiarse *vr* to take refuge.
refugio *m* refuge.
refunfuñar *vi* to grumble.
regadera *f* watering can.
regalar *vt* (*dar*) to give (as a present).
regaliz *m* liquorice, US licorice.
regalo *m* present.
regañadientes a regañadientes reluctantly.
regañar 1 *vt* to tell off. **2** *vi* to nag.
regar [1] *vt* to water.
regata *f* regatta.
regatear *vi* to haggle; (*in fútbol*) to dribble.
regazo *m* lap.
regeneración *f* regeneration.
régimen *m* (*pl* **regímenes**) regime; (*dieta*) diet; **estar a r.** to be on a diet.
regio,-a *a* (*real*) regal; *Am* (*magnífico*) majestic.
región *f* region.
regional *a* regional.

registrado,-a *a* **marca registrada** registered trademark.

registrar 1 *vt* (*examinar*) to inspect; (*cachear*) to frisk; (*inscribir*) to register. **2 registrarse** *vr* (*detectarse*) to be recorded; (*inscribirse*) to register.

registro *m* inspection; (*inscripción*) registration.

regla *f* (*norma*) rule; (*instrumento*) ruler; (*periodo*) period; **por r. general** as a (general) rule.

reglamentario,-a *a* statutory.

reglamento *m* regulations *pl*.

regocijar *vt* to delight.

regocijo *m* (*placer*) delight; (*alborozo*) rejoicing.

regresar *vi* to return.

regreso *m* return.

regular 1 *vt* to regulate; (*ajustar*) to adjust. **2** *a* regular; (*mediano*) so-so; **vuelo r.** scheduled flight. **3** *adv* so-so.

regularidad *f* regularity; **con r.** regularly.

regularizar [4] *vt* to regularize.

rehabilitar *vt* to rehabilitate; (*edificio*) to convert.

rehacer (*pp* **rehecho**) **1** *vt* to redo. **2 rehacerse** *vr* (*recuperarse*) to recover.

rehén *m* hostage.

rehogar [7] *vt* to brown.

rehuir *vt* to shun.

rehusar *vt* to refuse.

reina *f* queen.

reinar *vi* to reign.

reincidir *vi* to relapse (**en** into).

reincorporarse *vr* **r. al trabajo** to return to work.

reino *m* kingdom; **el R. Unido** the United Kingdom.

reír [6] *vi*, **reírse** *vr* to laugh (**de** at).

reiterar *vt* to reiterate.

reivindicación *f* demand.

reivindicar [1] *vt* to demand.

reja *f* (*de ventana*) grating.

rejilla *f* grill; (*de horno*) gridiron; (*para equipaje*) luggage rack.

rejoneador,-a *mf* bullfighter on horseback.

relación *f* relationship; (*conexión*) connection; **relaciones públicas** public relations.

relacionado,-a *a* related (**con** to).

relacionar 1 *vt* to relate (**con** to). **2 relacionarse** *vr* to be related; (*alternar*) to get acquainted.

relajación *f* relaxation.

relajar *vt*, **relajarse** *vr* to relax.

relamerse *vr* to lick one's lips.

relámpago *m* flash of lightning.

relatar *vt* to tell, relate.

relativo,-a *a* relative (**a** to).

relato *m* story.

relax *m* relaxation.

relegar [7] *vt* to relegate.

relevante *a* important.

relevar *vt* (*sustituir*) to take over from.

relevo *m* relief; (*en carrera*) relay.

religión *f* religion.

relinchar *vi* to neigh.

rellano *m* landing.

rellenar *vt* (*impreso etc*) to fill in; (*llenar*) to pack (**de** with).

relleno,-a **1** *m* (*de aves*) stuffing; (*de pasteles*) filling. **2** *a* stuffed.

reloj *m* clock; (*de pulsera*) watch.

relojería *f* (*tienda*) watchmaker's.

relucir *vi* to shine.

reluzco *indic pres de* **relucir**.

remache *m* rivet.

remangarse *vr* (*mangas, pantalones*) to roll up.

remar *vi* to row.

rematar *vt* to finish off.

remate *m* (*final*) finish; (*en fútbol*) shot at goal; **para r.** to crown it all; **de r.** utter.

remediar *vt* to remedy; (*enmendar*) to repair; **no pude remediarlo** I couldn't help it.

remedio *m* (*cura*) remedy; (*solución*) solution; **¡qué r.!** what else can I do!; **no hay más r.** there's no choice; **sin r.** without fail.

remendar [1] *vt* (*ropa*) to patch.

remesa *f* (*de mercancías*) consignment.

remiendo *m* (*arreglo*) mend; (*parche*) patch.

remilgado,-a *a* (*melindroso*) fussy.

remite *m* (*en carta*) sender's name and address.

remitente *mf* sender.

remitir **1** *vt* (*enviar*) to send. **2** *vi* (*fiebre, temporal*) to subside.

remo *m* oar.

remodelación *f* (*modificación*) reshaping; (*reorganización*) reorganization.

remojar *vt* to soak (**en** in).

remojón *m fam* **darse un r.** to go for a dip.

remolacha *f* beetroot, *US* red beet.

remolcador *m* tug.

remolcar [1] *vt* to tow.

remolino *m* (*de agua*) whirlpool; (*de aire*) whirlwind.

remolque *m* (*acción*) towing; (*vehículo*) trailer.

remordimiento *m* remorse.

remoto,-a *a* remote.

remover [4] *vt* (*tierra*) to turn over; (*líquido*) to shake up; (*comida etc*) to stir.

remuneración *f* remuneration.

remunerar *vt* to remunerate.

renacuajo *m* tadpole; *fam* (*niño pequeño*) shrimp.

rencor *m* resentment; **guardar r. a algn** to have a grudge against sb.

rencoroso,-a *a* resentful.

rendido,-a *a* (*muy cansado*) exhausted.

rendija *f* crack.

rendimiento *m* (*de máquina, motor*) performance.

rendir [6] **1** *vt* (*fruto, beneficios*) to yield; (*cansar*) to exhaust. **2** *vi* (*dar beneficios*) to pay. **3 rendirse** *vr* to surrender.

RENFE *abr de* **Red Nacional de Ferrocarriles Españoles** Spanish railway. *or US* railroad network.

renglón *m* line.

reno *m* reindeer.

renombre *m* renown.

renovación *f* (*de contrato, pasaporte*) renewal.

renovar [2] *vt* to renew; (*edificio*) to renovate.

renta *f* (*ingresos*) income; (*beneficio*) interest; (*alquiler*) rent.

rentable *a* profitable.

renunciar *vi* (*dimitir*) to resign; (*no aceptar*) to decline; **r. a** to give up.

reñido,-a *a* (*disputado*) hard-fought.

reñir [6] **1** *vt* (*regañar*) to tell off. **2** *vi* (*discutir*) to argue; (*pelear*) to fight.

reo *mf* (*acusado*) accused; (*culpable*) culprit.

reojo mirar algo de r. to look at sth out of the corner of one's eye.

reparar 1 *vt* to repair. **2** *vi* **r. en** (*darse cuenta de*) to notice.

reparo *m* **no tener reparos en** not to hesitate to; **me da r.** I feel embarrassed.

repartidor,-a *mf* distributor.

repartir *vt* (*dividir*) to share out; (*regalo, premio*) to give out; (*correo*) to deliver.

reparto *m* distribution; (*distribución*) handing out; (*de mercancías*) delivery; (*de actores*) cast.

repasar *vt* to revise.

repecho *m* short steep slope.
repeler *vt* (*repugnar*) to disgust.
repente de r. suddenly.
repentino,-a *a* sudden.
repercutir 1 *vt* (*subida de precio*) to pass on. **2** *vi* **r. en** to affect.
repertorio *m* repertoire.
repetición *f* repetition.
repetir [6] **1** *vt* to repeat; (*plato*) to have a second helping of. **2** *vi* (*en colegio*) to repeat a year. **3 repetirse** *vr* (*hecho*) to recur.
repicar [1] *vti* (*campanas*) to ring.
repisa *f* shelf.
replegarse [1] *vr* to fall back.
repleto,-a *a* full (up); **r. de** packed with.
réplica *f* answer; (*copia*) replica.
replicar [1] **1** *vt* (*objetar*) to argue. **2** *vi* to reply.
repollo *m* cabbage.
reponer 1 *vt* to replace. **2 reponerse** *vr* **reponerse de** to recover from.
reportaje *m* report; (*noticias*) news item.
reportero,-a *mf* reporter.
reposar *vti* to rest (**en** on).
reposo *m* rest.
repostar *vti* (*gasolina*) to fill up.
repostería *f* confectionery.
reprender *vt* to reprimand.
represalias *fpl* reprisals.
representante *mf* representative.
representar *vt* to represent; (*significar*) to mean; (*obra*) to perform.
represión *f* repression.
reprimenda *f* reprimand.
reprimir *vt* to repress.
reprochar *vt* **r. algo a algn** to reproach sb for sth.
reproducción *f* reproduction.
reproducir *vt*, **reproducirse** *vr* to reproduce.
reptil *m* reptile.
república *f* republic.
repuesto *m* (*recambio*) spare (part); **rueda de r.** spare wheel.
repugnante *a* disgusting.
repugnar *vt* to disgust.
repulsivo,-a *a* repulsive.
repuse *pt indef de* **reponer.**
reputación *f* reputation.
requesón *m* cottage cheese.

requisar *vt* to requisition.
requisito *m* requirement.
res *f* animal.
resaca *f* hangover.
resaltar *vi* (*sobresalir*) to project; *fig* to stand out.
resbaladizo,-a *a* slippery.
resbalar *vi*, **resbalarse** *vr* to slip.
resbalón *m* slip.
rescatar *vt* (*liberar*) to rescue.
rescate *m* rescue; (*dinero pagado*) ransom.
rescindir *vt* (*contrato*) to cancel.
rescoldo *m* embers *pl*.
reseco,-a *a* parched.
resentimiento *m* resentment.
reserva *f* (*de entradas etc*) booking; (*provisión*) reserve.
reservado,-a *a* reserved.
reservar *vt* (*billetes etc*) to reserve, book; (*guardar*) to keep.
resfriado,-a 1 *m* (*catarro*) cold; **coger un r.** to catch (a) cold. **2** *a* **estar r.**
to have a cold.
resfriarse *vr* to catch (a) cold.
resguardo *m* (*recibo*) receipt.
residencia *f* residence; **r. de ancianos** old people's home.
residir *vi* to reside (**en** in).
resignarse *vr* to resign oneself (**a** to).
resina *f* resin.
resistencia *f* resistance; (*aguante*) endurance; (*de bombilla etc*) element.
resistir 1 *vi* to resist; (*soportar*) to hold (out). **2** *vt* (*situación, persona*) to
put up with; (*tentación*) to resist. **3 resistirse** *vr* to resist; (*oponerse*) to
offer resistance; (*negarse*) to refuse.
resolver [4] (*pp* **resuelto**) **1** *vt* (*solucionar*) to solve; (*asunto*) to settle. **2**
resolverse *vr* (*solucionarse*) to be solved.
resonar [6] *vi* to resound; (*tener eco*) to echo.
resoplar *vi* (*respirar*) to breathe heavily; (*de cansancio*) to puff and pant.
resorte *m* (*muelle*) spring; (*medio*) means.
respaldo *m* (*de silla etc*) back.
respecto *m* **al r., a este r.** in this respect; **con r. a, r. a** with regard to.
respetable *a* respectable.
respetar *vt* to respect.
respeto *m* respect.
respetuoso,-a *a* respectful.
respingo *m* start.

respiración f (acción) breathing; (aliento) breath.

respirar vti to breathe.

resplandecer vi to shine.

resplandor m (brillo) brightness; (muy intenso) brilliance; (de fuego) blaze.

responder 1 vt to answer. **2** vi (a una carta) to reply; (reaccionar) to respond; (corresponder) to answer; (protestar) to answer back.

responsabilidad f responsibility.

responsabilizar [4] **1** vt to make resonible (de for); (culpar) hold responsible (de for). **2 responsabilizarse** vr to claim responsibility (de for).

responsable 1 a responsible. **2** mf **el/la r.** (de robo etc) the perpetrator.

respuesta f ánswer, reply; (reacción) response.

resquicio m chink.

resta f subtraction.

restablecer 1 vt to re-establish; (el orden) to restore. **2 restablecerse** vr (mejorarse) to recover.

restante a remaining.

restar vt to subtract.

restaurante m restaurant.

restaurar vt to réstore.

resto m rest; (en resta) remainder; **restos** remains; (de comida) leftovers.

restregar [1] vt to scrub.

restricción f restriction.

restringir [6] vt to restrict.

resucitar vti to revive.

resuello m gasp.

resultado m result; (consecuencia) outcome.

resultar vi (ser) to turn out; **me resultó fácil** it turned out to be easy for me.

resumen m summary; **en r.** in short.

resumir vt to sum up.

retaguardia f rearguard.

retahíla f series sing.

retal m (pedazo) scrap.

retar vt to challenge.

retazo m (pedazo) scrap.

retención f retention; **r. de tráfico** (traffic) hold-up.

retener vt (conservar) to retain; (detener) to detain.

retirada f withdrawal.

retirar 1 vt (apartar, alejar) to take away; (dinero) to withdraw. **2 retirarse** vr (apartarse) to withdraw; (irse, jubilarse) to retire.

retiro m (*lugar tranquilo*) retreat.

reto m challenge.

retoque m final touch.

retorcer [4] **1** vt (*cuerda, hilo*) to twist; (*ropa*) to wring (out). **2 retorcerse** vr to become twisted.

retorno m return.

retortijón m (*dolor*) stomach cramp.

retraído,-a a reserved.

retransmisión f broadcast.

retrasado,-a 1 a (*tren etc*) late; (*reloj*) slow; **estar r.** (*en el colegio*) to be behind. **2** mf **r. (mental)** mentally retarded person.

retrasar 1 vt (*retardar*) to slow down; (*atrasar*) to postpone; (*reloj*) to put back. **2 retrasarse** vr to be delayed; (*reloj*) to be slow.

retraso m (*demora*) delay; **con r.** late; **una hora de r.** an hour behind schedule.

retrato m (*pintura*) portrait; (*fotografía*) photograph.

retrete m toilet.

retribución f (*pago*) pay; (*recompensa*) reward.

retroceder vi to back away.

retroceso m (*movimiento*) backward movement.

retrospectivo,-a a & f retrospective.

retrovisor m rear-view mirror.

retumbar vi (*resonar*) to resound; (*tronar*) to thunder.

retuve pt indef de **retener**.

reúma, reumatismo m rheumatism.

reunión f meeting.

reunir 1 vt to gather together; (*dinero*) to raise; (*cualidades*) to possess; (*requisitos*) to fulfil. **2 reunirse** vr to meet.

revelar vt to reveal; (*película*) to develop.

reventar [1] vti, **reventarse** vr to burst.

reventón m (*de neumático*) blowout.

reverencia f (*de hombre*) bow; (*de mujer*) curtsy.

reversible a reversible.

reverso m back.

revés m (*reverso*) reverse; (*contrariedad*) setback; **al** o **del r.** (*al contario*) the other way round; (*la parte interior en el exterior*) inside out; (*boca abajo*) upside down; (*la parte de detrás delante*) back to front.

revisar vt to check; (*coche*) to service.

revisión f checking; (*de coche*) service; **r. médica** checkup.

revisor,-a mf ticket inspector.

revista f magazine.

revivir vti to revive.

revolcarse [2] *vr* to roll about.

revoltijo, revoltillo *m* jumble.

revoltoso,-a *a* (*travieso*) mischievous.

revolución *f* revolution.

revolver [4] (*pp* **revuelto**) **1** *vt* (*desordenar*) to mess up; **me revuelve el estómago** it turns my stomach. **2 revolverse** *vr* (*agitarse*) to roll; (*el mar*) to become rough.

revólver *m* (*pl* **revólveres**) revolver.

revuelo *m* (*agitación*) stir.

revuelto,-a *a* (*desordenado*) in a mess; (*tiempo*) unsettled; (*mar*) rough; (*huevos*) scrambled.

rey *m* king; (**el día de) Reyes** Epiphany, 6 January.

rezagarse *vr* to fall behind.

rezar [4] **1** *vi* (*orar*) to pray. **2** *vt* (*oración*) to say.

rezumar *vt* to ooze.

ría *f* estuary.

riada *f* flood.

ribera *f* (*de río*) bank; (*zona*) riverside.

rico,-a 1 *a* **ser r.** to be rich; **estar r.** (*delicioso*) to be delicious. **2** *mf* rich person; **los ricos** the rich.

ridiculizar [4] *vt* to ridicule.

ridículo,-a 1 *a* ridiculous. **2** *m* ridicule; **hacer el r., quedar en r.** to make a fool of oneself; **poner a algn en r.** to make a fool of sb.

riego *m* irrigation.

rienda *f* rein.

riesgo *m* risk; **correr el r. de** to run the risk of.

rifa *f* raffle.

rifle *m* rifle.

rigidez *f* rigidity; (*severidad*) inflexibility.

rigor *m* rigour; (*severidad*) severity.

rigurosamente *adv* rigorously; (*meticulosamente*) meticulously; (*severamente*) severely.

riguroso,-a *a* rigorous; (*severo*) severe.

rimar *vti* to rhyme (**con** with).

rímel *m* mascara.

rincón *m* corner.

rinoceronte *m* rhinoceros.

riña *f* (*pelea*) fight; (*discusión*) row.

riñón *m* kidney.

río *m* river; **r. abajo** downstream; **r. arriba** upstream.

riqueza *f* wealth.

risa *f* laugh; (*carcajadas*) laughter; **me da r.** it makes me laugh; **morirse o**

mondarse de r. to die laughing.
risueño,-a *a* (*sonriente*) smiling.
ritmo *m* rhythm; (*paso*) rate.
rival *a & mf* rival.
rivalizar [4] *vi* to rival (**en** in).
rizado,-a *a* (*pelo*) curly; (*mar*) choppy.
rizar [4] *vt*, **rizarse** *vr* (*pelo*) to curl.
rizo *m* (*de pelo*) curl.
robar *vt* (*objeto*) to steal; (*banco, persona*) to rob; (*casa*) to burgle.
roble *m* oak (tree).
robo *m* robbery, theft; (*en casa*) burglary; **r. a mano armada** armed robbery.
robot *m* (*pl* **robots**) robot; **r. de cocina** food processor.
robusto,-a *a* robust.
roca *f* rock.
roce *m* (*fricción*) friction; (*en la piel*) chafing; (*contacto ligero*) brush.
rociar *vt* to sprinkle.
rocío *m* dew.
rocoso,-a *a* rocky.
rodaja *f* slice.
rodaje *m* shooting.
rodar [2] **1** *vt* (*película etc*) to shoot. **2** *vi* to roll.
rodear 1 *vt* to surround. **2 rodearse** *vr* to surround oneself (**de** with).
rodeo *m* (*desvío*) detour; (*al hablar*) evasiveness; *Am* rodeo; **no andarse con rodeos** to get straight to the point.
rodilla *f* knee; **de rodillas** kneeling; **hincarse** *o* **ponerse de rodillas** to kneel down.
roer *vt* (*hueso*) to gnaw; (*galleta*) to nibble at.
rogar [2] *vt* (*pedir*) to ask; (*implorar*) to beg; **hacerse de r.** to play hard to get.
rojo,-a 1 *a* red; **estar en números rojos** to be in the red. **2** *m* (*color*) red.
rollizo,-a *a* chubby.
rollo *m* roll; *fam* (*pesadez*) drag.
romance *m* (*aventura amorosa*) romance.
romántico,-a *a & mf* romantic.
rombo *m* diamond; (*en geometría*) rhombus.
rompecabezas *m inv* (*juego*) (jigsaw) puzzle.
romper (*pp* **roto**) **1** *vt* to break; (*papel, tela*) to tear; (*vajilla, cristal*) to smash; (*pantalones*) to split; (*relaciones*) to break off. **2** *vi* to break; **r. a llorar** to burst out crying. **3 romperse** *vr* to break; (*papel, tela*) to tear; **romperse la cabeza** to rack one's brains.
ron *m* rum.

roncar [1] *vi* to snore.

roncha *f (en la piel)* swelling.

ronco,-a *a* hoarse; **quedarse r.** to lose one's voice.

ronda *f* round; *(patrulla)* patrol; *(carretera)* ring road; *(paseo)* avenue.

rondar *vti (merodear)* to prowl around; *(estar cerca de)* to be about.

ronquido *m* snore.

ronronear *vi* to purr.

roñoso,-a *a (mugriento)* filthy; *(tacaño)* mean.

ropa *f* clothes *pl*, clothing; **r. interior** underwear.

ropero *m (armario)* **r.** wardrobe, *US* (clothes) closet.

rosa 1 *a inv (color)* pink; **novela r.** romantic novel. **2** *f (flor)* rose. **3** *m (color)* pink.

rosado,-a 1 *a (color)* pink; *(vino)* rosé. **2** *m (vino)* rosé.

rosal *m* rosebush.

rosbif *m* roast beef.

rosco *m (pastel)* ring-shaped pastry.

rosquilla *f* ring-shaped pastry; **venderse como rosquillas** to sell like hot cakes.

rostro *m (cara)* face; *fam* **tener mucho r.** to have a lot of nerve.

roto,-a 1 *a* broken; *(papel)* torn; *(gastado)* worn out; *(ropa)* in tatters. **2** *m (agujero)* hole.

rótula *f* kneecap.

rotulador *m* felt-tip pen.

rótulo *m (letrero)* sign; *(titular)* heading.

rotundo,-a *a* categorical; **éxito r.** resounding success.

rotura *f (ruptura)* breaking; *(de hueso)* fracture.

rozadura *f* scratch.

rozar [4] **1** *vt* to brush against. **2** *vi* to rub. **3 rozarse** *vr* to brush (**con** against).

Rte. *abr de* **remite, remitente** sender.

rubí *m (pl* **rubíes)** ruby.

rubio,-a 1 *a (pelo, persona)* blond; **tabaco r.** Virginia tobacco. **2** *m* blond; *f* blonde.

ruborizarse [4] *vr* to blush.

rudimentario,-a *a* rudimentary.

rudo,-a *a* rough.

rueda *f* wheel; **r. de recambio** spare wheel; **r. de prensa** press conference.

ruedo *m* bullring.

ruego *m* request.

rugido *m (de animal)* roar.

rugir [6] *vi* to roar.

ruido *m* noise; *(sonido)* sound; **hacer r.** to make a noise.

ruidoso,-a *a* noisy.
ruin *a* (*vil*) vile; (*tacaño*) mean.
ruina *f* ruin.
ruiseñor *m* nightingale.
ruleta *f* roulette.
rulo *m* (*para el pelo*) roller.
rumba *f* rumba.
rumbo *m* direction; **(con) r. a** bound for.
rumor *m* rumour; (*murmullo*) murmur.
rumorearse *v impers* to be rumoured.
ruptura *f* breaking; (*de relaciones*) breaking-off.
rural *a* rural.
ruso,-a *a* & *mf* Russian.
rústico,-a *a* rustic.
ruta *f* route.
rutina *f* routine.

S

S.A. *abr de* **Sociedad Anónima** plc.

sábado *m* Saturday.

sábana *f* sheet; *fam* **se me pegaron las sábanas** I overslept.

sabañón *m* chilblain.

saber[1] *m* knowledge.

saber[2] **1** *vt* to know; (*tener habilidad*) to be able to; (*enterarse*) to learn; **que yo sepa** as far as I know; **vete tú a s.** goodness knows; **a s.** namely; **¿sabes cocinar?** can you cook? **2** *vi* (*tener sabor*) to taste (**a** of); *Am* (*soler*) to be accustomed to; **sabe a fresa** it tastes of strawberries.

sabiduría *f* wisdom.

sabio,-a 1 *a* (*prudente*) wise. **2** *mf* scholar.

sable *m* sabre.

sabor *m* (*gusto*) flavour; **con s. a limón** lemon-flavoured.

saborear *vt* (*degustar*) to taste.

sabotaje *m* sabotage.

sabré *indic fut de* **saber.**

sabroso,-a *a* tasty; (*delicioso*) delicious.

sacacorchos *m inv* corkscrew.

sacapuntas *m inv* pencil sharpener.

sacar [1] *vt* to take out; (*con más fuerza*) to pull out; (*obtener*) to get; (*conclusiones*) to draw; (*entrada*) to buy; (*libro, disco*) to bring out; (*fotografía*) to take; (*pelota, bola*) to kick off; **s. la lengua** to stick one's tongue out; **s. provecho de algo** to benefit from sth.

sacarina *f* saccharin.

sacerdote *m* priest.

saciar *vt* (*sed*) to quench; (*deseos, hambre*) to satisfy.

saco *m* sack; *Am* (*jersey*) pullover; **s. de dormir** sleeping bag.

sacrificar [1] **1** *vt* to sacrifice. **2 sacrificarse** *vr* to make sacrifices.

sacrificio *m* sacrifice.

sacudida *f* shake; (*espasmo*) jolt; (*de terremoto*) tremor.

sacudir *vt* (*agitar*) to shake; (*alfombra, sábana*) to shake out; (*arena, polvo*) to shake off; (*golpear*) to beat.

sádico,-a 1 *a* sadistic. **2** *mf* sadist.

saeta *f* (*dardo*) dart.

safari *m* (*cacería*) safari; (*parque*) safari park.

sagaz *a* (*listo*) clever; (*astuto*) shrewd.

sagrado,-a *a* sacred.

sal[1] *f* salt; **s. de mesa** table salt; **s. gorda** cooking salt.

sal[2] *imperativo de* **salir.**.

sala *f* room; (*en un hospital*) ward; **s. de estar** living room; **s. de espera**

waiting room; **s. de exposiciones** exhibition hall; **s. de fiestas** nightclub.

salado,-a *a* (*con sal*) salted; (*con exceso de sal*) salty; *Am* (*infortunado*) unlucky; **agua salada** salt water.

salario *m* salary.

salchicha *f* sausage.

salchichón *m* (*salami-type*) sausage.

saldar *vt* (*cuenta*) to settle; (*deuda*) to pay off.

saldo *m* (*de cuenta*) balance; **saldos** sales.

saldré *indic fut de* **salir**.

salero *m* (*recipiente*) saltcellar.

salgo *indic pres de* **salir**.

salida *f* (*partida*) departure; (*puerta etc*) exit, way out; (*de carrera*) start; (*de un astro*) rising; (*perspectiva*) opening; (*en ordenador*) output; **callejón sin s.** dead end; **s. de emergencia** emergency exit; **te vi a la s. del cine** I saw you leaving the cinema; **s. del sol** sunrise.

salir 1 *vi* (*de un sitio, tren etc*) to leave; (*venir de dentro, revista, disco*) to come out; (*novios*) to go out; (*aparecer*) to appear; (*ley*) to come in; (*trabajo, vacante*) to come up; (*resultar*) to turn out (to be); (*problema*) to work out; **salió de la habitación** she left the room; **¿cómo te salió el examen?** how did your exam go?; **s. ganando** to come out on top; **s. barato/caro** to work out cheap/expensive; **esta cuenta no me sale** I can't work this sum out. **2 salirse** *vr* (*líquido, gas*) to leak (out); **salirse de lo normal** to be out of the ordinary; **salirse con la suya** to get one's own way.

saliva *f* saliva.

salmón 1 *m* (*pescado*) salmon. **2** *a inv* (*color*) salmon pink.

salmonete *m* (*pescado*) red mullet.

salobre *a* (*agua*) brackish; (*gusto*) salty.

salón *m* (*en una casa*) lounge; **s. de actos** assembly hall; **s. de belleza** beauty salon; **s. del automóvil** motor show.

salpicar [1] *vt* (*rociar*) to splash; **me salpicó el abrigo de barro** he splashed mud on my coat.

salsa *f* sauce; (*de carne*) gravy.

saltamontes *m inv* grasshopper.

saltar 1 *vt* (*obstáculo, valla*) to jump (over). **2** *vi* to jump; (*romperse*) to break; (*plomos*) to blow; (*desprenderse*) to come off; **s. a la vista** to be obvious. **3 saltarse** *vr* (*omitir*) to skip; (*no hacer caso*) to ignore; **saltarse el semáforo** to jump the lights; **se me saltaron las lágrimas** tears came to my eyes.

salto *m* (*acción*) jump, leap; **a saltos** in leaps and bounds; **dar** *o* **pegar un s.** to jump, leap; **de un s.** in a flash; **s. de altura** high jump; **s. de longitud** long jump; **s. mortal** somersault.

salud *f* health; **beber a la s. de algn** to drink to sb's health; **¡s.!** cheers!

saludable *a* (*sano*) healthy.

saludar *vt* (*decir hola a*) to say hello to; **saluda de mi parte a** give my regards to; **le saluda atentamente** (*en una carta*) yours faithfully.

saludo *m* greeting; **un s. de** best wishes from.

salvado *m* bran.

salvaguardar *vt* to safeguard (**de** from).

salvaje *a* (*planta, animal*) wild; (*pueblo, tribu*) savage.

salvam(i)ento *m* rescue.

salvar 1 *vt* to save (**de** from); (*obstáculo*) to clear; (*dificultad*) to overcome. **2 salvarse** *vr* (*sobrevivir*) to survive; (*escaparse*) to escape (**de** from); **¡sálvese quien pueda!** every man for himself!

salvavidas *m inv* life belt.

salvo,-a 1 *a* safe; **a s. safe. 2** *adv* (*exceptuando*) except (for). **3** *conj* **s. que** unless.

san *a* saint; *ver* **santo,-a.**

sanar 1 *vt* (*curar*) to heal. **2** *vi* (*persona*) to recover; (*herida*) to heal.

sanción *f* sanction.

sancionar *vt* (*castigar*) to penalize.

sandalia *f* sandal.

sándalo *m* sandalwood.

sandía *f* watermelon.

sandwich *m* sandwich.

sangrar *vi* to bleed.

sangre *f* blood; **donar s.** to give blood; **a s. fría** in cold blood.

sangría *f* (*bebida*) sangria.

sangriento,-a *a* (*cruel*) cruel.

sanguíneo,-a *a* blood; **grupo s.** blood group.

sano,-a *a* healthy; **s. y salvo** safe and sound.

santiguarse *vr* to cross oneself.

santo,-a 1 *a* holy. **2** *mf* saint; (*día onomástico*) saint's day; **se me fue el s. al cielo** I clean forgot; **¿a s. de qué?** why on earth?

santuario *m* shrine.

sapo *m* toad.

saque *m* (*en tenis*) service; (*en fútbol*) **s. inicial** kick-off; **s. de esquina** corner kick.

saquear *vt* (*casas y tiendas*) to loot.

sarampión *m* measles.

sarcástico,-a *a* sarcastic.

sardina *f* sardine.

sargento *m* sergeant.

sarpullido *m* rash.

sarro *m* (*en los dientes*) tartar; (*en la lengua*) fur.

sartén *f* frying pan, US skillet.

sastre *m* tailor.

satélite *m* satellite; **televisión vía s.** satellite television.

satén *m* satin.

sátira *f* satire.

satisfacción *f* satisfaction.

satisfacer (*pp* **satisfecho**) *vt* to satisfy; (*deuda*) to pay.

satisfecho,-a *a* satisfied; **me doy por s.** that's good enough for me.

sauce *m* willow; **s. llorón** weeping willow.

sauna *f* sauna.

saxofón *m* saxophone.

sazonar *vt* to season.

se¹ *pron* (*reflexivo*) (*a él mismo*) himself; (*a ella misma*) herself; (*animal*) itself; (*a usted mismo*) yourself; (*a ellos/ellas mismos/mismas*) themselves; (*a ustedes mismos*) yourselves; **se afeitó** he shaved; **se compró un nuevo coche** he bought himself a new car. ‖ (*recíproco*) one another, each other. ‖ (*voz pasiva*) **el vino se guarda en cubas** wine is kept in casks. ‖ (*impersonal*) **nunca se sabe** you never know; **se habla inglés** English spoken; **se dice que ...** it is said that ...

se² *pron pers* (*a él*) (to *o* for) him; (*a ella*) (to *o* for) her; (*a usted o ustedes*) (to *o* for) you; (*a ellos*) (to *o* for) them; **se lo diré en cuanto les vea** I'll tell them as soon as I see them; **¿se lo explico?** shall I explain it to him/her *etc*?

sé¹ *indic pres de* **saber**.

sé² *imperativo de* **ser**.

sea *subj pres de* **ser**.

secador *m* dryer; **s. de pelo** hairdryer.

secadora *f* tumble dryer.

secar [1] **1** *vt* to dry. **2 secarse** *vr* to dry; (*marchitarse*) to dry up; **secarse las manos** to dry one's hands.

sección *f* section.

seco,-a *a* dry; (*tono*) curt; (*golpe, ruido*) sharp; **frutos secos** dried fruit; **limpieza en s.** dry-cleaning; **frenar en s.** to pull up sharply.

secretaría *f* (*oficina*) secretary's office.

secretario,-a *mf* secretary.

secreto,-a 1 *a* secret; **en s.** in secret. **2** *m* secret.

secta *f* sect.

sector *m* sector; (*zona*) area.

secuencia *f* sequence.

secuestrar *vt* (*persona*) to kidnap; (*avión*) to hijack.

secuestro *m* (*de persona*) kidnapping; (*de avión*) hijacking.

secundario,-a a secondary.
sed f thirst; **tener s.** to be thirsty.
seda f silk.
sedal m fishing line.
sedante a & m sedative.
sede f headquarters; (de gobierno) seat.
sedentario,-a a sedentary.
sedimento m sediment.
sedoso,-a a silky.
seducir vt to seduce.
seductor,-a 1 a seductive. **2** mf seducer.
segar [1] vt to cut.
seglar 1 a secular. **2** mf lay person; m layman; f laywoman.
segmento m segment.
seguida en s. immediately, straight away.
seguido adv straight; **todo s.** straight ahead.
seguir [6] **1** vt to follow; (camino) to continue. **2** vi to follow; **siguió hablando** he went on o kept on speaking; **sigo resfriado** I've still got the cold.
según 1 prep according to; (en función de) depending on; (tal como) just as; **estaba s. lo dejé** it was just as I had left it. **2** conj (a medida que) as; **s. iba leyendo ...** as I read on ... **3** adv ¿vendrás? - s. are you coming? – it depends.
segundo,-a[1] a second.
segundo[2] m (tiempo) second.
seguramente adv (probablemente) most probably; (seguro) surely.
seguridad f security; (física) safety; (confianza) confidence; (certeza) sureness; **s. en carretera** road safety; **s. en sí mismo** self-confidence; **con toda s.** most probably; **tener la s. de que ...** to be certain that ...; **S. Social** ≈ Social Security.
seguro,-a 1 a (cierto) sure; (libre de peligro) safe; (protegido) secure; (fiable) reliable; (firme) steady; **estoy s. de que ...** I am sure that ...; **está segura de ella misma** she has self-confidence. **2** m (de accidentes etc) insurance; (dispositivo) safety device; **s. de vida** life insurance. **3** adv definitely.
seis a & m inv six.
seiscientos,-as a & mf inv six hundred.
seleccionar vt to select.
selecto,-a a select.
self-service m self-service restaurant.
selva f jungle.
sello m (de correos) stamp; (para documentos) seal.

semáforo *m* traffic lights *pl.*

semana *f* week; **S. Santa** Holy Week.

semanal *a & m* weekly.

semanario *m* weekly magazine.

sembrar *vt* to sow; **s. el pánico** to spread panic.

semejante 1 *a* (*parecido*) similar. **2** *m* (*prójimo*) fellow being.

semestre *m* semester.

semifinal *f* semifinal.

semilla *f* seed.

seminario *m* (*en colegio*) seminar; (*para sacerdotes*) seminary.

sémola *f* semolina.

sencillo,-a *a* (*fácil*) simple; (*natural*) unaffected; (*billete*) single; (*sin adornos*) plain.

senda *f*, **sendero** *m* path.

seno *m* (*pecho*) breast; (*interior*) heart.

sensación *f* sensation; **tengo la s. de que ...** I have a feeling that ...; **causar s.** to cause a sensation.

sensacional *a* sensational.

sensato,-a *a* sensible.

sensible *a* sensitive; (*perceptible*) perceptible.

sensiblemente *adv* noticeably.

sensualidad *f* sensuality.

sentar [1] **1** *vt* to sit; (*establecer*) to establish. **2** *vi* (*color, ropa*) to suit; **el pelo corto te sienta mal** short hair doesn't suit you; **s. bien/mal a** (*comida*) to agree/disagree with; **la sopa te sentará bien** the soup will do you good. **3 sentarse** *vr* to sit (down).

sentencia *f* (*condena*) sentence.

sentido *m* sense; (*significado*) meaning; (*dirección*) direction; (*conciencia*) consciousness; **s. común** common sense; **no tiene s.** it doesn't make sense; **(de) s. único** one-way; **perder el s.** to faint.

sentimental 1 *a* sentimental; **vida s.** love life. **2** *mf* sentimental person.

sentimiento *m* feeling; (*pesar*) sorrow.

sentir [5] **1** *vt* to feel; (*lamentar*) to regret; **lo siento (mucho)** I'm (very) sorry; **siento molestarle** I'm sorry to bother you. **2 sentirse** *vr* to feel; **me siento mal** I feel ill.

seña *f* mark; (*gesto, indicio*) sign; **hacer señas a algn** to signal to sb; **señas** (*dirección*) address.

señal *f* sign; (*marca*) mark; (*vestigio*) trace; **s. de llamada** dialling *o* US dial tone; **s. de tráfico** road sign.

señalar *vt* (*indicar*) to indicate; (*identificar, comunicar*) to point out; **s. con el dedo** to point at.

señor *m* (*hombre*) man; (*caballero*) gentleman; (*con apellido*) Mr;

(*tratamiento de respeto*) sir; **el Sr. Gutiérrez** Mr Gutiérrez.

señora *f* (*mujer*) woman; (*trato formal*) lady; (*con apellido*) Mrs; (*tratamiento de respeto*) madam; (*esposa*) wife; **¡señoras y señores!** ladies and gentlemen!; **la Sra. Salinas** Mrs Salinas.

señorita *f* (*joven*) young woman; (*trato formal*) young lady; (*tratamiento de respeto*) Miss; **S. Padilla** Miss Padilla.

sepa *subj pres de* **saber.**

separación *f* separation; (*espacio*) space.

separar 1 *vt* to separate; (*desunir*) to detach; (*dividir*) to divide; (*apartar*) to move away. **2 separarse** *vr* to separate; (*apartarse*) to move away (**de** from).

septentrional *a* northern.

septiembre *m* September.

séptimo,-a *a & mf* seventh.

sepultura *f* grave.

sequía *f* drought.

séquito *m* entourage.

ser¹ *m* being; **s. humano** human being; **s. vivo** living being.

ser² *vi* to be; **ser músico** to be a musician; **s. de** (*procedencia*) to be from; (+ *material*) to be made of; (+ *poseedor*) to belong to; **el perro es de Miguel** the dog belongs to Miguel; **hoy es dos de noviembre** today is the second of November; **son las cinco de la tarde** it's five o'clock; **¿cuántos estaremos en la fiesta?** how many of us will there be at the party?; **¿cuánto es?** how much is it?; **el estreno será mañana** tomorrow is the opening night; **es que ...** it's just that ...; **como sea** anyhow; **lo que sea** whatever; **o sea** that is (to say); **por si fuera poco** to top it all; **sea como sea** be that as it may; **a no s. que** unless; **de no s. por ...** had it not been for ... ∥ (*auxiliar en pasiva*) to be; **fue asesinado** he was murdered.

sereno,-a *a* calm.

serial *m* serial.

serie *f* series *sing*; **fabricación en s.** mass production.

seriedad *f* (*severidad*) seriousness; (*gravedad*) gravity; **falta de s.** irresponsibility.

serio,-a *a* serious; **en s.** seriously.

sermón *m* sermon.

serpiente *f* snake; **s. de cascabel** rattlesnake; **s. pitón** python.

serrín *m* sawdust.

serrucho *m* handsaw.

servicial *a* helpful.

servicio *m* service; (*retrete*) toilet, *US* rest room; **s. a domicilio** delivery service; **s. militar** military service.

servidor *m* server.

servilleta *f* serviette.

servir [6] **1** *vt* to serve. **2** *vi* to serve; (*valer*) to be suitable; **ya no sirve** it's no use; **¿para qué sirve esto?** what is this (used) for?; **s. de** to serve as. **3 servirse** *vr* (*comida etc*) to help oneself.

sesenta *a & m inv* sixty.

sesión *f* (*reunión*) session; (*pase*) showing.

seso *m* brain.

seta *f* (*comestible*) mushroom; **s. venenosa** toadstool.

setecientos,-as *a & mf inv* seven hundred.

setenta *a & m inv* seventy.

setiembre *m* September.

seto *m* hedge.

seudónimo *m* pseudonym; (*de escritor*) pen name.

severidad *f* severity; (*rigurosidad*) strictness.

sexo *m* sex; (*órgano*) genitals *pl*.

sexto,-a *a & mf* sixth.

sexual *a* sexual; **vida s.** sex life.

si *conj* if; **como si** as if; **si no** if not; **me preguntó si me gustaba** he asked me if *o* whether I liked it.

sí[1] *pron pers* (*sing*) (*él*) himself; (*ella*) herself; (*cosa*) itself; (*pl*) themselves; (*uno mismo*) oneself; **por sí mismo** by himself.

sí[2] *adv* yes; **porque sí** just because; **¡que sí!** yes, I tell you!; **un día sí y otro no** every other day; (*uso enfático*) **sí que me gusta** of course I like it; **¡eso sí que no!** certainly not!

sico- = psico-.

SIDA *m* AIDS.

siderúrgico,-a *a* iron and steel.

sidra *f* cider.

siempre 1 *adv* always; **como s.** as usual; **a la hora de s.** at the usual time; **para s.** for ever. **2** *conj* **s. que** (*cada vez que*) whenever; (*a condición de que*) provided, as long as; **s. y cuando** provided, as long as.

sien *f* temple.

sierra *f* saw; (*montañosa*) mountain range.

siesta *f* siesta; **dormir la s.** to have a siesta.

siete *a & m inv* seven.

sigilo *m* secrecy.

sigilosamente *adv* (*secretamente*) secretly.

sigiloso,-a *a* secretive.

sigla *f* acronym.

siglo *m* century.

significado *m* meaning.

significar [1] *vt* to mean.

significativo,-a *a* significant; (*expresivo*) meaningful.

signo *m* sign; **s. de interrogación** question mark.

sigo *indic pres de* **seguir.**

siguiente *a* following, next; **al día s.** the following day.

sílaba *f* syllable.

silbar *vi* to whistle.

silbato *m* whistle.

silbido *m* whistle.

silencio *m* silence.

silencioso,-a *a* (*persona*) quiet; (*motor etc*) silent.

silicona *f* silicone.

silla *f* chair; (*de montura*) saddle; **s. de ruedas** wheelchair.

sillín *m* saddle.

sillón *m* armchair.

silueta *f* silhouette; (*de cuerpo*) figure.

silvestre *a* wild.

símbolo *m* symbol.

simétrico,-a *a* symmetrical.

simiente *f* seed.

similar *a* similar.

similitud *f* similarity.

simio *m* monkey.

simpatía *f* (*de persona, lugar*) charm; **tenerle s. a algn** to like sb.

simpático,-a *a* nice.

simpatizar [4] *vi* to sympathize (**con** with); (*llevarse bien*) to hit it off (**con** with).

simple 1 *a* simple; (*mero*) mere. **2** *m* (*persona*) simpleton.

simulacro *m* sham.

simular *vt* to simulate.

simultáneo,-a *a* simultaneous.

sin *prep* without; **cerveza s.** alcohol-free beer; **s. más ni más** without further ado.

sinagoga *f* synagogue.

sinceridad *f* sincerity.

sincero,-a *a* sincere.

sincronizar [4] *vt* to synchronize.

sindicato *m* trade union, *US* labor union.

sinfonía *f* symphony.

singular 1 *a* singular; (*excepcional*) exceptional; (*raro*) odd. **2** *m* (*número*) singular; **en s.** in the singular.

siniestro,-a 1 *a* sinister. **2** *m* disaster.

sino *conj* but; **nadie s. él** no-one but him; **no quiero s. que me oigan** I only want them to listen (to me).

sinónimo,-a 1 *a* synonymous. **2** *m* synonym.

sintético,-a *a* synthetic.

sintetizar [4] *vt* to synthesize.

síntoma *m* symptom.

sintonía *f* (*de programa*) tuning.

sintonizador *m* (*de radio*) tuning knob.

sintonizar [4] *vt* (*radio*) to tune in.

sinvergüenza 1 *a* (*desvergonzado*) shameless; (*descarado*) cheeky. **2** *mf* (*desvergonzado*) rogue; (*caradura*) cheeky devil.

siquiera *adv* (*por lo menos*) at least; **ni s.** not even.

sirena *f* mermaid; (*señal acústica*) siren.

sirviente,-a *mf* servant.

sistema *m* system; **por s.** as a rule; **s. nervioso** nervous system; **s. operativo** operating system.

sitio *m* (*lugar*) place; (*espacio*) room; **en cualquier s.** anywhere; **hacer s.** to make room.

situación *f* situation; (*ubicación*) location.

situar 1 *vt* to locate. **2 situarse** *vr* to be situated.

slogan *m* slogan.

smoking *m* dinner jacket, *US* tuxedo.

s/n. *abr de* **sin número.**

snob *a* & *mf* = **esnob.**

sobaco *m* armpit.

soberanía *f* sovereignty.

soberano,-a *a* & *mf* sovereign.

soberbio,-a *a* proud; (*magnífico*) splendid.

sobornar *vt* to bribe.

sobra *f* **de s.** (*no necesario*) superfluous; **tener de s.** to have plenty; **saber algo de s.** to know sth only too well; **sobras** (*restos*) leftovers.

sobrante 1 *a* remaining. **2** *m* surplus.

sobrar *vi* to be more than enough; (*quedar*) to be left over; **sobran tres sillas** there are three chairs too many; **ha sobrado carne** there's still some meat left (over).

sobrasada *f* sausage spread.

sobre¹ *m* (*para carta*) envelope; (*de sopa etc*) packet.

sobre² *prep* (*encima*) on, on top of; (*por encima*) over, above; (*acerca de*) about, on; (*aproximadamente*) about; **s. todo** above all.

sobrecogedor,-a *a* awesome.

sobredosis *f inv* overdose.

sobreentenderse *vr* **se sobreentiende** that goes without saying.

sobrehumano,-a *a* superhuman.

sobrenatural *a* supernatural.

sobrepasar 1 *vt* to exceed. **2 sobrepasarse** *vr* to go too far.

sobreponerse *vr* (*superar*) to overcome; (*animarse*) to pull oneself together.

sobresaliente 1 *m* (*nota*) A. **2** *a* (*que destaca*) excellent.

sobresalir *vi* to protrude; *fig* (*destacar*) to stand out.

sobresalto *m* (*movimiento*) start; (*susto*) fright.

sobrevenir *vi* to happen unexpectedly.

sobreviviente 1 *a* surviving. **2** *mf* survivor.

sobrevivir *vi* to survive.

sobrevolar [2] *vt* to fly over.

sobrina *f* niece.

sobrino *m* nephew.

sobrio,-a *a* sober.

socarrón,-ona *a* (*sarcástico*) sarcastic.

socavón *m* (*bache*) pothole.

sociable *a* sociable.

social *a* social.

socialista *a & mf* socialist.

sociedad *f* society; (*empresa*) company.

socio,-a *mf* (*miembro*) member; (*de empresa*) partner; **hacerse s. de un club** to join a club.

sociológico,-a *a* sociological.

socorrer *vt* to assist.

socorrista *mf* lifeguard.

socorro *m* assistance; **¡s.!** help!; **puesto de s.** first-aid post.

soda *f* (*bebida*) soda water.

soez *a* vulgar.

sofá *m* (*pl* **sofás**) sofa; **s. cama** sofa bed.

sofisticado,-a *a* **estar s.** to be out of breath; (*preocupado*) to be upset.

sofocado,-a *a* suffocated.

sofocante *a* stifling.

sofocar [1] **1** *vt* (*ahogar*) to suffocate; (*incendio*) to extinguish. **2 sofocarse** *vr* (*ahogarse*) to suffocate; (*irritarse*) to get upset.

soga *f* rope.

soja *f* soya bean, *US* soybean.

sol *m* sun; (*luz*) sunlight; (*luz y calor*) sunshine; **hace s.** it's sunny; **tomar el s.** to sunbathe; **al** *o* **bajo el s.** in the sun.

solamente *adv* only; **no s.** not only; **s. que ...** except that ...

solapa *f* (*de chaqueta*) lapel; (*de sobre, bolsillo, libro*) flap.

solar¹ *a* solar; **luz s.** sunlight.

solar² *m* (*terreno*) plot; (*en obras*) building site.

soldado *m* soldier.

soldar [2] *vt* (*cable*) to solder; (*chapa*) to weld.

soleado,-a *a* sunny.

soledad *f* (*estado*) solitude; (*sentimiento*) loneliness.

solemne *a* (*majestuoso*) solemn.

soler [4] *vi defectivo* to be in the habit of; **solemos ir en coche** we usually go by car; **solía pasear por aquí** he used to walk round here.

solicitar *vt* (*información etc*) to request; (*trabajo*) to apply for.

solicitud *f* (*petición*) request; (*de trabajo*) application.

solidaridad *f* solidarity.

sólido,-a *a* solid.

solitario,-a *a* (*que está solo*) solitary; (*que se siente solo*) lonely.

sollozar [4] *vi* to sob.

sollozo *m* sob.

solo,-a 1 *a* only; (*solitario*) lonely; **una sola vez** only once; **se enciende s.** it switches itself on automatically; **a solas** alone, by oneself. **2** *m* (*musical*) solo.

sólo *adv* only; **tan s.** only; **no s. ... sino (también)** not only ... but (also); **con s., (tan) s. con** just by.

solomillo *m* sirloin.

soltar [2] **1** *vt* (*desasir*) to let go of; (*prisionero*) to release; (*humo, olor*) to give off; (*carcajada*) to let out; **¡suéltame!** let me go! **2 soltarse** *vr* (*desatarse*) to come loose; (*perro etc*) to get loose; (*desprenderse*) to come off.

soltero,-a 1 *a* single. **2** *m* (*hombre*) bachelor. **3** *f* (*mujer*) single woman.

solterón,-ona 1 *m* (*hombre*) old bachelor. **2** *f* (*mujer*) old maid.

soluble *a* soluble; **café s.** instant coffee.

solución *f* solution.

solucionar *vt* to solve; (*arreglar*) to settle.

sombra *f* shade; (*silueta proyectada*) shadow; **s. de ojos** eyeshadow.

sombrero *m* (*prenda*) hat; **s. de copa** top hat; **s. hongo** bowler hat.

sombrilla *f* sunshade.

sombrío,-a *a* (*oscuro*) dark; (*tenebroso*) gloomy.

someter 1 *vt* to subject; (*rebeldes*) to put down; **s. a prueba** to put to the test. **2 someterse** *vr* (*subordinarse*) to submit; (*rendirse*) to surrender; **someterse a un tratamiento** to undergo treatment.

somnífero *m* sleeping pill.

somnoliento,-a *a* sleepy.

sonar [2] **1** *vi* to sound; (*timbre, teléfono*) to ring; **suena bien** it sounds good; **tu nombre/cara me suena** your name/face rings a bell. **2 sonarse** *vr* **sonarse (la nariz)** to blow one's nose.

sondeo *m* (*encuesta*) poll.

sonido *m* sound.

sonoro,-a *a* (*resonante*) resounding; **banda sonora** soundtrack.

sonreír [6] *vi*, **sonreírse** *vr* to smile; **me sonrió** he smiled at me.

sonrisa *f* smile.

sonrojarse *vr* to blush.

soñar [2] *vti* to dream; **s. con** to dream of *o* about.

soñoliento,-a *a* sleepy.

sopa *f* soup.

sopera *f* soup tureen.

soplar 1 *vi* (*viento*) to blow. **2** *vt* (*polvo etc*) to blow away; (*para enfriar*) to blow on; (*para apagar*) to blow out; (*para inflar*) to blow up.

soplo *m* (*acción*) puff; (*de viento*) gust.

soplón,-ona *mf fam* (*niño*) telltale; (*delator*) informer.

soportar *vt* (*sostener*) to support; (*tolerar*) to endure; (*aguantar*) to put up with.

soporte *m* support.

sorber *vt* (*beber*) to sip; (*absorber*) to soak up.

sorbete *m* sorbet.

sorbo *m* sip; (*trago*) gulp.

sórdido,-a *a* sordid.

sordo,-a 1 *a* (*persona*) deaf; (*ruido, dolor*) dull. **2** *mf* deaf person.

sordomudo,-a 1 *a* deaf and dumb. **2** *mf* deaf and dumb person.

sorprender *vt* to surprise; (*coger desprevenido*) to take by surprise.

sorpresa *f* surprise; **coger por s.** to take by surprise.

sorpresivo,-a *a Am* unexpected.

sortear *vt* to draw lots for; (*rifar*) to raffle (off).

sorteo *m* draw; (*rifa*) raffle.

sortija *f* ring.

sosegar [1] **1** *vt* to calm. **2 sosegarse** *vr* to calm down.

soso,-a *a* lacking in salt; (*persona*) dull.

sospechar 1 *vi* (*desconfiar*) to suspect; **s. de algn** to suspect sb. **2** *vt* (*pensar*) to suspect.

sospechoso,-a 1 *a* suspicious. **2** *mf* suspect.

sostén *m* (*apoyo*) support; (*prenda*) bra, brassiere.

sostener 1 *vt* to hold; (*sustentar*) to hold up; **s. que ...** to maintain that ... **2 sostenerse** *vr* (*mantenerse*) to support oneself; (*permanecer*) to remain.

sostuve *pt indef de* **sostener.**

sota *f* (*de baraja*) jack.

sotana *f* cassock.

sótano *m* basement.

soviético,-a *a* & *mf* Soviet; **la Unión Soviética** the Soviet Union.

soy *indic pres de* **ser.**

spray *m* (*pl* **sprays**) spray.

Sr. *abr de* **Señor** Mister, Mr.

Sra. *abr de* **Señora** Mrs.

Srta. *abr de* **Señorita** Miss.

standard *a & m* standard.

su *a pos* (*de él*) his; (*de ella*) her; (*de usted, ustedes*) your; (*de animales o cosas*) its; (*impersonal*) one's; (*de ellos*) their.

suave *a* smooth; (*luz, voz etc*) soft; (*templado*) mild.

suavizante *m* (*para el pelo*) (hair) conditioner; (*para la ropa*) fabric softener.

suavizar [4] **1** *vt* to smooth (out). **2 suavizarse** *vr* (*temperatura*) to get milder.

subalterno,-a *a & mf* subordinate.

subasta *f* auction.

subcampeón *m* runner-up.

subconsciente *a & m* subconscious.

subdesarrollado,-a *a* underdeveloped.

subdirector,-a *mf* assistant director.

súbdito,-a *mf* subject.

subestimar *vt* to underestimate.

subir **1** *vt* to go up; (*llevar arriba*) to take up, bring up; (*precio, salario, voz*) to raise; (*volumen*) to turn up. **2** *vi* (*ir arriba*) to go/come up; (*al autobús, barco etc*) to get on; (*aumentar*) to go up; **s. a** (*un coche*) to get into. **3 subirse** *vr* to climb up; (*al autobús, avión, tren, bici*) to get on; (*cremallera*) to do up; (*mangas*) to roll up; **s. a** (*un coche*) to get into.

súbitamente *adv* suddenly.

súbito,-a *a* sudden.

sublevarse *vr* to rebel.

sublime *a* sublime.

submarinismo *m* skin-diving.

submarino,-a **1** *a* underwater. **2** *m* submarine.

subnormal **1** *a* mentally handicapped. **2** *mf* mentally handicapped person.

subordinado,-a *a & mf* subordinate.

subrayar *vt* to underline; *fig* (*recalcar*) to stress.

subscripción *f* subscription.

subsecretario,-a *mf* undersecretary.

subsidiario,-a *a* subsidiary.

subsidio *m* allowance; **s. de desempleo** unemployment benefit.

subsistencia *f* subsistence.

subterráneo,-a *a* underground.

suburbio m (*barrio pobre*) slum; (*barrio periférico*) suburb.

subvención f subsidy.

suceder 1 vi (*ocurrir*) (*uso impers*) to happen; **¿qué sucede?** what's going on?; **s. a** (*seguir*) to follow. **2 sucederse** vr to follow one another.

sucesión f (*serie*) succession.

sucesivamente adv **y así s.** and so on.

sucesivo,-a a (*siguiente*) following; **en lo s.** from now on.

suceso m (*acontecimiento*) event; (*incidente*) incident.

sucesor,-a mf successor.

suciedad f dirt; (*calidad*) dirtiness.

sucio,-a a dirty.

suculento,-a a succulent.

sucumbir vi to succumb.

sucursal f (*de banco etc*) branch.

sudadera f sweatshirt.

sudafricano,-a a & mf South African.

sudamericano,-a a & mf South American.

sudar vti to sweat.

sudeste m southeast.

sudoeste m southwest.

sudor m sweat.

sueco,-a 1 a Swedish. **2** mf (*persona*) Swede. **3** m (*idioma*) Swedish.

suegra f mother-in-law.

suegro m father-in-law; **mis suegros** my in-laws.

suela f sole.

sueldo m wages pl.

suelo m (*superficie*) ground; (*de interior*) floor.

suelto,-a 1 a loose; (*en libertad*) free; (*huido*) at large; (*desatado*) undone; **dinero s.** loose change. **2** m (*dinero*) (loose) change.

sueño m sleepiness; (*cosa soñada*) dream; **tener s.** to be sleepy.

suerte f (*fortuna*) luck; **por s.** fortunately; **tener s.** to be lucky; **¡que tengas s.!** good luck!

suéter m sweater.

suficiente 1 a (*bastante*) sufficient, enough. **2** m (*nota*) pass.

suficientemente adv sufficiently; **no es lo s. rico como para ...** he isn't rich enough to ...

sufragio m (*voto*) vote.

sufrimiento m suffering.

sufrir 1 vi to suffer. **2** vt (*accidente*) to have; (*dificultades, cambios*) to experience; (*aguantar*) to put up with.

sugerencia f suggestion.

sugerir [5] vt to suggest.

sugestión *f* suggestion.
suicida 1 *mf* (*persona*) suicide. **2** *a* suicidal.
suicidarse *vr* to commit suicide.
suicidio *m* suicide.
suizo,-a 1 *a* Swiss. **2** *mf* (*persona*) Swiss. **3** *m* (*pastel*) eclair.
sujetador *m* (*prenda*) bra, brassiere.
sujetar 1 *vt* (*agarrar*) to hold; (*fijar*) to hold down; (*someter*) to restrain.
  2 sujetarse *vr* (*agarrarse*) to hold on.
sujeto,-a 1 *m* subject; (*individuo*) fellow. **2** *a* (*atado*) secure.
suma *f* (*cantidad*) sum; (*cálculo*) addition.
sumar *vt* (*cantidades*) to add (up).
sumergir [6] **1** *vt* to submerge; (*hundir*) to sink. **2 sumergirse** *vr* to
  submerge; (*hundirse*) to sink.
sumidero *m* drain.
suministrar *vt* to supply; **s. algo a algn** to supply sb with sth.
suministro *m* supply.
sumiso,-a *a* submissive.
supe *pt indef de* **saber.**
súper *m* (*gasolina*) 4 star, *US* premium; *fam* (*supermercado*) supermarket.
superar *vt* (*obstáculo etc*) to overcome; (*prueba*) to pass; (*aventajar*) to
  surpass.
superdotado,-a 1 *a* exceptionally gifted. **2** *mf* genius.
superficial *a* superficial.
superficie *f* surface; (*área*) area.
superfluo,-a *a* superfluous.
superior 1 *a* (*posición*) top, upper; (*cantidad*) greater (**a** than); (*calidad*)
  superior; (*estudios*) higher. **2** *m* (*jefe*) superior.
supermercado *m* supermarket.
supersónico,-a *a* supersonic.
supersticioso,-a *a* superstitious.
supervisar *vt* to supervise.
supervivencia *f* survival.
súpito,-a *a Am* sudden.
suplantar *vt* to supplant.
suplementario,-a *a* supplementary.
suplemento *m* supplement.
suplicar [1] *vt* to beg.
suplicio *m* (*tortura*) torture; (*tormento*) torment.
suplir *vt* (*reemplazar*) to replace; (*compensar*) to make up for.
suponer (*pp* **supuesto**) *vt* to suppose; (*significar*) to mean; (*implicar*) to
  entail; **supongo que sí** I suppose so.

supositorio *m* suppository.

supremo,-a *a* supreme.

suprimir *vt* (*ley*) to abolish; (*restricción*) to lift; (*palabra*) to delete.

supuesto,-a *a* (*asumido*) supposed; (*presunto*) alleged; **¡por s.!** of course!; **dar algo por s.** to take sth for granted.

supuse *pt indef de* **suponer.**

sur *m* south.

suramericano,-a *a & mf* South American.

surco *m* (*en tierra*) furrow; (*en disco*) groove.

sureste *a & m* southeast.

surf(ing) *m* surfing.

surgir [6] *vi* (*problema, dificultad*) to crop up; (*aparecer*) to arise.

suroeste *a & m* southwest.

surtido,-a 1 *a* (*variado*) assorted. **2** *m* selection.

surtidor *m* spout; **s. de gasolina** petrol *o US* gas pump.

susceptible *a* susceptible; (*quisquilloso*) touchy; **s. de** (*capaz*) capable of.

suscitar *vt* (*provocar*) to cause; (*rebelión*) to stir up; (*interés etc*) to arouse.

suscribirse *vr* to subscribe (**a** to).

suscripción *f* subscription.

suspender 1 *vt* (*reunión*) to adjourn; (*examen*) to fail; (*colgar*) to hang; **me han suspendido** I've failed (the exam). **2** *vi* (*en colegio*) **he suspendido** I've failed.

suspense *m* suspense; **novela/película de s.** thriller.

suspensión *f* (*levantamiento*) hanging (up); (*de coche*) suspension.

suspenso *m* (*nota*) fail.

suspicaz *a* suspicious; (*desconfiado*) distrustful.

suspirar *vi* to sigh.

suspiro *m* sigh.

sustancia *f* substance.

sustantivo,-a *m* noun.

sustento *m* (*alimento*) sustenance.

sustituir *vt* to substitute.

sustituto,-a *mf* substitute.

susto *m* fright; **llevarse** *o* **darse un s.** to get a fright.

sustraer *vt* to subtract; (*robar*) to steal.

susurrar *vi* to whisper.

sutil *a* (*diferencia, pregunta*) subtle; (*aroma*) delicate.

suyo,-a *a & pron pos* (*de él*) his; (*de ella*) hers; (*de animal o cosa*) its; (*de usted, ustedes*) yours; (*de ellos, ellas*) theirs.

T

tabaco *m* tobacco; (*cigarrillos*) cigarettes *pl*; **t. rubio** Virginia tobacco.

taberna *f* bar.

tabique *m* (*pared*) partition (wall).

tabla *f* board; (*de vestido*) pleat; (*de sumar etc*) table; **t. de surf** surfboard; **t. de windsurf** sailboard.

tablero *m* (*tablón*) panel; (*en juegos*) board; **t. de mandos** (*de coche*) dash(board).

tableta *f* (*de chocolate*) bar.

tablón *m* plank; (*en construcción*) beam; **t. de anuncios** notice *o* US bulletin board.

taburete *m* stool.

tacaño,-a 1 *a* mean. **2** *mf* miser.

tachar *vt* to cross out.

tacho *m* *Am* bucket.

taco *m* (*tarugo*) plug; (*de jamón, queso*) cube; (*palabrota*) swearword.

tacón *m* heel; **zapatos de t.** high-heeled shoes.

táctica *f* tactics *pl*.

táctico,-a *a* tactical.

tacto *m* (*sentido*) touch; (*delicadeza*) tact.

tajada *f* slice.

tal 1 *a* (*semejante*) such; (*más sustantivo singular contable*) such a; (*indeterminado*) such and such; **en tales condiciones** in such conditions; **nunca dije t. cosa** I never said such a thing; **t. vez** perhaps, maybe; **como si t. cosa** as if nothing had happened. **2** *adv* **t. (y) como** just as; **¿qué t.?** how are things?; **¿qué t. ese vino?** how do you find this wine? **3** *conj* as; **con t. (de) que** + *subjuntivo* so long as, provided. **4** *pron* (*cosa*) something; (*persona*) someone, somebody.

taladro *m* (*herramienta*) drill.

talante *m* (*carácter*) disposition; **de mal t.** unwillingly.

talar *vt* (*árboles*) to fell.

talco *m* talc; **polvos de t.** talcum powder.

talega *f* sack.

talento *m* talent.

Talgo *m* fast passenger train.

talla *f* (*de prenda*) size; (*estatura*) height.

tallar *vt* (*madera, piedra*) to carve; (*piedras preciosas*) to cut; (*metales*) to engrave.

tallarines *mpl* tagliatelle *sing*.

talle *m* (*cintura*) waist.

taller *m* (*obrador*) workshop; **t. de reparaciones** (*garaje*) garage.

tallo *m* stem.

talón *m* heel; (*cheque*) cheque, *US* check.

talonario *m* (*de cheques*) cheque *o US* check book.

tamaño *m* size; **de gran t.** large; **del t. de** as big as.

tambalearse *vr* (*persona*) to stagger; (*mesa*) to wobble.

también *adv* too, also; **yo t.** me too.

tambor *m* drum.

tampoco *adv* (*en afirmativas*) nor, neither; (*en negativas*) not . . . either; **no lo sé, – yo t.** I don't know, – neither *o* nor do I.

tampón *m* tampon.

tan *adv* so; **¡es t. listo!** he's so clever; **¡qué gente t. agradable!** such nice people; **¡qué vestido t. bonito!** such a beautiful dress. ‖ (*consecutivo*) so . . . (that); **iba t. deprisa que no lo ví** he was going so fast that I couldn't see him. ‖ (*comparativo*) **t. . . . como** as . . . as; **t. alto como tú** as tall as you (are). ‖ **t. sólo** only.

tango *m* tango.

tanque *m* tank.

tanto,-a 1 *m* (*punto*) point; **un t. para cada uno** so much for each; **t. por ciento** percentage; **estar al t.** (*informado*) to be informed; (*pendiente*) to be on the lookout. **2** *a* (+ *sing*) so much; (+ *pl*) so many; **t. dinero** so much money; **¡ha pasado t. tiempo!** it's been so long!; **tantas manzanas** so many apples; **cincuenta y tantas personas** fifty odd people; **t. . . . como** as much . . . as; **tantos,-as . . . como** as many . . . as. **3** *pron* (+ *sing*) so much; (+ *pl*) so many; **otro t.** the same again; **no es *o* hay para t.** it's not that bad; **otros tantos** as many again; **uno de tantos** run-of-the-mill. **4** *adv* (*cantidad*) so much; (*tiempo*) so long; (*frecuencia*) so often; **t. mejor/peor** so much the better/worse; **t. . . . como** both . . . and; **tú como yo** both you and I; **por lo t.** therefore.

tapa *f* (*cubierta*) lid; (*de libro*) cover; (*aperitivo*) appetizer.

tapadera *f* cover.

tapar 1 *vt* to cover; (*botella etc*) to put the lid on; (*con ropas o mantas*) to wrap up; (*ocultar*) to hide; (*vista*) to block. **2 taparse** *vr* (*cubrirse*) to cover oneself; (*abrigarse*) to wrap up.

tapete *m* (table) cover.

tapia *f* wall; (*cerca*) garden wall.

tapizar [4] *vt* to upholster.

tapón *m* (*de lavabo etc*) plug; (*de botella*) cap; (*de tráfico*) traffic jam.

taponar 1 *vt* (*tubería, hueco*) to plug; (*poner el tapón a*) to put the plug in. **2 taponarse** *vr* **se me han taponado los oídos** my ears are blocked up.

taquigrafía *f* shorthand.

taquilla *f* ticket office; (*de cine, teatro*) box-office.

tararear *vt* to hum.

tardar 1 *vt* **tardé dos horas en venir** it took me two hours to get here. **2** *vi* (*demorar*) to take long; **no tardes** don't be long; **a más t.** at the latest. **3 tardarse** *vr* **¿cuánto se tarda en llegar?** how long does it take to get there?

tarde 1 *f* (*hasta las cinco*) afternoon; (*después de las cinco*) evening. **2** *adv* late; **(más) t. o (más) temprano** sooner or later.

tarea *f* task; **tareas** (*de ama de casa*) housework *sing*; (*de estudiante*) homework *sing*.

tarifa *f* (*precio*) rate; (*en transportes*) fare; (*lista de precios*) price list.

tarjeta *f* card; **t. postal** postcard; **t. de crédito** credit card.

tarro *m* (*vasija*) jar; *Am* (*lata*) tin.

tarta *f* tart; (*pastel*) cake.

tartamudear *vi* to stutter, stammer.

tartamudo,-a 1 *a* stuttering, stammering. **2** *mf* stutterer, stammerer.

tartera *f* lunch box.

tasa *f* (*precio*) fee; (*impuesto*) tax; (*índice*) rate; **tasas académicas** course fees; **t. de natalidad/mortalidad** birth/death rate.

tasar *vt* (*valorar*) to value; (*poner precio*) to fix the price of.

tasca *f* bar.

tatarabuelo,-a *mf* (*hombre*) great-great-grandfather; (*mujer*) great-great-grandmother; **tatarabuelos** great-great-grandparents.

tataranieto,-a *mf* (*hombre*) great-great-grandson; (*mujer*) great-great-granddaughter; **tataranietos** great-great-grandchildren.

tatuaje *m* tattoo.

taurino,-a *a* bullfighting.

taxi *m* taxi.

taxista *mf* taxi driver.

taza *f* cup; **una t. de café** (*recipiente*) a coffee cup; (*contenido*) a cup of coffee.

tazón *m* bowl.

te *pron pers* **1** (*complemento directo*) you; (*complemento indirecto*) (to o for) you; (*reflexivo*) yourself; **no quiero verte** I don't want to see you; **te compraré uno** I'll buy you one; **te lo dije** I told you so; **lávate** wash yourself; **no te vayas** don't go.

té *m* (*pl* **tés**) tea.

teatro *m* theatre; **obra de t.** play.

tebeo *m* children's comic.

techo *m* (*de habitación*) ceiling; (*tejado*) roof.

tecla *f* key.

teclado *m* keyboard; **t. numérico** numeric keypad.

técnica *f* (*tecnología*) technology; (*método*) technique; (*habilidad*) skill.

técnico,-a 1 *a* technical. **2** *mf* technician.

tecnología *f* technology.

tedio *m* tedium.

teja *f* tile.

tejado *m* roof.

tejanos *mpl* jeans.

tejer *vt* (*en el telar*) to weave; (*hacer punto*) to knit.

tejido *m* fabric.

tela *f* cloth; **t. de araña** cobweb; **t. metálica** gauze.

telaraña *f* spider's web.

telecabina *f* cable car.

telediario *m* television news bulletin.

telefax *m* fax.

teleférico *m* rack and pinion railway; (*en pista de esquí*) cable car.

telefilm(e) *m* TV film.

telefonear *vti* to telephone, phone.

teléfono *m* telephone, phone; **t. portátil** portable telephone; **t. móvil** car phone; **te llamó por t.** she phoned you; **al t.** on the phone.

telegrama *m* telegram.

telenovela *f* television serial.

teleobjetivo *m* telephoto lens.

telescopio *m* telescope.

telesilla *m* chair lift.

telespectador,-a *mf* TV viewer.

telesquí *m* ski lift.

televidente *mf* TV viewer.

televisión *f* television; **ver la t.** to watch television.

televisivo,-a *a* television.

televisor *m* television.

télex *m inv* telex.

telón *m* curtain.

tema *m* subject.

temblar [1] *vi* (*de frío*) to shiver; (*de miedo*) to tremble (**de** with); (*voz, pulso*) to shake.

temblor *m* tremor; **t. de tierra** earth tremor.

temer 1 *vt* to fear. **2** *vi* to be afraid. **3 temerse** *vr* to fear; **¡me lo temía!** I was afraid this would happen!

temerario,-a *a* reckless.

temor *m* fear; (*recelo*) worry.

témpano *m* ice floe.

temperamento *m* temperament.

temperatura *f* temperature.

tempestad *f* storm.

templado,-a *a* (*agua*) lukewarm; (*clima*) mild.

templo *m* temple.

temporada *f* season; (*período*) period; **t. alta** high season; **t. baja** low season.

temporal 1 *a* temporary. **2** *m* storm.

temprano,-a *a & adv* early.

tenaz *a* tenacious.

tenaza *f,* **tenazas** *fpl* (*herramienta*) pliers.

tendencia *f* tendency.

tender [3] **1** *vt* (*extender*) to spread out; (*para secar*) to hang out; (*trampa*) to set; (*mano*) to hold out; (*tumbar*) to lay. **2** *vi* **t. a** to tend to. **3** **tenderse** *vr* to stretch out.

tendero,-a *mf* shopkeeper.

tendón *m* tendon.

tenebroso,-a *a* (*sombrío*) dark; (*siniestro*) sinister.

tenedor,-a *m* fork.

tener 1 *vt* to have, have got; **va a t. un niño** she's going to have a baby. ‖ (*sostener*) to hold; **tenme el bolso un momento** hold my bag a minute. ‖ **t. calor/frío** to be hot/cold; **t. cariño a algn** to be fond of sb; **t. miedo** to be frightened. ‖ (*edad*) to be; **tiene dieciocho (años)** he's eighteen (years old). ‖ (*medida*) **la casa tiene cien metros cuadrados** the house is 100 square metres. ‖ (*contener*) to hold. ‖ (*mantener*) to keep; **me tuvo despierto toda la noche** he kept me up all night. ‖ (*considerar*) to consider; **ten por seguro que lloverá** you can be sure it'll rain. ‖ **t. que** to have (got) to; **tengo que ...** I have to ..., I must ... **2 tenerse** *vr* **tenerse en pie** to stand (up).

tenga *subj pres de* **tener.**

tengo *indic pres de* **tener.**

teniente *m* lieutenant.

tenis *m* tennis.

tenor *m* tenor.

tensión *f* tension; (*eléctrica*) voltage; **t. arterial** blood pressure.

tenso,-a *a* (*cuerda, cable*) taut; (*persona, relaciones*) tense.

tentación *f* temptation.

tentar [1] *vt* (*incitar*) to tempt; (*atraer*) to attract.

tentativa *f* attempt.

tentempié *m* (*pl* **tentempiés**) (*comida*) snack; (*juguete*) tumbler.

tenue *a* (*luz, sonido*) faint.

teñir [6] **1** *vt* (*pelo etc*) to dye. **2 teñirse** *vr* **teñirse el pelo** to dye one's hair.

teoría *f* theory; **en t.** theoretically.

terapia *f* therapy.

tercer *a* third; **el t. mundo** the third world.

tercero,-a *a & mf* third.

tercio m (one) third; (de cerveza) medium-size bottle of beer.

terciopelo m velvet.

terco,-a a stubborn.

tergiversar vt to distort; (declaraciones) to twist.

terminal 1 a terminal. 2 f terminal; (de autobús) terminus. 3 m (de ordenador) terminal.

terminar 1 vt to finish. 2 vi (acabarse) to finish; (ir a parar) to end up (en in); **terminó por comprarlo** he ended up buying it. 3 **terminarse** vr to finish; (vino etc) to run out.

término m (final) end; (palabra) term; **en términos generales** generally speaking; **por t. medio** on average.

termo m thermos (flask).

termómetro m thermometer.

termostato m thermostat.

ternera f calf; (carne) veal.

ternura f tenderness.

terraplén m embankment.

terremoto m earthquake.

terreno m (tierra) land; (campo) field; (deportivo) ground; (ámbito) field.

terrestre a (de la tierra) terrestrial; (transporte, ruta) by land.

terrible a terrible.

territorio m territory.

terrón m (de azúcar) lump.

terror m terror; **película de t.** horror film.

terrorismo m terrorism.

terrorista a & mf terrorist.

terso,-a a (liso) smooth.

tertulia f get-together.

tesis f inv thesis; (opinión) point of view.

tesoro m treasure; (erario) exchequer.

test m test.

testamento m will; **hacer t.** to make one's will.

testarudo,-a a obstinate.

testificar [1] vi to testify.

testigo mf witness.

testimonio m testimony; (prueba) evidence.

tétano m tetanus.

tetera f teapot.

tetina f (rubber) teat.

texto m text; **libro de t.** textbook.

tez f complexion.

ti pron pers you; **es para ti** it's for you; **piensas demasiado en ti mismo** you think too much about yourself.

tía *f* aunt; *fam* (*mujer*) woman.

tibio,-a *a* tepid.

tiburón *m* shark.

tic *m* (*pl* **tiques**) twitch; **t. nervioso** nervous twitch.

tiempo *m* time; (*meteorológico*) weather; (*de partido*) half; (*verbal*) tense; **a t.** in time; **a su (debido) t.** in due course; **al mismo t.** at the same time; **al poco t.** soon afterwards; **con t.** in advance; **¿cuánto t.?** how long?; **¿cuánto t. hace?** how long ago?; **estar a t. de** to still have time to; **¿nos da t. de llegar?** have we got (enough) time to get there?; **t. libre** free time; **¿qué t. hace?** what's the weather like?; **hace buen/mal t.** the weather is good/bad.

tienda *f* shop, *US* store; **ir de tiendas** to go shopping; **t. (de campaña)** tent.

tienta *f* **a tientas** by touch; **andar a tientas** to feel one's way; **buscar (algo) a tientas** to grope (for sth).

tierno,-a *a* tender; (*reciente*) fresh.

tierra *f* land; (*planeta*) earth; (*suelo*) ground; **tocar t.** to land.

tieso,-a *a* (*rígido*) stiff; (*erguido*) upright.

tiesto *m* flowerpot.

tifus *m inv* typhus (fever).

tigre *m* tiger; *Am* jaguar.

tijeras *f* pair of scissors, scissors *pl*.

tila *f* lime tea.

timar *vt* to swindle.

timbre *m* (*de puerta*) bell; (*sonido*) timbre.

timidez *f* shyness.

tímido,-a *a* shy.

timo *m* swindle.

timón *m* (*de barco, avión*) rudder; *Am* (*de coche*) steering wheel.

tímpano *m* eardrum.

tinieblas *fpl* darkness.

tino *m* (*puntería*) **tener buen t.** to be a good shot.

tinta *f* ink; **t. china** Indian ink.

tinte *m* dye.

tintero *m* inkwell.

tintinear *vi* (*vidrio*) to clink; (*campana*) to tinkle.

tinto 1 *a* (*vino*) red. **2** *m* (*vino*) red wine.

tintorería *f* dry-cleaner's.

tío *m* uncle; *fam* guy; **mis tíos** (*tío y tía*) my uncle and aunt.

tiovivo *m* merry-go-round.

típico,-a *a* typical; (*baile, traje*) traditional.

tipo *m* (*clase*) type, kind; *fam* (*persona*) guy; (*figura*) (*de hombre*) build; (*de mujer*) figure; **jugarse el t.** to risk one's neck; **t. bancario** *o* **de descuento** bank rate; **t. de cambio/interés** exchange/interest rate.

tira *f* strip.

tirabuzón *m* ringlet.

tirachinas *m inv* catapult, *US* slingshot.

tirada *f* printrun.

tiranía *f* tyranny.

tirante 1 *a* (*cable etc*) taut. **2** *m* (*de vestido etc*) strap; **tirantes** braces, *US* suspenders.

tirar 1 *vt* (*echar*) to throw, fling; (*dejar caer*) to drop; (*desechar*) to throw away; (*derribar*) to knock down. **2** *vi* **t. de** (*cuerda, puerta*) to pull; (*disparar*) to shoot; **ir tirando** to get by; **tira a la izquierda** turn left. **3** **tirarse** *vr* (*lanzarse*) to throw oneself; (*tumbarse*) to lie down; **tirarse de cabeza al agua** to dive into the water.

tirita(R) *f* Elastoplast(R), *US* Band-aid(R).

tiritar *vi* to shiver.

tiro *m* (*lanzamiento*) throw; (*disparo, ruido*) shot; (*de chimenea*) draught, *US* draft; **t. al blanco** target shooting; **t. al plato** clay pigeon shooting.

tirón *m* pull; (*del bolso*) snatch; *fam* **de un t.** in one go.

titubear *vi* (*dudar*) to hesitate.

titular¹ **1** *mf* (*persona*) holder. **2** *m* (*de periódico*) headline.

titular² **1** *vt* (*poner título*) to call. **2** **titularse** *vr* (*película etc*) to be called.

título *m* title; (*diploma*) diploma; (*titular*) headline.

tiza *f* chalk.

tiznar *vt* to blacken (with soot).

toalla *f* towel.

toallero *m* towel rail.

tobillo *m* ankle.

tobogán *m* chute.

tocadiscos *m inv* record player; **t. digital** *o* **compacto** CD player.

tocador *m* (*mueble*) dressing table; (*habitación*) dressing room.

tocar [1] **1** *vt* to touch; (*instrumento, canción*) to play; (*timbre, campana*) to ring; (*bocina*) to blow; (*tema, asunto*) to touch on. **2** *vi* (*entrar en contacto*) to touch; **¿a quién le toca?** (*en juegos*) whose turn is it?; **me tocó el gordo** (*en rifa*) I won the jackpot. **3** **tocarse** *vr* (*una cosa con otra*) to touch each other.

tocino *m* lard; **t. de cielo** sweet made with egg yolk.

tocólogo,-a *m* obstetrician.

todavía *adv* (*aún*) still; (*en negativas*) yet; (*para reforzar*) even, still; **t. la quiere** he still loves her; **t. no** not yet; **t. más/menos** even more/less.

todo,-a 1 *a* all; (*cada*) every; **t. el mundo** everybody; **t. el día** all day, the whole day; **t. ciudadano de más de dieciocho años** every citizen over eighteen years of age; **todos,-as** all; **t. los niños** all the children; **t. los martes** every Tuesday. **2** *pron* all, everything; **t. aquél** *o* **el que quiera** anybody who wants (to); **todos,-as** all of them; **hablé con todos** I spoke to everybody; **todos aprobamos** we all passed; **ante t.** first of all; **del t.** completely; **después de t.** after all; **eso es t.** that's all; **hay de t.** there are all sorts; **lo sé t.** I know all about it; **t. lo contrario** quite the opposite; **t. lo más** at the most. **3** *adv* completely; **t. sucio** all dirty.

toldo *m* (*cubierta*) awning; (*en la playa*) sunshade; *Am* (*cabaña*) tent.

tolerar *vt* to tolerate.

toma *f* (*acción*) taking; **t. de corriente** socket.

tomar 1 *vt* to take; (*comer, beber*) to have; **toma** here (you are); **t. el sol** to sunbathe; **t. en serio/broma** to take seriously/as a joke. **2 tomarse** *vr* (*comer*) to eat; (*beber*) to drink; **no te lo tomes así** don't take it like that.

tomate *m* tomato; **salsa de t.** (*de lata*) tomato sauce; (*de botella*) ketchup.

tómbola *f* tombola.

tomo *m* volume.

tonel *m* cask.

tonelada *f* ton; **t. métrica** tonne.

tónico,-a 1 *m* tonic. **2** *f* (*bebida*) tonic (water); **tónica general** overall trend.

tono *m* tone; **un t. alto/bajo** a high/low pitch.

tontería *f* silliness; (*dicho, hecho*) silly thing; (*insignificancia*) trifle.

tonto,-a 1 *a* silly. **2** *mf* fool.

topacio *m* topaz.

toparse *vr* **t. con** to bump into; (*dificultades*) to run up against.

tope *m* (*límite*) limit; **estar hasta los topes** to be full up; **fecha t.** deadline.

tópico *m* cliché.

topo *m* mole.

topónimo *m* place name.

torbellino *m* (*de viento*) whirlwind.

torcer [4] **1** *vt* (*tobillo*) to sprain; (*esquina*) to turn; (*inclinar*) to slant. **2** *vi* to turn. **3 torcerse** *vr* (*doblarse*) to twist; (*tobillo, mano*) to sprain; (*desviarse*) to go off to the side.

torear *vi* to fight.

torero,-a *mf* bullfighter.

tormenta *f* storm.

tormento *m* (*tortura*) torture; (*padecimiento*) torment.

tornillo *m* screw.

torno *m* (*de alfarero*) wheel; **en t. a** around.

toro *m* bull; **¿te gustan los toros?** do you like bullfighting?

torpe *a* (*sin habilidad*) clumsy; (*tonto*) thick; (*movimiento*) slow.

torre *f* tower; (*en ajedrez*) rook.

torrente *m* torrent.

tórrido,-a *a* torrid.

torso *m* torso.

torta *f* (*pastel*) cake; (*golpe*) slap.

tortazo *m* (*bofetada*) slap.

tortícolis *f inv* crick in the neck.

tortilla *f* omelette, *US* omelet; *Am* tortilla; **t. francesa/española** (plain)/ potato omelette.

tortuga *f* (*de tierra*) tortoise, *US* turtle; (*de mar*) turtle.

tortura *f* torture.

tos *f* cough; **t. ferina** whooping cough.

tosco,-a *a* (*basto*) rough; (*persona*) uncouth.

toser *vi* to cough.

tostada *f* **una t.** some toast, a slice of toast.

tostador *m* toaster.

tostar [2] *vt* (*pan*) to toast; (*café*) to roast.

total 1 *a* total. **2** *m* (*todo*) whole; (*cantidad*) total; **en t.** in all. **3** *adv* anyway; (*para resumir*) in short.

totalidad *f* whole; **la t. de** all of; **en su t.** as a whole.

tóxico,-a 1 *a* toxic. **2** *m* poison.

toxicómano,-a 1 *a* addicted to drugs. **2** *mf* drug addict.

tozudo,-a *a* stubborn.

traba *f* (*obstáculo*) hindrance.

trabajador,-a 1 *mf* worker. **2** *a* hard-working.

trabajar 1 *vi* to work; **t. de camarera** to work as a waitress. **2** *vt* to work (on).

trabajo *m* work; (*esfuerzo*) effort; **un t.** a job; **t. eventual** casual labour; **trabajos manuales** arts and crafts.

trabalenguas *m inv* tongue twister.

trabar 1 *vt* (*conversación, amistad*) to start. **2 trabarse** *vr* **se le trabó la lengua** he got tongue-tied.

tractor *m* tractor.

tradición *f* tradition.

tradicional *a* traditional.

traducción *f* translation.

traducir 1 *vt* to translate (**a** into). **2 traducirse** *vr* to result (**en** in).

traductor,-a *mf* translator.

traer 1 *vt* to bring; (*llevar consigo*) to carry; (*problemas*) to cause; (*noticia*) to feature; **trae** give it to me. **2 traerse** *vr* (*llevar consigo*) to bring along.

traficante *mf* (*de drogas etc*) trafficker.
tráfico *m* traffic; **t. de drogas** drug traffic.
tragaperras *f inv* (**máquina**) **t.** slot machine.
tragar [7] *vt*, **tragarse** *vr* to swallow.
tragedia *f* tragedy.
trágico,-a *a* tragic.
trago *m* (*bebida*) swig; **de un t.** in one go; **pasar un mal t.** to have a bad time of it.
traición *f* betrayal.
traicionar *vt* to betray.
traidor,-a 1 *a* treacherous. **2** *mf* traitor.
traigo *indic pres de* **traer.**
traje[1] *m* (*de hombre*) suit; (*de mujer*) dress; **t. de baño** swimsuit; **t. de chaqueta** two-piece suit; **t. de novia** wedding dress.
traje[2] *pt indef de* **traer.**
trama *f* plot.
tramar *vt* to plot.
trámite *m* (*paso*) step; (*formalidad*) formality.
tramo *m* (*de carretera*) stretch; (*de escalera*) flight.
trampa *f* (*de caza*) trap; (*engaño*) fiddle; **hacer trampa(s)** to cheat.
trampilla *f* trap door.
trampolín *m* springboard.
tramposo,-a 1 *a* deceitful. **2** *mf* cheat.
tranquilizante *m* tranquillizer.
tranquilizar [4] **1** *vt* to calm down; **lo dijo para tranquilizarme** he said it to reassure me. **2 tranquilizarse** *vr* (*calmarse*) to calm down.
tranquilo,-a *a* (*persona, lugar*) calm; (*agua*) still; (*conciencia*) clear.
transatlántico,-a 1 *m* (*ocean*) liner. **2** *a* transatlantic.
transbordador *m* (*car*) ferry; **t. espacial** space shuttle.
transbordo *m* (*de trenes*) **hacer t.** to change.
transcurrir *vi* (*tiempo*) to pass, go by; (*acontecer*) to take place.
transcurso *m* **en el t. de** in the course of.
transeúnte *mf* (*peatón*) passer-by.
transferencia *f* transference; (*de dinero*) transfer; **t. bancaria** bank transfer.
transformación *f* transformation.
transformador *m* transformer.
transformar 1 *vt* to transform. **2 transformarse** *vr* to turn (**en** into).
transfusión *f* transfusion.
transición *f* transition.
transistor *m* transistor.
transitado,-a *a* (*carretera*) busy.

transitivo,-a *a* transitive.

tránsito *m* (*tráfico*) traffic; (*movimiento*) passage; **pasajeros en t.** passengers in transit.

transitorio,-a *a* transitory.

transmisión *f* transmission; (*emisión*) broadcast.

transmisor *m* transmitter.

transmitir *vt* to pass on; (*emitir*) to transmit.

transnochar *vi* to stay up (very) late.

transparentarse *vr* to be transparent; **se le transparentaban las bragas** you could see her panties.

transparente *a* transparent.

transpiración *f* perspiration.

transplante *m* transplant.

transportar *vt* to transport; (*pasajeros*) to carry; (*mercancías*) to ship.

transporte *m* transport.

transversal *a* cross.

tranvía *m* tram, *US* streetcar.

trapo *m* (*viejo, roto*) rag; (*bayeta*) cloth; **t. de cocina** dishcloth; **t. del polvo** duster.

tráquea *f* trachea.

tras *prep* (*después de*) after; (*detrás*) behind.

trascendencia *f* (*importancia*) significance.

trascendental, trascendente *a* significant.

trasero,-a **1** *a* back, rear; **en la parte trasera** at the back. **2** *m fam* bottom.

trasladar **1** *vt* (*cosa*) to move; (*trabajador*) to transfer. **2 trasladarse** *vr* to move.

traslado *m* (*de casa*) move; (*de personal*) transfer.

traspié *m* (*pl* **traspiés**) stumble; **dar un t.** to trip.

trastero *m* (**cuarto**) **t.** junk room.

trastienda *f* back shop.

trasto *m* thing; (*cosa inservible*) piece of junk.

trastornar **1** *vt* (*planes*) to disrupt; *fig* (*persona*) to unhinge. **2 trastornarse** *vr* (*enloquecer*) to go mad.

trastorno *m* (*molestia*) trouble; **t. mental** mental disorder.

tratado *m* (*pacto*) treaty; (*estudio*) treatise.

tratamiento *m* treatment; (*de textos etc*) processing.

tratar **1** *vt* to treat; (*asunto*) to discuss; (*manejar*) to handle; (*textos etc*) to process; **me trata de 'tú'** he calls me 'tu'. **2** *vi* **t. de** (*intentar*) to try to; **t. de** *o* **sobre** *o* **acerca** to be about. **3 tratarse** *vr* (*relacionarse*) to be on speaking terms; **se trata de** (*es cuestión de*) it's a question of; (*es*) it is.

trato *m* (*contacto*) contact; (*acuerdo*) agreement; (*comercial*) deal; **malos**

tratos ill-treatment; **¡t. hecho!** it's a deal!

traumático,-a *a* traumatic.

través 1 *prep* **a t. de** (*superficie*) across, over; (*agujero etc*) through; (*por medio de*) through; **a t. del periódico** through the newspaper. **2** *adv* **de t.** (*transversalmente*) crosswise; (*de lado*) sideways.

travesía *f* (*viaje*) crossing.

travestí, travesti *mf* transvestite.

travesura *f* mischief.

travieso,-a *a* mischievous.

trayecto *m* (*distancia*) distance; (*recorrido*) route; (*viaje*) journey.

trazar [4] *vt* (*línea*) to draw; (*plano*) to design.

trébol *m* trefoil; (*en naipes*) club.

trece *a & m inv* thirteen.

trecho *m* (*distancia*) distance; (*tramo*) stretch.

tregua *f* truce.

treinta *a & m inv* thirty.

tremendo,-a *a* (*terrible*) terrible; (*muy grande*) enormous; (*excelente*) tremendous.

tren *m* train.

trenca *f* (*prenda*) duffle coat.

trenza *f* (*de pelo*) plait, *US* braid.

trepar *vti* to climb.

tres *a & m inv* three; **t. en raya** noughts and crosses, *US* tick-tack-toe.

trescientos,-as *a & mf* three hundred.

tresillo *m* three-piece suite.

treta *f* ruse.

triángulo *m* triangle.

tribu *f* tribe.

tribuna *f* (*plataforma*) dais; (*en estadio*) stand.

tribunal *m* court; (*de examen*) board of examiners; **T. Supremo** High Court, *US* Supreme Court.

tributo *m* tax.

triciclo *m* tricycle.

trienio *m* three-year period.

trigésimo,-a *a & mf* thirtieth; **t. primero** thirty-first.

trigo *m* wheat.

trimestral *a* quarterly.

trimestre *m* quarter; (*escolar*) term.

trinchar *vt* (*carne*) to carve.

trinchera *f* trench.

trineo *m* sledge; (*grande*) sleigh.

tripa *f* (*intestino*) gut; *fam* tummy; **dolor de t.** stomachache.

triple *a & m* triple.

trípode *m* tripod.

tripulación *f* crew.

tripulante *mf* crew member.

tripular *vt* to man.

triquiñuela *f* dodge.

triste *a* (*infeliz*) sad; (*sombrío*) gloomy.

tristeza *f* sadness.

triturar *vt* to grind (up).

triunfador,-a 1 *a* winning. **2** *mf* winner.

triunfar *vi* to triumph.

triunfo *m* (*victoria*) triumph; (*deportiva*) win; (*éxito*) success.

trivial *a* trivial.

triza *f* **hacer trizas** to tear to shreds.

trocear *vt* to cut up (into pieces).

trofeo *m* trophy.

tromba *f* **t. de agua** violent downpour.

trombón *m* trombone.

trompa *f* (*instrumento*) horn; (*de elefante*) trunk; *fam* **estar t.** to be sloshed.

trompeta *f* trumpet.

tronchar 1 *vt* (*rama, tronco*) to cut down. **2 troncharse** *vr* **troncharse de risa** to split one's sides laughing.

tronco *m* (*torso, de árbol*) trunk; (*leño*) log.

trono *m* throne.

tropa *f* **tropas** troops *pl*.

tropel *m* **en t.** in a mad rush.

tropezar [1] *vi* (*trompicar*) to stumble (**con** on); **t. con algn/dificultades** to run into sb/difficulties.

tropezón *m* (*traspié*) stumble; **dar un t.** to trip.

tropical *a* tropical.

trópico *m* tropics *pl*.

tropiezo[1] *m* (*obstáculo*) trip.

tropiezo[2] *indic pres de* **tropezar.**

trotar *vi* to trot.

trote *m* trot; **al t.** at a trot.

trozo *m* piece.

truco *m* (*ardid*) trick; (*manera de hacer algo*) knack; **coger el t. (a algo)** to get the knack *o* hang (of sth).

trucha *f* trout.

trueno *m* thunder; **un t.** a thunderclap.

trufa *f* truffle.

tu *a pos* your; **tu libro** your book; **tus libros** your books.

tú *pron* you.

tubería *f* (*de agua*) pipes *pl*; (*de gas, petróleo*) pipeline.

tubo *m* tube; (*tubería*) pipe; **t. de ensayo** test tube; **t. de escape** exhaust (pipe).

tuerca *f* nut.

tuerto,-a 1 *a* blind in one eye. **2** *mf* person who is blind in one eye.

tuerzo *indic pres de* **torcer.**

tulipán *m* tulip.

tullido,-a *a* crippled.

tumba *f* grave.

tumbar 1 *vt* to knock down. **2 tumbarse** *vr* (*acostarse*) to lie down.

tumbona *f* easy chair; (*de lona*) deckchair.

tumor *m* tumour.

tumulto *m* commotion.

túnel *m* tunnel; **el t. del Canal de la Mancha** the Channel Tunnel.

túnica *f* tunic.

tupé *m* (*pl* **tupés**) (*flequillo*) fringe.

tupido,-a *a* thick.

turba *f* (*combustible*) peat.

turbado,-a *a* (*alterado*) disturbed; (*desconcertado*) confused.

turbar 1 *vt* (*alterar*) to unsettle; (*desconcertar*) to baffle. **2 turbarse** *vr* (*preocuparse*) to become upset; (*desconcertarse*) to become confused.

turbio,-a *a* (*agua*) cloudy; (*negocio etc*) dubious.

turbulencia *f* turbulence.

turco,-a 1 *a* Turkish. **2** *mf* (*persona*) Turk; *fig* **cabeza de t.** scapegoat. **3** *m* (*idioma*) Turkish.

turismo *m* tourism; (*coche*) car; **ir de t.** to go touring.

turista *mf* tourist.

turístico,-a *a* tourist; **de interés t.** of interest to tourists.

turnarse *vr* to take turns.

turno *m* (*en juegos etc*) turn; (*de trabajo*) shift; **t. de día/noche** day/night shift.

turquesa *a & f* turquoise.

turrón *m* nougat.

tutear 1 *vt* to address as 'tú'. **2 tutearse** *vr* to call (each other) 'tú'.

tutela *f* guidance.

tutor *m* (*de huérfano*) guardian; (*de estudiante*) tutor.

tuve *pt indef de* **tener.**

tuyo,-a 1 *a pos* (*con personas*) of yours; (*con objetos*) one of your; **¿es amigo t.?** is he a friend of yours?; **un libro t.** one of your books. **2** *pron pos* yours.

U

u *conj* (*before words beginning with* **o** *or* **ho**) or.

ubicación *f* location.

ubicar [1] **1** *vt* (*situar*) to locate. **2 ubicarse** *vr* (*en un lugar*) to be located.

Ud. *abr de* **usted** you.

Uds. *abr de* **ustedes** you.

úlcera *f* ulcer.

últimamente *adv* recently.

ultimar *vt* (*terminar*) to finalize; *Am* (*matar*) to finish off.

ultimátum *m* (*pl* **ultimátums**) ultimatum.

último,-a *a* last; (*más reciente*) latest; (*más alto*) top; (*más bajo*) lowest; (*definitivo*) final; (*más lejano*) back; **por ú.** finally; **a últimos de mes** at the end of the month; **últimas noticias** latest news; **el u. piso** the top flat; **el u. de la lista** the lowest in the list; **la última fila** the back row.

ultraderecha *f* extreme right.

ultramarinos *m* groceries; **tienda de u.** greengrocer.

ultrasónico,-a *a* ultrasonic.

ultravioleta *a inv* ultraviolet.

ulular *vi* (*viento*) to howl; (*búho*) to hoot.

umbral *m* threshold.

un,-a **1** *art indet* a, (*antes de vocal*) an; **unos,-as** some. **2** *a* (*delante de m sing*) one; **un chico y dos chicas** one boy and two girls.

unánime *a* unanimous.

unanimidad *f* unanimity; **por u.** unanimously.

undécimo,-a *a* eleventh.

únicamente *adv* only.

único,-a *a* (*solo*) only; (*extraordinario*) unique; **hijo ú.** only child; **lo ú. que quiero** the only thing I want.

unidad *f* unit; (*cohesión*) unity; **u. de disquete** disk drive.

unido,-a *a* united; **están muy unidos** they are very attached to one another; **una familia muy unida** a very close family.

unificación *f* unification.

uniforme **1** *m* (*prenda*) uniform. **2** *a* uniform; (*superficie*) even.

unilateral *a* unilateral.

unión *f* union.

unir *vt*, **unirse** *vr* to unite.

unísono *m* **al u.** in unison.

universal *a* universal.

universidad *f* university; **u. a distancia** ≈ Open University.

universitario,-a **1** *a* university. **2** *mf* university student.

universo *m* universe.

uno,-a 1 *m inv* one; **el u. de mayo** the first of May. **2** *f* (*hora*) **es la una** it's one o'clock. **3** *a* **unos,-as** some; **unas cajas** some boxes; **debe haber unos/unas veinte** there must be around twenty. **4** *pron* one; (*persona*) someone, somebody; (*impers*) you, one; **u. (de ellos), una (de ellas)** one of them; **unos cuantos** a few; **se miraron el u. al otro** they looked at each other; **de u. en u.** one by one; **u. tras otro** one after the other; **vive con u.** she's living with some man; **u. tiene que ...** you have to ...

untar *vt* to smear; (*mantequilla*) to spread.

uña *f* nail; **morderse** *o* **comerse las uñas** to bite one's nails.

uperizado,-a *a* **leche uperizada** UHT milk.

urbanismo *m* town planning.

urbanización *f* (*barrio*) housing estate; (*proceso*) urbanization.

urbano,-a *a* urban.

urbe *f* large city.

urgencia *f* urgency; (*emergencia*) emergency.

urgente *a* urgent; **correo u.** express mail.

urgir [6] *vi* to be urgent.

urna *f* (*para votos*) ballot box.

urraca *f* magpie.

uruguayo,-a *a* & *mf* Uruguayan.

usado,-a *a* (*ropa*) second-hand.

usar 1 *vt* to use; (*prenda*) to wear. **2 usarse** *vr* to be used.

usina *f* *Am* (*central eléctrica*) power station.

uso *m* use; **u. externo** for external use only; **u. tópico** local application; **haga u. del casco** wear a helmet.

usted (*pl* **ustedes**) *pron pers* you; **¿quién es u.?, ¿quiénes son ustedes?** who are you?

usual *a* usual.

usuario,-a *mf* user.

utensilio *m* utensil; (*herramienta*) tool.

útil *a* useful; (*día*) working.

utilidad *f* utility; **tener u.** to be useful.

utilitario,-a 1 *m* (*coche*) utility vehicle. **2** *a* utilitarian.

utilización *f* use.

utilizar [4] *vt* to use.

utópico,-a *a* & *mf* utopian.

uva *f* grape; **u. blanca** green grape.

UVI *f* *abr de* **unidad de vigilancia intensiva** intensive care unit.

V

vaca *f* cow; (*carne*) beef.

vacaciones *fpl* holidays *pl*, *US* vacation; (*viaje*) holiday; **estar/irse de v.** to be/go on holiday.

vacante 1 *a* vacant. **2** *f* vacancy.

vaciar *vt*, **vaciarse** *vr* to empty.

vacilar *vi* (*dudar*) to hesitate; (*voz*) to falter; **sin v.** without hesitation.

vacío,-a 1 *a* empty; (*hueco*) hollow; (*sin ocupar*) vacant. **2** *m* void; (*hueco*) gap; (*espacio*) (empty) space.

vacuna *f* vaccine.

vado *m* (*de un río*) ford; **'v. permanente'** 'keep clear'.

vagabundo,-a 1 *a* (*errante*) wandering. **2** *mf* wanderer; (*sin casa*) tramp, *US* hobo.

vagar [7] *vi* to wander about.

vago,-a 1 *a* (*perezoso*) lazy; (*indefinido*) vague. **2** *mf* (*holgazán*) lay-about.

vagón *m* (*para pasajeros*) carriage, *US* car; (*para mercancías*) wagon, *US* freight car.

vaho *m* (*de aliento*) breath; (*vapor*) vapour.

vaina *f* (*de guisante etc*) pod; *Am* (*molestia*) nuisance.

vainilla *f* vanilla.

vajilla *f* dishes *pl*.

valdré *indic fut de* **valer.**

vale[1] *interj* all right, OK.

vale[2] *m* (*comprobante*) voucher; (*pagaré*) IOU (I owe you).

valer 1 *vt* to be worth; (*costar*) to cost; **no vale nada** it is worthless; **no vale la pena (ir)** it's not worthwhile (going); **¿cuánto vale?** how much is it? **2** *vi* (*servir*) to be useful; (*ser válido*) to count; **más vale** it is better; **más vale que te vayas ya** you had better leave now. **3 valerse** *vr* **valerse por sí mismo** to be able to manage on one's own.

valgo *indic pres de* **valer.**

válido,-a *a* valid.

valiente *a* (*valeroso*) brave.

valioso,-a *a* valuable.

valor *m* value; (*precio*) price; (*valentía*) courage; **objetos de v.** valuables; **sin v.** worthless.

valoración *f* valuation.

valorar *vt* to value.

vals *m* waltz.

válvula *f* valve; **v. de seguridad** safety valve.

valla *f* (*cerca*) fence; (*muro*) wall; **v. publicitaria** hoarding, *US* billboard.

valle *m* valley.

vampiro *m* vampire.

vandalismo *m* vandalism.

vanguardia *f* vanguard; (*artística*) avant-garde.

vanidad *f* vanity.

vanidoso,-a *a* conceited.

vano,-a *a* (*vanidoso*) vain; (*esfuerzo, esperanza*) futile; **en v.** in vain.

vapor *m* (*de agua hirviendo*) steam; (*gas*) vapour; **al v.** steamed; **v. de agua** water vapour.

vaporizador *m* vaporizer.

vaquero,-a 1 *m* cowherd, *US* cowboy. **2** *a* **pantalón v.** jeans *pl*. **3** *mpl* **vaqueros** (*prenda*) jeans.

vara *f* rod.

variable *a & f* variable.

variado,-a *a* varied.

variante *f* (*carretera*) detour.

variar *vti* to vary; (*con ironía*) **para v.** just for a change.

varicela *f* chickenpox.

variedad *f* variety; (*espectáculo*) **variedades** variety show.

varilla *f* (*vara*) rod; (*de abanico, paraguas*) rib.

varios,-as *a* several.

variz *f* varicose vein.

varón *m* (*hombre*) man; (*chico*) boy.

vas *indic pres de* **ir.**

vascuence *m* (*idioma*) Basque.

vaselina *f* vaseline(R).

vasija *f* pot.

vaso *m* (*para beber*) glass.

vaticinar *vt* to predict.

vatio *m* watt.

vaya[1] *interj* **¡v. lío!** what a mess!

vaya[2] *subj pres de* **ir.**

Vd., Vds. *abr de* **usted, ustedes** you.

ve 1 *imperativo de* **ir.** **2** *indic pres de* **ver.**

vecindad *f*, **vecindario** *m* (*área*) neighbourhood; (*vecinos*) residents *pl*.

vecino,-a 1 *mf* (*persona*) neighbour; (*residente*) resident. **2** *a* neighbouring.

vega *f* fertile plain.

vegetación *f* vegetation; (*en nariz*) **vegetaciones** adenoids.

vegetal *a & m* vegetable.

vegetariano,-a *a & mf* vegetarian.

vehemente *a* vehement.

vehículo *m* vehicle.

veinte *a* & *m inv* twenty.

vejez *f* old age.

vejiga *f* bladder.

vela¹ *f* candle; **pasar la noche en v.** to have a sleepless night.

vela² *f* (*de barco*) sail.

velador *m Am* (*mesilla de noche*) bedside table.

velar *vt,* **velarse** *vr* to blur.

velatorio *m* vigil.

velero *m* sailing boat.

veleta *f* weather vane.

velo *m* veil.

velocidad *f* (*rapidez*) speed; (*marcha*) gear; **v. máxima** speed limit.

velocímetro *m* speedometer.

veloz *a* rapid.

vello *m* hair.

vena *f* vein.

venado *m* deer; (*carne*) venison.

vencedor,-a 1 *mf* winner. **2** *a* winning.

vencer [2] **1** *vt* to defeat; (*dificultad*) to overcome. **2** *vi* (*pago, deuda*) to be payable; (*plazo*) to expire.

vencido,-a *a* (*derrotado*) defeated; (*equipo etc*) beaten; **darse por v.** to give up.

venda *f* bandage.

vendaje *m* dressing.

vendar *vt* to bandage; **v. los ojos a algn** to blindfold sb.

vendaval *m* gale.

vendedor,-a *mf* seller; (*hombre*) salesman; (*mujer*) saleswoman.

vender *vt,* **venderse** *vr* to sell; **'se vende'** for sale.

vendimia *f* grape harvest.

vendré *indic fut de* **venir.**

veneno *m* poison; (*de serpiente*) venom.

venenoso,-a *a* poisonous.

venéreo,-a *a* venereal.

venezolano,-a *a* & *mf* Venezuelan.

venga *subj pres de* **venir.**

venganza *f* vengeance, revenge.

vengo *indic pres de* **venir.**

venir 1 *vi* to come; **el año que viene** next year; *fam* **¡venga ya!** (*expresa incredulidad*) come off it!; (*vamos*) come on!; **v. grande/pequeño** (*ropa*) to be too big/small; **v. mal/bien** to be inconvenient/convenient. ▌ (*en* *pasivas*) **esto vino provocado por ...** this was brought about by ... **| esto viene ocurriendo desde hace mucho tiempo** this has been going on for a long time now. **2 venirse** *vr* **venirse abajo** to collapse.

venta *f* sale; (*posada*) country inn; **en v.** for sale; **a la v.** on sale; **v. a plazos/al contado** credit/cash sale; **v. al por mayor/al por menor** wholesale/retail.

ventaja *f* advantage; **llevar v. a** to have the advantage over.

ventana *f* window; (*de la nariz*) nostril.

ventanilla *f* window; (*de la nariz*) nostril.

ventilador *m* ventilator; (*de coche*) fan.

ventilar *vt* to ventilate.

ventisca *f* blizzard; (*de nieve*) snowstorm.

ver 1 *vt* to see; (*televisión*) to watch; **a v.** let's see; **a v. si escribes** I hope you'll write; (**ya**) **veremos** we'll see; **no tener nada que v. con** to have nothing to do with. **2 verse** *vr* (*imagen etc*) to be seen; (*encontrarse con algn*) to see each other; **¡nos vemos!** see you later!; *Am* **te ves divina** you look divine.

veraneante *mf* holidaymaker, *US* (summer) vacationist.

veranear *vi* to spend one's summer holiday.

veraniego,-a *a* summer.

verano *m* summer.

veras de veras really.

verbena *f* street party.

verbo *m* verb.

verdad *f* truth; **es v.** it is true; **¡de v!** really!, truly!; **un amigo de v.** a real friend; (*en frase afirmativa*) **está muy bien, ¿(no es) v.?** it is very good, isn't it?; (*en frase negativa*) **no te gusta, ¿v.?** you don't like it, do you?

verdaderamente *adv* truly.

verdadero,-a *a* true.

verde 1 *a* green; (*fruta*) unripe; (*chiste, película*) blue. **2** *m* (*color*) green.

verdoso,-a *a* greenish.

verdura *f* vegetables *pl*.

vereda *f* path; *Am* (*acera*) pavement, *US* sidewalk.

veredicto *m* verdict.

vergonzoso,-a *a* (*penoso*) disgraceful; (*tímido*) shy.

vergüenza *f* shame; (*timidez*) shyness; **¿no te da v.?** aren't you ashamed?; **es una v.** it's a disgrace; **me da v.** I'm too embarrassed.

verificar [1] *vt* to check.

verja *f* (*reja*) grating; (*cerca*) railing; (*puerta*) iron gate.

vermut, vermú *m* (*pl* **vermús**) vermouth.

verosímil *a* probable, likely; (*creíble*) credible.

verruga *f* wart.

versión f version.

verso m (*poesía*) verse.

vertebrado,-a a & m vertebrate.

vertedero m (*de basura*) tip.

verter [3] vt to pour (out); (*basura*) to dump.

vertical a vertical.

vertiente f (*de montaña, tejado*) slope; *Am* (*manantial*) spring.

vertiginoso,-a a (*velocidad*) breakneck.

vértigo m vertigo; **me da v.** it makes me dizzy.

vespa(R) f (motor) scooter.

vespino(R) m moped.

vestíbulo m (*de casa*) hall; (*de edificio público*) foyer.

vestido,-a 1 m (*de mujer*) dress. **2** a dressed.

vestigio m trace.

vestir [6] **1** vt (*a alguien*) to dress; (*llevar puesto*) to wear. **2** vi to dress;
ropa de (mucho) v. formal dress. **3 vestirse** vr to get dressed, dress;
vestirse de to wear; (*disfrazarse*) to dress up as.

vestuario m (*conjunto de vestidos*) wardrobe; (*para teatro*) costumes pl;
(*camerino*) dressing room; (*en estadio*) changing room.

veterano,-a a & mf veteran.

veterinario,-a 1 mf vet, veterinary surgeon, *US* veterinarian. **2** f
veterinary medicine.

veto m veto.

vez f time; (*turno*) turn; **una v.** once; **dos veces** twice; **cinco veces** five times;
a o **algunas veces** sometimes; **cada v.** each o every time; **cada v. más** more
and more; **de v. en cuando** now and again; **¿le has visto alguna v.?** have
you ever seen him?; **otra v.** again; **a la v.** at the same time; **tal v.** perhaps,
maybe; **de una v.** in one go; **en v. de** instead of.

vía 1 f (*del tren*) track; (*camino*) road; **(por) v. oral** to be taken orally; **por
v. aérea/marítima** by air/sea. **2** prep (*a través de*) via.

viajar vi to travel.

viaje m journey, trip; (*largo, en barco*) voyage; **¡buen v.!** have a good
trip!; **estar de v.** to be away (on a trip); **v. de negocios** business trip; **v. de
novios** honeymoon.

viajero,-a 1 mf traveller; (*en transporte público*) passenger. **2** a **cheque v.**
traveller's cheque, *US* traveler's check.

víbora f viper.

vibración f vibration.

vibrar vti to vibrate.

vicepresidente,-a mf vice president; (*de compañía, comité*) (*hombre*)
vice-chairman, *US* vice president; (*mujer*) vice-chairwoman, *US* vice
president.

viceversa *adv* vice versa.

vicio *m* vice; (*mala costumbre*) bad habit.

vicioso,-a 1 *a* (*persona*) depraved; **círculo v.** vicious circle. **2** *mf* depraved person.

víctima *f* victim.

victoria *f* victory.

vid *f* vine.

vida *f* life; **en mi v.** never in my life; **ganarse la v.** to earn one's living; **¿qué es de tu v.?** how's life?

vídeo *m* video; **grabar en v.** to video.

videocámara *f* video camera.

videoclub *m* video club.

videojuego *m* video game.

vidriera *f* stained-glass window; *Am* (*escaparate*) shop window.

vidrio *m* glass.

viejo,-a 1 *a* old; **hacerse v.** to grow old; **un v. amigo** an old friend. **2** *mf* (*hombre*) old man; (*mujer*) old woman; **los viejos** old people.

viento *m* wind; **hace** *o* **sopla mucho v.** it is very windy.

vientre *m* belly.

viernes *m inv* Friday; **V. Santo** Good Friday.

vietnamita *a* & *mf* Vietnamese.

viga *f* (*de madera*) beam; (*de hierro*) girder.

vigencia *f* validity; **entrar en v.** to come into force.

vigésimo,-a *a* & *mf* twentieth.

vigilante *m* guard; (*nocturno*) night watchman.

vigilar 1 *vt* to watch; (*lugar*) to guard. **2** *vi* to keep watch.

vigor *m* vigour; (*fuerza*) strength; **en v.** in force.

vil *a* vile.

villa *f* (*población*) town; (*casa*) villa.

villancico *m* (Christmas) carol.

vinagre *m* vinegar.

vinagreras *fpl* oil and vinegar cruets.

vinagreta *f* vinaigrette sauce.

vincha *f Am* headband.

vínculo *m* link.

vine *pt indef de* **venir.**

vino *m* wine; **v. blanco/tinto** white/red wine; **v. rosado** rosé.

viña *f* vineyard.

viñedo *m* vineyard.

viñeta *f* illustration.

violación *f* (*de persona*) rape; (*de ley, derecho*) violation.

violar *vt* (*persona*) to rape; (*ley, derecho*) to violate.

violencia *f* violence.

violento,-a *a* violent; (*situación*) embarrassing; **sentirse v.** to feel awkward.

violeta 1 *a* violet. **2** *m* (*color*) violet. **3** *f* (*flor*) violet.

violín *m* violin.

violonc(h)elo *m* cello.

virar *vi* to turn round.

virgen *a* (*persona, selva*) virgin; (*aceite, lana*) pure; (*cinta*) blank.

viril *a* virile.

virtud *f* virtue; (*propiedad*) ability.

virtuoso,-a *a* virtuous; (*músico*) virtuoso.

viruela *f* smallpox.

virus *m inv* virus.

visa *f Am* visa.

visado *m* visa.

visera *f* (*de gorra*) peak; (*de casco*) visor.

visibilidad *f* visibility.

visible *adj* visible.

visillo *m* small net curtain.

visión *f* vision; (*vista*) sight.

visita *f* visit; (*invitado*) visitor; **hacer una v.** to pay a visit; **estar de v.** to be visiting.

visitante 1 *mf* visitor. **2** *a* (*equipo*) away.

visitar *vt* to visit.

vislumbrar *vt* to glimpse.

visón *m* mink.

víspera *f* (*día anterior*) day before; (*de festivo*) eve.

vista *f* sight; (*panorama*) view; **a la v.** visible; **a primera** *o* **simple v.** on the face of it; **en v. de** in view of, considering; **corto de v.** short-sighted; **conocer a algn de v.** to know sb by sight; **perder de v. a** to lose sight of; **¡hasta la v.!** see you!; **con vista(s) al mar** overlooking the sea.

vistazo *m* glance; **echar un v. a algo** (*ojear*) to have a (quick) look at sth.

visto,-a 1 *a* **está v. que ...** it is obvious that ...; **por lo v.** apparently; **estar bien v.** to be well looked upon; **estar mal v.** to be frowned upon. **2** *m* **v. bueno** approval.

vitalicio,-a *a* lifelong.

vitalidad *f* vitality.

vitamina *f* vitamin.

viticultor,-a *mf* wine grower.

vitorear *vt* to cheer.

vitrina *f* (*aparador*) display cabinet; (*de exposición*) showcase; *Am* (*escaparate*) shop window.

viudo,-a *mf* (*hombre*) widower; (*mujer*) widow.

viva *interj* hurrah!

vivaracho,-a *a* lively.

vivaz *a* vivacious; (*perspicaz*) quick-witted.

víveres *mpl* provisions.

vivero *m* (*de plantas*) nursery.

vivienda *f* housing; (*casa*) house; (*piso*) flat, *US* apartment.

vivir 1 *vi* to live. **2** *vt* (*guerra etc*) to live through.

vivo,-a *a* alive; (*vivaz*) lively; (*listo*) clever; (*color*) vivid; **en v.** (*programa*) live; **al rojo v.** red-hot.

vocabulario *m* vocabulary.

vocación *f* vocation.

vocal *f* vowel.

voceador,-a *mf Am* vendor.

vocero,-a *mf Am* spokesperson; (*hombre*) spokesman; (*mujer*) spokeswoman.

vociferar *vi* to shout.

vodka *m* vodka.

volandas en volandas flying through the air.

volante 1 *m* steering wheel; (*de vestido*) frill; **ir al v.** to be at the wheel. **2** *a* flying; **platillo v.** flying saucer.

volantín *m Am* (*cometa*) small kite.

volar [2] **1** *vi* to fly; *fam* **lo hizo volando** he did it in a flash. **2** *vt* (*explotar*) to blow up; (*caja fuerte*) to blow open; (*terreno*) to blast. **3 volarse** *vr* (*papel etc*) to be blown away.

volcán *m* volcano.

volcar [2] **1** *vt* (*cubo etc*) to knock over; (*barco, bote*) to capsize; (*vaciar*) to empty out. **2** *vi* (*coche*) to turn over; (*barca*) to capsize. **3 volcarse** *vr* (*vaso, jarra*) to fall over; (*coche*) to turn over; (*barca*) to capsize.

voleibol *m* volleyball.

voltaje *m* voltage.

voltereta *f* somersault.

voltio *m* volt.

volumen *m* volume.

voluminoso,-a *a* voluminous; (*enorme*) massive.

voluntad *f* will; **fuerza de v.** willpower; **tiene mucha v.** he is very strong-willed.

voluntario,-a 1 *a* voluntary; **ofrecerse v.** to volunteer. **2** *mf* volunteer.

volver [4] (*pp* **vuelto**) **1** *vi* to return; (*venir de vuelta*) to come back; (*ir de vuelta*) to go back; **v. en sí** to come round; **v. a hacer algo** to do sth again. **2** *vt* (*convertir*) to make; (*dar vuelta a*) to turn; (*boca abajo*) to turn upside down; (*de fuera adentro*) to turn inside out; (*de atrás adelante*) to turn back to front; (*cinta, disco*) to turn over; **volverle la espalda a algn** to turn one's back on sb; **al v. la esquina** on turning the corner. **3 volverse** *vr* to turn; (*venir de vuelta*) to come back; (*ir de vuelta*) to go back; (*convertirse*) to become; **volverse loco** to go mad.

vomitar 1 *vi* to vomit; **tengo ganas de v.** I feel sick. **2** *vt* to bring up.

voraz *a* voracious.

vosotros,-as *pron pers pl* you.

votación *f* (*voto*) vote; (*acción*) voting.

votante *mf* voter.

votar *vi* to vote; **v. a algn** to vote for sb.

voto *m* vote.

voy *indic pres de* **ir.**

voz *f* voice; (*grito*) shout; **en v. alta** aloud; **en v. baja** in a low voice; **a media v.** in a low voice; **a voces** shouting; **dar voces** to shout; **no tener ni v. ni voto** to have no say in the matter.

vuelo *m* flight; **v. chárter/regular** charter/scheduled flight; **una falda de v.** a full skirt.

vuelta *f* (*regreso*) return; (*viaje*) return journey; (*giro*) turn; (*en carreras*) lap; (*ciclista*) tour; (*dinero*) change; **a v. de correo** by return post; **estar de v.** to be back; **dar media v.** to turn round; **la cabeza me da vueltas** my head is spinning; **no le des más vueltas** stop worrying about it; **dar una v.** (*a pie*) to go for a walk; (*en coche*) to go for a drive.

vuestro,-a 1 *a pos* (*antes del sustantivo*) your; (*después del sustantivo*) of yours. **2** *pron pos* yours; **lo v.** what is yours.

vulgar *a* vulgar.

vulnerable *a* vulnerable.

WXY

walkman(R) *m* walkman(R).

wáter *m* (*pl* **wáteres**) toilet.

whisky *m* whisky; (*irlandés, US*) whiskey.

windsurf(ing) *m* windsurfing.

xenofobia *f* xenophobia.

y *conj* and; **son las tres y cuarto** it's a quarter past three; **¿y qué?** so what?;
¿y tú? what about you?; **¿y eso?** how come?; *ver* **e.**

ya 1 *adv* already; (*ahora mismo*) now; **ya lo sabía** I already knew; **¡hazlo
ya!** do it at once!; **ya mismo** right away; **ya hablaremos luego** we'll talk
about it later; **ya verás** you'll see; **ya no** no longer; **ya no viene por aquí** he
doesn't come round here any more; **ya era hora** about time too; **ya lo
creo** I should think so; **¡ya voy!** coming!; **¡ya está!** that's it! 2 *conj* **ya que**
since.

yacaré *m Am* alligator.

yacer *vi* to lie.

yacimiento *m* deposit.

yanqui 1 *a* Yankee. 2 *mf* Yank.

yarda *f* yard.

yate *m* yacht.

yedra *f* ivy.

yegua *f* mare.

yema *f* (*de huevo*) yolk; (*de planta*) bud; (*pastel*) sweet made from sugar
and egg yolk; **y. del dedo** fingertip.

yendo *gerundio de* **ir.**

yerba *f* = **hierba.**

yerbatero,-a *mf Am* (*curandero*) witch doctor who uses herbs.

yerno *m* son-in-law.

yerro *indic pres de* **errar.**

yeso *m* plaster.

yo *pron pers* I; **entre tú y yo** between you and me; **¿quién es? – soy yo** who
is it? – it's me; **yo no** not me; **yo que tú** if I were you; **yo mismo** I myself.

yoga *m* yoga.

yogur *m* yoghurt.

yuca *f* yucca.

yudo *m* judo.

yugo(e)slavo,-a *a & mf* Yugoslav, Yugoslavian.

Z

zafarse *vr* to get away (**de** from).

zafiro *m* sapphire.

zalamero,-a 1 *mf* crawler. **2** *a* crawling.

zamarra *f* (*prenda*) sheepskin jacket.

zambo,-a *a* knock-kneed; *Am* half Indian and half Negro.

zambullirse *vr* to jump.

zanahoria *f* carrot.

zancada *f* stride.

zancadilla *f* **ponerle la z. a algn** to trip sb up.

zanco *m* stilt.

zancudo *m Am* mosquito.

zanja *f* ditch.

zapatería *f* shoe shop.

zapatero,-a *mf* (*vendedor*) shoe shop owner; (*fabricante*) shoemaker; (*reparador*) cobbler.

zapatilla *f* slipper; **zapatillas de deporte** trainers.

zapato *m* shoe.

zarandear *vt* to shake.

zarcillo *m* (*pendiente*) earring.

zarpa *f* claw.

zarpar *vi* to set sail.

zarza *f* bramble.

zarzamora *f* (*zarza*) blackberry bush; (*fruto*) blackberry.

zarzuela *f* Spanish operetta; **la Z.** royal residence in Madrid.

zigzag *m* (*pl* **zigzags** *o* **zigzagues**) zigzag.

zócalo *m* (*de pared*) skirting board, *US* baseboard.

zodiaco, zodíaco *m* zodiac; **signo del z.** sign of the zodiac.

zona *f* zone.

zoo *m* zoo.

zoológico,-a 1 *a* zoological; **parque z.** zoo. **2** *m* zoo.

zopilote *m Am* buzzard.

zoquete *mf fam* blockhead.

zorra *f* vixen.

zorro *m* fox.

zueco *m* clog.

zumbar *vi* to buzz; **me zumban los oídos** my ears are buzzing.

zumbido *m* buzzing.

zumo *m* juice.

zurcir [3] *vt* to darn.

zurdo,-a 1 *mf* (*persona*) left-handed person. **2** *a* left-handed.

LOS NÚMEROS		NUMBERS
cero	0	nought
uno, una	1	one
dos	2	two
tres	3	three
cuatro	4	four
cinco	5	five
seis	6	six
siete	7	seven
ocho	8	eight
nueve	9	nine
diez	10	ten
once	11	eleven
doce	12	twelve
trece	13	thirteen
catorce	14	fourteen
quince	15	fifteen
dieciséis	16	sixteen
diecisiete	17	seventeen
dieciocho	18	eighteen
diecinueve	19	nineteen
veinte	20	twenty
veintiuno	21	twenty-one
veintidós	22	twenty-two
treinta	30	thirty
treinta y uno	31	thirty-one
treinta y dos	32	thirty-two
cuarenta	40	forty
cincuenta	50	fifty
sesenta	60	sixty
setenta	70	seventy
ochenta	80	eighty
noventa	90	ninety
cien	100	a or one hundred
ciento uno	101	a or one hundred and one
ciento diez	110	a or one hundred and ten
doscientos, doscientas	200	two hundred
quinientos, quinientas	500	five hundred
setecientos, setecientas	700	seven hundred
mil	1,000	a or one thousand
doscientos mil	200,000	two hundred thousand
un millón	1,000,000	a or one million